INSIDERS' GUIDE® SERIES

INSIDERS' GUIDE® TO

AUSTIN

FOURTH EDITION

CAM ROSSIE AND HILARY HYLTON

INSIDERS'GUIDE®

GUILFORD, CONNECTICUT

AN IMPRINT OF THE GLOBE PEQUOT PRESS

The prices and rates in this guidebook were confirmed at press time. We recommend, however, that you call establishments before traveling to obtain current information.

Publications from the Insiders' Guide® series are available at special discounts for bulk purchases for sales promotions, premiums, or fund-raisings. Special editions, including personalized covers, can be created in large quantities for special needs. For more information, please contact The Globe Pequot Press at (800) 962-0973.

INSIDERS'GUIDE®

Text design: LeAnna Weller Smith
Maps created by XNR Productions, Inc. © The Globe Pequot Press

ISSN 1533-5216
ISBN 0-7627-2997-X

Manufactured in the United States of America
Fourth Edition/Second Printing

Texas Capitol. AUSTIN CONVENTION AND VISITORS BUREAU/ J. GRIFFIS SMITH

Austin skyline. AUSTIN CONVENTION AND VISITORS BUREAU/J. GRIFFIS SMITH

Sixth Street. AUSTIN CONVENTION AND VISITORS BUREAU/J. GRIFFIS SMITH

Young musician. AUSTIN CONVENTION AND VISITORS BUREAU/J. GRIFFIS SMITH

Live music. AUSTIN CONVENTION AND VISITORS BUREAU/J. GRIFFIS SMITH

Sailing. AUSTIN CONVENTION AND VISITORS BUREAU/J. GRIFFIS SMITH

Lone Star *riverboat.* AUSTIN CONVENTION AND VISITORS BUREAU/BILL STOAGHTON

Governor's Mansion.   AUSTIN CONVENTION AND VISITORS BUREAU/J. GRIFFIS SMITH

Carriage ride. AUSTIN CONVENTION AND VISITORS BUREAU/J. GRIFFIS SMITH

University of Texas spirit. PETER A. SILVA

University of Texas sports. AUSTIN CONVENTION AND VISITORS BUREAU

[Top] *Zilker Playscape.* AUSTIN CONVENTION AND VISITORS BUREAU/J. GRIFFIS SMITH
[Bottom] *Pennybacker/360 Bridge.* AUSTIN CONVENTION AND VISITORS BUREAU/J. GRIFFIS SMITH

Austin Steam Train. AUSTIN CONVENTION AND VISITORS BUREAU/J. GRIFFIS SMITH

Goddess of Liberty atop the Texas Capitol. PETER A. SILVA

CONTENTS

CONTENTS

Directory of Maps

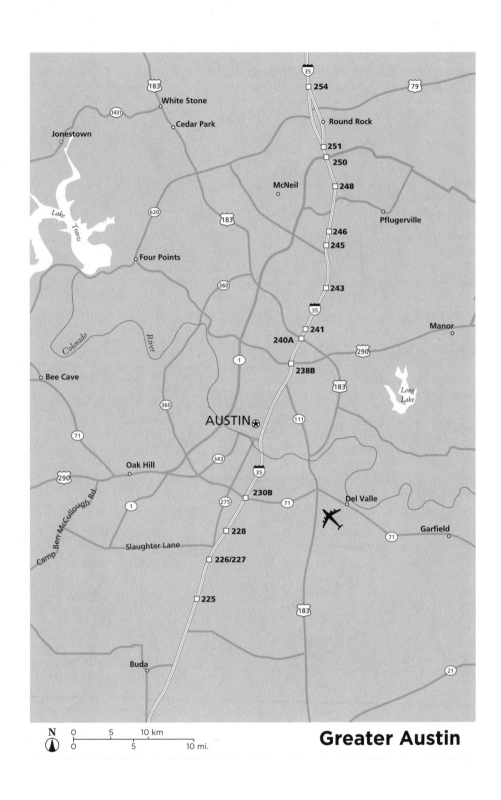

Greater Austin

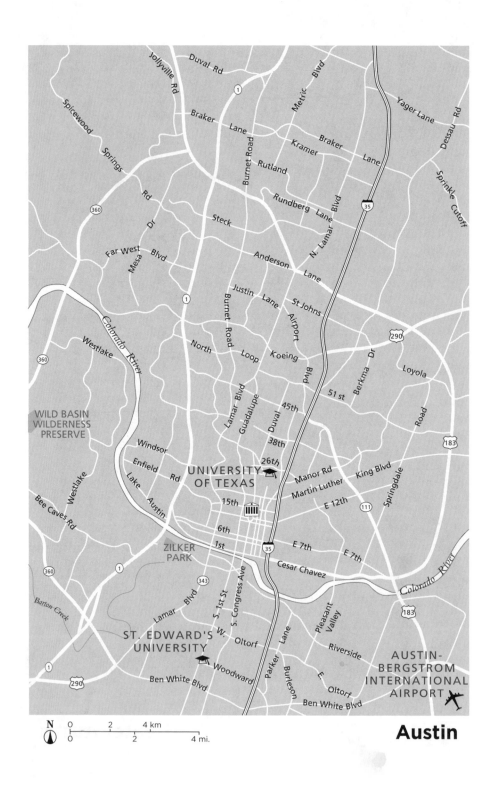

Austin

Jollyville Rd.
Duval Rd.
Metric Blvd
1
Yager Lane
Dessau Rd
Spicewood Springs
Braker Lane
Braker Lane
Kramer
Sprinkle Cutoff
Burnet Road
Rutland
Rundberg Lane
360
Rd
Steck
N. Lamar Blvd
35
Dr
Far West Blvd
Anderson Lane
Mesa
1
Justin Lane
St Johns
Burnet Road
Airport
290
Westlake
North Loop
Koeing Blvd
Berkma Dr
Loyola
360
Colorado River
Lamar Blvd
Guadalupe
45th
51 st
Road
WILD BASIN WILDERNESS PRESERVE
Duval
38th
183
Windsor
26th
UNIVERSITY OF TEXAS
Manor Rd
King Blvd
Enfield Rd
Martin Luther
Springdale
Westlake
Lake Austin
15th
E 12th
111
Bee Caves Rd
6th
E 7th
1st
E 7th
360
1
ZILKER PARK
35
Cesar Chavez
Colorado River
343
Barton Creek
Lamar Blvd
S. 1st St
S. Congress Ave
Pleasant Valley
183
1
S. W.
Oltorf
Riverside
AUSTIN-BERGSTROM INTERNATIONAL AIRPORT
290
ST. EDWARD'S UNIVERSITY
Woodward
Parker Lane
Burleson
E.
Ben White Blvd
Oltorf
Ben White Blvd

N
0   2   4 km
0   2   4 mi.

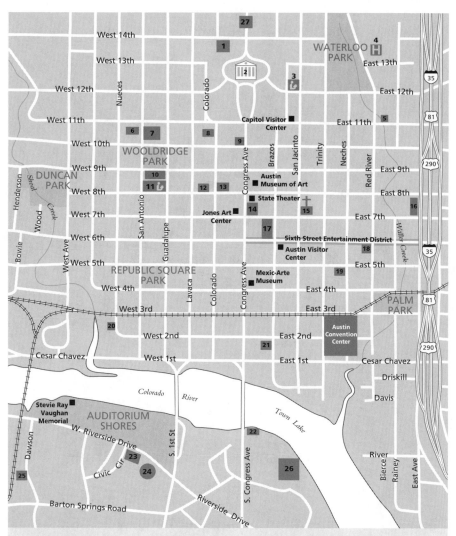

West 14th
West 13th
West 12th
West 11th
West 10th
West 9th
West 8th
West 7th
West 6th
West 5th
West 4th

27
1
2
3
4
WATERLOO PARK
East 13th
East 12th
East 11th
East 9th
East 8th
East 7th

Capitol Visitor Center

WOOLDRIDGE PARK

DUNCAN PARK

6 7
8
9
10
11
12 13
14
15
16
17
18
19

Austin Museum of Art
State Theater
Jones Art Center

Sixth Street Entertainment District
Austin Visitor Center

Mexic-Arte Museum

REPUBLIC SQUARE PARK
West 4th

Nueces
Colorado
Congress Ave
Brazos
San Jacinto
Trinity
Neches
Red River

Henderson
Shoal Creek
Wood
Bowie
West Ave
San Antonio
Guadalupe
Lavaca
Colorado
Congress Ave

Waller Creek

East 5th
East 4th

PALM PARK

West 3rd
East 3rd

20

West 2nd
East 2nd

Austin Convention Center

21

West 1st
East 1st

Cesar Chavez
Cesar Chavez
Driskill
Davis

Colorado River
Town Lake

Stevie Ray Vaughan Memorial
AUDITORIUM SHORES
W. Riverside Drive

22

Dawson
Civic Ctr
S. 1st St
S. Congress Ave

23
24
25
26

River
Bierce
Rainey
East Ave

Barton Springs Road
Riverside Drive

1. Supreme Court Building
2. State Capitol
3. Lorenzo De Zavala State Archives & Library
4. Brackenridge Hospital
5. Symphony Square
6. Courthouse Annex
7. Travis County Courthouse
8. Governor's Mansion
9. Old Bakery Emporium
10. Austin History Center
11. Main Library
12. U.S. Courthouse
13. Old City Hall
14. Paramount Theatre
15. St. David's Church
16. Police Headquarters
17. The Driskill
18. Esther's Follies
19. O. Henry Museum
20. Austin Music Hall
21. Chamber of Commerce
22. Bat Viewing Area
23. Palmer Events Center
24. Long Performing Arts Center
25. Dougherty Cultural Arts Center
26. Austin American-Statesman
27. Bob Bullock State History Museum

N
0   .1   .2 km
0   .1   .2 mi.

Downtown Austin

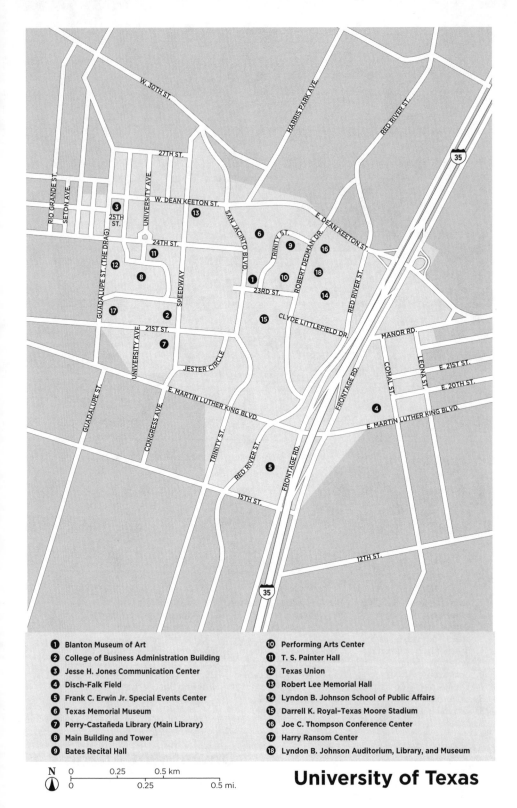

1 Blanton Museum of Art
2 College of Business Administration Building
3 Jesse H. Jones Communication Center
4 Disch-Falk Field
5 Frank C. Erwin Jr. Special Events Center
6 Texas Memorial Museum
7 Perry-Castañeda Library (Main Library)
8 Main Building and Tower
9 Bates Recital Hall
10 Performing Arts Center
11 T. S. Painter Hall
12 Texas Union
13 Robert Lee Memorial Hall
14 Lyndon B. Johnson School of Public Affairs
15 Darrell K. Royal–Texas Moore Stadium
16 Joe C. Thompson Conference Center
17 Harry Ransom Center
18 Lyndon B. Johnson Auditorium, Library, and Museum

N

0   0.25   0.5 km
0   0.25   0.5 mi.

University of Texas

PREFACE

Austin! Just the name evokes so many images. Music. High Tech. Universities. Government. Movies. Research. The Hills. The Lakes. The Springs. Independence! Opportunity! Austin is all those things and much more, as you'll soon discover.

Riding on nothing more than beauty, its perch on the edge of a wild frontier, and the determination of its citizens, Austin became the capital of the Republic and then of the state of Texas, a vast territory that reaches from the Mexican border almost halfway to Canada. Like other Texans, Austinites who shaped this region developed a kinship with the land and with one another. To be a Texan is a definite distinction. To add Austinite—now that's the shine on the star.

Like many other Austinites, we are not natives, although Austin is one city that quickly becomes your own, no matter where you've lived before. The familiar bumper sticker "I wasn't born in Texas, but I got here as soon as I could" goes double for Austin. We're speaking from experience when we give these words of caution, especially for you who've come for just a visit: Austin sneaks up on you unexpectedly, like a sudden shower on a hot summer day. It will capture your heart as quickly as a dry field blossoms into wildflowers. Once you've gotten swept up in the energy of this city or given in to our peaceful pastimes, it's hard to leave. Austin is clever that way. It's old, and it's new, and every minute it's got something different to offer you. That's part of the Austin mystique.

Perhaps you've come to see for yourself what it is about Austin that causes people to perk up when they hear the name. We hope you'll find this guide useful in that regard. Within these pages we've shared our ideas about the people and places, the sounds and the scenery that contribute to Austin's unique style. We've sought to give you a deeper understanding of who we are by telling you where Austin has been and where it's headed as this booming region endeavors to define its future and preserve its acclaimed quality of life.

It's hard to argue with the national magazines that have rated Austin among the top cities for living and conducting business. Citing Austin's "emergence as a hotbed for high-tech startup firms," the prestigious *Fortune* magazine has listed Austin as "The Best City for Business in North America." "Austin has always been the sort of town where the '60s never really died, where creativity was encouraged, and free spirits were nurtured," *Fortune* praised. In his 2002 book *The Rise of the Creative Class,* economist and author Richard Florida lists Austin as the "No. 2 Creative Hot Spot" in the nation. Indeed, Austinites are warmhearted, outgoing people who tolerate about anything but encroachment on our stunning natural environment or challenge to our way of life. Our music scene is so hot that we call ourselves "The Live Music Capital of the World." Our vibrant film industry, which includes local actors and directors who are making it big, is luring more and more internationally known stars and directors to Austin. At any given time there are a dozen or more stage productions to enjoy as well as art museums and galleries to visit and poetry readings to attend. Our countless sports enthusiasts, the bikers, boaters, runners, golfers, and swimmers, keep Austin humming with their passion.

The University of Texas contributes much more than character and economic drive. UT, along with our other colleges and universities, draws leading scholars and researchers to Austin and offers our students and the public countless educational opportunities and chances to hear world-renowned speakers. Our bookstores and libraries are abuzz day and night. It's no surprise, then, that Austin is considered a literary capital as well as the center of our massive state government. Along with thousands of jobs, the vigorous high-tech industry adds another dimension to Austin's intellectual community. The reward in living and working in Austin comes in knowing that no matter what challenges the day brings, there is a fascinating, fun, beautiful, easygoing city right outside the door.

Austin's amazing ability to combine that vitality—that feeling that anything is possible here—with a sense of tranquility is among its greatest attributes. There's plenty of space to get away: lying on the beach at Lake Travis, strolling along a wooded trail, flying a kite atop breathtaking Mount Bonnell, taking a cool dip in Barton Springs, picnicking at the park, exploring the natural wonders of the Hill Country, canoeing along Town Lake.

Don't take our word for it, though. Austin is a city that must be experienced firsthand. This book is meant to point you in the right directions. For those of you who've come to live, congratulations, you've chosen well. If you're here as a visitor, enjoy your Austin experience. Like we said, however, beware of its captivating charm.

ACKNOWLEDGMENTS

One of the perks of working on *Insiders' Guide to Austin* is the opportunity to talk with so many of the fascinating people whose drive and creative energy help make our city so vibrant. Through their eyes I always discover new dimensions of Austin and grow to appreciate the singularity of this region even more than before. For their excellent advice I am deeply obliged to John Kunz, owner of Waterloo Records, and to Beverly Horne, office administrator of the Writers' League of Texas. I also would like to thank the Austin Circle of Theaters, specifically Executive Director Latifah Taormina and Business Manager Heather Barfield, for taking the time to meet with me and for allowing me to share their resources. Brenda Johnson of the Austin Convention & Visitors Bureau offices of music and film was so kind to provide information about her areas of expertise. I am also grateful to Ellen Bartel of Dance Umbrella, Heather Brand at the Bob Bullock State History Museum, and Katie Cook of the Austin Convention & Visitors Bureau for their generous contributions to this edition. I am most appreciative of the editors and staff at The Globe Pequot Press who labor most diligently to make this book happen, and I would like especially to acknowledge my coauthor on this project, Hilary Hylton, an excellent journalist and friend and a true Austin Insider. Of course I am eternally grateful for my daughter, Quint Simon, who always provides pearls of wisdom and outstanding moral support.

—Cam Rossie

Working on this latest edition of our guide to Austin reinforced for me, once again, that this is a wonderful place to live. Austin continues to attract creative and interesting people and to nurture those of us who have called the city home for some time. This is a city that resists the cookie-cutter approach to urban life, and there is no shortage of characters, experts, eager amateurs, and cutting-edge professionals in the city's restaurants, stores, galleries, gardens, nightclubs, parks, and boulevards. One fast-growing facet of life in the capital has been the growth of virtual Austin—the city is as dynamic and fascinating in cyberspace as it is in the flesh. Thanks to my coauthor, Cam, whose enthusiasm and professionalism are unmatched; and thanks to my husband, Peter Silva, whose photographs appear in this book and whose insights into our hometown are invaluable.

—Hilary Hylton

HOW TO USE THIS BOOK

Whether you're planning to stay in Austin for a night, a fortnight, or the rest of your life, this book will guide you to, and through, the best the Capital City has to offer in more than two dozen areas of interest. *Insiders' Guide to Austin* is arranged by categories that appeal to both tourists and newcomers and can be useful whether you've just arrived or are only contemplating a visit or a move to Austin. Longtime residents may even discover a new thing or two about our city.

Our challenge in writing this book was to provide solid information and arrange it suitably so that you can map out a tour of Austin according to your own interests. It's up to you whether you take in these pages in one big gulp or choose to savor them slowly, chapter by chapter, as you make your way around town. Whatever your style, *Insiders' Guide to Austin* is meant to be used and used again as you delve deeper into the treasures of our Capital City. More than anything, we've designed this book to answer that age-old question: Where can I go to find . . . ?

Within these pages you'll encounter detailed descriptions of many of our most popular restaurants, attractions, hotels and motels, bed-and-breakfasts, and resorts as well as extensive listings of great places to shop and fun things to do with the kids. The chapter devoted to The Music Scene was a must, as you'll see, and we've dedicated another to Austin Nightlife. We've described our dynamic Literary Scene and given you an introduction to Austin's great Arts community. Nature lovers and outdoor types will discover the best that Austin has to offer in our chapter on Parks and Recreation.

For a wealth of information on our diverse periodicals, and radio and television stations, we've included a chapter on the Media. Newcomers will want to take special note of our chapters on Relocation, The Senior Scene, Worship, and Health Care and Wellness. Our chapter on Schools and Child Care includes information on private schools and all 10 public school districts in and around Austin, including those in our neighboring communities. Of course, no story of Austin would be complete without the Insiders' view of the capital's political personality. Don't miss our Politics and Perspectives chapter to find out what makes Austin tick.

Because much of the subject matter begs to be included in more than one chapter, we've noted where to look in the book for further information on a particular topic. Austin is loaded with resources, and we regret that we could not include every choice available in each chapter. We have, however, provided a solid foundation for you in all our categories and have pointed out additional resource materials that may provide more information. Also look for Insiders' Tips—marked with an ℹ️ —that let you in on local secrets.

Finding your way around town will probably be the first challenge you face upon arriving in Austin. While Austin does have some great natural and manufactured boundaries, such as the Colorado River and our main highway arteries, the layout can be confusing due to our unique Hill Country terrain and the fact that Austin isn't too keen on east-west thoroughfares. No two people agree exactly on how to divide Austin into geographic regions, especially now that the city has grown so much. (The area that is still referred to today as West Austin, for example, is now in Central Austin, while a new West Austin is, well, farther west.)

Start your tour of Austin by reading our Getting Here, Getting Around chapter. In this chapter we've explained the boundaries we use in this book to divide the city into 10 regions: Central, South Central, North, South, East, West, Northeast, Northwest, Southeast, and Southwest. In some chapters we've subdivided these regions even further. In the Hotels and Motels chapter, for instance, you will find an extensive listing for accommodations under the Interstate 35 Corridor heading. Because there are so many Attractions in Central Austin, we've divided that region into Downtown, The University of Texas, and Central Austin. Some chapters will also include an additional listing for Lake Travis, and you'll also find some information on Round Rock, Pflugerville, and Cedar Park. The boundaries we've described may not be universal boundaries, but they seemed the most realistic for us, and convenient for you. Refer to the maps we've provided to get started on your Austin adventure.

We've made every effort to provide you with the most accurate, up-to-date information in all categories. However, if you discover that your opinion differs from ours or that we've missed an important option, please feel free to send your comments or suggestions (see the contact information on page 579).

AREA OVERVIEW

"Where do you live?" folks on planes sometimes ask us. "Austin, Texas," we say. Nine times out of ten the questioner smiles, sighs, and says, "Lucky you."

Austin gets good press. In the past two decades, the city has been touted as a top place to live by numerous magazines. Perhaps the most overused adjective in all this positive coverage is "laid-back." But it fits. After all, this is a city where you can get by with one or two pairs of pantyhose a year or keep your tie rack in the back of the closet.

As former Mayor Kirk Watson once described Austin to us in an interview, "Austin is a city of boots and suits, hippies and nerds, all in the same boardroom . . . a city that allows almost ironic contradictions—at the same time we boast that we are the Live Music Capital of the World, we also boast we are Silicon Hills."

Laid-back, but on the high-tech cutting edge, cherishing the past, but charting the future. That dichotomy makes Austin an exciting, sometimes challenging place to live. We are embracing the future, yet looking longingly at the past, and, as the former mayor told us, so far each new wave of Austinites thinks they got here just in time to enjoy the real Austin.

Austin is a mecca for musicians and moviemakers, software engineers and hardware wizards, entrepreneurs and investors, artists and artisans, intellectuals and teachers, political activists and environmentalists, and lots of hardworking, everyday Texans who labor to make this city flourish. More than a million people call themselves Austinites these days, but there is still a neighborly feel about Austin and a notion that much of what goes on here is authentic.

As Austin has grown in both population and acreage, the pivotal question has been How can Austin stay Austin, yet flourish? The answer, so far, has come from within. Homegrown is the key here—whether it is homegrown businesses such as Dell Computer and Whole Foods Markets or homegrown restaurants such as Threadgill's and Jeffrey's, Austin's creative juices flow from the ground up. Franchise and chain operations, national corporations, and international businesses are represented in Austin, and they are growing in number; but, for the most part, they opt to adapt an Austin face, and often are overshadowed when viewed side by side with Austin originals.

This makes Austin a great place to live and to visit. Despite all its attributes, Austin has avoided being labeled a tourist town. Visitors are drawn to Austin not by a single, large attraction, a Disney World or a Fisherman's Wharf, but by the ambience of Austin. Consequently, we also are relatively free of touristy bric-a-brac, restaurants, and other sites that attract only out-of-towners. So whether you're visiting Sixth Street or stopping in for some spicy Tex-Mex food or barbecue, you will find yourself among the locals.

AUSTIN'S MANY FACES

The population of Austin is diverse and growing more so every year as new residents join the Austin melting pot. According to the U.S. Census Bureau, 12.4 percent of the city's residents are African-American, 23 percent Hispanic, and 3 percent Asian. Approximately 7 percent of the city's residents are older than 65. About 9 percent of Austin's residents are foreign-born, and 23 percent speak a language other than English at home.

The percentage of adults with college degrees stands at 35 percent, fourth place among 77 U.S. cities with a population of 200,000 or more. The median

Austin's Vital Statistics and Timeline

Founded: 1821 by Stephen F. Austin's colonists and named Waterloo; incorporated as Austin December 27, 1839

Mayor/Governor: Mayor Will Wynn; Governor Rick Perry

Population:
> Austin: 656,562
> Austin metropolitan statistical area: 1,249,763
> Texas: 18.4 million

Area:
> Austin: 232 square miles
> Austin metro area: 2,705 square miles

Counties in the Austin area (with major cities and county seats):
> Travis County (Austin is county seat and state capital)
> Williamson County (Round Rock; county seat Georgetown)
> Hays County (county seat San Marcos)
> Bastrop County (county seat Bastrop)
> Caldwell County (county seat Lockhart)

Major airports/interstates: Austin-Bergstrom International Airport; I-35, the Nafta Highway, runs through Austin

Nicknames: "Live Music Capital of the World," "Third Coast," and "City of the Violet Crown"

Average temperatures:
> Mean 68° F
> Mean low 58° F
> Mean high 79° F

Average annual precipitation: 32 inches

Annual days of sunshine: 200+

Major colleges and universities: Austin: University of Texas, Austin Community College, St. Edwards University, Texas State University—San Marcos, Southwestern University Georgetown, Concordia University of Austin, Huston-Tillotson College, Austin Presbyterian Seminary

Major area employers: University of Texas, Dell Computer, City of Austin, Austin Independent School District, Motorola, H-E-B Grocery Company, Seton Healthcare Network, IBM, Internal Revenue Service, State of Texas

Famous sons and daughters: (Some native; others, as they say in Texas, got here as fast as they could.) Lyndon Baines Johnson, Lady Bird Johnson, O. Henry, Dabney Coleman, Lou Ann Barton, Charles Umlauf, Michael Dell, Stevie Ray Vaughn, Earl Campbell, J. Frank Dobie, James Michener, Lance Armstrong, Ethan Hawke, Zachary Scott, Molly Ivins, Willie Nelson, Karl Rove, Linda Ellerbe, Ben Crenshaw, Nelly, Joe Ely, Roger Clemens, Tom Kite, Bud Schrake, Ann Richards, Steven Fromholz

Public transportation: Capital Metro operates buses and downtown 'Dillo buses.

Driving laws: Speed limits vary according to the size of the street or highway and its location. Generally, interstate speed limits are 70 mph, city freeways are 55 mph or 65 mph, and most neighborhood speed limits are 30 mph.

Alcohol laws:

- You must be 21 to purchase wine, beer, or liquor in bars, restaurants, and stores.
- Blood alcohol level at which one is presumed to be intoxicated is 0.08.
- Beer and wine may be purchased in grocery and convenience stores seven days a week. Fortified wines like port cannot be sold on Sunday, and liquor stores are closed on Sunday.
- Bars remain open until 2:00 A.M.

Daily newspapers: the *Austin American–Statesman,* the *Daily Texan*

Alternative newspaper: the *Austin Chronicle*

Taxes:

- State sales taxes vary in the Central Texas region but generally range around 8 percent. In the City of Austin the rate is 8.25 percent. Groceries are not taxed.
- Hotel-motel occupancy tax in Austin is 15 percent.

Chamber of commerce: Austin Chamber of Commerce, in the Lakeshore Tower building at 210 Barton Springs Road, Suite 400, Austin, TX 78704; (512) 478-9383, www.austin-chamber.org

Visitor center: Austin Convention and Visitors Bureau, 209 East Sixth Street; (512) 478-0098 or (800) 866-GOAUSTIN; www.austintexas.org

Time and weather:

- KVUE-TV operates a time and temperature service at (512) 451-2424.
- Fox Channel 7 has a live weather cam at www.fox7.com, and Cable Channel 8 has "weather on the eights" throughout the hour.
- National Weather Service: www.srh.noaa.gov/ewx

Notable events in Austin history:

1730: Spanish explorers establish a temporary mission at Barton Springs.

1821: Stephen F. Austin sends settlers to the banks of the Colorado River near Walnut Creek.

August 1833: The settlers are attacked by Indians.

1835: Jacob Harrell leaves Walnut Creek area and settles near the current site of the Congress Avenue Bridge.

March 2, 1836: Texas declares its independence from Mexico.

1837: William Barton settles on south bank of Colorado near artesian springs now named for him.

1838: Mirabeau Lamar, vice president of the Republic of Texas, goes on a buffalo hunt near the Colorado River and declares, "Here should reside the seat of the future empire."

May 1839: A one-story capitol building is erected at what is now Colorado and Eighth Streets.

August 1, 1839: The first city lots are sold.

November 1839: Waterloo is renamed Austin in honor of one of the founders of the Texas Republic.

December 27, 1839: Austin is incorporated.

December 1840: Jean Pierre Isidore Alphonse Dubois de Saligny builds the French Legation mission, Austin's oldest structure still intact.

March 5, 1842: As the Mexican Army takes San Antonio, President Sam Houston orders the Republic's archives moved to Houston.

December 29, 1842: The Archive War begins as Houston moves the capital to Washington-on-the-Brazos east of Austin and city residents refuse to move the archives to the new capital.

Summer 1845: A constitutional convention is held in Austin to ease the Republic's merger into the United States.

February 19, 1846: Texas joins the Union, and Austin is declared the state capital.

1850: A new capitol building is begun on the current site and completed in 1853.

February 1861: Austin and Travis County vote against secession from the Union, 704–450.

December 25, 1871: Houston and Texas Central Railroad reaches Austin, the most western railroad station in Texas, stimulating a decade-long boom.

1874: The first street lamps are placed along Austin's streets.

1876: David T. Lamme Sr. opens a candy store on Congress Avenue; the company is still in business in Austin.

1881: The city charters the University of Texas, which opens two years later. Tillotson Collegiate and Normal Institution opens to provide higher education to African Americans.

1885: St. Edward's College opens.

1886: The Driskill Hotel opens downtown.

May 16, 1888: The new pink granite capitol opens, replacing the first structure, which burned down.

1892: Celebrated European sculptor Elisabet Ney builds Formosa, her home and studio, in Hyde Park.

1893: Austin Dam, 60 feet high, is completed on the Colorado River.

1894: Writer O. Henry dubs Austin "The City of the Violet Crown" in a short story titled "Tictocq."

1895: Thirty-one so-called "moonlight towers" cast light throughout the night over the city.

April 7, 1900: Austin Dam collapses; eight die and the city is without power for months.

October 11, 1915: The Majestic Theatre opens on Congress Avenue. (Now completely restored and renamed the Paramount Theatre, it's a major performing arts venue.)

1918: Andrew Zilker's land, with iconic Barton Springs, becomes a city park named for its former owner.

1920: Austin's population reaches 34,876, but the city does not grow as fast as other regions of the state and ranks 10th in size.

1923: A major oil find in West Texas on land owned by the University of Texas sets the stage for the establishment of a permanent university fund.

October 14, 1930: Robert Mueller Municipal Airport opens.

December 6, 1933: Travis County Beer License No. 01 is issued to Kenneth Threadgill, whose little saloon would become a major magnet for musicians and help launch the city's modern-day music scene.

1937: The 27-story UT Tower is built, prompting J. Frank Dobie to ask why, with all the space in Texas, does a building here have to look like one in New York City.

1937: Lyndon Baines Johnson is elected to Congress, and his support for New Deal programs, including electrification of the Hill Country, helps Austin through the Great Depression.

July 2, 1939: KTBC–AM radio station opens; some of its notable staffers will include Nellie Connally and Bill Moyers.

1941: Mansfield Dam on Lake Travis is completed.

1942: Del Valle Air Force Base, later renamed Bergstrom, opens.

Thanksgiving Day 1952: Launched by Lyndon and Lady Bird Johnson, Central Texas's first television station, KTBC, makes its debut.

1956: The University of Texas is the first major Southern school to admit African-American undergraduates.

1963: Football Coach Darrell Royal leads the UT Longhorns to their first national championship.

November 10, 1964: James M. White opens the Broken Spoke, which has become one of the nation's best country music halls.

April 1, 1966: From his perch in the UT Tower, sniper Charles Whitman shoots, killing 16 and wounding 31.

1967: IBM locates in Austin.

1968: An African American is elected to the Austin school district; three years later the first African American is elected to the city council. Mexican-American candidates succeed in 1972 and 1975 to the same bodies.

1969: Texas Instruments opens in Austin.

August 7, 1970: The legendary Armadillo World Headquarters opens.

1971: The LBJ Presidential Library opens.

1974: Motorola opens facilities in Austin.

1974: KLRU–TV producer Bill Arhos proposes a new music show, *Austin City Limits;* Willie Nelson stars in the pilot.

July 15, 1975: Clifford Antone opens his first blues club on Sixth Street. Over the years, Antone's puts Austin blues on the national map.

1982: Lady Bird Johnson opens her wildflower research center.

1983: City political and business leaders push successfully for the MCC high-tech consortium to be located in Austin.

1984: Michael Dell starts his computer company and direct flights, "Nerd Birds," are launched between Austin and Silicon Valley.

1987: Leaders once again make a big catch, luring the Sematech consortium to the city. Dell is the top employer, with annual sales of $12 billion.

1994: A seismic shift takes place in state politics as Republicans dominate both U.S. Senate seats and most of the state's highest offices and judicial posts.

1998: Incumbent Governor George W. Bush leads his party to a sweep of all statewide offices.

November 7, 2000: Thousands of supporters and media stand in a cold downpour on Congress Avenue, watching the presidential election gridlock.

2000: By year-end the dot-com boom had gone bust, with start-ups like living.com and garden.com evaporating.

2001: The year of the lay-offs, with Dell letting 5,700 workers go and some 21,000 lay-offs citywide.

November 2002: The Republican surge continues as the GOP takes all three branches of state government.

May 28, 2003: Signs of life in downtown Austin as the city's newest landmark, the 33-story Frost Bank skyscraper, is topped.

November 2003: More signs of recovery; an estimated 3,000 apartments and lofts are under construction in the downtown area.

income in Austin in 2000 was $42,689, and only 4.5 percent of households received public assistance, ranking 72nd out of those 77 cities.

One startling statistic is that the Austin labor force increased 44 percent in the decade from 1980 to 1990, and in recent years, unemployment rates stood at less than 3 percent, dipping to 1.9 percent in mid-2001 and climbing to just under 6 percent in mid-2003. Austin residents are predominantly young, diverse,

dynamic, and hardworking; perhaps that is why the Austin lifestyle is characterized by a love for the outdoors and a lively interest in the latest music and art. But there is also a fondness for old Texas traditions; witness the abundance of annual events dedicated to cultural traditions (see our Annual Events and Festivals chapter).

While the past is celebrated, cultural diversity is unfolding at a furious pace in Austin. Restaurants and shops reflecting diverse cultural origins are growing in number. In a city where 25 years ago the choice of restaurants was relatively limited and dominated by Tex-Mex, barbecue, and homestyle cooking, residents and visitors can now choose from a wide variety of cuisines, often presented as "fusion" cuisine by one of the city's hot young chefs. There is a palpable sense of exploration in the air as the city adopts and absorbs a multitude of influences, translating them into an authentic Austin experience.

THE GREAT OUTDOORS

No description of Austin would be complete without an ode to the area's physical surroundings. Forget those clichéd Texas movie images you have seen in the Westerns. Austin is a city where trees and plants abound. Live oaks, pecans, cedar elms, and redbuds shade city streets, and city ordinances make it illegal to cut down trees of a certain diameter. Wildflowers, native plants, and grasses provide a year-round palette for both gardeners and Mother Nature as she paints the wild and natural areas of Central Texas.

Anyone who has visited Austin in the spring when the bluebonnets and Indian paintbrushes are in bloom leaves with a much-changed image of Texas. Hill Country pastures cry out for the brush of Monet, while the grassy banks along city freeways and country roads have been painted with a riot of color thanks to the state highway department's wildflower planting program.

The parade of wildflowers continues to bloom through summer and into fall. Every visitor and resident should make a pilgrimage to the Lady Bird Johnson Wildflower Center in Southwest Austin to take in the beauty, learn about native plants, and pay personal homage to the former First Lady who made saving American wildflowers a personal crusade (see our Attractions chapter).

Other examples of Austin natural wonders include Barton Springs, the spring-fed natural swimming pool that sits in the heart of the city's large downtown greenbelt, Zilker Park (see our Parks and Recreation chapter). Then there are the bats: North America's largest urban colony of Mexican freetail bats lives under the Congress Avenue bridge spring through fall, and their nightly flight in search of bug dinners draws crowds to the shores of Town Lake in downtown Austin (see our Attractions chapter). To the west of the city are the Highland Lakes, a chain of artificial lakes that stretch more than 150 miles, encompass 56,000 acres of water, and offer 700 miles of shoreline, making up the greatest concentration of fresh water in Texas. A network of lake and state parks, county and city parks, plus nature preserves and greenbelts surround Austin and provide green havens within the city limits (see our Parks and Recreation chapter).

In addition to a beautiful environment, Austinites also enjoy a generally benign climate. There are a few weeks in summer, notably late July and August, when the midday sun can take its toll, but since most buildings and cars in the city are air-conditioned, even those days are bearable. In winter there can be some brief spells of cold weather, but freezes are infrequent and snow is very rare, falling in any measurable amount about once every decade. One local tradition that new residents soon learn is the "plant shuffle"—hauling in all those patio plants that are sensitive to a hard freeze and then hauling them back out again a day or two later, but some winters pass without a single hard freeze.

The so-called "blue norther" is another Texas phenomenon that quickly becomes part of a newcomer's lexicon. These winter cold fronts often can be seen coming as the wind shifts to the north and the clouds are swept from the sky, allowing temperatures to fall into the 40s and 30s. Visitors often are astounded by how quickly the temperature falls, going from 70-something to 40-something literally in minutes—a good reason to carry a sweater in winter.

Spring is usually the rainy season, but Austin also enjoys spring days that border on the sublime, when residents can keep their windows open night and day. The average yearly rainfall is 32 inches, and there are on average 116 clear days, 114 partly cloudy days, 135 cloudy days, and 84 days with measurable rain. While winters are mild, sudden summer thunderstorms can be threatening. The Hill Country is riddled with what appear to be dry creekbeds, but after a sudden spring or summer rainfall they quickly become dangerous, as flash floods rage along their paths. Never try to drive across a flooded creekbed, and be aware of weather warnings about lightning storms and infrequent tornadoes.

For much of the year, the weather is benevolent and beautiful, allowing Austinites to spend their leisure time outdoors enjoying the many parks and recreational facilities in the area, perhaps a cup of coffee at an outdoor cafe, or a walk along Town Lake in the heart of downtown. But when the sun goes down they turn to other activities, enjoying the area's casual dining scene (see our Restaurants chapter) and the abundant nightlife.

THE MUSIC SCENE

Boasting the hottest live music scene in the country, Austin rocks day and night with just about any style of music imaginable: blues, country, jazz, folk, funk, punk, bluegrass, Tejano, rock and roll, alternative, and the savory sounds of our true Texas hybrids. Called a mecca for musical mavericks in 1998 by *Billboard* magazine, Austin is world renowned for its unique brands of original music and for attracting top-notch performers who would rather live and play in Austin than bend to the prevailing winds of musical fashion elsewhere. Home to the world's best-known country music outlaw, Willie Nelson, launching stage for late blues legend Stevie Ray Vaughan, a haven for scores of world-class artists and up-and-comers,

Austin is a paradise of live music. Read more about our music haven in The Music Scene chapter, which includes a close-up on Austin favorites, Willie and Stevie Ray.

THE ARTS

While they haven't earned equal billing with the Live Music Capital of the World, Austin's dynamic arts and literary scenes lend the cultural dimension that makes this city such an inviting place to live. Long known as a haven for artists and intellectuals, more and more talented artists have found inspiration in Austin over the past few decades. Today Austin offers more than 250 theater productions a year, including national touring shows and an excellent variety of local productions. There are numerous annual arts and music events throughout the year, including the SXSW (South-By-Southwest) music and media conference in spring and the Texas Book Festival in fall (see our Annual Events chapter). Our art museums, galleries, and bookstores abound with fresh voices in both the visual and literary arts. The city also is home to the Texas Film Commission, the state agency that has been successful in bringing many movie productions to what is affectionately called "The Third Coast." We give complete coverage to the art culture in our chapters on The Literary Scene and The Arts.

THE UNIVERSITY

Sprawling over 357 acres in the very heart of Central Austin, the University of Texas is an omnipresent force throughout this region. UT's contribution to Austin's economy and to its intellectual, political, and artistic development over the past 115-plus years has helped make Austin the envy of Texas and one of the coolest places in the land to live, work, study, and play. With about 50,000 students, UT gives Austin much of its youthful energy while bolstering its reputation as one of the country's hippest small cities. A breeding ground for intellectuals and a renowned research center, UT is one factor driving Austin's knowledge-intensive economy today. What's more, UT rewards Austinites almost daily by offering a rich variety of artistic, educational, and sporting events.

Although it's not considered one of the country's most beautiful campuses, UT nevertheless is a sight to behold. Towering shade trees, sculptures, and fountains by world-class artists, dozens of architectural wonders representing more than a century of development, and the 27-story UT Tower that soars as a landmark for all of Austin give the UT campus its unique flair. UT-Austin, the flagship of the system's 15 campuses spread throughout the state, is a source of pride for all Texans. Read about UT in our Attractions, Spectator Sports, The Arts, and Higher Education chapters and about its libraries in The Literary Scene chapter.

UT's size and importance to the economic development of Central Texas over the past century make UT Austin's most significant institute of higher learning. But our other colleges and universities— St. Edward's University in South Austin, Huston-Tillotson on the east side, Concordia University near UT, Southwestern University north of us in Georgetown, Texas State University south in San Marcos, and Austin Community College's campuses all over the region—combine to give Central Texas its fame as an educational Eden (see our Higher Education chapter).

GOVERNMENT

The Austin economy rests on three sectors: higher education, government, and the high-tech industry. The State of Texas employs approximately 50,000 people in the Austin area. As the state capital, the city is headquarters for many state agencies and, of course, the legislature and high courts.

The Texas legislature is convened on the second Tuesday of January in odd-

numbered years for a 120-day regular session. Special sessions are occasionally called at other times by the governor. During the biennial session Austin takes on a little different air as hotels and restaurants fill with politicians, their staffs, and lobbyists. But Austin is also a political city year-round, since many legislative staffers live here, along with those agency heads, judges, and state bureaucrats who live, eat, and breathe the political air of the city.

Austin is also known for its active local political scene where the environment and the fight to keep Austin true to itself are always center stage (see our Politics and Perspectives chapter).

HIGH-TECH

The third major pillar of the Austin economy is a relative newcomer. High-tech is now an integral part of the picture, and the three largest private-sector employers in Austin are technology companies— Dell Computer Corp., Motorola Inc., and IBM Corp. The vibrant music industry, a burgeoning film scene, and an up-and-coming multimedia sector have added to the diverse economic picture, giving Austin a much wider economic base and ensuring that it is not as subject to the whims of a single economic sector's ups and downs as it was in the past.

Austin's homegrown computer titan, Dell Computer Corp., along with other Fortune 500 companies that established Central Texas branches in the 1980s and 1990s, brought tens of thousands of jobs

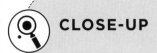

Texas Pronunciation Guide

"Texas—It's a whole other country!" Turns out the ad slogan used to promote Texas as a tourist destination is right, at least when it comes to the local lingo. Newcomers and visitors to Austin can be confounded by the local eccentricities in language, so we have developed this handy primer:

Balcones (Bal-CONE-niss) – A geological fault line that runs north-south through the city. This is just the first of several Spanish names that are not pronounced the way you were taught in high school Spanish.

Boerne (BURN-nee, rhymes with Bert and Ernie) – A small town southwest of Austin noted for its dude ranches. Just as many local names have their roots in Mexican culture, many also derive from the German settlers who made their homes in the Hill Country in the last century.

Bowie (BOO!-ee) – As in that buoy in the water. A hero of the Alamo, Jim Bowie gave his name to both a knife and an Austin high school.

Brazos (BRAA-ziss) – A Texas river that runs through Waco and the name of a downtown Austin street. All seven major Texas rivers give their names to downtown, north-south streets in Austin; memorize their names and their respective east-west position on the Texas map and you will know how to find them in downtown Austin (see our Getting Here, Getting Around chapter).

Buchanan (Buck-ANN-un) – Rhymes with buckin' bronco and is one of the Highland Lakes northwest of Austin. We have no explanation for why this Scottish name lost its "Byew" and became "Buck," except, of course, this is Texas.

Buda (BYEW-dah) – Rhymes with phew! This small town just south of Austin is noted for its small antiques and collectibles shops.

Bonnell (Bun-NELL) – That's Mount Bonnell, a popular spot to take in a view of Austin (see our Attractions chapter).

Burnet (BURN-it) – Rhymes with "durn it" and is a road in Austin and a Hill Country community.

Cameron Road (CAM-run) – Drop the middle syllable here, and you'll sound okay.

Coupland (COPE-land) – As in Aaron Copland, a musical connection that is appropriate since this is the home of the famous Coupland Dance Hall (see the Insiders' Tip in our Nightlife chapter).

Dessau (DESS-aw) – Dessau Lane is in North Austin.

Del Valle (Dell Valley) – Another Spanish word that has been anglicized, or Texas-ized, Del Valle is a community southeast of Austin near the Austin-Bergstrom International Airport.

Elgin (ELL-ghin) – No gin here (it rhymes with "kin"), or vermouth, just sausages. This small town east of Austin makes a famous German-style sausage that some barbecue aficionados regard as a mandatory element in any cookout.

Gruene (Green) – The German word for green and the name of a small town south of Austin known for its antiques shops and artists (see our Day Trips chapter).

Govalle (Go Valley) – Another Spanish word corrupted by gringo tongues? Surprise! No, this is derived from a Swedish phrase *go val* meaning "good grazing land," and Swedish settlers gave this name to fertile pastureland east of Austin along the Colorado River. A cabin built there in 1840 by S. M. Swenson, the first Swedish settler in Texas, is now found in the Zilker Park Garden Center (see our Attractions chapter).

Guadalupe (GWA-da-loop) – If you can remember Alley Oop, you will quickly get the hang of this street name. The portion of Gwadaloop that runs through the University of Texas campus is known as "The Drag."

Huston (HYOU-stun) – As in Sam Houston, and part of the name of Huston-Tillotson College (see our Higher Education chapter).

Jager (YAY-gahr) – That's Yeager as in Chuck "The Right Stuff" Yeager and the name of a lane, now a major roadway, in North Austin.

Koenig (KAY-nig) – Another German name that was given to a lane in North Austin and another of those "lanes" that is now a major thoroughfare.

Kreuz (Cry-tzz) – You don't really have to know how to pronounce this name if you have good sense of smell. Simply start sniffing as you approach Lockhart, and your nose will carry you to the famous barbecue spot (see our Annual Events and Festivals chapter).

Lavaca (La-VAH-cah) – One of the few Spanish names pronounced correctly here, it means "the cow" and is also the name of a famous Spanish explorer, an Austin street, and a Texas river.

Llano (LAN-oh) – The name means "plains" in Spanish, but historians believe the county and town of the same name northwest of Austin take their name from the Llano River in the plains west of the Hill Country.

Manchaca (MAN-shack) – Not only has this Spanish word been given the Texas treatment, but the spelling has been changed as well. Legend says a spring south of Austin was named for Colonel Jose Antonio Menchaca, scion of an old San Antonio family. The "e" was changed to an "a" over the years to become Manchaca, the name given the community that grew up around the spring south of Austin. The Manchaca community is now part of the growing Austin, but the elementary school there has been named for Menchaca with the original spelling.

Manor (MAY-ner) – Forget your "to the manor born" accent when pronouncing the name of this community east of Austin and opt for a down-home twang.

New Braunfels (New BRAWN-fells) – This is one of several picturesque Hill Country towns that owe much of their character to German settlers (see our Day Trips chapter).

Nueces (New-AY-sez) – The Spanish word means "nuts," but in Austin the Spanish "nway" becomes "new." It is one of those downtown streets named for a Texas river.

Pedernales (PUR-der-nal-liss) – This "purdy" river runs through the LBJ Ranch near Johnson City (see our Day Trips chapter).

Pflugerville (FLEW-ger-ville) – The "p" is silent here, but this small town northeast of Austin is not a quiet backwater anymore. It is a thriving vibrant community (see our Relocation chapter).

Rio Grande (REE-oh Grand) – If it was good enough for John Wayne, then it's good enough for those Austinites who drop the final syllable here. This is another of those downtown river streets.

San Antonio (San An-TONE) – Not everyone opts for this pronunciation, but it does have a Texas ring to it. Again, a downtown street named for this Texas river.

San Jacinto (San Jah-SIN-tow) – In Spanish it would be "San Hah-seen-toh," but locals opt for the hard "J" here when they pronounce the name of this downtown street, another one of those river streets.

San Marcos (San MAR-kiss) – Round vowels are not the preferred Texas pronunciation, especially when they come at the end of a word, like the name of this college town south of Austin.

Texans (TEX-uns) – It is the round vowel syndrome again.

Texas (TEX-us) – Yet again, flat is better than round.

to become the driving force behind this region's economy. What's more, it didn't take too long for the Texas spirit of adventure to emerge in a big way in the technology field, and venture capital has played a major role.

Oil wildcatters of earlier decades enhanced Texas's mystique as a hotbed of fiercely independent risk-takers, but a new breed of prospectors is leading Austin today. Armed with computer chips rather than drill bits, Austin's modern wildcatters are gambling on start-up technology companies in computers and especially in software development. Some have hit major gushers (see our Politics and Perspectives chapter), while others have gone bust.

GROWTH ISSUES

Long known as a low-growth region, Austin lived out its unique vision for more than 150 years without much concern for policies in then-far-off Round Rock, Cedar Park, Dripping Springs, and other neighboring communities. But as this booming region expands into one big metropolis, Austin now is faced with developing a plan for the future that encompasses all of Central Texas's concerns. Growth has been the No. 1 topic in Austin for the last two decades, and now those once-small, quiet communities like Cedar Park and Dripping Springs are wrestling with the same issue.

Growth has been a two-edged sword for the Austin area. It has brought economic stability and even boom times, but it also has put stress on the environment. It has led to more restaurants, more shops, more donations to the arts, and contributions to the cultural scene, but it also has put pressure on infrastructure and public resources. However, growth also has led to dynamic, creative solutions, has revitalized old neighborhoods, given downtown a new vibrancy, and brought people together in new ways.

AUSTIN OVERLOOK

We called this section Overlook because visitors get many of the grandest views of this city looking down from one of its many hills or from above: the first view of the city from an airplane, a tapestry of lights surrounding two distinctive land-marks, the capitol and the University of Texas tower; a view of the downtown sky-line from a scenic lookout point on Capital of Texas Highway west of the city; or the sun shimmering on Lake Travis at sunset, viewed from the deck of a lakeside restau-rant; the reflections of the downtown lights in Town Lake viewed from a high-rise hotel; the view of the city from a pic-nic site on Mount Bonnell.

But Austin is not a city to be experi-enced only from above—or from afar. To get the most of this city, walk among the people and the places that have made

Local weather forecasts are available from a variety of sources, including four local television stations: KTBC-TV, Channel 7; KVUE-TV, Channel 24; KXAN-TV, Channel 36; and KEYE-TV, Channel 42 (see our Media chapter). Time Warner Channel 8, a 24-hour news channel, has weather "on the eights" every hour.

Austin what it is today. So many of the places visitors find enjoyable are places the locals love to visit also.

By the time you're ready to leave Austin, if you can tear yourself away, you'll really know what it means when the locals bid you farewell with a "Y"all come back." You might even find yourself responding, "Y'all take care!"

POLITICS AND PERSPECTIVES

"All politics is local," former U.S. Speaker Tip O'Neill reportedly said, and in no place in Texas is that more true than Austin. Not only are city politics hard fought here, but this is also where the state's major parties have their headquarters. Austin is home to political spin doctors and policy wonks, lobbyists of all stripes, political scientists, and ardent grassroots volunteers, consultants, and image-makers.

No description of Austin would be complete without a discussion of politics. It is, after all, an Austin industry and one that flourishes year-round, coming into full bloom every other spring during the biennial sessions of the Texas Legislature. Most Texas politicians, no matter their political party, hold to a Texas version of the old saw: "What is good for the country is good for General Motors, and what's good for General Motors is good for the country." Just substitute Texas for country and "bidness" (Texan for "business") for GM, and you'll get the picture.

Economic development, business stimulation, and great public works (particularly roads and airports) are viewed as good public policy in Texas by the majority of state legislators. Not all their plans are welcomed by some of the citizens of Austin, and that is at the heart of a long-running love-hate relationship the city has with the legislature. Austin is well known as a "liberal" city, and the majority of voters within the city limits consistently vote for Democratic candidates, although the voter profile in the fast-growing suburbs is tending to be more Republican. However, Austin remains home to progressives and populists, a town where the most active political segment might be labeled the "Greens"—environmentalists, sometimes derided as "no-growthers"—who have been sounding a drumbeat of warnings about the need to limit growth, particularly in the Hill Country (see our Close-up on Barton Springs Pool in the Parks and Recreation chapter).

But the political picture is more complicated than that and, in some ways, getting more blurred as Austin's political profile changes. This is also the city that built the only new international airport in the country in the late 1990s, thanks to the clout of powerful Texas politicians such as retired Democratic Congressman JJ "Jake" Pickle, whose mentor was the biggest Texas politico of them all, President Lyndon B. Johnson. Austin residents can thank Johnson and other Texans with clout in Washington for the Highland Lakes, where so many residents and visitors head for recreation. Of course Austin also was home to President George W. Bush, further strengthening the Austin-Washington ties.

THE PARTNERSHIP

Government is a major employer in Austin, and it is also a major partner in the city's economic development. In the 1960s several visionary leaders in business and at the University of Texas began a campaign to bring industry to Austin. Not only did the city provide a pleasant cultural and social climate for new industry, they argued, but the university's engineering and science programs offered a valuable resource to major research operations. In 1966, the efforts paid off with the announcement that IBM was opening a new plant in Austin.

The move was a catalyst that resulted in Texas Instruments and Motorola opening up plants in the area to link to IBM. The efforts by community leaders had paid off, but they could not know what they had begun.

"IBM was both an end and a beginning—and it was the shape of things to come," Anthony M. Orum wrote in his book *Power, Money & the People: The Making of Modern Austin.*

Fast forward to 1983 when William Norris of Control Data Corporation came up with the notion that U.S. companies needed to form a consortium of private technology companies to design the fifth generation of computers. The consortium, which had to turn to the federal government for exemptions from antitrust laws, was named the Microelectronics and Computer Technology Corporation, or MCC for short, and Norris chose Admiral Bobby Ray Inman, a former deputy director of the Central Intelligence Agency, to head up the effort.

Dozens of U.S. cities joined the chase to bring MCC home. Several cities in Texas made the pitch, and Austin ended up on the short list. The city's business leaders, politicians, and the state leadership went into a full-court press.

Orum wrote: "By the time MCC officials set foot in Austin, the city's presentation did not include merely local officials, but was an orchestrated effort by major state figures to lure MCC. Governor (Mark) White had been persuaded that the economic future of the state lay with the development of a strong high-technology base of operations and he, in turn, helped to corral a number of other prominent state leaders including computer magnate H. Ross Perot, Houston banker Ben Love, former Governor Allan Shivers, and multibillionaire Perry Bass."

Austin won the prize. The reasons are disputed, but Orum credits the huge financial package Texas leaders and the university put together. The University of Texas (UT) committed to $15 million worth of endowed faculty chairs for 30 new positions in computer science and electrical engineering plus $1 million a year for

The Texas State Motto is "Friendship," and Texas is said to have been the Spanish pronunciation for a Caddo Indian word meaning "friends" or "allies."

research for each of these areas, grants for graduate students, money for equipment, and a lease at the university's Balcones Research Center for a nominal fee. The multimillion-dollar package prompted Atlanta Mayor Andrew Young to sniff that Austin had "bought" MCC.

Austin was on the high-tech map. Hadn't *Megatrends* author John Naisbitt predicted it in his best-seller? Suddenly the city was being profiled and touted in national magazines and newspapers. In 1984 Michael Dell began his computer company out of his UT dorm room. Four years later, city and state leaders turned to many of the same team members it had employed in the MCC hunt to lure Sematech, a semiconductor consortium, to town. One key player was Austin lawyer Pike Powers, a member of the powerful Fulbright & Jaworski law firm and a close friend and former top aide to Governor White. Powers and the rest of the team brought home the bacon again.

Austin was on a roll. At mid-decade the city's population stood at 436,188, a 26 percent gain since 1980. As the *Austin American–Statesman* noted, the city had gained as many people in five years as it had since World War II. In one of those typical Austin dichotomies, growth had fueled a real estate boom and that had prompted some of the city's most ardent liberals to become lobbyists and lawyers for development interests. Fortunes were being made, savings and loans were being chartered, and "flipping" real estate—buying it and quickly selling it—became the favorite game in town. At the same time, oil prices were sky-high, and since the oil and gas business still accounted for a third of the state's economy, the banks were flush with money to lend.

Then, the bottom fell out of the oil market, inflated land prices began to fall, and the Texas economy fell into recession. Some of the most well-known names in Austin declared bankruptcy, and a few went to jail. Texas languished and by all outward appearances was stuck in a rut. But behind the scenes, thanks to public policy and private know-how, the high-tech engines were churning and would soon reach a critical mass that would push both the Austin and Texas economy in a whole new direction.

HIGH-TECH RESCUE

The Austin economy began to turn around, and it became evident the new Austin was not dependent on real estate speculation and government growth for its economic well-being. In 1993 the *Austin American–Statesman* began to publish "Tech Monday," a business section that appears weekly and gives readers the latest news on the Austin technology scene (see our Media chapter). That also was the year young Michael Dell's company broke the $1 billion mark. By the end of 1997, Dell sales stood at $12 billion and the company was the area's largest private employer, with 12,000 people. (Dell is still the number-one private employer.) Along the way, several Dell employees had gone their own way and established their own businesses plus Dell's success had created hundreds of so-called Dellionaires who were savvy enough to buy Dell stock

when it first went public and hang on to it through several stock splits.

In 1994 the daily "Nerd Bird" flights began between Austin and Silicon Valley, California. The city that had called itself the Third Coast in the 1980s now was kicking around the name Silicon Hills. In 1995 Tivoli Systems issued stock, and Lockheed closed its doors in Austin—software was in, military hardware was out. That same year Austin's first Internet companies were created, including Ichat, Garden Escape, Deja News, and others. Within a year, Tivoli, which had raised $34 million in its initial stock offering, was sold to IBM for $743 million.

Samsung broke ground on its memory chip plant in Northeast Austin in 1996. Two years later, the $1.3 billion Samsung plant was in operation. The city had felt some minor bumps on the road as semiconductor prices fell and some ventures failed, but venture capital was being spread around, and new companies were forming weekly. According to the *Austin American–Statesman,* 33 companies raised $164 million in venture capital in 1997, up from $40 million by nine companies in 1995. Those numbers skyrocketed as Austin entered the year 2000. In the first quarter, the newspaper reported, Austin companies had raised and invested $562 million in venture capital—$100 million more than second-place Dallas and a whopping $500 million more than Houston.

The city saw unemployment rates drop to less than 3 percent as the 1990s ended and Austin was enjoying a secure, creative atmosphere for young workers, according to Angelos Angelou, an Austin economist. They flocked to Austin not to sign on for a benefits-loaded package with a traditional employer, but rather to venture forth on their own in Internet and dot-com companies.

"Internet-related companies being developed in Austin are siphoning off workers from the other technology companies. Multimedia software development—it's fashionable, if you are young and you can roommate with a number of

CLOSE-UP

Top Austin Employers

Government is a major factor in the Austin economy. Five state agencies are among the top 20 employers in Austin. However, as state agencies streamline and private sector employment grows, the government footprint is shrinking in Austin. The ranking changes according to the season and the source, but there is general agreement that Austin's Top 10 includes:

1. University of Texas, approximately 21,000 employees
2. Dell Computer, 16,000
3. City of Austin, 12,000
4. Austin Independent School District, 10,000
5. Motorola, 9,000
6. Seton Healthcare Network, 7,200
7. IBM, 6,300
8. H-E-B Grocery Company, 6,200
9. Internal Revenue Service, 5,000 year-round, but the payroll grows at tax time
10. Austin Community College (ACC), 4,600

people to cut costs. You can afford to join a start-up company and work for nothing," Angelos said.

For some, the ride was a roller coaster and a few dot-com ventures rode the wave, but overall the high-tech economy continued to grow and feed on burgeoning venture capital.

CHANGING OUTLOOK

By the mid-1990s the empty office towers built during the real estate boom were filling up—in some cases government had come to the rescue again with the state and city buying up the unused towers. The state's coffers were filling up as its economy strengthened, boosted in large part by the emerging high-tech sector and the boom in trade with Mexico, prompted by

the signing of the North American Free Trade Agreement (NAFTA) in 1994.

Support of NAFTA had been a bipartisan affair throughout the late 1980s and early '90s. It was a political sentiment and attitude reflected not only in Texas governor George Bush's 1994 campaign for governor, but also in the administration of his predecessors including Democratic governor Ann Richards and Republican governor William Clements. When some called for a ditch along the Texas-Mexico border during Clements's administration, the gruff, tough-talking governor, and independent oilman, said the United States should be "building bridges with Mexico, not ditches."

That attitude is rooted in both economic realities and cultural predispositions. Texas leads the states in trade with Mexico with more than $50 billion in annual exports, and the state's cultural, political, and social history is intertwined with Mexico's. Visitors and newcomers to Texas did not hear the same kind of divisive debate that occurred in California over such issues as illegal immigration and bilingual education, in part because of the stance taken by leaders in both parties on those issues.

After the peso devaluation in 1994, the number of illegal aliens increased. Federal officials estimated there were 357,000 undocumented workers in Texas—about 2 percent of the population. Texas ranked third in total number of undocumented workers. (California had about 1.4 million, 4.6 percent of its population; New York had 449,000, 2.4 percent of its population.) But while some economists tagged the cost of illegal immigrants to the U.S. economy, others tried to assess their contribution. Texas economist and author M. Ray Perryman estimated their contribution to the Texas economy in 1994 at $5.2 billion in a $471 billion economy.

Undocumented workers built new homes for Texans, baby-sat their children, picked their vegetables, and cooked for them. When the Immigration and Naturalization Service embarked on a series of raids on workplaces in Austin around July 4, 1996, public reaction was mixed, but some expressed the view that illegals with jobs should be left alone. Polls showed that Texans did not approve of illegal immigration, but most polls also showed it was not a major topic of concern for voters. A majority of Texans, including former governors Richards and Bush, have continued to support education for the children of illegal immigrants.

Sensitivity to Mexico and Hispanic heritage in Texas is a hallmark of both political parties. Governors Richards and Bush both developed diplomatic relations with Mexican leaders and governors south of the border. The political reality is that Hispanic voters have growing clout in Texas and in Austin. From 1980 to 1990, Texas's Hispanic population grew by 45 percent, and Hispanics make up some 25.6 percent of the

state's population and 23 percent in Austin. Overall, by 1990 Texas's minority population was more than 40 percent, compared with the national number, 25 percent. By 2010 Texas is predicted to be a minority majority state, with Hispanics making up the largest sector in that majority.

Demographers predict the Texas population will increase by 99 percent from 1990 to 2030—Anglo population will increase by 20 percent, African-American by 62 percent, and Hispanic by a whopping 258 percent.

Not only is the Hispanic vote significant in Texas, but so is Hispanic leadership. Texas leads the way nationally in the number of Hispanic officeholders. According to the National Association of Latino Elected and Appointed Officials (NALEO), before the 1994 elections, Hispanics held 5,466 seats across the country—2,215 of them in Texas. California had only 803, and New Mexico was next in line with 716.

The election and appointment of Hispanics in Texas is seen as a significant and necessary move. While the majority of Hispanic officeholders are Democrats, the Texas GOP has a Republican Hispanic Assembly aimed at boosting Republican membership among Hispanics.

POLITICAL CHANGES

In addition to demographic changes, Texas also has undergone significant political realignment, some say because of the influx of new residents, others because of historical changes in the two major political parties. The year 1994 marked a watershed in Texas politics as the Republican Party recorded several landmark achievements. Republican gubernatorial candidate George W. Bush defeated Democratic governor Ann Richards, who had achieved national celebrity status. The pundits opined it would be a tight race, but it was not, and Bush recorded the biggest gubernatorial win in 20 years. He continued to get high ratings from voters throughout his first term.

Bush had defeated the woman who once said of his father at the national Democratic Party convention, "Poor George. He can't help it. He was born with a silver foot in his mouth." (The president sent her a silver foot charm.) Richards, who had won the governor's race by attracting moderate Republican women in 1990, won counties in South Texas, several around her hometown of Waco, some rural counties in East and North Texas, and Travis County, where the capital city is located. Austin area voters had supported her 59 percent to 41 percent for Bush. Just to the north, in booming Williamson County, home of Round Rock and North Austin suburbs, the numbers were reversed—58 percent for Bush and 42 percent for Richards.

In the 1996 presidential race the numbers also showed the political differences between what might be called "old Austin" and "new Austin"—Travis County voted 53 percent for President Bill Clinton, 40 percent for U.S. Senator Bob Dole, and 6 percent for H. Ross Perot, while Williamson County voted 36 percent for Clinton, 56 percent for Dole, and 7 percent for Perot.

The 1994 state election also saw Republicans achieve several significant "firsts," identified by *Dallas Morning News* political writer Carolyn Barta: In the mid-1990s the state had two Republican senators for the first time in this century; a Republican majority on the highest civil court, the Texas Supreme Court; the Texas Railroad Commission, which regulates the state's oil and gas industries, had an all-Republican membership; and the State Board of Education was dominated by Republicans.

The Republican Party continued its rise in 1998 as incumbent governor George W. Bush led a historic sweep by his party of all the major statewide races. Bush made major inroads into the traditionally Democratic Hispanic vote, winning almost 50 percent of that electorate. By 2003 Republicans held all major statewide offices and majorities in both the Texas House and Senate.

One of the best times to see the state Legislature at work is on the final day of the biennial session—usually dubbed sine die, *the Latin term meaning the final day—and pronounced with a Texas twang as "sigh-knee dye." The Texas Legislature is convened on the second Tuesday of January in odd-numbered years for a 120-day regular session. Usually,* sine die *is a hectic day marked with last-minute debate, deal making, and parties in the halls and offices of the Capitol.*

In local politics, the battle between Republicans and Democrats has not reached the critical mass that it has on the state level. Typically, the political map in Austin looks a little like a doughnut, with the new outer suburbs voting Republican and the inner, older neighborhoods voting Democratic.

City elections are, on the surface, nonpartisan, but many of the political consultants who work state races can be found aligned with various factions in city politics—generally Republicans with pro-business candidates and Democrats with pro-environment groups. The world of city politics can be a Byzantine one for newcomers—one of the most frequent questions longtime residents hear is "Why doesn't Austin have single-member districts?" (That question ranks first, followed by "Why doesn't Austin have any east-west freeways?" See our Getting Here, Getting Around chapter.)

Unlike many other Southern cities where the U.S. Justice Department has required single-member city council districts be drawn to meet voting rights laws, Austin has managed to avoid federal oversight. For years there has been what is openly called "a gentlemen's agreement" that called for one seat on the council to be designated the Hispanic seat and another to be the African-American seat. That agreement has generally held, although there have been criticisms and some changes over the years. As the city grows and more newcomers arrive, more changes are likely. Austin city politics may be the ultimate "inside baseball" game, as politicos often call under-the-surface, behind-the-scenes political games.

While politics is a full-time business for many in Austin, voter turnout has fallen, as it has across the United States. With a population passing a half million in Travis County, fewer than 100,000 voted in the 1996 primaries—40,132 in the Democratic primary and 42,978 in the Republican primary. The numbers did rise in 2000, perhaps because a favorite son governor was on the ballot. City and school bond elections attract even fewer voters, but that has not stopped politics from being the talk of the town.

FULL CIRCLE

Karma—it's a word heard a lot in Austin, a city where political consultants study yoga and politicians seek psychic renewal from a swim in the city's famed Barton Springs Pool. Karma—consider the story of the Alamo Hotel.

The old brick hotel stood at the corner of Sixth and Guadalupe Streets, a few blocks west of Congress Avenue. For decades it had been home to traveling salespeople and visitors on a budget, and the street-level cafe had been a favorite place for breakfast and lunch among downtown workers and business owners. After World War II the hotel went into a slow decline, but longtime residents, including Sam Houston Johnson, brother to President Lyndon Baines Johnson, continued to call it home. By the early 1980s it was being used as a residence hotel by folks on a budget, and several welfare agencies issued room vouchers for those down and out of luck who needed a place to stay (among the hungry young artists who stayed here were comedian Harry Anderson and his friend Turk Pipkin, a mime, juggler, and writer).

During the real estate boom of the mid-1980s, Lamar Savings bought the property, and in 1984 the Savings and Loan (S&L) announced plans to tear the hotel down and build an office/hotel high-rise. Social activist Tony Hearn and others were dismayed, since the new plans would not accommodate the needy who had received shelter at the old hotel. Hearn called the local media and announced he would put a blood curse on the property. As television cameras rolled, Hearn circled the old hotel spreading a red liquid on the ground (not blood, but vinegar and red food coloring), murmuring incantations—unless the property was dedicated to meeting the needs of the poor, no one would ever make money from it.

The hotel was torn down, although the demolition crew was plagued by problems and equipment failures. The plans for the high-rise fell apart when the S&L crisis hit. The developer, Lamar chairman Stanley Adams, eventually went to federal prison for bank fraud. The northwest corner of Sixth and Guadalupe Streets stood empty.

In the mid-1990s, Sixth Street and the warehouse district brought new life to downtown. All around the old Alamo there were signs of renewal—a '50s era paint shop became a popular bar, and another storefront was turned into a hip bistro. Austin's downtown was turning into a lively place at all hours of the day and night.

But when the U.S. Post Office built a new facility across from where the Alamo had once stood, local critics decried its stern, stark exterior with its large parking lot and drive-through mailboxes—Austin needed a pedestrian-friendly downtown, advocates declared. City planners went on full alert. So when Extended Stay America Inc. announced plans to build a residence hotel on the site of the old Alamo, a city advisory board criticized the design, saying it did not embrace the spirit of downtown Austin.

The battle was engaged in late summer 1998, but Austin residents were sending signals that what they wanted was what the Alamo had once been—a friendly place where the smells of home cooking had wafted out to the street from the ground-floor cafe and where pedestrians could walk by the lobby and see friends meeting. Changes were made to the plans, but the new hotel was just the first of many changes in downtown Austin as several high-tech companies made the move to downtown as the city entered the new century.

The battles between newcomers and old-timers, the new suburbs and the older parts of the city continue. Changing demographics, economic diversification, and shifting political tides are altering the power structure in Austin, but there are some common threads that do bind—preserving the authentic Austin experience is one of them, and that means politics.

HISTORY

A NEW REPUBLIC AND ITS CAPITAL

Sam Houston rarely lost a fight. Of all the heroes who struggled for Texas's independence from Mexico, General Houston had been the one to lead the decisive bloody conflict. His troops had captured the ruthless Mexican dictator, General Antonio Lopez de Santa Anna, at the Battle of San Jacinto on April 26, 1836. As commander-in-chief of the Texas Army, he had altered the destiny of a continent.

Houston, a towering figure of a man, was born to lead. As a youth he had gone off on his own to live among the Indians and had been accepted as a son by a chief of the Cherokees. His Indian name, *Co-lon-neh,* meaning the Raven, would add luster to his legend. Houston had served as governor of Tennessee before striking out for the wilds of Texas. He was among the courageous leaders who had signed the Texas Declaration of Independence at Washington-on-the-Brazos on March 2, 1836. And he had already served a term as the first elected president of the fledgling Republic of Texas. In many ways he was the ultimate prototype of the new Texan: tall, independent, fearless, self-assured, every bit the maverick, a hero among heroes.

And he was furious. The year was 1839, and the new president of the Republic, Mirabeau Lamar, was suggesting that Texas's permanent capital be established in the tiny hamlet of Waterloo. What insanity! The hamlet, on the banks of the Colorado River, sat in the middle of nowhere, perched on the edge of a wild frontier. The U.S. border was 250 arduous miles east at the Sabine River, while the disputed Texas-Mexico boundary stood just half that distance away at the Nueces River. Comanche Indians occupied the hills nearby. Mexican marauders could invade at any time. Besides, Houston had already secured a pledge from the Texas government that the capital would remain, at least until 1840, in the town that bore his own name—or so he thought.

Lamar had other ideas. He envisioned a Texas empire that spread far into the west. Moving the capital to the center of the Republic, he believed, would give Texas a launching point from which to carve out its future. Lamar dreamed of the newly adopted Lone Star flag sailing one day over lands still controlled by Mexico and the Indians.

While camping near Waterloo on an excursion with Texas Rangers the year before, Lamar had awakened to shouts that a buffalo herd had been spotted nearby. He rode out and shot the biggest buffalo some had ever seen. As fate would have it, his prey had been standing right on the corner of what would become the heart of downtown Austin at Congress Avenue near Eighth Street. Lamar recalled the beautiful spot when it came time to assign a commission to select Texas's permanent capital.

The new capital was to be named Austin in honor of the "Father of Texas," Stephen F. Austin, who less than 20 years before had brought the first Anglo settlers to the territory. Citizens of Houston, Washington-on-the-Brazos, Matagorda, and other Texas towns lobbied hard for the capital. But there was something about Waterloo that drew out the romantic in the roughest of men. According to articles published in the *Austin American,* Indian fighter James Jones described the scene in letters to President Lamar in 1839. "We are marching through a beautiful country—its face presents a scene of grandeur and magnificence rarely, if ever witnessed," Jones wrote. "It is the most beautiful and sublime scene. Rome itself with all its famous hills could not surpass the natural scenery of Waterloo."

Equally infatuated, commissioners investigating potential capital sites filed this report: "The imagination of even the romantic will not be disappointed on viewing the valley of the Colorado, and the fertile and gracefully undulating woodlands and luxuriant prairies at a distance from it. The most skeptical will not doubt its healthiness, and the citizen's bosom must swell with honest pride when, standing in the portico of the capitol of this country, he looks abroad upon a region worthy only of being the home of the brave and free."

Waterloo, renamed Austin, got the nod in April 1839. For the next 33 years Austin would have a precarious grip on the seat of government.

Despite objections from Sam Houston and many others who believed it was madness to venture to the very brink of civilization, Lamar moved quickly to establish the new center of government. He dispatched a veteran of the Texas Revolution, Edwin Waller, to lay out the town and begin construction of its public buildings.

"Convinced that delay would give the opposition an opportunity to crystallize, Waller resolved to have Austin ready when Congress convened in November," Austin historian David C. Humphrey wrote in his book *Austin: An Illustrated History.* "Despite the frenzied pace, Waller planned his infant city in a manner that has pleased its citizens and visitors ever since."

Waller's popularity soared in the town he designed. In January 1840 he won unanimous election as mayor by the town's 187 voters.

As the capitol and other wooden public buildings took shape along Congress Avenue (the capitol was surrounded by stockades to protect it against Indian attack) more and more souls moved to Austin, many to take jobs as public servants in the fledgling government, some

to set up private professions and businesses, still others arriving with their owners as slaves. By 1840 Austin's population had grown to 856, according to an informal census taken by a resident, the Reverend Amos Roark. The population, by Roark's count, totaled 711 whites and 145 blacks and included 75 religious people, 35 mechanics, six doctors, four lawyers, and 20 gamblers.

Sam Houston, still seething over the transfer of power to Austin, made plans to end this wild experiment once and for all. Having been reelected president of the Republic, succeeding Lamar in September 1841, Houston was provided the perfect excuse when invading Mexicans briefly recaptured San Antonio in 1842— causing nearly the whole population of Austin to flee. He ordered the official papers be transferred from Austin to Washington-on-the-Brazos, the site Houston had selected for the interim capital. In what has gone down in history as the "Archive War," however, a group of the remaining Austinites fired a cannon at their Texas brethren, and then chased them into the night to recover the papers. The following day, December 31, 1842, the victors returned the archives to Austin. Sam Houston, ever the rebel, continued to conduct his presidential business at Washington-on-the-Brazos. Austin, with no reason for existence, slipped into decline as Comanche raids grew more frequent.

This was the darkness before the dawn, as it turned out. A constitutional convention held in Austin on July 4, 1845, voted to approve the United States' offer to annex Texas. Austin was again chosen the interim capital, this time of the State of Texas. In a poignant ceremony held at high noon on February 19, 1846, Texas President Anson Jones declared, "The Republic of Texas is no more." While the decade-long experiment in frontier democracy had come to an end, its legacy would live on in generations of proud Texans yet to be born.

THE 28TH STATE

With Texas representing the 28th star on the flag of the United States, Austin's tensions could ease somewhat. The Mexican-American War, fought largely on Mexican soil, settled the international boundary far south of Austin along the Rio Grande with the 1848 Treaty of Guadalupe Hidalgo. By 1850, when Austin won another 20-year term as the state capital, the city claimed just 629 residents. Ten years later, the population had grown to 3,494, nearly a third of them slaves, as the number of government jobs grew and the private sector expanded. While the threat of Indian attack remained strong in the new capital during those years, stalwart Austinites moved ahead to build a lasting city. Texas's first permanent state capitol was open for business by 1853, and the city's master builder, Abner Cook, completed the Governor's Mansion, still in use today, by 1856. The architecturally magnificent Texas Land Office Building, which today is the Capital Complex Visitors Center, was completed by 1857. The future looked bright. Then came the Civil War—and secession.

Sam Houston had envisioned Texas as part of the United States since the early days of the Republic. Now, as the 70-year-old governor of Texas, "Old Sam" denounced the idea of seceding from the Union, despite the incendiary slavery issue and other grievances about states' rights that increasingly angered the South. In the face of growing revolt against the Union, Houston departed the Austin Governor's Mansion and traveled around the state in an attempt to prevent secession. Houston biographer Marquis James reported in *The Raven* that the aging statesman faced an angry mob in Galveston and still would not back down. "Some of you laugh to scorn the idea of bloodshed as the result of secession," Houston told the throng. "But let me tell you what is coming. You may, after the sacrifice of countless millions of treasure and hundreds of thousands of lives, as a bare possibility, win Southern independence, but I doubt it."

In February 1861, Texas voted overwhelmingly to secede. On March 16, the ever-defiant Houston stepped down as governor rather than take the oath of allegiance to the Confederacy. Despite all his former ill-will toward Austin as the capital, Houston must have taken a small degree of pleasure in learning that Austin and Travis County, as well as neighboring Williamson County, also voted against secession at first. As historian Humphrey reports so well, Austin was a slave city just as Texas was a slave state, but Austinites, like Sam Houston, "opposed efforts to precipitate Texas 'into revolution.' " After war broke out in April, however, most of tolerant Austin accepted the secession and hundreds of local men and boys marched off to battle. Four years later, Houston's dire prediction came true when the South fell.

While Austin had grown by nearly 3,000 people between 1850 and 1860, the war had taken its toll. By 1870, when Union forces (commanded for a time by General George Armstrong Custer) ended a five-year occupation of Austin, the city claimed just 4,428 residents, not even a thousand more than a decade before. A good portion were freed slaves eager to start new lives. Clarksville, still on the west side of town today, became just one of several thriving black communities that grew up during this period (see our Relocation chapter).

Austin was set to take off. But first it had to battle the city of Houston once again. Austin's 20-year term as interim capital had expired, and the issue again was to be put to a vote. The debate raged across the miles as each side volleyed nasty remarks about its opposition. Houston, according to Austinites, was home to "fetid, green-scum-covered bayous," while Austin was called a "bleak, inhospitable rocky waste," Humphrey reports. In November 1872 Austin won the vote by nearly a 2-to-1 margin over its longtime rival. Four years later, the new state constitution designated Austin the permanent capital. At long last, the issue was settled.

A THRIVING CAPITAL

The years following the Civil War became a time of unprecedented growth for Austin and for Texas as a whole. Despite the enormous suffering brought by the war, the state remained physically undamaged. While much of the South was in shambles, Texas offered huge expanses of open frontier just awaiting settlement. Southern in heritage and yet so Western in character, Texas became the great Southwestern frontier as immigrants poured in. With the coming of the railroad in 1871, Austin surged full steam ahead. The city more than doubled its 1870 population within 10 years, growing to 11,013. The newcomers arrived largely from the South but also from Europe. Germans, more than any other European ethnic group, forged new lives here, but Swedes, English, Irish, Italians, and Poles, came too. Congress Avenue and Pecan Street (now Sixth Street) became the commercial and political center of this thriving region.

The Texas Constitution, which encouraged immigration, certainly contributed to the state's, and Austin's, open attitude toward diversity as both American and foreign-born newcomers discovered a warm climate of acceptance. Great homes and commercial buildings designed to last the ages appeared on the landscape. Scholz Garten, a restaurant and beer garden built by German immigrant August Scholz in 1866, would become a popular gathering spot for Austin citizens of all nationalities during these years—and remains so to this day. Allen Hall, the first building west of the Mississippi River dedicated to the higher education of blacks, rose up on Austin's east side at Tillotson College, chartered in 1877 and opened to students by 1881. Austin, meanwhile, rallied for its next important phase.

Back in 1839, President Lamar had gained recognition as the Father of Education when, at his urging, the Congress of the Republic set aside land in each existing county to be used for public education. In Austin, a 40-acre site named

College Hill had been designated for a university. But Texas in those early days lacked the resources for such a grand scheme, so education had been left to churches and private schools. In 1854 Governor Elisha Pease had signed a bill establishing the Texas Public School System. Now it was time to do something about a university. The Constitution of 1876 called for establishment of "a university of the first class." The location for the University of Texas was to be decided by a vote of the people.

College Hill had been standing by for nearly four decades. But with the location suddenly up for grabs, town leaders throughout the state quickly moved to claim the university as their own. Ten towns, including Waco, Lampasas, Tyler, and Matagorda, vied with Austin for the honor. But Austin had an ace in the hole in a man by the name of Alexander Penn Woolridge, a New Orleans–born, Yale-educated up-and-comer. As head of the Austin campaign, Woolridge, according to Humphrey, flooded Texas with pro-Austin literature, pointing out the city's beauty, healthfulness, central location, and the fact that Austin already had land ready and waiting. East Texas voters went solidly for Tyler, but Austin triumphed. And Woolridge went on to serve Austin in one capacity or another for four decades. A wonderful downtown city park (see our Parks and Recreation chapter) is named for him. On September 15, 1883, townspeople gathered for an inaugural ceremony in the unfinished Main Building on College Hill, right on the original 40-acre site. In 1885 St. Edward's opened as a Catholic college on Austin's southern edge.

Three years later, on May 16, 1888, the youngest son of Sam Houston dedicated the magnificent new Texas State Capitol with the words, "Here glitters a structure that shall stand as a sentinel of eternity to gaze upon the ages." Presiding majestically over the hill looking down Congress Avenue, the capitol was, indeed, a site to behold.

BUILDING A VIABLE ECONOMY

Seat of government. Center of education. The twin economic pillars for Austin's development stood as solidly as the glorious new structures that served as their symbols.

Instead of bringing instant wealth to Austin, however, the University of Texas struggled in its early years.

In fact, all of Austin struggled to define its economic future. Early dreams of a commercial center ushered in by the railroad failed to materialize as rail lines spread and shippers found other cities more convenient. The Colorado River proved unnavigable, dashing hopes for lucrative barge traffic. Factories were few and far between. Still, Austin remained the seat of political power in Texas. Along with important government jobs came the prestige of catering to the state's most influential men.

Besides, if jobs didn't come from huge factories or meccas of trade, enterprising Austinites would just invent their own. Retailers, lawyers, doctors, journalists, butchers, bakers, and brewers as well as operators of boarding houses, brothels, and saloons all found work in Austin. Builders certainly didn't lack work. Some of Austin's finest historic buildings today, including the regal hotel built by cattle baron Jesse Driskill, opened in the latter decades of the 19th century. The distinguished neighborhood of Hyde Park in then far North Austin, which touted electric street car service, got its start during this period and became Austin's first suburb (see our Relocation chapter), while celebrated European sculptor Elizabet Ney set about building her elegant Hyde Park studio. A few blocks west of Congress Avenue, a neighborhood of wealthy merchants and bankers rose up. Churches, hospitals, and a courthouse dotted the Austin landscape, along with two grand opera houses that served the growing population's desire for cultural entertainment. Contributing to that scene were locally formed bands as well as the Austin Saengerrunde, a singing society founded by the city's German immigrants in 1879.

By the late 1880s Austin's growing number of professors and students bestowed a scholarly touch on the region, while the presence of the artist Ney and the short-story writer who would later become famous as O. Henry foreshadowed future artistic and literary communities. O. Henry would later give Austin one of its most endearing nicknames, "the City of the Violet Crown," in honor of the purplish cast that emerges over the city at dusk. (Some say the color comes from the cedar pollen in the air.)

"Austin's diverse population grew like the town itself during these years," historian John Edward Weems wrote in the 1989 *Austin American–Statesman* supplement "Austin 1839–1989." "The diversity helped give the town a degree of tolerance that, however slight at first and however imperfect still today, broadened into an accommodation of people with a remarkable variety of beliefs and lifestyles."

Through it all, dreams of commerce and manufacturing remained strong among some of Austin's leaders. By 1893 Austinites gathered to celebrate the opening of a new million-dollar dam on the Colorado River and the beautiful lake it created. The dam was aimed at producing enough hydroelectric power for both the city and for the manufacturing plants city officials expected would come along to propel Austin to prosperity. Lake McDonald, named for John McDonald, the building contractor-turned-mayor who had championed the dam, quickly became the city's prime recreational center. Accompanied by their dapper escorts, fashionable ladies wearing flower-topped bonnets boarded the great steamers *Ben Hur* and the *Belle of Austin* for relaxing cruises on the lake by day and dances by night. Rowing regattas at the lake attracted sports enthusiasts from around the world. Sunbathers and swimmers relaxed on shore, while the town elite snapped up resort properties along the perimeter.

Despite its increasingly civilized appearance, Austin retained much of its frontier flavor during the last two decades of the 19th century. In 1881 Austinites exhibited a mixture of tolerance and plain common sense by electing Ben Thompson to the job of city marshal. Thompson, considered the best gunfighter in the West by many, was also one of Pecan Street's most notorious gamblers. "During his tenure as marshal, it was claimed that major crime dropped to an all-time low," wrote Larry Willoughby in his book, *Austin: An Historical Portrait.* Unfortunately, the colorful Thompson resigned in 1882 to face murder charges in San Antonio and was killed later in a saloon shoot-out. Well into the 1890s, according to Humphrey, "Cowboys were familiar figures, and horses tied to hitching posts lined dusty Congress Avenue. Along the east side of the Avenue the saloons, cowmen, and gamblers were so thick in the evenings that 'ladies' would not think of walking there."

Austin's red-light district grew into an enterprise during these years. Located west of Congress Avenue and called Guy Town, "it was not at all an unpopular part of town for many men—Austin residents, male visitors, and legislators," reported Weems. "It was said that additional women were brought in when the state government blossomed into full lawmaking activity."

THE 20TH CENTURY

Austin's Wild West spirit didn't disappear overnight, but the coming of the 20th century marked the beginning of its decline. By New Year's Day 1900 Austin's eyes were clearly focused on the future—and progress. Only one small item appeared on the front page of the local paper that day to indicate anything might be awry in the land of opportunity. "Saturday and yesterday some alarmists were busy circulating the report that there were great leaks in the powerhouse, in the dam, in the lake, and everywhere else out at the

power and light plant up the river," the article said. "Superintendent Patterson stated that they were without foundation." Austin got busy with its plans for the new century.

Whether those "alarmist" reports were true at the time mattered little just three months later when the skies unleashed a torrent of rain. On April 7, 1900, dreams of turning Austin into a manufacturing center were literally swept away along with the seven-year-old dam in a devastating flood that cost at least eight lives, destroyed everything in its path, and left Austin without power for several months. When Austin overcame the shock enough to take stock of its situation—no big business, no big industry—city leaders determined to make the best of it. Austin's economic future would be built on the twin pillars of education and government the city had fought so hard to win in the past. Besides, they reasoned, Austin was just a beautiful place to live.

Growth and progress were now the name of the game. Wide and stately, yet made of dirt for more than 60 years, Congress Avenue was finally paved with brick in 1905, while a new concrete bridge replaced a rickety iron bridge across the Colorado River at Congress. "By 1910, Austin had its own skyscrapers, the Scarbrough and Littlefield buildings. The horseless carriage was no longer considered an intrusion into the lives of 'civilized' people, and as early as 1910 the automobile was an invaluable part of Austin's lifestyle and economy. When the first airplane landed in Austin in 1911, the 20th century had really arrived," wrote Willoughby.

COLOR BARRIERS

While Austinites had always made time for leisure and cultural activities, the coming of the industrial age made those pursuits even easier. Austin's new Majestic Theater (now the Paramount) opened in 1915, hosting major touring acts from around the country. Two years later the Austin Symphony Orchestra presented its first concert. Human habitation at Barton Springs, the jewel in a town endowed by enormous natural beauty, has been traced back several thousand years, but the arrival of the automobile made trips to this glorious swimming hole easier for "modern" Austinites. In 1917 Colonel A. J. Zilker gave the city hundreds of acres around the springs for use as a park. UT football, first played in 1893, became a popular spectator sport in the 1900s, along with the horse races that thrilled the crowds in Hyde Park. Grand balls attended by the city's most fashionable citizens continued at the elegant Driskill Hotel, while the lovely Hyde Park Pavilion hosted other stylish affairs.

Hyde Park, however, was an exclusively Anglo community; its posh gatherings were barred to Austin's minorities, as was Barton Springs, to name just two. Austin's black citizens, who had enjoyed some acceptance during Reconstruction, were now subjected to segregation and discrimination. As far back as 1885 a group of citizens in one ward had formed an "Anti-Colored Movement" to block the reelection of a black city councilmember, Humphrey reported. During the first decade of the 1900s Austin's color barrier became as distinct as in many other cities throughout the South. While the white-robed Ku Klux Klan paraded through Austin streets undeterred, blacks sat in a separate section on streetcars, attended separate schools, drank from separate drinking fountains, and used separate public rest rooms—when such facilities could be found. They also increasingly congregated on Austin's east side, away from their Anglo oppressors. Austin's many black professionals—doctors, lawyers, dentists, pastors, as well as business owners—found a racially mixed district to work in but remained excluded from Austin "society." Not until 1950 would the first black student be admitted to the UT law school—under order from the U.S. Supreme Court.

Austin's small but growing Mexican-American population also faced treatment that would be considered despicable today. Most of the town's Mexicans had been chased out of town during the 1850s, while those that had followed found themselves still considered foreigners, despite their birthright. Even worse, some Austinites counted them as enemies because of the Texas Revolution, forgetting that many Mexicans living in the region during the war had fought—and died—for Texas.

By 1910 Austin claimed not quite 30,000 citizens. Houston, already a railroading and shipping center, witnessed huge industrial development following Texas's first great oil strike in the region in 1901. Its population had surged to nearly 79,000 by 1910. Dallas, enjoying success as a center for insurance, banking, commerce, and the cotton trade, had skyrocketed to 92,000 people. Following World War I, Austin's population had increased by just 5,000, while Houston and Dallas soared to 128,000 and 156,000, respectively.

Although not cash rich at the beginning of the Roaring '20s, the University of Texas did own a great deal of land, including 2 million acres in West Texas, some of it leased to oil speculators. On Monday morning, May 28, 1923, the Santa Rita oil well blew in a gusher of black gold. The Big Lake Oil Field out west would continue to pump riches into the Permanent University Fund for nearly seven decades. Wealthy for the first time in its 40-year history, UT went on a building spree.

THE "ATHENS OF THE WEST"

Now city officials really had something to brag about. Besides the rapidly growing UT, Austin also claimed St. Edward's University on the south side and two black colleges on the east. Austin was indeed becoming the center of culture, learning, and politics that leaders had envisioned. They began touting Austin as the "Athens of the West," and citizens responded by earmarking funds to develop the city. Parks and playgrounds, wide boulevards, and public buildings rose up. Austin's population more than doubled during the 1920s and 1930s, hitting nearly 88,000 by 1940.

UT's spending binge, coupled with an influx of local and federal funds, staved off the worst of the Great Depression for Austin, according to local historians. One of the city's most treasured landmarks today, the 27-story UT Tower, was among many buildings completed on campus during the 1920s and 1930s. President Roosevelt's New Deal, solidly backed by Austin's ubiquitous new mayor, Tom Miller, brought millions in construction funds to the area through the Works Progress Administration (WPA). Camp Mabry on Austin's west side, home to the Texas Volunteer Guard since 1891, mushroomed with new WPA construction, as did other areas of the city. By late 1936, when *Forbes* magazine reported that Austin was one of the "bright spots in the nation," it appeared the worst of the Depression was over. And yet Miller, along with Austin's newly elected U.S. Representative, Lyndon Johnson, won for Austin the country's first federal housing project, completed in 1939 for the city's rapidly expanding Mexican-American population.

Miller, who would remain at the forefront of Austin business and politics throughout the '30s, '40s, and even well into the '50s, was responsible in many ways for fashioning modern Austin. A liberal among liberal Democrats of the era, Miller was a master politician who worked to gain support from all three sectors of Austin's increasingly tri-racial community. Although he did support racial segregation (not unusual even for liberal Southerners of the era), Miller nonetheless promoted equal civil rights for all.

"Miller was one of those fairly numerous anomalies in the South—the good businessman, the deep Southerner, who also stood strong on behalf of much of Roosevelt's New Deal, and Truman's Fair

Deal, civil rights, and the like," according to Anthony M. Orum, author of *Power, Money & the People: The Making of Modern Austin*. Low-income housing extended to blacks and Mexican Americans under his reign, while Miller also saw to it that East Austin's black community received basic city services. The lovely Rosewood Park that remains today was commissioned by Miller. His broader vision, however, remained on the city's future growth.

Among Miller's greatest coups was his success—along with LBJ—in getting federal Depression-era funds to complete the Austin Dam (now named in his honor) by 1940. Two years later, construction of the Mansfield Dam that created Lake Travis wrapped up efforts around these parts to bring the unpredictable Colorado River under control.

SHAPING THE FUTURE

On December 7, 1941, the United States went to war. While Austin's youth waged battle on far-off fronts, loved ones remained at home, sharing with the rest of the country in the hardships of scarcity and rationing—and the fear that a knock on the door would mean a son, husband, brother, or even a daughter had paid the ultimate price. In 1943 Congressman Johnson and his wife, University of Texas graduate Lady Bird Johnson, bought small Austin radio station KTBC. Nine years later, on Thanksgiving Day 1952, KTBC became Central Texas's first television station. What more important event could have been chosen as a first broadcast during the heyday of the postwar years? The station aired the football game between arch rivals UT and Texas A&M. UT, of course, prevailed.

According to Humphrey, the seeds of Austin's eventual blossoming as a high-tech mecca were also planted in the 1940s with the creation of the Austin Area Economic Development Foundation. Established in 1948 with C. B. Smith as president, the council "foreshadowed and helped shape what was to come," Humphrey wrote. "Smith's foundation sought to diversify Austin's economy in a manner compatible with its 'way of life.' Research and development laboratories and high technology companies fit the bill."

Austin would also elect its first woman city council member in 1948. Interestingly, Emma Long was not just a female version of the reigning power elite but "an avowed enemy of the city establishment and a champion of the underdog," as Weems described her.

GAINING NEW SENSIBILITIES

Meanwhile, somewhere during the second half of the 1940s, Austin's population hit 100,000 as the city became one of the fastest growing cities in the Southwest. By 1950 the population had reached 132,459. While nowhere near the size of Houston or Dallas, or even San Antonio, Austin had nevertheless turned into a thriving metropolis.

The time to address some long-ignored social injustices had arrived. Heman Marion Sweatt's victorious Supreme Court battle to gain admission to the UT law school in 1950 opened UT's doors to other black graduate students. Six years later, by decree of the UT Board of Regents, the university admitted its first black undergraduates, while Austin's public schools began the excruciatingly slow process of integration. In 1954 UT graduate and social activist Ronnie Dugger debuted the *Texas Observer* in Austin. Within months the small biweekly magazine had established itself as the liberal voice in Texas media, reporting on lynchings in East Texas. (The *Observer* continues its mission as a liberal voice in Texas media to this day.) As the tide for racial equality swelled across the United States, students at UT and the city's other colleges spearheaded the Austin movement of the 1950s and 1960s.

The movement, however, reached beyond UT and the city's other campuses to extend deep into the community. As a result, Austin experienced nascent political and social enlightenment as established barriers against minorities slowly cracked. Black and Mexican-American communities began taking places in positions of power by the late '60s and into the '70s.

While UT "radical" politics reached back decades, the university boomed during the 1960s as a haven for serious social activists and the hippies who brought their music and their faith in flower power. Austin's antiwar protesters took to the streets throughout the decade as public opinion against the Vietnam War surged. (In May 1970 students led Austin's largest protest of the Vietnam era following the deaths of four students in Ohio during an antiwar demonstration at Kent State University.)

UT enrollment had swelled to more than 25,000 by 1966, although only about half remained on campus for the summer session. The morning of August 1, 1966, dawned like any other hot, lazy summer day in the city. A few hours later, Austin became the site of what was then the largest simultaneous mass murder in American history when a heavily armed 25-year-old UT student and ex-Marine climbed the beloved campus tower and commenced firing. Charles Whitman, who had murdered his mother and his wife the night before, fired round after round at unsuspecting victims below, killing 14 people and wounding 31 more before he was finally shot to death by Austin police. The 19-minute melee would spawn debate across the country over the issue of gun control.

At the epicenter of America's turbulent 1960s stood Lyndon Johnson, the former school teacher who had risen to political power from his boyhood home 50 miles southwest of Austin. A century had passed since Sam Houston stared Southern slave owners in the face—and lost. Now another tall Texan was storming the bastion of bigotry. He had already guided two civil rights measures through the Senate and as president was fighting for passage of a landmark civil rights act. Angry Southerners rebuked Johnson and Lady Bird at every turn, but the Texas leader prevailed. Johnson signed the Civil Rights Act of 1964 and the Voting Rights Act a year later. Johnson, however, would be judged at the time not for his efforts on behalf of human rights nor for the dozens of education bills and social reform measures he championed, but for drawing the United States further into the mire of the Vietnam War. Battered by public opinion against the war, Johnson chose not to seek reelection in 1968. He and Lady Bird returned home to their Central Texas ranch.

THE UPS AND DOWNS

While live music concerts had formed part of the Austin lifestyle since its earliest days, the 1960s would see the city boom with musicians of all kinds. Among UT's growing "folkie" music crowd was a shy freshman named Janis Joplin, who performed first on campus and later at a popular beer joint called Threadgill's. Later came the psychedelic sounds, rock and roll, the blues, and the country rock that would eventually turn Austin into the Live Music Capital of the World.

The '60s brought much more than music and social change, however. Attracted by UT's excellent reputation for research and development and by the city's attractive surroundings, high-tech manufacturers moved in. By the end of the decade, Austin claimed three major technology plants: IBM, Texas Instruments, and Tracor. The high-tech revolution had arrived.

By 1970 Austin's population topped a quarter million. UT had mushroomed to more than 40,000 students. The number of city, county, state, and federal government employees reached into the thousands, and high-tech firms had become the city's largest private employers. The Armadillo World Headquarters opened in 1970 and soon earned a nationwide reputation as a hot live music venue. Austin's cultural explosion during this decade extended into the areas of writing, theater, and visual arts as more and more artists found themselves drawn to the city.

In the summer of 1970, just a couple of months after UT students rallied 25,000 people for a march in protest of the Kent State shootings, a group of UT students gathered to map out a plan for Austin's future. Among the students was Jeffrey Friedman, a law school student who had taken a leadership role in the protest march. Armed with the knowledge that the voting age was about to be lowered from 21 to 18, and realizing that students could register by proclaiming they intended to remain in Austin after graduation, the group determined to register thousands of university students. That accomplished, Friedman and a slate of other liberal candidates decided to challenge the existing power structure.

Friedman, according to Orum, "wanted things to be better in East Austin for the browns and the blacks. He wanted the poor people to have better jobs and better housing. But he also wanted to bring down the forces of the Establishment. He wanted to bring down the rich and the powerful." For his part, Friedman's conservative opponent, Wick Fowler, ran on a platform "that hippies were unfit to hold public office."

While the conservative business sector claimed the majority of seats on the council that year, Friedman won his race to become the first student and youngest council member. Berl Handcox also won election, becoming the first African American to serve on the city council since the 1880s. Five years later Friedman became Austin's youngest mayor in what Orum called "the watershed council election of 1975, in which the majority of those elected were liberals." Among those voted in was John Trevino, Austin's first Mexican-American council member.

TREE HUGGERS UNITE

Apart from the frustration over establishment politics that colored the 1970s, Austin's population explosion became a source of increasing consternation.

Longtime residents mourned the good ol' days and expressed fears that Austin's scenic beauty was being bulldozed away to make way for expressways, shopping malls, housing developments, and sky-scrapers. The slogan "Keep Austin Austin" became a popular rallying cry during these years.

Austin's increasingly powerful environmental protection groups successfully thwarted major development in several environmentally sensitive areas, while helping to keep the protection of Austin's natural endowments on the minds of old-timers and newcomers alike—as well as on the front burner of local politics. Lady Bird Johnson, who divided her time between Austin and her ranch nearby, spearheaded a project to beautify Town Lake, which led to the planting of thousands of trees as well as construction of a hike-and-bike trail and gazebos. Austin had indeed changed radically from its days as a small, sleepy town. But of the nearly 94,000 new residents who would move into Austin during the '70s, the majority would still be left breathless by the city's natural appeal—and still are today.

By the mid-1980s nothing appeared to stand in the way of continued growth. The economy boomed as more high-tech industries moved into Central Texas, bringing investment dollars and plenty of jobs. Austinite Michael Dell started his own little computer company in 1984 to add to the high-tech landscape. Housing costs rose, then skyrocketed, as Austin's population continued to expand. Banks made exorbitant loans, with little money down, as real estate speculators and tycoon developers snapped up residential and commercial properties around the region.

Then the bubble burst. Downturns in oil prices—which had already hurt many parts of Texas—contributed to the problem, as did a slump in the technology field, but many economists pointed to the overheated real estate economy as the leading cause of Austin's recession. For a while during the second half of the decade, it appeared that more people were leaving the city than moving in. Real estate prices plummeted, businesses failed, bankruptcies became common, offices closed. By the end of the decade, according to reports, Austin led the country in the percentage of vacant office space and topped all other Texas cities for amount of indebtedness.

THE HIGH-TECH ERA IGNITES

Austin entered 1990 with a gloomy economic forecast. The United States as a whole was in recession, banks remained in turmoil, and another U.S. president who claimed Texas as home, George Bush, was preparing to declare war on Iraq. Despite earlier indications, however, Austin's population had grown by nearly 120,000 people during the past decade. In 1993 Apple Computer bought 129 acres in neighboring Williamson County for a financial services and customer support site. That same year, Motorola announced plans to build a $1 billion chip plant in Northeast Austin. Meanwhile, young Austinites Richard Linklater and Robert Rodriguez had each made a low-budget, wildly successful film (*Slacker* and *El Mariachi,* respectively) that was to skyrocket them to Hollywood—and help put the Austin film scene on the map. (See the Close-up in The Arts chapter). All the while, the beat of Austin music pulsated in every corner of the city.

By the end of the decade, Austin was riding the crest of another wave in growth and development as Central Texas solidified its reputation as one of the country's leading high-tech hubs. Dell Computer had grown to become the city's largest private employer and the world's third-largest maker of personal computers, with more than $12 billion in annual sales. Samsung built a $1.3 billion Austin plant. Computer manufacturers and chip makers, however, formed just part of the scene. Local start-up companies focusing on software development and the Internet also swelled during the '90s.

Along with the economic good times came increasing pressures. Rampant growth became the norm as the city expanded by about 1,500 inhabitants each month throughout the decade. Signs of the changing times were clearly visible everywhere as roads jammed, office space diminished, trees were sacrificed to make way for housing and commercial developments, and school districts scrambled to build new facilities to keep up with expanding enrollment.

As a result, a new phrase entered the Austin lexicon in 1998: "Smart Growth." Aiming to develop a city that grew "smart" as it grew fast, the Austin City Council and then-Mayor Kirk Watson presented a series of initiatives designed to protect the environment and to limit sprawl, especially into environmentally sensitive areas, by encouraging development inside the city. Race relations, often ignored in the past, also climbed on the city agenda as more enlightened leaders sought to bring some sense of community to a city that remained fractured in many respects—despite important strides among Austin's minority racial and ethnic groups over the past 40 years.

SINGING THE BLUES

If Austin ever really needed a reason to party, the dawn of the 21st century provided an excellent excuse. Indeed, on December 31, 1999, an estimated 260,000 revelers packed Austin's "A2K" downtown bash. And why not? These were technological boom times, and the venture capital was flowing as freely as the beer. If the U.S. economy was hot, Austin's was red hot. Jobs were plentiful, high-tech salaries soared, and the stock market skyrocketed. Locally, dot-coms glittered among the investment darlings of the "new" Internet economy, while the region's chip makers were selling their goods as fast and furious as Frito-Lay. To the enormous relief of tormented Austin techies, and the partygoers on Sixth Street, the ominously predicted Y2K bug never even hatched.

By March 2000, Austin officials had signed deals with two computer biggies, software manufacturer Computer Sciences Corp. (CSC) and Intel Corp., to build giant complexes downtown—the heart of Smart Growth territory. These were to be the first in a string of computer companies whose presence in the city center would create a "Downtown Digital District" and thus rejuvenate the entire area. The building boom extended even further as the construction of office towers, posh condominiums, and lofts changed the face of downtown forever.

True, Austin's $600 million annual music industry was feeling a pinch as musicians struggled to find affordable housing and clubs faced escalating costs. Austin already had lost three great music venues: Steamboat, the Electric Lounge, and, perhaps worst of all, Liberty Lunch. The Lunch, an Austin leader in live music for nearly a quarter of a century, was demolished to make room for the pending CSC complex and a proposed new City Hall. The city's poor also suffered. Not only had the number of poor increased, but the gap between the lowest- and highest-paid workers in the private sector had doubled. The basic cost of living increased as demands for goods and services by the area's high-salaried consumers—and the droves of new Central Texas residents—drove prices up. In fact, when census figures came in, the Austin Metropolitan Statistical area, which includes Austin's Travis County as well as neighboring Bastrop, Caldwell, Hays, and Williamson Counties, had burgeoned to nearly 1.25 million people—and still the people poured in.

The stock market rollover of April 14, 2000, caused little more than a sprinkle on the long-running Austin parade. By August another computer biggie, Austin's Vignette Corp., announced plans to spend more than $100 million on its new downtown complex. Meanwhile, the man living in the Austin Governor's Mansion, George W. Bush, had clinched the Republican nomination for president and would by year's end become the third U.S. president from Texas.

A year that had started on such a high note, however, then went flat. By the end of 2001 Austin musicians weren't the only ones singing the blues. The Central Texas economy had witnessed its worst downturn in a decade. The stock market plummeted, consumer confidence vanished, venture capital dried up, the chip industry melted, and many developers pulled the plug on downtown plans. To make matters worse, the entire nation was reeling from the September 11 terrorist attacks. The results of Austin's economic downturn included thousands of workers—especially high-wage earners—layed off, foreclosures on expensive homes and office buildings, shrinking retail sales, school districts scrambling to make ends meet, and cutbacks in state and local government budgets. These were the norm well into 2003. CSC did complete its downtown complex, and several other new public and private buildings graced the skyline. Fairly or not, however, Intel's abandoned skeleton of a high-rise stood for years as a grim reminder of better days. In 2003 Mayor Will Wynn and the Austin City Council quietly replaced the Smart Growth plan with a far more extensive economic development policy.

Still, the region's economic picture looked somewhat brighter by late in the year, and some economists—noting increases in venture capital, modest improvements in the high-tech industry, and a bottoming out in job losses—predicted that the worst of the recession was over.

THE BEAUTIFUL AND THE SUBLIME

As the new century builds up steam, debates over Austin's future rage on. Yet the city's heart and soul have managed to survive. Ever true to their eccentric roots, Austinites have embraced a new slogan: "Keep Austin Weird." The phrase, appearing on bumper stickers, T-shirts, event promos, and even on shot glasses, just about says it all. Austin is not the city some old-timers remember; but then again, the generations before them most likely said the same. For the thousands of newcomers who are seeing it for the first time, however, Austin remains one of the prettiest, most vibrant spots on the planet. Austin's once-forlorn downtown is experiencing a renaissance to become a thriving center for culture and entertainment. Live music pours from clubs all over greater downtown as the Live Music Capital of the World continues to attract the young, the restless, and the talented. UT's influence on the arts has helped spawn entire communities of performing and visual artists, writers, and filmmakers. Austin's enduring youthful spirit and creative energy add a luster that is as much a hallmark of this city as the State Capitol and the UT Tower.

The Texas pioneers who first laid eyes on this "beautiful and sublime scene" 165 years ago could not possibly have envisioned the Austin of today. And yet, in countless ways, Austin remains ever so sublime.

GETTING HERE, GETTING AROUND

X marks the spot, and smack dab in the middle of Texas is Austin. There is an old saying in the Lone Star State: "The sun has riz and the sun has set, and I ain't outta Texas yet." That says a lot about traversing the state. Austin is about a three-hour drive south of Dallas, a little less than a three-hour drive west of Houston, and a little more than an hour north of San Antonio. It is about a five-hour drive to Nuevo Laredo, Mexico; a five-hour drive to both the Louisiana and Oklahoma borders; and if you are heading west to New Mexico, plan on taking all day for the eight-hours-plus drive.

I-35, often called the Nafta Highway (a reference to the North American Free Trade Agreement), bisects the state from north to south, running from Laredo on the Mexican border up through the middle of the country to the Canadian border. I-10 runs from the Louisiana border through Houston, south of Austin through San Antonio and on to El Paso. U.S. 290 connects Houston to Austin and then joins I-35 for a short stretch, cuts west through the Oak Hill area of Austin and off into the Hill Country.

Austin is literally deep in the heart of Texas. Here are some tips on getting here—and getting around once you have arrived.

---

i *A variety of names were suggested for Austin's new international airport, but city officials decided to stick with the name given to the Air Force base that occupied the site. It was named in honor of Austin's first World War II casualty, Captain J. A. Bergstrom.*

AIRPORTS/COMMERCIAL

Austin-Bergstrom International Airport
3600 Presidential Boulevard
(512) 530–ABIA: General Information;
8:00 A.M. to 5:00 P.M., Monday–Friday
(512) 530–COPS: Airport Police and Lost and Found, 24-hour number
(512) 530–PAGE: Paging, 24-hour number
(512) 530–2242: Parking Information, 24-hour number
www.ci.austin.tx.us/austinairport
Austin was the only city in the United States to embark on a major airport building program as the 20th century drew to a close. In the spring of 1999, the city shut down the municipal airport near downtown Austin, Robert Mueller Municipal Airport, and opened a new international facility in the southeast sector of the city called Austin-Bergstrom International Airport.

The same airlines and rental car companies serve the new $690 million airport, but the facility is much larger with twice as many gates, two runways (as opposed to one) aptly named for two famous Texas politicians, President Lyndon Baines Johnson and Congressman JJ "Jake" Pickler, and a much larger terminal, named in honor of the late Texas congresswoman Barbara Jordan. Austin-Bergstrom has a two-level access road (one level for arrivals, the other for departures) and a three-level parking garage.

The site of the old airport is expected to be developed as a mixed-use community with homes, apartments, shops, businesses, and green spaces.

The designers and builders sought to evoke the spirit of Austin at the new facility by including a stage in the terminal for live music performances and Hill Country landscaping by using water elements, rocks, and native plants. The new terminal includes a business center, 12 restaurants and snack shops (some of them operated by local businesses such as Amy's Ice Cream, Book People, and the Salt Lick barbecue), retail shops, and bookstores. The restaurants and snack bars sell food at "street prices," rather than the inflated prices often found at airports. The retail stores feature regional items, including music by Austin musicians and works by local artists and crafters.

The airport also offers guided tours for groups of adults and children (five years and older). Reservations are necessary; call the program at (512) 530-2242. There is also an outdoor family viewing area (with a parking area and picnic tables) on the west side of Highway 71 East, near the east runway, where one acre has been set aside for visitors to watch planes take off and land.

The parking garage next to the terminal provides 2,419 covered short-term public parking spaces on the first and second levels. Car rental returns are located on the third level. There is a close-in surface parking lot (Lot A) near the terminal and several outlying long-term lots (Lots B, C, D, E, F, and G), providing 8,947 parking spaces. Shuttle buses run every 7 to 10 minutes and 24 hours a day from the parking lots. Airport shuttles from all surface parking lots pick up at shuttle stops within the lots and discharge departing passengers in front of the terminal on the lower baggage level. Airport parking shuttles pick up arriving passengers outside the lower baggage level in front of the terminal and take them to surface parking lots.

Wheelchair-accessible parking is available free for up to five days in the parking garage and up to ten days in all parking lots. Wheelchair-accessible parking spots are located on the first available row in the garage and near the shuttle stops in all surface parking lots. Shuttle buses are equipped with wheelchair lifts.

Transportation to and from the Airport

There is a transportation information desk on the ground floor of the terminal. Passengers arriving and departing from the airport have several options, in addition to rental cars and their own personal automobiles. SuperShuttle provides door-to-door minivan service for a fixed fee for one-way rides. Fees are determined by the zip code of destination or pickup. The shuttles also are available for groups at charter rates. Contact SuperShuttle at (512) 258-3826, or make reservations online at www.supershuttle.com.

Capital Metro (see listing below) also offers local bus service between downtown Austin and the airport, linking to other bus routes in the city; www.capmetro.austin.tx.us.

AIRPORTS/GENERAL AVIATION

There are two fixed-base operators at Austin-Bergstrom International Airport. Both provide general aviation terminals, hangars, maintenance, and fuel facilities and access to the adjacent instrumented 9,000-foot runway. They provide 170 spaces, including 50 T-hangar spaces for small aircraft.

Trajen Flight Support, L.P.
4309 General Aviation Avenue
(512) 530-7000
www.airnav.com/airport/KAUS/TRAJEN

The pink granite on the outer walls of the new Austin-Bergstrom International Airport comes from Marble Falls, west of the city, and is the same type of granite used at the State Capitol.

Signature Flight Support
4321 General Aviation Avenue
(512) 530-5451
www.airnav.com/airport/KAUS/
SIGNATURE

Lakeway
115 Flying Scott Road
(512) 261-4385
www.3r9.com
Operated by Lakeway Airpark Association, a cooperative, this private facility is non-profit and unattended. There is a 4,000-foot landing strip open from sunrise to sunset plus self-serve gas facilities. Overnight parking is $5.00, but that is waived with gas purchase. The landing strip is 15.5 statute miles from Austin. The association reminds pilots there is a noise ordinance in place, plus pilots should watch for the deer grazing near the landing strip.

AIR CHARTERS

Capitol Wings
4321 General Aviation Avenue
(512) 530-1700
www.capitolwings.com
Capitol Wings' fleet ranges from a Cessna 414 four-seater to a large Gulfstream III jet. The company, located in the general aviation area of Austin-Bergstrom International Airport, also provides turnkey aircraft management services, flight crews, tie-down services, hangar space, and maintenance management.

McRae Aviation
4309 General Aviation Avenue
(512) 385-9615
www.mcraeaviation.com
McRae offers jet charters and light cargo service from its location at the general aviation area of Austin-Bergstrom International Airport.

TRAIN STATIONS

There are several recreational trains for sight-seeing in the Austin area. (For more information on recreational trains, see our Attractions chapter).

Amtrak
250 North Lamar Boulevard
(512) 476-5684,
(800) 872-7245 reservations
www.amtrak.com
North/south service is available four times a week on the Amtrak Eagle. Northbound trains leave on Sunday, Tuesday, Wednesday, and Thursday mornings; southbound on Sunday, Wednesday, Friday, and Saturday evenings. The north route goes through Dallas to Chicago, the south route goes to San Antonio. Fares to San Antonio range from $9.00 to $17.00, depending on how close to departure time reservations are made; fares to Dallas range from $20 to $40. Children 2 to 15 travel for half price with an adult. East-west service is available from San Antonio; that route connects Los Angeles with Miami.

BUS SERVICES

Bus service within the city of Austin is covered in the Public Transportation section.

Greyhound
816 East Koenig Lane
(512) 458-4463, (800) 231-2222
www.greyhound.com
The intercity bus station is near Highland Mall, just west of the intersection of U.S. 290 East and I-35. Greyhound offers service to more than 2,500 U.S. cities.

Kerrville Bus Co., Inc.
(512) 389-0319, (800) 231-2222
This Texas-grown bus company is also served by the Greyhound station facility (see previous listing). Kerrville serves several Texas cities and small towns.

ROADWAYS

Austin sits at the crossroads of two major highways: I–35 and U.S. 290. That sounds simple, but as visitors and newcomers to Austin quickly discover, the picture gets muddied first by a local propensity for calling highways by names other than the state highway department designations, and second by the absence of any clear east-west routes in the center of the city.

In this section we'll give you a primer on the major roads, their official names and the names they are called by the locals, and then a discussion of Austin traffic and the peculiarities of getting around the city by car.

I–35 runs right through the middle of the city, heading south to San Antonio and on to the Mexican border, heading north to Waco, Dallas–Fort Worth, and points north.

U.S. 290 runs from Houston westward to the northeast section of Austin where it is called U.S. 290 East. It merges with I–35, emerging again in South Austin as U.S. 290 West, where it is called Ben White Boulevard.

Texas Highway 71 merges with U.S. 290 West at I–35 through the southern and southwestern section of the city, separating at what locals call the "Y" in Oak Hill. U.S. 290 West heads west to Johnson City, while Highway 71 heads northwest to Bee Cave and the Highland Lakes.

U.S. 183 runs diagonally through the city from northwest (at Cedar Park) to southeast (near the new Austin-Bergstrom International Airport). It has numerous names along its route (see discussion of east-west roads below).

The MoPac Expressway, called Loop 1 on all the highway signs, runs north-south through the western environs of the city. The locals just call it MoPac, as we do throughout this book.

Loop 360, or the Capital of Texas Highway, runs north-south through far West Austin. Businesses along this roadway use Capital of Texas Highway in their addresses, but the locals usually call it "360." We use both in this book.

R.M. 620 is a primarily north-south road that swings around Austin in the Hill Country west of Lake Austin and east of Lake Travis. Usually called just "620." The designation R.M. means Ranch-to-Market road, a leftover from the days when the state built highways so that farmers and ranchers could bring their goods and cattle to town. Some roads are called R.M., while others are F.M. (Farm-to-Market).

One thing you can count on in Austin: Whenever you hear people complaining about the traffic, economic times are good. When times are bad, folks have other things on their minds. There is also an ongoing major debate on whether a light rail should be developed in the greater Austin area.

Commute times have become longer as the city has grown, but they pale in comparison with commutes in some of America's larger cities. During morning and evening rush hours (6:30 to around 9:00 A.M. and 4:30 to 7:00 P.M.) traffic slows to a crawl on the area's major roadways, notably I–35, MoPac, and U.S. 183. At other times, driving in Austin is relatively easy.

Perhaps the biggest problem in navigating Austin streets is the fact that there is no major east-west freeway in the heart of the city. In the north, U.S 183 (at intervals called Research Boulevard, Anderson Lane, Ed Bluestein Boulevard, and Bastrop Highway) has been widened and improved, while in the southern end of the city U.S. 290 West (known as Ben White Boulevard for much of its length) has been widened and turned into a freeway from I–35 to Oak Hill. Construction on U.S. 290 has been completed through Oak Hill, but there is a daily afternoon bottleneck as U.S. 290 spills into the "Y" intersection at the western end of Oak Hill, where U.S. 290 heads west and Highway 71 heads northwest.

As for a midtown freeway, the issue has been a major political football for years as older central city neighborhoods have fought attempts to widen their streets. Koenig Lane, which becomes

Rural Route 2222 west of MoPac, has been touted as a possible route, but the idea is opposed by residents in that area. Enfield Road/15th Street, which leads from west of MoPac to the State Capitol, has been considered as another possible route. However, it goes through one of Austin's oldest, wealthiest, and most politically influential neighborhoods, so that idea has been a virtual nonstarter.

A third option for a midtown thoroughfare is Cesar Chavez Boulevard, which for part of its length is now one-way. Cesar Chavez Boulevard does link I-35 with MoPac, but it also runs along Town Lake, and citizens have been loath to speed up traffic adjacent to the city's premier park or sacrifice any park land just to widen a roadway.

When it comes to north-south streets, Austin does have several freeways that offer nonstop driving. The major roadway, and the one on which most visitors arrive, is I-35, often called the Nafta highway these days because it is a major route between the United States and Mexico. The highway is two-tiered as it passes through downtown Austin; the upper deck has fewer exits, while the bottom deck has entrance and exit ramps to neighborhoods from downtown to just south of U.S. 290 East.

MoPac was built parallel to the Missouri-Pacific Railroad on a north-south axis. There have been battles over the extension of MoPac, primarily at the southern end from Town Lake and beyond. That section passes over the recharge zone for the Edwards Aquifer, the underground water system that feeds Barton Springs (see Close-up on Barton Springs Pool in the Parks and Recreation chapter). Currently, MoPac runs from Slaughter Lane in far South Austin to Wells Branch in far North Austin. There are stoplights along the north and south portions. Many Austin drivers use MoPac as a way to avoid the I-35 bottlenecks in the center of the city.

There are plans for a north-south toll road east of the city parallel to the Missouri–Kansas railroad, to be named MoKan, which also will divert some traffic away from I-35.

Two major roadways serve the western environs, and with population growth they have become increasingly busy. Loop 360 (Capital of Texas Highway) roughly parallels MoPac but is farther west. Originally intended to be a scenic throughway, the road has been accumulating more and more traffic signals as suburbs and shopping centers spring up along its banks. R.M. 620 sweeps around Austin to the west and serves the Highland Lakes area. Although it is a wide roadway, like Loop 360 it has become busier as the area has grown and development has flourished.

Two scenic west-east roads feed into the city from the west: R.R. 2222 and Bee Caves Road (Rural Route 2244). The former spills into Northwest Austin, while the latter winds through West Lake Hills. A wide, four-lane roadway, R.R. 2222 can be dangerous, particularly on weekends when drivers who have been drinking at the lake drive too fast on the curving road. There have been many fatal accidents on R.R. 2222, and drivers should always be alert when driving it. Bee Caves Road is being widened in several areas, but West Lake Hills residents are concerned that any further widening could turn the roadway through their community into a fast throughway.

Growth and increasing trade with Mexico will continue to have an effect on Austin traffic, ensuring that it will be a hot topic of conversation and political wrangling in the future.

CAR RENTAL

Rental car counters are located on the ground floor of the airport terminal, with express service available on the third level of the parking garage immediately north of the terminal. In addition to airport-based rental car agencies, several companies offer rental car services in the city.

PARKING

Downtown parking can be hard to find—many meters allow only 30-minute parking, and two-hour meters are located several blocks away from Congress Avenue.

There are several parking garages in the downtown area, which are a good place to park if the weather is hot (shade is invaluable in the hot Texas summer) or at night when street parking can be hard to find. Other lots have attendants, and some have banks of boxes where patrons must deposit their fees. If you don't pay, you will be towed.

Parking around the capitol has improved with the opening of a new visitor parking garage on San Jacinto east of the capitol. There is a large parking garage under the capitol extension, but that is for legislators and their staffs. There are also parking spaces for legislators on the capitol grounds, and these are guarded by parking attendants.

Parking meters around the capitol are limited to two-hour stays, which is a hassle for anyone wanting to spend time touring the building or doing business at one of the many state buildings in the area. The idea behind this implementation is to discourage state workers from using street parking.

TAXIS

Taxi cabs line up to serve customers at the western end of the airport terminal. Cabs wait in a holding area at the airport and are dispatched into the pickup lane, which is immediately outside the terminal. *Note:* there is a $1.00 surcharge at the airport. Only at very slow times will a passenger have to call for a cab. Austin's taxi services are regulated by the city, which requires companies to operate both smoking and nonsmoking cabs plus wheelchair-accessible vehicles. The flag-drop charge is $1.75, and each mile is

$1.75. The charge from the airport to downtown ranges from around $20 to $30, depending on what part of downtown you need to reach. Taxi service is available throughout the city 24 hours a day, seven days a week. Taxis cruise downtown, particularly around the capitol area. Response time, especially downtown, is very good. Cabbies accept cash and credit cards. There are even pedicabs (roving bicycle cabbies) downtown; their Web site is www.Austinbikecabs.com.

American Yellow-Checker Cab Co.
(512) 452-9999,
(512) 835-7272 TTY

Austin Cab, (512) 478-2222

Checker Cab Co., (512) 434-7777

Taxi companies serving the Round Rock area:

Roy's Taxi of Round Rock Taxi,
(512) 218-8200

Round Rock Taxi,
(512) 733-8383

LIMOUSINES

There are several limousine operators in Austin, and, like taxi cab companies, they are regulated by city ordinances governing safety and business practices. Companies charge hourly rates, starting around $55 for four passengers. Most also add service and gratuity charges, usually 15 percent each, and many also charge more during the peak spring prom season and on holidays such as Halloween and New Year's Eve. Sedan limos used for hotel/airport pickups cost around $120 an hour.

The limo business is highly competitive, and there is frequent turnover. Several large chains also operate in Austin. For a complete listing, check the Yellow Pages.

PUBLIC TRANSPORTATION

**Capital Metro
106 East Eighth Street
(512) 474-1200, (512) 385-5872 TDD
www.capmetro.austin.tx.us**

One of the easiest ways to navigate the downtown area is to ride the 'Dillo, the free trolley-style buses that cruise the area from early morning to around 10:00 P.M. The 'Dillos are just one service of the Capital Metro public transportation service, a publicly funded agency that operates buses and shuttle services in the greater Austin area. Most of the major attractions in Austin are located on bus routes, including the museums and live music spots. Capital Metro also operates an airport-to-downtown bus line.

In addition to operating bus routes to many of the city's attractions and shopping centers, Capital Metro also runs the UT Shuttle, a bus service that takes students back and forth to the campus for 50 cents a ride—the same fare it charges on its regular city bus routes. The suburbs are served by flyers, which are nonstop buses that operate from park-and-ride stops in the outlying areas.

The Capital Metro bus system serves a 500-square-mile area that encompasses the cities of Austin, Cedar Park, Leander, Lago Vista, Jonestown, Pflugerville, Manor, and San Leanna. Capital Metro offers a comprehensive booklet of its policies and schedules that is available at all area H-E-B, Fiesta, Randall's and Albertson's grocery stores; Ace Cash Express; major shopping malls; and the agency's offices.

Capital Metro's Customer Information Center has operators on duty from 6:00 A.M. to 10:00 P.M. Monday through Saturday and 7:00 A.M. to 6:00 P.M. on Sunday. The agency operates a local toll-free number, (800) 474-1201, that allows customers to dial free from any local pay phone.

There are several methods of payment on Capital Metro buses. Ticket books are available at previously listed grocery stores and at the Capital Metro Customer Infor-

mation Center. Each ticket book has 20 tickets valued at 50 cents each for $5.00, a 50 percent savings on the regular ticket price of 50 cents. Passengers must have tickets or exact change to board the bus.

Seniors and mobility-impaired riders may ride free on city buses by obtaining a free ID at the information center or, in the case of seniors, by showing an ID with a birthdate. There are discounts for individuals who qualify for Special Transit Services, which provide transportation for those who cannot ride public buses. All city buses have bike racks and are equipped with wheelchair lifts.

The agency provides a variety of programs including park-and-ride services, a car-pooling program called Ridefinders, a special van service for seniors called Easyrider, and other programs tailored to the mobility impaired. Capital Metro often provides free public shuttles at major Austin events and festivals, and visitors and downtown workers can avail themselves of the free 'Dillo service, which runs from approximately 6:00 A.M. to 10:00 P.M. These modern trolley-like buses circulate the downtown area. Downtown-area bus stops have 'Dillo route maps.

BICYCLING

Austin is trying its best to be a bike-friendly city. The city even employs a Bicycle & Pedestrian Program Coordinator, who is charged with formulating a bicycle- and pedestrian-friendly transportation plan. The coordinator may be contacted at www.ci.austin.tx.us/bicycle/, by calling (512) 499-7240, or by writing to the Department of Public Works and Transportation, City of Austin, P.O. Box 1088, Austin, TX 78767. The city's Bicycle Planning policy is published by the city, and complimentary copies are available at the above address.

The city currently has approximately 62 miles of roadway with marked bicycle lanes. City ordinances also require bicyclists

17 and younger to wear a bicycle helmet. An ordinance to require all bicyclists to wear a helmet was amended after many free-spirited adults complained; however, given the city's busy streets, all riders are advised to wear a helmet in traffic.

Bicyclists 17 and younger must wear helmets in the city of Austin on all streets, bike trails, and in parks. Violation is a Class C misdemeanor punishable with a $20 fine for the first conviction and $40 for each subsequent conviction.

We provide more information on recreational biking and cycling in the Austin area in our Parks and Recreation chapter. A great resource Web site is www.bicycleaustin.com.

There are several organizations in Austin that promote bicycle awareness/commuting/safety. They include:

- **The Texas Bicycle Coalition**, (512) 476–RIDE, www.biketexas.org, a nonprofit advocacy organization
- **The Yellow Bike Program**, (512) 916–3553, a nonprofit group promoting community free-use bicycles, which are painted yellow and left at various locations, notably around the University of Texas campus
- **The Austin Cycling Association**, www.ccsi.com/~aca, a recreational riding club, P.O. Box 5993, Austin, TX 78763
- **Austin/Travis County Super Cyclist Program**, (512) 708–0513, a children's bicycle safety and education program
- **Austin Ridge Riders**, (512) 835–8411, www.austinridgeriders.com, a recreational mountain-biking club
- **The City of Austin Bicycle Program**, (512) 499–7240, the city's bicycle transportation planning effort
- **The University of Texas College Traffic Safety Program**, (512) 471–4441, a bicycle safety, education, and defensive-cycling course

- **Austin Triathletes**, (512) 314–5773, a recreational triathlon club.

WALKING

There are areas of Austin where walking can be a pleasure, notably Congress Avenue, the Town Lake Hike and Bike Trail, and in some of the neighborhood parks. There are also several popular Historic Walking Tours in the city. For more information on these opportunities, see the Attractions and Parks and Recreation chapters.

Walking in downtown Austin is a wonderful way to see the city. Visitors should, of course, always exercise caution. Street crime is not a problem in downtown Austin during daylight hours, but do avoid alleyways after dark. Always exhibit caution when using ATMs, and carry purses and wallets in a secure manner. The Austin Police Department operates both horseback patrols and bicycle patrols in the city's parks and downtown streets.

HORSE-DRAWN CARRIAGES

One of the most romantic ways to tour downtown Austin is in a horse-drawn carriage. Carriages are not permitted on East Sixth Street, and it's likely the horses would not appreciate the sometimes rowdy atmosphere on that stretch of Sixth between Congress Avenue and I-35, anyway.

Austin Carriage Service
(512) 243–0044
www.austincarriage.com
This service has Belgian and Percheron horses to pull the carriages, which take up positions near the capitol, usually around sunset. Fees are $60 an hour or $30 for a half-hour tour of the downtown area. The drivers are equipped with radios so that they can be summoned to a restaurant,

hotel, or nightclub, sometimes for an extra fee if it is far from the capitol. One pleasant ride is a tour of the Bremond Historic District downtown (see Attractions chapter) or a waterfront tour along Town Lake. Hours are Sunday through Thursday from just before sunset to around midnight and on Friday and Saturday from sunset to around 2:00 A.M.

Die Gelbe Rose Carriage
(512) 477–8824
www.angelfire.com/DieGelbeRose
Carriage
Headquartered near the Radisson Hotel at Cesar Chavez Street and Congress Avenue, this carriage company uses Clydesdale horses but also has one Belgian and one Percheron. Rates are $80 an hour or $40 for a half hour. A popular tour is along Congress Avenue to the capitol and past the Governor's Mansion. If he is in the garden, you may get a wave from Governor Rick Perry. Carriages are available from around sunset to midnight during the week and until 2:00 A.M. on weekends.

MOTORCYCLES

Go whole hog and hire a Harley-Davidson motorcycle. These three rental operations require a valid motorcycle driver's license, and rates are approximately $150 a day, depending on the day of the week. Longer rental periods also are available. Substantial deposits, charged to your credit card, are required. All have operations in other cities around the country and can arrange one-way rentals.

Austin Harley-Davidson/Buell
801 East William Cannon Drive
(512) 448–4294
www.austinharley-davidson.com
Rent an Electra Glide Classic, a Buell Blast, or one of eight other models at this South Austin rental agency.

Eaglerider Motorcycle Rental
2300 South Lamar Boulevard, Suite 105
(512) 442–7539, (877) 732–4531
www.EagleRider.com
Take a Fat Boy for a spin or have a royal ride on a Road King, two of the eight models available at this South Austin location.

Street Eagle
5120 Burnet Road
(512) 250–9010
www.streeteagle.com
This Harley rental business in north Austin offers a membership program for $500 a year that gives members a 50 percent reduction on rental rates.

HOTELS AND MOTELS

Are you the type of traveler who just wants a comfortable, clean, inexpensive place to fling your bags and rest your body so that you can spend all your time getting to know Austin? Or are you looking for a lodging that caters to your every business need? Do you prefer divided space to conduct private meetings or to give you some breathing room from the kids? Perhaps you're looking for accommodations that reflect the history of Austin and transport you back in time. Is luxury the key to your heart? Whether you're looking for a massage and a sauna, a morning jog along Town Lake, a view, shopping, or nightlife, you've come to the right place!

While Austin offers plenty of accommodations for the traveler who believes the best surprise is no surprise, there also is an ever-increasing number of rooms for those searching for the unique. If you're wishing to be transported, think of us as "OZ-tin," click your heels, make a reservation, and repeat, "There's no place like Texas."

The turn-of-the-21st-century building boom added several thousand new hotel and motel rooms to the city, many of them in the southeast and southern sectors in response to the opening of the Austin-Bergstrom Airport in that area but also in the north and northwest to keep up with the explosive growth of business and commerce. A number of chain hotels and motels also opened at the north and south ends of MoPac (see the Getting Here, Getting Around chapter). The newest area to see hotel growth was Southwest Austin, with chains like La Quinta and Extended Stay Suites opening facilities at the intersection of MoPac and U.S. 290. The majority of new rooms are in limited-service or extended-stay facilities.

In 1998, however, the grand dame of Austin hotels, the Driskill, underwent a historically accurate restoration estimated at

more than $10 million. Another classic Austin landmark, the long-vacant Stephen F. Austin Hotel, was restored to its earlier splendor, opening as part of the luxury Intercontinental chain in 2000. An exquisite piece of Austin history, the stately Goodall Wooten Mansion, was rescued in 2003 with the opening of downtown's luxury boutique hotel, the Mansion at Judge's Hill. A hip hotel on up-and-coming South Congress Avenue is the newly restored World War II–era Hotel San José. These hotels, and a few others scattered around the city, are Austin through and through. Many of the other major hotels have also created a Texas ambience, notably the Four Seasons Hotel, where the lobby bar has become a perfect people-watcher spot. Here, high-tech executives from around the world rub shoulders with lobbyists and world-famous musicians, actors, and film executives (see the Nightlife chapter). But travelers don't have to shell out big bucks to get a real Austin experience. Some of our locally owned, older motels are truly Austin—and a lot easier on the pocketbook.

Although the hotel industry thrives by catering to convention visitors and corporate travelers, Austin's casual tourists are also reaping the rewards, in the form of more and more lodging options and choices of amenities. Studio and suite hotels are springing up all over the area. They are often called "extended-stay" facilities because they entice long-term visitors by offering fully equipped kitchens and other amenities as well as reduced rates for longer stays. Austin is also seeing an explosion in the number of business express hotels, lower-priced limited-service versions of some of the luxury chains that cater to the busy executive—and to others.

While Austin may never see a return to the days when the grand hotel was the center of community activity, hotels are giving residents more and more reasons to check in. As a result, out-of-towners aren't the only ones to benefit from Austin's hotel industry. For weddings and other festivities, meetings, dining, socializing, or getaway weekends, Austinites are discovering the pleasures of our local hotels.

Whether you've come to live in Austin, or only wish you could, there are a few things you should know before making your hotel or motel reservation in Austin.

If this is your first visit to Austin, or you haven't had the pleasure of returning for a while, allow us to orient you to the lay of the land when it comes to accommodations. The majority of Austin's full-service and luxury hotels are clustered around downtown. However, you'll also find several noteworthy full-service hotels along the I-35 corridor. Another luxury lodging, the Renaissance Austin Hotel, is in Northwest Austin in the upscale Arboretum area. Northwest Austin, a beautiful area loaded with live oak trees, has seen tremendous growth in limited-service and suite hotels in the past few years, placing it among Austin's chief lodging locations today. Southeast Austin, anchored by the stately Omni Southpark Hotel, is another area that experienced a major boom in the number of hotels and motels with the opening of the new airport. Even Southwest Austin is beginning to see hotels move in, and more are likely to open in the coming years as business and resort development continues here.

A high concentration of Austin hotels and motels is found along I-35. Because this north-south artery bisects Austin, I-35 hotels and motels can accommodate travelers who want to stay in North, Northeast, East, Central, South, and Southeast Austin. For that reason, we've decided to include sections of I-35 in our geographical listings for those who prefer to stay close to this practical thoroughfare.

We've also tried to point out the best of the other hotels and motels scattered around the city. Although there aren't many of them, they can offer some interesting options and are certainly worth checking out. Of course, there are a number of resorts and bed-and-breakfast establishments in the Lake Travis area. (For information on those see the Resorts Close-up in this chapter and our chapter on Bed-and-Breakfasts and Country Inns.) Our neighboring communities of Round Rock, Cedar Park, and Pflugerville have yet to see construction of a full-service hotel, although they are witnessing a boom in construction of national chain motels and hotels. You'll find some of these properties in the listings of additional addresses we've provided for these chains and in the apartment hotels listings at the end of this chapter.

Austin is bustling, both during the week and often on the weekends, so it's advisable to make advance reservations, especially if you've got a specific hotel in mind. But don't give up the opportunity to stay at the hotel of your choice just because you're late in arriving or making a reservation. There's always a chance. Most often, however, you'll get a better rate with a reservation, as many hotels charge more if they're filling up—the old law of supply and demand. Of course, always ask about discounts or weekend packages the hotel may offer. The annual South by Southwest Music Festival (see our Annual Events and Festivals chapter), sessions of the Legislature, University of Texas football weekends, and other big UT events all draw crowds to Austin, so it's especially important to reserve your room for these times (see our Annual Events chapter).

Are you arriving by air? Travelers who prefer to stay close to the airport have a growing list of choices, including most of the major chain hotels.

The Americans with Disabilities Act led to important changes at hotels throughout the country. These days all but a few lodgings have accommodations for persons with special needs. Austin's Club Hotel by DoubleTree offers rooms for the hearing impaired, which feature a special door buzzer and a blinking light in the

Austin is a pretty laid-back city when it comes to dress. Shorts, T-shirts, and sandals are the standard uniform for summer and will get you in just about anywhere. Unless you've come for a gala, casual dress for evening is just perfect. While you can plan on it being hot during the summer, winter can be trickier. We can have 80-degree days and 20-degree days. Mostly, however, Austin's winters are pretty mild, especially compared with those up north. It's best to check the forecast.

room. However, since there are a limited number of these specially designed rooms at each hotel, it is crucial to make advance reservations.

Traveling with children, especially small ones, can bring the added concern of finding adequate baby-sitting so that you can enjoy a night on the town or an afternoon of work or play. Several of Austin's better hotels will recommend an in-room baby-sitting service for you to contact, or they will make the arrangements for you. This is a great option, since the hotel can vouch for the quality of service you are getting. If you choose to make baby-sitting arrangements yourself or need a day-care provider that will accept drop-ins, check out our Child Care chapter.

If Fido or Fluffy have accompanied you to Austin, it's important to note that some hotels and motels do accept your pet, but many charge a nonrefundable additional fee for the privilege. Others require a refundable deposit, while at some accommodations Fluffy stays free. However, this can get complicated, as your pet may be welcome only on certain floors or in certain rooms. Even if you prefer a top-floor room with a view, for example, your pet (and you) may be relegated to a lower floor. Always check with the hotel before bringing your pet.

Smokers should also check the smoking policy when making a reservation. All but one of the hotels and motels listed below have rooms for smokers, and the policy in many of the full-service hotels is to have smoking floors—many times the lower floors. Bring your smokes if you must, but don't always count on the room with the view. As noted in our Restaurants chapter, Austin bills itself as a smoke-free city and NO SMOKING signs dominate public facilities.

This chapter includes extensive listings of hotels and motels in Austin. It is not, however, a comprehensive list. Included here are some of Austin's best hotels, some that give you the most for your lodging dollar and, of course, some of our favorites. The listings include a dollar-sign code that will give you an idea of the hotel's rate for a one-night stay for two people in a standard room. Taxes are not included in the rates so when you're calculating the cost of your stay be sure to add 15 percent. A portion of the tax goes to support the arts in Austin. The rate information has been provided by the hotels themselves and is subject to change. Unless otherwise noted, all the hotels and motels listed accept major credit cards.

Now that you're armed with the basic facts, read on to learn about some of Austin's great lodgings. Enjoy your stay. We have a feeling you'll be back.

PRICE CODE

The following price code is based on the average room rate for double occupancy during peak business. These prices do not include taxes, which in Austin total 15 percent. Please note that prices may change without notice.

$	Less than $70
$$	$70 to $100
$$$	$101 to $150
$$$$	$151 to $200
$$$$$	More than $200

DOWNTOWN

Austin Marriott at the Capitol $$$$
701 East 11th Street
(512) 478–1111, (800) 228–9290
www.marriott.com

Guests of this Marriott might wonder why some hallways zig and zag instead of following a straight line as in most other hotels. The reason is a "capitol" one. The hotel is designed to give guests on the north side a view of Austin's majestic state capitol. The Marriott, next to I–35 and 4 blocks from the seat of Texas government, is, after all, very proud of its location and deservedly so. The State Capitol is one of the coolest views in Austin (see our chapter on Attractions). But there's more. Towering windows throughout the lobby and convention rooms also afford glimpses of the imposing pink-granite structure. The use of pink-toned steel and other building materials throughout the hotel is a stylish tribute to our capitol. This really is a lovely hotel, with rooms that are ideal for relaxation or for work. The hotel, which has 365 rooms and suites, was built in 1987 and all 16 floors were remodeled in 1998. The Marriott offers 14,000 square feet of meeting and convention space, including two "Capitol View" conference rooms. The hotel even features a separate registration desk for large conventions. This hotel offers something for everyone, from the fully equipped fitness center and two swimming pools for the fitness enthusiast to the "Sports Bar and Grill"—featuring a big-screen TV for those who prefer spectator sports. Allie's American Grille serves up American and Texas specialties for breakfast, lunch, and dinner. There's also a business center and a gift shop. And the Marriott's Concierge Lounge for the business traveler is one of the nicest we've seen in the city. Marriott also operates three Residence Inns in the Austin area, one northwest near the Arboretum, one south, and another in Round Rock; call (800) 331–3131 for information and reservations.

The Driskill Hotel $$$$
604 Brazos Street
(512) 474–5911, (800) 252–9367
www.driskillhotel.com

Cattle baron Jesse Driskill opened his stately hotel in downtown Austin on December 20, 1886, offering guests an architectural wonder and such modern conveniences as steam heat and gas lights. More than a century later, The Driskill adds timeless grandeur to the Sixth Street Historic District, where live music pours from the popular nightclubs and packed restaurants of Austin's most-visited strip. Guests leave all that commotion behind when they step into The Driskill's handsome marble-floored lobby. In 1997 and 1998 the hotel underwent a historically accurate multimillion-dollar renovation, and the results are outstanding. Each of the hotel's 180 rooms and suites is unique, designed to reflect the exceptional beauty of the 1880s Driskill. The hotel's famous Cattle Baron Suite, which features two bedrooms, a dining room, and an elegant living area, rents for $2,500 a night—for those who truly want to feel like barons. There's also a sitting room named the Maximilian Room, known for its eight gold-leaf mirrors called the Empress Carlota mirrors. These French mirrors were a wedding gift from Maximilian, briefly emperor of Mexico, to his bride Carlota. The story goes that these mirrors were discovered in crates in San Antonio in the 1930s. The two-story side of the hotel is the original hotel and features spacious, alluring rooms with nearly 14-foot ceilings. The tower side was built in the 1920s and has nine levels, offering guests better views of downtown Austin. Some rooms feature balconies for an even closer perspective on downtown. The ballroom, upper lobby piano bar, and restaurant also have been remodeled to accentuate the beauty of a bygone era. The piano bar, which features live music in the evenings, is also home to portraits of some of Austin's leading historical figures, including Stephen F. Austin, the Father of Texas (see

Don't forget to make The Driskill Hotel part of your walking tour of downtown Austin, even if you're lodging elsewhere. Look for The Driskill, A Walking Tour brochures in the hotel lobby, and learn about this historic site.

our History chapter for more on Stephen F. Austin). A captivating Western sculpture called *Widow Maker,* by the artist Barvo, adorns this lobby—a must see.

The gourmet restaurant is open daily for breakfast, lunch, and dinner. The Driskill has no swimming pool or fitness center on the premises, although guests can request free passes to use the World Gym across the street. Neither is there a parking garage on the premises. Guests use valet parking or park at the meters around the hotel.

Extended StayAmerica $$
600 Guadalupe Street
(512) 457-9994, (800) EXT-STAY
www.exstay.com

Finding a budget hotel downtown can be difficult, but this national chain offers reasonably priced rooms that can be rented by the night or the week. The rooms are small suites with kitchen facilities and desks, making them ideal for business visitors or families on a budget. There is a coin laundry on site. There are additional hotels from this chain in other parts of the city—one near the Arboretum (see our Shopping chapter) and two additional facilities planned for the north and south ends of MoPac. The downtown location is just 2 blocks from Congress Avenue and within easy walking distance of the Sixth Street entertainment district and the sights around the State Capitol complex. The hotel rests on a famous site, a corner once occupied by the Alamo Hotel (see our Politics and Perspectives chapter), a funky, famous hotel once well-known to traveling salesmen. Its demise is part of the Austin urban mythology, while the

opening of the new hotel reflects Austin's changing downtown area.

Four Seasons Hotel $$$$$
98 San Jacinto Boulevard
(512) 478-4500, (800) 332-3442
www.fourseasons.com

It doesn't take many steps past the lobby entrance to know you're in one of Austin's premier hotels. Carpeting so thick and plush that your shoes practically disappear leads down the stairs into The Cafe restaurant and terrace, offering a drop-dead-gorgeous view of Town Lake and of the hotel's own manicured lawns. The Four Seasons is just an extraordinary lodging. This hotel pampers you, your child, AND your pet. Yes, the Four Seasons not only accepts domestic pets of all sizes on certain floors, but it even provides treats. Children get cookies and milk or popcorn and sodas the evening of arrival. The hotel and its 292 exceptionally spacious rooms and suites—some offering stunning views of the lake—are designed with a sophisticated Southwestern flair that is both elegant and relaxing. The amenities and services go on and on: 24-hour room service, twice-daily housekeeping service, a heated outdoor pool overlooking Town Lake, a state-of-the-art health club that includes free weights and features a television on every bike, a spa with massage and body treatments offered, complimentary morning newspaper and overnight shoe shine, and one-hour pressing service. There's even a dock for sunning, splashing your feet in Town Lake or, if your rowing team is in town, heading out for training. And while you're outside, you can take advantage of the hotel's direct access to Austin's wonderful Hike and Bike Trail. The Four Seasons will even arrange a bicycle if you want.

La Quinta Inn $$
300 East 11th Street
(512) 476-1166, (800) 531-5900
www.laquinta.com

If you want to stay in downtown Austin, but don't need—or can't afford—all the amenities of Austin's upscale hotels, it's hard to beat the recently renovated La Quinta Inn. For comfort, location, and comparative price, La Quinta is an excellent choice. It offers valet parking, a real plus for a motel downtown, where finding parking on the street can be a nightmare. The 145 rooms and suites are spotless and comfortably sized. Nice touches have been added to spruce up the outdoor walkways, such as huge potted flowers and plants. Among the motel's many features are free continental breakfasts, in-room coffeemakers, and Nintendo games. The state capitol is just around the corner, Sixth Street is 5 blocks down the road, and the University of Texas is a mile away. During the week, La Quinta's guests are mostly professionals. Weekends tend to draw a college crowd.

Travelers who prefer staying at a La Quinta Inn will be happy to learn there are seven other Austin-area locations, including one in Southwest Austin near the intersection of MoPac and U.S. 290 West. The toll-free number for other locations is (800) 687–6667.

The Mansion at Judges' Hill $$$–$$$$$
1900 Rio Grande Street
(512) 495–1800, (800) 311–1619
www.mansionatjudgeshill.com
Small and ultrachic, the Mansion at Judges' Hill brings one of Austin's historic homes back to splendor—making it, perhaps, even better than during its prime. For more than a century the Goodall Wooten Mansion has stood just a few blocks from the University of Texas in the Judges' Hill neighborhood. But time had taken its toll on this graceful, stone-colonnaded structure. The once-luxurious residence had over the years been used as a dormitory, a sorority house, and finally a drug rehabilitation center. Owner William Gurasich, one of the founders of Austin's well-known GSD&M advertising agency and now a real estate developer, oversaw a complete renovation, paying special attention to the most minute details.

Opened in 2003 this 48-room luxury hotel and gourmet restaurant features rich colors and textures throughout. The large rooms, some with fireplaces, include antique and custom-made furniture, and each is uniquely designed to reflect a timeless quality. Even the spacious bathrooms are gorgeous. Three-room suites also are available. What mansion would be complete without its own private courtyard, library, and covered garage? Amenities include high-speed Internet access, custom bath products, twice-daily housekeeping service, deluxe bathrobes, in-room minibars, iron and ironing board, and Egyptian cotton linens. There are separate rates for the Mansion and the North Wing, the latter being somewhat less expensive. This is a perfect place for a wedding or special event.

The mansion, built in 1898, was a wedding gift to prominent Austin doctor Goodall Wooten, and his bride, Ella Newsome, from their fathers. Ella Wooten, widowed in 1942, sold the house after World War II. The Mansion at Judges' Hill is an exquisite Austin landmark—and an equally exquisite hotel property.

Omni Austin Hotel Downtown $$$$
700 San Jacinto
(512) 467–3700, (800) THE–OMNI
www.omnihotels.com
Enormous plate-glass windows supported by steel beams rise from the ground to the towering ceiling in this ultramodern hotel, which features huge abstract paintings and polished granite throughout the atrium-style lobby. Sunlight pours through the tremendous wall of glass and illuminates the sprawling lobby, which is home to Ancho's, the hotel restaurant featuring Southwest cuisine. The lobby bar next to Ancho's also has that airy look and is a nice place to relax and have a drink or a bite. The hotel, part of the Austin Centre office complex, has 314 rooms and suites in 14 floors of hotel space. Built in 1986, the hotel was remodeled in 1994. The modern, impeccable rooms offer superior comfort

and a cozy capital-city feel, with Texas stars scattered here and there throughout the hotel. Guests are treated to the ultimate in comfort in the hotel's large rooms, meeting and convention spaces, and ballroom. The upper floors provide excellent views of downtown Austin and across town.

Radisson Hotel & Suites on Town Lake $$$
111 Cesar Chavez Street
(512) 478-9611, (800) 333-3333
www.radisson.com

The tower addition to the Radisson Hotel opened in August of 1998, adding 135 suites to one of Austin's busiest hotels. A fabulous location on Town Lake just off the Congress Avenue bat-viewing bridge (see our Attractions chapter), great service, a lively staff, and inviting rooms add up to a great hotel experience. And the Radisson, whose 280 other rooms and suites were remodeled in 1997, is one of the most affordable of the high-quality downtown hotels.

Three huge tropical fish tanks delight guests upon arrival and add a colorful and relaxing touch to the lobby. The outdoor swimming pool, although not heated for winter swimming, is a wonderful place to unwind during Austin's long, hot summers. T.G.I. Friday's restaurant, on the premises, offers breakfast, lunch, and dinner starting at 6:00 A.M. Friday's large outdoor deck is a great, informal place to dine or have drinks while watching the evening bat show during spring and summer. The hotel also offers easy access to Austin's Hike and Bike Trail, one of the finest inner-city trails anywhere. One-half of the hotel's immaculate, charming rooms offer excellent views of Town Lake, and the view from the upper floors is far-reaching. The hotel does have a covered parking garage, a plus for a downtown hotel, but charges about $5.00 per day for its use.

Stephen F. Austin Hotel $$$$$
701 Congress Avenue
(512) 457-8800, (800) 327-0200
www.austin.intercontinental.com

"Austin's Dream Comes True with Brilliant Opening of New Hotel."

So read the *Austin American*'s front-page headline on May 20, 1924, the day following the grand opening of the Stephen F. Austin Hotel. Three-quarters of a century later, the hotel reopened in 2000 as Austin's newest luxury hotel. The hotel, vacant for more than a decade, underwent a complete renovation aimed at offering guests the latest in comfort and style while retaining the look and feel of the 1920s. That meant rooms were equipped with the latest technology, including multiline phones in the rooms, dataports and T-1 lines, amenities Austin's other luxury downtown hotels, the Driskill and the Four Seasons, also boast. The Stephen F. Austin also provides a service called CyberAssist, on-site tech support. But while the renovation installed the latest technology, it also revived the hotel's 1920s class. A grand staircase of marble and brass beguiles visitors as they enter the lobby and walk up to the Grand Ballroom. The 189 rooms and suites have a truly Texan ambience, with star emblems on some headboards and lots of wrought iron. Facilities include a state-of-the-art fitness center, an indoor swimming pool, a cigar bar, a cafe, and a restaurant for fine dining. Additionally, the hotel offers 6,000 square feet of meeting and convention space as well as special services for executive travelers, including a business center.

Modern amenities, however, are just part of the allure of this hotel. Austin and Texas history wafts through the halls and hangs like tapestries from the walls. Lyndon B. Johnson made this grand hotel his congressional campaign headquarters after World War II, and it seems as if everybody who had a hand in shaping modern Texas walked through its doors at one time or another. In 1984 the *Dallas Morning News* wrote this about the hotel: "To native Austinites and University of Texas Exes, she is known simply as 'the Stephen F.' The name has been adopted for the second story bar which features an outside balcony overlooking Congress

Avenue. And if walls could talk, they would relate fascinating tales of oil and cattle deals transacted over breakfast and a handshake, of political intrigue involving state legislators, and of romances begun during World War II." Who knows what tales will be told about the Stephen F. in the 21st century?

SOUTH CENTRAL

Austin Motel   **$$**
1220 South Congress Avenue
(512) 441-1157
www.austinmotel.com
Location, history, personality, and price combine to make the family-owned Austin Motel one of the city's most unique lodgings. As Congress Avenue gentrification spreads south of Town Lake, this motel is in the right spot at the right time, again. The main buildings were built in 1938 on Austin's central thoroughfare and way before the coming of the highway system. With its now classic red and white neon sign, this motel attracted travelers from near and far. When the traffic moved to the highways, so did much of the Austin Motel's business. South Congress, meanwhile, grew into a popular spot for prostitutes and drug dealers. These days South Congress is hip and happening, and the bad influences are long gone.

Today's Austin Motel, like many other businesses along this funky stretch, is attracting visitors who want to get a distinct feel for Austin. This is not a place for guests who like modern, cookie-cutter accommodations. Artists, musicians, and poets seem especially attracted to the Austin Motel's particular flair, as are others who put character before elegance. This motel has 41 rooms for 41 personalities, from small rooms for those who'd rather spend their time out on the town, to spacious executive suites, to rooms overlooking the large, newly renovated pool. A small, shaded garden just off the pool provides a great place for guests to gather. California wicker, New England

dark maple, Florida flamingos, Chinese fans, American red, white and blue, and Spanish traditional are just a few of the imaginative decor themes that make each visit interesting. Antiques are sprinkled liberally throughout the motel and, while many show their age, all add to the distinctiveness of each room. New owner Dottye Dean, who took over from her mother in 1993, undertook a massive remodeling project that has encompassed every room, including the addition built in the 1960s. Dean and her staff of artists paid special attention to the bathrooms; some feature original fixtures and tile; others have been updated to include marble Jacuzzi bathtubs. One room has a cultured marble shower with two showerheads and seating inside—perfect for a couple. El Sol Y La Luna, the Mexican restaurant next door that is leased from the hotel, is a popular spot for travelers and residents alike (see our Restaurants chapter).

Embassy Suites Downtown   **$$$$**
300 South Congress Avenue
(512) 469-9000, (800) EMBASSY
www.embassysuites.com
Just 3 blocks south of Town Lake on historic Congress Avenue, this all-suite hotel is perfectly located for the traveler who wants to take advantage of all downtown Austin's attractions—and have room to move around to boot. Each of the 262 suites in the nine-story Embassy features a bedroom with either a king-size bed or two double beds that is separated by a door from the meeting/living area, making each room perfect for a small meeting or gathering—or just a place to put the kids to bed while you relax or watch television. The Presidential Suite, for those who really want space, has two bedrooms and two baths as well as the living area. The suites come fully equipped. The hotel offers an indoor swimming pool and hot tub, an exercise room, a comfortable lobby lounge, and the Capital City Bistro restaurant that serves American-style meals beginning at 11:00 A.M. The Embassy

serves its famous complimentary cooked-to-order breakfast daily, just about the best free breakfast in town. And just across the street is Threadgill's World Headquarters (see Restaurants chapter). For music trivia buffs, this Threadgill's is near the site once occupied by the Armadillo World Headquarters (see The Music Scene chapter). For social or business gatherings of all kinds, the Embassy offers 2,300 square feet of space in five rooms. You might strain your eyes trying to catch the evening flight of the bats from the hotel, but the Congress Avenue Bridge is just steps away. Don't miss the show in spring and summer (see Attractions chapter). There are two additional Embassy Suites in Austin, one in far north Austin, the other in the Arboretum area.

Hotel San José $$-$$$$
1316 South Congress Avenue
(512) 444-7322, (800) 574-8897
www.sanjosehotel.com

"Hip" is the word most often used to describe this restored Congress Avenue motel, and not only does it suit the San José but also the neighborhood. No wonder it is favored by visiting musicians and artists, since it is just across the street from the famed Continental Club (see our Music Scene chapter) and in the midst of the funky South Congress gallery and junque shop scene (see our Shopping chapter). The hotel was built in 1939 as a "court hotel," the forerunner of the motel,

with rooms built around a central courtyard. There are 40 rooms and suites in assembled bungalows that make up the San José, all decorated in retro-style but with up-to-date conveniences like dataports. The courtyards and gardens have been decorated in Texas style with cactus, aloes and yuccas, gravel pathways, and outdoor seating areas. One public area of the hotel is dedicated to the works of local artists. An "artist in residence" is chosen every few months to display his or her works in the hotel gallery. The unique atmosphere here is also enhanced by the on-site Jo's coffeehouse, which sponsors Thursday evening movies in the courtyard. A local band hosts the entertainment and chooses the movie, and neighbors and guests are invited to BYOC (bring your own chair) and settle down for an outdoor movie. On Tuesday the hotel offers "steak night," grilled tuna and tenderloin in the courtyard. Prices have increased since the traveling salesmen days, but the hotel offers top-notch services including drycleaning, shoe shines, bike rental, access to a music and video library, plus a swimming pool and fitness center.

Hyatt Regency Austin $$$$
208 Barton Springs Road
(512) 477-1234, (800) 233-1234
www.hyatt.com

From the cowhide seat cushions in the lobby to the bed skirts stamped with a boot motif to the reproductions of historic maps and flags of Texas on the walls, this delightful hotel on the south bank of Town Lake radiates Texas charm. The Branchwater Lounge in the lobby has a stream running through it, and the bar opens out onto an inviting patio that offers an excellent view of Town Lake. Bat watching is one of the perks for spring and summer guests, although the view of the evening spectacle is not great from the lobby lounge or the lower rooms because the bats take off from the opposite side of the Congress Avenue Bridge (see our Attractions chapter). If you want to catch a glimpse of the bats, be sure to request an appropriate

The mall isn't the only place to get your Austin memorabilia or gifts to take home. Many locally owned restaurants sell T-shirts and other gifts with their own logos, and more. At some you can get locally produced CDs, Austin-made salsas, and other treats. When you see a gift shop or gift counter at a restaurant, don't just pass it by. It could have the perfect item for that loved one who didn't get to come to Austin.

room—perhaps one with a balcony—or take the elevator up to the 17th floor and watch from the huge picture window up there.

For the business traveler, the Hyatt offers the 16th floor, which offers two telephone lines and a fax machine in every room. A business lounge on this floor provides comfortable seating and the use of office equipment. The hotel also offers its Gold Passport floors for guests who want a little extra service while they rack up bonus points for frequent-flyer mileage and free hotel stays. The Hyatt has 23,000 square feet of meeting rooms, boardrooms, and ballrooms for every type and size of gathering. The hotel's La Vista restaurant serves breakfast, lunch, and dinner starting at 6:30 A.M. The Hyatt Regency, one of Austin's largest hotels with 446 rooms and suites, was built in 1982 and remodeled in 1996. The interior atrium, open from the lobby to the rooftop skylights, lends a very spacious look and feel. This hotel is stylish but comfortable and certainly deserving of the Hyatt Regency name. An outdoor swimming pool, fitness center, and easy access to Austin's exquisite Hike and Bike Trail along Town Lake provide excellent options for the fitness enthusiast.

SOUTHWEST

The Heart of Texas Motel $$
5303 U.S. 290 West
(512) 892-0644
www.heartoftexasmotel.com

Owned by the Osbon family since 1981, this 30-room motel draws a steady stream of regular customers and plenty of newcomers. The Osbons live on-site, and the care they take to maintain these rooms and the surrounding premises is obvious. The attractively decorated, good-size rooms all have microwaves, refrigerators, and coffeemakers. The motel also offers one Jacuzzi-suite room with a king-size four-poster bed. Other rooms have two double beds or a double bed with a sleeper sofa. Upper-level rooms have ceil-

ing fans, a real plus for Austin's long, hot summers. For those who like to spend their spare time outdoors, the Heart of Texas Motel has a putting green, a horseshoe pit, a basketball hoop, and a barbecue grill. For movie buffs, this motel has some interesting local history. Actor Matthew McConaughey shot a music video there before he became famous, and Loni Anderson filmed scenes for a TV movie at the Heart of Texas. On U.S. 290 near the junction with the MoPac Expressway, this motel offers easy access to many parts of town and to Austin-Bergstrom International airport. For travelers looking for affordable rooms, especially those who have business in this area or just want to stay with someone they can trust, the Heart of Texas Motel is a great choice.

AIRPORT

Hilton Austin Airport $$$
9515 New Airport Drive
(512) 385-6767, (800) 774-1500
www.hilton.com

While there are other chain hotels in the Austin-Bergstrom Airport area, this one is the closest—it's on-site. It also is the most "Austin." Housed in the former administration building and officers' headquarters of what was Bergstrom Air Force Base, the round building is affectionately known as "the donut." Totally remodeled and opened in 2001, the hotel offers all the amenities of a full-service hotel, including 262 well-appointed guest rooms, an outdoor swimming pool, state-of-the-art fitness center, jogging trails, a gift shop, lobby bar, and a casual restaurant, "The Creeks." For that really big party, there's also the Bergstrom Grand Ballroom, which holds up to 800 persons. Located two minutes from the passenger terminal, the hotel offers a free airport shuttle. It's 7 miles from downtown Austin and is also located quite conveniently close to the area's high-tech businesses.

For those wishing to stay at a full-service Hilton closer to downtown, the high-rise Hilton Austin–Convention Center opened in 2004 at 500 East Fourth Street. For more information, check the Hilton Web site.

LAKE TRAVIS

Mountain Star Lodge   **$$**
3573 Rural Route 620 South
(512) 263-2010, (888) 263-2010
www.mountainstar.citysearch.com
A great location near fabulous Lake Travis and a superb unobstructed view of the Texas Hill Country combine to make the Mountain Star Lodge an excellent choice in accommodations. From its vantage point on Ranch Road 620, the main thoroughfare to an abundance of lakeside recreational spots and restaurants, the lodge offers guests easy access to the community of Lakeway and to fishing, boating, skiing, and other outdoor activities. And yet it's just 1 mile north of Highway 71 in Southwest Austin.

Opened in 1997, the two-story Mountain Star Lodge is locally owned and operated. This lovely building of native limestone offers 20 nonsmoking rooms, each with a private patio or balcony overlooking the large outdoor swimming pool and the vast Canyon Lands Nature Preserve. The rooms, which feature outdoor access and parking just outside the rooms, are decorated in an early Texas theme. Each morning from 7:00 to 9:00 A.M. guests are treated to a complimentary continental breakfast in the large, inviting lobby, which is designed to reflect the look and feel of a mountain lodge. A large fireplace, a soaring wood-beam ceiling, and huge windows that take advantage of that gorgeous view make this a very cozy spot for relaxing, conducting small business conferences, or hosting parties or weddings. For those visiting town on business, the lodge offers fax service.

INTERSTATE 35 CORRIDOR—NORTH

Hotels in this area are north of the I-35—U.S. 290 East interchange. Because of the high concentration of hotels and motels along I-35, especially in this area, some of the following hotels are only a few blocks north of those listed under I-35 Corridor—Central lodgings.

Austin Chariot Resort Inn   **$$**
7300 North I-35
(512) 452-9371, (800) 432-9202
Do not let the dated front entrance to this motel fool you. We almost passed it by ourselves. But what a surprise awaited us! The two-acre manicured courtyard of this 157-room motel is one of the loveliest we've seen in Austin and certainly the best of any in this price range—on the inexpensive end of the scale we've provided. Here, among towering oaks, palm trees, and sprawling ivy, is a mini-oasis with a charming free-form swimming pool that winds around a gorgeous stone waterfall and under a footbridge. There's even a separate baby pool. Covered patio tables are scattered among the trees, and a spiral staircase leads up to the second-floor rooms. There's a nine-hole putting green, and out back is a sand volleyball court. Built around 1960, the Chariot Inn is certainly one of Austin's landmarks—there's even a rumor that Elvis slept here! But the inn was in need of repair when the Kochs family purchased it in 1996. Since then the family has invested more than $2 million to upgrade the facility and renovate rooms. They've created an attractive, comfortable, inexpensive place to stay in Austin. They haven't gotten around to redoing the front of the inn, however, choosing to invest first in guest facilities. The Chariot offers free continental breakfasts and coffeemakers in every room. HBO is included in the cable television package. Deluxe rooms are available

for guests requiring more space. A 3,000-square-foot ballroom, other meeting rooms, and a large breakfast room complete the facilities. On I-35 at the U.S. 183 intersection, the motel does get traffic noise, but it's also a fine location from which to discover Austin. Unless you're the kind of traveler who prefers to see your car out the window, request a room in the back near the pool. A security guard protects the premises at night.

DoubleTree Hotel $$$$
6505 North I-35
(512) 454-3737, (800) 222-TREE
www.doubletreehotels.com
An upscale hotel with a Mediterranean flair, the DoubleTree is designed with imposing archways, lots of stonework, and an exquisite multilevel courtyard filled with lush greenery and the gentle sound of flowing water. This palatial Spanish Colonial–style structure with 350 rooms and suites is an attractive Austin landmark along I-35 just 1 block north of U.S. 290. Minutes from downtown, the University of Texas campus, and important high-tech industries; across from major shopping centers; within walking distance of two popular Austin restaurants; and close to nearly two dozen more—the DoubleTree is perfectly situated for the traveler who wants to get to know Austin. Forget the little candy on the pillow. The DoubleTree offers guests a yummy chocolate-chip cookie upon arrival. For those requiring additional sustenance, the DoubleTree has its own Courtyard Cafe, which overlooks the lovely courtyard and serves continental cuisine with a Texas touch all day. The hotel's outdoor swimming pool is on a stunning tropical terrace, and the new state-of-the-art fitness center offers the serious health buff plenty of options. There's also a gift shop and the inviting Courtyard Lounge, which features a wide-screen TV, billiards table, and a cozy fireplace. This chain also operates the DoubleTree Guest Suites property in Cen-

tral Austin at 303 West 15th Street (512-478-7000), and the Club Hotel by Doubletree just east of downtown, listed later in this chapter.

Four Points Hotel Sheraton $$$
7800 North I-35
(512) 836-8520, (800) 325-3535
www.starwood.com
The landscaped 1½-acre courtyard, complete with swimming pool and lighted pavilion, lends an almost bucolic touch to this ITT Sheraton Hotel, even though the Four Points is at one of Austin's busiest junctions. At the interchange of I-35 and U.S. 183, and just north of U.S. 290, the Four Points serves as a launching point to all parts of the city. The interior guest rooms surrounding the courtyard all have functional balconies or patios, making them a perfect spot to relax in the evening. This is simply a lovely spot, impeccably maintained and well-deserving of the Sheraton name. You wouldn't guess the hotel is about 30 years old. The rooms and suites all come equipped with three telephones, desks, and comfortable seating areas. They are totally modern and spacious for fun or work. The elegant suites are huge and include great bathrooms with double-size Jacuzzi tubs. Stringfield's Restaurant serves a complimentary full breakfast buffet daily and is open for lunch and dinner. Stringfield's Club, the hotel lounge, is a great place for drinks and socializing. An exercise facility and indoor hot tub make a great duo for working out and then unwinding. The hotel features 7,000 square feet of space for large and small gatherings.

Habitat Suites Hotel $$$
500 Highland Mall Boulevard
(512) 467-6000, (800) 535-4663
www.habitatsuites.com
For the environmentally conscious traveler—or anyone who wants beautiful environs—the Habitat Suites Hotel is a miniature Eden in the heart of a bustling

A trip to Austin isn't complete without a visit to Amy's Ice Cream. This home-grown ice-cream shop, with six locations around the city (see our Restaurants chapter) plus another at the Austin-Bergstrom International Airport, draws crowds throughout the year. (They don't take reservations, however, so the wait in summer could be 10 minutes or more—but it's worth it.) The varieties of gourmet ice cream, some with liqueur added, are delicious by themselves. But don't forget to get your personalized "crush 'n": fresh strawberries, Oreo cookies, candies, and such folded into the ice cream of your choice at the moment you place your order. Yum!

commercial area. This 96-suite locally owned property in an apartment-like setting received Austin's "Best" award in 1996 as a Business for an Environmentally Sustainable Tomorrow. Everything from breakfast to bedtime is planned to protect and honor the earth's bounty. The complimentary full-course breakfast buffet includes healthful alternatives—soy milk, tofu migas, stone-ground tortillas, and black beans—as well as an entire range of traditional breakfast dishes. Nontoxic, phosphate-free cleansers are used to maintain the suites and clean the laundry, while the grounds are kept using natural fertilizers and pesticides. Ionizers are used to maintain clean air quality in all the suites, and the hotel uses biodegradable, recycled paper products and returns to the recycling bin all possible items. Habitat is "green" both figuratively and literally. The property is totally surrounded by native foliage and flowering plants that create a lush, inviting atmosphere, while they require the least amount of water. The hotel staff even grows a variety of fruits, vegetables, and herbs on the property. Habitat's outdoor swimming pool, also enveloped by greenery, uses ionized water and bromine instead of chlorine, better for the environ-

ment and for the skin. What's inside is also inviting. The spacious one- and two-bedroom suites, all with fully equipped kitchens, are tastefully decorated and include, of course, green plants. The rooms come equipped with irons and ironing boards, telephones with dataport connections, and cable televisions that include the premium channels; most have wood-burning fireplaces. No smoking is allowed in the rooms, but the hotel has plenty of outdoor benches and provides ashtrays and matches. The upper-level bedrooms in the two-bedroom units have their own private entrances. The hotel offers fax and copying services, express checkout, same-day dry cleaning and laundry service, a do-it-yourself laundry, and free newspapers. The 504-square-foot meeting room provides additional space for gatherings of all kinds. The hotel also treats guests to an evening social hour, with free drinks and snacks. While there's no fitness center on the premises, guests are given free passes to use the 24-hour World Gym facilities just down the street. This hotel is within a stone's throw of the Highland Mall shopping center, 16 movie theaters, and several popular restaurants. It's about a 10-minute drive from downtown Austin and offers easy access to all parts of town. This is the only I-35 corridor hotel that's not right on the highway. It's just a few blocks off but worth the extra effort to locate it.

Hawthorn Suites—Central $$$
935 La Posada Drive
(512) 459-3335, (800) 527-1133
www.hawthorn.com

Situated just across I-35 from a major shopping mall, with easy access to downtown and many high-tech industries, and nestled between two of Austin's luxury hotels, Hawthorn Suites can claim a great location as one of its major advantages. But there's much more. Hawthorn's 71 spacious one- and two-bedroom suites all have complete kitchens with full-size appliances, and they all feature patios or balconies, working fireplaces, and telephones equipped with dataports. A collapsible door separates the sleeping area from the living quarters in the one-bedroom studio unit and on the lower level of the two-bedroom lofts. For the business traveler, Hawthorn Suites offers a meeting room that can accommodate up to 50 people. This recently renovated lodging with a Southwestern flair serves a complimentary hot breakfast buffet daily and free cocktails and hors d'oeuvres Monday through Thursday from 5:00 to 7:00 P.M. Guests can unwind in the heated outdoor pool or soak in the hot tub. There's even a sports court for playing basketball and a half-size tennis court with rackets and balls available. Guests who really want a workout can pay $5.00 to use the World Gym facilities less than half a mile away. The Hawthorn has two other facilities in Austin, one northwest and one south. Call the "800" number above for information.

Holiday Inn Express   **$$–$$$**
7622 North I-35
(512) 467-1701, (800) HOLIDAY
www.basshotels.com/holiday-inn
A limited-service hotel that lives up to Holiday Inn standards, the Express offers 125 comfortable guest rooms, including junior and executive suites that come with refrigerators and microwaves. Each room has a coffeemaker and one telephone with a dataport hookup. Same-day laundry and dry cleaning is offered. The hotel features two meeting rooms that seat up to 35 people each. A free deluxe continental breakfast is served daily in the pleasant lobby cafe. On Wednesday evening from March through October, weather permitting, the hotel hosts a complimentary cookout on the patio near the swimming pool. Hot dogs and hamburgers are served along with chips and drinks. Monday through Thursday year-round is the evening reception from 5:00 to 6:30 P.M. Bennigan's Restaurant is next door and also provides room service from 2:00 until 11:00 P.M. daily. Located at the I-35 and U.S. 183 interchange, the Holiday Inn Express is 6 miles north of downtown and the capitol complex.

Motel 6—Austin North   **$**
9420B North I-35
(512) 339-6161, (800) 4-MOTEL 6
www.motel6.com
One of four Motel 6s in Austin for the budget-minded traveler, this North Austin location offers 158 guest rooms on two levels. Guests are treated to free HBO, and the motel's outdoor swimming pool is open from May through September. Complimentary coffee is served in the lobby from 7:00 to 10:00 A.M. This Motel 6 property, Austin's northernmost, offers easy access to I-35, U.S. 183, and U.S. 290. The capitol, University of Texas, and LBJ Library are 6 miles south. Major shopping centers are just a few miles south on I-35. Call the "800" number above for information on other Austin locations, all of which are located in the I-35 corridor.

INTERSTATE 35 CORRIDOR—CENTRAL

This area of I-35 is defined in our book as the area south of the I-35—U.S. 290 East junction and north of Town Lake. Hotels in this listing can be found on either side of the interstate or just a block or two away.

Club Hotel by DoubleTree   **$$$**
1617 North I-35
(512) 479-4000, (800) 444-CLUB
www.doubletreehotels.com
DoubleTree's innovative concept has taken the business traveler's hotel to a new level with its Club Hotel. A self-contained business environment—just like the office back home—has been created right off the lobby area for the use of hotel guests. Two private cubicles complete with reference materials and six well-lighted personal work stations create a functional and comfortable work setting. A private conference room in this space would seat three or four people comfortably. And just a step away, guests have access to a copier, a fax machine, and a printer for printing from your laptop computer. There is an extra charge for these services.

While this area is designed to create an "office-away-from-the-office" setting, the spacious lobby is fashioned to make guests feel as if they are at home. This is all just steps away from Au Bon Pain—The Bakery Cafe, the hotel's delicatessen-style restaurant serving fresh pastries, soups, sandwiches, and more. The limited-service hotel's 152 spacious and immaculate rooms of varying sizes all come equipped with desks, telephones with dataports, and coffeemakers. The hotel, which opened in September 1997, offers many other amenities, including an outdoor swimming pool, exercise room, guest laundry facilities, and an evening lounge. A larger meeting room on the premises holds up to 50 people. This hotel is conveniently located just across the interstate from the University of Texas, downtown Austin, and the Frank Erwin Center.

Days Inn University $$$
3105 North I–35
(512) 478-1631, (800) 725-ROOMS
www.daysinn.com
Recently renovated and redecorated, Days Inn University is a reasonable choice for the traveler on a budget who wants to be close to some of Austin's featured attractions. The motel is near the University of Texas and all its sports stadiums. This motel is right on the interstate, offering easy access to many parts of town. There could be some traffic noise, however. Rates are cheaper during the week. A second facility, Days Inn North, is at 820 East Anderson Lane, (512) 835-4311 or (800) DAYS INN.

Drury Inn—Highland Mall $$
919 East Koenig Lane
(512) 454-1144, (800) 325-8300
www.drury-inn.com
A large outdoor patio next to the swimming pool is a splendid place for get-togethers at this practical, well-situated inn. Near the intersection of I–35 and U.S. 290 East, the Drury offers easy access to many parts of town. For shoppers, the hotel is conveniently located half a mile

from Highland Mall and the Lincoln Village Shopping Center. Guests of the Drury Inn are treated to a full continental breakfast daily and evening cocktails, soft drinks, and snacks in the Drury's comfortable breakfast room. Coffee is available in the lobby 24 hours a day. The inn's four deluxe rooms are 1½ times the size of a normal room and feature microwave ovens, refrigerators, and coffeemakers. Austin's other Drury property is just up the street at 6711 I–35 North, (512) 467-9500.

Embassy Suites Hotel—North $$$
5901 North I–35
(512) 454-8004, (800) EMBASSY
www.embassy-suites.com
Palm trees and tropical plants abound in the Spanish-style indoor atrium of this lovely Embassy Suites. Ducks and fish keep an eye on guests from the delightful waterscape that weaves through the atrium, passing a cascading waterfall and under a footbridge. And that's just the beginning. The hotel, renovated in 1998, offers 260 spacious guest suites designed for the most comfortable of stays. Guests are treated to the Embassy's complimentary cooked-to-order breakfast daily and to the manager's reception in the evening, which includes soft drinks, cocktails, and snacks. The Embassy's classic two-room suites are designed to appeal both to the corporate traveler and to families. All rooms in the 10-floor hotel look out on the atrium, and some feature small balconies. The Embassy's Plaza Grill serves lunch and dinner, and the cozy Lynx lounge is a great place to unwind over drinks or a game of pool or Foosball. The heated indoor swimming pool and hot tub are great for year-round enjoyment. We especially like the pool area. It's just brimming with greenery of all kinds, and the patio is so spacious that you don't get that cramped feeling like you do around some indoor pools. Plenty of patio furniture allows guests to just sit and relax. There's even a unisex sauna nearby and a newly remodeled fitness

center on the second floor. In 1998 Embassy Suites opened its newest hotel in Northwest Austin at 9505 Stonelake Boulevard. Call (512) 372-8771.

Fairfield Inn—Austin North $$
959 Reinli Street
(512) 302-5550, (800) 228-2800
www.fairfieldinn.com

Comfort and hospitality are the hallmarks of the Fairfield Inn, the Marriott's most affordable lodging in Austin. The Fairfield's 63 attractive guest rooms are ideal for unwinding after a busy day—and the location is great for the traveler on the go. Situated near the junction of I-35 and U.S. 290 East, the Fairfield is close to major shopping centers, and within 3 miles of the University of Texas campus and the LBJ Library and Museum. Carrow's restaurant is adjacent to the hotel, and several other restaurants are within walking distance. The Fairfield offers complimentary continental breakfasts in its charming lobby cafe, while coffee and bowls brimming with fresh fruit are provided all day. The inn features a heated indoor pool and whirlpool, a handy exercise room, and guest laundry. All rooms are equipped with irons and ironing boards, Nintendo games, and cable TV, including HBO and pay-per-view movies. Marriott standards at an affordable price. What more could you ask? Austin's other Fairfield Inn, Austin South, is at 4525 South I-35, (512) 707-8899.

Holiday Inn—Town Lake $$$
20 North I-35
(512) 472-8211, (800) HOLIDAY
www.basshotels.com/holiday-inn

This 320-room property was designed to give guests the best possible view of Town Lake—and what a view it is. On Austin's central waterway, many of the hotel's sleeping quarters, meeting rooms, common areas, and the outdoor swimming pool provide stunning views of the lake. Large picture windows in the rooms maximize the view. The 14-floor, round "Capitol Tower" portion of this hotel was built in the 1960s, making it one of Austin's oldest full-service hotels. (The newer "Lake Tower" was built in the mid-1980s.) All the facilities are very well maintained, so it's hard to tell when you're in the older part. That, combined with a great location, services, and lower prices than some other full-service properties, make the Holiday Inn comfortable in many aspects. Guests looking for a workout can slip into the exercise room or head on down to the Hike and Bike Trail right outside the door. To relax afterward, there's the indoor hot tub and two saunas with private showers nearby. To catch a game on television, play a game of pool, or just relax, guests can head to Dabber's Bar, named for distinguished UT football recruiter Ken Dabber, who retired in 1995. Because this hotel is right on the lake, there's plenty of room to just enjoy being outdoors—and we saw some picnic tables not too far away. Other Holiday Inn Hotels can be found at 3401 South I-35, (512) 448-2444, and northwest at 8901 Business Park Drive, (512) 343-0888.

Quality Inn $$
909 East Koenig Lane
(512) 452-4200, (800) 228-5151
www.qualityinn.com

On the southwest corner of I-35 and U.S. 290, the affordably priced Quality Inn provides quick access to many parts of Austin. This 91-room motel offers free deluxe continental breakfasts to all guests and an evening reception, which includes mixed drinks, sodas, beer, and snacks from 5:00 to 7:00 P.M. Tuesday through Thursday. Remodeled in 1996, the Quality Inn is exceptionally clean and comfortable. Coffeemakers, free HBO and Cinemax, and dataport telephones are among the amenities guests can count on at this property. The Quality Inn also features larger executive rooms and a conference room that will accommodate up to 60 people. There are several restaurants within walking distance and, of course, many more Austin attractions within easy driving distance.

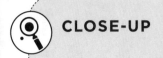

Austin's Resorts

The Texas Hill Country west of Austin is conducive to outdoor recreation and relaxation. The lakes and waterways, the natural beauty of the hills, the hospitable climate, and Texas hospitality have been combined to create several top-quality resorts that offer a variety of experiences. Two of the three listed here are noted golf resorts, and they are detailed in our Golf chapter. The third is a Hill Country spa that offers not only outdoor recreational activities but also all manner of therapies designed to relax both body and spirit.

Barton Creek Conference Resort and Country Club
8212 Barton Club Drive
(512) 329-4000, (800) 336-6157
www.bartoncreek.com
A topflight resort with four beautiful golf courses designed by the top names in the sport, Barton Creek is on some of the most beautiful land just west of Austin. Barton Creek wends its way through the hills here, creating not only a beautiful setting for golf but also for other activities, including tennis, skeet shooting, jogging on wonderful Hill Country trails, swimming, boating, fishing, and horseback riding. The resort also offers sightseeing and shopping tours, a spa, and even a Kid's Club where the youngsters can be entertained while Mom and Dad enjoy their own playtime.

The resort has several excellent dining facilities, for both casual meals and special occasions. (It has one of the few restaurants in Austin where a jacket is required.) The resort's spa offers an extensive menu of treatments from facials to salt rubs to aromatic loofah scrubs. There is also a fitness center in the resort complex. The resort maintains recreational facilities, including swimming and tennis, at Barton Creek Lakeside at nearby Lake Travis.

An additional 158 rooms have been added to the resort, bringing the total to 305, but despite the size the atmosphere is private and quiet. The rooms all have views of the golf course or the surrounding Hill Country. The resort offers a number of packages tailored to guest's interests. High season is from March to November; low season is December through February. Packages begin at around $270 per person per night in low season and $330 in high season. Room rates vary from around $230 to $1,100 for the presidential suite.

Lake Austin Spa Resort
1755 South Quinlan Park Road
(512) 372-7380, (800) 847-5637
www.lakeaustin.com
You can ask the concierge to fix you up for a round of golf. Or perhaps a set or two of tennis. A sailboat ride. A little water-skiing. But why would you? Wouldn't you rather just have another massage? This spa on the shores of Lake Austin aims to capture the essence of Austin and rid you of all those uptight urban ills. Readers of *Condé Nast Traveler* and *Travel and Leisure* magazines have named it one of the Top 10 spas in North America. Lake Austin Spa Resort offers a large variety

of spa services by the day or week. A three-night refresher package is a little more than $1,500 and includes two spa treatments of your choice, fitness classes and programs, a 30-minute personal fitness consultation, meals, and a deluxe private room. The seven-night ultimate pampering program costs approximately $3,000, and that includes a monogrammed robe.

Just reading the brochures is enough to make you long for a night or two of pampering. How about a Blue Lagoon massage—a body wrap of blue seaweed. Or a Texas two step—someone rubs your toes while you get an herbal facelift.

The spa also offers special programs throughout the year on diverse topics, including gardening, cooking, and nutrition. Guest speakers from all walks of life are invited to these presentations. One special package is dubbed "A Gathering of Wise Women" and featured experts on women's health issues.

If you really want to get more active, in addition to golf and tennis the spa offers a long list of outdoor activities, including watersports on adjacent Lake Travis and hiking in the hills.

The pool at Lake Austin Spa Resort offers an escape from the hubbub of the city.
COURTESY OF LAKE AUSTIN SPA RESORT

Lakeway Inn
101 Lakeway Drive
(512) 261-6600, (800) LAKEWAY
www.lakewayinn.com
This resort hotel on Lake Travis, west of the city, is a longtime favorite for visitors from around Texas and Mexico. The resort has topflight amenities for golfers and tennis players plus provides the facilities and equipment for a variety of watersports. Prime season is March to November; "value season" runs from December to February. The resort offers a variety of packages ranging in price from approximately $200 a couple per night in value season to $280 in prime season.

In addition to golf packages, the resort also offers romantic getaways, "lake escape" packages, and family packages and is a popular spot for catered events, including weddings and family reunions.

Rodeway Inn University   **$$**
2900 North I-35
(512) 477-6395, (800) 228-2000
www.rodeway.com

For the budget-minded traveler, Rodeway Inn University is one of the area's best buys, largely due to its proximity to the University of Texas campus, the state capitol, and downtown Austin. The 50-room motel is a locally owned franchise, and the owner spends a great deal of time on the premises. The rooms are clean and well maintained. The motel offers free coffee, juice, tea, and doughnuts from 6:00 to 9:30 in the morning. Coffeemakers in every room, fax and copying service, an outdoor pool, and cable television, including HBO and ESPN, complete the amenities. There is no restaurant on the premises, but next door is the Enchiladas y Mas restaurant, and there are many choices within walking or easy driving distance. The motel is right next to busy I-35, a plus for many travelers who like easy access, though there could be some traffic noise. Rodeway Inn University was built in 1965 and remodeled in 1997. Another Rodeway is located farther north at 5656 North I-35, (512) 452-1177.

INTERSTATE 35 CORRIDOR—SOUTH

The hotels in this area are on I-35 beginning on the south side of Town Lake and heading south. More national chain hotels are planned for this area, plus along Highway 71 from the Ben White Boulevard interchange on I-35 as it heads east to the airport.

Best Western Seville Plaza Inn   **$-$$**
4323 South I-35
(512) 447-5511, (800) 528-1234
www.bestwestern.com

One of three independently owned Best Western hotels in Austin and Round Rock, the Seville Plaza Inn offers 95 rooms, most with balconies. Located next to Celebration Station, one of Austin's favorite enter-tainment centers for children, the hotel is a great location for families, although it also attracts Austin visitors of all kinds. A free continental breakfast of pastries, fruit, juice, coffee, and tea is served daily in the lobby. All rooms have desks, irons, and coffeemakers, and the larger rooms come with love seats or recliners. There's also a self-service guest laundry room for those who like to return home with clean clothes. The hotel's restaurant, Saigon Kitchen, serves Vietnamese food for both lunch and dinner. A Subway sandwich shop is also on the property. Other Best Western properties are in Round Rock at 1831 North I-35, (512) 255-3222, and in Atrium North at 7928 Gessner Drive, (512) 339-7311.

Excel Inn   **$**
2711 South I-35
(512) 462-9201, (800) 367-3935
www.excelinns.com

For the traveler looking for an affordable room, the Excel Inn is a very nice choice. The inn features 90 rooms on three floors, including a deluxe room with a whirlpool bath. The rooms, all of which have writing desks with phones, are cute, comfortable, and well maintained. The Excel is close to St. Edward's University and within 3 miles of the state capitol, downtown Austin, and the Convention Center and just 4 miles from the University of Texas.

Omni Austin Southpark   **$$$**
4140 Governors Row
(512) 448-2222, (800) THE-OMNI
www.omnihotels.com

An enticing lobby designed with luxurious dark woods, marble, and subdued lighting greets guests upon arrival at the Omni Austin Southpark, I-35's southernmost full-service hotel in Austin, with access to nearby high-tech giant AMD. A unique and inviting horseshoe-shaped gourmet coffee and cocktail bar beckons visitors to "come, relax, unwind." The 313 rooms and suites in this 14-story giant are exceptionally large and comfortable and are well equipped with coffeemakers, hair dryers, irons and ironing boards, desks, and telephones with dataport connections. The upper-level floors on the north side offer the best views of downtown Austin and St. Edward's University. For those who prefer the outdoors, the hotel offers 24 rooms with walk-out balconies. We especially like the huge heated outdoor-indoor swim-ming pool, a wonderfully original concept. The outdoor portion of the pool is sur-rounded by a large deck and lovely garden area and then wraps around into the fit-ness center building. The fully equipped fitness center includes a sauna and a hot tub surrounded by tropical foliage—very relaxing. The Omni's Onion Creek Grille, popular with both travelers and local resi-dents, serves breakfast, lunch, and dinner beginning at 6:30 A.M. Don't miss the made-to-order pasta bar, open for lunch daily. After a full day of work or sight-seeing, the Republic of Texas Bar, designed with a Western flair, is a great place to watch a game on television or socialize. For business or social gatherings, the Omni offers 15,000 square feet of space, including a huge ballroom for large groups. The hotel also features a conference center with tiered seating for 30 people, a gift shop, and a full-service business center.

Super 8 Motel $
2525 South I-35
(512) 441-0143, (800) 800-8000
www.super8.com

Instead of the standard writing desk, the Super 8 Motel features a table with two chairs in its standard rooms that can work as both a desk and a dining table. This Super 8 features 79 functional, exceptionally clean guest rooms, including a huge deluxe room that offers plenty of space in addition to a refrigerator, microwave oven, and seat-ing area. For the budget-minded traveler, the Super 8 is a fine choice, both for quality and location. The motel is just a few min-utes' drive from downtown Austin and offers easy access to areas both north and south on I-35. Continental breakfast is free, and the motel provides irons and ironing boards. Faxing and copying services are

also available. Austin has two other Super 8 Motel locations at 6000 Middle Fiskville Road, (512) 467-8163, and 1201 North I-35, (512) 472-8331.

SOUTH

Ramada Inn—South $$
1212 West Ben White Boulevard
(512) 447-0151, (800) 272-6232
www.ramada.com

Clusters of Austin's famous live oak trees surround this newly remodeled Ramada Inn, providing shade and an inviting atmosphere for travelers.

Casual comfort is the hallmark of the Ramada, which features 103 guest rooms on six floors. As they say, the cream rises to the top, and the Ramada is no exception. For romantic getaways of all kinds, the Ramada features six Jacuzzi hot tub suites on the top floor. In each room, the double-sized Jacuzzi is up on risers in the center of the sleeping area and next to a picture win-dow that offers a stunning view of down-town Austin's skyline. What a way to get clean!! The hotel also offers six parlor suites in which the living area is divided by a door from the sleeping area. There also are patio rooms that lead directly to the Ramada's outdoor swimming pool. Coachman's Steakhouse serves breakfast, lunch, and dinner beginning at 6:30 A.M., and the lounge is open until around midnight. Guests staying Sunday through Thursday night get treated to a complete breakfast the following morning. While there's no fit-ness center on the premises, Ramada guests are offered discounted daily rates at three nearby fitness centers. The Ramada's ballroom seats up to 150 guests banquet style and can be divided to accommodate groups of all sizes. Smaller conference rooms are also available. The hotel, on Ben White Boulevard between MoPac and I-35, is about 3 miles south of downtown and its great entertainment venues. This Ramada is also closest to the international airport.

Austin has another Ramada Inn and two Ramada Limited hotels. There also is a Ramada Limited on I–35 in Round Rock. They can be reached by calling the "800" number listed above.

NORTHWEST

Hampton Inn $$
3908 West Braker Lane
(512) 349-9898, (800) HAMPTON
www.hamptoninn.com

Efficient and inviting, the Hampton Inn is one of several newer hotels in this part of town that cater to professionals, including many who work in the high-tech industries. Each of the hotel's 124 rooms is equipped with a small desk and telephone that features a dataport. The comfortably sized rooms feature coffeemakers and an iron and ironing board. The hotel also offers one-day valet laundry service and provides a fax service. For those who want to unwind after a busy day, there's an outdoor swimming pool and a small fitness center with a treadmill, stationary bike, and stair stepper. The Hampton offers a complimentary continental breakfast daily from 6:00 to 10:00 A.M. and coffee in the lobby throughout the day. The hotel doesn't leave guests feeling left out in the boonies. It is just off the MoPac Expressway and within a couple of minutes' drive to more than a dozen restaurants, three large movie theaters, several grocery stores, and some of Austin's choicest shops. Hampton Inn has five other properties in the area, including the airport and in Round Rock.

Homewood Suites—Northwest $$$
10925 Stonelake Boulevard
(512) 349-9966, (800) CALL-HOM
www.homewoodsuites.com

An exceedingly inviting lobby tastefully designed with a Southwest decor greets guests upon arrival at this all-suites hotel fashioned for both the business traveler and for families. Those traveling with children will especially like the solid door that divides the bedroom—or bedrooms—from the living area, so the children can sleep peacefully while the parents relax, entertain guests, or watch television. The apartment-style suites are stylish and very comfortable with fully equipped, full-sized kitchens that even include toaster ovens. Homewood offers one- and two-bedroom suites as well as a choice of bed sizes. Each suite has two 25-inch TVs and a video player as well as two dual-line telephones with dataport capabilities. A nice-size outdoor swimming pool is a great place to work out or relax. There's also a sports court and an exercise room. For serious exercisers, Homewood Suites offers free passes to The Q, a great fitness facility a few blocks away. The hotel offers complimentary continental breakfast and an evening social time off the lobby. There's also an executive center with a typewriter, copier, and a printer to print from your computer. Guests can use the do-it-yourself laundry facilities or take advantage of the valet laundry service. Homewood offers excellent access to Arboretum-area restaurants, shops, movie theaters, and grocery stores. Located between MoPac and U.S. 183, the hotel can claim easy access to areas both north and south. Daily rates are lower for extended-stay guests.

Homewood Suites has another hotel in Southeast Austin at 4143 Governors Row. Call (512) 445-5050.

Renaissance Austin Hotel $$$$
9721 Arboretum Boulevard
(512) 343-2626, (800) 468-3571
www.renaissancehotels.com

Northwest Austin's luxury hotel, the Renaissance Austin pampers each guest as it caters to nearly every whim and any need. Enter through the lobby into the immense pavilion, the airy indoor courtyard that reaches up 10 stories to the skylight. Here among trees and plants, attractive sculptures, and tremendous dangling mobiles, visitors will find the Garden Cafe, which serves breakfast and lunch. Across the pavilion is the hotel delicatessen, open 24 hours a day. Need a sandwich at three o'clock in the morning?

Stretch your legs for a walk to the pavilion, or just dial the phone and the hotel's 24-hour room service will send it up. Feel like dancing? Drop into Tangerine's, the hotel's nightclub. How about a gourmet Italian meal? The Trattoria Grande delivers excellent dining fare (see our Restaurants chapter). Swim indoors or outdoors, drop in to the fitness center, or walk next door or across the street to some of Austin's finest shops and a great selection of nearby restaurants. The rooms are ample and tasteful and, for those staying on the Hill Country side, afford excellent views of the trees and hillsides. This hotel, owned by Marriott, is the largest of Austin's luxury hotels, with 478 rooms and suites. The Renaissance, like many other topflight hotels in the area, offers a Club Floor for those guests wanting a little extra space and service. The hotel has an enormous amount of meeting and convention space, including an auditorium with tiered seating for 55 people, an exhibition hall, a 12,000-square-foot ballroom, and many other private rooms and halls. The executive traveler can pop downstairs to the Business Center, which offers copying, faxing, shipping, word processing, and a notary. The Renaissance is one of the farthest hotels from the airport, but its location near the junction of MoPac and U.S. 183 is great for the discriminating traveler who wants to be on the edge of Austin's beautiful Hill Country and yet have easy access to the high-tech industries in the north and other parts of town.

**Courtyard by Marriott—
Austin Northwest** $$$
**9409 Stonelake Boulevard
(512) 502-8100, (800) 321-2211
www.marriott.com**
A view of the indoor pool and the charming breakfast room, complete with fireplace, greets guests at this modern, efficient hotel designed for business travelers. Each of the hotel's 78 rooms features a coffeemaker, iron and ironing board, hair dryer, and two telephones, one conveniently located on a desk—a must

for travelers using computer modems. Fax service is available at the lobby desk. After a hectic business day, guests can flip on the television or work out in the fitness center, which features treadmills, bicycles, and other exercise equipment, or they can take a dip in the pool or a relaxing soak in the hot tub. Courtyard has no outdoor pool on the premises, but guests are allowed to use the pool at Marriott's Residence Inn next door. *USA Today* is delivered free to each room Monday through Friday, and other newspapers are available for purchase. A small do-it-yourself laundry room and a comfortable meeting room that holds about 25 adults complete the amenities. For guests desiring even more, upgraded rooms that include microwave ovens and small refrigerators are available, as are Executive King rooms that are about 1½ times the size of a normal room. The hotel has no restaurant on premises, but it's near restaurants and shopping centers in the area. A second Courtyard is located in north Austin at 5660 North I-35, (512) 458-2340.

APARTMENT HOTELS

While the vast majority of those who visit Austin and our surrounding communities stay less than a week, many people come for reasons that require them to stay much longer—a long-term business contract or the search for suitable housing, for example. While many of the establishments listed above provide

If you've decided to take a chance on Texas's multimillion-dollar lottery while you're in town, check the Austin American-Statesman's *"Metro & State" section on Thursday and Sunday for results, or visit the official site at www.txlottery.org. The Texas Lottery also runs other games, Cash 5 and Pick 3, as well as plenty of scratch-off games. Tickets can be purchased at dozens of places around town, mostly at gas stations and convenience stores. We haven't made our fortune this way, but maybe you'll have better luck.*

reduced rates for long-term stays, some travelers prefer to be in an apartment. For that reason, we're giving you the names of some companies that may be able to fulfill your needs. We have not provided a price code for these apartments, as rates can vary greatly. It's best to call for current rates.

Austin Executive Lodging
809 West Martin Luther King Jr. (main office)
(512) 478-0051, (800) 494-2261
www.austinlodging.com
This locally owned company has one-, two-, or three-bedroom fully furnished apartments at four locations in the Arboretum area of Northwest Austin. However, they can also provide apartments for temporary residents in other areas. The apartments come with washers and dryers, and the kitchens are complete. Complexes also have tennis courts, swimming pools, and fitness centers. Executive Lodging offers daily, weekly, and monthly rates.

Balcones Woods Apartments
11215 Research Boulevard
(512) 346-6850

A minimum seven-night stay is required at Balcones Woods Apartments, which offers completely furnished apartments for the temporary resident. The one- and two-bedroom apartments include fully equipped kitchens, washers, and dryers. Balcones Woods Apartments features swimming pools, spas, and a fully equipped weight room. Maid service is optional. Rates are by the week or the month.

Corporate Lodging
4815 West Braker Lane
(512) 345-8822, (800) 845-6343
www.corporate lodging.com
Corporate Lodging offers one- and two-bedroom apartment living for temporary lodgers at seven locations, six in the Arboretum area of Northwest Austin and one in South Austin. The apartments are fully furnished, including dishes, washers, and dryers and include membership to The Q Sports Club and guest privileges at two area country clubs. There also are swimming pools and workout facilities on-site. A hostess is available for errands. Daily, weekly, and monthly rates are available.

Pinnacle Suites—Round Rock
16601 F.M. 1325
(512) 218-4050, (800) 586-4050
www.pinnaclesuites.com
Located in Round Rock at I-35 and F.M. 1325, Pinnacle Suites offers new one-, two-, and three-bedroom furnished apartments in a gated community for guests staying a minimum of three nights. The full kitchens are fully equipped, and the complex includes two swimming pools, two hot tubs, a sand volleyball court, a tennis court and sport court, two picnic areas, a 1-kilometer jogging trail, a playground, a 24-hour fitness center, and a 24-hour business center. Guests can check out videos and sports equipment free of charge.

HOSTELS

Hostelling International $
2200 South Lakeshore Boulevard
(512) 444-2294, (800) 725-2331
www.hi-austin.org

Austin is a mecca for young travelers, especially those fascinated by the city's music scene. Finding a cheap place to stay can be a challenge, but the arrival of Hostelling International on the shores of Town Lake near the city's Hike and Bike Trail has made Austin affordable for travelers on a budget. There are 39 beds in four dormitories in the facility, and beds are assigned at check-in. Guests must show an ID with an address outside the Austin area, and guests who are members of Hostelling International pay a few dollars less for their accommodations. The central location is not far from the city's entertainment area, and the hostel even offers its own live music two nights a week. The hostel is located on city and University of Texas bus lines and is an easy walk to banks, grocery stores, and restaurants. There is a kitchen on premises, common areas, Internet access, and a laundry, and the hostel is air-conditioned and heated. Visitors also can rent canoes, kayaks, and bicycles. There are some rules—no alcoholic beverages on site, no smoking inside, and no sleeping bags. Reservations are recommended and can be made with a credit card or a Hostelling International membership card. Groups of up to 20 persons are accepted.

BED-AND-BREAKFASTS AND COUNTRY INNS

For a truly unique Austin experience, spend the night, or the week, in one of our incomparable bed-and-breakfast establishments. Austin provides an exciting range of possibilities for visitors searching for the unique. Among Austin's many bed-and-breakfasts today, you'll find some listed as historic landmarks; some wonderful examples of Victorian, Texas Colonial Revival, Mediterranean, and Greek Revival styles of architecture; as well as some vintage and more modern structures distinctive in their own way. Six of Austin's bed-and-breakfast establishments have been accepted for membership in the selective organization Historic Accommodations of Texas: Adams House, Austin's Governor's Inn, Austin's Wildflower Inn, Brook House, Carrington's Bluff, and Woodburn House.

Looking for a room with a view? Austin offers several. If you want to get away to a country retreat, Austin can answer that call. And if you're looking to escape to a bed-and-breakfast and yet remain close to the action of downtown, the UT campus, or Austin's other hot spots, there are plenty of inns from which to choose.

For distinctive special events, such as weddings, parties, and business gatherings, several of Austin's bed-and-breakfast establishments can fulfill all your needs by providing an original setting as well as taking care of all your music and catering arrangements. For that romantic interlude, some bed-and-breakfasts offer celebration packages that include champagne and other delights. With all these special services, it's no wonder more and more Austinites are discovering that they don't have to leave town to go on vacation.

The special people who operate these lodgings are, in many cases, sharing their own homes and their lives—not to mention their favorite breakfast recipes. Visitors will also find bed-and-breakfasts created for the exclusive use of their guests. One common denominator among all our bed-and-breakfasts, however, is the attention to detail paid to each of these properties. Character, style, charm. There's no better reason to choose a bed-and-breakfast than simply the desire to stay in a one-of-a-kind lodging.

Bed is just half the equation at these inns. There's also breakfast, of course, and you'll find that Austin's proprietors have put as much effort into the morning fare as they have into their homes. From quick and delightful self-serve continental breakfasts to full-scale seated gourmet meals, the menus are designed to please. What better way to wake up in the morning than to the inviting aroma of a feast someone else has prepared for you? Don't hesitate to tell your host or hostess about any dietary constraints or preferences that you may have, as most are willing to accommodate your needs. Some inns serve at specific times of the morning; others are more casual.

In this chapter you'll find a wide selection of the bed-and-breakfast establishments in Austin. Unless otherwise noted, the inns listed here accept major credit cards. The Americans with Disabilities Act does not require that these lodgings create wheelchair-accessible rooms, although you will find some with that amenity. Smoking is usually permitted outdoors only at these establishments. Guests should be aware that check-in times and cancellation policies at bed-and-breakfast establishments differ from those at hotels and motels and that some charge a cancellation fee. Please check with the individual establishment regarding the cancellation policy and check-in times when you make your reservation. And if you're planning to stay in Austin for a while, be sure to ask about extended-stay rates.

PRICE CODE

Our rate categories are based on a one-night stay for two people throughout the year. Because some bed-and-breakfasts offer a wide range of room sizes and amenities, their rates can vary greatly. In that case we have given you two dollar codes and you will expect to find rates within those spectrums. These rates do not include the 15 percent total Austin tax on lodgings. Nor do they take into account the extended-stay or other specialty rates available at many establishments.

$	Less than $70
$$	$70 to $110
$$$	$111 to $150
$$$$	More than $150

CENTRAL

1110 Carriage House Inn $$-$$$$
1110 West 22½ Street
(512) 472–2333
www.carriagehouseinn.org

This well-established, award-winning B&B is unique in that its six guest rooms and suites are housed in three different buildings on-site, each with its own special features and most with private entrances. The inn's location—on a quiet street yet minutes from downtown and the UT campus—is another pleasant anomaly. The main house, a beautifully restored 100-year-old colonial structure, is the home of proprietors Tressie and Jim Damron. The two lovely guest rooms in this building are upstairs via a private outdoor staircase, which ends at a large deck—perfect for looking down on the gazebo and koi pond below or up at the stars. There's a telescope if you'd like to find Cassiopeia. The

rooms here share a kitchen that, like the others at the inn, comes stocked with dishes, crystal, soft drinks, tea, and coffee.

Out back on the property is the Cottage, which houses two spacious suites. The Robinson Suite features a living room/kitchen and a separate bedroom highlighted by a queen-size poster bed. A queen-size sleigh bed is the focal point of the bedroom in the Garden Suite, which also has a comfortable living/kitchen area. Unlike the inn's other rooms, however, this suite has no phone—for those who wish to totally withdraw from the real world. Next door is the Guesthouse, a quaint gem made from lava rock from an inactive volcano near here! In addition to two well-appointed guest rooms, each with a queen-size bed and private bath, this building features a communal living room with extra half bath, microwave, and coffee and tea service. Each of these rooms also has its own private outdoor seating area.

The Guesthouse also is home to the B&B's contemporary Western-style breakfast room, accentuated by individual handmade cedar tables. The real treats, however, are the breakfasts Tressie puts on these tables. Homemade waffles with homemade whipped cream and fresh blueberries, rosemary breakfast tacos, chicken sausage, and homemade scones are among her guests' favorites.

The 1110 Carriage House Inn has received several honors from the industry trade publication *Arrington's Bed & Breakfast Journal*, including being listed among the top 15 most elegant inns in the country. Indeed, the inn is long on attributes. We especially like its many private decks, terraces and patios—and the large garden itself. Most notable, however, is the warm Texas charm of Tressie herself.

Adams House $$-$$$
4300 Avenue G
(512) 453–7696
www.theadamshouse.com

One of Austin's newer bed-and-breakfasts, Adams House opened for business in

1998. And what a house it is. Historic-preservation architect Gregory Free has restored this 1911 home in historic Hyde Park from top to bottom. He installed stylish gray slate floors in some areas and added a gray wash to the original hardwood floors in others. White woodwork, high ceilings, and wraparound sunrooms on two levels give this home a bright and airy look that adds to its beauty. The current resident owners, Sidney and John Lock, have added their own special touches, which give this old Colonial Revival house the look and feel of a classy modern dwelling—even with the many remarkable antiques throughout.

Adams House originally was built as a one-story bungalow. W. T. Adams and his family purchased the home in 1922 and added another level in 1931. The home, however, fell on hard times during the second half of the 20th century and was turned into apartments. Free and the Locks have done a wonderful job restoring the place. Original paintings, a baby grand piano, and a designer kitchen with granite counters all contribute to its charm. Adams House offers three rooms, all on the second floor. This inn does not accommodate children. And, sorry, no pets are allowed.

The superb King Suite features its own private sunroom with shuttered windows on three sides. The king-size four-poster bed, with a wonderfully high mattress, is draped in custom fabrics from a specialty shop in historic Fredericksburg. This room has a private bath with dual sinks and granite counters. The Queen Suite features a four-poster bed, another step-up mattress covered in custom linens, an antique armoire, and a walnut antique chest. The private bath in this room has a large walk-in shower and slate floor. Adams House also offers a double-bedroom suite, which can be used for a family or group of friends traveling together. These lovely rooms share a bath, or guests have the option of choosing just one of the rooms, with a private bath just steps away. All the rooms have private telephones. For watching television, socializing, or reading from the huge selection of books and magazines, guests are invited to use the comfortable sunroom on the main floor. There's also an office area, with the Locks' computer that guests can use to send e-mail if the need arises. Breakfast on weekdays is a serve-it-yourself continental affair, which includes muffins, croissants, fresh fruit, cereals, juice, and gourmet coffee. Weekends and special occasions are a treat at Adams House because a local chef often comes to prepare a full, seated breakfast especially for guests. Breakfast tacos, gourmet quiches and other egg dishes, pastries, and homemade breads are just some of the delicacies served.

Austin Folk House $$-$$$
506 West 22nd Street
(512) 472-6700, (866) 472-6700
www.austinfolkhouse.com

Some people stay at this great bed-and-breakfast just to enjoy the eclectic collection of folk art on display throughout the house. But don't come to feast your eyes on the art alone. Young University of Texas grads Sylvia and Chris Mackey have created a classy, Austin-hip inn that invites guests to settle in, relax, and stay awhile. This B&B got its name from the artwork (the collection is from Sylvia's family), but now a new dimension has been added to make it even "folkier." Once a month on Sunday evening, the Mackeys host a folk concert for their guests and the general public. How Austin is that?

The two-story establishment offers nine well-appointed rooms, including one designed for wheelchair accessibility. While all the rooms feature either queen- or king-size beds, each room is quite distinctive. Some are painted in vibrant red or olive tones; others are light and airy. There are sleigh beds, canopy beds, iron beds, and four-poster beds, each with a handmade spread that perfectly accentuates the decor. The romantic Room Seven upstairs is done in crimson and gold and features an exquisite Oriental carpet and an iron canopy draped with elegant fabric.

All rooms have private baths, most with tub and shower, phones, TVs, and VCRs.

Sylvia serves a full, hot buffet-style breakfast each morning. Migas, banana crepes, raspberry waffles, fresh fruit, and fresh-baked breads are among her guests' favorites. A word of warning, though: Her homemade cookies are addictive. The elegant dining room, another showcase for some intriguing paintings, consists of five individual pub tables. Guests also are invited to take their breakfast out to the spacious front porch. The porch, by the way, is a fine hangout any time of the day or night. The kitchen is always open for those who like to make a late-night cup of tea or grab a snack from the fridge.

The Folk House is perfectly located for easy access to downtown or the UT campus, although one trade-off for its central location is a bit of traffic noise. For that, there are soothing sound machines in each room. This B&B also has its own parking lot, a real plus for this neighborhood, and the free 'Dillo people mover stops right across the street. While the establishment does not accept pets, well-behaved children are welcome. Don't forget to ask Sylvia about the Folk House's own T-shirts and the special packages and treats she offers—like mimosas served in your room!

Austin's Governor's Inn $–$$$
611 West 22nd Street
(512) 477–0711, (800) 871–8908
www.austinbedandbreakfast.com
An elegant neoclassic Victorian home decorated in rich tones and romantic fabrics awaits guests at Austin's Governor's Inn, just a short walk from the UT campus. Lisa and Matt Weidermann, who run Brook House, also own this property. Like Brook House, Governor's Inn is listed with Historic Accommodations of Texas (the others are named in the introduction to this chapter). But these are two very distinct properties. This graceful home was chosen as one of three Texas bed-and-breakfasts to be featured on The Travel Channel's *Romantic Inns of America*. And no wonder.

Many of the bed-and-breakfast establishments we've listed are members of the Greater Austin Bed-and-Breakfast Association (GABBA), which operates a referral service among members. If you find that the bed-and-breakfast you prefer is booked, ask for the name and phone number of the member contact person that week. That person will be able to help you locate a bed-and-breakfast that is right for you from among GABBA members.

Built in 1897 and restored in 1993, this three-story inn is finished in white woodwork and wonderful Laura Ashley and Ralph Lauren fabrics and wall coverings. The dining room—with its high ceiling, wallpaper of white flowers on a bright red background, white damask tablecloths, and lace curtains—will transport visitors to another era. Here guests are offered a full hot breakfast on elegant china and crystal with silver tableware and serving pieces. Breakfast always include a delicious hot entree such as egg blossoms in puff pastry, quiche, fruit-stuffed French toast, or a delectable casserole. There's also homemade granola, fresh-baked muffins and breads, and fresh fruit.

The 10 rooms of Governor's Inn are just gorgeous. Four-poster beds draped in vibrant blue, white iron beds enveloped in delicate flowers with matching draperies, claw-foot bathtubs, and an abundance of period antiques are just some of the delights awaiting guests at this inn. It offers something for every romantic-at-heart. All the rooms come with private baths, telephones, cable television, bathrobes, and coffee and tea services. And there's always plenty of Texas-made Blue Bell ice cream in the freezer.

The home features five rooms with queen beds, four kings, and a cozy twin. Of course each room is named for a historic Texas governor. Lovers and children will delight in the third-floor Governor Ma and Pa Ferguson room. (Yes, they were

February through June and September through November are the busiest seasons for Austin's bed-and-breakfasts. We highly recommend making your reservations well in advance, especially if your heart is set on one particular establishment. The limited number of rooms in each inn can fill up quickly, especially during special events in Austin.

both governors of our state). This room, with a pitched ceiling and lots of cozy nooks and crannies, offers one king-size bed and two twins. The sit-down antique tub has a hand-held shower. Victorian rocking chairs and porch swings adorn the two wraparound verandas—perfect places to unwind or sit and watch the backpack-toting college kids on their way to and from the university. This is a marvelous place to hold a wedding or other special event, and the inn offers a full range of amenities for gatherings of all kinds.

Austin's Wildflower Inn $$$-$$$$
1200 West 22½ Street
(512) 477-9639
www.austinswildflowerinn.com

One of Austin's most well-established B&Bs, Austin's Wildflower Inn underwent an ownership change and a face-lift in 2003—and the results of both are simply marvelous. Native Texan Chris Sims is relying on his extensive background in both the hotel and the restaurant businesses to provide guests with the perfect combination of bed *and* breakfast. Of course he and business partner Gus Campman have an excellent property to work with. The two-story 1930s colonial-style home features a long front porch, complete with swing and wicker sofa, while the bilevel deck overlooking the beautifully designed back garden is a real Texas treat. Polished hardwood floors, a spacious living room, and a cozy dining room contribute to the charm of the inn's interior.

This B&B offers two bedrooms and one two-room suite, all with private baths. On the main floor is the Burnet Room, named in honor of David G. Burnet, one of the presidents of the Republic of Texas. This room features an elegant queen-size cherry bed, antique iron floor lamp, and white lace curtains. The centerpiece of the Walker Room is an impressive queen-size pine sleigh bed. Complimenting the decor are an antique desk, marble-top side table, and oak library chair. The Texas Country Suite has its own entrance and features a comfortable sitting room with a love seat that converts to a twin bed. This room, done in antique white wicker, offers a great option if you're traveling with children. The bedroom features a view of the back garden and is highlighted by a queen-size iron sleigh bed. Pets also may be accommodated at the inn, but check with Chris first, please.

Chris is your morning chef here at the Wildflower Inn. He serves a full hot breakfast at 8:00 A.M. on weekdays, 9:00 A.M. on weekends. Dutch apple pancakes, baked French toast, egg frittata, and Elgin sausage are among his specialties. Of course there's always plenty of fresh fruit, juice, and coffee; and guests are welcome to rustle up snacks and drinks from the kitchen.

Location is another plus here. The inn is on a quiet residential street but close to UT and downtown. This is a warm and inviting place to spend your time in Austin.

Brava House $$-$$$$
1108 Blanco Street
(512) 478-5034, (888) 545-8200
www.bravahouse.com

Blanco Street in downtown Austin is lined with many of Austin's Victorian-era homes, among them Brava House, built in the 1880s and now beautifully restored. The home is within easy walking distance of Austin's central city sights and nightlife. There are two guest rooms, two suites, and a large apartment, each named for the era the decor suggests. The Van Gogh

Room on the first floor off the garden has its own private entrance and is completely wheelchair-accessible. The room has a lovely bay window and features a queen-size bed with canopy netting. A beautiful four-poster bed is the centerpiece of the Moroccan-style Casablanca Room, which also has a sitting area by the large corner picture windows.

Fireplaces in both the parlor and the bedroom and an antique wooden queen bed add touches of romance to the Garbo Suite, which brings to mind the Hollywood of the 1930s. The spacious Fitzgerald Suite, named for F. Scott of course, has a 1920s Art Deco decor. This room is great for families; there's a sleeper sofa in the parlor, as well as a fireplace. The lovely bedroom has a queen-size bed. The Monroe Suite upstairs is a one-bedroom, fully equipped apartment of about 650 square feet. It features a wood-burning fireplace, full kitchen, and plenty of space in the living room to spread out. All the rooms and suites have private baths, phones, cable TV, coffeemakers, and minirefrigerators.

Sunday morning is special at Brava House—that's when this B&B offers its great champagne brunch, a full hot breakfast complete with mimosas and berries and cream. A hot breakfast buffet is also served on Saturday. On weekdays the breakfasts are continental. Trays are provided so that guests can eat in their rooms if they'd like or enjoy the morning air on the front porch or the exquisite back deck.

Brook House $$–$$$
609 West 33rd Street
(512) 477–0711, (800) 871–8908
www.austinbedandbreakfast.com

Variety is the spice of life at this charming bed-and-breakfast, which offers six unique rooms from which to choose. Brook House, built in 1922, features three rooms upstairs inside the home as well as more private lodgings in the Carriage House and the Cottage out back across the lawn. Owners Lisa and Matt Weidermann have created a cozy country inn with plenty of space both indoors and out for their

guests' enjoyment. There's a great covered back porch with large antique tables and ceiling fans where breakfast is served in nice weather. You'll always find a big bowl of fruit and homemade breads along with a main entree that can be an egg dish, waffles, French toast, or other tasty morning fare. Or guests may follow the short path to the gazebo and make themselves at home at one of the patio tables there. Post oaks and elm trees shade this attractive backyard area.

The home itself has high ceilings and lots of windows that bathe the rooms in light. All guest rooms are delightfully adorned with antiques and feature cable television, telephone, and private baths. The stately Green Room, featuring an antique oak king-size bed, matching armoire and bath stand, and an extra large bathroom, offers an attached screened sitting porch with wicker chairs. The Blue Room also has a wonderful sitting porch shaded by a 100-year-old Spanish oak. This room is especially light and airy and features an elevated mahogany queen-size four-poster bed and antique rocking chair. The bathroom is right outside the door. A classic fainting couch highlights the romantic Rose Room. Or guests may choose to "faint" on the antique pine king-size bed or relax in the antique claw-foot tub. The rooms in the Carriage House and the Cottage have private entrances. The spacious Upper Carriage, with high-pitched ceilings, dormer windows, a large walk-in closet and kitchen facilities, is decorated with antique furnishings and a queen-size iron bed. Four persons can sleep comfortably in this room. The cozy Lower Carriage features a secluded deck, queen-size brass bed, sofa, and desk.

The Cottage is just delightful. This suite has a separate sleeping area with an antique oak queen-size bed. There's also a daybed with trundle in the sitting area for extra guests. Children and pets are welcome to stay in this lovely cottage, which also features kitchen facilities with refrigerator, microwave, and coffeemaker as well as an antique oak table and chairs.

This cottage is perfect for a small family or anyone who requires a little extra space. Of course, all guests are invited into the cozy living room to watch television, read a book, socialize, or just relax.

Carrington's Bluff $$-$$$
1900 David Street
(512) 479-0638, (888) 290-6090
www.carringtonsbluff.com

A 500-year-old native oak is just one of the many trees that shade the one-acre bluff where this attractive bed-and-breakfast stands. Operated by resident owner Phoebe Williams, this English Country–style home got a face-lift in 2003, so now it really shines. The Main House, built in 1877, features five guest rooms with elegant king- or queen-size beds, most decorated with floral fabrics and featuring American and English antiques. The large covered porch is a great place to rock and relax while enjoying the view of the garden and gazebo, where many Austin couples have been married. The Writers' Cottage just across the lawn has its own kitchen and living area, as well as three additional guest rooms, including one especially large room that holds two queen-size beds. This cottage is a great place for family retreats or for those who want to feel like they're off on their own, to work or just to unwind. All the rooms have private bathrooms and come with guest bathrobes, irons and ironing boards, TVs, VCRs, and telephones.

Every morning Phoebe serves a complete buffet-style hot breakfast in the dining room of the Main House. The menu always includes one of her specialties, such as a Gouda cheese and bacon frittata, crepes with fresh raspberries, or a green-chile and cheese casserole. Children of all ages are invited to Carrington's Bluff, and so is the family pet. Just give Phoebe a call first.

Carrington's Bluff, part of an original 22-acre homestead of the Republic of Texas, is just above busy Lamar Boulevard, but it's nestled so well amid the lush greenery and flower gardens that it's hard to tell. Guests feel isolated here, even though they're minutes from downtown—and just 7 blocks from the University of Texas. For those who really want to pamper themselves, Phoebe can arrange on-site spa services, including massages and manicures, but do let her know in advance so that she can accommodate you. She also offers some great special packages, such as candles, flowers and chocolates, and breakfast in bed.

The Inn at Pearl Street $$-$$$$
809 West Martin Luther King Jr. Boulevard
(512) 478-0051, (800) 494-2261
www.innpearl.com

This gorgeous Greek Revival–style mansion was selected as the 1995 Designer Showhouse by the Austin Symphony League. And it shows. The turn-of-the-20th-century property, completely restored in 1995 and decorated by some of Austin's finest designers, is among the city's most elegant bed-and-breakfast establishments. Each of the eight rooms and the many common areas are luxuriously decorated to reflect Old World radiance. The inn also offers one cottage and one apartment. Sumptuous designer fabrics and wallpapers throughout this cozy home add the perfect touch to each room. The French Room, decorated in shades of yellow and gold, features French antique furniture, a stylish four-poster iron bed, a crystal chandelier, and a claw-foot bath. The European Room exudes the utmost in Old World charm, with its king-size bed, billowy-topped floral chintz draperies, and unique furnishings. The Far East Room, decorated in shades of salmon and featuring a beautiful Oriental screen and armoire, offers the perfect escape. Here guests will discover a lovely private balcony and a fabulous private bathroom.

The Gothic Suite, with a separate dayroom and Jacuzzi bath, is perfect for a special occasion, or just a special treat. A glorious cathedral-inspired bed highlights this room, decorated in sage greens, pale reds, and coppery metals. The Gothic Suite includes a refrigerator, coffeemaker, and complimentary toiletries. The common areas also are a feast for the eyes. The music room is especially attractive, with its ivory-lacquered grand piano, mirrored pedestals, and antique fireplace. The large outdoor deck, surrounded by oak and pecan trees, is perfect for a wedding or a special gathering of any nature. This is one place that begs to be discovered.

The Inn at Pearl Street offers an elaborate European-style self-serve breakfast during the week from as early as you request it until about 10:30 A.M. Cereals, muffins, fruit, bagels, and more are presented along with cold cuts and cheeses to give breakfast that European flair. A full-service breakfast is offered on weekends from 9:00 to 9:30 A.M. While the table service is exquisite every day of the week, the inn pulls out all stops on Sunday with full china and silver service, tantalizing entrees, and mimosas. A house specialty is the wonderful egg soufflé served with smoked ham and fresh bread. For an extra fee and advance notice, you can request breakfast on your private balcony. There is coffee and tea service on both floors. And for those truly special occasions, the Inn at Pearl offers a celebration package, which includes a bottle of champagne on arrival and breakfast in bed. For that special occasion, make arrangements in advance for the Inn's Twilight Dinner: an elegant five- or six-course meal served by candlelight for an extra fee. This bed-and-breakfast is on busy Martin Luther King Boulevard Jr. at Pearl Street, just blocks from the UT campus and close to downtown entertainment of all kinds. Children age 12 and up are invited to stay at this historic inn.

Strickland Arms Bed & Breakfast $$
604 East 47th Street
(512) 454-4426
www.stricklandarmstexas.com
Judge John McCamy Patterson built his home in Austin's premier turn-of-the-20th-century neighborhood, Hyde Park, in 1904. This historic neighborhood located just north of the university has maintained its unique character over the years, and many fortunate and dedicated homeowners have restored homes and battled to retain the charm of the neighborhood, including Jim and Barbara Strickland, owners of the Strickland Arms. (See our Relocation chapter.) This neighborhood B&B is within walking distance of the Elisabet Ney Museum, as well as several popular restaurants and neighborhood coffee shops and is about a 10-minute drive to downtown. Built of native limestone, the 5,000-square-foot home has 12-foot ceilings, formal dining and living areas, and a wraparound Antebellum-style porch with rattan swings. Much care has been given to the gardens, which are enclosed in an old-fashioned wrought-iron fence and shaded by huge oak and pecan trees. Two Great Dane statues guard the front door, and Barbara Strickland's stained-glass panels decorate the front windows. Inside, guests will find four guest suites named in medieval style after knights and their ladies. All the rooms have cable TVs and VCRs, private telephone lines, and antique wardrobes and chests of drawers. Two of the suites have four-poster beds, and all have private baths.

Woodburn House $$–$$$
4401 Avenue D
(512) 458–4335
www.woodburnhouse.com
This gracious Austin Landmark features two wonderful wraparound verandas, spacious rooms tastefully adorned with antique quilts and family heirlooms, and the allure of historic Hyde Park. (See our Relocation and Attractions chapters.) This 1909 two-story bed-and-breakfast, one of

The smaller towns in Central Texas claim a growing number of B&Bs and country inns. Check out the Historic Accommodations of Texas Web site at www.hat .org for a listing of some of our favorites.

six bed-and-breakfasts in Austin listed as a Historic Accommodation of Texas (see the introduction to this chapter for a list of the others), is named for Bettie Hamilton Woodburn, who bought the house in 1920. Mrs. Woodburn is the daughter of Andrew Jackson Hamilton, who was chosen provisional governor of Texas following the Civil War and was a personal friend of Abraham Lincoln.

This great structure narrowly escaped the wrecking ball in the late 1970s, when artist George Boutwell, a former Hyde Park resident, bought the house for $1.00 and had it moved to its present location. Now beautifully restored, Woodburn House is the home of Herb and Sandra Dickson, who have created a bed-and-breakfast that exudes Texas charm. This beautifully understated home features original Louisiana longleaf pine woodwork and hardwood floors.

Woodburn House offers four guest rooms on the second floor and one suite on the third floor, all with private baths. The Bettie Hamilton Room features an antique Jenny Lind queen-size bed and a beautiful Oriental rug. Our Mother's Room is stylishly decorated with quilts made by Herb's grandmother and also features a queen-size Jenny Lind bed. The H. Dickson Room offers direct access to the wonderful second-floor veranda, where guests can unwind and enjoy the Hyde Park breeze. This room also features a king-size bed and a shower and claw-foot tub. The Frank Woodburn Room can comfortably accommodate three people with a queen-size and twin beds. The third-floor suite, aptly named the Treehouse Suite, features

a king-size bed, a sitting room with television, and a bath with his and hers lavatories and whirlpool tub for two. A third person can be accommodated on a twin bed in the sitting room.

Woodburn House guests are treated to a full hot breakfast each morning cooked up by Herb himself. The menu is quite varied and exciting here, including such delicacies as spinach-feta cheese quiche, migas, German pancakes, blueberry-pecan French toast, and sun-dried tomato-basil egg frittata as well as plenty of muffins and fresh ground coffee the Dicksons purchase themselves in Mexico. Seating times are flexible, but breakfast is usually served around 9:00 A.M. on weekends. The large table in the dining room is the perfect place to gather, meet other guests, and become part of the family. The Dicksons want their guests to feel like they're home—but, please, don't get up to wash the dishes. Guests are invited to use the very comfortable living room to listen to music or watch television or a video. And for those who just want some quiet, there's a formal front parlor. Woodburn House accepts children age 10 and up. Sorry, no pets please. A minimum two-night stay is required on holidays and during special events.

SOUTH CENTRAL

1888 Miller-Crockett House $$-$$$$
112 Academy Drive
(512) 441-1600, (888) 441-1641
www.millercrockett.com

There are so many reasons to visit the 1888 Miller-Crockett House: fabulous New Orleans–style Victorian architecture, a location and view that can't be beat, great guest rooms, incredible gourmet breakfasts, and, perhaps most of all, the bubbling personality of owner Kathleen Mooney. Built in 1888, the house is one of just 12 homes built south of the river during that time period—and one of only five left standing. No wonder that it's now a designated Texas landmark—and was

 No matter which bed-and-breakfast you choose in Austin, you'll be staying close to one of our wonderful lakes or parks. Be sure to ask your host about the nearest outdoor oasis, and check out our Parks and Recreation chapter for details.

featured in the 1998 film *The Newton Boys,* starring Matthew McConaughey.

The 1888 Miller-Crockett House features an exquisite wraparound veranda, an inviting parlor with 12-foot-high original pressed-tin ceiling, and a spacious tree-filled lawn that is very popular for outdoor weddings and special events. There's even a lovely grape arbor on top of the carport, which is fast becoming popular for outdoor parties and meetings. Just south of the Congress Avenue Bridge, a few minutes from downtown, the house is distinctive for its outstanding view of the downtown skyline. Kathleen offers two rooms and a suite in the main house and two more suites in bungalows across the lawn.

The Blues Quarters, named in honor of the band Blues Traveler, which stayed here while recording an album in Austin, takes up the entire first floor of the estate. It features a king-size bed, Saltillo-tile floors, fully equipped kitchen, a sitting room with a full-size bed, and a lovely patio. The stunning Lydia Marguerite Room has a queen-size Victorian mahogany bed, polished-wood floors, and a private bath. Caroline's Room, with its queen-size iron-and-brass bed, private bath, and lovely deck that offers a great skyline view, is a delightful spot. Across the lawn is Bungalow Bill's, a gorgeous Southwestern-stye bungalow with both a queen-size bed and a queen sleeper sofa. It also features a kitchen and private bath. There's also a lovely patio and garden off this suite. La Casita is decorated with eclectic artwork and Saltillo tile. It, too, features a queen bed and sleeper sofa, kitchen, bath, and a garden deck.

Breakfast is a gourmet affair on weekends, a delicious hot buffet on weekdays. Green-chile and cheese quiche, blueberry pancakes, exotic fresh fruits, homemade muffins, and gourmet coffee are just a few of the treats Kathleen serves her guests. If you've overdone it on breakfast, there are plenty of mountain bikes for guests' use. Therapeutic massages can also be arranged.

Lazy Oak Inn $$-$$$
211 West Live Oak Street
(512) 447-8873
www.lazyoakbandb.com

A great country kitchen, original shiplap walls, and turquoise-painted wooden floors in the common areas give this 1911 plantation-style home a very casual and comfy feel. And resident hosts Renee and Kevin Buck were voted "Best Down-Homey Hosts" in an *Austin Chronicle* critics' poll. This two-story bed-and-breakfast, for adults and young people age 15 and up, features a wonderful covered porch on the second floor where guests can sit and survey the residential neighborhood, just blocks from the funky South Congress Avenue shopping and dining district and close to downtown Austin. Stairs leading down from this porch allow guests to come and go as they please. The five rooms, each with cable television, telephones, and private baths, are detailed with great antiques and original artwork by some of Austin's most interesting artists. And no wonder. The Bucks are great supporters of the city's artists and regularly host shows in their home. There's even a lovely gift shop on the back porch area, where guests can find some small antiques, collectibles, and artwork by Central Texas artists.

This house, which the Bucks renovated in 1996, has an open design, with high ceilings and carpeted, nice-size rooms. The large, exposed kitchen on the main floor has huge windows adorned with wall-to-wall country shelves, and a fireplace that's just covered in lush potted plants. Renee prepares a breakfast buffet for her guests each morning, with cereals, muffins, fruits, yogurt, and luscious gourmet coffee as well as a hot specialty of the day, sometimes an egg soufflé or a homemade fruit cobbler. Yum.

The inviting parlor across from the kitchen comes complete with books, collectibles, and a guitar for the musically inclined. A wide, carpeted staircase leads to the four second-story rooms, all with the look and feel of a modern country house. Here, guests can choose from among the king and queen rooms, or the room that features two double beds with a private bath just across the hall. The king room features a neat Art Deco armoire and an especially roomy bathroom. The cozy room on the main floor stands out for its fascinating antique queen bed, with three-dimensional cherubs carved into the footboard. The Lazy Oak Inn has been open since just 1997, but it's rapidly becoming a popular South Austin bed-and-breakfast.

LAKE TRAVIS

La Villa Vista $$$-$$$$
6701 Oasis Pass
(512) 266-6000
www.lavillavista.com

The view of Lake Travis is simply stunning from La Villa Vista's hillside perch. In fact, unless you visit the Oasis, a popular bar and restaurant nearby, or happen to have friends who own a home overlooking the lake, this vista is as good as it gets. Built in 1984 as a vacation home, the villa was designed with just that panorama in mind. And that's not all. This B&B features a gorgeous swimming pool, complete with flagstone deck and waterfall, that also overlooks the lake. It's no wonder La Villa Vista is a popular spot for outdoor weddings and parties.

The large living/breakfast room features floor-to-ceiling windows as well as a spacious covered terrace, and all four guest rooms look out over the lake. Only the Milan Suite on the lower level foregoes the view, but it offers some great amenities in exchange, such as a fully equipped full-size kitchen, big-screen TV, washer and dryer, Jacuzzi tub, two double beds, and easy access to the six-person hot tub outside. The Serengeti and Tuscany Rooms are on the second level. The Serengeti, whose theme is African, of course, has a king-size bed complete with leopard-print spread. This very spacious room includes a sofa and desk, a walk-in closet, and a large vanity with two sinks. There's even a window in the shower, in case you want yet another peak at the lake. The Tuscany Room is designed for romance and comes complete with a gas fireplace and a Jacuzzi tub with a view of the lake. These two rooms are connected by a cozy private living room, complete with television, minifridge, and coffeemaker, making them a perfect choice for a family or friends traveling together. The entire third floor is the B&B's common area, and the kitchen is open 24/7. Two smaller perchlike rooms are upstairs off the third floor. We especially like the Sunset Room, the highest room in the house, because it has its own private terrace that offers a panoramic view of the lake and the tree-covered hills. There's also a minifridge and microwave in the out-of-the-way wet bar. The only drawback here is that the bathroom, although private, is downstairs.

Breakfasts are quite casual at La Villa Vista. A full continental breakfast is arranged on the breakfast bar, and guests are free to serve themselves at the hour they prefer. There are always plenty of soft drinks and juice in the fridge, and guests are welcome to use the stove if they prefer something more substantial. All the rooms have TV and cable, and some come with VCRs. The B&B's one telephone is in the common area, athough there are phone jacks in the rooms.

Because this is such a popular spot for events, weekend bookings can be a bit of a problem—so plan your trip to the lake for midweek. While this property is not right on the lake, beaches and boat ramps are just minutes away. The Villa Vista is owned and operated by Myra Ratliff.

Robin's Nest $$$-$$$$
1007 Stewart Cove
(512) 266-3413
www.robinsnestlaketravis.com

Resident owner Robin Maisel celebrates the great outdoors with this casual, eclectically furnished bed-and-breakfast on a small Lake Travis cove. She has converted 50-

year-old fishing cabins into a fascinating assortment of guest rooms, offering the perfect spot for families traveling with children, couples wanting a little romance, or individuals looking for a peaceful getaway.

Offering nine guest rooms and suites, including a cheery three-bedroom cottage with a fully equipped kitchen that can be rented as a whole or by the room, Robin's Nest aims to please. Those looking for an intimate setting may like the Robin's Perch, which feautures an antique sleigh bed of burled wood, cozy chairs, cable TV, and a large covered deck overlooking the lake. The private bathroom has a large soaker tub, with plenty of room for placing candles or incense. The compact Biscuit's Room is cheery and light, with a queen-size brass bed, antique school desk, and oak armoire. It has a small private terrace and a bathroom equipped with a double-seated shower. A Western theme prevails in the spacious Windy Lindy's Guesthouse: The drapes are hung on antlers, the antique rockers are done in cowhide, and the king-size bed is made of cedar posts. There's a whirlpool tub in the bath and a 12-foot covered deck. This room is just beautiful. The room, Old Blue Two, has one of the most unique pieces of furniture we've ever seen: an antique table that converts to a love seat. This room also features a small dayroom with a bed, cable television with VCR, and a nice patio just outside.

This waterfront property, located next to the Yacht Harbor Marina, has a huge front lawn, plenty of patios and decks for enjoying the view, a soft hot tub, and its own large dock—a great place to take in some sun or to take a cool dip in the lake. There are telephones in every room. Four of the rooms are near the water, and five have lake views. Two of the rooms feature working fireplaces for a romantic evening— or a chilly weather stay, when room prices are a bit less.

Breakfasts are sit-down family-style affairs. If you prefer more privacy, a breakfast basket can be delivered to your room. Robin offers fresh breads and homemade

Migas are a specialty item on the break-fast menu of several Austin B&Bs. For those of you not from these parts, migas are sliced corn tortillas fried up with eggs and cheese and, perhaps, onion, chile peppers, cilantro, toma-toes—or whatever else inspires the chef.

bran muffins, a daily meat course or smoked salmon with bagels, and fresh fruit. On Sunday she like to cook up one of her specialties, which include shrimp migas and homemade beans, Italian eggs, and blueberry French toast. Breakfast is served at the main house on the outdoor terrace.

While Robin's Nest is secluded, it's not far from the Oasis, one of the most popular dining and partying spots in the area (see our Attractions chapter). Downtown and Sixth Street are less than 25 minutes away.

DRIPPING SPRINGS

The Cabin on Barton Creek, $$
P.O. Box 414, Dripping Springs 78620
(512) 858-4407, (888) 511-8400
www.bbonline.com/tx/bartoncreek
You will have to call or write to owners Richard and Susan Stark for directions to their Hill Country hideaway. Lots of bed-and-breakfasts and hotels promise a hide-away, but this one really delivers. The cabin is located above the banks of Barton Creek, one of the most treasured water-ways in central Texas, near Dripping Springs west of Austin on U.S. 290 West. This is the creek that wends over and under the Edwards Aquifer and feeds the cool springs of Barton Springs in Austin (see our Close-up in the Parks and Recreation chapter). The cabin is handcrafted from old cedar fence posts (juniper wood is called cedar by the locals), native stone, and lumber gathered from old Texas barns. It is situated not far from the creek and surrounded by oak, pecan, and walnut trees, a rustic retreat from the noise of the

ever-encroaching city. The Starks wanted their cabin to reflect their pioneer roots but also provide a comfortable retreat for visitors eager to celebrate the natural wonders of the Texas Hill Country—wildflowers and native grasses that paint an ever-changing picture with the seasons and wildlife including deer, birds, and small animals that roam the pastures and hills nearby. There is a swing near the creek, two tennis courts nearby, and a swimming pool. Guests can also try their hand at fishing in the creek. The cabin has a front porch where guests can take their morning coffee, plus a fully equipped kitchen and a barbecue grill. Continental breakfast is served, but guests can create other meals in the quiet of the cabin. There are two bedrooms, one with a queen-size bed, the second with a twin bed. No children or pets are allowed. No smoking inside. In addition to the cabin, the Starks have a bunkhouse on their property that sleeps 30 and a kitchen/dining room that seats up to 50 people—a great way to celebrate a family reunion. Dripping Springs is a 30-minute drive from Austin, and guests also can drive within an hour or less to Wimberley, Johnson City (the LBJ Ranch; see our Day Trips chapter), Fredericksburg, and San Antonio.

RESTAURANTS

If there is one rule on the Austin restaurant scene it likely is this: You got a shirt, you got shoes or sandals, you got service! There is not a restaurant in town (maybe a private club or two) where a tie is required. Ties are just targets for bean dribbles and spaghetti spills. This is a city where dining is supposed to be fun, not an exercise in tailored torture. But as Austin grows, the question being asked is will things stay this way? As the number of upscale restaurants increases and more and more restaurants are demanding that diners make reservations, there is a fear that Austin's dining scene will lose some of that wonderful casual flavor.

In the past two decades, the Austin restaurant scene has ridden the same economic roller coaster as the real estate sector, falling into the doldrums in the mid-1980s only to rise from the ashes like the proverbial phoenix. In 1998 the phoenix began to soar with restaurants popping up in converted bungalows in old Austin neighborhoods, sprouting on street corners, and slipping into strip shopping centers whenever a storefront became available. That trend has continued as more and more restaurants, some of them small, exciting spots, open around the city. With the dot-com bust, the pace slowed somewhat. Some of the new, high-priced restaurants have come up with innovative ways to maintain their clientele—some introducing prix-fixe menus and some opening only for lunch. Nevertheless, the Austin dining scene remains an exciting one where changes can be swift. For that reason, we suggest you call ahead before heading out for a special dinner.

Some of the new restaurants are franchises or outlets for a national chain, but many are homegrown. There has been a dramatic increase in the number of Asian restaurants in the city as immigrants from that continent have found a home here.

Several long-established local restaurants have opened second, third, and fourth locations, often in the burgeoning northwest section of the city. One of the coolest trends has been the emergence of young, dynamic chefs, eager to take advantage of the wide variety of fresh foods in the city and the willingness of Austin diners to try new things.

There is no such thing as "Austin cuisine." But there are certain signature cuisines that do have a connection to Texas culture. Given the fact that Texas once was part of Mexico and Mexican-American life is vibrant and very much a part of the state's cultural weave, it is only natural that Mexico's culinary influence is felt in a number of ways. There's Tex-Mex, Nuevo Tex-Mex, South Texas/Northern Mexico, New Mexican, Interior Mexican, and Latin American, even South American.

Tex-Mex is probably the most prevalent and recognizable. Standard fare includes enchiladas, tacos, chalupas, and refried beans. An easy way to spot Tex-Mex is whether the dish includes yellow cheese instead of the traditional white farmer's-style cheese found in true Mexican cuisine. That's not to put Tex-Mex down. David Garrido, chef at one of Austin's finest restaurants, Jeffrey's, and a native of Mexico, published *Nuevo Tex-Mex* in the spring of 1998, and the book includes an introduction by one of Texas's top chefs, Stephan Pyles, who remembers that Tex-Mex was everyday fare when he grew up in West Texas.

Pyles notes the processed yellow-cheese phenomenon: "Over the years, processed cheese food and other shortcuts have found their way into many Tex-Mex cocinas (kitchens) and compromised the integrity of their cuisine. But in every Texas city, there are still Tex-Mex restaurants that have remained true to their time-honored cooking traditions—traditions rooted firmly in the peasant culture of Texas."

In our listings we have included a variety of Tex-Mex and other Mexican/Latino restaurants in an effort to give readers a good cross section of that multifaceted cuisine. Just as many of us get a hankering for an old-fashioned burger once in a while, yellow-cheese Tex-Mex has its appeal and a loyal following. But readers who want to go beyond that point have a wide variety of restaurants to choose from, including several that celebrate interior Mexican culinary traditions. Those unfamiliar with that territory should not hesitate to explore. Not all Mexican food is spicy hot. The chile pepper is a staple of the Mexican kitchen, but not all peppers are hot, and many are served in rich sauces, called moles, that blend the pepper with herbs, spices, even chocolate to create multinuanced tastes.

Most Austinites have their favorite Mexican restaurant, particularly when it comes to weekend brunch. A popular traditional dish is migas, eggs scrambled with tortilla chips, diced chiles, and tomatoes. Given the city's late nightlife, weekend breakfast is often served into midafternoon. During the week, breakfast tacos are the early-morning order of the day, economical and easy to eat—simply flour tortillas stuffed with combinations of eggs, chorizo (sausage), potatoes, bacon, and salsa.

A menu staple in Austin and, now, beyond is fajitas. This dish had its origins in South Texas and Northern Mexico when vaqueros (Mexican cowboys) would grill skirt steak, a cheap cut taken off the ribs, over coals, perhaps marinating it first in a little beer or simply with salt and pepper. The meat was then cut up or shredded, topped with a salsa cruda—a fiery uncooked mix of tomatoes, onions, serranos or jalapeños, and cilantro—and folded into a tortilla. The name comes from the Mexican word *faja*, meaning belt—hence, "little belts," a play on the appearance of the meat and its location on the body of the cow.

Fajitas are now made from the traditional skirt steak or a fancier cut of flank steak, chicken, shrimp, even catfish, and customers are given a choice of corn or flour tortillas (flour tortillas predominate in Northern Mexico and South Texas cuisine, whereas corn are more familiar in the southern parts of Mexico). Sometimes frijoles borrachos, or drunken beans, a Northern Mexican favorite concocted from pinto beans, salt, bacon, onions, peppers, and beer, are served, but other restaurants serve their fajitas with refried black or pinto beans. (Pinto beans are preferred in Northern Mexico and South Texas, while black beans are favored in the southern regions of Mexico.)

Another star in the Texas culinary pantheon is, of course, barbecue. It's a subject, like religion and politics, that should be discussed carefully and with great consideration for individual beliefs—even the spelling of barbecue promotes debate. Generally speaking, Texas barbecue is slow-cooked with indirect heat over wood coals, often mesquite—a quite delicate-looking tree with a gnarled trunk that is the bane of ranchers since it spreads like a weed and sucks up water. Brisket is the most popular cut of meat to be slow-cooked, and most cooks "marinate" with a dry rub of spices and sometimes herbs.

(This is treacherous ground, because already some aficionados are saying, "No! No!")

Barbecue is usually served with pinto beans, potato salad, perhaps coleslaw, certainly sliced raw white onions (or sweet 1015 Texas Onions), pickles, plain old white bread, and barbecue sauce—often the ingredient by which a barbecue joint is judged.

Some of the best barbecue can be found in the small towns of Texas, among them four communities just a short drive from Austin. Most barbecue joints are open all day but close around 6:00 P.M.—earlier on Sunday afternoon. We recommend calling ahead to check on hours of operation. But as you drive through the small towns of Central Texas, you can also follow your nose; sometimes roadside stands serve up fine barbecue. Here are just a few of the most famous and popular joints in the area beyond Austin's city limits; other barbecue cafes within the Austin city limits and environs are included in the restaurant listings in this chapter.

Lockhart, which touts itself as the barbecue capital of Texas, is home to several barbecue joints. For years the most famous of these was Kreuz, where years of smoke had blackened the walls of an old brick building on the main street of this small town southeast of Austin. But in 2002, with the death of "Smitty" Schmidt, the fabled owner of Kreuz Market, a family feud erupted. Smitty had left the business to his sons and the building to his daughter. The battle even made national headlines and only quieted when the brothers moved Kreuz Market to a new building nearby at 619 Colorado Street (512-398-2361), while the founder's daughter started selling barbecue in the original building at 208 South Commerce Street (512-398-9344) under the new label, Smitty's. A third popular restaurant is Black's Barbecue, 215 North Main Street (512-398-2712).

Luling is famous for its annual Watermelon Thump festival (see Annual Events chapter), but barbecue aficionados also flock to Luling City Market in this small town southeast of Austin. Along with the barbecue aroma emanating from the market at 633 East Davis Street (830-875-9019), occasionally the smell of natural gas wafts over town. But the locals don't complain; in fact, they even decorate the rocker well pumps that dot the community with cutouts of Uncle Sam and cartoon characters.

Northeast of Austin, the town of Taylor is home to two of the legends of Texas barbecue: Louie Mueller's at 206 West Second Street (512-352-6206) and Rudy Mikeska's, at 300 West Second Street (512-365-3722).

One of the most popular items to toss on the barbecue in Central Texas is Elgin sausage, and the original can be found in the small town of the same name just east of Austin. Visitors can watch the sausage

being made just as it has been since 1882 and then sit down to a feast at Elgin Southside Market, 1212 U.S. 290 (512-281-4650). The owners also have opened a second location, Meyers Elgin Smokehouse, at 188 U.S. 290 East (512-281-3331).

Almost as revered as barbecue is chicken-fried steak, a staple of the home-style restaurants and sure to be a blue plate special at most country-cooking restaurants. The meat fried is usually a Salisbury steak, pounded thin to tenderize the meat, then covered with bread crumbs or flour mixed with salt and pepper, and then deep fried, just like chicken—hence the name. Some of Austin's upscale restaurants are treating other cuts of meat in this fashion—Z'Tejas (see our Central listings) serves a chicken-fried rib-eye.

Another hallmark of Austin cuisine is the emergence of native homegrown foods. Texas is home to a large variety of foodstuffs, including exotic game, prime beef, fresh seafood, onions, chiles, fruits, handcrafted cheeses, and special blends of rice. The Texas Department of Agriculture has an aggressive promotional program, and we have taken a look at this and locally crafted foodstuffs in our Close-up in this chapter, Texas Cuisine: Not Just a Bunch of Beef.

The multitude of cultural influences, the availability of a great variety of ingredients, and the innovative abilities of local chefs has led to a wide number of restaurants featuring "fusion" cuisine. Dishes on one menu might exhibit Mexican, Asian, Italian, and Mediterranean influences. But there are also a number of restaurants and cafes serving homestyle cooking. In a phrase, there is something for every taste these days in Austin.

A word or two about local customs. As noted above, casual attire is fine at most Austin restaurants, and even the most upscale allow customers to wear jeans and golf shirts—pressed jeans and clean golf shirts, of course. Smoking is a crime in Austin, as the late Timothy Leary, LSD guru, found out when he lit up in the Austin airport. A banner there reminds visitors AUSTIN IS A CLEAN AIR CITY. Some restaurants do have a smoking area if they have a bar or outdoor patio, but you will not be asked "Smoking or nonsmoking?" in the Austin city limits when you ask for a table. Outside the city limits, most restaurants do have designated smoking areas.

Many restaurants are open for major holidays, except Christmas. It is wise to call ahead. Most restaurants do not take reservations except for parties of six or more. We have noted where reservations are advised or required. All restaurants listed accept major credit cards, except where noted. A few take local checks, but that custom is fading as the city grows. More and more restaurants are staying open later to accommodate Austin's penchant for late-night noshing after the movies or theater, but most close at 10:00 P.M. during the week and 11:00 P.M. on weekends. Some stay open throughout the afternoon to serve late lunch or afternoon snacks, since many Austin businesspeople, particularly the city's large self-employed population, utilize favorite local restaurants as a conference room or an office away from their home office. We have noted restaurants that stay open beyond the usual hours.

Our restaurant listings are arranged by area of town. Where a local restaurant has more than one location, refer to the first listing for menu information. For the most part, well-known national chains are not listed, although a couple of Texas restaurant groups with a major presence in Dallas or Houston have been included, since

they are likely not familiar to out-of-state visitors.

One final note: Austin is growing at such a great rate that new restaurants are opening virtually every week, and, given the competitive nature of the business, sometimes others close. Generally those listed here have been open for at least a year or have achieved such success and popularity that they warrant listing.

PRICE CODE

The price key symbol in each listing gives the range for the cost of a meal for two, an entree and beverage, but not including alcoholic beverages, appetizer, or dessert. Since some restaurants serve three meals a day, or have a wide range of entree prices, the range is noted by the symbols.

$	Less than $20
$$	$20 to $40
$$$	$41 to $60
$$$$	More than $60

CENTRAL

Aquarelle $$-$$$
606 Rio Grande Street
(512) 479-8117

Austin has seen the proliferation of small boutique restaurants that evoke their European cousins, intimate places where the food is a work of art. The inspiration at this topflight restaurant is French with an emphasis on fresh American ingredients. Patrons are offered a choice of fixed-price dinners or a la carte, and main courses might include fresh fish and seafood, veal, rabbit, game, and other dishes evocative of French dining. Drawing on European tradition, Aquarelle offers little bites, perhaps cheese straws or miniature vegetable tarts, as appetite teasers while patrons study the menu, and dinner ends with what the French call a "mignardise," a selection of small bites of cookies or candies. Aquarelle consistently ranks among Austin's best. Dinner only; closed Sunday.

Asti Trattoria $$-$$$
408-C East 43rd Street
(512) 451-1218
www.astiaustin.com

Anyone who is familiar with the Tuscan countryside can't help but see echoes of the Italian landscape in the limestone hills and oak trees of Central Texas. Some Texans have even created a new style of Tuscan-Texas architecture that embraces natural stone, handmade tiles, and rough-hewn lumber. The affinity for things Tuscan doesn't stop there. Rural entrepreneurs producing wine, goat cheese, olive oil, and herbs proliferate in the Hill Country. Emmett and Lisa Fox are long-time fixtures on the Austin culinary scene and key contributors to the successful Texas Hill Country Wine and Food Festival (see our Annual Events chapter). They know all about this affinity, and they celebrate it at their neighborhood trattoria. Reflecting its Hyde Park location, this is a friendly place where the food evokes the cafe menus found in the hillside towns of northern Italy: grilled steaks served with arugula, mussels roasted in wine and herbs, squash stuffed with chestnuts, roasted chicken, pastas, pizzas, and homemade breads. The trattoria is housed in a converted drugstore, the long, narrow store now fitted with sleek fixtures, small tables, and dimmed lighting. Some customers come by simply for coffee and dessert, conjured up by Lisa Fox, a noted pastry chef. Others have a simple dinner of salad and pizza. The trattoria is open Monday through Friday for lunch and dinner, Saturday for dinner only. Closed Sunday.

**Austin Land and
Cattle Company** $$$-$$$$
Enfield Shopping Center,
1205 North Lamar Boulevard
(512) 472-1813

Steakhouse—the term usually brings to mind leather banquettes, red walls, and dark wood paneling—but this locally owned steakhouse in a small, quiet shopping center a few blocks from downtown has a lighter touch. The soft, cool palette acts as a foil to the hearty fare found here. The menu features steak and top-quality seafood, complemented with Southwestern touches, including grilled chile strips. A house specialty is the beer-battered mushrooms made with dark Shiner bock beer from the Central Texas brewery in the town of that name. (See our Annual Events chapter for the annual Shiner picnic.) Open daily for dinner.

Bitter End Bistro and Brewery $$-$$$
311 Colorado Street
(512) 478-2337

One name that surfaces with some regularity in any compendium of Austin restaurants is Clemons. Reed and Betsy Clemons are responsible for some of Austin's most popular restaurants, including the Bitter End across the street from another Clemons's favorite, Mezzaluna, in the downtown warehouse district. A combination brewpub (read more about Austin's brewpubs in our Nightlife chapter), the Bitter End is the sort of hip bistro favored by Austin's young (and not so young) movers and shakers. The menu is a mix of Italian, Mediterranean, American, and French. A wood-fired oven produces a large selection of pizzas and breads, while the salad menu includes a wonderful salade Niçoise with fresh grilled tuna. The wood-roasted trout is popular, and the hamburgers are huge and satisfying. Grilled dishes are included on the menu plus several yummy appetizers—calamari, roasted vegetables, steamed mussels. Light dishes are served in the bar, which overlooks the restaurant floor. In addition to a reasonable wine list, the Bitter End serves selections of its made-on-the-premises beers. Next door is the B-side lounge, also owned by the Clemons restaurant group, where blues and jazz bands play (see our Nightlife chapter). There is also a cigar room on the premises. Lunch, dinner, and late-night snacks are served daily in this restored warehouse space.

Want to eat out in? Call EatOutIn, (512) 346-9990, www.eatoutin.com, a local delivery company that brings the food of some 20 local restaurants to your door for a fee. The service will fax you a menu, you can ask them to mail you a brochure, or they can brief you on your choices.

Boiling Pot $-$$
700 East Sixth Street
(512) 472-0985

The tablecloths are made of butcher paper at this Sixth Street cafe just west of the interstate in downtown Austin. The napkins are large rolls of paper towels. The patrons are swathed in bibs and then armed with mallets, sure signs that dinner will be a messy, finger-sucking affair. A popular item on the menu is the Cajun Combo, made up of boiled crab, shrimp, sausage, corn, and potatoes; or try a platter of snow crab legs. This is a good place for a family feast or an early evening dinner before embarking on a tour of Sixth Street nightlife. Open Monday through Thursday for dinner, Wednesday through Sunday for all-day lunch and dinner.

Brick Oven $
1209 Red River Street
(512) 447-7006
1608 West 35th Street
(512) 453-4330
www.brickoven.citysearch.com

Just east of the capitol on Red River Street is one of Austin's most popular pizza restaurants, noted and named for its wood-fired pies. The menu has a pizza for every taste—thick and thin crust, a variety of toppings, even an all-garlic pizza for those who believe in its efficacy and are not afraid to indulge. In addition to being near the capitol, the Brick Oven is just a few blocks south of the University of Texas Special Events Center, so it is popular among concertgoers and basketball fans. Pizza dominates the menu, but there are other offerings, including a vegetarian stromboli. See the Northwest Austin section for two other Brick Oven locations. Lunch and dinner are served daily.

The 35th Street restaurant is a relatively new branch of the Brick Oven pizza restaurants. It is in a converted home in the 35th Street shopping district.

Cafe at the Four Seasons $$$$
98 San Jacinto Boulevard
(512) 478-4500

Elegant is the word most critics apply to this hotel restaurant, where the menu is a tribute to the best European traditions touched by Southwestern flair as divined by Chef Elmar Prambs. This is the place for a power lunch, power dinner, or divine brunch. The hotel is a favorite among movie stars in town for filming, high-tech wunderkind in town for networking, and politicians in town to be taken to dinner by lobbyists. That said, you never can tell who might be grazing on field greens at the next table. The menu is a wondrous combination of elegant dishes, some of them with Texas connections—nachos with smoked lamb, grilled duck salad with black-eyed pea chili—plus bistro fare such as roasted chicken and healthy, low-fat choices, all concocted in high style. The cafe, decorated in the same beiges and subdued pastels as the rest of the hotel, features topflight service and an extensive wine list. One of the best and most affordable ways to experience the cafe is to sample brunch at the Four Seasons. A groaning board of omelettes, blintzes, salmon, caviar, desserts, and fresh fruits abounds. The restaurant offers a good view of the nightly summer bat flight from under the Congress Avenue Bridge, although the tab for your dinner will be considerably more than the bats are going to pay for their bug supper. Lunch and dinner are served daily, plus a prix-fixe brunch. Reservations are recommended.

Cafe Josie $$-$$$
1200-B West Sixth Street
(512) 322-9226

This is one of those Austin cafes that lie hidden behind unassuming storefronts and in back of other businesses where young chefs are exploring the world of fusion cuisine. Here the emphasis is on Caribbean flavors, with dishes like redfish tacos with lime cilantro aioli and mesquite-grilled jerk pork tenderloin created by chef-owner Charles Mayes. The restaurant is tucked behind Portabla, a gourmet food shop (see Shopping chapter) in the West Sixth Street shopping district, and has a small indoor dining room plus a comfy outdoor patio. Open for lunch and dinner daily.

Cafe Piccolo $-$$
2828 Rio Grande Street
(512) 476-5600

This Italian cafe near the university is popular with both students and families for its affordable, fresh fare. The large covered patio is a favorite dining spot where guests can enjoy a variety of antipasti, including fried calamari and mozzarella sticks, pizzas, and pastas. The restaurant offers a daily ravioli special plus homemade soups, all in a colorful, casual setting. Open daily from lunch through dinner. Closed Sunday.

Carmelo's $$-$$$
504 East Fifth Street
(512) 477-7497
www.carmelosrestaurant.com

An old favorite just east of downtown and 1 block south of Sixth Street, Carmelo's serves large portions of rich Italian-American food with flair and drama. Steak Diane is flambéed tableside, while lobster-stuffed veal is presented with a flourish and a side order of fettucine Alfredo. Another house favorite is pollo Carmelo, cooked with olives, mushrooms, herbs, and garlic and served with mashed potatoes flavored with olives. The restaurant is housed in an old limestone building that once served as the Depot Hotel. Lunch and dinner daily.

Casita Jorge's $-$$
2203 Hancock Drive
(512) 454-1980

For the grown-ups there are frozen margaritas topped with a "blast of Cointreau" and for the kids, nachos. Tex-Mex with a tropical flair is the order of the day here, so the margaritas also come in raspberry, strawberry, peach, and banana flavors. The restaurant has an indoor dining room decorated in bright colors, a patio lined with banana palms to continue that tropical theme, and an arcade for kids. Entrees include enchiladas, fajitas, tacos—all the standard Tex-Mex fare—plus daily specials. The menu includes both crispy tacos and soft tacos, the latter made with flour tortillas. Open for lunch and dinner daily.

Castle Hill Cafe $$-$$$
1101 West Fifth Street
(512) 476-0728
www.castlehillcafe.com

Where's the castle? Where's the hill? Old-timers know that this popular cafe began as a tiny, tiny restaurant a few blocks north of its current location near the West Sixth Street shopping district. That spot is now occupied by Wink, see below.

Just to the west of the original tiny restaurant is a well-known landmark, a home on a hill that looks like a castle—hence the name. Castle Hill outgrew its original location but continues to draw crowds, especially on weekends. The food here is a delightful mix of Southwestern, Asian, and Mediterranean with a touch of Caribbean thrown in, perhaps even Indian, created by chef/co-owner David Daley, described by *Austin American–Statesman* critic Dale Rice as the "most admired chef in Austin." There are fixed items on the menu, but new dishes are constantly being introduced. Some of the longtime favorites include Lucinda's basil cheese torta, an appetizer that was inspired by well-known Austin writer and herbal expert Lucinda Hutson. Another staple on the menu is the spicy sausage and duck

RESTAURANTS

gumbo. The restaurant is airy and deco-rated with Oaxacan folk art, a far cry from the tiny, cramped quarters it once occu-pied. One thing the larger location does share with the old is the air of culinary excitement. Lunch and dinner daily. Reser-vations recommended on weekends.

Central Market   **$**
4001 North Lamar Boulevard
(512) 206-1020
www.centralmarket.com
Most of us go to the grocery store to shop, not to eat, or not eat substantially, perhaps a munch or two along the way. But Austin's showcase grocery store and top tourist spot (see our Close-up in the Shopping chapter) is a favorite lunch and early dinner spot, particularly among par-ents and grandparents. The store has added a breakfast/brunch bar and pre-pares breakfast tacos to go. Central Mar-ket Cafe features several "restaurants"—a bistro, an Italian cafe, and a bakery—housed in the southern wing of the store and aimed at satisfying a variety of tastes. Mom and Dad can order a roast beef sandwich or a salad, and the kids can peel the cheese off a pizza. The cafe is under the direction of a top chef, and the menu reflects Austin's tastes for a mix of tradi-tional, nouvelle, and fusion dishes. Dishes are reasonably priced, and customers can either graze or dig into a hearty meal. There is a large indoor dining room, flanked by a wide wooden deck looking out over the greenbelt. Kids can race around outside, dogs can sit in the shade while their owners nosh, and families can enjoy nightly live music concerts featuring a wide variety of musicians. The eateries are open daily from 7:00 A.M. to 10:00 P.M. A second Central Market is described in our Southwest Austin restaurant listings.

Chez Nous   **$$-$$$**
510 Neches Street
(512) 473-2413
www.cheznous.citysearch.com
Since 1982, Chez Nous has been serving authentic French bistro fare at this cozy

restaurant half a block south of Sixth Street. Bistro is a word much bandied about these days, but Chez Nous is as close to the real thing as you can get in Austin, with traditional dishes like oven-roasted chicken and homemade pâtés. There is a menu du jour, daily chef's spe-cials, plus lighter fare including crepes. The wine list features French wines, of course. The interior evokes the cozy bistros of Paris, and here friends and lovers can enjoy a quiet moment or two but yet be just a stone's throw from the frenzy of Sixth Street. The bistro is open for lunch and dinner Tuesday through Fri-day; dinner only on the weekends.

Clay Pit   **$$-$$$**
1601 Guadalupe Street
(512) 322-5131
www.claypit.com
It was only natural that as Austin became more and more high-tech, the number of good Indian restaurants would increase in the city. The high-tech sector has recruited many Indian engineers to work here, and their cultural influence is being felt. The Clay Pit occupies a historic stone building not far from the capitol, and after several culinary incarnations it has emerged as a much-praised Indian dining spot, including plaudits from *Bon Appetit* magazine. The owners brought a highly rated chef who had worked at a leading Indian hotel, among other top spots on his résumé, and local critics have praised the results. Many traditional Indian dishes have been updated to give them a contempo-rary feel, but devotees of Indian staples, particularly the country's flavorful breads, will be satisfied. Both vegetarian and meat dishes are on the menu. Open Monday through Friday for lunch and dinner.

Crimson   **$$-$$$**
407 Colorado Street
(512) 473-2700
www.crimsonaustin.com
Dubbed the "Warehouse District," the area just west of Congress Avenue and around Fourth Street has become a hangout for

the young and beautiful, particularly on weekend nights. Crimson makes its pitch to that demographic with its "naughty and nice" menu, featuring what it calls upscale Southern food. The nice entrees might include grilled fish, while naughty options include butter-broiled steak or pork chops with macaroni and cheese. The restaurant also offers half-off appetizers during happy hour and has a drink menu that features concoctions named after the seven deadly sins. Due to the parking headaches in this part of downtown, Crimson offers valet parking. Open daily for lunch and dinner.

Dan McKluskey's $$$
301 East Sixth Street
(512) 473-8924

Hand-cut steaks are the featured item at this restaurant in the heart of the Sixth Street club scene, just 3 blocks east of Congress Avenue. The menu lists a 20-ounce rib-eye but notes that the house butcher will cut a steak to any size. In addition to steaks, fish and chicken dishes are offered, also smoked pork chops, a mixed grill, baby back ribs, and all the appropriate side orders—onion rings, sautéed mushrooms, baked potatoes, etc. Lighter fare also is available. The restaurant has a traditional steakhouse aura: dark woods, polished brass. Open for lunch and dinner daily. Given its location, there is a late-night menu on weekends. There's a second location in Northwest Austin at the Arboretum.

Dirty Martin's Place $
2808 Guadalupe Street
(512) 477-3173

In this day of image-makers and spin doctors, who would ever name a restaurant "Dirty's"? This is a restaurant that has roots back to the '20s, but the story of the name has been lost in time. Some call this campus-area hamburger joint "Martin's Kumback"—and that is what the sign says—but the majority refer to it as "Dirty's." That name has stuck both in the popular imagination and the phone book.

The fare is fry-cook simple here: hamburgers off the grill with fries and onions, a cold beer or soda. Dirty's is open daily for lunch and dinner, but the menu doesn't change when the sun goes down.

Dog and Duck Pub $-$$
406 West 17th Street
(512) 479-0598
www.dogandduckpub.com

Pub grub is the order of the day in this downtown bar and restaurant that has all the comfy, familiar shabbiness of an old British public house. The walls are decorated with a mishmash of souvenirs, trophy cups (there's a dartboard, of course), tankards, and ye olde London street signs. The menu is a mix of English pub favorites, including fish-and-chips, shepherd's pie, bangers and mash (the staff will translate—sausage and mashed potatoes), plus dishes the Yanks love such as hamburgers, tacos, chicken-fried steak, even lasagna and macaroni and cheese. The bar serves a wide variety of beers plus has a great selection of British, Irish, Canadian, Australian, and American beers and ales on tap. The pub is open daily for breakfast, lunch, and dinner plus late-night snacks.

Driskill Grill $$$-$$$$
Driskill Hotel
604 Brazos Street
(512) 391-7162
www.driskillgrill.com

The venerable Driskill Hotel underwent a renovation in 1999 to emerge in 2000 as even more luxurious and evocative of Texas turn-of-the-20th-century luxury than before. (See our Hotels and Motels chapter.) The Grill, with its polished wooden walls and soft lighting, is one of the best places in Austin for a special dinner—a place where the setting and the food combine to create a wonderful experience. The star of the Driskill Grill is Executive Chef David J. Bull, variously described as "boy wonder," "wunderkind chef," and, in 2003, Best New Executive Chef in the United States by *Food & Wine* magazine. Bull, who is now in his midtwenties, began working at age 19 for Chef Dean Fearing at his much-praised Mansion on Turtle Creek in Dallas. He rose through the ranks quickly and now has brought all manner of accolades to the Driskill Grill, including its being named one of the top 50 hotel restaurants in the country by *Food & Wine*. The Grill serves dinner only, and menus are posted on the restaurant's Web site. Bull seeks out the highest quality ingredients, employs classic techniques, and adds a touch of Southwestern flavor in an homage to the Driskill Hotel's Texas history. His barbecued duck burrito, a specialty, has drawn rave reviews. He also serves duck confit in a focaccia club sandwich, and that same confit appears with a crispy duck in a dual duck entree. Other stars include beef, perhaps a rib-eye served with braised beef ribs in a tamarind and chile glaze or lobster tails with a lobster and mushroom polenta with truffled cognac butter. The desserts are also luxurious, and to take the edge off the hefty bill, diners are served a selection of chocolate truffles. There is no doubt that Driskill Grill is an Austin favorite for celebrating a special occasion—or simply experiencing the art and craft of one of the country's top chefs. Open for dinner daily.

Eddie V's Edgewater Grille $$$-$$$$
301 East 15th Street
(512) 472-1860
www.eddiev.com
As the Austin culinary scene has matured, seafood has finally taken pride of place at the table in a number of top dining spots. Eddie V's two locations, one downtown and the other northwest, are the creation of two veterans of the local culinary scene, Larry Foles and Guy Villavaso (Z'Tejas creators), and they have chosen to focus on seafood prepared in classic, simple ways. One of the favorites on the menu is the batter-fried lobster tail; another is the crispy Szechwan-style catfish. Gulf snapper is served grilled and topped with crabmeat. For meat-lovers

there are also steakhouse offerings on the menu. In addition to an oyster bar, Eddie V's also has a relaxing piano bar. Open daily for dinner.

El Arroyo $
1624 West Fifth Street
(512) 474-1222
www.ditch.com
The hallmark of this West Sixth Street–area restaurant is the large sign out front that offers pithy, scathing, and sometimes self-deprecating comments on a daily basis. Commuters making their way downtown off MoPac are entertained by the political humor of the El Arroyo folks every day. (The restaurant's Web site offers visitors a chance to design a sign on-line. The name of the Web site celebrates the location of the original El Arroyo, overlooking a drainage ditch.) El Arroyo is one of several home-grown restaurants whose success had led to expansion, and there are now three additional branches, one in Northwest Austin, another west, and a third in Round Rock (see listings). The restaurant offers standard Tex-Mex fare, and the owner-humorists have been known to cast aspersions on their own culinary efforts, but that does not stop the crowds from coming. In addition to Tex-Mex, the restaurant serves barbecued chicken. Customers love the funky atmosphere, the cheeky waiters, and the lively bar scene featuring "floaters": margaritas topped with liqueurs. When the restaurant was burned down by an arsonist in early 1998, the faithful customers showed up to help rebuild the structure, including the outdoor deck under the live oaks. El Arroyo is open daily for lunch and dinner.

El Mercado Restaurant & Cantina $-$$
1702 Lavaca Street
(512) 477-7689
One of three El Mercados in the city, this restaurant serves up generous portions of Tex-Mex staples—enchiladas, chimichangas, and tacos. Some of the dishes

have a Texas slant with barbecued meat featured in the brisket tacos and chicken enchiladas. There are low-fat and vegetarian Tex-Mex dishes on the menu, including mushroom and spinach enchiladas. The decor includes huge sombreros and multicolored, stylized parrots. The Mexican background music adds to the fiesta feel. Open daily for lunch and dinner and on weekends for breakfast.

Fadó's Irish Pub $$-$$$
214 West Fourth Street
(512) 457-0172

The food is filling and the noise level high at this take on an Irish pub. The decorations are a little like "Disney does pub," but the place is popular, particularly among enthusiasts for all things Irish, including sports, music, and brews. The restaurant serves breakfast all day, an Irish version with bangers (sausages), rashers of bacon, eggs, black and white puddings, brown bread, baked beans, and fried tomatoes. Other typical pub offerings at Fadó include fish-and-chips, Irish potato pancakes, and "ploughman's lunch," a selection of cheeses and bread. The pub has late-night food service. Open daily for lunch through late-night dinner.

Fleming's $$-$$$$
320 East Second Street
(512) 457-1500
www.flemingssteakhouse.com

Time was, a steak in downtown Austin meant heading to the Hoffbrau, a venerable diner-style cafe where the meat is grilled diner-style and the side orders consist of iceberg lettuce and slices of white bread. (The Hoffbrau appears later in this section of the Central listings.) But as Austin has grown, so has the number of classic steakhouses, several added in the past few years to meet the demand for high-style food in classy settings. Part of a national chain founded in California and with a heavy presence on the East Coast, Fleming's has opened in a restored warehouse near the convention center and offers prime beef, lamb, veal, and top-

quality seafood dishes. The restaurant features an exhibition kitchen in a sophisticated setting. One thoughtful touch is an extensive wine-by-the-glass menu, 100 offerings that also can be ordered by flight (three small selections in one serving). Open daily for dinner.

Frank & Angie's Pizza $
508 West Avenue
(512) 472-3534
www.frankandangies.citysearch.com

Just around the corner from its sister restaurant, Hut's, famed for its hamburgers, this pizzeria pays homage to another American favorite. New York–style pizzas, noted for their thin crusts, are featured here. Everything is homemade, including the house minestrone, the salad dressings, and the focaccia used in the sandwiches. In addition to pizza, whole or by the slice, there are sandwiches and calzones and for dessert homemade cannoli, cheesecake, and fruit pizzas. This pizza joint, which has a deck overlooking Shoal Creek, opens for breakfast with special early-morning pizzas. There is a coffee bar, plus wine and beer are served. Open for breakfast, lunch, and dinner daily.

Frisco Shop $
5819 Burnet Road
(512) 459-6279

There used to be several Night Hawk diners in Austin, but the hometown chain has gone out of the restaurant business, although its frozen dinners are sold in Texas grocery stores—perhaps the most famous being a chopped steak dinner. The Frisco Shop is no longer owned by Night Hawk, but the memories and some of the waitresses remain at this traditional diner on the northern edge of our Central district. Breakfasts feature huge homemade biscuits, and the dinner menu retains the famous chopped steak special. For dessert, there are homemade pies. It is typical American diner fare here, served in a Western motif setting. Breakfast, lunch, and dinner are served daily.

Gumbo's $$-$$$$
710 Colorado Street
(512) 480-8053

The trend in Austin usually follows a pattern—a restaurant becomes a hit in downtown Austin and then takes that success to the suburbs. Gumbo's has bucked that trend by first finding success in Round Rock (see our listings toward the end of this chapter) and then moving downtown. the restaurant chose to move into one of the most interesting buildings downtown, the Brown Building. It was built in 1938 by Herman Brown, one of the founders of Brown & Root, the legendary Houston construction company that parlayed its close political ties to President Lyndon B. Johnson and others into worldwide ventures. In 1998 the owners, the LBJ Company (guess which prominent Texas political family owns the company), transformed the building into a loft project. Gumbo's occupies a ground-floor space where it serves up a menu with a Louisiana flair. The tenderloin is topped with crabmeat, the pastas have a Cajun touch and, of course, there is gumbo. Open weekdays for lunch, daily for dinner. Closed Sunday.

Granite Cafe $$-$$$
2905 San Gabriel Street
(512) 472-6483

This was the original restaurant opened by Austin entrepreneurs Reed and Betsy Clemons (see the Bitter End listing). The Granite Cafe brought the California-style open-kitchen model featured in several Napa Valley restaurants to Austin, and the Clemonses gave the walls and furniture a Southwestern touch. After a successful few years, Granite Cafe fell into a slump, but local critics have high praise for the cafe's new co-owner and chef Sam Dickey. From the outset, the cafe has relied on local ingredients, and the menu has returned to its Southwestern roots after wandering the globe. Dickey and his wife, who are parents, have introduced a kids' menu that goes beyond the old staples so that little would-be

epicures can get an early start. The cafe utilizes local ingredients, notably vegetables, goat cheese, and sausage, plus fresh fish, homemade pastas, and flavorful chiles from spicy to hot to mellow. A wood-fired oven produces a variety of pizzas. The weekend brunch is popular here. The restaurant is housed in a small, modern brick shopping center not far from the University of Texas campus and some of Austin's most prestigious neighborhoods. The second-floor dining room is surrounded by a large, airy veranda, which is a great place to enjoy daily lunch, dinner, or brunch in spring and fall.

Hickory Street Bar & Grille $
800 Congress Avenue
(512) 477-8968

Outdoor dining has become popular in Austin, except on those few days when rain, heat, or cold drives folks indoors. While some downtown restaurants had to seek special City Council approval for sidewalk setups, this Congress Avenue restaurant has a large patio set back from the sidewalk and just 4 blocks from the capitol. A focal point of the menu is a large selection of salads, including a jerk chicken salad, or customers can visit the salad buffet to build their own. There are daily soup specials and chili for colder days. The restaurant opens very early during the week for breakfast, and the weekend brunch features a variety of egg dishes plus such New Orleans touches as beignets and café au lait. Open daily for breakfast, lunch, and dinner.

Hut's Hamburgers $
807 West Sixth Street
(512) 472-0693
www.hutshamburgers.citysearch.com

There are 20 types of burgers on the menu here, plus chicken-fried steak, fried chicken, and meat loaf—in a word, all the stuff you want to eat, and you did back when cholesterol was just a gleam in the Surgeon General's eye. The daily blue plate specials attract a faithful crowd. Burgers can be ordered to match your particular tastes, or you can simply pick one off the menu. The Wolfman Jack features sour cream, diced green chilies, and jack cheese. The Ritchie Valens has guacamole, grated cheese, jalapeño mayo, chopped tomatoes, and mustard. The list of possibilities goes on, including the Beach Boy's favorite with pineapple, Swiss cheese, mayo, lettuce, and bell peppers. Don't pass on the onion rings and french fries. The decor here is '50s diner, and the walls are decorated with college sports memorabilia. Hut's is open for lunch and dinner daily.

Hyde Park Bar & Grill $-$$
4206 Duval Street
(512) 458-3168

Look for the two-story giant fork out front and the potato truck parked out back. According to local lore, the grill goes through one and a quarter tons of potatoes a week making its famous spicy, battered fries. They are dipped in buttermilk and rolled in peppered flour before being deep-fried (in healthy canola oil) and then served with a mayonnaise flavored with peppers and onions, a Texas take on the European tradition of serving fries with mayo. The restaurant also serves a huge chicken-fried steak plate plus burgers. But not all the fare is hearty—grilled fish and salads are also offered. The restaurant is open daily for lunch and dinner, with late-night hours on Friday and Saturday. It occupies a large, old home in the Hyde Park neighborhood, the historic heart of Austin just north of the university campus.

Iron Works Barbecue $$
100 Red River Street
(512) 478-4855
www.ironworksbbq.com

Home to the Weigl Iron Works for years, this converted workshop just east of the city's convention center is now a popular barbecue spot, particularly during week-day lunch hours. The Weigl family's iron-work can be seen on several buildings around town, including the History Center at 810 Guadalupe Street. Now the walls of

the Weigl workshop are decorated with branding irons, an appropriate motif for a restaurant serving all manner of Texas barbecue—chicken, pork ribs, pork loin, beef, brisket, and sausage. Side orders of beans, potato salad, and baked potatoes are offered. Diners can sit inside or on an outdoor deck. Lunch and dinner are served daily.

Jeffrey's $$$$
1204 West Lynn Street
(512) 477-5584
www.jeffreysofaustin.com

This is perhaps the quintessential and one of the best Austin restaurants—a longtime favorite of Austinites and the place where President George W. Bush and First Lady Laura Bush loved to take friends when they occupied the Governor's Mansion. Founded in the 1970s by three University of Texas friends (one of them a childhood friend of the First Lady), Jeffrey's was creating top-flight cuisine in an unassuming, quiet atmosphere when most Austin restaurants were serving up everyday fare. Jeffrey's took another bold step following the 2000 Presidential election (at least when it was clear who would be inaugurated) and opened a branch of Jeffrey's in the Watergate in Washington, D.C. The restaurant's home is a restored house in Clarksville, one of the city's revered

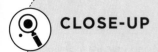

Texas Cuisine:
Not Just a Bunch of Beef

Thanks to Hollywood, people around the world know that ranching is big business in Texas, so it comes as no surprise that many unfamiliar with the state's culinary pantheon think a typical Texas meal features a large chunk of beef.

But Texas beef is just one part of the picture. Texas chefs, both professional and amateur, create a wide variety of dishes drawing on several cultural traditions and a multitude of homegrown food products.

Agribusiness is important to the state, making up about 12 percent of the state's gross state product, and behind that number is an incredible diversity of products. Texas farmers produce rice, grains, citrus fruits, nuts, pears, apricots, strawberries, and avocados; they raise pigs, dairy cows, goats, chickens, and, of course, cattle; and food companies, small and large, are engaged in developing products that tout their Texas origins—everything from axis venison to zucchini flowers.

The Texas Department of Agriculture has developed four programs that give consumers, both home cooks and restaurant chefs, a way to identify and label Texas goods, and the department has launched a "Buy Texas" program that is touted on billboards and in media ads around the state. The program has four components—Taste of Texas, Naturally Texas, Texas Grown, and Vintage Texas—and these labels can be found on food and agricultural products.

For example, salsas, barbecue sauces, salad dressings, cheeses, fresh meats, organically produced vegetables, several varieties of rice, and hundreds of other goods bear the Taste of Texas label. The Naturally Texas program promotes the state's cotton, wool, mohair, and leather production. Texas grows one-third of the cotton in the United States, and there are approximately two million angora goats in the Hill Country southwest of San Antonio producing about 15 million pounds of mohair each year. Herbs and garden plants grown in Texas bear the Texas Grown label, while Vintage Texas promotes Texas wine production.

Visitors and newcomers to the Austin area can find Texas food products at local grocery stores and in area farmers' markets (see our Shopping chapter), or they can visit one of the local farms to pick their own produce or buy it at a farmhouse or roadside stand. The *Austin American–Statesman* Wednesday food section lists information on seasonal foods and pick-your-own locations. Another excellent way to become familiar with Texas foods, and the chefs who are creating new dishes with them, is to join in the Texas Hill Country Wine & Food Festival, held each April in Austin (see our Annual Events and Festivals chapter).

Within a few miles of Austin, farmers and ranchers are producing apples, peaches (see our Annual Events and Festivals chapter for peach festivals), herbs, organic vegetables, blackberries, pecans, chile peppers, heirloom tomatoes and beans, and more. Inside the city, many

Texas beef. Enough said. PETER A. SILVA

entrepreneurs have taken home recipes to the marketplace, and their salsas, barbecue sauces, tamales, pestos, salad dressings, and sauces now line the shelves of local grocery stores and specialty shops. Others have headed for the countryside to produce gourmet foods such as Texas goat cheese, a mini-industry in Dripping Springs southwest of Austin. Some of these businesses are small boutique operations, while others are large and well-known, such as Blue Bell Ice Cream, made in Brenham east of Austin, a Texas favorite.

Central Texas also has attracted microbreweries (see our Nightlife chapter) and is home to Shiner Brewery in the town of the same name southeast of Austin, with roots going back to 19th-century German settlers. Visit Shiner in May during the Annual Catholic Church Picnic (see our Annual Events and Festivals chapter).

Texas beers are not alone in winning kudos. The state also produces several award-winning wines, a fact that draws snickers only among those who have not sampled the wares. Texas is emerging as one of the top-producing wine states in the country, and recent warm summers have led to bumper crops. Several areas of the state have microclimates that are very conducive to grape growing, a fact that was not lost on Spanish settlers who planted the first vines in Texas during the 17th century. There are over a dozen wineries in the hills surrounding Austin, some close to the city and easily reached in an hour, others farther afield but easily accessible for a day trip. October is Texas Wine Month and is a great time to visit, but most are open year-round. Two close to Austin are listed below. For a look at more Texas wineries, check out www.texaswinetrail.com or www.winetrails.com. The Austin Convention and Visitors Bureau has a brochure and map detailing Texas Wine Country trails. The Texas Department of Agriculture (www.gotexan.org) also is cheerleader for the industry.

Fall Creek Vineyards
Tow
(915) 379-5361
www.fcv.com
Fall Creek has won national awards for its wines and has established a firm reputation as one of the state's leading wineries. The vineyards, some 65 acres, are on the hills above Lake Buchanan, one of the Highland Lakes, about 70 miles northwest of Austin. Founder Ed Auler got the inspiration to start his vineyard while traveling in France 25 years ago when he noticed the wine country terrain matched the land on his Hill Country ranch. The Aulers experienced great success with their wines—President George Bush served them at the White House and took Fall Creek wines with him to Beijing, China, for an official dinner during a state visit.

Tastings, tours, and sales are conducted March through October. There are no vineyard tours during the week, but the cellars are open for tastings and sales from 11:00 A.M. to 4:00 P.M. Tours, tastings, and sales are offered on the weekend, on Saturday from noon to 5:00 P.M. and on Sunday from noon to 4:00 P.M. In August Fall Creek hosts a weekend Grape Stomp (see our Annual Events chapter) when the whole family can jump into a grape vat and crush grapes the old-fashioned way. To reach Tow, take Highway 1431 from Marble Falls, northwest of Austin, until it dead-ends into Highway 261, then take Farm-to-Market Route 2241 to Tow. Drive through the community; the road ends at Fall Creek. The winery also has an Austin office where visitors can inquire about special tours and sales, 1111 Guadalupe Street, (512) 476-4477. For more information about the vineyard area, see the Highland Lakes section of the Day Trips chapter.

Slaughter Leftwich Vineyards
4209 Eck Lane, Austin
(512) 266-3331
www.slaughterleftwich.com
Wines from Lubbock? Forget any clichéd notions you might have about the Texas High Plains; there are several excellent grape-growing microclimates in West Texas. Slaughter Leftwich has had particular success with Chardonnay grapes there. In order to bring its wines to as many people as possible, the owners decided to grow their grapes in Lubbock and build a winery in Austin. Eck Lane is at the intersection of Hudson Bend Road and Rural Route 620, near Lake Travis west of Austin. Tastings are available daily Tuesday through Sunday from 1:00 to 5:00 P.M. Tours are offered on Friday through Sunday at 1:30 and 3:30 P.M., except in the busy summer months, June through September, when tours are held Wednesday through Sunday.

central city neighborhoods (see our Relocation chapter). The founders took over a space occupied by a small wine shop, put up an inconspicuous sign outside and the work of local artists inside, and embarked on a culinary journey that draws on the world's cuisines but has Hill Country roots. Dinner items are added and updated regularly, but recent offerings include a duck and shrimp dish with black bean ravioli and shiitake mushroom sauce, crispy oysters on yucca root chips with habanero-honey aioli, and grilled sturgeon on champagne mushroom risotto with Roquefort and port wine glaze. Chef David Garrido is now in charge of the restaurant's fare. Garrido formerly worked as assistant chef to famed Texas chef Stephan Pyles at the Routh Street Cafe in Dallas. He also coauthored a fun cookbook published by Chronicle Books in 1998, called *Nuevo Tex-Mex,* which features "festive" food that can be cooked at home, not the complex culinary masterpieces served up at Jeffrey's nightly except Sunday.

Katz's   **$–$$**
618 West Sixth Street
(512) 472-2037
www.katznevercloses.com
The slogan is "Katz's never Kloses"—and it doesn't, making this downtown deli a very popular late-night spot. In the wee hours, customers are likely to look around and think they may have fallen into an intergalactic bar, since the clientele is so varied—country music fans, heavy metal types, boomers, Gen-Xers, you name it. All have come for the New York deli fare: corned beef sandwiches, bagels with lox, pickle barrels on every table, and blintzes for those who need a late-night sugar rush. Katz's also delivers via Yellow Cab to areas close to downtown.

Kaya Blue   **$$–$$$**
621A East Sixth Street
(512) 478-8788
Kaya Blue takes the concept of fusion cuisine to explosive, exciting heights. Take the Kaya paella, where Spain meets Thailand and some points in between with a mixture of seafood steamed in coconut milk with saffron rice, tasso ham, and kaffir lime leaves. How about scallops wrapped in a wasabi mousse on a bed of black-eyed peas? Or sweet-and-sour tortilla soup? Perhaps beef tenderloin in a Cuban adobo sauce with sweet potato pancakes? Other dishes gain inspiration

from China, the Caribbean, and the Mediterranean. The setting at this small downtown restaurant is as exciting as the food, with deep, jewel-tone colors and blue waves swept onto the walls, velvet drapery, dimmed lights, candles everywhere, and bold artwork. The lunch menu is lighter but just as stimulating to the tastebuds. Lunch is served weekdays, dinner nightly. Closed Sunday.

Kenichi   **$$–$$$$**
419 Colorado Street
(512) 320-9993
Who would have thought that Austin would ever have a restaurant that attracted the "beautiful people"? Yet that's how one local critic described the clientele when this Japanese-American import from Aspen arrived in Austin. The minimalist setting outside gives way to a high-fashion black-on-black interior. Austinites cling to their casual dress style, although a new terminology has crept into the lexicon—"business casual." Could it have slipped in from Aspen, inspired by places like Kenichi? The menu offers beautifully presented sushi, plus American specialties such as steak, lamb, ribs, and seafood for heartier appetites. Dinner daily.

Kerbey Lane Cafe   **$–$$**
3704 Kerbey Lane
(512) 451-1436
www.kerbeylanecafe.com
The original Kerbey Lane Cafe now has two sister restaurants, one south and another northwest, testimony to the concept that homemade, healthful food is a necessity 24 hours a day. Many of the cafe's dishes are Tex-Mex in origin, but the emphasis is on fresh local ingredients. The menu also features burgers, sandwiches, omelettes, pancakes, and desserts.

Kyoto   **$$–$$$**
315 Congress Avenue
(512) 482-9010
Named for the ancient Japanese imperial city, Kyoto is tucked away in a narrow, stone building on Congress Avenue. There

are two dining rooms upstairs: one a sushi bar with counter seating and western-style tables, the second a traditional area with tatami mats and low Japanese tables. In addition to sushi, the restaurant serves yakitori and kushiyaki dishes (tiny grilled shish kebabs of meat, fish, and vegetables) plus noodle dishes, tempura, and other traditional Japanese offerings. The restaurant offers lunch Tuesday through Saturday and dinner Monday through Saturday. There is a second Kyoto location; see our Northwest section.

La Madeleine $
3418 North Lamar Boulevard
(512) 302-1485
www.lamadeleine.com
There are three La Madeleine restaurants in Austin, one in a converted bookstore (northwest), another in a new shopping mall (west), and this one in a building that has housed several restaurants over the years. All three share the atmosphere of a French bakery and bistro, so don't be discouraged when you read that service is cafeteria-style. The menu features soups, salads, sandwiches, quiche, pizzas, and light dinner entrees that are posted on the blackboard, plus an array of breads, desserts, pies, cakes, and cookies from the on-site bakery. The restaurants serve breakfast, lunch, dinner, midmorning and midafternoon coffee, and snacks daily.

Las Manitas Avenue Cafe $
211 Congress Avenue
(512) 472-9357
The menu features both interior Mexican and South Texas-Mexican dishes plus a healthy dose of Austin art and Austin politics. Breakfast tacos reflect the cuisine of South Texas, while other breakfast fare reflects South of the Border traditions. The huevos Motuleños has its roots in the city of Motul, Yucatan—fried eggs atop tortillas dressed with beans, peas, ham, and farm cheese. Lunch dishes include carne guisada, a South Texas–Northern Mexico stew, or a tamal vegetariano, tradi-

tional corn tamales stuffed with carrots, broccoli, and eggplant with a cream cheese sauce and sprinkled with nuts and raisins, an Austin concoction. The enchiladas reflect regional differences in Mexico. The enchiladas Zacatecas are made with poblano peppers and tomatillos; the enchiladas Morelianos are dressed in an ancho chile sauce. The cafe is housed in a storefront on the lower end of Congress Avenue, next door to Tesoro's folk art shop (see our Shopping chapter). The window is plastered with posters advertising cultural and political happenings, and a bench inside is loaded with alternative newspapers and news of Latin American political movements. Open daily for breakfast and lunch only.

La Traviata Italian Bistro $$-$$$
314 Congress Avenue
(512) 479-8131
A relatively new addition to the downtown dining scene, Marion Gillcrist, who learned her profession under Stephen Pyles and the winner of the *Austin Chronicle* Readers' Poll "best female chef" in 2001, opened this small, intimate restaurant determined to produce authentic Italian cuisine. The menu offers her interpretation of classic dishes like polenta with Gorgonzola sauce and spaghetti bolognese, and features top-quality Italian ingredients like prosciutto and famous Italian cheeses. Open for lunch Monday through Friday and for dinner nightly, except Sunday.

Louie's 106 $$$$
106 Sixth Street
(512) 476-1997
www.louies106.net
Housed in the historic Littlefield Building at the busy northwest corner of Sixth Street and Congress Avenue, Louie's has the aura of a grand old restaurant in a European capital. The menu leans toward classical Spanish with lots of Mediterranean and European touches. Tapas, Spanish noshes, are offered here, and patrons can simply drop in to the bar for a round of snacks or

sample some before dinner. Dishes include a traditional Valencian paella plus grilled meats, fish, risottos, and bouillabaisse. There is a cigar room plus an extensive wine, single-malt whisky, and brandy list. Open weekdays for lunch and daily for dinner. Given its busy downtown location, Louie's offers curbside valet parking.

Malaga Wine and Tapas Bar $-$$
208 West Fourth Street
(512) 236-8020

A delightful cross between a restaurant and a bar, Malaga's is an Austin version of a Spanish tapas bar, a place to gather and nibble tasty snacks while sipping wine or sherry. Malaga's is next door to a popular jazz and cigar bar, Cedar Street (see our Nightlife chapter), and occupies a narrow, old warehouse space. The floors are hardwood; the walls are limestone and lined with wine racks. Among the tapas offerings are traditional Spanish omelettes, called "tortillas" in Spain, stuffed with savory ingredients and served at room temperature, plus ham and sausage, olives and cheese. Malaga's opens at 4:00 P.M. during the week for after-work conviviality and closes daily at 2:00 A.M., except Sunday when it closes at midnight. On the weekend it opens at 6:00 P.M.

Mansion at Judges' Hill $$-$$$
1900 Rio Grande Street
(512) 495-1800
www.mansionatjudgeshill.com

The dining room at this restored mansion not far from the capitol and the University of Texas campus is one of the most sophisticated and refined in Austin. The restaurant echoes the elegant decor of the boutique hotel (see listings in our Hotels and Motels chapter) and is a fitting setting for the refined cuisine created by Chef John Maxwell, who previously led the creative team at Zoot, one of Austin's favorite restaurants (see listing later in this chapter). Maxwell has taken the freshest of ingredients—some local, others like lobster and imported foie gras—and created sophisticated dishes that Maxwell

Two local writers are indispensable when it comes to understanding vital ingredients in Texas food. Jean Andrews, often called the "Pepper Lady," has written a couple of books on the genus Capsicum *and her text, recipes, and beautiful drawings of peppers are invaluable to food fans and cooks. Another local expert with several books in print is herb and tequila expert Lucinda Hutson.*

describes as "modern American cuisine with classical French influences." Maxwell trained at the famed Culinary Institute of America in Hyde Park, New York, and honed his skills at Mark Miller's Red Sage restaurant in Washington, D.C.

Manuel's $-$$$
310 Congress Avenue
(512) 472-7555
www.manuelsdowntown.citysearch.com

The setting is sleek and modern, with black booths, neon signs, and hip jazz music at this downtown restaurant, but the food is light, saucy, and evocative of interior Mexican classics. Chile rellenos are made as they are in Mexico, stuffed with spicy and fruit-studded meat filling then topped with almond sauce. Fish is served Veracruzano-style with tomatoes and peppers, and enchiladas banderas reflect the red, green, and white of the Mexican flag. Gorditas, small cakes of corn masa and potato, are topped with a homemade venison chorizo (sausage). Manuel's is open for lunch and dinner and has a jazz brunch on Sunday. There is a late-night snack menu. A second location has been opened in Northwest Austin.

Mars $$-$$$
1610 San Antonio Street
(512) 472-3901
www.marsaustin.com

Fusion cuisine is a much-used term these days, but it fits the picture at Mars, a place where lovers of spicy food congregate to celebrate a world of flavors. The restaurant was formerly the home of Oat Willie's, the city's famous "head shop," west of the capitol. After several incarnations, it evolved into Mars, where dishes from several cultures have landed. Dishes and techniques are borrowed from the Middle East, Africa, India, Thailand, the Caribbean, and Mexico. Tandoori meats are served with pomegranate sauce, while stuffed grape leaves sit alongside potstickers on an appetizer tray. Thai curries and noodle dishes take up another section of the menu, and many patrons return for a house specialty, Thai bouillabaisse. Other popular dishes include grilled salmon in wasabi sauce and a jerked pork tenderloin. The food is spicy, the walls red, the lights dim, and the 2,000-square-foot restaurant crowded. As one critic said, this is not the place to propose marriage unless you want several adjacent diners to accept or decline. But it is a fun place for lively food and conversation, so expect a wait on weekends. Mars is open for dinner daily. Reservations are recommended for large parties.

Mezzaluna $$$
310 Colorado Street
(512) 472–6770
www.mezzalunaaustin.com
One of the nightlife pioneers in the warehouse district west of Congress Avenue, Mezzaluna can be spotted by its large sign shaped like a mezzaluna, a half-moon-shaped cutting tool used in Italian cuisine. Yet another restaurant creation by Reed and Betsy Clemons (their Bitter End is across the street), Mezzaluna has been a roaring success since it opened. On weekend nights it continues to draw crowds, especially the bar, where the concrete counters are home to dozens of hip elbows. The menu is nouvelle fare with Italian roots and American know-how. Antipasti are made from fresh, local ingredients, including sausage served atop polenta. Diners can choose a light supper of salad and antipasti or sample a pizza or

a pasta dish. They can enjoy a grand three-course meal, Italian-style, with antipasti, pasta and an entree or perhaps lasagna with smoked chicken or grilled salmon flavored with chiles and basil. The extensive wine list offers many American and Italian wines by the glass and a selection of grappas, the Italian brandy distilled from the grape pomace that packs a punch. Mezzaluna is open for lunch during the week and dinner nightly. There is late-night service on weekends.

Mongolian Barbecue $
117 San Jacinto Boulevard
(512) 476–3938
Not far from the city's convention center is a restaurant favored by families and folks on a budget. The menu is simple at this Asian-style buffet: Simply head for the cafeteria-style line and pick out the ingredients you want the chef to stir up in the giant wok behind the counter. Vegetarians, meat and fish eaters, and finicky kids can all find something to put on their plate. Customers also can select their seasonings and sauce from sweet and sour to spicy Szechwan. Open for dinner daily and lunch on weekdays.

Mother's Cafe and Garden $–$$
4215 Duval Street
(512) 451–3994
www.motherscafe.citysearch.com
Vegetarian food with international inspiration is served at this neighborhood cafe. Tex-Mex dishes are given a vegetarian translation here, while stir-fries draw on Asian inspiration. The menu has low-fat and vegan options, and local beers and Texas wines are featured. The cafe is in the heart of the Hyde Park neighborhood and features a large outdoor patio. Open daily for lunch and dinner and serves weekend brunch.

Mother Egan's Irish Pub $–$$
715 West Sixth Street
(512) 478–7747
The fish-and-chips here pass muster with British expatriates, and Guinness is the

beverage of choice at this "Irish pub." The menu also features other pub staples, including shepherd's pie, potato skins slathered in cheese, and an American take on an Irish staple: a corned beef and cabbage hoagie. Open daily for lunch and dinner.

Nau Enfield Drug $
1115 West Lynn Street
(512) 476-1221
An old-fashioned drugstore in the historic Clarksville neighborhood, Nau's serves up sandwiches, burgers, malts, and breakfast dishes daily (see our Attractions chapter). Breakfast is a busy time for Nau's, when breakfast tacos, omelettes, and huevos rancheros are on the menu. The atmosphere here is authentic and draws customers from both the neighborhood and downtown to the booths and bar daily for breakfast and lunch.

Ninfa's Mexican Restaurant $$-$$$
612 West Sixth Street
(512) 476-0612
Ninfa Lorenzo was a legendary businesswoman in Houston, where she took a single small Mexican restaurant and built it into a food empire. This West Sixth Street location is next door to Katz's deli, within the ever-expanding shopping and nightlife district west of downtown, and is one of two Ninfa's in Austin. The fare is a take on traditional Tex-Mex and Mexican fare with an uptown touch; for example, smoked quail marinated in salsa negra, fresh fish tacos, camarones ajillo (shrimp in a garlic sauce), and pollo asado (roasted chicken). Lunch and dinner are served daily, plus there is a late-night menu on the weekends.

Old Pecan Street Cafe $$-$$$
310 East Sixth Street
(512) 478-2491
The changing face of Sixth Street embraces the history of Austin. Back in 1971, this small cafe was one of the first businesses to stir talk of a Sixth Street revival. Throughout the decades, the cafe

has withstood the changes and continues to attract faithful customers despite the sometimes rambunctious street life beyond the shutters. The historic building gives the cafe an ambience reminiscent of an Old World restaurant with its fieldstone walls and wooden floors. It is particularly cozy on a quiet Sunday afternoon or on a cold winter night, when a cup of the house kaffe mit schlag, coffee with cream and kahlua, warms the hands and the heart. The menu features light cafe-style entrees, crepes, quiche, sandwiches, soups, and salads. But it is the cafe's cakes that bring customers back, particularly the Italian cream cake. The cafe is open daily for lunch, dinner, and brunch.

Opal Divine's Freehouse $-$$
700 West Sixth Street
(512) 477-3308
www.opaldivines.com
Housed in a 19th-century limestone building, Opal Divine's is a Texas pub named for the owner's fun-loving grandmother. There is live music several nights a week, and the place is also a popular spot to wait out the downtown rush hour. The menu features both snacks and full meals, including standby Tex-Mex dishes, nachos, salads, Philly cheese steaks and hoagies, chicken-fried steak, German bratwurst, and pub sandwiches. Patrons can eat indoors or out on the balcony, although the view is of a busy street. The bar features a special Scotch menu and special tasting sessions are sometimes offered; reservations recommended. Open daily from lunch to bar closing time, 2:00 A.M.

P. F. Chang's China Bistro $$-$$$
201 San Jacinto Boulevard
(512) 457-8300
www.pfchangs.com
The Austin Convention Center and other downtown commercial developments have boosted the number of restaurants in downtown Austin, most of them homegrown, and a few, like P. F. Chang's and nearby Fleming's (see above), good representatives of national chains. Chang's is

popular for both its sophisticated atmosphere and its menu of fresh Chinese dishes. Vegetarians and lovers of spicy food will appreciate the variety on the menu. Unlike many other Chinese restaurants, P. F. Chang's offers a wide selection of wines. Open for lunch and dinner.

Pok-E-Jo's Smokehouse $$
1603 West Fifth Street
(512) 320-1541
www.pokejos.com

There are four Pok-E-Jo's in the Austin area, serving a variety of smoked and barbecued meats, including ribs, pork, beef, ham, pork loin, sausage, turkey, and chicken. Meats are mesquite-smoked, and the restaurant serves the usual variety of side orders: beans, potato salad, pickles, and onions. The Fifth Street location is housed in a small building that looks a little like a country cabin, with simple wooden tables. Take-out is a large part of the restaurant's business. Open daily for lunch and dinner.

Ray's Steakhouse $$-$$$$
3010 Guadalupe Street
(512) 478-0000
www.rays-steaks.com

When the Ruth's Chris restaurant (see below) moved downtown, Austin caterer Ray LeMay decided to open his own steakhouse in this historic building just north of the university "Drag," the main thoroughfare through the University of Texas campus. This is a meat-eater's dream; even the appetizers carry out the theme. Among the most popular are the little cheeseburgers, little mouthfuls that are about as big as a quarter. The menu,

---

Looking for a picnic site? Two of the easiest to access are Town Lake and the capitol grounds, where you may have to share with the squirrels (look for the famous albino squirrel at the capitol). For other inspirations check the Parks and Recreation chapter.

---

of course, features steak, including a 26-ounce T-bone and even a buffalo meat rib-eye. There are also chicken, lamb, and seafood offerings. Open for lunch Monday through Friday and dinner every day.

Roppolo's Pizzeria $
316 East Sixth Street
(512) 476-1490

This Austin pizza restaurant with several area locations has been named best pizza in town by readers of the *Austin Chronicle* in several annual surveys. In addition to selling whole pizza pies to eat on the premises or to go, Roppolo's also sells pizza by the slice so that strollers along Sixth Street can munch as they watch the street scene. The menu also includes stromboli, calzone, pasta with meatballs or Sicilian meat sauce, garden vermicelli, and meat and veggie lasagna. Roppolo's is open daily for lunch and dinner.

Roy's Austin $$-$$$
340 East Second Street
(512) 391-1500
www.roysrestaurant.com

This Austin branch of Chef Roy Yamaguchi's Hawaiian Fusion group of restaurants is one of the new faces around the city's convention center. Yamaguchi has won accolades from *Condé Nast Traveler* magazine and others for his blending of Asian and Hawaiian cuisines, and foodies will also know him from his appearance on the Food-TV Network's *Iron Chef* series. Seafood is the star of the menu at Roy's, with dishes like mahi-mahi encrusted with macadamia nuts and grilled shrimp with Korean kim chee pickles. There are also chicken satays, honey-fruit glazed ribs, and grilled lamb chops. The decor is sophisticated, with a splash of island motifs. Open daily for dinner.

Ruth's Chris $$$
107 West Sixth Street
(512) 477-RUTH
www.ruthchris.com

When it comes to steakhouses the national Ruth's Chris chain is noted as one of the best. While we don't usually list chain restaurants since they are familiar to our readers, the Austin Ruth's Chris steakhouse is very popular, particularly among the political crowd that gathers every two years in Austin for the legislative session. The restaurant moved from its campus-area location into the historic Scarbrough Building, 1 block west of Congress Avenue, in 1999 and offers valet parking for patrons. The menu features thick-cut steaks simmered in butter made famous by Ruth Fartel, founder of the restaurant chain. Chicken and fish dinners are also on the menu. Reservations are recommended, particularly when the legislature is in session—in the odd years from January to May, except for specially called sessions.

Saba Blue Water Cafe $-$$$
212 West Fourth Street
(512) 478-7222
www.sabacafe.com

Like its neighbor Malaga's (see above), Saba's is a combination bar-restaurant, an Austin munchie and meet spot, but unlike its neighbor, where Spanish tapas are the bite-sized goodies, the menu here reflects Yucatecan–Caribbean–Pacific Rim influences. Housed in a 1907 building but decorated with modern art, including a wonderful blue glass wall, the design was created by Austin's noted urban artist Sinclair Black, whose offices sit above Malaga's next door. While patrons drink one of the house special drinks, try the Cuban Mojito, they can nibble on cilantro shrimp potstickers or salmon miso. Most of the dishes are munchie-sized, but there are some more substantial offerings during dinner. Open daily for lunch, dinner, and late-night snacks, with special prices during happy hour.

Scholz Garten $
1607 San Jacinto Boulevard
(512) 474-1958
www.scholzgarten.com

Political junkies regard this old German beer garden as something of a shrine, a place that serves as a favorite watering hole and meeting place for political types, their staffers, and supporters (particularly Democrats). Hillary and Bill Clinton hung out here during their days as workers for the George McGovern presidential campaign. The beer garden is also featured in the 1962 novel about Texas politics, *The Gay Place,* by Billy Lee Brammer. The beer hall, which dates back to 1866, is east of the capitol and is owned by the Austin Saengerrunde, a German-American fraternal organization. The tree-shaded beer garden is a favorite lunchtime spot for state workers, politicians, and pre- and postgame fans of UT football and basketball. The restaurant features German food and typical American down-home fare: burgers, chicken, sandwiches, Tex-Mex specials, and beer, of course. Scholz's is open for lunch and dinner. Closed Sunday.

Serrano's Cafe & Cantina $$
Symphony Square, 1105 Red River Street
(512) 322-9080
www.serranos.com

There are nine (and growing) Serrano's cafes in various regions of the city, but this one has the best setting—in the small historic complex saved by the Austin Symphony (see our Attractions chapter). The Jeremiah Hamilton home is original to the site here, east of the capitol. Hamilton was a carpenter and legislative delegate to the Republican convention in 1873 when he built the triangular house in the small complex, which now houses a Tex-Mex restaurant. Hamilton's home has seen lively occupants before, serving as a grocery store, saloon, barber shop, and music club. Now customers can order fajita nachos, deep-fried jalapeños stuffed with cheese, and a variety of entrees, including enchiladas, Tex-Mex plates, grilled meat and chicken, plus fajita platters. Open daily for lunch and dinner.

Shoreline Grill $$$$
98 San Jacinto Boulevard
(512) 477-3300
www.shorelinegrill.com

Tucked into a prime location on Town

Lake, just west of the Four Seasons, the Shoreline is known for its fish and seafood creations and the great view of the nightly summer evening exodus of Austin's famous bat colony. The menu changes seasonally, but dishes include semolina-crusted oysters, crab cakes with roasted pepper relish, grilled salmon, and a variety of fresh fish from the Gulf of Mexico. The restaurant also serves a variety of meat and pasta dishes plus a good selection of salads. The best bat viewing is on the restaurant's patio, but seating is first-come, first-served there. Reservations can be made for the indoor rooms. Open daily for lunch and dinner.

Stubb's Bar-B-Q $-$$
801 Red River Street
(512) 480-8341
www.stubbsaustin.com
The late C. B. Stubblefield is the soul of this restaurant, and his portrait hangs here as an homage to his vision of bar-becue and home cooking plus the blues. Barbecue—beef, sausage, brisket, chicken, ribs, turkey—is served with old-fashioned potatoes, beans, and greens. (Stubb's barbecue sauce is used in-house and can be found in Austin grocery stores.) The menu also includes chicken-fried steak, corn on the cob, okra, and squash. This is the kind of food Stubble-field grew up on back in Lubbock, Texas. In addition to serving lunch and dinner and offering live music nightly except Sunday (see The Music Scene chapter), Stubb's also serves a Sunday Gospel Brunch with typical Southern breakfast fare—hash browns, grits, biscuits and gravy, plus pancakes and syrup and a live gospel band.

Sullivan's $$$-$$$$
300 Colorado Street
(512) 495-6504
www.sullivanssteakhouse.com
Just when you think you have Austin fig-ured out as a town where the hallmark is natural and laid-back, you walk into Sulli-van's, where the menu is red meat, red meat, red meat, and the atmosphere reeks of confidence and power. Stand in the lobby during the legislative session and you could get a quorum. Chat with the parking valet, and you will hear tales of movie stars and directors who love to eat here. Sullivan's is in the heart of the down-town warehouse district, but while neigh-bors offer bistro fare and nouvelle Italian dishes, it touts itself as a "Chicago-style steakhouse." The beef is top-quality here and is served with a variety of side orders, including delicious potatoes au gratin. For dessert, waiters try to entice diners with individual soufflés. The atmosphere is clubby and definitely alpha male. Reserva-tions are recommended. Dinner is served daily.

Sweetish Hill Bakery $
1120 West Sixth Street
(512) 472-1347
98 San Jacinto Boulevard, Suite 170
(512) 472-2411
www.sweetishhill.com
The lemon bars are addictive, but since no one can live by sweets alone, Sweetish Hill also serves up a popular lunch menu that finds inspiration in several quarters. The eggplant and Brie sandwich served on a French baguette is a favorite; the Italian panini brings back memories of Assisi; and the Hero is a fresh take on an old favorite. There is also a wide variety of meat and vegetable sandwiches served on the bakery's various grain and herb breads, plus daily homemade soups, sal-ads, and side orders of fruit and potato salad. The bakery (see our Shopping chapter) is well known for its pastries and breads, so few eat lunch without getting a cookie or loaf to go. Since the bakery is in the middle of the West Sixth Street dis-trict, it is usually busy all morning and into late afternoon as Austinites move to their own internal clocks, eating breakfast and lunch at their own pace. Food can be enjoyed on the premises, inside or on the small sidewalk cafe area, or it can be

packed for an afternoon picnic. The bakery also has a smaller operation near the convention center.

Texas Chili Parlor $
1409 Lavaca Street
(512) 472-2828
www.cactushill.com

The Texas equivalent of a neighborhood pub, this bar and restaurant attracts a loyal clientele, many of them state workers, attorneys, and political types from the nearby capitol. The ambience is funky bar meets roadhouse. The highlight of the menu is, of course, chili, served at varying degrees of heat and completely without beans (beans are a Yankee aberration). Sandwiches, tacos, and burgers are also on the menu, plus something called a Frito Pie, a Texas original—the recipe begins, "Take one bag of Fritos . . . " Open for lunch and dinner daily.

Texas French Bread $
2900 Rio Grande Street
(512) 499-0544
3213 Red River Street
(512) 478-8796
1722 South Congress Avenue
(512) 440-1122
www.texasfrenchbread.com

This popular Austin bakery chain is expanding quickly in the city. The Rio Grande Street location is just north of the university campus and next door to Breed Hardware (see our Shopping chapter). The bakery serves a variety of sandwiches, including the Niçoise sandwich that reflects Mediterranean flavors—tuna is melded with capers, olives, tomatoes, and onions on French bread. Customers can order any sandwich on the bread of their choice: Tuscan, French, cracked rye, white, or whole wheat. The menu also features a variety of soups—tortilla soup, cold borscht, Mediterranean vegetable, white bean, and pesto. Of course, the bakery also features a large selection of pastries and cookies. Coffee, herbal tea, and a pile of free newspapers make this a favorite spot for an early-morning stop on the way to work or school. Open daily for breakfast and lunch.

Thai Passion $$
620 Congress Avenue, Suite 105
(512) 472-1244
www.thaipassion.com

Thai Passion is an elegant downtown restaurant that features the cuisine of Thailand, with its contrasting flavors of spice, heat, and herbs. The menu features curries, noodle dishes, and traditional pad Thai. Some dishes are vegetarian. Open daily for lunch and dinner.

The Hoffbrau $-$$
613 West Sixth Street
(512) 472-0822

Since 1934 they have been serving meat off the grill at this West Sixth Street simple, no-frills restaurant. The decor here has been minimalist before minimalist got a name. The tables are simple orange Formica, and the wall decorations include a print of the Alamo, an old photograph or two, and a proclamation from former state representative Sarah Weddington (attorney in the *Roe v. Wade* case) praising the joint. In 1934 a T-bone steak was 35 cents, and a bottle of beer was a dime. Prices have risen, but the menu has remained the same—steak or, in a concession to modern times, grilled chicken breast. Salad is extra, but don't expect field greens. On the side there is white bread and saltines. The Hoffbrau is open weekdays for lunch and early dinner and closed on weekends.

Tres Amigos $$
26 Doors, 1206 West 38th Street
(512) 453-0026
www.tresamigos.com

Many Austin residents have been taking family and friends to the four Tres Amigos restaurants for years, knowing they can be assured of dependable Tex-Mex cooking and friendly service. The restaurant offers tacos, fajitas, and all the familiar Tex-Mex fare—don't miss the house specialty, mango ice cream.

This branch in the 26 Doors shopping center evokes Old Mexico in the design and decoration. Open daily for lunch and dinner.

Trulucks $$-$$$
400 Colorado Street
(512) 482-9000
www.trulucks.com

It is all about seafood at Trulucks, one of four restaurants that share the name in Texas. The ingredients are flown in from both coasts and the Gulf, ensuring high quality. Seasonal favorites like stone crab legs make appearances on the menu, and some dishes have a distinctive Texas touch, like the jalapeño salmon béarnaise. Texas Gulf snapper, another regional star, also is featured on the menu. For seafood purists, a "naked fish" menu features a selection of fresh fish simply grilled and served with a touch of lemon butter. Oyster aficionados will enjoy a selection of classic raw and cooked oyster dishes, but meat-eaters will not feel left out, with a variety of steak dishes also on the menu. Like other restaurants in the Warehouse District, Trulucks offers valet parking. The decor might be dubbed sophisticated supper club. Open for lunch Monday through Friday and for dinner nightly.

Upper Crust Bakery $
4508 Burnet Road
(512) 467-0102
www.uppercrustbakery.com

The city has several neighborhood bakeries that serve as gathering places for friends and a comfy spot to enjoy a breakfast croissant or midmorning break. In addition to sandwiches, soups, and breads, Upper Crust has a selection of croissants, both sweet and savory, that can be enjoyed while perusing the morning papers. Open daily for breakfast, lunch, and afternoon snacks.

Waterloo Ice House $
600 North Lamar Boulevard
(512) 472-5400
26 Doors, 1106 West 38th Street
(512) 451-5245

This hamburger joint serves a variety of American fare. In addition to burgers, customers can order tacos and chicken-fried steaks. The Lamar Boulevard Waterloo is next door to one of the city's most noted record stores, Waterloo Records, in the West Sixth Street shopping district (see The Music Scene chapter). You'll find two other Waterloo locations under our West and North sections, including one at the popular live music venue the Backyard (see The Music Scene chapter).

West Lynn Cafe $-$$
1110 West Lynn Street
(512) 482-0950
www.westlynn.citysearch.com

A totally vegetarian restaurant that has a reputation as a chic dining spot? Those who think vegetarian means boring have not visited West Lynn Cafe, the Clarksville (see our Relocation chapter) restaurant that won a national architectural design award. The menu draws on influences from Asia, Mexico, India, and the Mediterranean for lunch, dinner, and brunch daily. Some of the offerings are labeled zero-cholesterol and/or nondairy. Just to prove that not all sybaritic pleasures are verboten, the restaurant has a good wine list.

Wink $$$-$$$$
1014 North Lamar Boulevard
(512) 482-8868
www.winkrestaurant.com

Blink and you might miss Wink, but you would be missing a small jewel of a restaurant that has wowed locals. The small 15-table restaurant is located in what is in Austin culinary history a blessed spot. Castle Hill Cafe (see above) was born here, as was Cafe Spiazzo (Northwest listings). Austin chefs Stewart Scruggs and Mark Paul have created a popular, if crowded, foodie hotspot. The aim is to create a degustation menu—simply put, several smaller portions to allow diners to sample a variety of delicacies. The chefs and their staff shop daily for the best ingredients they can find, which might include Kobe beef sliced into carpaccio or seared foie

A Word about Ice Cream

It's hard to beat a cold cup of ice cream on a balmy night as a fitting end to an evening out. Several Austin small businesses offer "handmade" ice cream. Perhaps the most famous is Amy's, which began as a single store but now has five outlets and packs ice cream for sale in local shops and restaurants. Patrons pick their flavor and toppings and watch as they are hand-beaten to a yummy, creamy, but cold consistency on marble counters.

All five locations are open late; the two downtown at Sixth Street and Guadalupe Street are open until 1:00 A.M. on weekends. Look for the big moving cows on the outer wall of Amy's at 1012 West Sixth Street, (512) 480-0673. Other locations are in the Westgate Mall, home of Central Market at Westgate; in Southwest Austin at South Lamar and Ben White Boulevards, (512) 891-0573; 3500 Guadalupe Street, (512) 458-6895; 10000 Research Boulevard at the Arboretum in Northwest Austin, (512) 345-1006; and 3300 Bee Caves Road in West Austin, (512) 328-9859.

The Hyde Park neighborhood in Central Austin is home to the Dolce Vita Gelato and Espresso Bar, 4222 Duval Street, (512) 323-2686. This neighborhood coffee shop and Italian-style gelateria opens early for breakfast and stays open late for gelato.

Dolce Vita also is a great spot for an after-dinner drink, perhaps coffee and a liqueur, or one of the 35 grappas the cafe has on hand. In addition to gelato, the menu includes wonderful tarts with traditional Italian flavors like hazelnut and walnut. The cafe has a small indoor space plus an outdoor area with tables and chairs.

Another addition to the ice cream scene in Austin is Babbo's Gelato in the 26 Doors Shopping Center near Central Market in Central Austin. Babbo's features authentic Italian ices and gelatos made by owner Matthew Fry, who trained in Italy. The shop, which also houses a small coffee shop featuring Italian beans, opens early—around 6:00 A.M. on weekdays, a little later on weekends—and stays open until late evening daily except Sunday, when the cafe shuts down around 9:00 P.M. Babbo's is located at 1206 West 38th Street, Suite 1204-B, (512) 451-9555, www.babbosgelato.com.

gras on pistachio shortbread or placed atop a black currant tart. Other dishes might focus on top-rated ahi tuna or duck confit. Chef Paul's desserts have won raves—one local critic called his Lemon Meringue Pots (meringue shells filled with lemon curd, candied lemon, and fresh berries) a "lemon lover's dream dessert."

She also raved over his Chocolate Zin, a play on words to describe a sinfully rich dessert made from cherries soaked in chocolate and Zinfandel and then layered in phyllo pastry. The food is the focus here, and the tiny restaurant does bubble with enthusiasm, or noise if you are inclined to view it that way, which makes it hard to keep a secret from the folks at the next table. Reservations are accepted and recommended, given its size and popularity. Open daily for dinner; closed Sunday.

Zoot $$$-$$$$
506 Hearn Street
www.zootdining.com
(512) 477-6535

Gourmet magazine has praised Zoot's executive chef John Maxwell for creating some of the "most exciting food" in Austin. In 2001 Zoot celebrated its tenth anniversary and has consistently ranked as one of the city's best restaurants. Located just west of MoPac, strictly speaking Zoot should be listed in our West section, but it is so close to downtown that we have listed it here in the Central section. The small restaurant, housed in a converted bungalow, also captures the spirit of Austin with its relaxed atmosphere and emphasis on the best ingredients, many of them produced in Texas. The menu changes with the seasons, and there are daily specials. Offerings might include chickpea-crusted Gulf oysters, seared duck breast with duck confit, a New York strip served with Gorgonzola-creamed potatoes, or perhaps a wood-grilled Atlantic salmon with a potato-celery root gallete and frisee salad, apple-leek compote, and sage oil. A vegetarian entree is usually on the menu, perhaps eggplant prepared osso buco-style. The restaurant also offers a prix-fixe pre-theater menu for early diners. Given the restaurant's size and popularity, reservations are recommended. Open daily for dinner.

Z'Tejas Grill $$-$$$
1110 West Sixth Street
(512) 478-5355
www.ztejas.com

There are two Z'Tejas restaurants in Austin—the original in the West Sixth Street shopping/restaurant district and a second in Northwest Austin near the Arboretum—and perhaps a visit to both is the best way to get a quick fix on old

Austin and new Austin. Both serve much the same menu, but the original Z'Tejas is housed in a converted home where the garage doors can be opened, exposing diners to the elements. (Read about the Northwest location in that section.) The interior of the West Sixth Street location is decorated in the bright colors of the Southwest, and the outdoor patio serves as a lazy-day refuge just a few blocks from downtown or a place to relax during rush hour and enjoy the restaurant's "appetizer happy hour." The menu is sometimes described as Santa Fe meets Texas, with a dash of Louisiana thrown in. The restaurant's gumbo is offered at lunch and dinner; appetizers include oyster "shooters" (fried oysters with chipotle cream), catfish beignets, and quesadillas; entrees include Navajo tacos (crisp fried flour tortillas topped with deep-fried spinach, beans, onions, and chicken), smoked pork tenderloin, smoked duck enchiladas, and grilled salmon and trout. But don't pass on the restaurant's most famous dessert, Ancho chile fudge pie, which is made with just a touch of ancho chile powder, adding richness to the dish, not spice. Chocolate and chiles are vital components of one of Mexico's most famous dishes, mole poblano, so it is no surprise the chef took inspiration from south of the border. The recipe, by the way, is framed on the wall at the entrance to the restaurant. Open daily for lunch through dinner, plus Sunday brunch.

SOUTH CENTRAL

Artz Rib House $
2230 South Lamar Boulevard
(512) 442-8283
www.artzribhouse.citysearch.com

Live music and Texas barbecue are on the menu at this South Austin restaurant, but just to make sure no one feels left out, the menu also offers vegetarian dishes, including a grilled vegetable platter. The barbecue fare includes a combination plate made up of your choice of brisket, chicken, or sausage plus baby back ribs; all are served with coleslaw, pinto beans, pickles, bread, and spicy potato salad. There is live music seven nights a week at Artz, with regulars playing on certain nights. The Old Time Texas Fiddlers perform on Tuesday; on Sunday afternoon the Central Texas Bluegrass Club performs. The restaurant has both indoor dining and a screened-in porch with ceiling fans. Open daily for lunch and dinner.

Baby Acapulco $-$$
1628 Barton Springs Road
(512) 474-8774
www.babyacapulco.com
A favorite with young, downtown workers, this restaurant on the Barton Springs strip is usually packed on weekends, especially when the weather conjures up margarita fantasies. The menu includes more than a dozen kinds of margaritas, including banana, pink passion, strawberry, and pineapple, and has been named as serving the best margaritas in town several times in the *Austin Chronicle*'s reader's poll. The Tex-Mex menu offers the usual fare, including 14 types of enchiladas. The outdoor patio is the heart of the action on balmy days, and inside there is a casual, colorful atmosphere. Open for lunch and dinner daily.

Chuy's $-$$
1728 Barton Springs Road
(512) 474-4452
www.chuys.com
Chuy's is perhaps the most famous restaurant on the Barton Springs Road strip and one of the most colorful in Austin. Where else would you find a shrine to Elvis? Or more than 1,000 wooden fish hanging from the ceiling? The decor is a mixture of fantasy and kitsch, with iguanas and lava lamps setting the theme. The food is a mixture of Tex-Mex and New Mexico. When the harvest comes in, New Mexico chiles are grilled out front on a large metal barbecue rig. One house specialty is the Chuychanga, a 12-inch flour tortilla stuffed with cheese, chicken,

cilantro, and green chiles, and then deep-fried and topped with sour cream and salsa. There are also Chuy's Special Enchiladas made with smoked chicken and blue corn tortillas. There are now three Chuy's in Austin: this one, one in North Austin and another in Northwest Austin (see below). The lively atmosphere makes this a popular family spot. The restaurant also sponsors a Christmas Parade (see our Annual Events chapter). Chuy's is open for lunch and dinner daily.

Curra's Grill $-$$
614 East Oltorf Street
(512) 444-0012
www.currasgrill.citysearch.com
Austin abounds in small family restaurants that bring the flavors of Mexico home in a variety of ways. Curra's signature is a variety of salsas—borracho, which means "drunken" in Mexico, is made with tomatoes and a touch of beer; pasilla takes its name from the smokey rich taste of the pasilla chile; verde is a green sauce made from tomatillos, sometimes called green tomatoes but really no relation—in fact, tomatillos, which are covered in a papery husk, are actually related to gooseberries. Other sauces include allende, a nutty cream sauce; and chipotle, the name given to smoked jalapeños. The menu features all-day breakfast tacos, enchiladas and carne guisada, a slow-simmered stew, and other traditional Mexican dishes, including several delicious Yucatean offerings. Open daily for breakfast, lunch, and dinner, and you can buy the restaurant's tamales on-line.

El Mercado Restaurant and Cantina $-$$
1302 South First Street
(512) 447-7445
This South Central location, one of three El Mercados in Austin (see the others under Central and North), serves up the same generous proportions of Tex-Mex favorites in a lively, colorful setting. The restaurant is open daily for breakfast, lunch, and dinner.

El Nopalito $
2809 South First Street
(512) 326-2026

This typical Mexican cafe near St.
Edward's University is popular with the
working-class neighbors, students, and
foodies who love homemade Mexican
food. The small restaurant—its name
means "little cactus"—serves breakfast
and lunch only. Popular dishes include
tacos and migas (eggs scrambled with
tomatoes, onions, chiles, and strips of corn
tortillas), the homemade flan, and, on
weekends, menudo. Touted as a hangover
cure, menudo is a tripe and hominy stew
that is an acquired taste. No credit cards.

El Sol y La Luna $-$$
1224 South Congress Avenue
(512) 444-7770

An old motel coffee shop has been revived
as a Mexican cantina as part of the changing face of South Congress Avenue. With
so many good Mexican restaurants in
town, opening a new venture is not always
easy, but El Sol y La Luna (The Sun and
the Moon) quickly developed a loyal following, particularly on weekend mornings,
when a leisurely breakfast of migas (eggs
scrambled with peppers and onions) or
huevos rancheros is local custom. The outdoor patio with its rustic Mexican furniture
is a favorite place to have a late breakfast.
The menu also features Latin American
and Central American dishes, but for an
introduction to classic Mexican cuisine try
the house mole poblano, a spicy chocolate
sauce with more than two dozen ingredients that is served over meat and enchiladas. Open daily for breakfast, lunch, and
dinner.

Green Mesquite $-$$
1400 Barton Springs Road
(512) 479-0485
www.greenmesquite.com

Texas barbecue and Louisiana Cajun fare
are the specialties here. For avowed meat
lovers the barbecue dishes include
sausage, turkey, brisket, and ribs, but there
are also chicken-fried steaks, hamburgers,

and sandwiches. On the Cajun side, the
spicy gumbo and jambalaya are favorites,
and there is catfish. The pies are homemade, and there is live music on weekends.
A second location is found in Southwest
Austin (see below). Green Mesquite is
open daily for lunch and dinner.

Green Pastures $$$-$$$$
811 West Live Oak Road
(512) 444-1888
www.greenpastures.citysearch.com

In 1945 the Koock family decided to turn
their family mansion into a restaurant,
and ever since Green Pastures has been a
quiet, elegant place to celebrate special
events and family gatherings. The mansion was built in 1894 and has been in the
Koock family since 1916. Surrounded by a
large garden with more than 200 live oak
trees, the mansion is hidden away in an
everyday South Austin neighborhood.
Patrons can begin their dining experience
with a glass of milk punch out on the
veranda, watch the peacocks stroll on the
lawn, and listen to music being played on
the restaurant's grand piano. The goal at
Green Pastures is to re-create the hospitality of the Old South while offering continental cuisine with touches of Texas.
The dinner menu includes duck Texana,
duck breasts wrapped in bacon and
dressed with blackberry sauce, or snapper Florentine and lobster crepes. The
desserts echo the traditions of the past:
flaming bananas Foster, bread pudding,
and the Texas pecan ball, a take on a traditional hot fudge sundae. The restaurant
serves lunch and dinner daily, but one
highlight of the week is the Sunday
brunch, when Green Pastures sets a table
that astounds both the eye and the
palate. The brunch includes cheese
boards, a savory table with bowls of
boiled shrimp, huge silver chafing dishes
filled with egg dishes and entrees, plus a
large standing rib roast. A large dessert
table is also part of the brunch picture.
Reservations are recommended for
brunch and for lunch and dinner on
weekends.

Güero's $-$$
1412 South Congress Avenue
(512) 447-7688

The stretch of South Congress Avenue that rises from Town Lake and up the hill to the horizon is undergoing great change as funky shops and restaurants (see our Shopping chapter) convert old buildings to new uses. Architectural ingenuity has turned an old feed store on the avenue into Güero's, where the food reflects both Tex-Mex and Mexican influences. The interior has been decorated with Mexican tiles, old photographs from the Mexican Revolution, and a picture of former President Bill Clinton, who has eaten here when visiting Austin. First Lady Laura Bush sometimes drops by. A portion of the kitchen is open, and diners can watch tacos and salsas being made. Breakfast tacos are a bargain here and are served all day, although the restaurant is not open for breakfast during the week. Some of the entrees are taken from the Mexican pantheon—dishes like chicken al carbon, a Yucatecan dish that features grilled chicken breasts spiced with chiles and achiote. Steak a la Tampiqueña and snapper a la Veracruzano are on the dinner menu. The steak is grilled and served with grilled vegetables and salsa; the fish is cooked with tomatoes and green olives. On weekends Güero's opens early for breakfast, featuring tacos, migas, huevos rancheros, and other popular Tex-Mex favorites. There is usually live music on Sunday afternoon.

Kerbey Lane Cafe $-$$
2700 South Lamar Boulevard
(512) 445-4451

This is the South Austin location of a very popular local cafe that serves homemade, healthful food 24 hours a day. The menu features sandwiches, salads, Tex-Mex favorites, breakfast specials (available all day and night), omelettes, pancakes, and homemade desserts.

Lamberts American Kitchen $-$$
1716 South Congress Avenue
(512) 383-8877

Lou Lambert grew up in West Texas, worked for a time as a charcuterie cook for Wolfgang Puck in California, and then ran Liberty Pie, an Austin catering company, before converting his workspace in a small, though often packed, restaurant south of the river, near downtown Austin. They call this funky strip of South Congress "SoCo," and in the past few years it has developed a unique atmosphere—a mix of hip restaurants and funky shops. Lamberts' menu is what has come to be known in Austin as American bistro with a Southwestern flair. But the descriptions of some of the dishes are not an exercise in cultural navigation; for example, his roasted chicken is simple, fresh, and made to order. For dessert try Lambert's coconut cream pie, a not-to-be-ignored "leftover" from his catering days. Lamberts is open daily for dinner; closed Sunday.

La Reyna Mexican Bakery $-$$
1816 South First Street
(512) 443-6369

When the owners of the original bakery, La Reyna (named for the picture of the Virgin Mary whose image hangs on a wall of the bakery), retired, they sold the business to one of their longtime bakers, Jesus Becerra, who still gets to work at midnight to begin baking. The bakery and cafe is in the heart of one of Austin's predominantly Mexican-American neighborhoods, but it's a neighborhood that, like much of Austin, is changing and trying to hold on to its authentic atmosphere. The cafe is a meeting place for neighbors, local politicians, artists, and those who appreciate the homey atmosphere of the long-established South Austin restaurant. Over 70 different kinds of Mexican sweet breads are offered, and the staff will help you learn their names. Coffee and Mexican hot chocolate are good accompaniments. Be sure to take home a bag of Mexican pastries and cookies—the conchas, a sweet bread with a whirled shell design in sugar, are a favorite. But eat them the same day: Mexican pastries have no preservatives and little salt, so they do not stay fresh for long. The cafe is open daily from 6:00 A.M. to 8:30 P.M.

Magnolia Cafe South $
1920 South Congress Avenue
(512) 445–0000

There are two Magnolia Cafes, this one in South Austin and the original in West Austin. The cafe is open 24 hours a day, seven days a week, and serves a home-style menu featuring breakfast dishes no matter the hour, sandwiches, fajitas, and salads, all in a homey atmosphere.

Matt's Famous El Rancho $$
2613 South Lamar Boulevard
(512) 462–9333

In 2002 Matt's celebrated its 50th anniversary. The Martinez family has been in the restaurant business for longer than that, but in 1952 Matt Martinez opened up the first El Rancho, now operating in a new, large building south of downtown. President Lyndon B. Johnson ate here before he was president, and lots of other Austin notables have come here for a regular Tex-Mex fix. The guacamole, cheese, and meat dip is named for former Texas Land Commissioner Bob Armstrong, who went on to serve in the Clinton administration. The menu includes all the old faithful standbys: enchiladas, fajitas, tacos, chile rellenos, and grilled shrimp. The hacienda-style restaurant can seat 500, but there is always a line on weekends at peak dining hours. Open for lunch and dinner daily, except Tuesday.

PizzaNizza $
1600 Barton Springs Road
(512) 474–7470

A fixture on the Barton Springs Road restaurant row, this pizza restaurant forgoes the red and white checkered tablecloths for a livelier decor with yellow walls and primary color accents. The pizza joint

was opened by one of the founders of the Whole Food Markets (see our Shopping chapter) and offers a wide variety of pies aimed at matching a diversity of tastes. Diners can design their own pizza, choosing from several sauces—some spicy, others light—and then dress them with the toppings of their choice. Open daily for lunch and dinner.

Romeo's $$
1500 Barton Springs Road
(512) 476–1090
www.romeos.citysearch.com

From the concrete stone swan planters in front to the plastic grapevines inside, the owners of Romeo's have managed to re-create the kitschy atmosphere of a neighborhood Italian-American cafe. This Barton Springs Road restaurant row cafe offers patrons a taste of those old, familiar restaurants as well. Sausage sandwiches, pepperoni pizza, manicotti, and eggplant Parmesan are on the menu, but there are a few Texas touches also. Chipotle chicken is a spicy dish served with black beans and fresh cilantro. There are also a few nouvelle Italian dishes that have crept onto the menu—grilled pesto chicken on focaccia, grilled portobello mushrooms, and a pasta salad. The atmosphere and the prices make this a great date restaurant. Open daily for lunch and dinner plus a Sunday brunch featuring vegetarian and meat fritattas, Italian eggs Benedict, and, of course, migas, the Tex-Mex breakfast must.

Schlotzsky's Marketplace/
Bread Alone Bakery $
218 South Lamar Boulevard
(512) 476–2867
www.schlotzskys.com

Schlotzsky's is a chain sandwich shop that was founded in Austin and has grown worldwide, including an outpost in Beijing. There are almost two dozen outlets in Austin, but this special branch just south of Town Lake is notable for its breezy atmosphere, airy architecture, and its on-site partner, Bread Alone Bakery. The famous sandwiches are sold here—the Original is made with special bread (grilled sourdough buns) stuffed with salami, ham, several cheeses, olives, onions, lettuce, and tomato—plus soups, salads, and small pizzas. The bakery offers whole loaves of specialty bread, cakes, cookies, desserts, and coffees. This is a good place to put together lunch or afternoon snacks for an impromptu picnic on the shores of Town Lake. Open daily for breakfast, lunch, and dinner and offers wireless connections.

Shady Grove   **$-$$**
1624 Barton Springs Road
(512) 474-9991
www.theshadygrove.com
This Texas roadhouse–style restaurant takes its name from the pecan grove that shades the patio and the parking lot. There is seating inside, but many patrons prefer to sit outside and watch the squirrels race around harvesting pecans or begging for crumbs. The food here is the sort served in roadhouses across America back in the days before interstate highways brought chain food to the crossroads. Hamburgers are a staple, or try a Frito pie (Fritos topped with chili and cheese). For vegetarians there is a variety of salads and a Hippie Sandwich made with grilled eggplant and other vegetables. The Airstream Chili is hot and named for the Airstream trailer that sits in the garden. During summer, Shady Grove features live music evenings and even movies on the patio. Open daily for lunch and dinner.

Taco Xpress   **$**
2529 South Lamar Boulevard
(512) 444-0261
www.tacoxpress.com
The bumper stickers in this part of Austin often say KEEP AUSTIN WEIRD, and funkiness is a point of pride in South Austin. At this—what else—funky cafe the patio features a shrine to Santa Taqueria Austin del Sur, and the menu has literally dozens of taco combos. Owner and chef Maria Corbalon is noted for her roasted meats,

which evoke memories of those tacos savored by travelers in the Yucatan and other regions of Mexico. The cafe is open daily for breakfast and lunch, closes midafternoon on Monday and Sunday, and stays open until midevening on other nights. No credit cards.

Threadgill's World Headquarters
Restaurant   **$$**
301 West Riverside Drive
(512) 472-9304
www.threadgills.com
Eddie Wilson founded the Armadillo World Headquarters (see The Music Scene chapter) and now owns Threadgill's, the two Austin restaurants that cherish home-cooking and celebrate the Austin music scene. The original Threadgill's is in North Austin (see North section), but this downtown restaurant has carried the Threadgill's banner back to the block where the legendary Armadillo stood. The restaurant celebrates the past by decorating the walls with Armadillo memorabilia. Much larger than the original Threadgill's, the downtown venue is nevertheless packed, especially at lunchtime. The food here is down-home diner-style with entrees like meat loaf, chicken-fried steak, fried chicken, and sandwiches. Side dishes include Cajun eggplant, garlic cheese grits, jalapeño jambalaya, and squash casserole, some of which can be found in grocery supermarket freezer cases in Austin. There is live music here and a Sunday gospel brunch. Open daily for lunch and dinner.

The Paggi House   **$$$**
200 Lee Barton Drive
(512) 478-1121
www.paggihouse.citysearch.com
It is easy to miss the Paggi House, tucked away as it is on a wooded lot just south of Town Lake, but this graceful little restaurant has been a fixture on the Austin restaurant scene for a couple of decades. The restaurant serves a continental-style menu—dishes such as cannelloni stuffed with chicken, walnuts, and peppers and

topped with Gorgonzola cream sauce, plus grilled meats and fresh fish. The building dates back to the 1840s, the earliest days of Austin's history, and the walls and floors have a patina imparted by history. Reservations are recommended for dinner, which is served Monday through Saturday. Lunch is offered on weekdays.

Uchi $$–$$$
801 South Lamar Boulevard
(512) 916–4808

An old South Austin bungalow that has been home to several culinary incarnations is now a sushi restaurant. Amidst the fabled funkiness of South Austin, the bungalow is now a quiet retreat with Zen-like decor, touches of bamboo, and an ordered garden. The sushi chef at this new addition to the south-of-the-river dining scene hails from one of the city's top sushi restaurants in North Austin. Open daily for dinner; closed on Sunday.

Vespaio $$–$$$$
1610 South Congress Avenue
(512) 441–6100

This Italian-inspired restaurant in the heart of the hot South Congress Avenue corridor (see our Shopping chapter) represents all that is both good and bad about the Austin restaurant scene these days. The food is inspired, the atmosphere lively, but the wait can be long! A small restaurant, Vespaio rocketed to fame soon after it opened. Created by Chef Alan Lazurus, the menu here allows patrons to dine in a small dining area with a view of the kitchen or to sit in the bar area and simply nosh for an hour or two on a wide selection of antipasti—perhaps quail eggs or prosciutto and figs. The antipasti case sits at the entrance to the restaurant, giving patrons a view of the day's offerings. The food here is Italian-inspired and diners can choose to indulge in four courses—antipasti, pasta, entree, and dessert—or simply opt for a lighter dinner. Many of the dishes reflect Italian classics like Tuscan grilled steak and mussels in wine sauce; others are inspirations that draw on

top Texas food products prepared in the Italian manner and in tune with the seasons. Vespaio is open Tuesday through Sunday for dinner.

SOUTH

Cherry Creek Catfish Co. $$
5712 Manchaca Road
(512) 440–8810
www.cherrycreek.citysearch.com

The decor is designed to re-create a Louisiana wharf, but the menu is both Cajun and Texan, with barbecue and seafood holding center stage. On the Cajun side is gumbo, frog legs, blackened catfish, crawfish, shrimp, and oysters plus po'boys. You'll also find fried green tomatoes, a dish found throughout the South. Meat lovers can try barbecue ribs, hamburgers, or chicken-fried steak. The restaurant also offers family packs of their food to go. Open daily for lunch and dinner.

El Gallo $–$$
2910 South Congress Avenue
(512) 444–2205

A popular Tex-Mex eatery that offers servings of enchiladas, tacos, chalupa, and fajitas so generous that no one leaves hungry. The dinner menu also features several dishes that are typical of South Texas cookery, including cabrito (roasted baby goat) and chicken mole, the rich, complex chocolate and chile-based sauce that legend says was created by nuns in Puebla, Mexico, in honor of a visiting bishop. The restaurant is located in a colorful building across the street from St. Edward's University. Open daily from lunch through dinner.

Evita's Botanitas Mexican Restaurant $–$$
6400 South First Street
(512) 441–2424

Tex-Mex eateries abound in Austin, but this far-south Austin cafe serves the sort of food you might encounter south of the border at family restaurants. The salsas are the stars here, and four small containers arrive with a preliminary basket of tortilla chips, a typical "botanita," or appetizer. The salsas include a black bean–chipotle sauce, a tomatillo and roasted pepper variety, garlic and chile salsa, plus a fresh uncooked sauce usually called "salsa cruda," a mix of chopped tomatoes, onions, chiles, and cilantro. Evita's also opts for authentic ingredients like Mexican queso, the white, mozzarella-like cheese that is used traditionally in Mexico. Dinner entrees include chicken breast stuffed with chorizo (Mexican sausage), and shrimp stuffed with jalapeños and wrapped in bacon with chipotle sauce on the side. Evita's is open all day, breakfast through dinner.

Tres Amigos $$
1807 West Slaughter Lane at Manchaca Road
(512) 292-1001
www.tresamigos.com

This is the South Austin entry of this hometown three-location chain. The menu is classic Tex-Mex and includes tacos, fajitas, and enchiladas. Don't pass on the house mango ice cream.

SOUTHWEST

Alpenhof's Steak Haus $$$
16018 Hamilton Pool Road
(512) 263-9875

A romantic spot on a quiet country road in the hills southwest of Austin, this small restaurant is out of the way but worth a visit. The natural stone walls are luminous at night with light cast by hundreds of tiny lights and candles. The room has two fireplaces and a few hunting trophies hanging on the wall to give the place a rustic Texas Hill Country air. The menu focuses on steak with some Swiss touches, such as the cheese tartlets offered as an appetizer. Hamilton Pool Road leads west off Highway 71 west of Austin and near the village of Bee Cave. (See our Parks and Recreation chapter for information about Hamil-

ton Pool Preserve with its nature trails and natural swimming hole.) Open daily for dinner; closed Monday.

Austin Pizza Garden $-$$
6266 U.S. 290 West
(512) 891-9980
www.austinpizzagarden.com

It took 19 years for James Patton to finish the Old Rock Store in Oak Hill; chances are it won't take much more than 19 minutes for you to get your pizza in the restaurant now housed in the historic building. Patton (the local elementary school is named for him) finished the store in 1898, and it has served as home to a variety of businesses over the years. Patton, whose father came to Texas in 1836 and fought in the Texas Revolution, served as postmaster of Oak Hill until the branch closed in 1910. He was known as the "Mayor of Oak Hill," despite the fact the city never incorporated. Now Oak Hill is a suburb of Austin, and a major freeway has wiped out many of the small stores that once lined the old highway. But Patton's stone structure is a registered historic building, and even the highway had to shift south to preserve history. Pizza is the major focus of the restaurant now occupying the site. There are almost two dozen choices on the menu, from quattro formaggio (four cheese) to Texas fajita, a Cajun pizza dubbed Tchoupitoulas with andouille sausage, shrimp, red onions, green and red peppers, and garlic, or a Neptune with crab, shrimp, and artichoke hearts. The restaurant also offers take-out service. Open daily for lunch and dinner.

Central Market at Westgate $-$$
4477 South Lamar Boulevard, Westgate Mall
(512) 899-4300
www.centralmarket.com

Just as the cafe at the original Central Market (see Central Austin) is a popular spot for family dining, this second location has proved to be a favorite place to take the whole family. The varied menu offers sandwiches, home-style entrees, gourmet

Austin abounds with bakeries where a last-minute picnic can be put together for outdoor (or indoor) munching. Several are listed here in the Restaurants chapter, but also check out the Food/Gourmet/Kitchenware section of our Shopping chapter.

salads, pizza, burgers, soups, and sandwiches, ensuring that everyone in the group will find something to suit his or her fancy. The cafe also opens early for breakfast, and there is free live music on the patio at night. Open daily 7:00 A.M. to 10:00 P.M., until 11:00 P.M. on Friday and Saturday. A drive-through, Rotisserie Express, serves breakfast, lunch, and dinner from 7:00 A.M. to 9:00 P.M.

Flipnotics Satellite Cafe   **$-$$**
7101 Highway 71 West
(512) 301-1883
www.flipnotics.com
The cafe is a spin-off of the popular Barton Springs Road Flipnotics coffeehouse and vintage clothing shop in South Central Austin (see both our Shopping and Nightlife chapters). With the growth of Southwest Austin and the presence of a branch of Austin Community College located nearby, Flipnotics Satellite Cafe has found a niche in the 'burbs, serving breakfast, lunch, and dinner, plus acoustic music on the deck on the weekends. Breakfast dishes include pancakes, migas, breakfast tacos, and Flipnotics' coffee, of course. Sandwiches, wraps, pastas, and salads appear on the lunch menu. Dinner choices include steaks, pastas, grilled dishes, and burgers. Open daily.

Green Mesquite   **$-$$**
7010 Highway 71 West
(512) 288-8300
www.greenmesquite.com
Fortunately for residents of Southwest Austin, they don't have to go down to "restaurant row" on Barton Springs Road

(see South Central above) to enjoy Green Mesquite's barbecue. This sister restaurant is inconspicuously tucked away in the HEB shopping center at the Y, the divergence of U.S. 71 West and U.S. 290 West in Oak Hill. The fare is the same—barbecue with all the fixin's. Open daily for lunch and dinner.

Nutty Brown Cafe   **$-$$$**
12225 U.S. 290 West
(512) 301-4648
One of the hottest growth areas of Austin has been the southwest region and the once-sleepy community of Dripping Springs down the road from what the locals call the Y at Oak Hill (see our Relocation chapter for a guide to Austin neighborhoods). The Nutty Brown Cafe is, according to its mailing address, in Dripping Springs, but the two communities are fast becoming merged, as evidenced by all the growth along U.S. 290. This is a popular family restaurant, especially on the weekends, when there is live music on the patio. The menu features Mexican food, salads, and sandwiches. On Friday night there is a free taco bar, and on Sunday morning breakfast is served, which makes it a good stop on the way to a Hill Country day trip. Open daily from lunch through dinner; open earlier on Sunday.

Serrano's Cafe & Cantina   **$$**
6510 U.S. 290 West
(512) 891-0000
One of nine Serrano's in Austin, this one in Oak Hill is housed in what was once a steakhouse. The walls are decorated with historic pictures and artifacts from the days when the hill across the street from the restaurant was dubbed "Convict Hill." There, convict laborers worked cutting stone for the interior walls of the capitol building. Several are reputed to be buried on the hill, but their graves have been lost. The menu here is typical Tex-Mex and includes fajitas, enchiladas, tacos, and generously sized appetizers.

The Salt Lick $$
Rural Route 1826,
Camp Ben McCullough Road, Driftwood
(512) 858-4959
www.saltlickbbq.com

One of the most atmospheric barbecue restaurants in the area, the Salt Lick occupies a rural site about 12 miles south of U.S. 290 West on R.R. 1826, known as Camp Ben McCullough Road. Set in a Hill Country pasture, the Salt Lick has garnered a worldwide reputation, thanks to its mail-order food shipments, corporate parties by some of Austin's top employers, and coverage in national and international publications. To get there, take R.R. 1826, just past the Y in Oak Hill, and head south for 12 miles—or until you smell the smoke from the smokehouse. There are picnic tables inside and out, and the place is always busy. In winter a large fireplace inside warms diners. The menu includes brisket, chicken, ribs, sausage, homemade pickles, and peach and berry cobblers. Open daily for lunch and dinner. Reservations are suggested for large groups. The Salt Lick is located in a dry area of Hays County, so no beer, wine, or liquor is served; however, patrons can bring their own alcoholic beverages. No credit cards.

Y Bar and Grill $$-$$$
7720 Highway 71 West
(512) 394-0220
www.ybargrill.com

For 14 years Jean-Pierre Piaget ran an elegant continental restaurant in Central Austin called Jean-Pierre's Upstairs. Then he decided in 2001 to change his focus, at least geographically, and opened his new restaurant in Southwest Austin at what is locally known as the Y because it is where U.S. 290 West and Highway 71 West part company, one heading west to the hills, the other northwest to the lakes. Southwest Austin has become a fast-growing section of the city and the location at the Y is convenient for both southwest Austinites and Hill Country residents to the west and northwest. The menu is contemporary American, and these days that means diverse influences reflected on the menu—from blue cornmeal crabcakes to macadamia-encrusted shrimp, honey-ancho duck, jerk meatballs, plus steak, seafood, and vegetarian dishes. Piaget encourages patrons to drop by for a glass of wine and a snack on the outdoor patio. Open daily for lunch and dinner; brunch served on weekends.

WEST

Baby Acapulco's $-$$
1705 South Lakeshore Boulevard
(512) 447-1339

The West Austin branch of the Barton Springs restaurant row hot spot. See our South Central listings for details.

Belgian Restaurant L'Estro
Armonico $$-$$$
3520 Bee Caves Road
(512) 328-0580

One of the most romantic places for a special evening, this West Lake Hills cozy restaurant features Belgian cuisine and continental service. Female diners are presented with a rose at the end of the meal, and no matter what your gender, you'll get a Belgian chocolate with the bill. The restaurant offers a prix-fixe menu plus an array of changing entrees, which might include duck in green peppercorn sauce or with dark cherries or grilled fish topped with sautéed leeks. Given the chef's Belgian roots, desserts featuring chocolates are a specialty—try the chocolate mousse. Open for lunch and dinner Monday through Friday, dinner only on weekends. Reservations are recommended.

Bistro 88 $$-$$$
2712 Bee Caves Road
(512) 328-8888
www.bistro88.com

Touted as Pacific Rim cuisine with Euro-Asian flare, the menu here is the creation of three partners who have operated top restaurants in Mexico and China. *Austin Chronicle* readers lauded this West Austin restaurant with its sophisticated menu and decor as "The Best New Restaurant in 2000." Dishes include such fusion creations as hot-and-sour seafood gumbo, roast lamb with a curried Asian pasta, mussels with a black bean sauce, plus entrees featuring top-quality seafood and Texas game. Open for lunch Sunday through Friday, dinner daily.

Canyon Cafe $$
701 South Loop 360 (Capital of Texas Highway)
(512) 329-0400
www.canyoncafe.com
Every effort has been made in this West Lake Hills shopping center restaurant to re-create the feeling of dining in a large mountain lodge somewhere in the Southwest. The menu reflects this same theme, with variations on traditional Tex-Mex fare, pastas with a spicy touch, grilled chicken, beef, and fish, plus house specialties like chicken-fried tuna. Open for lunch and dinner daily and Sunday brunch.

Canyonside Cafe and Grille $$-$$$
3595 Rural Route 620 South
(512) 263-4205
The view of the hills from this second-story restaurant is an added bonus for diners who enjoy the classic American food here, including steak and seafood selections and a popular Sunday brunch. On the first and third Wednesdays of the month, the restaurant presents the Capital City Mystery Players, a lighthearted dinner theater group. (For information on the schedule and ticket prices call 512-404-9123.) The view and the quiet atmosphere here make it a popular spot for sunset dining. Open daily for dinner, brunch only on Sunday.

Chinatown $$
3300 Bee Caves Road
(512) 327-6588
www.chinatownaustin.citysearch.com
Among the most popular items on the menu at this West Lake Hills restaurant

are several searing dishes, Thai pepper basil shrimp, and jalapeño chicken with black bean sauce—a reflection of the spicy Szechwan-style Chinese cuisine featured at Chinatown. Of course not all the dishes are spicy, but diners with a taste for the fiery can turn up the heat on request. Chinatown is open daily for lunch and dinner.

Ciola's $$-$$$
1310 Rural Route 620 South, Suite C-2
Lakeway Plaza
(512) 263-9936
www.ciolas.com
Fusion, nouvelle, northern Italian—all descriptions that get bandied about these days in descriptions of culinary trends. But sometimes we all get a hankering for the food we remember from the past. Finding the kind of traditional Italian dishes that used to be featured in small cafes with checkered tablecloths and Chianti-bottle candles can be hard. Dan and LeAnne Ciola watch over Ciola's, where patrons hungry after a day of water-skiing or sight-seeing in the Highland Lakes can find those evergreen favorites. Uncle Dominick opened the first Ciola's in Virginia Beach back in 1949, his dishes based on family recipes from Abruzzi, Italy. All the familiar favorites are here, including lasagna, fettucine Alfredo, even spaghetti and meatballs. There are also meat, chicken, and seafood dishes on the menu. Many dishes can be ordered family-style on large platters to be shared by everyone at the table. Open weekdays for lunch and dinner, weekends for dinner only.

County Line on the Hill $$-$$$
6500 Bee Caves Road
(512) 327-1742
www.countylinehill.citysearch.com
Upscale barbecue is the order of the day at this hillside restaurant. Over the years, the view from the hilltop patio has changed as Austin has grown and homeowners have headed for the hills. One of the highlights of the menu is the smoked

prime rib, served with baked potato, coleslaw, and beans. Barbecued ribs, brisket, chicken, sausage, pork, and baby back ribs are available by the plate or by the pound. The restaurant is open for lunch during the week and for dinner daily.

Hang Town Grill $
701 South Loop 360 (Capital of Texas Highway)
(512) 347-1039

This is an Austin favorite among the soccer-mom set because it not only feeds the kids what they want—burgers and pizza—but also gives mom a chance to nibble on salads and entrees with an Asian touch. Hang Town is yet another Clemons' creation (see Bitter End and Granite Cafe listings), which they describe as a "galactic salad/pizza/burger bar for all ages." This is a very popular family dining spot, especially for boomers with toddlers and preteens. The Rowdy Burger comes dressed with jalapeños, grilled onions, hickory sauce, and lots of napkins. Another popular sandwich features vegetables grilled in the wood-fired oven, dressed with red onions, pesto, feta cheese, and calamata olives. The Thai hacked chicken salad appeals to fans of spicy Asian dishes. The menu also features a variety of pizzas; for dessert try one of the house milk shakes.

Hill Country Pasta House $$-$$$
3519 Rural Route 620 North
(512) 266-9445
www.pastahouse.citysearch.com

This Lake Travis–area restaurant offers a variety of pastas and Italian-inspired entrees. The wood-fired oven produces pizza and focaccia, and there are grilled offerings, including steaks. The restaurant is kid-friendly, and crayons come with the menu so that the kiddies can be occupied while parents ruminate on the choices. Because it is close to the lake, many patrons come in after a day of boating or swimming, so the dress code is relaxed. Open daily for lunch and dinner.

Hudson's-on-the-Bend $$$$
3509 Rural Route 620
(512) 266-1369
www.hudsonsonthebend.com

Chef/owner Jeff Blank and executive chef Becky Barsch Fischer have built a wide-ranging reputation as innovators in Texas cuisine from their base near the shores of Lake Travis. *Condé Nast Traveler* magazine has named it one of the best 50 restaurants in the United States. The restaurant is housed in and around a small Hill Country cottage. On the grounds are a smokehouse and an herb garden that offers a hint of what Hudson's has to offer. Much of the menu is devoted to showcasing exotic game and ingredients—one of the popular appetizers is Omar's Rattlesnake Cakes with chipotle cream sauce. Other dishes utilize venison, javelina (a South Texas wild boar), and Axis antelope raised on Hill Country ranches. For the less adventurous there are top-quality steaks, veal, seafood, and pasta dishes. The restaurant's sauces, both savory and sweet, garnered such a devoted following they are now sold on specialty food store shelves and by mail order. (Look for them at Central Market, and look for Central Market in our Shopping chapter.) The atmosphere at Hudson's is intimate, although the series of small dining rooms when packed with customers can be fashionably noisy. Diners can eat or wait for a table on a balmy evening in the garden decorated with twinkling lights. Weekends are especially busy, so reservations are recommended. The restaurant is open daily for dinner but closes a little earlier in winter, so it is wise to call ahead. Hudson's also offers cooking classes.

La Madeleine $
701 South Loop 360 (Capital of Texas Highway)
(512) 306-1998
www.lamadeleine.com

Unlike the other two Austin locations, which are housed in buildings originally designed for other businesses, this latest addition was built for the French bistro-bakery in a West Austin shopping center. Despite the shopping mall location, the interior is a cozy rendition of a French cafe. See the Central Austin listing for details on the menu.

Las Palomas $$
3201 Bee Caves Road
(512) 327-9889

Tucked away in the corner of a fairly nondescript strip shopping center, this Mexican restaurant serves delicious interior food in a light, airy setting. Specialties from various Mexican states are featured, including pork pibil, inspired by Yucatecan cuisine, shrimp a la Veracruzana (green olives, tomatoes, and capers), and the much-praised mole poblano, a complex sauce made from chiles, chocolate, spice, and herbs. The restaurant features live mariachi music on the weekends to add to the ambience. Las Palomas is open for lunch and dinner daily.

Magnolia Cafe $
2304 Lake Austin Boulevard
(512) 478-8645

This is a homey, comfortable diner where gingerbread pancakes rank as comfort food 24 hours a day, seven days a week. The cafe is not far from downtown, just west of MoPac, and serves breakfast dishes, sandwiches, even fajitas whenever you want them, no matter the hour.

Rosie's Tamale House $
13436 Highway 71, Bee Cave
(512) 263-5245

Willie Nelson ate here so often they named a plate after him—Willie's Plate with a taco, enchilada, guacamole, and chile con queso. Willie must have tipped rather well, too, since Rosie's moved from a small building to a big new home a few years ago in the Bee Cave neighborhood. (Careful readers will note it is Bee Caves Road, but Bee Cave neighborhood—the community prefers the singular appellation.) A stop at Rosie's is a regular event for Austinites frolicking at the lake on the weekend. If they don't stop for lunch or

dinner, they are sure to drop in for an order or two of tamales to go.

Rudy's Bar-B-Q $–$$$
2451 Capital of Texas Highway
(Loop 360)
(512) 329-5554
www.rudys.com

You can gas up your car and grab a grocery bag of barbecue at this popular small Texas chain. Rudy's touts itself as serving "the worst barbecue in Texas," but obviously that's a gimmick, judging from the crowd. The gas station is not one of those small town stations; this is an up-to-date copy that simply reminds patrons that good barbecue originated in small town country stores. Patrons can eat in or get food to go, and Rudy's opens early to serve breakfast tacos. Open daily for breakfast, lunch, and dinner.

The Emerald Restaurant $$$–$$$$
13614 Highway 71 West
(512) 263-2147

Step inside this Hill Country cottage and you will think you have crossed the threshold of an Irish country cottage. The walls are decorated with shamrock wallpaper, the tablecloths and curtains are lace, and there are cozy nooks and crannies where diners can enjoy an intimate dinner. The Kinsella family, whose matriarch hails from County Mayo, runs this little Irish gem near Lake Travis. The evening begins here with orders of Irish soda bread and English treacle loaf (made with molasses) served with whipped strawberry butter and goes on from there to embrace roast pork in puff pastry, chateaubriand for two, roast lamb, grilled salmon inspired by Irish and continental influences. The desserts are rich, and Irish coffee is almost an obligatory end to dinner. The Emerald is open daily for dinner.

Tres Amigos $$
1801 South Loop 360
(Capital of Texas Highway)
(512) 327-1776
www.tresamigos.com

A longtime fixture on the Westlake Hills scene, Tres Amigos serves familiar Tex-Mex favorites such as enchiladas and tacos, fajitas, and Mexican plates. Some of the waitresses have been on the job for years and have watched as families grew up, nourished by the kind of food all Texans hanker for regularly. The setting is a pleasant evocation of Old Mexico. Try the homemade mango ice cream. Tres Amigos is open for lunch and dinner daily.

Waterloo Ice House at
The Backyard $
13101 Highway 71 West
(512) 263-5400
www.waterloomaster.citysearch.com
The Backyard, with its natural open-air stage under the live oak trees (see The Music Scene chapter), attracts large crowds on concert nights, but the branch of the Waterloo Ice House that is part of the site here is open for lunch and dinner daily. In addition to Waterloo, which features burgers, sandwiches, and chicken-fried steak, there is also a branch of Iron Works barbecue (see our Central listings), where barbecued beef, ribs, chicken, pork, and all the fixin's are served.

NORTHWEST

Bellagio $$-$$$
6507 Jester Boulevard
(512) 346-8228
www.bellagioitalianbistro.com
This family-owned restaurant, named for a picturesque small town in Lombardy, northern Italy, draws big crowds, especially on the weekends. The Loiacono family is dedicated to serving Italian classics in a sophisticated setting. All the pasta is handmade at the restaurant. The menu features classics like osso buco, calamari, and pasta dishes reflecting many different regions of Italy. Dinner served daily except Sunday.

Brick Oven Restaurant $
10710 Research Boulevard
(512) 345-6181

The latest addition to the hometown Brick Oven chain, this Northwest location features pizza baked in a wood-fired oven. Customers can choose from a variety of toppings, thin or thick crust, even an all-garlic pizza. The menu also features other Italian-American staples and salads. Open daily for lunch and nightly for dinner.

Cafe Spiazzo $$-$$$
5416 Parkcrest Drive, Suite 700
(512) 459-9960
Never judge a book by its cover or a restaurant by the outside appearance. Spiazzo is tucked away inside a typical neighborhood shopping center just west of MoPac, but inside the atmosphere of a modern Italian cafe has been re-created with lots of vibrant colors. Appetizers are light and include Sicilian caponata, a mix of eggplant, bell peppers, tomatoes, onions, olives, and capers plus goat cheese fritti—medallions of breaded, fried cheese topped with roasted tomato-basil sauce. Both the bread and the pizzas are cooked in a wood-fired oven; a variety of salads feature roasted vegetables, pasta, and fresh tomatoes and herbs; and the pastas vary from the simple to the rich and creamy. There is a special section of the menu dubbed "Italy SXSW" featuring Italian-style dishes with Southwestern touches—spicy chipotle cappellini, which gets its kick from the chipotle pepper (a smoked jalapeño), and spaghetti with Shiner Bock meatballs. Spiazzo is open daily for lunch and dinner. Closed Sunday.

Catfish Parlour $$
11910 Research Boulevard
(512) 258-1853
The original Catfish Parlour is in Southeast Austin (see our listing), but its popularity led to a new branch in Northwest Austin. Patrons can enjoy all-you-can-eat catfish and more, including both baked and fried catfish, chicken, and shrimp. Cajun touches on the menu include gumbo, plus there is a large salad bar. Catfish is open Monday through Saturday for lunch and dinner.

RESTAURANTS

As Austin grows, its population becomes more diverse, and that means more variety in the city's restaurants. Looking for Brazilian food? Try Sampaio's, 2809 San Jacinto Boulevard (512-469-9988) near the university. French bread and Vietnamese noodles? Head to Ba Le Vietnamese Bakery and Deli in North Austin at 8624 North Lamar Boulevard (512-491-9188). Or how about Colombian food from Dona Emilia's in East Austin, 1411 East Seventh Street, (512-478-2520)?

Chez Zee $$-$$$
5406 Balcones Drive
(512) 454-2666
www.chez-zee.com

This stylish bistro, with a large outdoor patio, art-studded walls, and a baby grand where customers can work a jigsaw puzzle while listening to cafe music, is a fixture on the Austin scene. The menu features both American and continental specialties, including sandwiches, pastas, salads, and grilled entrees, but it is the breakfast and weekend brunch menus that get rave reviews, particularly the crème brûlée French toast made from challah, soaked with custard, and topped with caramelized sugar. Brunch is served into midafternoon on weekends, breakfast begins early during the week, and lunch and dinner are served daily.

Chinatown $$
3407 Greystone Drive
(512) 343-9307

The original Chinatown opened in Westlake Hills, but this branch in Northwest Austin is equally popular. The restaurant offers many familiar Chinese dishes plus several chef's specialties that cater to Texas tastes for hot and spicy foods. Thai pepper basil shrimp and Szechwan spicy duck are two of the spicy offerings. Open daily for lunch and dinner.

Chuy's $-$$
11680 Research Boulevard
(512) 342-0011

The Northwest branch of the popular downtown favorite, see South Central Austin. The menu features Tex-Mex and New Mexico cuisine. Open daily for lunch and dinner.

County Line on the Lake $$-$$$
5204 F.M. 2222
(512) 346-3664
www.countylinelake.citysearch.com

This Northwest branch of a popular upscale barbecue restaurant (see West Austin) is situated along a creekbed. Diners can wait for a table or enjoy a drink on the outdoor deck under the trees. One word of warning: F.M. 2222 is a wide, winding road that leads to Highland Lakes, making it very busy on weekends. There have been serious accidents here, many involving alcohol; visitors should designate a driver if they plan to drink with dinner. Open daily for lunch and dinner.

Dan McKluskey's $$$
The Arboretum,
10000 Research Boulevard
(512) 346-0780

This steakhouse specializes in hand-cut steaks but also caters to lighter appetites by offering several fish and grilled chicken entrees. The setting is classic steakhouse: dark wood, brass fittings, and subdued lighting. The bar stays open late on the weekends for late-night customers, who can snack on appetizers and listen to live jazz music. Open daily for lunch and dinner.

Eddie V's Edgewater Grille $$$-$$$$
9400-B Arboretum Boulevard
(512) 342-2642

This is the Northwest branch of the downtown restaurant of the same name. See our Central listing for details.

El Arroyo   **$**
7032 Wood Hollow Drive
(512) 345-8226
www.ditch.com
The Northwest branch of the popular
downtown Tex-Mex joint. See our Central
listings for details.

Iguana Grill   **$$**
2900 Rural Route 620
(512) 266-8439
www.virtual-restaurants.com/iguana
A great view of Lake Travis plus a fresh take
on Tex-Mex—dubbed "Lake-Mex" by the
restaurant—has made the Iguana Grill a
favorite for leisurely dining, particularly on
weekends. The fajitas are marinated in
pineapple juice and beer, one of the signa-
ture touches that makes the food here a lit-
tle different from the average Tex-Mex fare.
A good choice on warm days is the ceviche,
marinated fresh fish with peppers and
tomatoes, topped with onions and cilantro.
The atmosphere is very casual, and no one
rushes lunch or dinner here. Open daily for
lunch and dinner, Sunday for brunch.

Kerbey Lane Cafe   **$-$$**
12602 Research Boulevard
(512) 258-7757
Northwest Austin is where successful
longtime Austin institutions break new
ground. Kerbey Lane Cafe operates a
branch of its popular Central Austin cafe
in this fast-growing section of Austin. The
same old-faithful staples are on the menu,
including Tex-Mex, burgers, sandwiches,
salads, and breakfast dishes. The cafe is
open seven days a week, 24 hours a day.

La Madeleine   **$**
9828 Great Hills Trail
(512) 502-2474
www.lamadeleine.com
You would never guess this French cafe
once was a bookstore. The decor has
been designed to create the atmosphere
of a French neighborhood bakery, and the
menu enhances that impression. Soups,

salads, quiche, pizzas, and light dinner
entrees are on the menu, with daily specials posted on the blackboard. Save room
for dessert. The bakery is open daily for
breakfast, lunch, and dinner plus midmorning and midafternoon breaks.

Manuel's   **$-$$$**
10201 Jollyville Road
(512) 345-1042
The same great Mexican food, inspired by
interior Mexican classics, found at the
original downtown location (see Central
listings) is found at this newer location. In
summer try the campechana seafood
cocktail, fresh seafood served in a spicy
tomato sauce with cilantro and fresh
limes. In fall try chile relleno en nogada, a
stuffed ancho chile served in a creamy
white walnut sauce. The decor is colorful,
and there is outdoor dining on a walled
patio. Open daily for lunch and dinner.

Mirabelle   **$$-$$$**
8127 Mesa Drive
(512) 346-7900
www.mirabellerestaurant
Don't be fooled by the location; Mirabelle
is one of Austin's best restaurants.
Located in Northwest Austin, a neighbor-
hood of town homes and innocuous, small
strip shopping centers, Mirabelle consis-
tently ranks as one of Austin's most cre-
ative places to dine. The restaurant is the
creation of Michael Vilim and Cathe Dailey,
two restaurateurs with credits at some of
the city's favorite places. Chef David
Apthorpe also has been touted in popu-
lous polls by the *Austin Chronicle*. The
goal of the kitchen here is to take top-
quality regional ingredients and concen-
trate the flavor using time-honored
techniques—for example, the espresso-
rubbed venison. While the restaurant
evokes the name of Provence in its
pitches, it also relies on Southwestern
touches and emphasizes the role of wine
in its cuisine. Open weekdays for lunch,
daily for dinner; closed Sunday.

Musashino Sushi Dokoro $$-$$$
3407 Greystone Drive
(512) 795-8593

The extensive menu at this Northwest Austin sushi bar (housed in the same building as Chinatown) features traditional offerings and some hybrid American takes on Japanese classics. The latter are listed under the "Born in the USA" section of the menu and include favorites such as California rolls topped with fresh tuna, shrimp, and salmon. Authentic Japanese offerings include seaweed and wild vegetable salads plus an array of sushi and sashimi. The atmosphere is quietly elegant. Open daily except Monday for dinner only.

North by Northwest $$-$$$
10010 Capital of Texas Highway
(512) 467-6969

This classy brewpub and restaurant was hailed by the locals as a much-needed addition to what some dub the Silicon Hills region of Austin. The building is sleek and modern, with that "Hill Country" look derived from local limestone and lots of natural light. There is a large bar inside, plus a dining area overlooking the brewery rooms where the House beers are concocted. The menu features grilled meats, fish, salads, sandwiches, and wood-fired pizzas. Some give a nod to Texas, like the grilled Texas quail appetizer; others look to the Mediterranean or Asia for inspiration. The grilled duck breast served with caramelized onion mashed potatoes is popular, as are the pan-seared crab cakes. Open daily for lunch through dinner.

P. F. Chang's China Bistro $$-$$$
10114 Jollyville Road
(512) 231-0208

The Northwest location of this sophisticated, popular Chinese restaurant. See Central listings for details.

Pok-E-Jo's Smokehouse $-$$
9828 Great Hills Trail
(512) 338-1990
www.pokejos.com

One of four Pok-E-Jo's in Austin, this one helps satisfy cravings for Texas barbecue in Northwest Austin. The meats here are mesquite-smoked and include ribs, beef, ham, pork loin, sausage, turkey, and chicken. Take-out is popular here. Open daily for lunch and dinner.

Reed's Jazz & Supper Club $$-$$$
9901 North Capital of Texas Highway
Gateway Plaza
(512) 342-7977
www.reedssupperclub.com

There is a sort of mythical Mason-Dixon line in Austin, and it's creeping north—or maybe it's just floating around in people's heads. At one time Town Lake, a.k.a. the Colorado River, was the demarcation line for what was funky old Austin versus the constrained Austin. Then the border marched north to around 35th, maybe 38th Street. These days, some say they never drive beyond Koenig Lane into what they call "south Dallas." But when they do, adventurers are often amazed to see miles and miles of new Austin, plus some hip places to enjoy an evening on the town. After a few years as the northern branch of Mezzaluna, the popular downtown restaurant, this Northwest restaurant threw in the towel and decided to assume its own identity. It has emerged as a sophisticated supper club with good food, great martinis, and jazz. The menu is straight out of a sophisticated New York club of the 1950s, the decor subdued and plush, the restaurant discreet, the bar boisterous—overall, a hit. Open for dinner daily, late nights on Friday and Saturday; closed Sunday.

Rosie's Tamale House No. 2 $
13776 Research Boulevard
(512) 219-7793

Associated with Rosie's at Bee Cave (see West Austin), this sister restaurant serves similar Tex-Mex fare.

Rudy's Bar-B-Q $$
11570 Research Boulevard
(512) 418-9898
www.rudys.com

With so many barbecue restaurants it can be hard to stand out. Rudy's makes the effort by calling itself "the worst barbecue in Texas," but that belies the packed parking lot. The atmosphere is old country store with gas pumps outside and picnic tables inside, and the menu features all the expected Texas items, including prime rib, smoked pork loin, chicken, and chopped beef. Rudy's opens early to serve breakfast tacos and offers lunch and dinner daily.

Siena $$$-$$$$
6203 North Capital of Texas Highway (Loop 360)
(512) 349-7667
www.sienarestaurant.com
The goal here was to create a restaurant evocative of grand dining in Italy, notably northern Italy and the Tuscan countryside, and place it at one of Austin's busiest intersections, Loop 360 and R.R. 2222. Judging from local reviews, Siena has fulfilled that mission. The decor is enough to make patrons imagine they are dining in an Italian villa, and the menu with its extensive wine list enhances that feeling. Dishes include pheasant ravioli and pappardelle with wild boar. In addition to pasta dishes, there are seafood, game, and meat entrees that all draw on Italian inspiration. A popular restaurant, reservations are recommended. Open Monday through Saturday for lunch and nightly for dinner.

Z'Tejas Grill $$-$$$
9400 Arboretum Boulevard
(512) 346-3506
Anyone who wants to get a view of how Austin has evolved in the past two decades should visit both branches of Z'Tejas Grill (see our Central Austin listings for the original restaurant). The original Z is on West Sixth Street and captures with its menu and atmosphere the much-touted, laid-back Austin lifestyle. The second Z'Tejas is in a new Santa Fe–style building near the Arboretum, and its atmosphere reflects the lively, booming lifestyle of Northwest Austin, where many of the newer city residents and high-tech

businesses have located. The menu is almost the same—a mix of Southwestern meets European, with a touch of Asian (seared sesame tuna and ancho-rubbed pork tenderloin)—but the restaurant does not serve breakfast like the original cafe. Open daily for lunch and dinner, late nights on Friday and Saturday.

NORTH

Baby Acapulco $-$$
5610 North I-35
(512) 302-1366
13609 North I-35
(corner of Howard Lane)
(512) 670-9111
Two branches of the popular downtown Tex-Mex hot spot, favored for margarita quaffing. See South Central listings for details.

Chuy's $-$$
10520 North Lamar Boulevard
(512) 836-3218
Chuy's is Tex-Mex with attitude. Just like the original down on Barton Springs Road (see our South Central listings), this location is a great mix of good food, lively atmosphere, and outrageous decor. Lava lamps and primary colors are Chuy's hallmarks. The menu features burritos, tacos, enchiladas, fajitas, and lots of variations on the nacho theme. Chuy's also offers several sauces, which can be ordered to accompany any entree. Parents like Chuy's because of the great finger food here—a plate of nachos can keep any four-year-old occupied—and the easygoing atmosphere. Chuy's is open daily for lunch and dinner.

El Mercado Restaurant & Cantina $-$$
7414 Burnet Road
(512) 454-2500
One of three El Mercados in town, this North Austin branch serves the same generous portions of Tex-Mex favorites in a lively, colorful setting. The restaurant is open daily for breakfast, lunch, and dinner.

Fonda San Miguel $$$-$$$$
2330 West North Loop Boulevard
(512) 459-4121
www.fondasanmiguel.com

Some of Austin's finest restaurants are found in unexpected places. Fonda San Miguel is situated in an everyday neighborhood, but once you step over the threshold it is easy to assume you are in Old Mexico. This is an accurate rendition of both Mexican architectural style and food. Designed to evoke the atmosphere of an old hacienda, the entrance to the restaurant, is a small court-yard complete with fountain and plants. Inside, the walls are decorated with antiques and ceramics representative of Colonial Mexico, including Talavera tiles, vases from Guanajuato, clay cooking pots from Puebla, and ollas (large water vessels) from Oaxaca.

Until recently, the cuisine of Mexico has been highly underrated and, among those not familiar with its complexities, there are misconceptions that it is simply a version of Tex-Mex. It's not, and this is the place to come to understand why. The menu features regional specialties from throughout the country. The doyenne of Mexican cooking, Diana Kennedy, has held cooking classes here. It is another misconception that all Mexican food is hot; many of the chiles and spices used south of the border are nuanced, not fiery. Some dishes are simple fare—steak served a la Tampiqueña, a grilled beef tenderloin. Others are more exotic, such as quesadillas made with huitlacoche (*wheet-laa-koh-chay*), the fungus that grows on the ears of corn at certain times of the year and has a mushroom-truffle taste. The menu also features seafood served in Yucatecan and Veracruzano styles, some spicy, others more Spanish in flavor. And there are several moles, the rich, complex sauces usually called by their color—verde (green), negro (black)—or by their geographical origin, such as poblano (from Puebla). The latter is the most famous, made from more than two dozen ingredients, including bitter chocolate, spices, herbs, and chiles. A good way to sample a variety of fare is to make a reservation for Sunday brunch. This meal evokes the Sunday custom in Mexico, where families sit down for a long, leisurely meal comprising snacks, entrees, desserts, coffee, and long conversation. The restaurant is open daily for dinner and on Sunday for brunch. Reservations are recommended.

Kim Phung $
7601 North Lamar Boulevard
(512) 451-2464

Asian noodle aficionados tout this humble-looking cafe as one of the best places in town to sample a wide variety of the Vietnamese specialty. There are more than 40 varieties of noodle dishes on the menu, including 19 varieties of beef noodle soup plus stir-fried and cold noodles. Thai coffee, made with canned evaporated milk, has become part of the coffee craze, and Kim Phung serves this also. The restaurant is in a strip shopping center, and the surroundings are plain. Open from midmorning to evening daily.

Koreana Grill and Sushi Bar $-$$
12196 North MoPac
(512) 835-8888

The shopping mall exterior of this popular restaurant belies the friendly, gracious restaurant inside, where the dining rooms include a sushi bar and a tearoom. Korean specialties, notably the national barbecue dubbed "bulgogi" here, are on the menu, plus "gimbab," the Korean equivalent of sushi. Open daily for lunch and dinner.

Korea House $-$$
Village Shopping Center,
2700 West Anderson Lane, #501
(512) 458-2477

Garlic, sesame, ginger, and peppers are key ingredients in Korean cuisine. Dishes such as Bul Go Ki (different spelling, but same dish as served above at Koreana Grill), a national favorite, is made with beef, chicken, or pork, thinly sliced and marinated in a sauce made from onions, soy sauce, garlic, sesame, pepper, sake, and grated fruit. The dish is sautéed quickly and served with a variety of garnishes, including kim chee, the potent Korean pickle. That is the sort of dish served at Korea House, a restaurant in the Village Shopping Center east of MoPac on Anderson Lane. The small restaurant has a view of an inner courtyard, which adds to the Oriental design. In addition to Korean specialties, the restaurant serves sushi. Open daily for lunch and dinner.

Ninfa's Mexican Restaurant $$-$$$
214 East Anderson Lane
(512) 832-1833

There are two Ninfa's in Austin, one downtown and this second location, both featuring the creations of Houston entrepreneur Ninfa Lorenzo. The food is described as "uptown" Tex-Mex with entrees such as smoked quail in salsa negra, shrimp in garlic sauce, and pollo asado (roasted chicken). There are also Mexican dishes on the menu featuring some classics from south of the border. Expect to pay more than the usual Tex-Mex prices here. Lunch and dinner are served daily.

Pok-E-Jo's Smokehouse $-$$
2121 West Parmer Lane
(512) 491-0434
www.pokejos.com

One of four Pok-E-Jo's in Austin, this one helps satisfy cravings for Texas barbecue in North Austin. The meats here are mesquite-smoked and include ribs, beef, ham, pork loin, sausage, turkey, and chicken. Take-out is popular here. Open daily for lunch and nightly for dinner.

Satay $$
Shoal Creek Plaza,
3202 West Anderson Lane
(512) 467-6731
www.satayusa.com

The spice trade was a two-way affair, bringing spices from the countries in South Asia to Europe and importing Dutch, British, Spanish, and Portuguese customs to the region. Satay celebrates

that trade with a menu that reflects Indonesian, Thai, Vietnamese, and Malaysian dishes. Dutch traders adopted the Indonesian custom of serving a variety of dishes at one course, dubbing it "rijsttafel," or rice table. At Satay it is a great way to share a meal with several friends. Another regional specialty is celebrated in the restaurant's name—satay is a Malaysian shish kebab. The menu also features curries, both Thai and Indian-inspired. Satay is well known not only for its diverse menu but also its food products, including a peanut sauce served with satay, which are sold in local food stores. The restaurant is in the Shoal Creek Plaza shopping center, but inside the decor is exotic and features artwork from the South China Seas region. Satay's sauces and food products are sold in local grocery stores and online at their Web site. Open daily for lunch and dinner.

Sea Dragon $-$$
Grand Central Shopping Center
8776-B Research Boulevard
(512) 451-5051

This Vietnamese restaurant also offers Chinese dishes on an extensive menu and, given Vietnam's geography, many of the dishes feature fresh seafood. The chef also creates daily specials featuring seasonal foods. Duck is a house specialty and is prepared in a number of ways, including stir-fried with leeks and ginger or tea-smoked. Open daily for lunch and dinner.

Taj Palace $$
6700 Middle Fiskville Road
(512) 452-9959

Both vegetarians and meat-eaters will find an abundant selection at this traditional Indian restaurant near Highland Mall. The vegetarian specialties include saag paneer, a homemade cheese and spinach sauté, and malai kofta, cheese and vegetable dumplings simmered in a cream and almond sauce. Carnivores can dig into tandoori dishes such as barra kabab, lamb marinated in spiced yogurt and then grilled. The menu also features a variety of curries with varying degrees of heat, and the tandoor oven-baked breads are not to be missed—aloo parantha is stuffed with potatoes, green peas, and spices. The restaurant is decorated with images of Indian gods and weavings from the subcontinent. There is an all-you-can-eat daily lunch buffet. Open for dinner daily.

Texas French Bread $
7719 Burnet Road
(512) 419-0184

Austinites love their bakeries, and this multibranched bakery ranks among Austin's favorite restaurants. On the menu for breakfast, muffins, croissants, and pastries, while lunch features a variety of sandwiches showcasing the bakery's French, Italian, and American breads. Open daily for breakfast and lunch.

Threadgill's Restaurant $$
6416 North Lamar Boulevard
(512) 451-5440

Janis Joplin sang here at the legendary (a much overused word, but justified) restaurant and club founded by Kenneth Threadgill on a mundane section of North Lamar Boulevard. Of course, back when Threadgill got a liquor license for the former Gulf gas station, this was the far northern reaches of Austin, practically a rural outpost. "There's music on the menu" is the boast these days, and the mix of Southern hospitality, music, and homestyle cooking packs 'em in. A second Threadgill's has opened near downtown (see our South Central listings), and both locations offer similar food: old-fashioned favorites such as chicken-fried steak, fried chicken, meat loaf, hamburgers, and lots of veggies. Open daily for lunch and dinner and until midnight on Friday and Saturday. (Read more about the Threadgill's legacy in The Music Scene chapter.)

Tien Hong $$
8301 Burnet Road
(512) 459-2263

Dim sum is Chinese for brunch, and every Saturday and Sunday this North Austin restaurant is packed as patrons enjoy a variety of what might be called Asian noshes. Waiters roam the dining room with steam carts filled with a variety of dumplings, steamed buns, savory tidbits, deep-fried nuggets of meat and seafood, and tiny sweet creations. Hot tea is the preferred beverage. In addition to the offerings created at the whim of the chef, there is a menu, printed in Chinese, Vietnamese, and English. Most patrons, and many hail from Austin's growing Asian community, simply look over the carts and point to their choice, but that can be risky for those unfamiliar with dim sum—one delicacy is fried chicken feet. Tien Hong also serves a familiar Chinese menu at lunch and dinner daily. Dim sum is served usually from midmorning to midafternoon on the weekend.

Waterloo Ice House $
8600 Burnet Road
(512) 458-6544
www.waterloonorth.citysearch.com

This is another homegrown restaurant chain with four locations in the Austin area. This branch of Waterloo features the same all-American menu of burgers, chicken-fried steak, and tacos. Open daily for lunch and dinner.

NORTHEAST

Tres Amigos $$
7535 U.S. 290 East
(512) 926-4441
www.tresamigos.com

The name means "three friends," and that is appropriate for the three Austin locations of this homegrown restaurant. All are touted by longtime Austin residents as friendly restaurants where both the menu and the staff are familiar. Tex-Mex is the theme here, and the surroundings evoke Old Mexico. Open daily for lunch and dinner.

La Palapa $-$$
6640 U.S. 290 East
(512) 459-8729
The thatched roof is a reminder of La Palapa's roots south of the border—a palapa is a thatched shelter in Mexico. The restaurant has ties to two La Palapas, one in Laredo, the other in Nuevo Laredo, Mexico. Under the thatch, patrons will find several variations on the fajita theme plus enchiladas and Tex-Mex fare. On Saturday night the restaurant features an all-you-can-eat fajita bar, and Sunday there is an all-you-can-eat lunch buffet. The restaurant's cantina has live music and karaoke on Wednesday, Friday, and Saturday nights. La Palapa is open daily for lunch and dinner.

EAST

Arkie's Grill $
4827 East Cesar Chavez Street
(512) 385-2986
This old-fashioned diner in a working-class neighborhood on the edge of East Austin serves breakfast and lunch. The cooking is homestyle with generous servings, especially those luncheon side dishes of home-cooked vegetables. The cooking attracts a wide variety of faithful customers. No credit cards.

Calabash $$
2015 Manor Road
(512) 478-4857
Just east of the university campus and I-35, this neighborhood cafe offers customers a chance to sample Caribbean fare. Dishes include jerk chicken and Jamaican-style patties (turnovers), served with such island staples as fried plantains and pigeon peas. Open for dinner Monday through Saturday.

Cisco's $
1511 East Sixth Street
(512) 478-2420
Rudy "Cisco" Cisneros is no longer with us, but his east-side cafe where the likes of President Lyndon B. Johnson took breakfast is still a fixture. The small bakery and restaurant continues to attract the powerful for breakfast or lunch, and the walls are plastered with photos of both current and former politicos. The menu is not extensive; simple Tex-Mex fare is offered along with sweet rolls and cookies from the bakery. Cisco was something of a humorist so the walls are covered with cartoons, jokes, and even a sign hung on an old gasoline pump that says: OUT OF GASOLINE, WE SELL BEANS. Cisco's is open for breakfast and lunch only.

Eastside Cafe $-$$
2113 Manor Road
(512) 476-5858
www.eastsidecafe.citysearch.com
Those looking for ways to revive older neighborhoods should visit this cafe east of the interstate in an area of the city that is economically depressed. A small, homey cottage has been turned into a thriving enterprise that includes a large kitchen and herb garden plus a cooking and garden shop. The house has been divided into small, cozy dining rooms, while outside there are tables on the patio. Visitors can stroll through the kitchen garden before or after brunch, lunch, or dinner. The menu is a variety of pastas, enchiladas, grilled fish and chicken dinners, and sandwiches and salads. Brunch begins with mimosas (champagne and orange juice) or poinsettias (champagne and cranberry juice), and then patrons can choose from rich waffle dishes or classics such as eggs Florentine, poached eggs on wilted spinach and topped with hollandaise sauce. After dining here, wander through the on-site store, where the house salad dressings are sold plus cookware and garden tools. Eastside is open daily for lunch and dinner, brunch on the weekends.

El Azteca $-$$
2600 East Seventh Street
(512) 477-4701

Wander the Mexican-American neighbor-hoods of South Texas and you will find family-owned restaurants like El Azteca, where the menu goes beyond the familiar Tex-Mex as served up by many chain restaurants. The Guerra family has run El Azteca for 40 years. Cabrito, spit-roasted baby goat, is a house specialty at this East Austin restaurant, about a mile and a half east of the interstate. Another popular dish is the barbacoa de cabeza (barbecued beef head), but don't wince until you have sampled the meat; the moist and tender cheek meat is touted as the best for folding inside a soft flour tortilla. El Azteca also serves carne guisada, a slow-simmered stew that is served with flour tortillas for a lick-your-fingers meal, and chicken mole enchiladas, dressed in the rich chocolate-chile mole sauce. The menu also features vegetarian dishes. The walls are hung with portraits honoring Mexican president Benito Juarez and American presidents Abraham Lincoln and John F. Kennedy plus Senator Robert F. Kennedy. The cafe is open for lunch and dinner every day except Sunday.

Hoover's Cooking $-$$
2002 Manor Road
(512) 479-5006

When you can't get home to Mom and you need a comfort food fix, Hoover's is the place. Hoover's doesn't look like much inside or out—it occupies a storefront in a neighborhood where working folks live—but the food is down-home good. Chicken-fried steak is a specialty, as it should be since it occupies a special place in the pantheon of Texas homestyle cooking, plus pork roast, macaroni and cheese, catfish, and barbecued ribs. Open Monday through Friday for lunch and dinner, weekends for breakfast, lunch, and dinner.

Nuevo Leon $-$$
1209 East Seventh Street
(512) 479-0097

Nuevo Leon offers pink walls, green booths, and a menu that pays homage to the cooking of Northern Mexico and the state of Nuevo Leon. The dishes make it plain that Texas once was part of Old Mexico, and many of the featured items are found on South Texas Mexican cafe menus—beef and vegetable caldo (soup), fajitas, rib-eye steak with ranchero sauce, and a burrito dressed with chili. Lunch and dinner are served weekdays; breakfast, lunch, and dinner on weekends.

Sam's Bar-B-Cue $
2000 East 12th Street
(512) 478-0378

Sam's biggest fan was famed guitarist Stevie Ray Vaughan, and the walls of this authentic barbecue joint are an homage to the late musician with pictures and newspaper clippings. The menu is simple: brisket, chicken, sausage, and ribs plus spicy beans, and potato salad. Take-out is available at this humble neighborhood cafe. Lunch and dinner are served daily. Open to 4:00 A.M. on Friday and Saturday. No credit cards.

SOUTHEAST

Catfish Parlour $$
4705 East Ben White Boulevard
(512) 443-1698

For more than two decades Catfish Parlour has been pulling in the crowds for all-you-can-eat catfish and more. Both baked and fried catfish are served, plus fried shrimp and chicken. The menu has Cajun touches with hush puppies and gumbo, plus there is a large salad bar. Open daily for lunch and dinner.

Marisco's Seafood $
1504 Town Creek Drive
(512) 462-9119

In search of an authentic neighborhood restaurant? Marisco's is housed in an A-frame building east of I-35 on a busy street. The food here is very cheap and simple; seafood entrees are simply pre-pared, either boiled, fried, or broiled, but there are Mexican touches such as the vuelve la vida (back to the good life) seafood cocktail, ceviche, and seafood soup. Marisco's is open daily for lunch and dinner.

ROUND ROCK

Antonio's Tex-Mex Mexican
Restaurant & Cantina $-$$
16912 North I-35, Round Rock
(512) 238-8969

There's live music at this lively Mexican restaurant, where traditional Tex-Mex fare has a few new twists. The restaurant touts its pechugas de pollo (chicken breasts) that are served stuffed with a variety of ingredients. The most requested is the pechugas Antonio, stuffed with Monterey jack cheese, mush-rooms, and bacon; breaded and deep fried; and then topped with chile con queso. Antonio's has an adjoining bar with big-screen TV and live music on Fri-day and Saturday. Take-out is popular here. Open daily for lunch and dinner.

El Arroyo $
301 West Taylor Street
(512) 310-1992

The Round Rock branch of Austin's funky downtown restaurant. See our Central list-ings for details.

Gumbo's $$-$$$$
901 Round Rock Avenue
(512) 671-7925
www.gumbos.citysearch.com

As noted in the Central listings, Gumbo's originated in Round Rock and moved into downtown Austin, contrary to most restaurant trends in the city. The original Round Rock serves the same Louisiana-inspired dishes in a more intimate setting. Unlike the classy, brassy downtown Austin restaurant in the Brown Building loft development, Gumbo's in Round

Rock is decorated in white and light col-ors, with natural stone walls offering a cozy feel. Both locations offer take-out. Open daily for lunch and dinner; closed Sunday.

Main Street Grill $$-$$$
118 East Main Street
(512) 244-7525
www.mainstreetgrill.citysearch.com

Residents of Round Rock have lovingly restored many of the old homes and businesses in their community, particu-larly the small downtown buildings that stand at the heart of what was once a small Texas town. (See our Relocation chapter.) The Grill occupies an old bank building on Main Street, and private par-ties can even reserve the vault dining room. Self-described as "American Conti-nental Grill," the Grill features prime rib, grilled fish, steaks, pastas, and salads. The Grill's salad dressings—maple bal-samic vinaigrette, and creamy cilantro pumpkinseed—have become so popular the restaurant sells them on-site and at Central Market, Austin's hip grocery store (see Close-up in our Shopping chapter). Main Street also offers "jazz on the patio" on certain nights and special wine tasting evenings. Open for lunch and din-ner during the week; dinner on Saturday. Closed Sunday.

While some folks have a hankerin' for those national-brand donuts, locals know to look for Round Rock donuts. At first there was only one place to get them—Lone Star Bakery in Round Rock at 106 Liberty Avenue (512-255-3629)— but now the word has spread, and those secret-recipe donuts are being delivered to gas stations and convenience stores around the area, where their presence is proclaimed in big letters on street signs. Check out www.roundrockdonuts.com.

Mom's Cafe $
1829 North Mays Street
(512) 255-6291

Locals swear this neighborhood cafe offers the best breakfast in town as well as a great homestyle lunch. The cafe is run by mother and daughter Martina and Janet Coker, and the sign out front says MOM'S CAFE, MOM'S MINI STORAGE, but the focus here is obviously on home cooking. The cafe boasts that it serves breakfast, lunch, and dinner, even though it closes in midafternoon, but then some folks work odd hours these days and need dinner in the middle of the day. Open at 6:00 A.M. daily for breakfast when huevos rancheros, cranberry pancakes, and cinnamon raisin oatcakes are popular; lunch follows with daily blue plate specials. Open daily.

Pok-E-Jo's Smokehouse $-$$
1202 North I-35, Round Rock
(512) 388-7578

The Round Rock branch of a popular Austin barbecue chain, Pok-E-Jo's serves mesquite-smoked meats, including ribs, beef, ham, pork loin, sausage, turkey, and chicken.

Rudy's Bar-B-Q $-$$$
2400 North I-35, Round Rock
(512) 244-2936

The Round Rock location of a popular drive-up or dine-in barbecue restaurant. See our West listings for a complete description.

Serrano's Cafe & Cantina $$
910 Round Rock Avenue, Round Rock
(512) 218-8880

Given the proliferation and popularity of Serrano's in Austin, it was inevitable they would open a Round Rock branch. The same Tex-Mex dishes are served here in a lively atmosphere. House specialties include several kinds of fajitas including, pork, shrimp, beef, chicken, and veggie. Open daily for lunch and dinner.

Yoli's Jambalaya $$-$$$
14735 Bratton Lane, Suite 310
(512) 670-2788

Yoli and Michael Amr were the original founders of Gumbo's (see above). After they sold it in 1999, they launched Yoli's. Again, seafood was the focus of many of the dishes, but this time the inspiration came not from Louisiana but the Mediterranean. But the bayou called, and Yoli's has gone back to its Cajun roots with gumbo, jambalaya, and seafood classics. The restaurant offers a wide range of wines by the glass. Open Tuesday through Saturday for dinner.

CEDAR PARK

Brick Oven Restaurant $
11200 Lakeline Mall, Cedar Park
(512) 335-5445

This new location of an old Austin favorite is a popular gathering spot for moviegoers at the nearby Lakeline Mall. The menu features pizza baked in a wood-fired oven. Customers can choose from a variety of toppings, thin or thick crust, even an all-garlic pizza. The menu also features other Italian-American staples and salads. Open daily for lunch and dinner.

China Cafe $-$$
13729 North U.S. 183, Cedar Park
(512) 331-7747

How about a movie and Chinese for dinner? The cafe's location near the Lake Creek cinema complex makes this a popular spot for a pre- or postmovie dinner. The menu features a variety of well-known Chinese dishes with an emphasis on spicy dishes. There are also low-fat and vegetarian entrees, and the cafe offers take-out and delivery within a 3-mile radius. Open daily for lunch and dinner.

Reale's Pizza & Cafe $-$$
13450 North U.S. 183, Cedar Park
(512) 335-5115

Resident Yankees at the *Austin Chronicle* have hailed the pizza here as the closest they have found in Austin to New York–style pizza with its yeasty crust. There are other old faithfuls on the menu, including pasta dishes, and on weekends there can be a wait for a table. The restaurant is just south of Cedar Park and north of what the locals call Jollyville. Open for lunch Monday through Saturday.

Saccone's Pizza $
2701-A U.S. 183, Leander
(512) 259–1882
13812 Research Boulevard
(512) 257–1200
www.saccones.com
There must be something about the northwest edge of Austin that attracts northerners, specifically pizza makers. Just as Reale's is hailed for its New

York–style pizza, Saccone's has been described as "a slice of Hoboken." The small, spartan cafe is just beyond Cedar Park on the edge of Leander, but it attracts the faithful from early morning to night. There is a second location near the intersection of R.R. 620 and U.S. 183 (Research Boulevard). The menu also features hot and cold subs, calzones, and stromboli. Open for breakfast, lunch, and dinner daily.

Serrano's Cafe & Cantina $$
12233 Rural Route 620, Cedar Park
(512) 918–8181
Another of the popular chain, this Serrano's serves the same Tex-Mex dishes in a lively atmosphere. Specialties include several kinds of fajitas including pork, shrimp, beef, chicken, and veggie. Open daily for lunch and dinner.

NIGHTLIFE ⓨ

Austin's nightlife is so vibrant we had to divide it into two chapters: The second, The Music Scene, is a comprehensive look at the musicians and clubs that have made it possible for Austin to claim the title Live Music Capital of the World. This chapter also lists a great many music and dance venues and takes a look at some of the other spots where residents and visitors gather after the sun goes down.

Some places are swanky, some are funky, others reflect old Texas traditions, and still others swing to a Latin beat. Austin after dark can be a quiet glass of wine in a subdued, sophisticated setting; or a cold brew among friends at a cheery pub; perhaps a shot of tequila and a salsa dance; a glass of sherry with tapas; a beach blanket bingo movie with Coke and pizza; or an evening of satire with Austin's favorite comedy troupe, Esther's Follies.

One thing that is constant about the Austin nightlife scene is it is evolving and growing by leaps and bounds. Every month there are new faces on the evening scene as the menu of choices grows. The historic center of the city's night scene is, of course, Sixth Street, sometimes called Austin's Bourbon Street. The scene there has evolved over the past three decades (check the Close-up in this chapter). There are nightspots throughout the city and beyond—perhaps an evening of country dance at the Gruene Music Hall (see our Day Trips chapter). However, the liveliest nightlife is to be found downtown around Sixth Street; in the Warehouse District just west of Congress Avenue; and south of the river in SoCo, the South Congress Avenue neighborhood, which is a mix of restaurants, bars, cafes, shops, and street theater. SoCo is particularly lively on the first Thursday of every month (www.firstthursday.info), when stores stay open late and street vendors and per-formers make the wide avenue a very popular place for a stroll, leisurely shopping, a late night latte, or a festive dinner.

Two of the best places to keep track of the city's evolving nightlife are the *Austin Chronicle,* the city's popular alternative newspaper, and the XLent section of the *Austin American–Statesman,* which appears in the daily paper every Thursday (see our Media chapter). We have divided this chapter into Bars—further subdivided into Sixth Street Bars and Sports Bars—Brewpubs and Pubs; Coffeehouses; Comedy Clubs; Dance Clubs and Nightclubs; The Gay Nightlife Scene; and Movie Houses.

Austin swings every night, and most clubs and bars are open every day, except where we have noted in the listings. Where there is music, either live or electronic, there is likely to be a cover charge of a few dollars, but rarely do those covers top $10. Bars must stop serving alcohol at 2:00 A.M. by Texas law and no one younger than 21 can be served, though some clubs do admit them. Driving-while-intoxicated laws are very strict, and bar owners are also held responsible under the state's liquor licensing laws for making sure customers do not overindulge. Taxis cruise the city's major nightlife areas, and patrons who overindulge are wise to take a ride home.

Given the vast and growing number of nightspots in Austin, it is impossible to list them all. Here we have attempted to give an overview, a wide sampling of nightspots both residents and visitors enjoy.

BARS

The Brown Bar
201 West Eighth Street
(512) 480–8330

The renovation of the historic Brown Building in downtown Austin has created not only an architectural gem where lucky loft owners can hang their hat but also has given birth to one of the city's best bars. Touted in 2001 by the *Austin Chronicle* readers' poll as having "the best bar ambience," the Brown Bar with its, yes, brown walls, brown ceilings, and dark furnishings has a comfy, yet sophisticated feel. The specialties are classics like single malt whiskies, martinis, mojitos, cosmopolitans, and margaritas. The clientele is a mix of hip 20-somethings and downtown powerbrokers, lobbyists, and lawyers.

Cedar Door
Second and Brazos Streets
(512) 473-3712
www.cedardooraustin.com
When they built the Cedar Door, they should have put wheels on the building. That would have saved this cherished neighborhood-style bar some money. The Door has moved, literally, several times—the first location is now occupied by a high-rise on 12th Street downtown. Originally a typical Austin cottage-turned-bar, its last home was on stilts on what was a landfill at the corner of Cesar Chavez Street and Lamar Boulevard, just north of Town Lake—but wait, another move came about when developers eyed the property. No matter, the Cedar Door pledged to roll on and survive, and now it lives west of the city's convention center. A popular watering hole for bureaucrats, politicos, and journalists, it has all the hallmarks of an old favorite with mismatched chairs and tables, old prints and posters, plus bartenders who know their regulars well.

Cedar Street Courtyard
208 West Fourth Street
(512) 495-9669
The patio of this hip bar, dubbed "the king of gin joints," is a few steps down from the elevated sidewalks that once served as loading docks in the Warehouse District, east of Congress Avenue. Live music

One way to give new meaning to the term "pub crawl" is to take one of Austin's pedicabs from nightspot to nightspot. Revolution Bike Taxi operates in the downtown area; (512) 203-3369, www.austinbiketaxi.com.

fills the air most nights, often jazz music, and the patio is flanked by two dark, cool indoor bars that make a nice retreat on steamy nights. The renovated buildings were designed by one of Austin's most noted architects, Sinclair Black, who still has his offices on the second floor, and the courtyard still bears the mark of a master designer with restored limestone walls and sculpture. Jazz, martinis, and, of course, cigars are on the menu here.

Chambers Bar
700 San Jacinto Street
(512) 476-3700
This is a posh cigar bar in the Omni Hotel, just west of Congress Avenue in the heart of downtown Austin. The sophisticated bar offers whiskey, cognac, and other appropriate accompaniments to a grand stogie, all served in a modern, sophisticated, quiet setting.

The Cloak Room
1300 Colorado Street
(512) 478-2622
You will have to look hard for this little bar tucked away in the basement of an old building immediately west of the west door of the capitol. Inside is a cozy piano bar, just the place to gather after a hard day of doing the "people's business," which is why it is so popular with workers at the capitol. It is also a refuge on hot days and a good place to rest after touring the capitol grounds.

Club DeVille
900 Red River Street
(512) 457-0900
The exterior of Club DeVille looks vaguely 1950s, definitely funky, and is certainly

Austin, with its mix of patrons, some dressed up for a posh night on the town, others in jeans and sandals. The guys who founded this Sixth Street–district club did so because they needed a place to hold their regular weekend cocktail parties. One of the owners is Mark McKinnon, a former *Daily Texan* editor and former Democratic political consultant who amazed his friends and political cohorts when he signed on with then Governor George W. Bush as a media consultant. One newspaper critic has described the decor as "hanging out in Grandma's basement while she's in Florida." But instead of turning on Grandma's reading lamps, there are candles on the table and you can actually hear what your table mate is saying. There is also a large outdoor deck equipped with funky furniture and blankets for chilly nights. The bar does get busy on the weekends, but the relaxed atmosphere is constant.

Driskill Hotel Lobby Bar
117 East Seventh Street
(512) 474–5911
www.driskillhotel.com

The venerable Driskill Hotel (see our Hotels chapter) is like an island of style amid the cacophony of Sixth Street. The lobby's cool marble floors and pillars, ornate gilt mirrors, and chairs a person can sink into make for a plush surrounding for the hotel's piano bar. Happy hour draws people in, and they often stay to unwind to the sounds of classic lounge hits played on the grand piano. Later in the evening, folks gather around and even join in as the old romantic hits are played.

The Elephant Room
315 Congress Avenue
(512) 473–2279
www.arthive.net/elephant

This smoky, dark basement bar in the heart of downtown is a longtime gathering spot for jazz aficionados. For more information about the jazz scene at the Elephant Room, see The Music Scene chapter.

Four Seasons Lobby Bar
98 San Jacinto Boulevard
(512) 478–4500
www.fourseasons.com

The lobby bar of this downtown luxury hotel (see our Hotels chapter) is a great place to people-watch. The patrons here might be top Texas businesspeople, foreign investors, high-tech wizards, top-name musicians and movie stars, politicians, or media personalities. The color palette is a gentle range of beige and neutral tones, and the furniture is a mix of rustic antiques and luxurious Southwestern pieces, some covered in leather or cowhide. During the biennial legislative session, many of the state's political leaders take advantage of the hotel's extended lease terms and hang their hats here for the duration of the 120-day session. That ensures that a great deal of politicking and lobbying goes on here as folks work the room, passing from table to table. The bar offers an extensive list of single malt whiskey and cognac plus wine and snacks, none of them inexpensive. In the afternoons, tea and sandwiches are available.

Louie's 106
106 East Sixth Street
(512) 476–2010

Unlike many of the other bars on Sixth Street, which appeal to the shots and longnecks crowd, the bar at Louie's 106 is as sophisticated as the restaurant (see our Restaurants chapter). Like its neighbor, the Driskill Hotel, Louie's 106 is a classy haven far from the rowdy spirit of Sixth Street. In addition to being a popular, top-notch restaurant, Louie's is also home to a cigar bar and a tapas bar. There are several tapas bars in Austin, but Louie's was the first—tapas are those Spanish noshes served after the sun goes down and intended to feed body and spirit until dinnertime (around 11:00 P.M. or midnight in Spain). Tapas might include a variety of olives, room-temperature savory omelettes called tortillas in Spain, or a selection of Spanish ham and sausages, all of which can be nibbled along with a glass of sherry or wine. Louie's has a wide selection of wine, whiskey, and cognac to go along with either tapas or a fine cigar.

Malaga's Wine and Tapas Bar
208 West Fourth Street
(512) 236-8020
www.malagatapasbar.com

A recent entry to the warehouse district scene, this wine and tapas bar is inspired by the wonderful Spanish tradition of nibbling on savories while drinking sherry or wine. Malaga's occupies an airy, narrow limestone-walled space next door to Cedar Street Courtyard. There is a full bar, and noshes can be ordered until 2:00 A.M. on weekends and midnight during the week and Sunday.

Manuel's
310 Congress Avenue
(512) 472-7555
www.manuels.com

This Congress Avenue restaurant (see our Restaurants chapter) is also a good place to end a workday with their half-price appetizer happy hour, or wind up an evening with a late night snack at the bar. There is also jazz music, either live or on tape, and an atmosphere that is hip and relaxed.

Oceans 11 Tiki Bar
720 Red River Street
(512) 708-1722
www.oceans11austin.com

Tiki bar afficionados abound around the world—just do an Internet search and you will find a multitude of sites dedicated to the Tiki way of life. Born in the years right after World War II, Tiki bars flourished in the 1950s and 1960s and then languished. But Tiki fans are dedicated to their survival. Among them is Mr. Fabulous, the Austin big band singer also known as Dino Lee in his Elvis days, who operates Austin's only Tiki Bar just north of Sixth Street. The glow-in-the-dark drinks, Tiki mugs, pu-pu platters, and shrunken coconut heads are all part of the scene

here. During the week there are Frank Sinatra happy hours, and on Saturday the Dean Martin happy hour is celebrated. Their music likely is on the turntable no matter what hour you visit.

Star Bar
600 West Sixth Street
(512) 477-8550

Just beyond the downtown warehouse district, West Sixth Street is developing into the hottest spot in town for new restaurants and bars. Star Bar once was a paint shop, but the '50s-style building is now a very hip place to be seen and to watch Austin's 20-something set at play. The store's big plate-glass window looks out on a small street-side patio, while inside the low ceiling and retro furnishings give the place an intimate, jazzy sort of feel. Martinis and cocktails are the order of the day, and sipping a gin sling is quite the thing.

Vespaio
16103 South Congress Avenue
(512) 441-6100

Some of the most sophisticated bars in Austin can be found in the city's top restaurants. This popular Italian restaurant in the heart of the SoCo district has a small, but very popular bar where patrons can enjoy a Negroni or glass of wine while noshing on a variety of Italian antipasti.

SPORTS BARS

In addition to the sports bars listed here, check the Brewpub section, since many local pubs also turn on the TV when there is a hot sports event.

Aussie's Volleyball and Grill
306 Barton Springs Road
(512) 480-0952

Volleyball takes center stage at this South Central Austin bar and grill (see our Restaurants chapter), but sports enthusiasts also gather at the bar to watch sporting events on several television sets. A favorite drink is, of course, Foster's—the national beer of Australia, mate.

BW-3
218 East Sixth Street
(512) 472-7227

Buffalo wings and football; buffalo wings and baseball; buffalo wings and basketball. You get the picture. (Hence the name BW-3.) This Sixth Street bar is known for its variety of buffalo (chicken) wings and friendly, laid-back atmosphere. There are 17 television sets and three big-screens for sports viewing. In addition to buffalo wings, the bar has other all-American food offerings to go along with the 23-ounce beers. BW-3 is popular at lunch and crowded in the evenings.

Legend's
8901 Business Park Drive
(512) 343-0888

Housed in the Holiday Inn in Northwest Austin, Legend's focus is simply sports, cold beer, and all-American fare. This is the quintessential sports bar: The 22 televisions are always tuned to sports, and the menu features food like hamburgers and steaks. Occasionally there is a cover charge when special sports broadcasts are scheduled.

Player's Sports Bar & Billiards
1779 Wells Branch Parkway
(512) 252-3056

This North Austin bar caters to sports fans from the nearby Wells Branch neighborhood, who enjoy watching games with friends and a cold beer. The bar also has several billiards tables and hosts darts games on Monday night.

Shoal Creek Saloon and Sports Parlor
909 North Lamar Boulevard
(512) 477-0600

New Orleans Saints fans are drawn to this Central Austin sports bar, perhaps because the pub's menu features Cajun dishes like gumbo and fried catfish. If the Saints are not winning, patrons can at least eat well.

The Tavern
12th Street and Lamar Boulevard
(512) 320-8377
www.austintavern.com

In 2003 it looked as though this venerable bar might close, but supporters rallied and the building was restored, the bar kept open, and the pool tables were busy once again. Opened in 1916 as a grocery store on what was then the edge of the city, the building has had several incarnations including, legend has it, serving as home to a brothel. After Prohibition, the Tavern came into its present life and is now a popular place for friends to gather for a burger, a game of pool, or a beer or two during a football game on the big screen.

Texas Sports Palace
9504 North I-35
(512) 837-1671

Housed inside Showplace Lanes, a North Austin bowling alley, the Texas Sports Palace offers patrons the next best thing to being at the game. Several big-screen televisions and a state-of-the art sound system add to your experience of the event, be it a regularly scheduled game or a pay-for-view event, all in cool, dark surroundings.

Warehouse Saloon & Billiards
509 East Ben White Boulevard
(512) 443-8799
www.warehousesaloon.com

This large pool hall is also home to a sports bar where patrons can watch regularly televised events or pay-for-view specials. In addition to 25 tables, the Warehouse also offers video games, pinball, and shuffleboard.

BREWPUBS AND PUBS

In 1993 the Texas Legislature permitted homemade brew products to be sold in public bars, despite the opposition of the big breweries and beer distributors. Microbreweries are as fashionable as coffeehouses these days, and Austin has its share. One prominent local brewer is Celis, where visitors can tour the facility of this Belgian-style brewery and sample the product (see our Attractions chapter).

B.D. Riley's Pub
204 East Sixth Street
(512) 494–1335
www.bdrileys.com

This is a real Irish pub that was built in Dublin and shipped over to Austin by owner John Erwin, whose grandmother Bessie D. Riley gave her name to the joint. Beer here is served in Imperial pints for two-fisted drinkers, and the pub grub is some of the best in Texas. In addition to being home of the Austin branch of the Notre Dame club, Riley's offers music, football nights, and pub quiz nights, a popular tradition in the old country.

The Bitter End Bistro and Brewery
311 Colorado Street
(512) 478–2337

A brewpub that has a classy, urban air, the Bitter End is also a popular bistro (see our Restaurants chapter) and offers patrons an opportunity to nibble on some great appetizers, along with a sampler tray of house brews. The bar overlooks the bistro, and the pub's brewing equipment stands in front of the bistro and can be seen through the front window, adding an interesting design element to this converted warehouse. There is a sophisticated but relaxed atmosphere here, attracting crowds on the weekends. The pub brews several English-style beers and two specialty brews, including EZ Wheat, the pub's biggest seller; Aberdeen Amber, a Scottish-style export; Bitter End Bitter; Austin Pale Ale; and Honey Mead Ale. Not all brews are available all the time, but there are always several choices on hand. The snack menu includes calamari, grilled vegetables with French bread, a smoked meat sampler, plus wood-fired pizzas. The adjoining Bitter End B Side bar is a cozy, quiet basement bar.

The Southwest Brewing News, *(512–443-3607 or 800–474-7291), publishes the latest brew news in the Southwest. Features on new pubs, awards, and taste tests are included in the paper, which can be found in several Austin pubs.*

The Blind Pig Pub
317 East Sixth Street
(512) 472–0809
www.blindpigpub.com

Thirty varieties of beer and ale are offered at this pub-cum-sports bar on Sixth Street. The pub has a small beer garden, Foosball, and pool tables, plus big screen televisions for watching sports events.

Copper Tank Brewing Company
504 Trinity Street
(512) 478–8444
www.coppertank.com

This Sixth Street brewpub attracts a diverse crowd, including a large college contingent and sports fans, drawn by the bank of big-screen televisions. Local brewery critics give Copper Tank high marks for its brews like Big Dog Brown Ale and Firehouse Stout. Lighter fare is offered, including White Tail Pale Ale, Copper Lite, and River City Raspberry. Happy hour on Wednesday draws a large crowd, and the bar is popular among downtown workers who want a cold one on hot days.

The Crown & Anchor
2911 San Jacinto Boulevard
(512) 322–9168

This UT campus–area pub is popular among students and perennial campus habitués. The aim here is to re-create an English pub, hence the dartboards and the wide selection of beers. Patrons can play pinball, Foosball, and video games and order a burger if they get hungry after a lively game. In balmy weather, patrons can enjoy a beer on the patio.

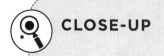

Sixth Street

Long before Jell-o shots and nachos became a staple of the college diet, Austin's Sixth Street was a social hub of the city. When Austinites refer to Sixth Street, they generally mean the stretch of downtown street that runs west from I-35 to Congress Avenue, but over the years Sixth Street has sent ripples west into the Warehouse District and beyond to the cultural and commercial district that centers on the Sixth Street and Lamar Boulevard nexus.

In 1886 the Driskill Hotel opened on Sixth Street, a bold architectural statement that captured the panache of Texas cattle barons. The Driskill is still a favorite refuge for visitors who enjoy the city's nightlife. One block east, at 209 East Sixth Street, on the south side stands an old building that once housed Grove Drugstore. In 1894 a young man named William Sydney Porter worked here, sleeping on the floor at night and writing short stories under his pen name—O. Henry.

Originally the east-west streets in downtown Austin were named for trees, and Sixth was known as Pecan Street, hence the music and craft gatherings held here twice a year are known as the Old Pecan Street Festivals (see our Annual Events chapter). The festivals are part of an attempt by Sixth Street merchants and property owners to give the entertainment district a more family-friendly face, to step back from the "Bourbonization" of the street that has caused some Austinites to avoid the area.

This so-called Bourbonization began in the mid-1970s. In 1975 Clifford Antone opened a live music venue at Sixth and Brazos, and others quickly followed. (Antone's has moved west into the Warehouse District, where it still serves up legendary blues and fresh new faces; see our Music Scene chapter.) Throughout the 1970s, Sixth Street was a mix of old and new, with small cafes, antiques shops, fern bars, a genuine Mexican conjunto joint, and even a few upstairs apartments with rooftop gardens. In recognition of this vital downtown area, it was designated a National Registered Historic District.

But things began to change on Sixth as more and more buildings were turned into nightclubs and bars. Now, on any given weekend there are likely to be 20,000 patrons cruising the 7-block area, where more than 30 bars try to entice them with games, shots, Imperial pints, frozen margaritas, music, and tons of nachos. Many of the bars reinvent themselves with fierce regularity, changing names and decor to fit the fad of the moment.

Some of the venerable Sixth Street institutions remain amid the proliferation of shot bars and sports pubs. Esther's Follies (see Comedy Clubs in this chapter) is home to the city's favorite comedy troupe. Other notable survivors include Pecan Street Cafe (see Restaurants chapter) and Joe's Generic Bar at 315 East Sixth Street, a comfy bar noted for its blues music. Then there is the Paradise Cafe at 401 East Sixth Street, the original fern bar that has been here since the mid-1970s.

Most of the bars along the street now feature cover bands. One of the last

Sixth Street bar. AUSTIN CONVENTION AND VISITORS BUREAU/J. GRIFFIS SMITH

famous live music venues to close was the Black Cat Lounge, in July 2002 following a fire. That's not to say Sixth Street should be avoided, but visitors should be aware that this is Austin's version of Bourbon Street, with its rowdy, shoulder-bumping atmosphere. On special holidays, notably Halloween and Mardi Gras, the crowds increase and police erect barriers to block traffic, allowing revelers to roam in a ritual circle dance.

Because the street has emerged as party central, there have been some law-enforcement problems, including a small riot on Mardi Gras in 2001, and occasional crimes of violence and drug sales in the alleys behind the clubs. Visitors should avoid the alleys and remain vigilant about their personal safety, but the Austin Police Department maintains a high pro-

file on the street with foot, bicycle, and horse patrols.

Most hotels offer brochure guides to Sixth Street and Warehouse District clubs, plus the City of Austin maintains a guide to the street on its Web site: www.ci. austin.tx.us/downtown/sixthmap.htm. The Austin Chronicle and its Web site (www.austinchronicle.com) publish updated listings for the changing bar scene and weekly music calendars.

A walk along Sixth Street at night is a ritual for visitors, but be sure to visit Sixth Street during the day and look in two directions—down at the sidewalk where brass stars honor famous Texans and skyward to the buildings that reflect the turn-of-the-20th-century architecture favored by German and other immigrant merchants who helped build the capital city.

The Dog & Duck Pub
406 West 17th Street
(512) 479-0598

This Central Austin bar is as close as Austin gets to an authentic English pub. The food here reflects a mix of English pub grub and popular American dishes (see our Restaurants chapter), and the bar offers, like any English pub, a wide variety of beers on tap and in bottles. The atmosphere here is authentic, also—the dartboard is busy, and the bar is decorated with an assortment of mugs, bottles, knickknacks and souvenirs, and the bartenders are friendly. Many of the patrons are regulars. This is an especially good place to go on a rainy, cold afternoon, sip a Guinness, order some fish-and-chips, and imagine you're back in the Old Country.

The Draught Horse Pub and Brewery
4112 Medical Parkway
(512) 452-MALT

This pub is a neighborhood fixture in Central Austin, just north of the 35th Street medical and shopping district. From the outside it looks like a reproduction of an English country town pub. Inside, the cozy atmosphere attracts a loyal clientele. In addition to stocking 80 different beer brands, the pub has been experimenting with several homemade brews, including a stout produced from an 1850 India Pale Ale recipe from Guinness. Other brews include Old Knucklehead, a traditional-style ale; Midland Cream Ale, a light draft; and Hammerhead Super Stout, a hearty stout that lives up to its name.

Fadó Irish Pub
214 West Fourth Street
(512) 457-0172
www.fadoirishpub.com

Stepping into this Irish pub in the downtown Warehouse District, you almost expect to see John Wayne and Maureen O'Hara at the next table. It's not because the place looks like an old Irish pub, but because it looks more like the Hollywood-set version of an Irish pub. In addition to a menu of Irish-inspired dishes (see our

Restaurants chapter), the bar offers a wide selection of beer and whiskey, and the televisions in the bar tune in to satellite transmissions of rugby games, Gaelic football, hurling, and other interesting sports.

The Ginger Man
303 West Fourth Street
(512) 473-8801
www.gingermanpub.com

A favorite pub for those who want a quiet spot downtown, the Ginger Man has a large selection of beers on tap, which can be quaffed in the cozy, dark interior or out on the patio in back of the bar. Inside, customers can sip their suds while settled on one of the couches, just like home. True to pub tradition, there is a dartboard. Local bands perform on the weekends on the outdoor patio.

Lovejoy's Tap Room and Brewery
604 Neches Street
(512) 477-1268

The tables here are created from manhole covers, a coffin serves as a coffee table, and the walls are covered with the work of local artists. The seating ranges from comfy couches to tables and chairs where patrons can enjoy bar food including empanadas, Cornish pasties (meat and potato–filled turnovers), tamales, and pretzels. Some of the food items are hearty enough to qualify as lunch. This downtown pub also has two pool tables for a leisurely game. Beer lovers will find an extensive menu of bottled beers plus several homemade brews. A house specialty is Insomnia Coffee Stout, a strong brew made with coffee. Coffee lovers who don't want beer in their brew can avail themselves of espresso drinks. Other crafted brews include Harper Valley IPA (India Pale Ale) and Samson's Best Draft Ale, named after the owner's dog.

Maggie Mae's Long Bar
512 Trinity Street
(512) 478-8541

This well-known Sixth Street bar has grown with the years from a narrow, single-room pub noted for its live-music offerings (see The Music Scene chapter) to a major presence in the downtown nightlife scene. The pub has taken over adjacent buildings and has a rooftop patio for Sixth Street viewing and plans to add a grill. The bar has a publike atmosphere and offers a large variety of beers from around the world.

Mother Egan's Irish Pub
715 West Sixth Street
(512) 478-7747
www.motheregansirishpub.com

Imperial pints and frozen margaritas—no place but Texas! Mother Egan's has the feel of an Irish pub, with its wooden floors, cozy nooks, and dark paneled walls, but it also has an outdoor deck and large back room where patrons gather for bluegrass Sunday brunches, Celtic music, pub trivia games, and fish-n-chips nights—buy one, get one free.

North by Northwest Restaurant and Brewery
10010 North Capital of Texas Highway
(512) 467-6969

Located just behind the Gateway Shopping Center in northwest Austin, this sleek, sophisticated restaurant and bar features several seasonal brews made on the premises. The glass-and-stone surroundings reflect the quality of the food and the on-premises brews. (See our Restaurants chapter.) North by Northwest also offers beer to go.

Old Pecan Street Ale House & Soccer Bar
310 East Sixth Street
(512) 474-6722
www.alehouseaustin.com

The name says it all here at this cozy Sixth Street alley pub, where the emphasis is on soccer. The pub, which is under the same roof as Pecan Street Cafe, is one of the earliest entries in the Sixth Street renaissance. It serves a variety of beers, mixed drinks, and snacks in the same surroundings as the cafe—old limestone walls and well-worn

floors, cozy seating, and dimmed lighting. The pub's television sets feature national and international soccer games.

Opal Divine's Freehouse
700 West Sixth Street
(512) 477-3308
www.opaldivines.com

Housed in an old stone building on Sixth Street, next door to Austin's 24-hour deli, Katz's, this pub is named in honor of the owner's ancestor, who apparently enjoyed the good life as represented by pub food, a wide selection of single malt whiskies, and a large variety of beers. The pub has both indoor and outdoor seating and offers live music several nights a week.

Scholz Garten
1607 San Jacinto Boulevard
(512) 474-1958

This old German beer garden is many things to many people. In addition to being a popular restaurant (see our Restaurants chapter), a historical landmark, a favorite postgame gathering spot for University of Texas sports fans, and a political watering hole, the old stage in the shaded garden is also a music venue. A variety of live music is offered here. Check local listings in the *Austin Chronicle* and the *Austin American–Statesman*.

COFFEEHOUSES

Austin's coffeehouses reflect their surroundings and the city's artistic, kooky, innovative population. Some are funky neighborhood hangouts, others serve as showplaces for local artists, while still others are favored by political activists.

Austin Java Company
1206 Parkway
(512) 476-1829

Austin old-timers and returning visitors may remember the large, revolving bug that twirled on a pole outside an extermination company near 12th Street and Lamar Boulevard. The colorful bug has

For a map of WiFi nodes, many of them in coffeehouses, log on to www.austin wireless.net.

gone, and now a popular coffeehouse occupies the spot. Inside and out Austin Java Company has a relaxed feel, with picnic tables on the deck outside for those who enjoy a little sunshine with their coffee. Among the house specialties here are Vietnamese coffee, mocha shakes, and mochachinos, little mocha lattes described by an *Austin American–Statesman* critic as tasting like chocolate cream pie. The cafe has expanded its menu from snacks and pastries and now serves sandwiches, salads, and pasta dishes. Austin Java Company is open daily for breakfast, lunch, and dinner. The coffeehouse also offers a late-night menu until 4:00 A.M. on weekends.

Bouldin Creek Coffee House & Cafe
1501 South First Street
(512) 416-1601

This south-of-the-river coffeehouse caters to the local neighborhoods that are a mix of old and new Austin (see our Neighborhoods chapter). The bright green exterior is in step with this part of the city where old Austin funky meets new Austin gentry. Inside old Austin hippie artists lucky enough to have hung on to their once modest, now high-priced homes rub shoulders with dot-commers. Patrons come here to read, play games, and feed their coffee habit. The cafe also offers an all-day vegetarian menu.

Cafe Mundi
1704 East Fifth Street
(512) 236-8034
www.cafemundi.com

The *Austin Chronicle,* which is almost mandatory reading in the city's coffeehouses, has described Cafe Mundi as Parisian-like and an oasis. There is a quirkiness about this quiet eastside coffeehouse that sits amidst a small arts district along the abandoned railroad tracks in the city's eastside barrio, near downtown. The menu features the usual wide variety of coffees, chais and teas, plus breakfast, sandwiches, and salads. Small music groups also perform in the garden; the schedule is posted on the cafe's Web site.

Crescent City Beignets
1211 West Sixth Street
(512) 472-9622

Tucked back from the busy street, this small restaurant is open from early morning to late evening, serving Cajun specialties in addition to those air-filled beignets coated in powdery sugar that are a hallmark of life in New Orleans. The coffee menu also includes that chicory-coffee blend that is a natural accompaniment to a midmorning beignet.

Dolce Vita Gelato and Espresso Bar
4222 Duval Street
(512) 323-2686

The name means the sweet life, and there are layers of meaning to that phrase for this Hyde Park–area coffeehouse. The menu is rich with sweets, many with an Italian flavor—gelato, sorbet, granitas, tiramisu, cannoli—and there is also a relaxed, easy-living European atmosphere at this neighborhood cafe. The menu also features Italian sodas, coffees, a full bar, and a variety of cognac, whiskey, liqueur, and wine. Dolce Vita opens early for breakfast and stays open late for after-theater snacks.

Flight Path Coffeehouse
5011 Duval Street
(512) 458-4472

So what's with the name? Old Austin hands know that this small, neighborhood coffeehouse was once in the flight path for planes landing at what used to be the city's main airport, Robert Mueller Municipal Airport. The planes are high above now on their way to the new Austin-Bergstrom International Airport. Located in the heart of the Hyde Park neighborhood at 51st Street and Duval, the Flight Path is a popular gathering spot for families, students, and artists, some of whom exhibit their work here.

Flipnotics
1601 Barton Springs Road
(512) 482-8533
www.flipnotics.com

If the oversized café au lait doesn't make you flip for Flipnotics, nothing will. Made from whole milk and condensed milk and served in a cup as big as a soup bowl, this coffee treat is "mmm-mmm good!" The coffeehouse is on the second floor of a building on Barton Springs restaurant row, not far from Zilker Park (see our Parks and Recreation and Attractions chapters). Downstairs is a vintage clothing store while Flipnotics occupies the upstairs space and has a large shaded deck in the back on the hillside. Decorated in a space-theme motif, the cafe offers a light menu of sandwiches, muffins and bagels, wine, beer, and coffee, of course. In the evening, local musicians often perform. It is open until midnight every night except Sunday, when it closes at 11:00 P.M.

Green Muse
503 West Oltorf Street
(512) 462-0804

There is a relaxed, laid-back feel to this South Austin java joint not far from the St. Edward's University campus. The exterior is decorated with murals; inside, the couches, bookcases, and assorted tables give the place a true coffeehouse aura— dare we say groovy? Some come here for a quick jolt, others to ponder the Muse, or just to chat and relax with friends. There is a patio out back where customers can enjoy a cup of coffee or a beer. Light snacks are on the menu. Given its location near St. Ed's, it is busy in the morning. The coffeehouse is open daily and closes at midnight Sunday through Thursday, and 1:00 A.M. on weekends.

Jo's Coffee
1300 South Congress Avenue
(512) 441-3627

A small coffeehouse on a big street, Jo's is a true neighborhood hangout in SoCo. The front porch is where the locals gather to gossip, read, or hang out. The staff at Jo's is tuned into neighborhood happenings and art events. They even conjure up special happenings like the Average Jo's Fashion Show, held in the neighboring Hotel San Jose (see our Hotels chapter) parking lot, featuring retro chic clothes and aimed at raising money for animal rescue groups.

Little City Espresso Bar and Cafe
916 Congress Avenue
(512) 476-CITY
3403 Guadalupe Street
(512) 467-BEAN

Just a few blocks from the capitol, the Congress Avenue coffeehouse helped give new meaning to the word "avenue." The French know an avenue as a place to stroll, sit, and watch the world go by. Little City was among the first downtown cafes to promote that idea by putting tables and chairs on the wide sidewalks that line the city's main street. This is a popular meeting place for all manner of people who have business, are visiting, or simply want to feel the pulse of the city. The cafe serves coffee, tea, juices, granitas (flavored, shaved ices, sort of Italian snow cones), breakfast items like bagels and muffins, and lunch and snack food, including sandwiches and savory pastries. There is a second Little City on The Drag, but here the premises are much smaller. Frappes, a mixture of coffee and fruit juices, are a specialty at this cozy shop. Coffee beans also are offered for sale here. Little City is open at both locations until midnight during the week, until 1:00 A.M. on Friday and Saturday, and until 9:00 P.M. on Sunday.

Metro Espresso Bar
2222 Guadalupe Street
(512) 474-5730

This is the only coffeehouse in Austin that is open all the time, and that means the scene is always changing as the customers come and go. The decor is dark and industrial, with an atmosphere that might have existed in a German cafe between the wars. Upstairs is dedicated to smokers who have a hard time finding a place to puff in Austin, given the city's public smoking laws. The menu includes a variety of coffees, including the popular House Rocket Shake, made with Amy's chocolate ice cream.

Mojo's Daily Grind
2714 Guadalupe Street
(512) 477-6656
A coffee shop with a bohemian bent, Mojo's is popular with UT students and campus habitués. The 19th-century-home-turned-cafe is open 24 hours daily except Sunday. The purple neon lights and the giant coffee mug sign mark the spot. There is a small outdoor seating area in front, and inside the wooden floors and comfy furniture create a cozy atmosphere. Mojo's prides itself on presenting the work of cutting-edge, and sometimes contro-versial, artists working in a variety of mediums including photography, painting, and collage. There are also poetry events held at the cafe; check the listings section of the *Austin Chronicle*. The popular house drink is the Iced Mojo, a cold, creamy brew. Munchie offerings include coffeehouse-style eggs steamed at the espresso machine, bagels, muffins, oat-meal, pastries, and empanadas. Beer is also served at Mojo's.

Mozart's Coffee Roasters
3826 Lake Austin Boulevard
(512) 477-2900
www.mozartscoffee.com
Europe meets Texas at this West Austin cafe, which boasts a large deck overlook-ing Lake Austin, a good spot for a late-afternoon cappuccino or a late-night espresso. On Wednesday and Saturday local artists perform contemporary music under the stars on the deck, which seats 350 people. In addition to an extensive coffee bar menu, the cafe also serves iced, herbal, flavored and chai (soy-based) teas, granitas, Italian soda, pastries, and snacks. There is a juice bar on the premises as well

as a bookstore specializing in arts, travel, and literature. Mozart's also roasts and sells a variety of coffee beans. Mozart's is open until 11:00 P.M. during the week and on Sun-day, 1:00 A.M. on Friday and Saturday.

Quack's 43rd Street Bakery
411 East 43rd Street
(512) 453-3399
Quack's, as the UT students call it, was a fixture on The Drag but has moved to the Hyde Park neighborhood, north of the campus. Lively and sometimes noisy at night, Quack's also offers work areas for aspiring poets and playwrights to plug in their laptops. The cafe hosts a weekly poetry workshop under the auspices of Austin Poets At Large (APAL). The work of local artists is featured on the walls, and classical music plays in the back-ground. In addition to work areas, Quack's also has comfy conversation areas where friends can gather for breakfast, lunch, and late-night snacks. On the menu are muffins, pastries, soups, and sandwiches. Quack's is open until midnight Sunday through Thursday and until 1:00 A.M. on Friday and Saturday nights.

Ruta Maya Coffee Company
3601 South Congress Avenue
(512) 707-9637
www.rutamaya.net
If there was a single coffeehouse that cap-tured the mood and spirit of Austin, it was Ruta Maya, which occupied an old build-ing in the heart of the warehouse district west of Congress Avenue in downtown Austin. The patrons here were a true Austin mix, and on any given night you could see young professionals, aging hip-pies, Jack Kerouac wannabes, even a spin-ning yogi chanting mantras on a rotating platform.

Why do we speak in the past tense? Because Ruta Maya closed down at its old location in early 2002, and Austinites held their breath to see if it would maintain its fabled ambience at a new location near St. Edwards University. Some of the funkiness has gone, but the new industrial-style building offers lots of wallspace for art and space for cultural and political gatherings. In fact, Vermont Governor Howard Dean held a fund-raiser here in October 2003.

Ruta Maya serves coffees produced in Latin America. In 1990 the company was formed to help Latin American farmers sell their products and make a fair return. The guiding principle of the company is "Oportunidades para Las Americas"—opportunities for the Americas. Funds from the sale of coffee help support cultural and educational studies of Mayan language and culture.

Ruta Maya Negra Lager Beer, brewed in El Salvador at La Constancia Brewery, is sold at the coffeehouse. In addition to coffee, the cafe serves soups and snacks. There are regular music events and poetry readings. The walls of the coffeehouse are covered in local artwork and notices on all manner of cultural and political events. Ruta Maya is open until 2:00 A.M. on weekends and 1:00 A.M. during the week and on Sunday.

Saradora's Coffeehouse & Emporium
101 East Main Street, Round Rock
(512) 310-1200

Not all the coffeehouse action is in Austin. This Round Rock cafe is housed in an old building in the heart of the town's historic district. Local artists sell their jewelry and artwork here, and there is live music several nights a week plus open-mike poetry night on Wednesday. The vintage coffee grinder churns out beans for a variety of coffee drinks, which patrons can sip in comfortable surroundings decorated with antiques. Saradora's is open until 10:00 P.M. during the week and midnight on Friday and Saturday.

Spider House
2908 Fruth Street
(512) 480-9562
www.spiderhousecafe.com

This coffeehouse just north of the University of Texas campus is packed with old stuff—not really antiques and not really junk, just old stuff like Christmas lights

Many of Austin's coffeehouses are pet-friendly, particularly those with outdoor decks. For a list of where Fido can curl up with a bowl of latte, check out www.dogfriendly.com.

and soft drink machines, old radios, and a miscellany of chairs and tables. The large outdoor deck is a stage for local musicians; inside, an assortment of seating arrangements offers students a chance to sit and ponder life or chat with friends. The low prices attract students—one house specialty is the Spider Bite, a giant cup of coffee with a jolt of espresso. The menu features a variety of coffee drinks, of course, plus Italian sodas, smoothies, and a large selection of beer. Late-night noshes include tamales and pasta dishes.

COMEDY CLUBS

Austin is well known as a funny place—especially when the State Legislature is in session. There is not a session that goes by without some Texas legislator making national headlines for offering one wacky proposal or another. The city also boasts several natural humorists, such as Austin's answer to Rush Limbaugh, progressive liberal talk show host and former Texas agriculture commissioner Jim Hightower, who broadcasts from Threadgill's restaurant downtown (see our Restaurants chapter). Hightower's signature phrase is "The only thing in the middle of the road are yellow stripes and dead armadillos."

Visitors will find political humor is high on the agenda at local comedy outposts, notably Esther's Follies, a longtime Austin troupe that takes aim at both local and national politicians. There are only a handful of nightclubs dedicated to comedy alone, but a few of the city's live music venues also take a comedy break now and then. That list expands greatly during the annual Big Stinkin' International Improv and Sketch Comedy festival held in April each year (see our Annual Events and Festivals chapter). The 1998 festival, known in festival shorthand as BS3, featured a wide variety of talent both national and home-grown at over 20 local venues.

Capitol City Comedy Club
8120 Research Boulevard
(512) 467-2333
www.capcitycomedy.com
This Northwest Austin club has pulled in some of the big names in comedy, including Ellen DeGeneres, Jeff Foxworthy, and Bobcat Goldthwait. While nationally known comics appear on Friday and Saturday nights, up-and-coming comedians, including local talent, are featured on other nights.

Esther's Follies/Esther's Pool
525 East Sixth Street
(512) 320-0553
www.esthersfollies.com
Like Barton Springs and the old Armadillo World Headquarters, Esther's Follies is part of the fabric of Austin. The comedy troupe performs every Thursday, Friday, and Saturday at Esther's Pool on Sixth Street on a stage where the backdrop is three floor-to-ceiling windows looking out on the street. The audience can watch the antics of the troupe and their interactions with the passersby on Sixth Street.

Esther's is named for Esther Williams, the actress and water ballet artist who made all those swimming movies in the 1950s. The group took that name in the 1970s when they performed skits between music sets at another legendary spot, Liberty Lunch (see The Music Scene chapter). Founders Michael Shelton and Shannon Sedwick (he is co-owner of Esther's and the announcer, she is a star of the troupe and co-owner) say they chose the name because the troupe would perform in the Texas heat wearing swimsuits and get cooled by the stage sprinklers.

Satire and outrageous, campy comedy are the troupe's mainstays. National and local politicians are spoofed, caricatured,

and mimicked. (Before you go you might want to brush up on local and state issues in our Politics and Perspectives chapter.) The show changes routines regularly and puts on special holiday shows, so repeat visitors are never disappointed. There are no reservations taken, and on Friday and Saturday it is wise to arrive early to ensure a seat. Performances are at 8:00 P.M. on Thursday and 8:00 P.M. and 10:00 P.M. Friday and Saturday. Tickets are $14, $10 for students.

Velveeta Room
521 East Sixth Street
(512) 469-9116
If Esther's Follies is the jewel in the crown of the Austin comedy scene, then the Velveeta Room is the jester. Housed on Sixth Street, next door to Esther's Pool, local and visiting comic talent try out some of their more outrageous and irreverent routines here. Sketches and improvisations are performed Thursday, Friday, and Saturday nights. There is a $5.00 admission charge.

DANCE CLUBS AND NIGHTCLUBS

Whether it is the Texas two-step, salsa, merengue, swing, even the Lindy hop, there is a club in Austin where dancers can strut their stuff. Even disco, heaven forbid, is alive and well as the 20-something crowd explores retro fashions. Those looking for a Texas experience should consider visiting one of the city's country dance spots, notably the Broken Spoke, which has been described as the best example of a Texas honky-tonk in Austin. But don't miss out on another important cultural experience: dancing to the Latino beat, ranging from tango to Tejano. Austin's Mexican-American residents have supported several Latino clubs over the years, but recently non-Hispanics are discovering the excitement of salsa music.

The 311 Club
311 East Fifth Street
(512) 477-1630

The *Austin Chronicle* calls this Sixth Street–area club the "Wal-Mart of dance clubs," suggesting it is both popular and cheap. It is always packed on the weekends and is popular with the college crowd. Paradox also stays open after the bars close at 2:00 A.M. The Wal-Mart designation aside, there is a dress code here (primarily on Friday and Saturday). Guys may get turned away at the door if their jeans are too ragged or their T-shirts have gaping holes.

Abratto's
318 East Fifth Street
(512) 477-1641

This is where the young and the beautiful hang out until the wee hours. A dance club where the sounds are a mix of house music and techno, Abratto's stays open until 4:00 A.M. for those who want to keep dancing even after the bars close. The *Austin Chronicle* says, "Abratto's seven years on Fifth prove vanity has yet to go out of style."

Atomic Cafe
705 Red River Street
(512) 457-0644

The outside of this downtown nightclub looks as grungy as the inside, but that is part of its charm for the metalhead fans who gather here. The club serves up hard rock nightly, and there are special fetish nights for those who want to show off their chains, piercings, and tattoos.

Azucar
400 Lavaca Street
(512) 478-5650

Salsa and merengue continue to be hot trends on the Austin dance scene. This downtown club touts itself as "the only 100 percent salsa and merengue club" in Austin. Salsa is not only an exotic way to get a great physical workout, it can be a good opportunity to spot some of the city's "stars," since many of the Hollywood

Want to experience a real Texas country dance hall? Head for The Coupland Dance Hall, (512) 856-2226, on Highway 95 between Taylor and Elgin, east of Austin. On weekends this old dance hall is "just a two-step back in time," as its slogan says.

types enjoy a salsa workout when they are in town, notably film star Sandra Bullock.

B-Side
311 Colorado Street
(512) 478-2337

The name is a play on the fact that its next-door neighbor and corporate sibling is the Bitter End, an upscale brewpub and restaurant. While the A-side offers top-notch food, wine, and beer, the B-Side serves up jazz and rock music in a casual atmosphere.

Broken Spoke
3201 South Lamar Boulevard
(512) 442-6189

An original honky-tonk that merits the description "legendary" (hence its inclusion in The Music Scene chapter), the Spoke is also a great place to dance a little, drink a little, and eat a lot. There is live music here Tuesday through Saturday, and the cover charges vary. The low ceiling, the tall men in big hats, and the wooden dance floor give this place the feel of an authentic Texas roadhouse. No visit to Austin should end without dropping by the Spoke in South Austin for a longneck.

Club Carnaval
2237 East Riverside Drive
(512) 444-6396

Southeast of downtown, along East Riverside Drive, there are several authentic Hispanic nightclubs that celebrate Mexican-American and Latin dance traditions. Club Carnaval is noted for its norteño dances, which originated in Northern Mexico and flourish in South Texas. Male dancers don Western wear, including large belt buckles, tight pressed jeans, and white cowboy

The latest hot dancing trend in Austin is the tango. Austin Tango Connection, (512) 480-9899, is dedicated to spreading the word and has information about classes, practices, and dance locations.

hats, while the women dance in full skirts or jeans and Western shirts. Some of the top names in norteño music play here in a setting that has an Aztec motif. In addition to norteño music, the club also features salsa, Tejano, merengue, and cumbia music. Cover charges vary.

Dallas
7113 Burnet Road
(512) 452-2801

Disco meets country at this North Austin nightclub. Much of the music is piped-in country hits with occasional top rock songs. Cheap drinks on Wednesday and Thursday attract a younger crowd, but older couples in their 30s and 40s also enjoy the dancing here.

Desperado's
9515 North Lamar Boulevard
(512) 834-2640

There are several different kinds of Latino music, but the homegrown kind here in Texas is called Tejano—the state was, after all, named "Tejas" when it was part of Mexico. The music has a fast-paced swing, a sort of cross between country and salsa. The outfit of choice celebrates the "vaquero," the northern Mexican cowboy whose dress influenced cowboys north of the border. Both men and women wear cowboy boots and the men wear cowboy hats, while the women wear either Western-style skirts or jeans. This 11,000-square-foot dance club has three full-service bars.

El Borinquen
2728 South Congress Avenue
(512) 443-4252

This tiny restaurant and bar re-creates the atmosphere of Old San Juan. The food

and drinks are Puerto Rican, as are many of the customers, but the dance floor also draws a diverse crowd that enjoys dancing to salsa and merengue sounds on Friday and Saturday nights.

Element Nightclub
301 West Fifth Street
(512) 480-9888

This warehouse district club rocks on after 2:00 A.M., the time when Texas bars close down. Techno and rave are the themes here, and the 1,600-square-foot dance floor is packed into the wee hours. The goal, the owners say, is to create a "hip, big city club," and to that end they have spent $2 million renovating the joint.

Flamingo Cantina
515 East Sixth Street
(512) 494-9336

The Flamingo gets consistently good reviews for its music, and the club also offers rock and reggae that keeps the place packed on weekends. The decor and the sounds are designed to evoke the Caribbean with a grass-thatched roof over the stage and pictures of Bob Marley on the walls.

Le Privilege
912 Red River Street
(512) 476-4441

Formerly the Caucus Club, this corner club has undergone several incarnations. Once a political hangout, then a cigar bar, now described by its owners as "elegant." Patrons are privileged to enjoy martinis and jazz in a refined setting. There is even a waterfall on the patio.

Miguel's La Bodega
415 Colorado Street
(512) 472-2369

Miguel's is the hot spot in the downtown Warehouse District for the Latino dance scene. Salsa and merengue rule here, and the uninitiated can take midweek lessons on the premises. Live bands on the weekends provide a constant salsa beat, and just to make sure you stay in a south-of-the-border mood, the club serves a Latino menu.

Meneo
217 Congress Avenue
(512) 479–5002
A combination Mexican restaurant and dance club, this Congress Avenue club features a variety of music including merengue, salsa, and Mexican rock. Customers dress in stylized salsa fashion with women wearing incredibly high heels and sexy skirts. When not dancing, they are drinking the house bombaritas. On the weekends there is also live mariachi music to set the mood. Happy hour features a free food buffet.

Polly Ester's '70s Disco and the Culture Club
404 Colorado Street
(512) 472–1975
Those of us who lived through the '70s (crushed-velvet bell bottoms and white go-go boots!?) just don't get it, but retro is in, and this warehouse district dance club is living proof. Packed on weekends, Polly Ester's is part of a national chain of dance clubs catering to this nostalgia for the decade—the club's ads even feature Pac Man and big daisy graphics. Others are based in Boca Raton, Denver, Washington, New York, and Chicago. The club offers Disco Fever Happy Hour on Friday and Saturday, and Thursday is Ladies Night. Polly's is popular with the college crowd.

Reeds Jazz and Supper Club
9901 Capital of Texas Highway North
(512) 342–7977
Reed Clemons, a noted Austin restaurateur, tried a northern branch of his popular downtown Austin restaurant, Mezzaluna, but it never quite clicked. But Clemons has hit the high notes with this popular supper club in Northwest Austin. The jazz is cool, the martinis dry, and guests can make an evening of dinner and music just as the Rat Pack did back in the golden age of nightclubs. The club is located in the Gateway Shopping Center.

Ringside at Sullivan's
300 Colorado Street
(512) 474–1870
The limos line up outside Sullivan's, the Chicago-style steakhouse (see our Restaurants chapter) and this adjoining jazz club. The atmosphere is upscale and glamorous with lots of big cigars and cold martinis in view. The adjacent restaurant bar usually is just as crowded and as smoky, especially during the biennial legislative session when lobbyists are picking up the tab for lawmakers and their staff.

Ritz Lounge
320 East Sixth Street
(512) 474–9574
You will find several listings for the Ritz in our Nightlife chapter since this important Sixth Street facility operates in a variety of guises. Once a posh downtown movie theater, the Ritz fell on hard times and became a porno palace. In the last two decades it has worn several faces as a music venue, but has emerged as a nightclub/dance club/lounge/comedy club and movie theater. Inside, you will find a lounge atmosphere in what was the balcony of the movie theater. The atmosphere is swanky, especially on Thursday when Latin dancing is featured: Tango is a big draw here. On other nights the music might be jazz or swing, very hip. It is a favorite late-night spot for some of Austin's young chefs and kitchen wizards who gather here after hours.

Speakeasy
412 Congress Avenue
(512) 476–8017
Listed in The Music Scene chapter, Speakeasy is also a classy spot for a martini or glass of wine. Housed in one of Congress Avenue's older buildings, recently a used appliance store, the renovation has produced one of the fancier nightspots. A mezzanine overlooks the dance floor, and an old elevator has been

restored to give the club that '20s feel. The whole place has a Prohibition theme, hence the emphasis on jazz and gin.

Tangerine's
9721 Arboretum Boulevard
(512) 343-2626
This upscale disco is on the Renaissance Hotel campus at the Arboretum. The crowd here is upwardly mobile, urban, professional—particularly on weekends. Open nightly except Sunday, Tangerine's plays music until midnight during the week and until 2:00 A.M. on weekends.

Tejano Ranch
7601 North Lamar Boulevard
(512) 453-6616
Tejano music is designed for dancing, and some of the biggest acts in the genre appear at this North Austin nightclub, notably on the weekends. The crowd here is generally older than 30 and familiar with the Tejano scene. The club has a South Texas atmosphere with neon mustangs outside and a large Selena mural inside, plus the chairs are covered in cowhide.

GAY NIGHTCLUB SCENE

The gay nightlife scene in Austin seems to divide into two categories—sophisticated downtown clubs where beautiful people gather and country swing clubs. However, there are also a couple of neighborhood bars that offer relaxing atmosphere after work hours.

1920's Club
918 Congress Avenue
(512) 479-7979
A recent addition to the gay nightlife scene, this Congress Avenue club, 3 blocks south of the capitol, has a '20s theme. Dubbed a "speakeasy," the club features jazz music and martinis, but there is also a food menu.

'Bout Time
9601 North I-35
(512) 832-5339
Gay patrons, both men and women, are attracted to this nightclub that aims for a neighborhood tavern theme. Indoors there are pool tables and darts, while outdoors there are sand volleyball courts. The bar also features a big-screen television and video games.

Boyz Cellar
213 West Fourth Street
(512) 479-8482
www.boyzcellar.com
This warehouse district club has two bars and a large dance floor. The club also features strippers, movie nights, and special musical events.

Chain Drive
504 Willow Street
(512) 480-9017
This Central Austin bar is described as Austin's only "leather bar," but this is soft and cuddly leather. Chain Drive is headquarters for a group calling itself the Heart of Texas Bears, a self-described social group for masculine, bearded, and/or hairy gay men and their admirers. The bar has pool tables and a small dance floor and is open daily from early afternoon until 2:00 A.M.

Charlie's
1301 Lavaca Street
(512) 474-6481
A longtime fixture on the gay scene, Charlie's is noted for its clubby atmosphere and party mood on weekends. On Sunday night, the downtown club hosts drag shows, while on Tuesday the steak and chicken dinners draw regular patrons. There is a dance floor, dartboards, pool tables, two bars, and television sets for special programming. The outdoor patio is a popular gathering spot when the weather cooperates.

Dick's Deja Disco
113 San Jacinto Boulevard
(512) 457-8010

The gay and lesbian community comes to this downtown club to kick up its collective heels and dance to the top country sounds or the retro sounds of disco music.

The Forum
408 Congress Avenue
(512) 476-2900

A relatively new addition to the gay nightlife scene in Austin, the Forum attracts an upscale, mature crowd. An upstairs patio offers respite from the busy dance floor and where patrons dance to Top 40 hits, country, and hip hop.

Oilcan Harry's
211 West Fourth Street
(512) 320-8823
www.oilcans.com

Some have dubbed this warehouse district bar a neighborhood bar for Austin's gay, beautiful set. The large bar is a major feature of the club, but the dance floor is the focal point. A patio in the back of the club offers a retreat from the frenzy of the dance floor. Although the majority of the customers are gay, straight patrons also enjoy the atmosphere here—and the dancing.

Rascal's Nightclub
305 West Fifth Street
(512) 472-5288

Country and western music is the order of the day at this downtown gay dance club and bar. During the week, patrons can take dance classes. In addition to two bars, there are areas set aside for darts and pool, and on Sunday customers can enjoy a large buffet.

MOVIES

There are movie complexes in all areas of the city, and several new facilities featuring stadium seating and other state-of-

the-art features have been added to the list in 1998. Check the daily *Austin American-Statesman* and the weekly *Austin Chronicle* for featured movies. The following movie houses feature classic, foreign, and independent films.

Alamo Draft House
409 Colorado Street
Alamo Draft House North
2700 Anderson Lane
(512) 476-1320
www.drafthouse.com

Tired of sitting in movie theaters where the average age of the audience is younger than your family dog? Try the Alamo Draft House, where there is no sticky Coke on the floor and munchie choices go beyond dill pickles and Butterfingers. This warehouse-district movie theater features cult favorites and classics, everything from beach movies to horror flicks served in a nightclub setting where you can order beer, wine, and food to accompany the evening's celluloid offerings. On the weekends there are midnight flicks and sometimes the movie house puts on special presentations, such as a presentation of the movie *Like Water for Chocolate* featuring dishes mentioned in the book. The theater's newest location is found on Anderson Lane in north Austin.

Arbor Cinema at Great Hills
9828 Great Hills Trail
(800) FANDANGO, ext. 684
www.regmovies.com

Movie fans were distraught when the Arboretum Cinema was shut down to

The Capital City Murder Mystery Theatre appears at various restaurants around Austin offering a dinner theater experience. The group also performs at private parties. Call (512) 404-9123 for more information.

make way for a Cheesecake Factory, a popular chain restaurant. In addition to mainstream new releases, the Arboretum theaters had featured arts and foreign films. To serve those Northwest Austin movie fans, Regal Movies took over a bank of screens at the Great Hills location, updated the furniture and equipment, and now serves up a mix of classics, foreign flicks, and art films.

Dobie Theatre
2021 Guadalupe Street
(512) 472–FILM (3456)
www.landmarktheatres.com
If you're looking for an independent release, foreign film, or art movie, check out the listings for this UT campus-area movie complex. The Dobie is housed in the large and ugly tower at the southern end of The Drag that serves as a residence hall and shopping center for students. Richard Linklater screened *Slacker* here.

Paramount Theatre for the Performing Arts
713 Congress Avenue
(512) 472-5411
www.austintheatrealliance.org
The beautifully restored theater on the city's main avenue hosts a summer film festival featuring the great classics of Hollywood. Also, given Austin's emergence as a movie-making venue (see our Close-up in The Arts chapter), premieres are held at the downtown theater.

Westgate 11
Westgate Shopping Center
South Lamar and Ben White Boulevards
(800) FANDANGO, ext. 369
www.regmovies.com
Regal Movies operates this modern cinema complex in the shopping center anchored by Central Market (see our Shopping chapter) in Southwest Austin. The 11 screens feature a mix of mainstream and art films.

THE MUSIC SCENE

If this chapter were set to the tune of Austin music, the savory sounds of country, blues, folk, funk, punk, pop, jazz, bluegrass, Tejano, and rock 'n' roll would waft off these pages and fill the air like a Saturday night on Sixth Street. While we can't reproduce the sounds, we can tell you about some of the artists, the venues, the free concerts, and the record stores that constitute the Live Music Capital of the World. So whether you're a music lover eager to explore the sounds of Austin or you've arrived with a guitar on your back and a pocketful of songs, get ready to enter a truly remarkable realm.

No matter what you may have heard about Austin's live music scene, there really is nothing that prepares newcomers for the jolt of firsthand experience. Music is, indeed, here, there, and everywhere in Austin. On any given Friday night, music lovers can choose from among well over 90 venues offering just about any style of music you can imagine, including those exotic strains created by our true Texas hybrids. No weekend-warrior music mentality exists here, however, as our club scene rocks seven nights a week. From national touring shows and top local acts to the most exciting up-and-coming artists and youngsters (some barely past puberty) taking the stage for the very first time, Austin is tuned in to music.

You'll find live music in record stores and bookstores. There's live music to accompany your Sunday brunch and live music to stir your evening coffee. Austin's premier gourmet grocery offers live music at its two locations on the patio (see our Close-up on Central Market in the Shopping chapter). You can listen to live music in our museums and art galleries, and there's live music in our parks and on our sidewalks. Austin's Sixth Street is an entire district dedicated to live music and dance halls, while our own nationally televised music TV show has celebrated Austin music for nearly a quarter of a century. *Austin City Limits,* which has been called the city's cultural calling card to the world, is Austin's top showcase for musical talent. We also have our own 24-hour music channel, the Austin Music Network, which serves up a steady stream of local and national acts on Time Warner Cable Channel 15 (see our Media chapter). Our city also hosts one of the most important live music festivals in the country, South by Southwest (see our Close-up in the Annual Events and Festivals chapter).

Though Austin took the motto "The Live Music Capital of the World" in the early 1990s, it gained prominence long before that as a haven for artists seeking to follow their own music and create their own sounds without much interference from the commercial establishment based in L.A., New York, and Nashville. *Billboard* magazine has called Austin a "mecca for musical mavericks," saying Austin is known as "a creative oasis, a place that puts music first and career far behind." For local consumption, Austin music critics have a less sympathetic description of this phenomenon, calling it the "Austin Curse," which they define as Austin's seeming inability to translate good music into commercial success. While it's true that many artists are drawn to Austin for its no-strings-attached spirit, so to speak, it is also true that some current and former Austin regulars have found the magic formula that cracks the charts, including Willie Nelson, the late Stevie Ray Vaughan, Pat Green, Shawn Colvin, Jerry Jeff Walker, Christopher Cross, Fastball, and others.

In fact, Austin is one of the few cities in the United States where young musicians can go from learning to play, to having a garage band, to performing in a club, to burning their own CDs, to getting an independent record contract, to earning a major-label deal without ever moving their base of operations. Austin claims several important recording studios as well as almost a hundred independent record labels, including a handful of prestigious names such as Freedom, Antone's, and Lazy SOB that actively promote Austin talent—and distribute their music around the country. (While the major label Arista/Austin was established here a couple of years ago, company executives later relocated the offices to Nashville.)

About 15 years ago, the City Council commissioned a survey that showed Austin had a higher number of people involved in the music business per capita than anywhere else in the United States. Our population has grown since then, but so has our music scene. By conservative estimates today, more than 9,000 people earn a living from Austin's music business, including producers, club staff, recording studios and record companies, music stores and record shops, music teachers, instrument makers, and, of course, the artists themselves.

Austin's music scene appears as dynamic today as ever, as more and more young musicians pour into town seeking the freedom to explore their music and the comfort of Austin's appreciative audiences. The constantly changing array of artists on stage—our classic legends and old mainstays combined with young newcomers and emerging talents—renews Austin's status as a musical mecca each and every night. So whether you prefer a lone singer on stage strumming a folk tune on an acoustic guitar or a 10-piece band rocking off the roof, you'll find that Austin has a sound all its own—the sound of originality.

CATCH 'EM IF YOU CAN

With an entire city of musical artists determined to travel to the beat of their own drummers, it's no wonder Austin offers so many choices for the music lover. A city that reestablishes itself as the

world's live music capital seven nights a week makes it hard on those of us trying to assemble a list of all the must-see acts. There are just so many talented musicians worthy of mention. The artists listed here are among Austin's favorites, but don't think for a minute that this list is all-inclusive. A little experimentation and willingness to explore the live music scene will bring its own reward.

Among the many artists we've mentioned here, you'll find a number we call Texas hybrids. These artists are the most difficult to categorize because they combine many musical styles. So you'll find artists described as country/folk/rock, bluesy-folk/country, Tex-Mex rock, alternative country, and several other such amalgamations. However you describe them, the voices will have you feeling like you've taken a tour across Texas and across the ages during the course of one song.

We've called this section Catch 'em if You Can because Austin's favorite artists are often the most in demand for concerts around the country and around the world. So catch them while they're here. You can't go wrong.

Asleep at the Wheel: Led by founder/singer/songwriter/guitarist Ray Benson, Asleep at the Wheel has perhaps done more to preserve and expand the Western Swing sound popularized by the legendary Bob Wills than any other band. From the group's 1973 debut record *Coming Right at Ya* to its 2003 release, *Asleep at the Wheel Live at Billy Bob's Texas,* this band has continued to impress fans with its fiddle- and steel guitar–driven sound. One of the group's landmark works, *Asleep at the Wheel Tribute to the Music of Bob Wills and the Texas Playboys,* won three Grammys. Benson and band came to Austin in 1974 at Willie Nelson's urging and have remained ever since—when they're not off touring, that is.

Asylum Street Spankers: *Spanks for the Memories* is our favorite CD title by this seven-piece band that eschews demon electricity in favor of an all-acoustic, string-dominated sound. But with a host of musical voices and a gaggle of instruments among them, who needs a speaker blasting at ya? The Spankers take their name from the original name of Austin's happening Guadalupe Street and the fact that the players "spank" their instruments. They produce original songs that incorporate the sounds of blues, bluegrass, country, and swing, and they would have been right at home in the '20s, '30s, and '40s. They've got ukuleles, kazoos, banjos, mandolins, flatpick and gypsy swing guitars, a washboard, an upright bass, a clarinet, and other instruments. The show, often hilarious, sometimes downright rowdy, is always unique—and you just know the Spankers are having as much fun as the audience.

Austin Lounge Lizards: With song titles that include "Jesus Loves Me (But He Can't Stand You)," "Put the Oak Ridge Boys in the Slammer," and "Shallow End of the Gene Pool," it's no wonder this group has earned a reputation for its inventive, and quite entertaining, style of satirical bluegrass, which has won them a number of regional awards as well as national touring dates. Hank Card and Conrad Deisler, former Princeton University and later University of Texas songwriting partners, formed the Lounge Lizards in 1980. Three years later, the Lizards won a Best Band award at the Kerrville Bluegrass Festival. This band, known for its stellar vocal harmonies and lyrical barbs at just about everything, remains an Austin favorite.

Marcia Ball: *CD Review* called Ball's 1994 release, *Blue House,* "another gusto-filled collection of tunes informed by the grit of Texas honky-tonk, the stomp of Louisiana Delta rhythms, and the soul of New Orleans–style blues." This piano-playing dynamo with a full-bodied, earthy voice continues to enchant audiences across the country. Born into a family of musicians in the small southern Louisiana town of Vinton, Ball learned to play the piano at an

early age. She moved to Austin in 1970 just as the local music scene was really taking off, played in a progressive country band called Freda and the Firedogs, and then hit the road for blues clubs, honky-tonks, and blues festivals throughout the South and Southwest. In 1998, Rounder Records released the celebrated *Sing It,* featuring Ball and two other R&B experts, Irma Thomas and Tracy Nelson. Ball's other albums include *Soulful Dress, Hot Tamale Baby,* and *Gatorhythms.* In 1998 Ball won a Handy Award for Contemporary Blues Female Artist of the Year.

Lou Ann Barton: It's the voice that gets 'em every time. Austin blues luminary Lou Ann Barton's full-throated voice and scorching on-stage performances have been packing clubs in Austin and around the country for years. *Rolling Stone* called her "the most commanding white female belter to erupt out of Texas since Janis Joplin—a singer to whom, in terms of vocal sophistication and emotion, Barton is far, far superior." A native of Fort Worth, Barton performed on stage in R&B clubs before she was 20. Her performance in a New York City club in 1980 so impressed legendary soul/blues producer Jerry Wexler that he signed Barton practically on the spot. *Old Enough* was released in 1982 to rave reviews. Barton's rich musical past includes stints with the late Stevie Ray Vaughan in the Triple Threat Revue and with the Fabulous Thunderbirds. Her other albums include *Forbidden Tones, Read My Lips,* and *Dreams Come True,* this last one with musical standouts Marcia Ball and Angela Strehli.

Junior Brown: There are guitar players—and then there are GUITAR players. Junior Brown couldn't find an instrument that could produce the sounds his mind was hearing—so he invented one. With his deep voice and trademark double-neck "guit-steel," a combination six-string and steel guitar, Brown produces a sound he calls "free-range country," and his fans call just plain out of sight. His music has been labeled country/rock, alternative country, and whatever else label-makers can think of. However you classify it, the sound is a little bit country, a little bit rock 'n' roll with blues, surfer music, and Hawaiian threads thrown in. No wonder Austin loves his four-member band, which includes his wife, Tanya Rae, at rhythm guitar. Born Jamieson Brown in Cottonwood, Arizona, in 1952, Brown eventually found his way to Austin and the spotlight. His albums include *12 Shades of Brown* and *Guit with It.*

Stephen Bruton: Inducted into the Texas Music Hall of Fame in 2003, this guy has done it all since his guitar talents were discovered by Kris Kristofferson in Bruton's hometown of Fort Worth. Kristofferson, who called Bruton "one very devil on the guitar," added the young musician to his band back in 1972, while Bruton was still in his 20s. Since then, Bruton has performed two years as lead guitarist for Bonnie Raitt, written a slew of great songs, and spent much of his professional life as a journeyman guitarist and session player. He also has produced a couple of acclaimed albums, Alejandro Escovedo's *Gravity* and Jimmie Dale Gilmore's *After Awhile.* Bruton's blend of country, soul, rock 'n' roll, R&B, and blues makes him a true Texas hybrid, and one of the most original musicians living and working in Austin today. He's produced several solo albums, including *Nothing but the Truth.*

W. C. Clark: Few living artists epitomize

Austin blues better than W. C. Clark. Born on Austin's east side on November 16, 1939, Clark developed his musical style playing bass and then guitar with the likes of T. B. Bell and Blues Boy Hubbard at the landmark Victory Grill, Charlie's Playhouse, and other black blues clubs of the era. Though he seldom toured and cut his first nationally distributed record, *Heart of Gold,* just a few years ago, Clark became a mentor for up-and-coming white musicians like Stevie Ray Vaughan and Denny Freeman. In 1976 Clark teamed with Vaughan and Lou Ann Barton in the band Triple Threat Revue. The past few years he's put out an album every other year, including *Lover's Plea.* Clark, a member of the Texas Music Hall of Fame, was honored in 1989 with an *Austin City Limits* tribute on his 50th birthday.

Shawn Colvin: With *A Few Small Repairs,* Austin's gem of the New Folk scene solidified her reputation as an important singer/songwriter. Colvin's first platinum album, *Repairs,* produced the single "Sunny Came Home," which won two 1997 Grammys for Record of the Year and Song of the Year and proved to the world what her fans have known all along: This songwriter can play the guitar and owns a set of provocative pipes to boot. Born in 1956 in Vermillion, South Dakota, Colvin started playing the guitar at age 10. She lived in Austin in the mid-1970s and performed with the Dixie Diesels before heading to San Francisco, New York, and Boston. Back in Austin since the early 1990s, Colvin's debut album for Columbia Records, *Steady On,* promptly won a Grammy for Best Contemporary Folk Recording. *Fat City* includes a wonderful version of her classic song "I Don't Know Why."

Alvin Crow: At home in Carnegie Hall as much as in honky-tonks and clubs around the country and in Europe, this classically trained musician, who earned a seat with the Oklahoma City Symphony as its youngest violinist, is one of Austin's great fiddlers in the Western Swing tradition of

---

Club hopping between Sixth Street and the Warehouse District downtown can wear a person out. Why not make it easy on yourself and call a bike taxi? These people-powered, bicycle-drawn carriages usually operate Wednesday through Sunday evenings. Try Austin Bike Cabs at (512) 591-7588 or Capital Pedicabs at (512) 851-2227.

Bob Wills and the Texas Playboys. Western Swing is just one dimension of an Alvin Crow show, however. He tosses in plenty of Cajun music, rockabilly, and classic country as well as his own originals. Born in 1950 and raised in Western Oklahoma, Crow has been a fixture on the music scene for nearly 30 years. Alvin Crow and his band, the Pleasant Valley Band, have released eight albums over the years, including *Texas Classics* on Austin's Broken Spoke record label. The *New York Times* has said Crow represents the "finest flower of Austin's club and concert scene." His other albums include *Pure Country, Honky Tonk Trail,* and *Long Texas Nights.*

Del Castillo: "Our music is kind of like the band, we all come with our own influences," Del Castillo percussionist Mark Holeman told the *Austin Chronicle* in 2003. "We got a Gipsy Kings/flamenco groove, but then we've got this Steven Tyler–Mick Jagger lead singer out there. It was either going to work or be the biggest train wreck of our lives. Luckily for us, it works." Austin agrees. This six-member Spanish-language band took home a slew of Austin Music awards in 2003, including Austin Band of the Year and Best Mexican/Traditional Band. It's a testament to the growing popularity of Latin music around these parts. (Or is it that Latin music is getting hotter around here *because* of groups like Del Castillo?) Brothers Rick and Mark del Castillo started this local phenomenon. For more Latin rhythms around Austin, check out the bands Vallejo, Los Lonely Boys, and Grupo Fantasma.

The Derailers: Combining the country sounds of Buck Owens, Merle Haggard, and others of the Bakersfield Sound era with influences of rock, R&B, and pop, the Derailers are making a major contribution to the music scene in Austin, and now around the country. This four-piece ensemble with slicked-back pompadour hairdos and those '60s-era suits got together in Austin in the early 1990s. Led by frontmen and guitarists Tony Villanueva and Brian Hofeldt, who came to play country music from, of all places, Oregon, the Derailers can always be trusted to provide a dang good, foot-stomping, made-for-dancing good time. Their debut album, *Live Tracks,* was recorded live at Austin's KUT–FM radio station on the local Freedom Records label. They followed up with *Jackpot* on the Watermelon label and a year later got their major-label break when Sire Records teamed up with Watermelon to release *Reverb Deluxe.* Their 2003 release is *Genuine.* That's *gen-u-WHINE.*

Alejandro Escovedo: It's hard to believe that a guy who launched his musical career by playing in his own student film about a rock band that couldn't play could have come so far. He has. A founding member of the 1970s landmark San Francisco punk band The Nuns, a member of Texas's influential country-punk band Rank and File, and later part of the electrifying rock band True Believers, Escovedo has already left his mark on American music. One of 12 children born in San Antonio into a family of musicians, Escovedo and family left Texas for California in the 1960s. The teenage Escovedo immersed himself in the flourishing music scene and later discovered his own unique voice. His songs, according to his biography, "blend lyrical strings and woodwinds with the gritty sound of crunching, sawed-off guitars and pumping pianos." We couldn't have said it better. Escovedo has a few records under his own name, including *With Gravity* and *13 Years,* as well as albums by his other musical manifestations, The Setters and Buick MacKane. Escovedo plays with a number of different bands around town.

Fastball: This pop trio had been paying its dues—writing the songs and driving the required hundreds of miles to gigs where a handful of folks, not fans per se, would show up. In Austin, finally, they were getting some notice, despite the fact that their 1996 debut CD for Hollywood Records,

Make Your Mama Proud, pretty much flopped. Then in 1998 Fastball became an overnight sensation with the release of the trio's second album, *All the Pain Money Can Buy,* which *CMJ New Music Monthly,* in a feature article on the group, called "measurably more ambitious than the punk-inspired, straightforward pop that had made the trio a local favorite in Austin." The album's infectious lead single, "The Way," got plenty of air play, while the album's other songs, including "Warm Fuzzy Feeling," also have a lot to offer. While not too crazy about the "pop" categorization—they insist they're a rock 'n' roll band—Fastball is a hit. The trio includes native Austinite Joey Shuffield on drums and songwriters Miles Zuniga on guitar and Tony Scalzo on bass. Look for their 2002 greatest hits album, *Painting the Corners.*

The Flatlanders: The flatlands of West Texas have produced some of our state's most inspired musicians. Buddy Holly, Roy Orbison, and Waylon Jennings all hail from that sparse outpost of pure Texas. In 1972 Jimmie Dale Gilmore and fellow Lubbock singer/songwriters Joe Ely and Butch Hancock formed a little acoustic band called the Flatlanders and recorded *One Road More* in Nashville. When the album fizzled, so did the band. Little did they know the album was to become a collector's item. It was later rereleased under the more appropriate title *More a Legend Than a Band.* All three went on to form successful solo careers and got together once in a while for a show or two. Fans everywhere got a real treat when the Flatlanders reunited in 2001 for shows across the United States and over into Europe. The three have been performing gigs together ever since, and there's finally a new CD out: *Now Again.* They also make musical magic in records and performances as solo artists—so catch them, if you can.

Ruthie Foster: This Texas born and raised singer/songwriter has a voice that embodies the Lone Star State in so many ways.

A hybrid of blues, gospel, roots, and folk music flows like a backcountry stream whenever she opens her mouth in song. "If music that sounds as if it were naturally fermented from the bayous, cricks, and back porches of rural America is what you seek, then look no further than Ruthie Foster's *Runaway Soul.*" That's what the *Houston Press* had to say about her 2002 album, recorded at the Hit Shack in Austin. Since the release in 1997 of her first CD of original songs, *Full Circle,* Foster has earned a place in Austin's heart. She often tours with her manager/partner, Cyd Cassone, whose roots are with gospel and folk groups.

Kevin Fowler Band: This hot Austin band plays the real stuff: traditional country music that its leader says is for "pickup driving, Wrangler wearing, everyday working-class people like me." We'll wager there are plenty of Hilfiger-wearing fans out there, too, as his star is on the rise on the local music scene. The 2003 Austin Music Awards named the Amarillo-raised Fowler Austin Musician of the Year and Best Songwriter, and his band tied with Del Castillo for Best Album of the Year, with *High on the Hog.* Before that, Fowler hit it big with *Beer, Bait & Ammo,* his 2000 self-released CD. Y'all need to get your tickets to a Kevin Fowler show pretty darn fast. He plays big joints these days, and they do sell out.

Davíd Garza: "His future's so bright, he's gotta wear shades." That's what the *Austin American–Statesman* said, quoting Austin group Timbuk3 about this pop singer/songwriter following the release of his 1998 major-label debut *This Euphoria.* Garza, who attended UT on a classical guitar scholarship, has had several musical incarnations. As a member of the now infamous pop trio Twang-Twang-Shock-a-Boom, a group he started when he was just 17, Garza became a favorite on the college circuit and sold thousands of self-produced albums from the trunk of his car. His other musical incarnations,

Dah-Veed and the Love Beads, went a long way toward establishing this young man as a new voice in the music world. His music, rooted in quirky yet alluring rock/pop melodies and lyrics, is sort of early Beatles but freshened for the times. Born one of five children of Mexican-American parents from Texas's Rio Grande Valley, Garza was raised near Dallas. He came to Austin more than a decade ago to launch his musical career. It seems he's succeeding.

The Geezinslaws: This musical act has become one of Austin's favorite country music attractions. Sammy Allred (also famous in Austin for cohosting KVET–FM's popular morning radio show), Dewayne "Son" Smith, and a band of four won a 1993 Austin Music Award for Single of the Year for their rap crossover "Help I'm White and I Can't Get Down," on the hit CD *Feelin' Good, Gettin' Up, Gettin' Down.* With song titles like "Help I'm White," "Daddy Don't Live in Heaven (He's in Houston)," and "Five Dollar Fine for Whining," it's no wonder this group has a reputation for humor. Their musical talents are impressive, too, and have earned them touring dates across the country as well as in Europe and Canada. Sammy and Son, both native Austinites, have been performing together since high school—that would be close to 50 years by our estimate.

Johnny Gimble: Still one of the greatest living exponents of the Texas fiddle tradition, Gimble was a member of the legendary country swing band Bob Wills and the Texas Playboys back in the 1940s and 1950s and is featured on Wills's biggest hit, "Faded Love." In the late 1960s, Gimble moved to Nashville, where he spent many years as a much-in-demand studio musician before returning to Texas in 1978. Since then the fiddlemeister has recorded *Under the 'X' in Texas, Still Fiddling Around,* and other albums with his Texas Swing band. Named nine times as the Academy of Country Music Fiddler of the Year and recipient of several other CMA

and Grammy awards, Gimble is a favorite around the country as well as here in Austin. Gimble has played in various reunion bands with other ex-Playboys and also has been featured on many recordings with the likes of Willie Nelson and George Strait. Now almost 80 years old, the venerable fiddler hasn't lost his touch.

The Gourds: The music of Austin's rollickin', good-timin' country/rock band is just impossible to describe. No one can ever tell quite where it's going, but everyone knows they're having a grand time anyway. They've been making dang good music around these parts—and around the country—for some time now. This five-member group showcases the talents of Jimmy Smith, Kevin Russell, Claude Bernard, Keith Langford, and Max Johnston. Their CDs, *Dem's Good Beeble* and its calmer follow-up *Stadium Blitzer,* both earned excellent reviews and helped the Gourds establish themselves as a force on the national and international music scenes. But there are many more worth collecting. This band, famous for its infectious live performances, will have you singing and dancing along in no time.

Pat Green: In 1995, using money borrowed from friends and family, Green released his first self-published album of original songs, *Dancehall Dreamer.* At the time, Green was still a student at Texas Tech University in Lubbock. A lot has happened for this up-and-coming country artist since then. His second major-label album, 2003's *Wave on Wave,* which hit No. 1 on Country Music Television's Top 20 Countdown, and an appearance on *Austin City Limits* helped Green's well-deserved fame spread beyond the Texas border, and now he's packing auditoriums all over the place. This blond, boyish-looking singer/songwriter has taken a cue from the Texas music idols he listened to as a teen, including Willie Nelson and Waylon Jennings. His music is personal, and he's found success by doing things his own way.

Patty Griffin: *Billboard* magazine called Griffin's 2002 album, *1000 Kisses,* "the most magnetic album yet by one of the most compelling recording artists in popular music." Of course, her legions of fans here in Austin and across the country were already well aware of this singer/songwriter's amazing talents. Her two previous commercially released albums, *Living with Ghosts* and *Flaming Red,* had established Griffin as one of the most compelling performers of her generation. Her songs have been recorded by Linda Ronstadt, Bette Midler, the Dixie Chicks, and Emmylou Harris, to name a few. She tours alone or with the Chicks, Harris, and others. Born in Maine in 1964, Griffin has paved her own road to success. "I emptied my savings account of $55 when I was 16 and bought a used Honer guitar because I wanted to do what Rickie Lee Jones could do," she told *Billboard*. Her live album, *A Kiss in Time,* was released in 2003.

Sara Hickman: A superb live performer, Hickman is an acoustic rock 'n' roller who mixes folk sweetness with open-eyed humor—and not just a touch of mischievousness. This is another Austin artist who breaks the female singer/songwriter mold—due, perhaps, to the fact that she is inspired by all kinds of music. The *Dallas Times–Herald* called her live act "a cross between a stand-up comedy routine and group therapy, with great music as an added bonus." Hickman, who was raised in Houston and graduated from the High School for the Performing and Visual Arts, received her bachelor of arts degree in painting from North Texas State University in Denton. But music was her calling, so she headed to Dallas and the music scene there. Her first CD, *Equal Scary People,* released by an independent label, earned her a contract with Elektra Entertainment, which rereleased *Scary People* and its follow-up, *Shortstop.* She and Elektra later parted ways, and Hickman raised thousands of dollars from loyal fans to buy back an unreleased album, which she later

released as *Necessary Angels,* in tribute to the angels who helped her. Hickman's 1998 album, *Two Kinds of Laughter,* is filled with musical marvels. This outstanding performer also has a well-deserved reputation as a humanitarian who spends a good deal of her time performing in hospitals and working for social causes.

Tish Hinojosa: Born the last of 13 first-generation Mexican-American children, Leticia "Tish" Hinojosa grew up in San Antonio listening with one ear to the Spanish-language music her parents played on the radio and with the other ear to the popular American and British recording artists of the '60s. The result was a bilingual singer/songwriter with a remarkable ability to weave both languages into her songs. Her rich-textured music and poetic lyrics have earned her a place in Texas musical history. This guitar-playing songstress has received an Austin Music Award for Best Female Vocalist, Best Folk Artist, Best Latino Record, and Best Mexican American Folk, which demonstrates her ability to crisscross genres. All of her albums are gems, but our favorites include *Destiny's Gate, Dreaming from the Labyrinth/Soñar del Labertino,* and her 1996 children's recording *Cada Niño/Every Child.*

Eric Johnson: Guitar-player extraordinaire and Grammy Award winner Eric Johnson is one of those rare Austin musicians who actually was born here. This tall Texan won his Grammy in 1991 for Best Rock Instrumental Performance for his song "Cliffs of Dover" on the *Ah Via Musicom* album, which proved to the country that lyrics aren't an essential part of rock music. Of course Johnson also sings and writes, but guitar is his forte. In fact, Austin music legend Stevie Ray Vaughan once said Johnson "does incredible things with all kinds of guitars." Born in 1954, Johnson developed his style while working Texas's club circuit for years. In the 1970s he formed part of the Austin supergroup Electromagnets. (See our Close-up on the Music Biz in this chapter.) In 1986 Johnson recorded *Tones,* which got national airplay and turned into a successful commercial album. He won *Guitar Player* magazine's 1986 award for Best New Guitarist and in 1992 was named the magazine's Best Overall Guitarist. No stranger to the *Austin City Limits* stage, Johnson is a hometown favorite.

Jimmy LaFave: *Buffalo Returns to the Plains* is one of the best albums ever released by LaFave, whose talents as a singer, songwriter, and guitarist have catapulted him to the top ranks of Austin musicians. The Texas-born LaFave started his musical career in Stillwater, Oklahoma, where he joined a group that labeled its bluesy, folk rock style "red dirt' music. This poetic lyricist with a wonderfully raspy voice (that *Rolling Stone* magazine compared to a *Gasoline Alley*–era Rod Stewart) alternates easily between rock numbers and romantic ballads. LaFave discovered Austin in 1985, started out playing acoustic sets around town, and later added a band. While he has released four CDs for the Colorado-based Bohemia Beat Records, including 1997's *Road Novel,* it's still much more fun to see him perform live.

Los Lonely Boys: "Texican rock 'n' roll." That's how this young rock/blues/country/Mexican band describes its unique sound. This hit trio, which composes original songs in both English and Spanish, is made up of the Garza brothers: Henry (guitar), JoJo (bass), and Ringo (drums, of course). "See, we've got this musical burrito theory," Henry told the *Boston Globe* in 2003. "We're like the tortilla, and inside the tortilla we put the knowledge that we've gathered from all the greats—Stevie Ray Vaughan, Carlos Santana, B.B. King, Ritchie Valens, Willie Nelson, the Beatles, Chuck Berry, and Fats Domino. It goes on and on. We throw it all in this tortilla, roll it up, and feed it to the world. And, hopefully, everyone likes it and comes back for seconds." Willie Nelson is one fan who

In the old days Austin's downtown east-west streets were named for trees. Sixth Street was called Pecan Street, which is why you still see references to Pecan Street in business names or in our annual Old Pecan Street Festival. The street names were changed to numbers around 1897.

wanted extra helpings. He invited Los Boys to record their 2003 self-titled CD at his own Pedernales Studio in Austin.

James McMurtry: If that last name sounds familiar to all you fans of the books *Lonesome Dove, Terms of Endearment,* and other modern classics, you're on the right track. James is the son of novelist Larry McMurtry. This McMurtry, however, has taken a different writing path. As a singer/songwriter known for his intelligent, narrative-oriented rock 'n' roll songs, McMurtry tells stories his own way. Born in Fort Worth in 1962, McMurtry started out performing cover tunes in clubs around the country when he was still in his teens. Later, with a stack of his own songs, McMurtry entered the New Folk songwriting contest in the Kerrville Folk Festival and came away a winner. His CDs include *Too Long in the Wasteland, Candyland, Where'd You Hide the Body,* and *Saint Mary of the Woods.*

Abra Moore: This reed-thin beauty with the strikingly breathy voice scored a hit with her 1997 major-label debut on Arista/Austin, *Strangest Places,* which featured the catchy lead single "Four Leaf Clover." Before that came along, however, Moore had established herself as a voice to be reckoned with on the alternative pop scene. A founding member of the band Poi Dog Pondering, Moore released her critically acclaimed solo debut album, *Sing,* in 1995. Her passion on that album was described by one critic as that of an "angry young Bob Dylan." Born in 1969 in Mission Bay, California, Moore composed her first song

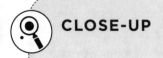
Two Voices

The Red Headed Stranger has turned gray before our eyes. The Guitar God will remain forever young in our minds. One became guru of Austin's explosive country rock movement. A decade later, the other put Austin blues on the map. Two Austin music icons. Two international superstars. Two musical styles. Two distinct stories.

Twenty-one years apart in age, Willie Nelson and Stevie Ray Vaughan were both on the run when they discovered Austin in the early 1970s. After a decade of rejection as a performer in Nashville, Willie took it as a sign when his Tennessee home burned to the ground in 1970. The 37-year-old musical outlaw decided to return to his native Texas. Here, at least, he wouldn't be tormented for refusing to bend with the winds of Nashville musical fashion—and certainly no one would bother him if he wanted to grow his hair long or tie a red bandana hippie-style around his forehead. Stevie, a scrawny 17-year-old when he hit town in 1972, was on the lam from the stifling prison of high school and the watchful eye of his parents in their working-class Dallas suburb of Oak Cliff.

Willie's and Stevie's timing couldn't have been better. Austin was perched to take the music world by storm. (See our Close-up on The Music Biz in this chapter.)

Willie's star would be the first to shine. Born April 30, 1933, in the tiny north central Texas town of Abbott, Willie and his sister, Bobbie (now a member of his band), learned music through mail-order courses taught by the grandparents who raised them after their parents divorced. When he wasn't picking cotton, the young Willie spent his childhood glued to the radio, listening to the Grand Ole Opry, New Orleans jazz, black blues from the South, Frank Sinatra, Big Band singers, and Western Swing, especially the sound pioneered by the famous Bob Wills. He became a member of a bohemian polka band at age 10 and as a young man worked selling encyclopedias, Bibles, and vacuum cleaners door to door. In an effort to get closer to the music he loved, Willie wheedled his way into his first job as a disc jockey in San Antonio, and later took his talents to Washington State. In 1956, while working as a DJ in Vancouver, Washington, he financed his first recording, "No Place for Me," and sold copies at a dollar each to his radio listeners.

The toddler born Stephen Ray Vaughan on October 3, 1954, meanwhile, was just learning to talk.

Willie returned to Texas in the late 1950s to work as a DJ and musical performer. While in Houston, he wrote some of his most memorable work, including "Night Life" and "Family Bible." He was so broke that he sold both songs for a mere $200, then set out to seek his fortune in Nashville.

In 1961 Patsy Cline recorded Willie's monumental song "Crazy" in Nashville and took it to No. 1 on the charts. Shortly thereafter, Faron Young scored a No. 1 hit with Willie's "Hello Walls." (Stevie, just seven years old back in Texas, had not yet picked up a guitar.)

While Willie attained extraordinary success as a country songwriter in Nashville and even made his own Grand Ole Opry debut in 1964, Nashville never warmed up to him as a performer. "The hobo funk of Jimmy Rodgers was gone from country music. It was polished, packaged and sold like any other form of commercial music . . ." wrote Austinite Jan Reid in his book *The Improbable Rise of Redneck Rock.* "All along the real Nashville rebel was Willie Nelson. He made enough money to sit back and be grateful, but he never toed the Nashville line." When his house burned, Willie and family decided to get out of Dodge.

Stevie, who by 1971 was a 16-year-old, guitar-playing radical with a blossoming drug habit, had determined that music would be his ticket out of Oak Cliff. His older brother, Jimmie, had proven it could be done when he'd split for Austin a couple of years earlier. Like Willie, Stevie and Jimmie Vaughan were raised on radio. But instead of Bob Wills, the Vaughan boys listened to blues artists such as Muddy Waters, Howlin' Wolf, and Bobby "Blue" Bland. When Jimmie broke his collarbone playing football at age 12, a family friend gave him a guitar to help him pass the time. Nine-year-old Stevie heard his big brother playing that guitar like he'd been born with it, and was instantly hooked.

As Stevie later explained, his was the classic, "Wow, me too," reaction of a younger brother. As it turned out, they were both naturals. The older Vaughan had the guitar and enough allowance money to amass a huge record collection that included the likes of B. B. King, Albert King, Lonnie Mack, Otis Rush, and Jimi Hendrix. Despite constant threats from his brother, Stevie couldn't keep his hands off either Jimmie's guitar or his record collection.

"I'd come home with a B. B. King album and try to learn all the leads and beginnings and ends, because I was so into the guitar," Jimmie told *Guitar Player* magazine in 1991. "And Stevie was there. He'd play the record over and over, trying to figure out, "What is he doing here?' . . . I'd put the guitar down and go in the other room, and he'd pick it up . . . We discovered how it worked together."

As the years passed, Jimmie went on to become a blues star in his own right. "Both matured into very distinct blues stylists," according to *Guitar Player.* "In a nutshell, Jimmie became the ultimate minimalist, a master of subtlety, economy, and simplicity; Stevie, three and a half years his junior, played every solo as if it were his last, as though he couldn't rest until he'd said his piece. And he had a lot to say."

Stevie had a lot of dues to pay before he would earn those accolades, however. In 1972, four months shy of graduation, Stevie dropped out of high school and headed for the Austin music oasis with his band, Blackbird. He was just 17. "For a Dallas kid bound and determined to play guitar for a living, moving to Austin was better than dying and going to heaven," wrote Joe Nick Patoski and Bill Crawford in their book, *Stevie Ray Vaughan: Caught in the Crossfire.* "Pursuing your art was the name of the game."

Pursuing his art is exactly what Willie had been doing since he had come home to Texas the year before. By August 12, 1972, when Willie first appeared on stage at the Armadillo World Headquarters, it was obvious he had something.

"Who in his right mind could have predicted that the same audience that got turned on by B. B. King and Jerry Garcia would also go nuts for Willie Nelson?" Gary Cartwright wrote in a 1998 *Texas Monthly* article. "This Abbott cotton picker had merged blues, rock and country into something altogether original and evocative." In 1973, the Nashville exile recorded his breakthrough album, *Shotgun Willie*.

Austin, meanwhile, became the epicenter of a trail-blazing movement in country music as other artists battered by the musical establishment found themselves drawn by the city's mounting musical charm. Alternately labeled progressive country, country rock, and redneck rock—because radio stations, the music press, and others didn't quite know what to make of this country music laced with rock and blues—the style created an enormous new class of country-fried hippies. (See our Music Biz Close-up in this chapter.)

In 1975, Willie recorded the album that would put him over the top: *The Red Headed Stranger*. Featuring the single "Blues Eyes Crying in the Rain," the album established Willie as a country music great. The following year RCA Records packaged previously issued material by Willie, Waylon Jennings, and others on the album *Wanted: The Outlaws*. It became the first country album to sell a million records, sparked a musical revolution, and finally branded Willie as a true outlaw. All the while Austin's "ropers and dopers" worshipped their hometown hero.

Stevie, who saw no use for Willie's outlaws, spent his early years in Austin getting high on the drugs that flowed freely and honing his considerable guitar skills at clubs such as the One Knite and the Soap Creek Saloon. The Soap Creek was "the place where he would develop the sophisticated yet hard-driving style that would become the basis of his legacy," wrote Patoski and Crawford.

In 1975, the year Willie accepted the first of his five Grammy Awards, a blues buff by the name of Clifford Antone decided to open a club to draw some of the country's blues greats to town. Austin finally had a home for the blues. At Antone's, Stevie would receive the thrill of his young life when his hero, Albert King, invited him on stage to play.

"Stevie worked the strings with such brute power and brash confidence, King was taken aback. It was like the young boy had just twisted the cap off the bottle that contained the secrets of all blues and poured every guitar lick known to man right out on stage," Patoski and Crawford wrote.

Stevie Ray went on to form Triple Threat Revue and then Double Trouble, the band that would skyrocket him to stardom. In 1983, the year the National Academy of Popular Music honored its first-ever country artist—Willie Nelson, of course—with a Lifetime Achievement Award, Epic Records released Double Trouble's first album *Texas Flood*. An international guitar hero was born. Double Trouble's second album, *Couldn't Stand the Weather,* went platinum and was followed by *Soul to Soul*. Double Trouble, fronted by the scrawny young man sporting his trademark flat-brimmed black hat and battered Stratocaster, landed prestigious international touring gigs, an appearance at Carnegie Hall, and legions of worshippers. Through it all, Stevie Ray remained a humble, gentle man who never failed to give credit to his musical mentors or his fellow artists. But Stevie Ray's addiction to drugs and alcohol was literally killing him. He collapsed while on tour in Europe.

Stevie Ray's commitment to beating his addictions and his willingness to share the secrets of his new-found sobriety with others are now legendary within the music industry. He checked himself into a London Clinic in 1986 and emerged from treatment a new man and an even better artist. He moved home to Dallas to renew ties with his mother while he cut a new album with Double Trouble. *In Step,* released in 1988, went platinum and earned the group a Grammy—one of six Stevie would win for his music.

In 1990 Stevie Ray and Jimmie finally got together musically for a Grammy-winning album, *Family Style.* It was released two weeks after Stevie Ray's tragic death. In the early morning hours of August 27, 1990, Stevie Ray Vaughan, blues player extraordinaire, was killed in a helicopter crash while returning to Chicago from an Alpine Valley concert in East Troy, Wisconsin. He was 35 years old.

For Willie, the 1990s brought a mixed bag of professional triumphs and personal hardships. His 33-year-old son, Billy (one of Willie's seven children), hanged himself in 1991. The tragedy came on the heels of Willie's major clash with the Internal Revenue Service and his arrest on a misdemeanor marijuana possession charge. In 1990, claiming he owed nearly $17 million in back taxes and interest, the IRS seized Nelson's bank accounts and property in Texas and around the country.

The crisis brought fans and friends rushing to his rescue—some donating change to a "Where There's a Willie, There's a Way" fund set up in Austin, other wealthier supporters going so far as to buy his ranch outside Austin and his treasured Pedernales Recording Studio, returning one to Willie outright and leasing the other to the artist for, well, a song. Willie himself made light of the calamity by marketing a CD called *Who'll Buy These Memories - The IRS Tapes* and eventually settled with the IRS for $9 million. The marijuana charge, meanwhile, was later dismissed. Nelson, who never has concealed the fact that he smokes pot (he once smoked a joint on the roof of President Carter's White House), has always publicly maintained the government has no business regulating an "herb."

Through it all, Willie has remained one of country music's most revered performers. In 1993 Willie broke out of a creative lull and released the exceptional album *Across the Borderline. Spirit,* his 1996 album, featured a whole new batch of originals. In 1998 Willie's latest CD, *Teatro,* made its debut. Among Willie's more than 100 albums are many that have gone multi-platinum, including his classics *Red Headed Stranger, Stardust,* and *Always on My Mind.* Over the years, Willie turned the Fourth of July into one of Texas' greatest musical celebrations with the continuation of the annual concerts he started in 1973.

The Farm Aid concerts Willie stages have raised thousands of dollars for farmers and called attention to the plight of family-owned farms across the country while the acting career he launched in 1980 with *Electric Horseman* is going strong. Just recently Willie launched the

Outlaw Music Channel in conjunction with the Kickapoo Indian tribe of Kansas. The cable channel, not yet available in Austin, showcases vintage country music programs, classic performances by Willie and other music greats and includes Indian dance and history programs. Today, his sprawling ranch outside Austin, known as Willie World, includes his home, recording studio, a golf course (for another of his passions), and even a Western movie set.

While Willie tours constantly, he always makes time for his hometown audience, and his Austin concerts invariably wind up as sold-out, standing-room-only events. With only a few chords of "Mamas Don't Let Your Babies Grow Up to Be Cowboys," "Angel Flying too Close to the Ground," "On the Road Again," and countless other classics, his shows turn into a sing-along. After all, every single person in the crowd knows the lyrics by heart.

"When I was working those cotton fields as a kid in Abbott, Texas, I had no idea the ride would be this long or this successful," Willie said in a published 1998 interview. "At that time, success was anywhere except in that cotton patch."

His face may be chiseled by the years, by the whiskey, and by a life spent on the road, but his music remains as fresh and as gut-wrenchingly powerful as it was when he started out more than four decades ago. He has definitely kept us satisfied.

Stevie Ray, the man who's been called the soul of Austin, lives on through his music and, as such, remains a beloved icon of this city. His phenomenal guitar talents continue to set the standard by which other Austin musicians are judged. A memorial statue of the late blues rocker, erected in 1993, stands by Town Lake as an eternal reminder of the gentle man and his far-out music. He is always on our minds.

when she was six and living in Hawaii. She studied piano while living in New York City and began playing small clubs while living in Europe. She switches between piano and guitar as easily as her passionate original songs shift from rock to blues to folk rhythms. Now a distinguished member of the Austin music scene, Moore won a whopping four Austin Music Awards in 1998, including Musician of the Year. She tours quite often but can still be found playing her favorite Austin venues.

Trish Murphy: A former member, with her brother, of the Trish & Darin group, one of Houston's successful club bands, Murphy went solo in 1995 and has since become one of Austin's most popular singer/songwriters. In this case, however, singer/songwriter doesn't always translate into folk music. Murphy, whose voice leans potently toward a Bonnie Raitt–style country, produces a fresh pop/rock sound that has managed to gain her an excellent following. Perhaps it's her guitar-playing technique that separates her from the typical female folk singer. "I thrash my guitar, I don't strum," she has said. Today she's as comfortable playing with a band as without. Born into a family of musicians (her father was a pop songwriter), Murphy learned to play guitar at age 11 by practicing on Bob Dylan and John Prine songs. She earned a psychology degree in Dallas, then turned down a job with the *Wall Street Journal* in Europe to pursue her music. Murphy arrived in Austin in 1996 with an acoustic EP of all-new songs and released her first solo CD, *Crooked Mile,* on her own label in 1997. "Running Out of Tomorrows,'" one of the cuts off *Crooked Mile,* features the line, "I'd rather go hungry than starve my dreams." Starving is not one of Murphy's concerns any longer.

Omar & the Howlers: This dynamite rockin' blues band is one of those quintessential Austin groups that just shouldn't be missed. Omar Dykes and the Howlers, bassist Paul Junior and drummer Steve Kilmer, have produced more than 15 albums (try *World Wide Open, Monkey Land,* or *The Screamin' Cat* for starters), any one of which will serve as a great introduction to this trio, but to see them perform live on stage is to delve delightfully into the Austin music scene. Dykes, a big man with an even bigger gravelly voice that howls, is simply a superb blues guitarist. Together, this trio electrifies the stage. Born in Bo Diddley's hometown of McComb, Mississippi, Dykes absorbed the blues as a youngster hanging out in McComb's black blues clubs. He developed his talents on the road and arrived in Austin in 1976 ready to wail. Omar & the Howlers soon carved a niche for themselves in the Austin club scene. They started recording in 1980 and haven't stopped yet. Interestingly, this trio has an incredible following overseas, especially in Scandinavia.

Overlord: It wasn't always the case, but Austin knows a great rap/hip-hop artist when it hears one, and way at the top of the heap is Overlord. This band seems to always win Best Hip-Hop Act at the Austin Music Awards (eight times already.) Overlord (a.k.a. Donnell Robinson) arrived on the Austin scene in 1987 and immediately set about teaching this city what hip-hop is all about. Now considered a pioneer of

the Austin rap scene, Overlord has paved the way for other young artists of the genre, including Megatron Bomb Squad and Mingo Fishtrap. *Billboard* magazine has called Overlord ". . . one of Austin Texas's best unsigned acts." Look for his albums *All Good Things, Back At Ya,* and 2003's *The Re-Up.*

Toni Price: Price is a rarity among Austin's divas: She neither writes her own songs nor plays an instrument. But can she sing! This blues/folk/country singer is so popular in Austin that she rarely has to leave to find a gig. She walked away from the Austin Music Awards with Album of the Year and Best Female Vocalist honors three years in a row—and captured yet another Best Female Vocalist award in 1998. Price is a terrific singer who "torches whatever she touches," said *Blues Access.* Price was born in Philadelphia in 1961 and raised in Nashville. But while other musicians were flocking to the Music City hoping for fame and fortune, Price was heading for Austin. She came for the South by Southwest music festival in 1989, fell in love with Austin, and has remained ever since, performing in major venues all over town. Price has been described as a "southern-fried Bonnie Raitt," a comparison we're sure she enjoys, since Price has been hooked on Raitt's music since discovering her nearly 20 years ago. Price released her first CD, *Swim Away,* in 1993. Since then, she's released *Hey, Sol Power, Low Down & Up,* and *Midnight Pumpkin,* the Austin Music Awards' Album of the Year in 2002.

Pushmonkey: This five-member rock band has been a staple on the Austin club circuit and a top contender for Rock Band of the Year in the Austin Music Awards since the 1990s. (They won the award in 2002 for Best Metal/Industrial Band). Not bad for a band that got its start with an ad in UT's *Daily Texan* student newspaper. "Valedictorian, band trombone geek, Kiss and Elvis fan looking for bad asses for rock and roll . . . ," read the ad placed by ℹ️ *For information related to just about any facet of the music business in the state, contact the Texas Music Office right here in Austin at (512) 463-6666. The music office is under the Governor's Office and its Web site is a goldmine of listings and information: www.governor.state.tx.us/music.*

Pat Fogarty, according to the band's bio. The band includes Darwin Keys (drums), Howie Behrens (guitar), Pat Fogarty (bass), Tony Park (lead vocals/trumpet), and Will Hoffman (guitar). Look for their latest, the self-produced *El Bitche'*. These singers/songwriters/rockers have got something.

Reckless Kelly: "Reckless Kelly, the most promising band to come out of Austin in the past year, could do for alternative-country what Nirvana did for grunge," the *Houston Chronicle* said in 1997. Austin definitely was—and still is—impressed with this new group, awarding the quintet several Austin Music Awards for Best New Band and Best Roots Rock Band, flocking to the group's spirited live shows, and snapping up their albums, which include *Millican* and *Under the Table and Above the Sun*. Formed in Oregon in 1995 and named for an Australian outlaw, just for fun, the group came to Austin in 1996 to share what it calls its "hick-rock" music. This smashing group comprises brothers Willie Braun (singer/songwriter) and Cody Braun (fiddle/mandolin) and most recently Jay Nazz (drums), David Abeyta (guitar), and Jimmy McFeeley (bass).

Bob Schneider: The driving force behind three distinctly unique and very popular Austin party bands, Schneider launched a solo career with the self-released CD *Lonelyland* a few years ago—and came in with a bang. He swept the 2000 Austin Music Awards with prizes for Musician of the Year, Band of the Year, Best Male

Vocals, Songwriter of the Year, and Best Funk Band. Then he topped those honors with an appearance on the *Tonight Show* with Jay Leno. He's won many more Austin Music Awards since then and continues to be a hot live act around the city—and the country. *Lonelyland,* meanwhile, remained at the top of Waterloo Records' list of best-selling Texas albums for eons. *The Galaxy Kings* is his newest release. With his solo career blossoming, and his continuing performances with the Scabs, this former leader of the Ugly Americans and Joe Rockhead has very little time to be lonely.

Charlie and Will Sexton: These two brothers, both of whom made major-label record deals when they were just teenagers and then spent more than a decade each developing separate musical identities, formed a musical family in 1997 when younger brother Will joined the Charlie Sexton Sextet. Guitar star Charlie, a child prodigy who was playing on stage with W. C. Clark when he was just 10 years old, recorded 1985's *Pictures for Pleasure* when he was 16 and then went on to play with David Bowie, Bob Dylan, Keith Richards, and Don Henley while barely out of his teens. He is a former member of the highly touted Arc Angels band, a blues-based hard-rocking band. The Charlie Sexton Sextet garnered critical success with its 1995 MCA Records release *Under the Wishing Tree.* Will, who, like his brother, is a guitar-playing singer/songwriter, formed the group Will & the Cannonballs as a teen and later recorded the album *Will and the Kill* in 1989. Will, whose musical collaborations keep him hopping, returned to his own work after a while and is no longer with the Sextet. These brothers are great performers and worth waiting for.

South Austin Jug Band: Okay, this quintet lives in South Austin, so that part of the name makes sense. But jug band when there's no "jug" in the band? Come to find out, that part comes from the Muppets movie, *Emmett Otter's Jug-Band Christmas.* Now that we've settled the name, how about the music that has Austin fans flocking to their shows? We'll just let them describe it: "Call the music . . . whatever you like: bluegrass or newgrass, neo-jug, acoustic country-folk, Texas roots unplugged, swinging Lone Star beatnik country, or anything else that strikes you." That comes from their own Web site. Their 2003 CD is titled *South Austin Jug Band*—of course.

Darden Smith: UT alumnus Darden Smith is a singer/songwriter who, like Lyle Lovett, had a hard time finding his niche. For a while record executives put him on country music labels as one of those new country artists, but Smith's sound was too urbane, the lyrics too complex, to attract a large country following. His music was country in name only. Then in 1989 Smith recorded the collaborative album *Evidence* with English singer/songwriter Boo Hewerdine. The disc earned some excellent critical reviews and helped establish Smith as a pop artist. Recording on pop labels for the past few years, Smith seems to have found his groove. His sound strongly reflects his Austin folk scene roots—more acoustic rock and ballads—in which the story is the heart of it all. Now in his mid-30s, Smith has perfected his on-stage act and possesses an excellent singing voice belting out his own, often bittersweet lyrics like only a songwriter could. *Deep Fantastic Blue* was released on Plump Records in 1996. Look also for *Trouble No More* on Columbia Records and others, including Smith's first album, *Native Soil.*

Jimmie Vaughan: Vaughan was a teenage rock star in Dallas when the Beatles first ruled the world, opened for Jimi Hendrix in Houston, and partied with Janis Joplin just about everywhere else—all before he was 20. Since those days, Vaughan has managed to become a virtual deity—"a living legend with a guitar style so deep that it defies description," according to *Guitar Player* magazine. Jimmie, older brother and mentor to late blues star Stevie Ray (read about Stevie Ray in our Close-up in this chapter), has been devoting himself full time to the blues since he dropped out of his Dallas high school in the mid-1960s and shortly thereafter headed for Austin. He formed the Fabulous Thunderbirds nearly 25 years ago, signed on as the house band for a new Austin blues club called Antone's, and headed straight for the history books. Vaughan has toured the world with ZZ Top, the Rolling Stones, B. B. King, and Eric Clapton. *Family Style,* an album he recorded with Stevie Ray shortly before the younger Vaughan's death in 1990, received rave reviews, won a Grammy Award for Best Contemporary Blues Recording, went platinum, and continues to be a coveted disc for blues fans everywhere. Vaughan has released *Strange Pleasure, Out There,* and the 2002 Grammy Award-winning *Do You Get the Blues?* If you happen to be in town when Vaughan is performing, your trip is made.

Don Walser: Nicknamed the "Pavarotti of the Plains," Don Walser possesses a talent as big as Texas. This country singer, who once opened for a kid named Buddy Holly, can yodel a cowboy tune like none other. Unfortunately for all of us, he retired in 2003, winding up a performing career that spanned 50 years. We just didn't have the heart to drop him from our list. You can still hear him on CD. Try *Down at the Sky-Vue Drive-In,* for one.

Vallejo: Perennial hometown favorites and Band of the Year and Best Rock Band at the 2001 Austin Music Awards, Vallejo is a rock band with a Latin beat. Brothers A. J., Alejandro, and Omar Vallejo, raised in Texas and Alabama by Mexican/Guatemalan–descended parents, team up with Diego Simmons and Heath Clark to produce a full-bodied, cross-cultural sound that makes them a top club draw. In 2002 the *Austin Chronicle* had this to say about Vallejo's new album: "With their latest, the independently released *Stereo,* the Vallejo crew has finally tipped the bottle all the way back and ingested the worm at the bottom."

Kelly Willis: Country crooner and darling of the Austin club circuit, Willis is one of those performers who make your jaw drop the minute she hits her first note. First, that powerful voice of hers comes charging at you like a bull on wings. Then you realize this young woman is mixing up some of the best traditional country sounds with a perfect dose of rock 'n' roll. Born in Lawton, Oklahoma, Kelly lived in North Carolina and then Virginia as a youngster. She was barely 18 when she convinced her parents to let her come to Austin with her rockabilly act Kelly and the Fireballs. When that broke up, Kelly went out on her own. In 1999 Willis signed a deal with Rykodisc and released *What I Deserve,* earning her rave reviews and the best-selling CD of her career up to then. Her second Rykodisc album, *Easy,* came out in 2002. Look also for her earlier albums, *Bang, Bang* and *Fading Fast.*

THE STAGES

Janis Joplin overcame her insecurities and launched her singing career in the early 1960s in an Austin beer joint. George Strait was a relative unknown when he first started singing around town. Stevie Ray Vaughan was just another teenager with a used guitar and a dream when he found a stage here. Austin's own Willie Nelson is a regular on our club and music hall scene. While not every artist who performs on an Austin stage goes on to fame and fortune, many of the hottest acts on the nation's club scene today got their start on an Austin stage.

From dark, intimate clubs to big concert halls to superb outdoor venues, Austin's club scene swings seven nights a week, bringing a wide array of live music from around Austin and around the country. Few other cities in the nation come close to Austin in the number of live acts performed on stage every night.

If Austin is the Live Music Capital of the World, then downtown is the Live Music Capital of Austin. The lively strip known simply as Sixth Street, on East Sixth between Congress Avenue and Interstate 35, touts nearly a score of live music venues, plus restaurants, comedy clubs, T-shirt shops, and tattoo parlors. (See our Close-up in the Nightlife chapter.) Because of its national reputation, Sixth Street often gives tourists their first taste of Austin's music scene, but downtown also has the popular Warehouse District, a growing list of venues on Red River Street just off Sixth, and some good clubs on Congress Avenue. While some of the clubs and restaurants that line East Sixth present hot acts and fascinating up-and-comers, this street also offers plenty of cover bands, DJs, and unproven performers. So experience the awesome Sixth Street scene, but check out downtown's other great clubs and music halls, as well as those scattered around Austin.

Of course, what would Austin be without music by the side of the lake? Several spots are known for presenting great live bands—some that cover popular songs and old favorites and others doing original stuff. While the places listed here under The Shore are mainly known as restaurants, we couldn't miss out on telling you about them in this section. Austin music and the lakes are meant to be together like a singer and a guitar.

While there are just too many clubs around Austin to list them all, we've provided you with information about some of Austin's favorites, as well as some of our own. For news about who's playng where, check the listings in the *Austin Chronicle* and the *Austin American–Statesman.* An encyclopedic list of clubs, venues, and events can be found on the Governor of Texas Web site: www.governor.state.tx.us/music.

We're not providing specific information on cover charges, because these can vary greatly, depending on the night of the week, the artist on stage, or, it seems, the alignment of the stars in the heavens. Hours vary, too, so check with the club. Some clubs admit minors; many don't. Again, check with the club. The drinking age in Texas is 21. Most clubs sell tickets at the door only. We've noted where you can go or call to purchase advance tickets when they're available.

Around Town

Antone's
213 West Fifth Street
(512) 263–4146,
(512) 469–SHOW (box office)
www.antones.net

If there's one existing local club practically the whole world has heard of, it's Antone's, Austin's home of the blues. Since 1975 this club, now in its fourth Austin location, has featured some of Austin's best blues performers as well as top blues artists from around the country. (See our History of the Music Scene in this chapter.) Since management of the club was taken over in 2003 by Tim O'Connor's Direct Events (see the next listing), Antone's lineup has expanded to include rock, pop, and country acts also. This Austin institution swings with live music almost every night of the week, offering a continuous parade of some of the best live music from Austin and around the country. Each year Antone's holds an anniversary week that draws some of the top names in blues. Yet Antone's continues its tradition of presenting some of Austin's most promising up-and-comers. Antone's also operates a record store (see our listing in this chapter) as well as a quality record label.

Clifford Antone opened his first club on Sixth Street on July 15, 1975. Its fourth Austin location opened at the corner of Fifth and Lavaca Streets downtown in 1997. Despite its renown, Antone's has had a long history of financial and legal problems, and Antone twice served prison terms on drug convictions. Although the club has been owned since 1985 by Clifford's sister, Susan Antone, he remains the heart and soul behind this operation. In fact, he is the recipient of the National Blues Foundation's "Lifetime Achievement Award" for his contributions to the genre.

Austin Music Hall
208 Nueces Street
(512) 263–4146,
(512) 469–SHOW (box office)
www.austinmusichall.com

One of Austin's premier venues for national touring shows, the Austin Music Hall's contribution to the local music scene is enormous. Outstanding performing artists from around the country have performed at this 2,400-seat venue, including Bruce Springsteen, the Neville Brothers, Sarah McLachlan, and John Fogerty. This hall, which is indeed a big hall with folding chairs for seats, also hosts the annual Austin Music Awards and other South by Southwest events, the annual Armadillo Christmas Bazaar, as well as a number of benefit events throughout the year. It's also a great place for private parties. The Music Hall has been operated since 1994 by Austinite Tim O'Connor's Direct Events, Inc., which also operates La Zona Rosa, the Backyard, and now Antone's (see listings in this chapter). O'Connor's experience in the Austin club scene goes back more than three decades, and it shows in the way he operates these clubs. O'Connor opened a club called Castle Creek in the early 1970s, which quickly gained a reputation for great touring shows. Later O'Connor opened the Austin Opera House, which often featured partner Willie Nelson as a performer. Direct Events also produces Willie Nelson's wildly popular annual Fourth of July Picnic, most recently in Luckenbach.

The Backyard
13101 West U.S. 71
(512) 263–4146,
(512) 469–SHOW (box office)
www.thebackyard.net

This delightful open-air venue surrounded by 500-year-old oak trees has become an

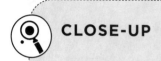

The Music Biz: Cold Beer and Hot Tunes

Austin luminary Eddie Wilson responds matter-of-factly when asked what launched the spectacular music scene we know today. "Cold beer and cheap pot," he says with a laugh. Wilson, however, humbly neglects to mention his own contributions to Austin's rise as a music mecca. As a founder of the renowned Armadillo World Headquarters in 1970, Wilson helped catapult Austin to the big time.

Of course, the collective talent of the hundreds of artists who have illuminated Austin stages over these many years goes without saying. But Wilson points out, too, that the sizable number of sofas offered to musicians during the '60s and '70s allowed brother and sister performers to find, if not a home, at least a place to bed down.

We're getting way ahead of ourselves, though. Austin's music history goes back much further than the 1960s—all the way back to the dance hall pickers, cowboy crooners, and black blues belters who were making music around Austin for eons. Some performed as far back as the 1800s and would continue to fill our city with their own sound of music despite the various musical invasions that followed.

Some say Austin's modern music scene started with Travis County Beer License No. 01, issued to one Kenneth Threadgill on December 6, 1933. Threadgill, a singer and yodeler who sold gasoline from the front side of the Gulf station he operated and bootleg whiskey out the back, stood in line all night to be the first to get a beer license after the county voted to go "wet" following Prohibition. Over the years, this little station evolved into a beer joint and haven for music makers. By the early 1960s the ongoing hootenanny at Threadgill's was attracting University of Texas "folkie" musicians, including a freshman named Janis Joplin, who gathered for the regular Wednesday night jam sessions. "The folkie invasion of Threadgill's was a brave move given the general attitude about hippies, beatniks, and long-haired men among the rednecks of the era," Wilson wrote in his book *Threadgill's: The Cookbook*. (As things turned out, however, Threadgill's was just the test kitchen for this bizarre social concoction. A decade later, the Armadillo would perfect the recipe when it became a melting pot of blue-haired grannies, bikers, rednecks, and hippies.) Threadgill's proved that the music, not the costume, mattered most.

As the '60s stoked up, Joplin joined up with a few budding UT musicians to form the Waller Creek Boys, a folk group that could play just about any kind of music the Threadgill's crowd demanded: blues, country, bluegrass, whatever. Other musicians soon began arriving in Austin, and finding their way to Threadgill's (now a popular restaurant and music spot—see our Restaurants chapter). Meanwhile, a few joints near UT, including the Jade Room and the New Orleans Club, were making names for themselves by offering Austin's flower children the kind of live music that appealed to them.

UT's hippies may have invaded Austin, but this was still TEXAS as sure as shootin', and no amount of folk, blues, or rock 'n' roll could wean this town off good old country and western music. In 1964, a young Austinite fresh from service in the Army established a little roadhouse on the southern outskirts of town. The Broken Spoke, as James White would call his restaurant and club, would become a hub for some of the best country bands in Austin and around the country—and remains so to this day.

By 1965 Joplin had split for San Francisco (being voted the ugliest "male" on campus perhaps hastened the move) and Austin was ripe for a band that could turn on the masses. In the fall of '65 a band called the 13th Floor Elevators burst on the scene at a Jade Room performance. Fronted by a young, good-looking singer/guitarist named Roky Erickson, the Elevators would go on to record two magical albums, break into the top 40, and carve a lasting place for themselves in the collective consciousness of Austin music disciples. (Unfortunately, before the Elevators' genius could spread, Erickson was arrested in 1969 for possession of one joint of marijuana, pleaded insane to avoid prison and was sent to a mental hospital, where he was given shock treatments and heavy-duty drugs. He was never quite the same again, although he did record the 1995 album *All That May Do My Rhyme.*)

Despite Austin's own psychedelic sounds, the blossoming of the counterculture revolution, and the drugs that fueled the movement, Austin at that time was still firmly rooted in Bible Belt mores and morality. By the fall of 1967 "there wasn't a hint of the now-bustling music biz in our town," Spencer Perskin, a member of another notable Austin band of the time, Shiva's Headband, wrote in the *Austin Chronicle* in 1993. "To perform only original material was considered almost outrageous by our musician friends, and there was zero tolerance for us at the few bars around town (serving beer-only at the time). Only the opening of the Vulcan Gas Company gave us the foothold we would need."

The Vulcan Gas Company, Austin's first musical haunt for hippies, opened in 1967 at 400 Congress Avenue, just 10 blocks from the state capitol. "The Vulcan presented a mixed bag of music on its small stage, embellishing the sounds with the first and most creative light show in the state," wrote Joe Nick Patoski and Bill Crawford in the book *Stevie Ray Vaughan: Caught in the Crossfire.* The 13th Floor Elevators, Shiva's Headband, and another esteemed Austin band called the Conqueroo all found a home at the Vulcan, while "groundbreaking acts such as the Velvet Underground, Moby Grape, and the Fugs would have bypassed the entire state of Texas if not for the Vulcan," according to Patoski and Crawford. The experiment lasted only three years. The Vulcan closed in 1970. As the new decade dawned, however, Austin was set to explode onto the national music stage.

On August 1, 1970, Armadillo World Headquarters opened as a counterculture concert hall. Wilson, a former regular at Threadgill's who was managing Shiva's Headband, says the inspiration for creating the Armadillo came to him one night after an evening at a South Austin honky-tonk called the Cactus Cafe. Responding to the call of nature, Wilson slipped outside to attend to business. That's when he saw it: the big, abandoned National Guard Armory, just sitting there awaiting its future. It took a whole group of people to get the Armadillo to fly, including a graphic artist by the name of Jim Franklin, who created the image of the nine-banded armadillo on ingenious posters that are now collectibles. Wilson took charge as majordomo.

"We wanted to create an entertainment facility that was different from anything Austin had ever seen," Wilson told the *Insiders' Guide*. Indeed. Despite early wobblings, the Armadillo succeeded in drawing throngs of fans desperate to hear top touring bands and even more of the original music that was by then the "in" thing. As the music grew better and better and the number of fans multiplied, talented musicians from around the country started appearing at the Armadillo. Other entrepreneurs riding the coattails of the Armadillo's success began opening clubs all over town.

"Through the interest of a curious national press and word-of-mouth communication by touring musicians, Austin gained almost overnight a reputation as one of the most exciting centers of music activity in the country," Austinite Jan Reid wrote in his book *The Improbable Rise of Redneck Rock*.

Still, the list of ingredients that went into Austin's magical musical brew was far from complete. Willie Nelson's return to his native Texas led the way for a rising tide of young musicians whose music was labeled progressive country, country rock, and redneck rock (see our Close-up on Nelson and Stevie Ray Vaughan in this chapter). A young country rock group led by Marcia Ball called Freda and the Firedogs catered to this new breed of music listeners. San Antonio native Doug Sahm, who'd found musical success on the West Coast, came home to Texas while Jerry Jeff Walker also settled in. Michael Murphey released his album *Cosmic Cowboy Souvenirs* in 1973, which unwittingly gave a name to the musical rebels. With the arrival of these and other "cosmic cowboys," Austin burst on the national scene as the hub of the redneck rock movement.

Suddenly, hippies and rednecks found themselves bonded by a common sound, rock- and blues-infused country and western music. Local radio station KOKE–FM began exalting the new sound, calling it "progressive country." The pickup truck became the preferred mode of transportation, while no self-respecting, long-haired, cowboy-hatted "goat roper" would be caught dead drinking anything but a longneck beer.

"This was a direct reversal of the previous decade's attitudes, when the city's young pacesetters, rebelliously rejecting haircuts while embracing rock, folk, and blues, would have preferred to drink muddy water and sleep in a hollow log rather than betray affinity with their hillbilly cousins," Clifford Endres wrote in his book, *Austin City Limits*.

Before long, however, Willie was on to his next incarnation as a musical outlaw and Austin moved on to new sounds.

The time had come for Austin's music scene to go national. With Willie Nelson as a featured act, Austin's own country music program, *Austin City Limits*, hit the airwaves in the spring of 1975. The program, still aired on Public Broadcasting Stations around the country, features the best-known acts in music today. In its nearly quarter-century of existence, ACL has taken its place among the city's music legends (see our Media chapter).

The cosmic cowboys may have dominated the music scene for a good spell during the 1970s, but theirs wasn't the only sound in town. Down at the Broken Spoke, fans of traditional country music found a refuge away from the city's invading hippies. (Austin lore has it that boys with hair longer than their date's were refused service at the Spoke during these years.)

On other stages, a band that included a young guitarist by the name of Eric Johnson (see the listing in the Catch 'em If You Can section in this chapter) blasted out a radically different tune. The Electromagnets, as the quartet called itself, "generated fan reaction proportional to the volume of its music, gathering an intense, almost worshipful, fan base that seemed to expand with each live date," *Austin American–Statesman* music critic Michael Point wrote in an 1998 article celebrating the reissue of the Electromagnets self-titled album. "Rarely singing and even more rarely acknowledging commercial sensibilities of any sort, the band . . . (dazzled) its fans while dazing and confusing the 'cosmic cowboy' contingent who never knew what hit them," Point wrote. As it goes in the music biz, however, the band broke up in 1977, leaving behind just the one album for adoring fans.

A group of West Texas singer/songwriters also migrated to Austin during the 1970s. Joe Ely, Butch Hancock, and Jimmie Dale Gilmore (see them collectively as the Flatlanders in the Catch 'em listings in this chapter) found Austin audiences receptive to the original music they wanted to make—and stayed to make a contribution. So did a teenage Dallas transplant named Jimmie Vaughan. Vaughan's group, Storm, would be just the beginning of the blues tradition Vaughan would help to inspire in his new hometown. Austin's musical tree, it appeared, was destined to produce many different branches.

Yet another Austinite geared up in the '70s to take his place in music history. Clifford Antone, a Port Arthur, Texas, native of Lebanese descent, came to Austin at age 19 to run the family gourmet grocery business. In 1973 the tiny back room of Antone's Imports became the unofficial launching pad for a group of blues artists that included Jimmie Vaughan's little brother, Stevie Ray. Antone opened his first club on Sixth Street on July 15, 1975, featuring such blues greats as Muddy Waters, Albert King, and Sunnyland Slim—in just its first year. Antone's is credited with helping to develop a blues tradition in Austin where none existed before, at least not in the predominantly white area west of I-35.

Antone's has provided a home, and a source of inspiration, for up-and-coming blues artists for almost 25 years. Another of Jimmie Vaughan's bands, The Fabulous Thunderbirds, got its start at Antone's and became the house band when its members were in their 20s. Stevie Ray perfected his talents at Antone's, and went on to be an international superstar. (See the Two Voices Close-up in this chapter.)

By the time Armadillo World Headquarters closed in 1980, Austin's status as a "mecca for musical mavericks" had solidified. And there was still more to come.

A star among Austin's rebels during this time was a lanky Texan by the name of Townes Van Zandt. Born in 1944 to a prominent Fort Worth oil family, Van Zandt had rejected the easy life to become a singer/songwriter. His poetic lyrics would inspire Austin's Steve Earle to proclaim, "Townes Van Zandt is the best songwriter in the whole world, and I'll stand on Bob Dylan's coffee table in my cowboy boots and say that." The writer of such country hits as "Pancho and Lefty," recorded by Willie Nelson and Merle Haggard, and Emmylou Harris's "If I Needed You," Van Zandt's work would influence a generation of Texas songwriters. Despite his near-constant struggles with alcohol, his own recording career spanned more than a quarter of a century from 1968's *For the Sake of the Song* (now sold as *First Album*) until 1994's *No Deeper Blue*. During his many years living and performing in Austin, Van Zandt became one of our city's most revered musicians—and a magnet for other musical storytellers. In fact, it's been said that he helped establish the "couch circuit" for drifting musicians. "I really, honestly believe Townes was one of the main reasons Austin received a reputation for quality," Jimmie Dale Gilmore told the *Austin American–Statesman* after Van Zandt's death, at age 52, in 1997. Van Zandt had died of a heart attack while recovering from hip surgery in Tennessee. His music lives on, however, and there have been many posthumous releases of his work.

While Austin's live music scene went ballistic in the '70s, the city's hottest acts continued to record elsewhere, according to Casey Monahan, director of the Texas Music Office. "Most of the artists that had major label money did not record in Austin. Most opted to go to wherever their producer wanted to record, usually L.A. or Nashville," Monahan told the *Insiders' Guide*. By the mid-1980s, however, Austin was singing a new tune, as more and more artists found they could record albums right here at home. Today, Monahan says, Austin claims more than 130 recording studios, including about two dozen that are competitive with Nashville and Los Angeles. Among the elite is Willie Nelson's Pedernales Studios, the only studio launched by an artist, as well as other top-notch studios operated by entrepreneurs, including Cedar Creek Recording, Austin Recording Studios, and Arlyn Studio.

The Sixth Street music scene, which had taken root in the 1970s, fired up in the 1980s and has since become a dominant district for live music and dancing. Well-established Sixth Street hangouts like Maggie Mae's, saw the once-tranquil strip turn into a frenzy of clubs turning out live music seven nights a week and now the greater downtown area packs in more outstanding live music than anyone could ever experience in a short visit here. Many of Austin's most notable live clubs, including Antone's, La Zona Rosa, Hole in the Wall, and the Continental Club can all be found in greater downtown. Wilson himself went on to revive the old Threadgill's saloon, turning it into one of Austin's most illustrious restaurants (featuring live music, of course). Threadgill's now touts two Austin locations, including one near the spot of the former Armadillo and appropriately named Threadgill's World Headquarters (see our Restaurants chapter).

Austin's star on the world stage continues to rise as more and more young artists flock to The Live Musical Capital of the World yearning to make a name for themselves. In what's been called "the second coming of the outlaw attitude," this century has witnessed a stunning national revival in Texas's unique brand of country music. Hot, hot, hot among the cities showcasing the talents of hometown "Texas Music" artists is Austin. Pat Green, Kevin Fowler, and other young artists are just the latest links in Austin's talent-heavy outlaw chain. Of course the Austin beat goes on in so many other musical realms as well. As Wilson told us, "There are many more quality musicians and 10 times more music in Austin today than there was during the days of the Armadillo."

Indeed.

Austin favorite since it opened in 1993 on a stretch of highway just west of town. Jonny Lang, Bonnie Raitt, Gypsy Kings, the Indigo Girls, Willie Nelson, the Allman Brothers, and many, many more national touring shows favor the Backyard during its March to November season. The Backyard amphitheater offers both seated concerts for about 2,400 people and more laid-back affairs in which people bring blankets to sit on. This venue is also popular for a number of family-oriented musical events, including a Father's Day show, giant Easter egg hunt, and the Bee Cave Chili Cookoff.

This venue is operated by Tim O'Connor's Direct Events, Inc. For really popular shows, get your tickets early, as these events sell out fast. So do the great barbeque sandwiches and wraps on sale along with the drinks during the shows.

Broken Spoke
3201 South Lamar Boulevard
(512) 442-6189

Willie Nelson calls the Broken Spoke his favorite watering hole. *Texas Highways* magazine has called it the Best Honky-Tonk in Texas, while *Entertainment Weekly* has said it's the best country dance hall in the country. The Broken Spoke has appeared in a host of movies, documentaries, and commercials (including one for Foster's beer that made the Spoke a household name in Australia). Since 1964 the Broken Spoke has been dishing up a steady stream of the best country music Austin has to offer— along with a full menu of down-home Texas cookin'. Alvin Crow, Asleep at the Wheel, Don Walser, Willie Nelson, the Derailers, and the Geezinslaws are some of the local luminaries that make regular appearances here. Bob Wills and the Texas Playboys, George Strait, Tex Ritter, Ernest Tubb, and other country stars past and present have become part of the Spoke's big family.

The hub of this operation is James M. White. Just 25 years old and fresh out of the Army, White spied a patch of land adorned by a big live oak tree on the southern outskirts of Austin, just a couple

miles from his boyhood home. On November 10, 1964, he opened the Broken Spoke. The dance hall was added a year later. Since then, White and his wife, Annetta, have raised two daughters and a whole generation of country music fans. White even wrote his own theme song, "Broken Spoke Legend." Crow recorded it on his *Pure Country* album on the Broken Spoke's own record label. Whether you come to the Broken Spoke to eat, to dance, or just listen to the music, be sure to allow time to visit the two rooms packed with country music memorabilia and mementos from the music stars and film celebrities who've made the Broken Spoke an Austin landmark. This ain't no fancy dancer. The low ceiling leaks in places (though White has devised his own intricate system to divert the runoff), and the stage is just a small rise above the dance floor. But, hey, nobody comes to the Spoke because they've seen it in *Architectural Digest*. They come because it's a good-timin', down-home Texas tradition.

Cactus Cafe
Texas Union Building
24th and Guadalupe Streets
(512) 475-6515
www.utexas.edu/student/txunion/ae/cactus

This excellent club in the Student Union on the University of Texas campus has been serving up live music for more than 70 years. Opened in 1933 as the Chuck Wagon, the club was among Austin's first hippie hangouts in the 1960s, catering to an emerging group of "folkie" musicians that included a young Janis Joplin. After going through a few names, the club was renamed the Cactus Cafe in 1977 but continues to be one of Austin's prime venues for singer/songwriters presenting acoustic performances. You can also find some bluegrass, swing, jazz, and an occasional rock act here. This nonsmoking venue is a popular daytime hangout for UT students, faculty, and staff. Evening shows draw both students and members of the public.

Carousel Lounge
1110 East 52nd Street
(512) 452-6790

Located just east of I-35, the Carousel Lounge has been serving up drinks and music since 1963 when Cecil and Myrtle Meier opened the place and decorated it with a whimsical circus decor. Now operated by their daughter, Nicki Mebane, the Carousel features an eclectic range of live music—usually swing, jazz, big band, country, rock, or lounge acts—Tuesday through Sunday nights. The lounge looks much as it did a quarter century ago, with those miniature jukeboxes (not in service) over the tables, an aqua-colored padded bar, and a big jukebox that's loaded with lots of old music. Huge circus-theme murals adorn both walls and the backstage area.

The Carousel serves beer and wine only but features a good list of microbrewed and imported beers. Additionally, this is a brown bag bar, meaning patrons can bring their own hard liquor and then order the soft drink and ice that goes with it. This treasured Austin landmark is now being discovered by a whole new generation of music fans.

Cedar Street Courtyard
208 West Fourth Street
(512) 495-9669

Jazz under the trees. Since Cedar Street opened in 1994, this lovely outdoor venue loaded with live oak trees has gained a reputation for featuring excellent local jazz musicians as well as acts from around the country. Tucked between two buildings a few steps down from sidewalk level in the Warehouse District, this intimate setting is the perfect place for live music. There also are indoor bars along the sides, so the music just moves inside when it rains. Malaga, a tapas restaurant and wine bar, is also here (see our Restaurants chapter).

Continental Club
1315 South Congress Avenue
(512) 441-2444
www.continentalclub.com

Perhaps it's the perennial odor of day-old beer and stale cigarettes that lends this club its primo atmosphere. More likely, it's the long, long list of top Austin acts that have earned their musical wings at the Continental Club over the years that gives it such an excellent reputation among Austin's music lovers. There's generally always somebody worth seeing within these dark walls.

Elephant Room
315 Congress Avenue
(512) 473-2279
www.arthive.net/elephant

Voted Best Jazz Bar in Austin seven years in a row by the Clarksville Jazz Festival, the Elephant Room presents a wide variety of live jazz, including Latin jazz, fusion, traditional, and funk. This cozy basement club, opened in 1991, presents an excellent assortment of Austin bands as well as bands from around the country. Audiences are treated to the cool sounds of live jazz seven nights a week. (Yes, some of the artists and members of the audience do don sunglasses—it's that cool.) The Elephant Room also features happy hour shows Tuesday through Friday from 6:00 to 8:00 P.M. You'll find this club below Kyoto's Restaurant on Congress (see our Restaurants chapter).

Emo's
603 Red River Street
(512) 477-3667
www.emosaustin.com

This newer Austin club just off Sixth Street is drawing oodles of fans for its eclectic mix of underground music. With two stages, one inside and one outside, there always seems to be an act worth seeing—sometimes two at once. If it's punk/indie/

electronica/garage/emo stuff you like, Emo's is your place. They also sport a beer garden.

Frank Erwin Center
1701 Red River Street
(512) 471-7744,
(512) 477-6060 (Texas box office)
www.uterwincenter.com

Austin's largest venue for national touring musicians is also home to University of Texas basketball as well as Disney on Ice shows, circuses, and scores of other events throughout the year. When it comes to music, however, there just isn't any space in Austin as large or as comfortable for the crowds that have turned out to see such top acts as Elton John, Garth Brooks, Kiss, Madonna, Julio Iglesias, Van Halen, Paul Simon, Crosby, Stills and Nash, and many more world-class musical performers, including, of course, many Austin music legends. The Erwin Center also hosts plenty of classical musical performers. Depending on the stage setup, the Erwin Center can hold anywhere from 4,000 to 18,000 fans. Performances are announced well in advance in the local press. The Erwin Center was built in 1977 and named in 1981 for the beloved University of Texas regent and chairman who had been crucial in getting this popular UT facility built.

Hanovers Draught House
108 East Main Street, Pflugerville
(512) 670-9617
www.hanovers.net

The suburbs have grown and grown around historic downtown Pflugerville, once a small, quiet Central Texas town (see our Relocation chapter), but not only has new life come to the fields surrounding downtown, there also has been new life for some of the town's old buildings. Once a saloon, then a hardware store, this 1899 stone building is alive again with the sounds of Texas, as famed artists like Joe Ely and Don Walser perform here. The bar features 76 types of beer. In addition to the music stage, there is a back room with pool tables and dart boards, plus a large outdoor beer garden in the back that can seat up to 1,000. For nourishment, there is barbecue, of course.

Hill's Cafe
4700 South Congress Avenue
(512) 851-9300
www.hillscafe.com

The chicken-fried steak isn't the only thing on the menu at this South Austin landmark. How about a helping of Kevin Fowler, Cory Morrow, or any one of the many other down-home country performers who are giving this place a reputation for presenting great live music? Hill's is owned in part by popular Austin radio personality Bob Cole, half of the morning drive duo of "Sammy and Bob" on FM country station KVET. So it stands to reason that Hills would attract some of Austin's best country singers. There's live music most nights, but the schedule varies. The original Hill's Cafe was built in 1947 and for decades was a Southside institution. Cole and his business partner renovated the abandoned building and reopened Hill's in 2001. Yes, there's "cole" slaw on the menu, too.

Hole in the Wall
2538 Guadalupe Street
(512) 477-4747

This Austin institution almost didn't make it to its 30th anniversary in 2003. Closed for nearly a year while the building was up for sale, the local Austin Pizza chain revived the space and returned the 200-capacity venue to its original configuration. Bands now play in the front; the back room has pool tables, pinball machines, and a jukebox. Located on The Drag near the University of Texas campus, this IS just a hole in the wall. But over its three decades in business, this club and eatery has earned a reputation for presenting excellent up-and-coming as well as established bands. Fastball used to play here for free on Sunday night. In fact, Fastball guitarist Miles Zuniga once told Jay Leno's *Tonight Show* viewers about how the entire Hole in the Wall crowd went chasing after a thief who'd tried to steal his guitar. Is this family or what? Although known mostly for presenting alternative bands, leaning toward punk, Hole in the Wall has also presented bluegrass, pop, acoustic, and country.

La Zona Rosa
612 West Fourth Street
(512) 463-4146
www.lazonarosa.com
A longtime Austin tradition, formerly a quaint Mexican eatery and music hall, La Zona Rosa now concentrates on outstanding live music. Owned by Direct Events, Inc., it is high on the list of hot Austin clubs known for providing consistent quality entertainment. La Zona Rosa presents both national touring shows and some of Austin's favorite artists. Its two rooms can be made into one for shows that seat up to 1,200 people. It's also perfect for catered private parties.

Liberty Lunch
Formerly at 405 West Second Street
We couldn't bear to drop this famed venue from our listings, even though it is no more. After decades of resistance to moving this hallowed club, it fell prey to the powerful downtown development trend, a victim of dot-com power. A high-tech office building took over this spot. Few live music venues have captured Austin's affection like Liberty Lunch. This large, airy space (half of it is out under the trees through huge garage-type doors) hosted some of the best music in the city. Lyle Lovett, Blues Traveler, Hootie and the Blowfish, as well as Austin's own Willie Nelson, Nanci Griffith, and Trish Murphy played the Lunch. This venue, officially called Liberty Lunch and Wagon Yard, dates back to the 1800s when it really was the town wagon yard,

located next to the Schneider Store, Austin's first grocery store. By the early 1900s, the building sat amidst Guy Town, Austin's red-light district, and then went through a series of incarnations, including a drive-through lumber yard. Austin's famous Esther's Follies (see our Nightlife chapter) turned it into a performance venue in the 1970s. Later it went musical. At one point in the 1980s, there was talk of building a City Hall complex with an Italian-style piazza facing Town Lake down here. Liberty Lunch would have been a major feature of the piazza, but its grassroots clientele rebelled, refusing any sort of change to their funky Liberty Lunch. The plan was nixed, but Liberty Lunch advocates could not hold back the 21st century.

Momo's
618 West Sixth Street
(512) 479-8848
www.momosclub.com
One of the best things about this downtown club is the view from the rooftop patio, which offers a view over the city and a look at the inside stage and dance floor. Formerly known as the Top of the Marc, the club underwent a transformation in 2000 and reemerged with little emphasis on sophisticated sounds and now leans more to Top 40/funk and soul sounds. The decor also evokes the 1930s gangster era, a popular decorating theme at some Austin clubs these days. The club is upstairs from Katz's, the 24-hour deli that is a very popular spot for late-night/early-morning noshing.

Red Eyed Fly
715 Red River Street
(512) 474-1084
www.redeyedfly.com
Austin's own band Pushmonkey is among the wide variety of hometown and national acts that play this exciting club, on increasingly busy Red River Street, just off Sixth. The emphasis seems to be on rock and funk here, but really it's an electrically eclectic mix of great sounds, with

some heavy metal and a bit of country rock tossed in the mix. There's definitely some musical experimentation going on here. Red Eyed Fly, which opened in 2002, has two stages, both worth checking out. Advance tickets are available for the bigger acts.

Riverbend Centre
4214 North Loop 360 (Capital of Texas Highway)
(512) 327-9416,
(512) 469-SHOW (Star Tickets)
www.riverbendcentre.com
Bluegrass singer Alison Krauss, pop star Kenny Loggins, country crooner Larry Gatlin, and the Austin Symphony Orchestra have all performed at this stunning 2,300-seat venue since the part-time house of worship opened as a performance venue in 2002 (see The Arts chapter, Main Stages).

Room 710
710 Red River Street
(512) 476-0997
www.room710.com
Austin American–Statesman critic Chris Riemenschneider credits Woody Wiedeman, a top booking agent, with bringing some of the hippest new bands to his club. The music here focuses on indie rock, punk, country, jazz—a little bit of everything. One side of the club is free, but the open bar between the two sides allows tantalizing sounds to waft over from the other side, where there is a cover charge.

Saxon Pub
1320 South Lamar Boulevard
(512) 448-2552
www.thesaxonpub.com
Saxon Pub started out as a folk music club when it opened in South Central Austin in 1990. While owner Joe Ables still books acoustic acts, Saxon is now gaining a reputation as a great blues club. Country and rock bands also have found a home here. Ables books mainly hot Austin acts, but he has been known

to book some national touring shows in addition to the local talent. To the delight of music fans, some of the country's most popular musicians also have been known to drop in for a jam session or two. Bonnie Raitt, Kris Kristofferson, Michael Martin Murphey, and others make occasional unannounced appearances. This club has had many owners and many names throughout the years, but "Saxon Pub" is the name that has caught Austin's attention.

Speakeasy
412 Congress Avenue
(512) 476-8017
Opened in 1997, the Speakeasy quickly joined the ranks of Austin's popular nightspots. This upscale club—real carpeting on the floors, fresh flowers, and cozy booths—features live music on most nights. This is the place to play billiards and hear bands play some great standards from the '30s and '40s as well as some original music. The Speakeasy offers plenty of blues, jazz, salsa, lounge music, swing, and some country tunes. The rooftop deck, which offers a great view of downtown, features world beat contemporary CDs. This club, run by Austin's Flamingos XCVI Corp., has a happy hour buffet Monday through Friday. While the address for this club is Congress Avenue, the entrance is around back in the alley. It's easy to find.

Getting free tickets to a taping of Austin City Limits requires stamina—and lots of luck. Call the hot line at (512) 475-9077 for taping dates. Then, one to three days prior to a taping, tune in to radio stations mentioned on the hot line to find out when tickets will be given away. Tickets are distributed at the KLRU-TV studios near UT. Holding a ticket doesn't always guarantee admittance, though. ACL tapes shows from midsummer through winter.

Stubb's
801 Red River Street
(512) 480-8341
www.stubbsaustin.com
www.frontgatetickets.com
It's hard to say which is more enticing at this Austin hangout, the excellent barbecue or the live music acts that perform six days a week on both the indoor and outdoor stages. The building itself is a historical gem. Built in the 1850s of native limestone, the building has been remodeled into a 6,000-square-foot two-level restaurant with mahogany and cherry bars that date to the 1870s. Outdoors, two decks and bars overlook the stage. In modern times this was the location of an earlier Austin hotspot, the One Knite. Today, Stubb's presents live music on Monday through Saturday nights as well as a Sunday gospel brunch and occasional Sunday night shows. C. B. "Stubb" Stubblefield is the barbecue king behind this operation, having operated barbecue joints in Lubbock and around Texas for more than 40 years. Today Stubb's showcases both national touring acts and some of Austin's finest musicians.

Sixth Street

The Chuggin' Monkey
219 East Sixth Street
(512) 476-5015
www.thechugginmonkey.com
With a name like Chuggin' Monkey, this club was destined for Sixth Street. If it hadn't been for efforts to revive Austin's venerated Steamboat nightclub in a new location (which, sadly, failed), the Chuggin' Monkey would have earned the title Best New Club in the 2002–03 *Chronicle* Readers' Poll.

Flamingo Cantina
515 East Sixth Street
(512) 494-9336
www.flamingocantina.com
Calling itself "Austin's Good Vibes Club," this place is where Austin goes to hear the city's best reggae music. Carpeted bleachers line two walls, offering great views of the band on stage. Of course there's a dance floor, for when swaying in your seat just isn't enough, and an upstairs open-air deck for dancing under the stars. The Flamingo Cantina features music six nights a week. There's also a back deck for just hanging out. Advance tickets are available at the club or at places like Waterloo Records.

Maggie Mae's
323 East Sixth Street
(512) 478-8541
With three different stages offering simultaneous music on weekends, an airy rooftop bar upstairs, and private courtyard downstairs, Maggie Mae's has no trouble drawing a crowd. Named for a famous London lady of the evening, Maggie Mae's offers live music most nights. One band is featured during the week, but on Friday and Saturday this two-story club rocks with different types of music in three different rooms, including at least two live bands. The building, originally a general store built in 1874, predates Sixth Street's historic Driskill Hotel by a dozen years. Maggie Mae's, one of this strip's longest running and most successful clubs, is also acclaimed for its extensive beer selection and the beer tastings it holds.

The Parish
214 East Sixth Street
(512) 478-6372
www.myplanetmercury.com
www.frontgatetickets.com
Formerly known as the Mercury, this has been a hot Sixth Street nightclub for quite some time. *Austin American–Statesman* music critic Michael Corcoran has called it "one of the last places to hear live original music on Sixth Street" and "Austin's most handsome room." The music biz got a scare in 2003 when it was announced that the Mercury had lost its lease. The lease was renewed after all, and the name changed to the Parish. In fact, it won the *Austin Chronicle*'s 2003 critics' award for

Best Non-Club-Closing. All sorts of bands play in this acoustically excellent space.

The 311 Club
311 East Sixth Street
(512) 477-1630

R&B star Joe Valentine is not just one of the 311 Club's owners, he's also the featured attraction here several nights a week. The New Orleans–born Valentine started playing professionally at age 12. By age 16, Valentine was opening for Ray Charles. Valentine has toured the world with his own bands, opened for acts like Ike and Tina Turner, written songs for James Brown Productions, scored his own hit in 1968 with "I Can't Stand to See You Go," and was the band leader for the Joe Tex Revue. This singer/songwriter/keyboardist is a longtime Austin club owner. When Joe Valentine and the Imperials aren't on stage, other blues and R&B bands from around Austin and around the country perform.

The Vibe
508 East Sixth Street
(512) 474-0632
www.liveatthevibe.com

It didn't take long for word to get out about this new club, which took over the space formerly occupied by Fat Tuesday and features a variety of live music. The crowd is multigenerational, multicultural—and everybody is here to have a good time. Friday happy hour shows from 6:00 to 8:00 P.M. have included some of Austin's up-and-coming solo performers.

The Shores

Music snobs may reckon that venues known primarily as lakeside eateries are unworthy of mention in the same listing with such Austin classics as Antone's, the Broken Spoke, and others. You might not always hear original music at these restaurants, but sometimes you will. Besides, even the cover bands we've heard at several of these places beat the music many

visitors will find at home. And you get to enjoy being out on the lakes at the same time. Water and music—now that's an unbeatable Austin combination. This is just one more dimension of the Live Music Capital of the World. To find more about most of these eateries, see our Restaurants chapter.

Carlos 'n Charlie's
5793 Hiline Road
(512) 266-1683
www.cncaustin.com

This popular Tex-Mex eatery was destroyed by rushing flood waters on Lake Travis in the summer of 1997. Now rebuilt—to float—the new, bigger location sacrifices much of the charm of the old place but makes up for it with a huge dance hall on the lower level. So you can have your dinner upstairs overlooking the lake and then descend the stairs for a night of music and dancing. There's live music Thursday through Sunday.

Johnny Fin's
16405 Marina Point Road
(512) 266-2811
www.johnnyfins.com

Dance on your boat or come on in for food, fun, and, of course, live music six nights a week. Sam Hill, on Lake Travis, serves live music Tuesday through Sunday and also offers one of the best beach menus on the lake—burgers, steaks, prime rib, seafood, pastas, salads, and more. You'll pay more here than at some other eateries, but the food is good, and so is the atmosphere when the boating crowd gathers round to hear the tunes.

The Pier
1701 River Hills Drive
(512) 327-4562
www.pierlakeaustin.com

A huge stage shaded by 60-foot elms, a large concrete slab of a dance floor, and plenty of picnic tables for dining and drinking make this one great place to hear all varieties of music, including cover bands and Austin acts playing original music. You can even drive your boat right up to the dock on Lake Austin and listen from there or join the crowds that gather for the show. The food is typical lakeside fare—fried foods, sandwiches, salads, grilled food, and snacks—but the bar is fully stocked, and the frozen margaritas and rum runners flow. This place also has a lighted sand volleyball court.

Ski Shores Waterfront Cafe
3101 Pearce Street
(512) 346-5915
www.skishores.com
Getting raves from Austin crowds since 1954, this is another supercasual place where you can just boat right up to the dock and hop in for a burger, a beer, or an evening of live music. Located on Lake Austin, Ski Shores is one of our favorite outdoor eateries. The stage, presenting Austin singer/songwriters during the summer, is so close to the water that the wake from the boats going by could almost serve as the rhythm section.

Starlight Terrace at The Oasis
6550 Comanche Trail
(512) 266-2441
www.oasis-austin.com
Situated high above Lake Travis, the Oasis is famous for its fabulous view of the sunset. But the multilayered outdoor decks are also perfect for dining—and for listening to live music Thursday through Sunday evenings on the Starlight Terrace. The bands play all kinds of music, including Top 40, jazz, salsa, and much more. Salsa lessons also are offered. Austin bands, performing both original hits and popular contemporary music, make this place a must-stop for those who want to experience the outdoor music scene in Austin. They've also got a great selection of frozen margaritas, a full bar, and a generous menu.

Free Concerts

Austin's Fourth of July Picnic
Auditorium Shores, Riverside Drive and South First Street
(512) 476-6064
www.austinsymphony.org
Austin's biggest free concert is the performance by the Austin Symphony Orchestra at the annual July Fourth Concert and Fireworks Show on the shores of Town Lake. See our Annual Events and Festivals chapter for more on this giant concert/picnic/party.

Fall Concert Series
Frost Bank Plaza
816 Congress Avenue
(512) 442-BAND (2263)
Members of the Austin Federation of Musicians, in conjunction with the Downtown Austin Alliance, offer free outdoor concerts on Friday from noon to 1:00 P.M. at this downtown outdoor venue. The series runs from mid-September to early November. Bring your lunch along and enjoy a taste of Austin.

Waterloo Park Concert Series
Waterloo Park, 403 East 15th Street
(512) 442-BAND (2263)
Formerly held at Auditorium Shores on Town Lake, this popular series of summer concerts has featured some of Austin's top performers over the years. These concerts, a typical Austin mix of music styles, are fun for the whole family and offer and excellent opportunity to get acquainted with the Austin music scene. Shows are held each Wednesday night from 7:00 to 9:00 P.M. from the end of April through June. This is another project by the Austin Federation of Musicians.

i

The Austin American-Statesman *features a daily "Best Bets" column on page 2 of the Arts section that can include recommended performances for that evening. The* Austin Chronicle *and the* Statesman's *XLent section, both published on Thursday, offer the weekly lineup of live music shows.*

Zilker Hillside Theater Concerts
2206 William Barton Drive
(512) 477-5335
www.ci.austin.tx.us/zilker/hillside.htm
The fabulous natural amphitheater near Barton Springs Pool in Zilker Park presents an array of free concerts during its season, which runs from late March to mid-October. Perfomances are given by the Austin Symphony, the Austin Civic Orchestra, the Ausic Civic Wind Ensemble, and many other groups. Special events include the Mother's Day, Pops, and Earth Day Concerts. This site also hosts dance and theater productions, including the popular Zilker Theater Productions' Summer Musical, and Shakespeare in the Park (see The Arts chapter). Admission is free to all these events, but there is a $2.00 parking fee. Call, or check the Web site for a schedule of events.

MUSIC STORES

Record stores, both independents and chains, are flourishing throughout Austin these days, some extending into new parts of town as the city grows. An extensive list can be found online at the Texas Music Office Web site: www.governor.state.tx.us/music/recordstores-austin.htm. These shops, which add yet another dimension to the city's music scene, feature a wide variety of music from jazz to Tejano, hip-hop to blues, classical to funk, and of course, Austin's own local artists. Furthermore, some of these stores go out of their way to promote Austin's music scene by sponsoring live in-store performances, setting aside special sections featuring CDs by local musicians, and offering advice and tips on the Live Music Capital of the World. Stop in any of the shops we've listed here for a taste of Austin.

Alien Records
1114 West Fifth Street
(512) 477-3909
www.alienrecords.net
This Central Austin store specializes in techno and hip-hop music. The store is a mecca for club DJs, who tout its extensive collection of electronic dance music.

Antone's Record Shop
2928 Guadalupe Street
(512) 322-0660
Reflecting the music played at the venerable Austin club of the same name (see the listing in this chapter), Antone's focuses on blues music. There is also a large selection of Texas and Cajun music, country sounds, soul, vintage rock 'n' roll, rockabilly, and jazz at this Central Austin store. Customers can buy, sell, and trade here. This is also the place to buy advance tickets to shows at Antone's club (see The Stages section of this chapter).

Barnes & Noble Booksellers
10000 Research Boulevard
(512) 418-8985
www.barnesandnoble.com
The name doesn't tout the record store within, but this Barnes & Noble location in the Arboretum Shopping Center in Northwest Austin, and most of the chain's other locations, stock an impressive selection of CDs, including the classics, show tunes, pop artists, and more. The fine collection of books about music and musicians just outside the music section whet the appetite for the tunes within.

Borders Books & Music
10225 Research Boulevard
(512) 795-9553
4477 South Lamar Boulevard
(512) 891-8974
Not all of Austin's best record stores are downtown, and not all are homegrown. Those living or visiting up in the 'burbs of Northwest Austin and in the Southwest sector of the city will be pleased to learn that when Borders says it has books AND music, it really means the music part. This national chain offers an enormous selection of CDs and tapes in all categories of music. The store has gone out of its way to prominently display the products of

Austin musicians, and includes a good selection of Austin artists among its music samplings. Borders also regularly hosts live music in the store.

Cheapo Discs
914 North Lamar Boulevard
(512) 477-4499
www.cheapotexas.com
Housed in the old Whole Foods store, just north of the West Sixth shopping district, not far from downtown in Central Austin, Cheapo features used CDs, one of the largest selections in Austin. The shop buys used CDs. Technically, Cheapo is part of a small Minnesota-based chain, but it retains the atmosphere of an independent outfit.

Half Price Books
Records and Magazines
8868 Research Boulevard
(512) 454-3664
13492 North Highway 183
(512) 335-5759
3110 Guadalupe Street
(512) 451-4463
2929 South Lamar Boulevard
(512) 443-3138
There are three locations of this hometown bookstore/record shop—one in Northwest Austin, the original location in Central Austin, just north of The Drag, and a third in South Austin. The music variety changes, but the stores buy and sell CDs, LPs, vinyl, and cassettes.

Jupiter Records
1000 East 41st Street, Suite 220
(512) 454-5678
www.jupiterrecords.com
Locally owned and operated by brothers Jason and Ryan Enright, Jupiter Records stocks a huge selection of new and used CDs, vinyl, and DVDs in all genres and styles, including a broad selection of Austin musical artists—and customers are invited to listen to anything in the store. Jupiter also has an extensive

inventory of rare, collectable, hard-to-find, and out-of-print items and pays good prices to those who wish to sell and trade music. Jupiter presents live in-store performances by Austin musicians on Friday evening. It's located on the east side of historic Hyde Park at the corner of 41st Street and Red River in the Hancock Center.

Musicmania
3909-D North I-35
(512) 451-3361
East of the interstate in the Fiesta grocery store center, this East Austin record store has a reputation for one of the best R&B and rap music collections in the country. In addition to CDs, the store has a large collection of vinyl records, posters, magazines, and music-related merchandise.

Sound Exchange
2100-A Guadalupe Street
(512) 476-2274
www.soundexchangeaustin.com
The store, which appeared as a hip hangout on MTV's *Austin Stories,* features a wide variety of records in all formats—mainstream, techno, jazz, punk. The store also sells posters and T-shirts.

Technophilia
2418 Guadalupe Street
(512) 477-1812
The name suggests the musical emphasis at this two-story store on The Drag in Central Austin. The upstairs area is dubbed the Vinyl Attic; downstairs shoppers, can find a large variety of new and used CDs.

Tesaneta
2207 East Seventh Street
(512) 478-0020
This East Austin record store touts itself as the oldest record shop in Austin—it was called Maldonado's until a name change in 2000. The flavor here is Latin,

with a large collection of conjunto, norteño (Northern Mexican music), Tejano music, and traditional imported Mexican music.

Thirty-Three Degrees
4017 Guadalupe Street
(512) 302-5233

Called the "most unusual record store in Town" by the *Austin American–Statesman*, this music shop features rare discs and CDs in all genres from punk classic to local artists.

Tower Records
2402 Guadalupe Street
(512) 478-5711
www.towerrecords.com

If any current UT student can remember when this popular chain store first went in on The Drag near the university, it's definitely time to graduate and join the real world. Its prominent and convenient location in the heart of The Drag has made this store a favorite among the university crowd, and just us regular folk, since it opened in 1990, replacing the old Varsity movie theater. Of course, Tower Records offers an outstanding collection of CDs, including world music, local artists, Latin, Cajun, and the classics. That could have something to do with its appeal. This huge store also has an excellent book section dedicated to music and musicians, pop culture, erotica, film, cyberculture, and more. There's also an extensive magazine rack and plenty of paraphernalia for your sound system.

Turntable Records
507 West Mary Street
(512) 462-2568

Just west of South Congress Avenue's funky shopping district, this small store sells breakbeat, retro, disco, Top 40, and other sounds, including both domestic and imported albums and singles.

The Austin City Council, the same body that proclaimed Austin the Live Music Capital of the World, has slapped a noise ordinance on Sixth Street clubs. So if you're expecting to be blasted away by the music on Sixth, you may be surprised by the softer tones wafting out of the clubs. Of course that all changes once you open the doors. Did somebody say, "Party"?

Waterloo Records
600-A North Lamar Boulevard
(512) 474-2500
www.waterloorecords.com

Consistently voted the Best Record Store in town in the annual *Austin Chronicle* Readers' Poll, Waterloo is at the heart of the West Sixth Street shopping district. The shop has a fabulous selection of records and CDs reflecting a wide variety of styles and sounds, and there are plenty of listening stations to sample the music. In-house performances and CD-release concerts are held regularly to highlight the work of popular artists, both up-and-coming and well known. Waterloo arranges its records alphabetically instead of by music type, which makes this store extremely user-friendly. Waterloo also stocks lots of other music-related items. Trying to decide what band to hear when you're in town—and you can't find any on our "Catch 'em If You Can" list? Stop in to Waterloo and ask the advice of owner John Kunz or any other member of the knowledgeable sales staff. Waterloo is also one place to purchase tickets for shows around town and for wristbands or individual tickets for SXSW events and the Austin City Limits Music Festival (see our Annual Events and Festivals chapter). It's no wonder this store has been going strong since 1982.

SHOPPING ⊛

You can never be too adventurous to enjoy shopping in Austin. Sure there are big malls with big parking lots to match, but while they provide Austin shoppers with the opportunity to buy appliances at national discount chain prices, local merchants present a dazzling array of arts, crafts, collectibles, folk art, funk, vintage redux, and just plain fun items.

Our aim in this chapter is to give you a feel for what is available in Austin—a sampler tray, if you will. We give you the big, the bold, and the beautiful. First is a look at the city's shopping districts, then a brief overview of the area's major malls and outlet stores. This is followed by listings, by category and area, of shops in the Austin area. It is impossible to list every noteworthy and intriguing shop in the city, but this list aims to give the reader the flavor of the shopping scene in Austin, plus tips at finding shops that are unique to the city.

Three significant categories of shops are not included here—bookstores appear in our chapter on The Literary Scene, art galleries are showcased in the Arts chapter, and music stores are featured in The Music Scene. In addition, sporting goods that cater to a specific sport are found in our Parks and Recreation chapter.

In recent years there has been a blossoming of retail in Austin. On the one hand, national giants such as Whole Foods Market and Dell Computer have emerged from the Austin earth; on the other hand, the personal has flourished. Older boulevards and city streets in Austin have seen small, unique shops sprout like cabbages as young Austin goes in search of expression and joy.

Years ago, Texas was like many other states that forced shops to close on Sunday, but the so-called Blue Laws have been revoked, and most shops are open seven days a week. Monday through Saturday most stores open around 9:00 A.M. On Sunday specialty shops and mall stores open around noon and close at 6:00 P.M. Closing hours vary. Smaller shops close at 6:00 P.M., while the malls close at 9:00 or 10:00 P.M. Monday through Saturday. Many stores, particularly discount chains and grocery stores, stay open 24 hours a day.

Given Austin's lively night scene, many bookstores and specialty food shops keep late hours. The burgeoning shopping scene along South Congress Avenue is one example of a late-night shopping district—some of the stores stay open until midnight, particularly on weekends. On the first Thursday of each month, the South Congress shopping district has a shopping, eating, and drinking celebration called "First Thursday" (see our Close-up in the Nightlife chapter). During the Christmas holiday season, many stores and malls extend their hours.

SHOPPING DISTRICTS

One of the liveliest shopping districts is on South Congress Avenue, in the neighborhood called "SoCo," south of Town Lake in South Central Austin. Congress Avenue is wide and magnificent here, but for many years the shops and businesses along the street decayed and stagnated. Now there is new life on the avenue and resale shops featuring vintage clothing, toy emporiums, retro furnishing stores, and folk art shops flourish—some staying open in the night hours to give the street an after-dark vitality. Mixed in with the new stores are a couple of old standbys that have been revived by the activity.

Not far from the South Congress shopping district is South Lamar Boulevard, where some of the city's really funky stores can be found. Vintage clothing stores, "junque" shops, antiques stores, and several thrift stores are located on this road to downtown Austin.

The nexus of West Sixth and North Lamar Boulevard is fast becoming the hippest shopping district in Austin. At its heart is the Whole Foods Market, the natural foods grocery store that is a leitmotiv for the Austin economy. Founded more than 20 years ago as a natural foods store by a couple of hippies with a vision, it now serves as the anchor of the country's largest natural foods grocery store empire. Next door is Austin's quintessential bookstore, Book People, a place where incense fills the air, and the titles outnumber any chain store in town. In 2003 Whole Foods broke ground on a site immediately to the south of the current store. The new 80,000-square-foot store will be a flagship for the chain and will anchor an urban shopping center that is scheduled to open in 2005.

There are big plans for West Sixth, but even without the proposed new inner city, people-friendly European-style shopping centers that will replace car lots, this area is packed with small stores and emporiums designed to lead the walking visitor from door to door.

Another shopping district in the making is the area along Burnet Road leading from North Austin down into Central Austin. This is a mix of antiques shops, ethnic bakeries and grocery stores, and crafts stores catering to potters and glassmakers.

One of the city's most enticing shopping corridors lies east of MoPac along 35th Street, flowing into 38th Street and then north on Lamar Boulevard to Central Park, home of the city's second-biggest tourist draw, Central Market (see our Close-up in this chapter), a grocery store that belies its pedestrian name. This corridor is marked by shops dedicated to excellence, be it in gardening, clock repair, pasta making, clothes design, or the art of photography. There are no big signs here, but Austin residents know this is where they can find some of the best shops in Austin.

To the northwest along U.S. 183 is the Arboretum, the Rodeo Drive of Austin. This is where some of the top merchandising names in the country have a foothold. Back in the city is The Drag, the section of Guadalupe Street that runs alongside the University of Texas campus. Here there is a odd mix of hip fashion stores and Vietnamese egg roll stands, old hippie vendors and souvenir shops selling all things Longhorn.

The Austin ethos dictates that nobody shops simply to shop; Austinites shop to find, to discover, to enjoy. If these listings are packed with stores selling folk art, food, and plants, it is an indication that Austin residents are sensual folk who love to dip into the unknown, find the new, and enjoy the past.

MALLS

We have it on good authority that when the Queen of England came to Austin, her staff and ladies-in-waiting ventured to a local shopping mall to sample the wares. Austin is booming and strip centers, plus malls at major intersections around the city, are blooming. There are some local merchants in the area's malls, but like much of America, the shopping mall is the home of chain stores, big-name department stores, and fashionable merchants of the moment.

The malls are open seven days a week, usually from 9:00 A.M. to 9:00 or 10:00 P.M. Monday through Saturday and from noon to 6:00 P.M. on Sunday, although hours are extended greatly during the Christmas shopping season and for special promotional sales.

The major shopping malls include The Arboretum (10000 Research Boulevard) in northwest Austin, an open-air mall that is home to many upscale national stores. Barton Creek Square, a large indoor mall, sits atop a hill in West Austin at 2901 Loop 360 (Capital of Texas Highway) and is home to several department stores, including Foley's,

Nordstrom's, Sears, Dillard's, and JCPenney. Lakeline Mall (11200 Lakeline Mall) is Austin's newest mall and serves the fast-growing northwest greater Austin area. It also is home to such major department stores as Foley's, Sears, Dillard's, and JCPenney. Highland Mall (6001 Airport Boulevard) was Austin's first mall in what was then far North Austin and is now considered the edge of Central Austin, near the intersection of I-35 and U.S. 290. It has several major department stores on the premises.

Shoppers who love to hunt for bargains at outlet stores have a major source of pleasure in San Marcos, about 45 minutes south of Austin. Both sides of I-35 are lined with outlet stores located in two malls, Prime Outlet Mall and Tanger Outlet Center, both located at exit 200 on the interstate.

ANTIQUES/COLLECTIBLES/FOLK ART
Central

Anjely
500 North Lamar Boulevard, Suite 140
(512) 482-0600
www.anjely.com
Boasting Austin's largest collection of African masks and tribal art, Anjely's is another addition to the shopping scene around Whit Hanks Antiques center. But the mix here goes beyond African tribal art to include European antiques and treasure from the Indian subcontinent.

Architects & Heroes
1809 West 35th Street
(512) 467-9393
Architectural elements are a popular decorative tool these days, and this store features stone and wooden decorative pieces that have been rescued from old homes and gardens. The store also sells antique furniture pieces, wrought iron, and textiles.

Bob Larson's Old Timer Clock Shop
1803 West 35th Street
(512) 451-5016
www.bobsclocks.com
The Old Timer Shop has been a treasured resource for years for Austin residents. The shop not only sells beautiful old clocks and watches but also offers a fine repair service.

Dreyfus Antiques Brocante
1901 North Lamar Boulevard
(512) 473-2443
The large wrought-iron replica of the Eiffel Tower is a surefire tip to what shoppers will find inside—a selection of 18th- and 19th-century French antiques, including armoires, tapestries, tables, architectural pieces, and chairs.

Eclectic
700 North Lamar Boulevard
(512) 477-1816
A longtime Austin shop and gallery that sells crafts from around the world, including Africa, Mexico, Latin America, and the Far East. The store lives up to its name and is a veritable bazaar, packed with large and small items—some costly, others bargains. Eclectic sells primitive and Southwest furniture, clothing, decorative items, pottery, textiles, and ceramics. The large jewelry section is very popular. Among the rare items are Zuni fetishes and an antique bottle collection, some of the glassware dating back to Roman times.

El Interior
1009 West Lynn Street
(512) 474-8680
www.elinteriormex.com
This Clarksville store is one of the best and oldest folk art stores in Austin. The owners really know where to find the best pottery, jewelry, and textiles south of the border. The selection of Oaxacan ceramics is notable, and the store also stocks Guatemalan fabric by the yard.

Fortney's
1116 West Sixth Street
(512) 495-6505

The collectibles, associated bric-a-brac, and oddities often tumble out over the sidewalk, coaxing passersby inside. There might be a bigger-than-life equestrian statue, a door from an Asian temple, a planter the size of a coffee table, or a wrought-iron fence. The store also specializes in Southwestern-style furniture and garden ornaments. Always an interesting browse.

Kerbey Lane Doll Shoppe
3706 Kerbey Lane
(512) 452-7086

This store sells both antique dolls aimed at the collectors' market and exquisite, new dolls for that special niece or granddaughter. The owners also offer on-site doll repair.

La Cosecha
3703 Kerbey Lane
(512) 450-0650

A popular store in the Kerbey Lane shopping scene, part of the 35th through 38th Street corridor, this store features Latin American folk art and clothing, hats, and jewelry, plus custom designed fashions and accessories by local Austin artists.

Tesoros Trading Co.
209 Congress Avenue
(512) 479-8377
www.tesoros.com

Tesoros is one of our favorite Austin stores. It features a wide selection of Mexican and Latin American folk art, jewelry, specialty pieces such as doorposts from Peru, African baskets, Day of the Dead tableaux, amulets, loteria art, old Mexican postcards, Moroccan mirrors, jewelry from all over the world, purses made in Vietnam from old Pepsi cans, Mexican grocery store calendars, retablos, Peruvian good luck pigs, etc., etc. The store's Christmas ornaments, particularly those from Latin America, are popular Austin collectibles. Look out for the occasional warehouse sales advertised in the local press. This downtown store is one of those must-see stops for any visitor. Next door is a unique restaurant, Las Manitas (see the listing in our Restaurants chapter).

Whit Hanks Antiques and Decorative Arts
1009 West Sixth Street
(512) 478-2101

More than 70 antiques and arts dealers can be found under one roof at Whit Hanks, an antiques showcase on West Sixth Street at the heart of one of Austin's burgeoning shopping districts. From the large, Tuscan-style pottery urns on its lawn to the myriad collectibles inside, this is one of the most pleasant and amenable antiques venues in Austin. The building, located next door to Treaty Oak (see our Attractions chapter), is a popular spot for a weekend outing. The dealers are friendly and ready to educate visitors about their collections, and there is a wide variety of antiques and collectibles—Oriental, European, Southwest, primitive, plus china, antique tile and pottery, household wrought iron, garden decorations and

Antiques collectors from across the nation and beyond gather in the tiny Texas community of Round Top, an hour's drive northeast of Austin, twice a year (usually April and October) for what Country Home *magazine has named "one of the 10 best antiques fairs in the country" (see the Day Trips and Weekend Getaways chapter). If you cannot visit during the fairs, you can still enjoy all the antiques shops and sights the community has to offer either on a day trip or on an overnight stay; the town has several bed-and-breakfast accommodations. In addition to shopping, Round Top is a center of culture, with concerts, plays, and historical sights.*

pots. Several Austin artisans display their original iron, ceramic, and woodworking pieces here also.

Zanzibar
1009 West Sixth Street
(512) 472-9234
www.zanzibarhome.com

The West Sixth area is evolving into one of the hippest shopping districts in Austin. A new area of shops has been built adjacent to the Whit Hanks Antiques center in what has been named the Courtyard. Named for the great African port, this store evokes the spirit of an old bazaar with a melange of Chinese furniture, kilim rugs, Arabic-style lamps, tribal baskets, ethnic jewelry, and primitive cooking utensils, pots, and tools.

South Central

Antigua
1508 South Congress Avenue
(512) 912-1475

Fossils, dream pillows, tile and tin mirrors, stained glass, suncatchers, decorative items from Thailand and Bali, Mexico and Guatemala are packed into this store in the South Congress shopping district. Two items worth looking for are the santos, carved figures of saints used in Southwest and Latin American churches, and nichos, household shrines popular in those regions also.

Aqua Fever
1415 South Congress Avenue
(512) 916-8800
www.aquamodern.com

Looking for a turquoise and orange ashtray for your Sixties-style Danish Modern coffee table, then this is the place to start your search. This South Congress shopping district store features those retro looks from the Fifties, Sixties and Seventies—the kind of furniture seen on Nick at Nite shows.

McLaren's Antiques & Interiors
517 South Lamar Boulevard
(512) 442-0361

Dubbing itself an antiques department store, this Austin branch of a well-known Houston shop also has links to stores in Europe. McLaren's touts itself as the largest independently owned antiques and interior store in Texas. Housed in what was formerly a office supply chain store, the aisles are filled with European antiques and accessories from around the world.

Mi Casa
1700A South Congress Avenue
(512) 707-9797
www.micasagallery.com

The entrance to this rabbit's warren of treasures is actually on West Milton, just half a block off Congress Avenue. Room after tiny room features rustic ranch and primitive furniture, while the walls hang with Southwestern and Mexican folk art. Texans have long known that Mexico and countries farther south are a treasure trove of finds and Mi Casa features a fine selection. In addition to furniture and art-work, the store also sells textiles and cotton clothing from Mexico and Guatemala.

Pieces of the Past
411 West Monroe Street
(512) 326-5141
www.pieces-of-the-past.com

Just 4 blocks west of the South Congress shopping area, this old warehouse is home to a selection of architectural pieces for the garden and home, including a large grouping of Mexican doors. There are also pieces of old iron fences, hardware, and stained-glass windows. The store also features the work of several Austin artists whose work reflects the funky South Austin style.

Rue's Antiques
1500 South Congress Avenue
(512) 442-1775
www.ruesantiques.com

Rue's has been operating at various locations in Austin for decades. Now housed in the South Congress shopping district, Rue's features antiques, old furniture, and what might be simply called junque items.

Finds run the gamut from wonderful old bedroom vanities to chipped china. The store also offers refinishing services and brass and copper polishing.

The Armadillo
1712 South Congress Avenue
(512) 443-7552

Hand-carved furniture takes center stage here, but the store also sells antique furniture pieces, jewelry, pottery, and ceramics that capture the spirit of Texas and the Southwest.

Thornton Road Studio Complex
2311 Thornton Road
(512) 443-1611

A gathering of 10 artists maintains studios in a small complex located on Thornton Road behind the Office Depot store at the corner of South Lamar Boulevard and Oltorf Street. Painters, sculptors, jewelry-makers, ironworkers, and mosaic artists have their studios here. Three maintain Web sites: www.studioglass.com, www.katsudesigns.com, and www.johntoole.com. The studio complex holds a sale each December, offering patrons a great way to buy unique gifts—the fantasy animal night-lights by Katsu, for example—at cut prices.

Tinhorn Traders
1608 South Congress Avenue
(512) 444-3644

The owner likes to call himself a "single dealer with multiple personalities," and the stock shows it—everything from funky to folk art here. Some of the most interesting items are planters and architectural elements rescued from old buildings.

Uncommon Objects
1512 South Congress Avenue
(512) 442-4000

There seems to be a competition in the South Congress shopping district to see which store can qualify for the Best Stuff award. Here, Mexican doors, architectural elements, lamps, and clothing all compete for attention.

West Mary Antiques
910 West Mary Street
(512) 916-9561

While some of the stores in the South Congress shopping district lean more toward the funky than the classic, this small store is the exception. The antiques here are antiques and not simply grandma's vintage pieces.

North

Adobe Pueblo
9070 Research Boulevard, Suite 203
(512) 323-0894

Western, Southwestern, and Mexican furniture pieces are sold here, plus Zapotec rugs from Oaxaca, dhurrie rugs from India, and kilims from Turkey. The store also has a collection of Native American pottery and Hopi kachina dolls.

Austin Antique Mall
8822 McCann Drive
(512) 459-5900
www.antiquetexas.com

Housed in a large warehouse, this is the Austin cousin to the Antique Mall of Texas in Round Rock (see listing later in this section). A little smaller than its Round Rock cousin, the large facility still has room for 100 vendors, who sell a wide variety of antiques, collectibles, and good stuff. The large building is visible from Research Boulevard but is accessible via Burnet Road.

Antique Marketplace
5350 Burnet Road
(512) 452-1000

In 1989 Antique Marketplace opened in a 19,000-square-foot former grocery store in North Austin. The large space is now a treasure trove of antiques, collectible, and arts and crafts stalls, featuring a variety of items, some expensive, others at bargain-basement prices. There is a relaxed, down-home atmosphere here, and strolling the aisles can turn into a afternoon adventure.

Courtyard Shops
5453 Burnet Road
(512) 477-1616

Several antiques dealers and crafters are creating a small shopping and craft center on Burnet Road, all part of the spontaneous revival of this street as a place to roam for special items and bargains. Negrel (www.negrel.com), one of the tenants, features furniture and household decorative objects from the south of France and has a second location at Whit Hanks (above) on West Sixth Street. Other tenants include Halbert Antiques, L'Elysee Antiques, and Austin Brass. The center of the shopping area is a small courtyard decorated by garden artist Bud Twilley. He uses old garden stoneware from Europe and Mexico to create fountains, topiaries, and garden art.

Dragon's Lair Comics & Fantasy
4910 Burnet Road
(512) 454-2399
117 Louis Henna Boulevard,
Suite 140
Round Rock
(512) 279-8888

Comic books, games, fantasy fiction, and videos, particularly those featuring the work of John Wu and Jackie Chan, are sold here. Japanese comic books are particularly popular. The Austin Board Game Group meets here every month, as the store hosts games on-site.

Turquoise Trading Post
6009 Burnet Road
(512) 323-5011
(888) 887-7864
www.texasttp.com

In addition to offering a wide selection of contemporary and traditional Native American jewelry, the store also has a collection of Zuni fetishes and Navajo kachinas, plus pottery and sculpture from the Southwest.

West

The Market
The Village Shopping Center at
Westlake, Loop 360 (Capital of Texas
Highway) and Bee Caves Road
(512) 327-8866

Decorators working on creating that classic English or French look can find antiques from those two countries here, plus top-quality modern pieces from the Ralph Lauren, Henredon, and Hickory Chair Furniture collections.

Round Rock

The Antique Mall of Texas
1601 South I-35
(512) 218-4290

More than 200 dealers are housed in this mall, selling a wide assortment of collectibles and antiques. The mall is run by the folks who operate the Austin Antique Mall, and it has the same down-home, comfortable atmosphere that engenders leisurely shopping and browsing.

ARTS AND CRAFTS
Central

Bydee Arts & Gifts
412 East Sixth Street
(512) 474-4343
www.bydee.com

Transplanted from the Caribbean to Austin, Brian "Bydee Man" Joseph has created a friendly new breed—the Bydee people. He describes them as happy, fun-loving, and laid back, and they have become an Austin symbol. Bydee stands for "Bringing You Delightful Entertaining Experiences." Joseph, who has a master's degree in urban studies, began painting while recuperating from surgery, and now his Bydee people can be found on posters, T-shirts, and note cards. His work is also sold at the airport gift shop.

Clarksville Pottery & Galleries
Central Park, 4001 North Lamar
Boulevard, Suite 200
(512) 454-9079
9722 Great Hills Terrace, Suite 380
(512) 794-8580
www.clarksvillepottery.com
This pottery shop found life in the old Central Austin neighborhood of Clarksville (hence the name); however, this shop and gallery now has two locations, one in Central Park on North Lamar Boulevard and the other in the Arboretum area. Both stores feature pottery by local artists, including decorative pieces and very practical, sturdy everyday ware; also stone fountains, lamps, beautiful wooden boxes, and hummingbird feeders. The store has a large selection of jewelry and wind chimes. (No kid can resist the large outdoor chimes on the deck at the Central Park store.)

Kerbey Lane Dollhouses and Miniatures
3503 Kerbey Lane
(512) 454-4287
www.kerbeylanedollhouses.com
Granddads looking for wallpaper, roof shingles, or carpet for that dollhouse project can find it here. The store also features a large collection of dollhouse furniture along with tiny household accessories—kitchen soap, flower arrangements, plates, cups, and saucers.

Renaissance Market
West 23rd and Guadalupe Streets
Some folks joke that Austin is an elephant's graveyard for old hippies, and Renaissance Market may be evidence of that. This small plaza on The Drag is home to a variety of crafters and artists who specialize in Woodstock-era items—tie-dyed shirts and skirts, silver jewelry, suncatchers, leather pouches and purses, etc. The outdoor market also attracts jugglers and mimes. A mural, dubbed "Austintatious," shows the city's life in the hippie heyday. Despite its laissez-faire atmosphere, the market is tightly regulated, and the operation is under the auspices of a special city oversight committee that makes sure only authentic hippie stuff is sold here. No place but Austin!

Many of the communities surrounding Austin hold spring and summer festivals celebrating local history and culture. Check out our Annual Events chapter for events such as the Old Gruene Market Days for an opportunity to find arts and crafts.

Silk Road
3910 North Lamar Boulevard
(512) 302-0844
www.srfabrics.com
A plain-looking, small building across from Central Market houses this store that sells natural fabrics from around the world, including cottons, silks, linens, batiks, and velvets. The store has an unusual collection of bone, glass, jet, pewter, and wood buttons.

The Needleworks
26 Doors, 1206 West 38th Street
(512) 451-6931
www.theneedleworks.com
A mecca for needlework enthusiasts, this store in the 26 Doors shopping center features all manner of needlework supplies and kits, including traditional yarns, specialty fibers, accessories, books, instruction, and finishing.

South Central

Fanny's Outlet Fabric Store
1150 South Lamar Boulevard
(512) 442-8255
The antithesis of an outlet, this small, friendly south Central Austin neighborhood shop features an assortment of fabrics and samples, plus decorating staples such as wide linen and Egyptian cotton.

Southwest

Cowgirls and Lace
1111 U.S. 290 West, Dripping Springs
(512) 858-4186
(800) 982-7424
www.cowgirlsandlace.com
A 15-minute drive from the Austin city limits along U.S. 290 West in Southwest Austin, this outlet store sells designer fabrics at wholesale prices. In addition to over 1,000 bolts of designer fabrics at discount prices, Cowgirls and Lace also stocks 100-inch-wide designer sheeting fabric so that you can become your own sheetmaker.

North

El Taller Gallery
8015 Shoal Creek Boulevard, #109
(512) 302-0100
www.eltallergallery.com
Amado Peña was an Austin art teacher who sold his paintings and prints on the arts and crafts circuit for years before being discovered. Peña's work features cultural themes reflecting life in the Southwestern United States and Mexico. His stylized figures, notably women in profile with long streaming black hair, large, oval eyes and colorful costumes, are presented in a variety of mediums. Peña's work has been featured on posters advertising annual events in Austin, and his prints and paintings can be seen in Austin homes and businesses. Now his work is featured at this popular gallery, which also sells works by other noted Southwest artists, including R. C. Gorman. In addition to prints, the gallery also sells Southwest-style jewelry and Mexican textiles. (For more information, see our listing for the gallery in the Arts chapter.)

Feats of Clay
4630 Burnet Road
(512) 453-2111
Local potters buy supplies at this Central Austin store, plus the store offers kiln firing for homemade pieces. The store also features stoneware, earthenware, and porcelain by local potters. Pieces include dinnerware, batter bowls, large tureens, teapots, and bird feeders.

Renaissance Glass Company
5200 Burnet Road
(512) 451-3971
Specializing in stained glass, this arts and crafts store also sells supplies for stained glass artists. It is a good place to find tools for cutting glass and metal foil tapes for picture frames.

East

Fire Island Hot Glass Studio, Inc.
3401 East Fourth Street
(512) 389-1100
www.fireisland.com
Owners and artists Matthew LaBarbera and Teresa Uelschey create fine art pieces, custom designs, and small items for sale at their East Austin studio. The smaller items include perfume bottles and paperweights. The artists also offer demonstrations on Saturday morning September through January and March through May.

Mitchie's
Fine Black Art Gallery and Bookstore
5706 Manor Road, Suite B-1
(512) 323-6901
www.mitchie.com
Mitchie's celebrates African-American, African, and Caribbean culture, selling arts, crafts, and books that illustrate these regions and the work of the people who live there. The store has a large print collection celebrating the lives of sports figures, cultural and religious heroes, historical figures from the American Civil Rights movement, and celebrations of African and African-American life and art.

CLOTHING/FASHION
Central

Capra & Cavelli
3500 Jefferson Street, Suite 110
(512) 450-1919
www.capraandcavelli.citysearch.com
This men's boutique features classic looks
and design, casual wear or button-down
office outfits. The aim is to provide personal service to customers who want to
look their best and be comfortable in the
Austin climate.

By George
524 North Lamar Boulevard, Suite 103
(512) 472-5951
2324 Guadalupe Street
(512) 472-2731
2346 Guadalupe Street
(512) 472-5536
The three By George shops are a favorite
among young, hip, and well-heeled
dressers. The look is simple and very modern; the price tag not so simple. There are
three locations—the younger set heads for
the stores on The Drag (Guadalupe) where
a women's store and men's store stand
side by side featuring labels such as
Romeo Gigli, Calvin Klein, and Massimo.
The older Gen-Xers and hip baby boomers
head for the San Gabriel location on North
Lamar Boulevard. All three sites also sell
personal care items and accessories.

Emeralds
624 Lamar Boulevard
(512) 476-4496
Emeralds is a favorite shopping spot for
hip young women looking for simple, well-
designed fashions. The store also has a
shoe collection and a variety of modern
accessories, plus decorative items for the
home.

Fetish
1112 North Lamar Boulevard
(512) 457-1007
Sexy, smart, sleek shoes by designers like
Isaac Mizrahi and Cynthia Rowley are sold
here. The shop also stocks fashions to
match, with designs by the likes of Diane
von Furstenberg and Laundry.

InStep
3105 Guadalupe Street
(512) 476-5110
www.instepaustin.com
This shoe store next door to Wheatsville
Co-op features Birkenstock shoes and
sandals, a mandatory item for the correctly dressed Austinite—chinos or khaki
shorts, a wrinkled linen shirt or faded T-
shirt, Birkenstocks. If your trusty Birkenstocks ever need fixing, this is the place; a
repair shop is on site.

Julian Gold
1214 West Sixth Street
(512) 473-2493
www.juliangold.com
Catering to well-dressed, well-heeled
(both in the bucks and the shoes departments) Texas women, Julian Gold has four
stores in the state, its newest one in
Austin. Clothes by designers like Escada,
Bill Blass, and Valentino can be found
here, plus popular collections created by
Ellen Tracy, Missoni, and others. Top
names including Ferragamo, Anne Klein,
and Isaac are featured in the shoe department and there are bridal, fur, evening
wear, and cosmetic departments also.

Scarbrough's
Central Park, 4001 North Lamar
Boulevard
(512) 452-4220
For more than 100 years this family-
owned business has operated in Austin.
The original downtown location opened
in 1894 and, for many years, the Scarbrough building at the southwest corner
of Sixth and Congress was home for the
traditional downtown department store.
Now, the family runs this upscale clothing
store with a wide variety of evening, day,

and resort wear in the Central Park Shopping Center.

T. Kennedy
1011 West Lynn Street
(512) 478-0545
The emphasis is on natural women's clothing here—easy, natural design and natural fabrics including linen, cotton, and flax. Batik clothing is a specialty, and the store also features jewelry and accessories.

Tropical Tantrum
Central Park, 4001 North Lamar Boulevard, Suite 520
(512) 302-9888
Headed for an island getaway or just a backyard luau? Then check out the clothes at this small Central Park shop. The comfortable wear for both men and women includes hand-painted clothing and batiks for tropical nights and days on the Seychelles or Sixth Street.

The Texas Clothier
2905 San Gabriel Street
(512) 478-4956
www.texasclothier.com
Owners Dain and LaDonna Higdon have survived the economic roller coaster in 20 years of business in Austin. After working for years in retail, Dain Higdon started his own store in 1976, and ever since Austin's busy, top businessmen and attorneys have turned to him for fashion advice. Higdon's clients insist on quality and are willing to pay for it.

South Central

Therapy
1113 South Congress Avenue, SoCo Center
(512) 326-2331
www.therapyclothing.com
So-called SoCo is alive with shops, including several vintage clothing stores (see listings later in this chapter). While some of the fabrics used for Therapy's featured

designs might be vintage, the creations are contemporary works by talented Austin designers. Owner Jyl Kutsche looks to local talent for clothing and accessories, notably handbags, and also imports smart, urban designs from New York and elsewhere. The store's Web site maintains a dialogue with customers and offers news on the latest fashions featured at the store.

North

Last Call
Brodie Oaks Shopping Center, 4115 South Loop 360 (Capital of Texas Highway)
(512) 447-0701
This is Neiman Marcus without the posh surroundings and posh prices. The famous department store has its discount store at this location in a small mall in Southwest Austin. The store features men's, women's, and children's fashions, shoes, some small decorative furniture items, and a few household items including sheets, pillows, and knickknacks. Savvy shoppers can find last season's designer fashions at greatly reduced prices. Sometimes when you find them, you wonder what all the fuss was about, while sometimes you discover a classic design that will survive both the vagaries of fashion dictates and the demands of your pocketbook. Items are discounted up to 70 percent.

Sue Patrick
5222 Burnet Road, Suite 150
(512) 452-7701
www.suepatrick.com
Dressing comfortably and smartly in Austin's climate can be a challenge given the hot summer weather and sudden temperature changes in the winter. Sue Patrick offers a wide variety of casual and dressier fashions well suited to the Austin lifestyle. Some of the casual but comfortable fashions often have a hint of Texas in their cut or design.

CLOTHING/KIDS
Central

Bright Beginnings
1006 West 38th Street
(512) 454-KIDS
701 South Capital of Texas Highway
(Loop 360)
(512) 328-8989
www.bestdressedkids.com
Owner Sally Whitehouse keeps the Austin lifestyle in mind when stocking her store. Just like their elders, Austin kids like to play, and that means casual clothes, preferably in natural fabrics. Even the dress-up clothes here emphasize easy wearing and easy caring. Jumpers are a big favorite for girls, while boys can often emulate Dad in a vest, but in place of gray worsted, the kid's version is emblazoned with dinosaurs.

Picket Fences and Down Cherry Lane
1003 West 34th Street
(512) 458-2565
More than a kids clothing store, Picket Fences features (hence the name) picket-fence kids beds, plus nursery necessities, baby books, baby bags, decorative accents for the nursery or playroom, fabrics by the yard, window treatments, comfy nursery chairs for Mom or Dad, and maternity clothes. Down Cherry Lane, at the same address, offers hand-painted furnishings for nursery or playroom, rocking chairs, and vintage armoires. Custom orders are welcomed.

Wild Child and Wild Child Too!
1600 West 38th Street
(512) 451-0455, (512) 453-4335
Wild Child features "fashion-forward" clothing and shoes for infants and kids through size 6X, Wild Child Too! has the same hip clothing for preteen and junior kids. The store also stocks "preppy" clothes for preteens. including madras shirts, twill pants, and simple T-shirts.

South Central

Dragonsnaps
1700 South Congress Avenue
(512) 445-4497
Owned by the same folks who own Terra Toys (see our Toys section in this chapter), Dragonsnaps seeks to bring the Terra Toys free spirit to kid's clothing. The clothes are easy to wear, fun, and eye-catching.

West

Lambs-e-Divey
Tarrytown Center,
2415 A&B Exposition Boulevard
(512) 479-6619
This West Austin store features both casual wear for kids and outfits for those special occasions, such as Easter, Christmas, and family weddings. Owner Wendy Yarbrough says the store specializes in helping moms coordinate the family's wardrobe so that Joe and Jane Jr. can stand out in a crowd. Kids also can find designer togs here, including Ralph Lauren polos and khakis, and there are very traditional pretty girl dresses decorated with lace and smocking just like Grandma likes. But don't look for any little leather shoes here, since the owner of Tarrytown Center is an avowed animal rights advocate and does not allow her tenants to sell animal products. That stance has made national headlines over the past couple of years.

CLOTHING/WESTERN

The late Texas State Senator Peyton McKnight was an oilman who strode the floor of the Texas Capitol in legendary style, wearing a silver and gold belt buckle the size of a dinner plate and a pair of boots etched with a map of Texas. To mark his hometown of Tyler on the leather map, there was a large diamond smack in the middle of East Texas—one on each boot.

There is an old saying in Texas: "That boy is all hat," meaning, of course, there's too much image and not much substance. If you are going to don Western wear, you have to have the panache and, perhaps, some of the bucks of Senator McKnight. Good boots, a well-made hat, and a sturdy leather belt with a finely made belt buckle do not come cheap.

Not everyone in Texas dresses Western-style; in fact, "cowboys" come in various styles across the state. In Houston and Dallas you are more likely to see a business-man in a Brooks Brothers suit with a finely made pair of cowboy boots. In Amarillo or Midland, you might see a lawyer, cattle-man, or oilman dressed for a business meeting in a Western-cut suit, a bolo tie, and boots. In the state's smaller towns and on farms and ranches you are sure to see well-worn boots and traditional cowboy hats, while in El Paso and the Rio Grande Valley the influence of Mexico's vaqueros (literally cowboys) can be seen in the design of belt buckles and boots.

In Austin, Western attire is not seen as much as in other parts of the state, although at some Western and Mexican dance clubs (see our Nightlife chapter) you will see both men and women dressed in fine Western wear. While you won't see a lot of Stetsons in Austin (out-side the dance halls), you will see boots, particularly well-worn, much loved old boots, usually worn with jeans or a long skirt. Boots with no hat is okay, but a hat and no boots is a social faux pas. Nothing says Yankee like a guy in a cowboy hat and a pair of loafers.

There are several boot outlet stores in Austin, listed below, but the well-heeled will turn to one of the city's master boot makers or specialty shops for a custom-made pair—well-heeled because a good pair of boots can run to several hundred dollars. If you can't afford a pair, settle for a kerchief or two. A faded cotton kerchief, dipped in cold water and tied around your neck on a hot day, is an authentic cowboy tradition.

Texas Hatters
5003 Overpass Road, Buda
P.O. Box 100, Buda
(512) 295-4287, (800) 421-4287
www.texashatters.com
What does Prince Charles have in common with Willie Nelson? They both own hats created by one of the most famous Western wear artists in the United States, the late Manny Gammage. For decades, country western music stars, politicians, presidents, and future kings have worn what are generically called "cowboy hats." The walls of Gammage's workshop and store in the small community of Buda, just south of Austin off I-35, are covered with photos of famous folks. Gammage, like his father before him, blocked his hats by hand rather than by machine. Gammage passed away in 1995, but his family has carried on the tradition.

Central

Capitol Saddlery
1614 Lavaca Street
(512) 478-9309
www.capitolsaddlery.com
Singer Jerry Jeff Walker made this leather shop famous when he sang about the talents of late master boot maker Charlie Dunn. The store has an old-fashioned air, with boots, saddles, tack, and assorted leather wear stacked everywhere. Look for the large boot-shaped sign hanging outside the old building.

South Central

Allen Boots
1522 South Congress Avenue
(512) 447-1413
This Western wear store has been on South Congress for years and now finds itself in the midst of a South Austin shopping revival. This is a great place to find Western wear and boots at reasonable

prices. Enjoy the ambience. This is a Western wear shop without the glitz and urban cowboy atmosphere found in some other large Texas cities.

North

Sheplers
6001 Middle Fiskville Road
(512) 454-3000
www.sheplers.com
Looking for a cowboy hat or boots to take home or wear to the office barbecue? Check out this branch of Sheplers, a chain store with a large selection, located near Highland Mall.

COMPUTERS

Austin has more computer stores than Los Angeles has car dealers. Perhaps not factually true, but metaphorically speaking it captures the tech mood in Austin. In addition to several major chain operations including Computer City and CompUSA, there is an ever-growing subculture of small stores and resale outlets in Austin. Judging from the ads in the technology section of the *Austin American–Statesman,* it might appear that there's more money in motherboards than mother's old Buick. However, putting a system together from bits of this and that is easily done in Austin, provided you know your bytes from bits. Keep track of the ads, know who is a fixture on the landscape as opposed to a fly-by-night operation, and ask questions. Here is one unique Austin store for geeks:

Goodwill Computer Works
8701 Research Boulevard
(512) 835-8839
Whether you're looking for a cheap PC or an old classic Mac, this may be the place. Given Austin's intense high-tech industry growth and level of computer ownership, the town's closets are filled with old models. So Goodwill decided to provide a home for the abandoned. Old computers are donated to the shop, fixed up, and sold at bargain-basement prices. It's a great place to find a computer for a schoolchild or grandma without spending a fortune. There is an informal "museum" on site, also.

FLEA MARKETS
Central

Austin City-Wide Garage Sales
Palmer Events Center
900 Barton Springs Road
(512) 441-2828
Every month the Palmer Events Center on Town Lake is host to a large sale featuring more than 180 vendors selling a variety of flea market merchandise. Dates vary, so check the *Austin American–Statesman* for each monthly sale.

Northeast

Austin Country Flea Market
9500 U.S. 290 East
(512) 928-2795
This is the real thing: an old-fashioned, take-your-chances flea market. A jumble of clothing, rugs, pottery, tools, records, furniture, CDs and videos, and sporting goods—all under one roof so that you can wander around, rain or shine. Beware, some of the "brand-name" items may not be the real thing, but nevertheless there are lots of bargains; at least they seem bargains until you get home and wonder, "Why did I buy a set of TV tray tables?" The market's Mexican herb stalls and Latino music stands give the market a south-of-the-border flavor. You also can have your palm or tarot cards read, or enjoy a snow cone and a barbecue sandwich. The market is approximately 5 miles east of I-35 and is open only on weekends.

Southwest

Market Day
Lions Field, Wimberley
(512) 847-2201
www.visitwimberley.com/marketdays
On the first Saturday of the month, April
through December, flea market mavens
flock to Wimberley, southwest of Austin,
to comb the multitude of stalls at the
famed Wimberley Market Day. Vendors
number in the hundreds, and the wise get
there early—to get first choice get there
by 7:30 A.M. Take U.S. 290 west out of
Austin to Dripping Springs, then head
south on RR 12 into Wimberley—about a
45-minute drive. When you reach the fork
in the road in the heart of the community,
take the right fork about 4 blocks to Lions
Field. The Lions Club sells sausage wraps
for breakfast and barbecue later in the
day, plus a couple of local churches operate cake and cookie stands.

FARMERS' MARKETS

A good resource for keeping track of local
farmers' market activities and the status of
locally produced vegetables and fruits is
the *Austin American–Statesman* food section, published each Thursday. The Texas
Department of Agriculture's Web site is an
invaluable resource: www.agr.state.tx.us.

Central

Austin Farmers' Market
422 Guadalupe Street
(512) 236-0074
www.austinfarmersmarket.org
The downtown market is the latest addition to the farmers' market scene in
Austin, turning Republic Square, 2 blocks
west of Congress Avenue, into a busy mix
of food stalls and craftspeople every Saturday morning from 8:00 A.M. to noon.
The market's Web site lists many of the
vendors and links to their Web sites, offering information on Texas goat cheese,

Oaxacan tamales, herbs, locally smoked
salmon, mesquite spoons, and longhorn
beef. The Web site also lists Capital Metro
bus information.

Whole Foods Farmers Market
601 North Lamar Boulevard
(512) 476-1206
www.wholefoods.com
The downtown Whole Foods Market flagship store holds a weekly afternoon farmers' market in front of the store. The
market is usually held on Wednesday
afternoon from spring through fall, but
check with the store for times.

North

Austin's Historic Farmers' Market
6701 Burnet Road
(512) 454-1002
The Austin's Historic Farmers' Market has a
permanent home in North Austin that
remains open all year, although the peak
vegetable- and fruit-selling season runs
from spring to fall. Throughout the year the
market celebrates the seasons and the various harvests with festivals, cook-offs, and
fiestas. In spring, Hill Country peaches are
featured, followed by the June tomato
crop. Fourth of July brings a watermelon
patch. In September the Green Chile Pepper festival is held, and chile roasters, large
barbecue-like contraptions, are on hand to
roast the end-of-summer crop of New
Mexico–style chiles. In October the market
has a large pumpkin patch. The market also
has a Mexican restaurant on the premises
(see our Restaurants chapter), a gift shop
featuring Texas foods, a coffee-roasting
company, and, of course, a barbecue joint.

South

South Austin Farmers' Market
2910 South Congress Avenue
Local farmers set up shop in the parking
lot of the El Gallo restaurant on Saturday
morning from spring to fall.

West

Westlake Farmers' Market
4100 Westbank Drive
www.westlakefarmersmarket.com
The Westlake market is held year-round on Saturday morning in the parking lot of Westlake High School. In addition to local produce, Bottega della Pasta, a popular local wholesale pasta producer, sets up a stall at the market. Italian gelato is also sold, and there are crafts, kids' activities, and community events.

Northwest

Whole Foods Farmers' Market
Gateway Shopping Center,
9607 Research Boulevard
(512) 345-5003
www.wholefoods.com
Whole Foods at Gateway holds a seasonal farmers' market spring through fall, usually on Monday afternoon. Call the store for times.

East

Boggy Creek Farm
3414 Lyons Road
(512) 926-4650
www.boggycreekfarm.com
It is almost unbelievable that just 2½ miles east of downtown Austin in an old East Austin neighborhood is a five-acre organic farm that offers its products for sale every Wednesday and Saturday morning throughout the year. Boggy Creek Farm is noted for its fruit and vegetable crops, particularly its tomatoes. Owners Larry Butler and Carol Ann Sayle send out a weekly e-mail to customers, announcing what is in season. But there's more; the e-mail also includes wonderfully written glimpses into farm life that offer busy urbanites a moment's pause for reflection.

Round Rock

Round Rock Farmers' Market
221 East Main Street
Every Saturday from spring to fall, farmers and growers set up stalls in the city hall garage on Saturday morning.

One of the largest farmers' markets in Central Texas is held on the town square in historic Georgetown, a 15-minute ride north of Round Rock on I-35. The market is held on Thursday afternoon spring through fall.

FOOD/GOURMET/ KITCHENWARE

Austin is a city that considers food a significant part of life, not in a highfalutin way, although the city's restaurants boast a fair number of top-notch chefs, but in a way that celebrates the mix of food and friends, new tastes and familiar comforts. It is no surprise that when out-of-town visitors arrive, many Austinites take them on a discovery tour of the city's food stores.

Central

Ace Mart Restaurant Supply Co.
1025 West Fifth Street
(512) 482-8700
www.acemart.com
A little-known secret in cooking circles is that many restaurant supply companies are open to the public. Ace sells both to the trade and to the individual customer. Thrifty cooks and hostesses will check out the price of plates, glasses, silverware, and party ware here. Good buys are aprons, kitchen towels, oversized cooking pans, and stockpots. Ardent cooks are certain to find something they must have at this warehouse just west of Lamar Boulevard.

Anderson Coffee Company
Jefferson Square
(512) 453-1533

Jefferson Square, just off West 35th Street near Kerbey Lane, is a collection of small, older homes turned into cozy shops, a fitting setting for Anderson Coffee Company, which sells coffees, teas, mugs and teapots, plus culinary spices—comfort stuff. Singer-songwriter Lyle Lovett is said to be a fan of Anderson's coffee.

Breed & Co.
718 West 29th Street
(512) 474-6679
3663 Bee Caves Road
(512) 328-3960
www.breedandco.com

This is the kind of store that actually can bring couples closer together, even heal marriages. One partner can stroll the nuts and bolts section, while the other daydreams about the days when the entire collection of cooking equipment will find its way to his or her kitchen. Austinites will drive in from the outer reaches of town to shop at this compact, some might say small, hardware store compared with today's megastores. Breed proves the old adage that good things come in small containers. The store stocks hard-to-find and everyday hardware and paint supplies, cleaning solutions for every surface, china and crystal, a perfumery, a specialty food section, garden supplies, picture frames, decorative accessories, throw rugs, coffee beans, bird feeders, knives, cutting boards, and all manner of cookware. A second Breed has opened in West Lake Hills on Bee Caves Road.

Central Market
Central Park, 40th Street and Lamar Boulevard
(512) 216-1000
Westgate, Ben White and South Lamar Boulevards
(512) 899-4300
www.centralmarket.com

Urban myth says the original Central Market grocery store in Central Park is second only to the capitol in terms of tourists. On a Saturday afternoon as you struggle to bag a few habañero peppers or wait in line for the to-die-for imported prosciutto, it's easy to believe. The second location in Southwest Austin is just as popular. See our Close-up in this chapter to find out what it's all about.

Chef's Tool Box
6004 North Lamar Boulevard
(512) 467-1994
www.chefstoolbox.com

Both the professional and the amateur chef will admire the knives at this Austin store. You'll find kitchen tools, chef's uniforms, coffee, cigars, gadgets, pastry supplies, and, for anyone who loves to cook but hates standing for hours on end, comfortable chef's clogs from Sweden.

Cipollina
1213 West Lynn Street
(512) 477-1237
www.jeffreysofaustin.com

The name is Italian for a special, small sweet onion, often grilled or roasted in a sweet balsamic vinegar, and it is a fitting symbol for this popular take-out deli in the Clarksville neighborhood created by the owners of one of Austin's favorite restaurants, Jeffrey's (see our Restaurants chapter). The menu might include oak-roasted ducks, those caramelized cipollinas, roasted vegetables, panini sandwiches, osso buco, pesto chicken salad, and tuna salad made from fresh, not canned, tuna. A great place to stop for picnic fare or a take-home dinner feast.

Dr. Chocolate
Central Park, 4001 North Lamar Boulevard
(512) 454-0555
www.drchocolateonline.com

Addicted to chocolate? Consult the doctor. The prescription is, of course, chocolate in the form of flowers, hand-dipped chocolates, chocolate ice cream, chocolate pizza, chocolate cakes, chocolate-dipped strawberries, chocolate fudge. . . . The doctor has no shame.

Fabulous Cheesecakes
26 Doors, 1206 West 38th Street
(512) 389-1960
For 13 years, this specialty store has been cooking up 50 flavors of cheesecake for special occasions, birthdays, anniversaries, or just everyday noshing. The shop sells bite-sized and mini-sized cheesecakes for instant gratification. Orders can be placed ahead of time for special events, or customers can pick up a full-sized cheesecake and have it decorated for last-minute celebrations.

Portabla
1200 West Sixth Street
(512) 481-TOGO (8646)
www.sweetishhill.com
Casual eating is a hallmark of the Austin scene, and this take-out deli (affiliated with nearby Sweetish Hill Bakery; see below) offers a variety of dishes, many with a Mediterranean flavor. Pasta salads, foccacia sandwiches, roasted vegetables and salads, plus pies, pastries, and fruit desserts are on the menu. Portabla also caters small and large parties. During football season, there is a tailgate menu offered to feed the fans in style. Closed Sunday.

Pasta & Co.
3502 Kerbey Lane
(512) 453-0633
Pasta to go is the theme here. The company makes numerous kinds of pasta and sauces, including jalapeño fettucine, wild-mushroom ravioli, and ancho-pecan pesto. For those who can't bring themselves to boil a pot of water, the store also features ready-cooked pasta dishes that simply need reheating.

Texas French Bread
2900 Rio Grande Street
(512) 499-0355
www.frenchbread.com

A successful Texas bakery that has taken its success citywide, Texas French Bread is headquartered at this central city location, next door to Breed Hardware (see our listing in this chapter). Its breads, which present the best of European and American breadmaking traditions, are now sold to grocery stores and restaurants throughout the city. One of the most popular is a delicious breakfast bread made with pecans. (See our Restaurants chapter for more.)

Sweetish Hill Bakery
1120 West Sixth Street
(512) 472-1347
98 San Jacinto Boulevard
(512) 472-1347
www.sweetishhill.com
One of Austin's most noted bakeries, Sweetish Hill is famed for its breads, cookies (the lemon bars are addictive), and European-style pastries. This is a great place to order a special birthday cake and many Austinites insist on a chocolate or mocha buche de noel (a French cake shaped and decorated like a log, complete with meringue mushrooms) at Christmas time. The bakery is also a popular breakfast and lunch spot (see our Restaurants chapter).

Upper Crust Bakery
4508 Burnet Road
(512) 467-0102
Upper Crust is a neighborhood European-style bakery that serves up a daily feast of fresh breads, croissants, muffins, cookies, and tarts. The shop is also a popular neighborhood cafe (see our Restaurants chapter).

Wheatsville Food Co-op
3101 Guadalupe Street
(512) 478-2667
www.wheatsville.com
Wheatsville is an old-fashioned cooperative grocery store where the customers own the store. Members pay a nominal annual fee or purchase a share, but anyone can shop here. The co-op specializes in natural foods, and there is a vegetarian deli.

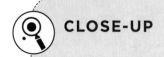

Central Market:
Austin's Feeding Frenzy

One surefire way to judge how people regard their hometown is to ask them where they take out-of-town visitors for an Insider's view of their city. Austin residents are lucky. The list of favorite spots is long and varied, but three spots appear on most short lists—Barton Springs Pool, the State Capitol, and Central Market.

Central Market? A grocery store? Yep. This central city grocery store now ranks among the city's most visited landmarks, and it has become a living symbol of the city's lifestyle. Since it opened in January 1994, Central Market has been a popular spot to give visitors a real peek at the Austin approach to living. On any given weekend, when the store is at its busiest, it is possible to see Austinites from all parts of the city, of all ages and backgrounds, speaking a variety of languages. They will be meandering through the store's aisles, tasting this, sampling that, and finding all manner of ingredients, some familiar, others exotic. Many are eagerly showing out-of-town guests or relatives the bounty at hand.

So popular was the original Central Market, a second has opened in Southwest Austin—Central Market Westgate.

On the eve of holidays such as July Fourth, Thanksgiving, and Christmas, finding a parking place at either of the shopping centers can be an exercise in patience. What draws the crowds to these central Austin grocery stores? It is a combination of ambience, incredible variety, and the notion that cuisine is an integral part of the Austin lifestyle, particularly on

weekends when Austinites light their barbecues, fire up their smokers, pack their picnic baskets, and fill up their ice chests.

The Central Market concept is the creation of the H-E-B grocery store chain, a family-owned South Texas chain now headquartered in restored buildings in the historic King William District in San Antonio (see our Day Trips chapter). H-E-B has been an innovator, both in its concept developments and its growth; in fact, the company has opened grocery stores in northern Mexico and is enjoying success in that country. The original Central Market in Austin is the model for others around the state, where residents quickly demanded to get their own Central Markets. However, each one is a little different in design and content. The concept may be duplicated, but these are not cookie-cutter stores. For example, the two Austin stores were developed from different pieces of real estate.

In the early '90s, the state legislature gave state agencies the go-ahead to lease state lands to private enterprise. One prime piece of state property was in the heart of Austin at 35th Street between Lamar Boulevard and Guadalupe Street. The state leased the property to a developer who then built the shopping center with Central Market as its anchor. Several state buildings still occupy part of the site, and the beautiful roses growing along Lamar Boulevard are a reminder that gardeners employed by the state nurtured this area for many years.

Central Market Westgate was developed on the site of an old shopping mall

The fishmonger's catch is lined up for gourmet buyers.
PETER A. SILVA

that had lost its appeal for many shoppers. An old H-E-B grocery store that had stood vacant for years was gutted and retooled along the Central Market concept of several markets under one roof. Just as other small shops opened around the original Central Market, the Westgate center is developing as a popular place to stroll—outdoors, that is, since this is not an enclosed mall. Some Austinites have jokingly taken to referring to Westgate as the Bubbaretum, as opposed to the upscale Arboretum, the trendy outdoor shopping mall in Northwest Austin, an acknowledgment that South Austin is a different place than North Austin neighborhoods (see our Relocation chapter).

Observers have credited other Austin grocery stores, including Whole Foods Market and the Wheatsville Food Co-op (see our listings in this chapter) with inspiring part of the Central Market concept. Certainly the emphasis on organic products and bulk items such as coffee beans, spices, beans, and grains were made popular by Austin's original health food stores. But H-E-B has developed a grocery-store concept that goes beyond catering to shoppers' requests for organic foods or specific ingredients; Central Market is designed to stimulate the imagination, educate the shopper and broaden his or her horizons. In doing so, the store captured the hearts (and pocketbooks) of Austin foodies—although it should be noted that while luxury items do abound here, prices for everyday items are competitive with neighborhood grocery stores.

The operative word here is "market"—Central Market is designed to evoke the spirit of an Old World marketplace. Visitors enter a vegetable and fruit market first, then proceed to a fish and meat market, a wine shop, a specialty food area, a bakery, a deli and cheese shop, finally reaching the front of the store, where a flower shop stands. The original Central Market building itself is a blend of local materials and design elements taken from 19th-century Texas buildings with a hint of Italian inspiration. The limestone walls and tin roof reflect buildings from the Texas frontier, while the terra-cotta columns evoke Tuscan architecture. A large tile mural by Austin artist Malou Flato at the front of the store depicts Barton Springs pool. The second location also borrows Austin icons, and there is a replica of the city's moonlight towers (see our Attractions chapter) out front, plus more tile murals of wildflowers by Flato.

Among Central Market's most crowded spots on the weekend are the butcher shop and fishmonger. The meat market features aged premium choice beef, lamb, veal, naturally raised pork, and poultry raised on organic grains, as well as 48 varieties of custom-made sausage. Special cuts of meat can be ordered, and many Austinites put in their orders for holiday turkeys or rib roasts.

The 75-foot-long seafood counter at the original store offers up to 100 varieties of both saltwater and freshwater fish, shellfish, and sushi, plus up to six varieties of fresh salmon in season. The second location has an equally impressive offering of fresh seafood, plus a boiling pot section where customers can buy shrimp and lobster ready to eat. The market also offers marinades created by local chefs. These can be added to the seafood to marinate on the ride home. Central Market is one of only two retailers in the nation that has been approved by the federal government to participate in a voluntary, intensive seafood inspection and safety program known as HACCP—Hazard Analysis of Critical Control Points.

The store's wine and beer shop offers 2,700 domestic and imported wines and more than 330 varieties of beer produced by American microbreweries and foreign brewers. Many of the wine selections are available for less than $10, and the store's wine shop has been voted Austin's best by the *Austin Chronicle* several years in a row.

The specialty foods section of the store features more than 175 olive oils, 165 varieties of vinegar, 60 varieties of barbecue sauce—and the list goes on. Freezers hold Indian and Chinese foods and sorbets made from exotic fruits; the dairy case is filled with butter from Europe and milk in glass bottles from Texas cows. The coffee and tea shop has coffee beans from Africa, Brazil, Mexico, and Hawaii; teas from the Himalayas; biscotti from Italy. Then there is the bakery, where French baguettes are baked daily (along with a large variety of other breads including a personal favorite, southern

Whole Foods Market
601 North Lamar Boulevard
(512) 476-1206
9607 Research Boulevard
(512) 345-5003
www.wholefoods.com
Take the Austin trivia test: Where was the first Whole Foods Market, and when did Michael Dell graduate from the University of Texas? Answers: 914 North Lamar Boulevard, and he didn't—the high-tech billionaire dropped out after his computer business could no longer be run from his dorm room. If there are two indicators for Austin's growth and development, they are Dell Computers and Whole Foods Markets. Both are now the hottest stocks around, and Austinites who bought both

Burgundy walnut bread), and fresh tortillas roll off the conveyer belt of the tortilla machine.

The deli has prosciuttos from Italy, smoked salmon from Scotland, pâtés, and organic cold cuts. Then there is the pasta shop, where shoppers can match handmade pasta with fresh sauces or pestos, and the cheese shop with cheeses from the best producers in the United States and Europe. Across the way is the salsa, pickle, olive, and antipasto bar. One final stop—the flower shop at the front of the market. Here shoppers can find a wide variety of ready-made bouquets, including Hill Country wildflower bouquets in season, special holiday arrangements, and dried-flower creations. You can also get custom-designed bouquets for any occasion.

On the second floor of the original store is the Central Market Cooking School, where internationally known chefs as well as top Austin chefs have taught, including Paul Prudhomme and Caprial Pence. There are 25 classes each month, including classes for kids. Cooking class gift certificates make a great Christmas present.

Both stores also feature a Central Market Cafe (see our Restaurants and Kidstuff chapters), a popular family gathering spot where patrons can eat inside or listen to a variety of local musicians while eating on the deck.

A gift shop offers a special assembly and packing service. A basket filled with Texas-made goodies is a great souvenir. Out-of-town shoppers can have their purchases packed in ice for the ride home, and dry ice is available for extended chilling. Around holiday time, Central Market also produces a gift catalog for mailing cheeses, seafood, meats, specialty sausages, and grocery items across the country.

The original location at 4001 North Lamar Boulevard is open from 9:00 A.M. to 9:00 P.M. daily, and the cafe is open from 7:00 A.M. to 10:00 P.M. daily. Call (512) 206-1000 for general information, (512) 206-1013 for the meat market, (512) 206-1012 for the seafood market, and (512) 458-3068 for the cooking school. The Westgate location at 4477 South Lamar Boulevard is open from 9:00 A.M. to 9:00 P.M. daily, and the cafe from 7:00 A.M. to 10:00 P.M. daily. Call (512) 899-4300 for all departments. During the holidays, notably Thanksgiving and Christmas, both stores extend their hours in the evening. For more information, check out www.centralmarket.com.

are now zillionaires. Whole Foods Market has expanded from a hippie-dippie, natural foods store to the largest natural foods retailer in the country with $1 billion in sales and a store just a few blocks from L.A.'s Rodeo Drive. It's been a bumpy ride, and founders John Mackey (who once drove around in a blue postal van painted with dancing vegetables) and Peter Roy have been criticized by natural foodies and some union activists along the way, but the bottom line is Whole Foods is an unparalleled success.

Whole Foods remains a popular icon on the local landscape, a place where you are just as likely to find a tie-dyed, would-be street mime shopping side by side with a Texas Supreme Court justice.

It has always been that kind of place. There's tofu and high-priced Bourdeaux, tabbouleh and hormone-free, top-grade fillet of beef, organic apple juice and high-priced balsamic vinegars. The 38,000-square-foot flagship store, adjacent to the company's corporate offices, opened in 1995 and features both organic and top-grade vegetables and fruit, a wide variety of bulk food, hormone-free beef and chicken, excellent fish, a broad selection of beer, wine, cheese, a deli, an extensive vitamin and supplements department, plus a bakery, sandwich shop, and on-site restaurant and masseuse. Construction is under way on an even larger homebase just south of the flagship store on North Lamar. A second location is in the Gateway shopping center in Northwest Austin.

Wiggy's
1130 West Sixth Street
(512) 474-WINE (9463)

If you are picking up a picnic at nearby Portabla, Cipollina, or Sweetish Hill (see above), this is a good place to find a wine to complement your menu. The staff is knowledgeable and the shop offers a wide range of wines, some bargains, others more expensive. The store also has a large selection of cigars and spirits.

North

Asahi Imports
100 West North Loop Boulevard
(512) 453-1850

It is easy to miss this store with its unassuming storefront in a strip shopping center, but its selection of everyday Japanese ceramics, sake sets, rice bowls, teapots, plus origami kits and Japanese food items (tea, rice candy, plum wine) is well worth seeking out, both for price and quality.

Grape Vine Market
7938 Great Northern Boulevard
(512) 323-2900
www.grapevinemarket.com

This 18,000-square-foot gourmet food and wine shop also offers classes, wine tastings, and has a rare-wine room where exceptional wines can be bought for special occasions. The store also designs gift baskets, sells gourmet foods and special take-out dishes, offers a bridal registry, and has a large selection of cigars and spirits. The store is located just east of MoPac off Anderson Lane. Closed Sunday.

Lamme's Candies
5330 Airport Boulevard
(512) 310-2223, (800) 252-1885
www.lammes.com

The Lamme family has been making candies in Austin since 1885. Famed for Texas Chewie Pecan Pralines, Lamme's also heralds the early summer with its chocolate-dipped strawberries. The company's headquarters is on Airport Boulevard, but there are other locations around the area: Lamar Village at 38th Street in Central Austin, downtown at Sixth and Congress, Northcross Mall in North Austin, Barton Creek Mall in West Austin, Highland Mall in North Austin, Lakeline Mall in Northwest Austin, R.R. 620 and I-35 in Round Rock, and at San Marcos Factory Outlet stores.

La Victoria Bakery
5425 Burnet Road
(512) 458-1898

Owner Anita Becerra creates Mexican specialties at this small bakery on Burnet Road. One seasonal item worth seeking out is her pan de muerto or Day of the Dead bread, which celebrates the annual Mexican holiday on All Souls Day. (See our Annual Events chapter for more on All Souls Day.)

Hong Kong Supermarket
8557 Research Boulevard
(512) 339-2068

A stroll around this North Austin supermarket is like a culinary tour of Asia. Formerly a neighborhood grocery store, the owners took over the facility and filled it with Asian foodstuffs, fresh, frozen, and canned to meet the needs of Austin's growing Asian population. The meat and fresh fish section features cuts and types of fish and fowl popular among Oriental cooks. There is a cooked meat section with barbecued ducks and meats, plus several aisles featuring kitchen and household goods. It is a good place to buy noodles, tea, and rice in bulk.

MGM Indian Foods
7427 Burnet Road
(512) 459-5353
www.mgmindianfoods.com
This is the city's oldest Indian grocery, stocking herbs, vegetables, dried fruits and nuts, and other vital ingredients for Indian cuisine. Recently the owner, who hails from the state of Kerala in India, has added foods from Ghana and Nigeria to meet customer demands.

My Thanh Oriental Market
7601 North Lamar Boulevard
(512) 454-4805
This Thai market sells curries, noodles, spices and herbs, Thai peppers, fish sauce, coconut milk—all the necessities for cooking a Thai feast, plus the utensils to do it, including woks and rice cookers, and the serving ware to bring it to the table.

Saigon Oriental Market
8610 North Lamar Boulevard
(512) 837-6641
This grocery stocks a full line of Vietnamese ingredients and also sells cooking utensils, incense, and traditional festival decorations.

East

El Milagro
910 East Sixth Street
(512) 477-6476
El Milagro—the Miracle—is an authentic tortilla factory that sells both wholesale to Austin grocery stores and restaurants and retail to the walk-in customers. Buying from the source can be fun, and it gives

you an opportunity to see the inner workings of an authentic culinary tradition both south of the border and in Texas. Ambitious cooks who plan to follow a Texas tradition and make Christmas tamales can buy freshly ground masa (cornmeal) from the factory.

Callahan's General Store
501 U.S. 183
(512) 385-3452, (800) 950-8602
220 South Bell Boulevard, Cedar Park
(512) 335-8585
The closest thing to an old-fashioned general store in Austin, Callahan's sells sausage-stuffing machines, canning equipment, and all manner of supplies for cooks. In addition, there is Western wear, boots, saddles, and supplies for the farm and ranch.

Fiesta Mart
3909 North I-35
(512) 406-3900
www.fiestamart.com
A branch of the Houston supermarket chain, Fiesta takes a multicultural approach to the grocery store business. Everything from banana leaves for tamales to British custard mixes can be found on the shelves here. If your Puerto Rican pen pal or your great aunt from Australia is coming to town, check the shelves here for those grocery essentials.

South Central

La Mexicana Bakery
1924 South First Street
(512) 443-6369
Mexican pastries are intended to be mood-lifters, a little sweet bite to accompany midmorning coffee, or a late night snack with a cup of hot Mexican chocolate. Many contain no salt or preservatives, so they are best eaten the day they are made. La Mexicana offers a variety of cookies and cakes, empanadas stuffed with pumpkin, gingerbread pigs, and sugarcoated conchas (shell-shaped

cakes). Be sure to ask the names of the varieties—often they are a wonderful play on the shape, ingredients, or taste of the item. The bakery also sells Mexican sodas.

Phoenicia Bakery & Deli
2912 South Lamar Boulevard
(512) 447-4444
4701 Burnet Road
(512) 323-6770
Phoenicia is a deli specializing in imported foods from those countries and regions that ring the Mediterranean, including Greece, Spain, Italy, North Africa, and the Middle East. In addition to olives, olive oils, peppers, spices, sauces, pasta, and grains, the store also sells cold cuts such as salami and mortadella, plus cheeses from the region, pickles, stuffed grape leaves, freshly made tahini, and hummus. There is a frozen food section where bakers can find phyllo dough. The deli also makes sandwiches (see our Restaurants chapter) and has a small bakery selling pita bread and baklava, plus other regional delights. In addition to the original location in South Central Austin, a second, larger new store has opened in North Austin on Burnet Road.

Southwest

Oak Hill Hardware
7010 Highway 71 West
(512) 288-7223
More than a hardware store, this friendly neighborhood store in Southwest Austin has a wide collection of kitchen and household goods that make great wedding or special occasion gifts. Many of the kitchen and cookware items celebrate Texas and Mexican themes and are especially suitable for serving Southwestern fare.

West

Great Harvest Bakery
3201 Bee Caves Road
(512) 329-9216
4815 West Braker Lane
(512) 345-0588
Noted for their crusty, rustic, flavorful European-style breads, Great Harvest has two locations and also sells its breads to local restaurants and grocery stores.

Trianon Coffee Roasters
3201 Bee Caves Road
(512) 328-4033
3742 Far West Boulevard
(512) 346-9636
4815 Braker Lane
(512) 349-7758
This French-style coffee boutique sells freshly roasted beans, pastries, chocolate, and candies. The other locations are in Northwest Austin.

Northwest

Williams-Sonoma
Arboretum Market, 9722 Great Hills Trail
(512) 338-4080
www.williamssonoma.com
Cooking enthusiasts are familiar with the Williams-Sonoma catalog, and many of those items can be found at this Arboretum-area store in Northwest Austin. In addition to top-quality small appliances and bakeware, the store stocks imported foods, plus numerous kitchen gadgets, dinner and glassware.

Round Rock

Lone Star Bakery
106 West Liberty
(512) 255-3629
www.roundrockdonuts.com

Lone Star claims to make the best dough-nuts in Texas, and there is no harm in test-ing their claim, even coming back for seconds or thirds to make sure the boast is true. The bakery celebrated its 75th anniversary in 2001 and also sells cakes, cookies, and kolaches (Czech pastries).

Saradora's Coffeehouse & Emporium
101 East Main Street
(512) 310-1200
In addition to a coffee bar, this store in the historic town center sells roasted beans, fresh breads, and pastries to go, plus homemade fudge and Austin's own Amy's ice cream.

GARDENING
Central

Gardens
18118 West 35th Street
(512) 451-5490
www.gardens-austin.com
The small garden in front of this Central Austin garden shop is living proof that wonderful gardens can be created not only in small spaces but also in the Austin climate, where summer heat and drought can be a challenge. Don't be fooled by the outward appearance of this shop in the 35th Street shopping corridor; it may look small, but inside there is a mother lode of resources for serious gardeners—imported pottery from Italy, Japanese garden ele-ments, English garden tools, books, seeds, and an outdoor nursery of herbs and plants, many of them unusual and eye-catching. This is a must-stop for any ardent gardener.

South Central

Floribunda
2401-B South Lamar Boulevard
(512) 441-6145
Tucked behind a bead shop and a vintage clothing store, Floribunda is like a small

magic garden. Austin-friendly plants, vibrant pots, seeds, tools, and garden ornaments are arranged artfully in this hidden garden. Ivan Spaller, a young Austin garden artist who once worked at the Bush Kennebunkport, Maine, home, has designed several garden follies, including a literal lawn chair—an over-sized lawn-covered sofa that sits in one corner of the garden—and a four-poster lawn "bed."

The Great Outdoors
3730 South Congress Avenue
(512) 448-2992
www.gardenadventures.com
Huge live oaks cover this South Austin nursery across from the St. Edward's Uni-versity campus, making it a pleasant place to meander while choosing plants and daydreaming about garden projects. The garden center offers advice on growing in the challenging Austin climate and has special tips on bamboo, fruit trees, banana palms, and other tropicals that can toler-ate both hot summers and sudden cold snaps. Another attraction is the on-site outdoor cafe, the Mad Bird Juice Garden, where smoothies, coffee, muffins, cookies, and sandwiches are served amid the hor-ticultural surroundings.

South

It's About Thyme
11726 Manchaca Road
(512) 280-1192
www.itsaboutthyme.com
Newcomers to Austin who enjoy garden-ing may be frustrated if they try to grow plants that flourish in cooler, northern climes, but they won't be disappointed if they stick to native plants and those herbs that do well in Mediterranean countries—rosemary, oregano, basil, and thyme. This South Austin herb nursery, 2 miles south of Slaughter Lane, has a wide selection of herbs and related items. The shop also sells antique roses, which do quite well in the Austin climate.

Marbridge Farms Greenhouse
F.M. 1626 and Bliss Spillar Road
(512) 282-5504

Marbridge Ranch is a residential facility for mentally handicapped men who earn a living tending the greenhouses that house hundreds of plants. Many Austinites head here for reasonably priced plants for the garden and the vegetable plot. The farm is in far South Austin on the outer edge of the city, but the wide variety and the worthy cause attract a great deal of gardeners.

Southwest

The Natural Gardener
8648 Old Bee Caves Road
(512) 288-6113
www.naturalgardeneraustin.com

Owner John Dromgole is a well-known radio personality who preaches the benefits of organic gardening every Saturday morning on KLBJ-AM. The nursery, tucked away on a country road in Southwest Austin, is always busy on the weekends as Austin gardeners flock here for plants, flowers, vegetables, seeds, and a wonderful variety of tools and garden ornaments. There is an antique rose collection, plus xeriscape plants for low water–maintenance gardens. The nursery also sells a line of soils and fertilizers, including Dillo Dirt, a soil enhancer made from recycled Austin sewage wastes. Shoppers can bag their soils or have large amounts delivered.

West

Barton Springs Nursery
3601 Bee Caves Road
(512) 328-6655

This West Lake Hills nursery features an extensive collection of native plants. Newcomers soon learn that native is often the best way to go in the Austin climate, and many varieties and species can be found here. The owners and staff have a warehouse of knowledge to help gardeners overcome the challenges of Hill Country

gardening. The center also has a collection of wildflower seeds and garden ornaments.

Pots and Plants
5902 Bee Caves Road
(512) 327-4564

"That crazy flamingo place" is how you will hear radio ads refer to this West Austin garden center. Austin gardeners know spring is on the way when a few pink flamingos show up on the front lawn of Pots and Plants at the intersection of Bee Caves Road and Loop 360. Later, the rest of the pink plastic flock arrives and Austin gardeners know the planting season goes into full swing. A few years ago, some zealous West Lake Hills citizens wanted to ban the flamingos because they thought they were tacky and flew in the face of the community's sign ordinance; but other citizens came to the rescue and the birds are now considered high-class yard art. The garden center has a wide selection of native plants, plus deer-resistant varieties.

Northwest

Smith & Hawken Garden
Gateway Courtyard,
9901 Loop 360 (Capital of Texas Highway)
(512) 345-8700
www.smith-hawken.com

Gardening enthusiasts likely are familiar with the Smith & Hawken catalog that features some of the best garden tools, well-designed pottery, and gardener's clothing. With the opening of this store, Austin gardeners have the opportunity to browse through the same collection of much-admired garden accoutrements featured in the popular catalog.

Round Rock

Pitchforks and Tablespoons
2113 Manor Road
(512) 476-5858

They grow their own vegetables and herbs at the Eastside Cafe (see our Restaurants chapter), so it was only logical that a small food and garden shop open on-site at this—the name says it all—eastside cafe. In addition to gourmet and homestyle pantry items, patrons can find balm to soothe those garden-stressed hands, birdhouses and butterfly kits, herbs, and natural fertilizers.

GIFTS
Central

Atomic City
1700 San Antonio Street
(512) 477-0293
Toys are us—for grown-ups that is. Atomic City is the place to find Godzillas that spit fire, fighting nuns, and other Japanese toys to keep on the desk for those moments when the brain bombs. The store also has a large collection of tin toys, lava lamps, Hawaiian shirts, even boots and shoes to add just the right sartorial touch to a toy player's tropical outfit.

Capitol Complex Visitors Center
112 East 11th Street, Capitol Annex
(512) 305-8400
The capitol police report the occasional ardent tourist attempting to remove part of the capitol's wrought-iron fence, a doorknob, or door hinge as a memento. But law-abiding visitors head to the capitol's gift shop where gifts reflecting these architectural elements can be bought without risking arrest. Replicas of the capitol's door hinges serve as bookends; other architectural elements are reproduced in paperweights. The store has a first-class collection of posters, flags, and books about Texas flora, fauna, travel, and history. The small shop also sells Texas foods and T-shirts.

Congress Avenue Souvenirs
615 Congress Avenue
(512) 478-1663
Looking for something that says "I went to Texas, and all I bought you was this bluebonnet soap holder"? This is the place. Items, both practical and fanciful, decorated with the Lone Star, the Texas flag, an armadillo or two, and the ubiquitous bluebonnet can be found here. Postcards, bumper stickers, stickers for kids, and coffee mugs are popular, reasonably priced gift items to send the Texas message.

Cowgirls and Flowers
508 Walsh Street
(512) 478-4626
www.cowgirlsandflowers.com
More than one of the most popular flower shops in the central city, Cowgirls is noted for its jewelry and craft items. If you are looking for a very artsy flower presentation, plus a special gift, check out this Central Austin store.

The Menagerie
1601 West 38th Street, Suite 7
(512) 453-4644
Bucatelli, Christofle, Saint Louis, and Wedgwood are just some of the top names in crystal, china, and silver that can be found at this small, elegant Jefferson Square shop. The bridal registry is a favorite among some of Austin's old families. The shop also sells jewelry and collectibles.

Morning Star Trading Company
1117 West Fifth Street
(512) 476-1727
The major trade here is in oils and essences aimed at making folks feel better. The store sells massage, relaxation, and bath oils, plus other body-care products—all designed to enhance both the skin and the soul. In addition to personal products, the store also features jewelry.

Necessities and Temptations
1202-A West Sixth Street
(512) 473-8334
Contemporary Southwestern jewelry and Texas souvenirs are among the items sold at this small gift shop that is part of

the Sixth Street strolling strip west of Lamar Boulevard. The store also features Brazilian slate fountains and falling rain chime boxes.

Oat Willie's
617 West 29th Street
(512) 482-0630

Remember the term "head shop"? A visit to Oat Willie's is a jaunt down memory lane for anyone who grew up in the '60s. Whenever you see an "Onward through the Fog" bumper sticker, you are a looking at an Austin hallmark—this was Oat Willie's (Yes, Virginia, there was an Oat Willie) slogan. Oat Willie once ran for President, and his T-shirts are now collectors' items. T-shirts are still sold at Oat Willie's, along with comic books, videos, toys, and clothing. Bongs (pipes, for the noninitiated) are no longer sold at Oat Willie's, but street vendors still sell them on The Drag (Guadalupe Street).

Old Bakery and Emporium
1006 Congress Avenue
(512) 477-5961

Austin's senior citizens sell their crafts in this old store just a block south of the capitol (see our Attractions chapter). The seniors also sell homebaked cookies and breads that are a good accompaniment to a stroll down Congress Avenue or a minipicnic on the capitol grounds.

Paper Place
4001 North Lamar Boulevard, Suite 540
(512) 451-6531

The stock here goes beyond invitations, celebratory cards for all occasions, and stationery to include a large stock of handmade papers that can be used in a variety of crafts. Japanese papers for calligraphy work, Italian marbleized papers to line journal covers, and thick natural-fiber papers to construct lampshade covers all can be found at Paper Place. Scrapbook enthusiasts, artists, diarists, and kids with sticker fever also shop here.

Pecan Square Emporium
1122 West Sixth Street
(512) 477-4900
www.pecansquare.com

A popular spot for Christmas shoppers— the local merchants decorate this stretch of Sixth Street with luminarias during the season—Pecan Street Emporium is noted for its selection of music boxes, German pottery collectibles, and nutcrackers. The shop also has a large collection of tiny boxes, plus jewelry, toys, and a great card collection. The back room of the store houses a large collection of Christmas ornaments and villages during the holidays.

Positive Images
1118 West Sixth Street
(512) 472-1831

Part of the so-called West End shopping district, this store has a delightful mix of handcrafted jewelry, wooden boxes, and glass art. The store also sells fantastical furniture—carved, painted, and decorated with inspirational and witty sayings— woodland animals, pastoral scenes, and fairy-tale fantasies.

The Cadeau
2316 Guadalupe Street
(512) 477-7276
Central Park, 4001 North Lamar
Boulevard
(512) 453-6988

This wonderful shop—in both locations—is more than a gift shop. Since 1952 the Cadeau has been presenting Austin shoppers with a wide variety of gifts, home furnishings, clothes, decorative items, toys, china, and crystal. Both the original store on The Drag and the new store in Central Park feature home furnishings by top designers, including Versace, Calvin Klein, Baccarat, and Kosta Boda. Not all the items are high-priced, and shoppers with a budget can find inexpensive but unique items. The store also has a good selection of cards and wrapping paper. The location on The Drag also has a selection of kitchenware and cookbooks.

Things Celtic
1806 West 35th Street
(512) 472-2358
www.thingsceltic.com
The name says it all here. The shop features arts, crafts, and food items from the Celtic world—Scotland, Ireland, Wales, Cornwall—and Celtic artists in the United States. Celtic lace, Bewley china, Waterford crystal, and Irish tea are sold in this small shop in the 35th Street shopping area. The shop also sells kilts, socks, walking sticks, and Celtic jewelry. The shop's operators have information on the Austin Celtic Association, which holds an annual festival in October (see our Annual Events chapter). The Web site offers on-line shopping and a link to the association.

University Co-op
2244 Guadalupe Street
(512) 476-7211
www.coop-bookstore.com
If God isn't a Longhorn, why did he paint the sunset burnt orange and then fill this store on The Drag with all that burnt-orange stuff? That philosophical question needs no answer in Austin. UT fans can find just about anything in their team colors here, from the theological burnt-orange question on a bumper sticker to windsocks. The co-op also has a bookstore (see our Literary Austin chapter), plus a camera shop.

Wild About Music
721 Congress Avenue
(512) 708-1700
www.wildaboutmusic.com
If you're looking for a gift that says Texas music, check out this downtown store. All the gifts at Wild About Music have a musical theme, including T-shirts, posters, jewelry, books, and knickknacks. The store also sells aquariums made from converted television sets by Austin artist Larry Plitz.

North

Source Menagerie
8015 Shoal Creek Boulevard, Suite 103
(512) 452-2756
www.dogstuff.com
Doggone it, they've got everything under the sun that has a dog motif—from life-size stone statues of labs to fluffy, stuffed Bridget the Border Collie, jigsaw puzzles with a doggy theme, car mats, even a salt and pepper set that has three items—a pepper grinder, a salt shaker, and a dog hair shaker. The store also has a catalog business; just call (888) 702-WOOF.

South Central

Off the Wall
1704 South Congress Avenue
(512) 445-4701
Animal theme gifts are the order of the day here. The store also sells antique clocks, ceramics, and occasional pieces of furniture.

The Herb Bar
200 West Mary Street
(512) 444-6251
Herbs, both culinary and medicinal, can be found here, plus tinctures and body oils designed to soothe what ails you.

Round Rock

Paper Dragon Etc.
34 Round Rock Avenue
(512) 255-2227
Only friendly dragons hang out here among the bears, angels, candles, and jelly beans. This store in Round Rock's historic center also sells jewelry and other gift items.

HOME FURNISHINGS
Central

Bella Home
1221 West Sixth Street
(512) 474-1157
Sixth Street just west of Lamar Boulevard is a great place to look for unique home furnishings with its mix of antiques and import shops. Bella Home is for lovers of modern Italian design—classic, sophisticated 20th- and 21st-century pieces that are imported after annual visits to Europe by owner Dante Bini.

Cities
524 North Lamar Boulevard
(512) 236-1200
In addition to the plethora of antiques shops in the West Sixth-North Lamar shopping area, new stores have been erected where used car dealerships once stood. For those with modern taste, this shop features simply elegant furniture, home accessories, and a collection of funny, wacky, playful gift items.

Cush Cush
500 North Lamar Boulevard
(512) 236-0068
Plush plush cush cush; the luxurious, tactile and exotic fabrics that fill the store make you want to touch touch. Fabrics can be purchased by the yard, or the store's workrooms will create window treatments, bedroom designs, cushions, throws, and slipcovers. The store also stocks a similarly exotic and wonderful collection of trims, feathers, tassels, and bows.

Eleganté
500 North Lamar Boulevard
(512) 236-0068
www.elegante-online.com
Those looking to evoke the spirit of a Mexican hacienda will enjoy a visit to this store in the shopping district around Whit Hanks Antique center. Large paintings depict the hacienda life or reflect on Latin America's rich religious art. Mexican antique and reproduction furniture, candleholders, and other decorative accessories including textiles are also featured.

Jaya
902 North Lamar Boulevard
(512) 457-1255
David and Jacque Hooks travel to China, India, and Southeast Asia to bring back exotic furniture and home furnishings for their central Austin store. They also take special orders that craftsmen in faraway places construct to meet your needs. Many of them are built from old woods to modern specifications.

Marco Polo's Attic
1105 North Lamar Boulevard
(512) 236-1320
www.marcopolosattic.com
The "attic" is located in a modern building near the Lamar Boulevard and West Sixth shopping district, but once inside, the visitor is transported to dozens of exotic places and times. Tibetan gongs and bells, carousel horses, teak furniture from the tropics, stone deities (there is a deities page on the store's Web site), linens and textiles from around the world, doors from palaces and temples, pillars and pots to decorate the garden are just a few of the finds here.

Tipler's Lamp Shop
1204 West Fifth Street
(512) 472-5007
Looking for a 1930's lamp to hang above your dining room table? Tipler's has a selection of hanging lamps from the 1900s to 1940s, plus a large variety of antique and custom-made lamps. The store also has an extensive selection of lampshades and provides repair and restoration services.

Wildflower
908 North Lamar Boulevard
(512) 320-0449
Natural is the keyword at this home furnishings boutique in the North Lamar–West

Sixth shopping district. Natural bedding, shabby slipcovers, organic cotton mattresses, and furniture from reclaimed wood are among the items for sale in this boutique. The store also sells natural clothing for the whole family, including babies.

South Central

Your Living Room
220 South Congress Avenue
(512) 320-9909
www.yourlivingroom.com
The Colorado River divides downtown Austin from what is now being dubbed SoCo, the hip neighborhood that lines South Congress Avenue as it rises to the south. The first store on the south side of the bridge (the famous "bat bridge"; see our Attractions chapter) is Your Living Room. One glimpse in the storefront window offers an idea of what SoCo is all about—hip, modern, with a splash of retro and a sense of humor. The contemporary furniture and lighting in the store embraces both the future and classics from the past.

West

Furniture Brokers of Westlake
4201 Westbank Drive
(512) 329-8421
The showroom for this upscale furniture consignment store is in a small shopping center across from Westlake High School. Given its West Austin location, much of the furniture here comes from some of Austin's more affluent residents. The store also sells collectibles and artwork.

North

Cierra
5502 Burnet Road
(512) 454-8603
Cierra presents primitive folk art and furnishings from the Southwest and Mexico,

including rustic tables, wrought-iron lamps and candleholders, cabinets, and chairs evocative of Old Mexico.

Christmas shopping takes on special meaning in Austin because of two popular annual events: the Austin Junior League Christmas Affair in late November and the Armadillo Christmas Bazaar in December. Check our Annual Events chapter for details.

East

Provencal Home and Garden
The Village at Westlake Shopping Center, Loop 360 (Capital of Texas Highway) and Bee Caves Road
(512) 306-9449
Looking to bring a touch of the South of France to your home? Here is where you can find French china, beautiful crystal, fabulous linens, and custom fabrics. The store also sells rustic furniture for both inside and outside the home.

JEWELRY
Central

Gallerie Estate Jewelers
3500 Jefferson Street, Suite 105
(512) 451-3889
Antique and estate sale jewelry is sold at this Jefferson Square–area jeweler. The store also accepts consignments.

Nomadic Notions
2426 Guadalupe Street
(512) 478-6200
2438 West Anderson Lane
(512) 454-0001
With two stores, one in the central area, the other in North Austin, Nomadic Notions sells beads from more than 35

countries, some 5,000 varieties ranging in price from pennies to around $50 apiece. The stores also sell jewelers' supplies and offer instruction to those eager to make their own distinctive jewelry. The stores also sell African bead strands and Egyptian blown-glass perfume bottles.

Russell Korman
3806 North Lamar Boulevard
(512) 451-9292
This is another Austin success story. Back in the '70s, Korman worked on The Drag near the university selling beads; now he is selling custom-made pieces made from precious metals and jewels.

South Central

The Turquoise Door
1204 South Congress Avenue
(512) 480-0618
Silver jewelry and Latin American and Southwestern folk art are sold at this downtown store next door to Mezzaluna Restaurant. The sign in the window says Axl Rose and Vanessa Redgrave have shopped here, and it's easy to see why. The turquoise and amber jewelry is particularly beautiful. In addition to top-quality Mexican folk art, the store has a small collection of folk art books.

PHOTOGRAPHY
Central

Precision Camera and Video
3810 North Lamar Street
(512) 467-7676
www.precision-camera.com
A favorite among Austin's professional and amateur photographers, Precision has grown from a small shop near the university to this large store just north of 35th Street. Services include film processing, camera rental, and repair. Check out the store's used-camera department.

South Central

Camera Co/Op
1718 South Congress Avenue
(512) 804-2668
The shelves are lined with some unique antique cameras, but camera buffs also can find new and used equipment here, along with photographic supplies.

Holland Photo
1221 South Lamar Boulevard
(512) 442-4274
www.hollandphoto.com
This is a full-service photographic lab used by many of Austin's professional photographers. It offers a variety of services to both professionals and amateurs alike, including two-hour E-6 processing, computer imaging, custom enlargements, and film and photo supplies.

RESALE SHOPS/CHARITY

Recycling is a subject close to Austin's heart, so it is no wonder that resale shops abound. Many are dedicated to raising money for charity; others seek to extend the life of bell-bottoms well beyond their expected life span. Goodwill, the Salvation Army, the MaryLee Foundation, the Junior League, St. Vincent de Paul, and other worthy institutions all operate thrift stores in Austin. Donations are encouraged, and listings for the stores can be found in the Yellow Pages. Here we have listed those charity stores with a specific mission or those with a unique presence in Austin.

Central

Junior League of Austin Resale Shop
6555 Burnet Road
(512) 459-4592
One of several fund-raising efforts by the Junior League (the popular Christmas Affair show is another; see our Annual Events chapter). The store is a good place

to find children's clothing, and it can be just one stop along Burnet Road, which boasts several resale shops selling clothing, furniture, and home furnishings.

Next to New
5308 Burnet Road
(512) 459-1288
The Next to New shop is a nonprofit organization sponsored by St. David's Episcopal Church. Staffed by community volunteers, the store's profits go to community outreach programs and to the restoration of historic church buildings.

Top Drawer Thrift
4902 Burnet Road
(512) 454-5161
This store supports people living with HIV/AIDS. Proceeds from the sale of donated merchandise benefit Project Transitions, which provides a homelike environment to meet the physical, emotional, and spiritual needs of persons experiencing the dying process.

East

Habitat for Humanity Re-Store
310 Comal Street
(512) 478-2165
7434 North Lamar Boulevard
(512) 225-9264
www.re-store.com
The large Comal Street warehouse features donated household fittings such as faucets, miniblinds, bathroom cabinets, stove tops, even the kitchen sink, plus doors, windows, and construction lumber. Many of the items are used and have been donated by homeowners and builders upgrading or replacing older items, but some are new. All proceeds benefit Habitat for Humanity, the organization that builds homes in low-income neighborhoods. A second Habitat store is located in North Austin on Lamar Boulevard.

Bargain hunters can spend Saturday morning roaming Austin neighborhoods to check out local garage sales. Often, neighbors will band together and have a multifamily sale. Check the classified section of the Austin American-Statesman *late in the week for ads, and keep your eye on busy intersections or entrances to subdivisions, where neighbors post notices of weekend sales.*

RESALE/VINTAGE CLOTHING AND STUFF

Vintage clothing stores abound in Austin, so much so that the Austin Convention and Visitors Bureau provides a "treasure map" of vintage stores around town. There are four general areas where the stores can be found: the South Congress Avenue shopping district (see the chapter introduction), on South Lamar Boulevard between Barton Springs Road and Oltorf Street, along "The Drag," Guadalupe Street near the university campus, and around North Loop Street and 51st Street in North Austin.

Central

Banana Bay Trading Company
2908 San Gabriel Street
(512) 479-8608
Banana Bay is Austin's version of an Army-Navy store. Located on a triangle of land east of Lamar and just north of 29th Street, Banana Bay features a variety of military clothing, including Commie stuff such as ammo boxes, tents, and survival kits.

Hog Wild
100A East North Loop Boulevard
(512) 467-6515
Is this a toy store or a clothing emporium? It's both, thanks to joint owners

with different interests. On the clothing side, customers find Hawaiian shirts, velvet bell-bottoms, miniskirts, and leisure suits, all divided by decade. On the toy/collectible side there are *Star Wars* toys, Barbies, even *Welcome Back Kotter* games. This is a retro store that goes hog wild.

Rethreads
1806 West 35th Street
(512) 459-3325
Consistently voted one of Austin's top resale shops by the readers of the *Austin Chronicle*, this unassuming (at least on the outside) shop sells top-name designer labels placed here by some of Austin's wealthier residents who live in the western enclaves of the city. The store also sells jewelry on consignment.

South Central

Big Bertha's Bargain Basement
1050 South Lamar Boulevard
(512) 444-5908
It is not in a basement, but it is in an old shopping center that seems to capture the essence of South Austin (see our Relocation chapter). The word *funky* is overused in Austin, but this is one case where it fits. The funky shopping center is home to several resale shops, a classic gym, a Salvation Army store, a music store, and this clothing resale store that owner Henry Tarin calls "extreme vintage." The store has a wild assortment of clothes that attracts retro fans and the theatrical community in Austin.

Bitch'in Threads
1030-D South Lamar Boulevard
(512) 441-9955
Grace Faulkner is a diminutive woman with a small treasure trove of a shop, located near her good friend Henry Tarin's Big Bertha's (see above). A native of Australia, she relies on an old school chum to ship her pre–World War II kimono (she will politely tell you that the plural of kimono is *kimono,* not kimonos) from Japan. Col-

lectors come from throughout the country to see what she is offering. In addition to kimono, Grace also sells "top-quality" vintage fashion, suits, cocktail dresses, evening gowns, shoes, and purses, classy enough to clad Audrey Hepburn on a world cruise.

Bohemia Retro-Resale
1606 South Congress Avenue
(512) 326-1238
Good junk from every era is the boast here. The ever-changing stock includes clothes, furniture, and housewares. Like other South Congress stores, Bohemia keeps late hours to encourage after-dinner browsing.

Flashback
2047 South Lamar Boulevard
(512) 445-6906
The shops along the 1000 and 2000 blocks of South Lamar Boulevard are tucked between businesses, bus stops, car washes, and apartment homes, and, if anything, they are even funkier than those found on the burgeoning South Congress Avenue shopping strip. This vintage clothing store is one of the longtime fixtures in this area and boasts a large selection of shoes.

Let's Dish
1102 South Lamar Boulevard
(512) 444-9801
The vintage clothing at Let's Dish ranges from the turn of the 20th century through the ever-popular '70s disco style. The store also has an extensive vintage jewelry collection and sells pottery, dishware, and maps dating from the 1920s to the 1950s.

Electric Ladyland
1506 South Congress Avenue
(512) 444-2002
The emphasis here is theatrical, with both gorilla suits and French maid's uniforms in stock. Disco wear also is big, and the store boasts that Bob Dylan shopped here. The shop's "formal" name is Lucy in Disguise with Diamonds and Electric Ladyland.

Flipnotics
1603 Barton Springs Road
(512) 322-9011
If the retro clothes here smell a little more like coffee than the usual thrift shop aroma, it is because there is a coffee shop with the same name on the premises. Among the finds here are surfer shirts, fifties-style rock 'n' roll wear, and fanciful little cocktail dresses.

Under The Sun
1323 South Congress Avenue
(512) 442-1308
Vintage clothing stores abound in Austin, particularly in the South Congress Avenue shopping district, but this one is a little different since it specializes in old Western-style clothes and boots. A great place to get your cowboy duds.

North

It's New to Me
7719 Burnet Road
(512) 451-0388
A variety of furniture is displayed in the store's 8,000-square-foot showroom, including some good-quality pieces from furniture producers such as Henredon. This is a consignment shop where Austin residents sell their quality furniture.

TOYS
Central

Hog Wild
100 East North Loop Boulevard
(512) 467-9453
These toys are for grown-ups who long for their childhood years—retro toys at a retro clothing store (see above under Resale/Vintage Clothing).

Kids-N-Cats
5808-A Burnet Road
(512) 458-6369
All things feline here—toys, jewelry, china cats, pens shaped like kitties, posters, cards, and kitty knickknacks. Despite its name, the store also has other sections devoted to dinosaurs, horses, and spacemen—in other words, all things kids hold dear. The shop is also a good resource for party favors.

Momoko's
705 West 24th Street
(512) 223-9801
www.momoko.citysearch.com
This small store and bubble tea shop sells all things by Sanrio. If you don't know Sanrio, then likely you don't know any preteen girls. The star of the Sanrio line is Hello Kitty, the little white-faced kitten whose face is plastered on backpacks, pens, notepads, bracelets, socks, etc., etc. The store, near the University of Texas, has a small tearoom that sells "bubble tea," a frothy, flavored concoction that first took off in popularity among Asian school kids. There is also a sushi restaurant in the store.

Rootin' Ridge
26 Doors, 1206 West 38th Street
(512) 453-2604
Georgean and Paul Kyle have been making toys since 1975, and their store in 26 Doors features their own creations, plus handcrafted quality wooden toys, puzzles, and musical instruments.

Toy Joy
2900 Guadalupe Street
(512) 320-0090
"You are never too old to play" might be the motto of this store, which boasts of selling toys for kids and grown-ups. Japanese toys are a specialty, plus there is a large selection of lava lamps, stickers, novelty items, and puppets.

North

World Wind Kite Shop
7208 McNeil Drive
(512) 250-9454
The store's slogan is "A Hobby to Some. A Way of Life to Us!" Listing it under "toys"

may be misleading, since this shop sells not only indestructible kid kites but also high-grade kites for competition. The store also offers repair services and kite-flying lessons.

East

Piñata Party Palace
2017 East Cesar Chavez Boulevard
(512) 322-9150
Custom-made piñatas for parties, particularly kid's birthday parties, can be ordered here. Piñatas are papier-mâché forms, covered with colorful tissue paper and stuffed with candies and little toys. The piñata is strung up over a tree limb and the birthday boy or girl blindfolded, given a baseball bat to take whacks at the piñata until it breaks open—then there is a mad scramble for the candy and toys. The store also sells ready-to-go piñatas.

South Central

Anna's Toy Depot
2620 South Lamar Boulevard, Suite B
(512) 447-8697
www.annastoydepot.com
None of the frenzy of a modern toy shop here. Anna's sells traditional toys, some of them gently used. It also caters to special-needs children and youngsters who can benefit from play-therapy toys.

Terra Toys
1708 South Congress Avenue
(512) 445-4489
A favorite place for shopping for stocking stuffers at Christmas, Terra Toys is hard to wrap up in a small word package. There is a wide selection of toys here, including Steiff teddy bears, educational toys, books, miniatures, dolls, tin soldiers, chemistry sets, and fingerpaints.

TRAVEL/ADVENTURE/ OUTDOORS

For sporting goods stores focused on a particular sport (e.g., soccer or cycling), see our Parks and Recreation chapter.

Armadillo Sport
1806 Barton Springs Road
(512) 478-4128
An Austin surf shop? This is the place to buy a surfboard for your trip to the Texas Coast, where the waves can get high if there is a major storm whipping up in the Gulf of Mexico. Housed in a former diner-style restaurant along the Barton Springs restaurant row (see our Restaurants chapter), Armadillo also sells sports equipment that you can use in nearby Zilker Park, including in-line skates, wakeboards, swimsuits, and lacrosse equipment.

The Austin Angler
312 Congress Avenue
(512) 472-4553
www.austinangler.com
Tucked away in an old downtown building, the store offers top-notch advice and sells top-quality equipment. It is so well regarded, it was featured in a national ad campaign for Visa.

McBride's Guns
30th Street and North Lamar Boulevard
(512) 472-3532
Popular among hunters, anglers, and collectors, McBride's is noted for its extensive collection of antique guns. The store also sells archery equipment and provides gunsmithing services. The store also has a complete line of fishing tackle and lures.

REI
9901 North Loop 360 (Capital of Texas Highway)
(512) 343-5550
www.rei.com

This store is a valuable resource for outdoors enthusiasts in Northwest Austin. REI sells and rents outdoor equipment and has an extensive line of clothing and supplies for outdoor activities including camping, hiking, and mountain climbing. The store sponsors nature and outdoor trips, provides information about the outdoor life in Texas, and brings in speakers to give their insights on how to enjoy life under the sky.

Rooster Andrews
3901 Guadalupe Street
(512) 454-9631
8650 Spicewood Springs Road
(512) 258-3488
www.roosterandrews.com
He stands 5 feet tall, but Rooster Andrews is a giant in University of Texas folklore. His real name is William Andrews, but the diminutive man has been called "Rooster" since his World War II days as a manager for the UT Longhorns football team. Andrews owns two sporting goods stores in Austin and continues to be a major organizer and booster of UT sports. His stores sell sports equipment and shoes, offer sports services such as racket restringing and custom T-shirt printing, and stock all the burnt orange Longhorn sportswear any UT fan could want.

Whole Earth Provision Co.
2410 San Antonio Street
(512) 478-1577
1014 North Lamar Boulevard
(512) 476-1414
Westgate Shopping Center,
4477 South Lamar Boulevard
(512) 899-0992
www.wholeearth.citysearch.com
Before Austinites head for the hills, they head for Whole Earth. Not only does the store sell the top labels in camping, hiking, diving, biking, and kayaking gear, it also has wonderful rainwear and sweaters, plus imported clothes from Latin America. The shoe shop has everyday, sturdy wear and great hiking boots. Whole Earth also sells tents, backpacks, climbing gear, toys, guidebooks, knives, flashlights, freeze-dried foods, desktop Zen gardens, and telescopes. If you are not sure you want to buy a tent, you can rent one here.

Golfsmith
11000 North I-35
(512) 837-4810
www.golfsmith.com
This North Austin outlet is a mecca for golf enthusiasts. The facility boasts that it has the largest golf inventory in the world, where shoppers can buy Golfsmith and Harvey Penick golf clubs. The store has a snack bar, computerized swing analyzer, and educational and practice facilities. In addition, visitors can take a factory tour. There is a second, smaller store at the Arboretum.

Oshman's Supersports
2525 West Anderson Lane
(512) 459-6541
www.oshmans.com
Whether you are looking for a new pair of tennis shoes or a set of skis, Oshman's has it. The store also features several sports arenas where you can try out your new gear before taking it home. Oshman's features a snow ski deck (and ski lessons year-round), a children's and an adult's basketball court, a racquetball court, a golf cage with simulated screen, a batting cage with simulated screen, an archery room, and a tennis court.

ATTRACTIONS

First, a word of appreciation to our sponsor: Nature.

It is, after all, our greatest attraction. The bluebonnets in springtime; the sparkle of sunlight on the lakes; the limestone cliffs and green rolling hills; the crisp, rushing creeks; the fresh air; the fauna; the fault and the foliage. Austin's natural beauty and bounty attracted our first visitors, drew our first settlers, and continue to entice our newest arrivals. Nature was Austin's greatest artist, perhaps an inspiration to the others who came to create some of the phenomena that give Austin its individuality. So while you're busy enjoying the production that is Austin, take a moment to acknowledge the set design.

While some of the sites below come to us courtesy of nature, we've devoted much of this chapter to giving you a tour of the landscape of invention, the visual sensations contributed by the ingenuity of Austin's own people over the past 150 years or so. Here you'll find attractions to tickle your fancy, tease your brain, touch your heart and, perhaps, stir your own imagination. Among these curiosities, historic treasures, and modern marvels you'll discover a provocative portion of Austin's story.

The Austin Museum Partnership was formed in 1998 by 31 Austin-area museums. The consortium promotes collaborations for the mutual benefit of the public and the museums. The membership includes art and science museums, historic sites, nature habitats and preserves, the University of Texas library and art repositories, a children's museum, and a Presidential library and museum. In the fall, the partnership hosts a citywide museum day that attracts thousands of visitors to the various facilities. The partnership's Web site, www.austinmuseums.org, is a treasure trove of information about area attractions.

We've pointed out some of our most interesting pieces of public art. Here, you'll receive an introduction to a few of the sculptures, statues, paintings, murals, and fountains that are on view for all to appreciate. These artistic creations enhance Austin's natural beauty and provide a window into the city itself.

Of course, Austin wouldn't be Austin without the many spots dedicated to celebrating our unique natural habitat. So for many more outdoor attractions, don't miss our chapter on Parks and Recreation, where we've introduced you to Lake Travis, Town Lake, and many, many other alfresco wonderlands. If you still yearn for more things to see and do, check out our chapters on The Arts, Kidstuff, The Music Scene, Nightlife, and Spectator Sports. Come to think of it, much of this book is dedicated to Austin attractions, in one form or another. *Note:* Because of the high concentration of Attractions in Central Austin, we've divided this section into three smaller parts to make it easier for you: Downtown, The University of Texas, and Central.

DOWNTOWN

Art at the Austin Convention Center
500 East Cesar Chavez Street
(512) 404-4000
www.austinconventioncenter.com
Even if you're not in town for a convention, stop in here to see artwork by six Austin-area artists. One of those artists, Damian Priour, raised some eyebrows with his sculpture *The Waller Creek Shelves*, made of limestone, glass, metal, and found objects. Priour used material collected at Waller Creek by homeless people. (Some of Austin's transients were displaced when the Convention Center was built in 1992.) Priour nevertheless

proceeded with his plan, and the results are fascinating. A wall-mounted installation of 400 powder-coated geometrically shaped metal components titled *Index for Contemplation* is the work of artist Margo Sawyer. The paintings of Rolando Braseño comprise a series of 12 triptychs, the result of the artist's investigation into the relationship between the natural and cultural worlds in a work titled *Macro-Micro Culture*. John A. Yancey with Steve Jones created *Riffs and Rhythms*, a broken-tile wall mosaic, and Jill Bedgood has contributed 20 oil paintings, called *Texas Botanicals*. These six artists have made a significant contribution to the center's appeal and to Austin's Art in Public Places program. The doors are open during the fairly constant stream of events at the center. However, visitors should check first to make sure the building is open. For a 24-hour listing of events at the convention center and Palmer Events Center, call the hot line at (512) 404-4404.

The Austin History Center
810 Guadalupe Street
No phone
www.cityofaustin.org/library/ahc
While Austin was among the last major Texas cities to build a public library, the city made up for its delay by constructing a facility that was both inspiring and advanced in its design. This Moderne-influenced, Classical Revival–style building opened in 1933 to replace the city's temporary public library, a wooden structure built in 1926. A showcase for some of Austin's finest crafters in its day, the building features loggia frescoes, a carved mantel, and ornamental ironwork balconies. The ironwork was done by a noted family of ironworkers, the Weigl's, whose workshop is now a barbecue restaurant, Iron Works Barbecue (see our Restaurants chapter). The History Center building, which served as the city's library for nearly 50 years, now houses the leading local history collections in the state. Here, visitors will find more than one million

items documenting the history of Austin from before it was founded to the present day. The center has received national recognition for its collection of more than 600,000 photographic images, which document the people, events, architecture, and social customs of this region. The center also has more than 1,000 maps of Austin and Travis County from the mid-1800s to the present as well as 25,500 drawings and documents from local architectural projects. The History Center serves as the official repository for the records of the City of Austin as well as those of Travis County. This is also the place to come to find issues of local newspapers dating back more than a century. The center also features regular temporary exhibits of interest to the Austin community. The History Center, part of the Austin Public Library system, is next door to Austin's main public library at the corner of Ninth and Guadalupe Streets in downtown Austin. It is open from 10:00 A.M. to 9:00 P.M. Monday through Wednesday, from 10:00 A.M. to 6:00 P.M. Saturday, and from noon to 6:00 P.M. on Sunday. The library also has a Web site featuring on-line exhibits: www.cityofaustin.org/library/ahc/austin_treasures.htm.

The Bats
Congress Avenue Bridge at Town Lake
Get your cooler and a comfy blanket and head out to Town Lake for a truly unique Austin experience. The largest urban bat colony in North America—as many as 1.5 million Mexican free-tails—resides in the crevices beneath the Congress Avenue Bridge for nearly eight months of the year. When they take off from under the bridge

for their evening flight for food, the spectacle is astounding. On their nightly forage the bats devour up to 30,000 pounds of insects. August is the best month for viewing the bats because they often come out before sunset. But they can be seen at other times during their stay here, from about mid-March to early November. You can see the bats from either side of Town Lake under the bridge, or from the top of the bridge. Check out our chapter on Hotels and Motels for the hotels in the area that also provide great bat views. Information kiosks are at the *Austin American-Statesman*'s information center on the south shore and on the north bank below the Four Seasons Hotel. The *Statesman* also operates a bat phone, (512-416-5700; category 3636) with estimated time for the nightly flight. Austin was scandalized when the huge colony first took up residence here in the early 1980s, even going so far as to petition to have the colony eradicated. But when citizens learned that the bats consume so many insects—thus cutting down the need for chemical insecticides—and that the bats pose no danger to the community, Austin changed its mind in a big way. Today our bat colony is a welcome addition to Austin. Our new hockey team is called the Ice Bats (see our Spectator Sports chapter). Of course, no one should ever try to handle a bat.

For more information on these nocturnal creatures, read the information provided at the kiosks, or contact Bat Conservation International in Austin at (512) 327-9721, www.batcon.org/discover/congress.

The Bob Bullock Texas State History Museum
1800 North Congress Avenue
(512) 936-8746
www.thestoryoftexas.com

This museum was Bob Bullock's dream. Who was he? Perhaps the most quintessential Texas politician of the last half of the 20th century. Bullock rose to be the state's lieutenant governor and was known for his tough politics and his unmitigated love of all things Texas. President George W. Bush, a Republican, has credited Bullock, a Democrat, with being a major influence on his political life and the two men grew to be very close. They sometimes disagreed, but they also were committed friends, in fact Bush was with Bullock during his final hours. When "Governor Bullock"—all lieutenant governors in Texas are called "Governor"—set a goal, nothing could stop him. He decided the great state of Texas needed a museum, just as he decided the Texas State Cemetery where he now rests needed a much needed restoration (see later in this chapter). The building echoes the colors, textures, and style of the nearby Texas Capitol, and its huge star out front says "This is Texas!" There are three floors inside, the first named "Encounters on the Land" where the ancient cultures and pre-Republic days are celebrated. The second floor is dubbed "Building the Lone Star Identity" and takes visitors through the volatile days of the Republic of Texas, followed by admission to the Union and the tragedy of the Civil War. "Creating Opportunity" is the theme on the third floor, where all the energy that has made modern Texas is chronicled.

In addition to permanent exhibits, the museum has rotating exhibits on each floor, borrowing art and artifacts from around the state. There is an IMAX theater, plus the Texas Spirit Theater that echoes the traditional Texas town opera house and where an electronic Sam Houston introduces the audience to a colorful history of Texas. There is even a cafe with an outdoor dining deck in the museum and a museum store. No visitor to Austin should miss a tour of this wonderfull addition to the historic center of the city. The museum is open from 9:00 A.M. to 6:00 P.M. Monday through Saturday and from 1:00 to 6:00 P.M. on Sunday. Parking is available nearby or for a fee in the underground parking lot. Ticket prices are affordable. There are additional admission prices for the IMAX Theatre and Texas Spirit Theater.

Capitol Complex Visitor Center
112 East 11th Street
(512) 305-8400
www.tspb.state.tx.us
The Capitol Complex Visitor Center definitely must be added to any list of places to visit while in Austin, for both what it was and what it is today. Built in 1856 and 1857, this is the oldest remaining state office building in Texas and, both for its architectural and historic values, one of the most significant properties owned by the state. Designed by German-born architect Christopher Conrad Stremme for use as the Texas General Land Office, the building is an excellent example of Medieval-inspired architecture and is listed on the National Register of Historic Places. Professor Stremme's design is a unique blending of the German Rundbogenstil (round-arch style) and the Anglo-American Norman style. Today, the two-story "castle" hosts a variety of exhibits relating to the State Capitol and to the history of the Old Land Office itself.

We recommend stopping here before taking a tour of the Capitol. For one thing, the 20-minute film *Lone Star Legacy: A History of the Capitol,* narrated by Walter Cronkite, will serve as a great initiation to the capitol tour itself. There's also a wonderful exhibit on the massive restoration and extension of the State Capitol and grounds completed in 1997. And don't miss the space next to the "small, dark spiral stairway" dedicated to William Sydney Porter, better known as O. Henry. (See our listing for the O. Henry Museum in this chapter.) The famous short-story writer worked as a draftsman in the Land Office from 1887 to 1891, and two of his stories are set in the Land Office, "Georgia's Ruling" and "Bexar Scrip No. 2692," in which he refers to the spiral stairway.

Upstairs in the wing dedicated to the history of the Land Office, visitors will find two surveyor's transits—those scopes we see surveyors using on the side of the road. Peek through a transit to get a perfect close-up view of the Goddess of Liberty who stands so regally on top of the Capitol Rotunda. (Remember, her features are exaggerated to be seen from afar.) The gift shop here is great and so are the people who work as information assistants just inside the front entrance.

The Capitol Complex Visitor Center is open 9:00 A.M. to 5:00 P.M. Monday through Saturday and noon to 5:00 P.M. on Sunday.

Dewitt C. Greer Building
125 East 11th Street
What with the splendor of the State Capitol, this building just across the street is easy to miss. But take a moment to enjoy its wonderful Art Deco architecture. Built in 1933, the building features three bronze panels over the main entrance depicting changes in Austin's modes of transportation. The first shows a Native American on horseback, the second is a covered wagon, and the third an automobile. There are also two stylized eagles over the entrance and a number of other details from the era that are worth a look. The building houses the administrative offices of the Texas Transportation Commission and was named for Greer, a former state highway engineer and commissioner from 1969 to 1981.

The Driskill Hotel
122 East Sixth Street
(512) 474-5911
www.driskillhotel.com
Built in 1886 for cattle baron Jesse Driskill, the Driskill Hotel was restored in 1998 to its original splendor. This Richardsonian Romanesque–style hotel is uniquely Austin and should not be missed. (See our chapter on Hotels and Motels for more details.)

Governor's Mansion
1010 Colorado Street
(512) 463-5516
www.governor.state.tx.us/mansion
Home to every Texas governor since 1856, this awesome Greek Revival–style structure is the fourth-oldest continuously used governor's mansion in the United States and is

listed on the National Register of Historic Places. If walls could talk, this stately mansion, reminiscent of a Southern plantation home, would tell the tales of the fabulous galas and famous leaders it has hosted, of the turmoil it has witnessed as Texas governors ponder the issues that have shaped Texas for going on 150 years, and of the "ghost" that roamed its halls after the suicide of Governor Murrah Pendleton's nephew more than 100 years ago. Governor Sam Houston lived here until he made the monumental decision in 1861 to reject the oath of allegiance to the Confederate States of America. Governor W. Lee O'Daniel invited all Texans to the mansion to celebrate his second inauguration—and 19,000 people came for lunch. Governor James Hogg's four children liked to slide down the spiral banister that graces the entryway, until one fell off. The 100-year-old holes, from the nails that Governor Hogg pounded into the banister to end the joy rides and prevent further mishaps, can still be seen in the curving wood.

Austin's master builder Abner Cook won the contract to build this home on a small hilltop 1 block southwest of the State Capitol. The home, facing east to catch prevailing winds during Austin's long hot summers, features six 29-foot fluted columns topped with Greek Ionic capitals below the roofline. Cook selected a simple, square design with four rooms upstairs and four rooms downstairs. In 1914 a conservatory was added and a new kitchen wing was built. Today the two-story brick structure, painted white with black trim, stands majestically among the trees and flowers on the 1-block lot. Inside, the home is filled with original furnishings and artwork from the era, as well as some more modern Texas treasures, some added during the $4 million restoration led by First Lady Rita Clements in the early 1980s. Visitors are shown only the grounds and the first-floor rooms—two gorgeous parlors rising 16 feet to the ceiling, the library, the conservatory, and the state dining room. The second level is the private home of the current governor. Free guided tours are held every 20 minutes from 10:00 A.M. to 11:40 A.M. Monday through Thursday. Guests are received on a first-come, first-served basis, and it is important to arrive early, as the tours are limited to 25 people and do fill up.

Lorenzo de Zavala
State Archives and Library Building
1201 Brazos Street
(512) 936-INFO
www.tsl.state.tx.us/arc

Make the Lorenzo de Zavala building a stop on your tour of Austin, even if you're in a hurry. Just inside, visitors will find the huge mural *Texas Moves Toward Statehood.* This epic work, 55 feet long by 18 feet high, depicts 400 years of Lone Star State history. Painted by English artist Peter Rogers and his father-in-law, well-known Western artist Peter Hurd, the mural features some of Texas' leading historical figures, including Stephen F. Austin, Sam Houston, and Mirabeau B. Lamar, and portrays events in history from the first encounters between Native Americans and European explorers to the emergence of the oil industry. This building, however, offers much more. This is the home of the Texas State Library and Archives Commission. Housed here is the official history of Texas government, including documents dating back to the 18th century. The Genealogy Collection includes most U.S. Census reports from 1790 to 1920 as well

You've most likely heard of the legendary Texas Rangers. But have you heard of the Downtown Rangers? These friendly folks roam the greater downtown area, offering help, advice, and making sure all is well. These rangers are not police and do not carry weapons, but they use two-way radios that allow them to contact authorities if anyone needs help.

as many other significant holdings. The building, completed in 1961, was named in 1972 in honor of Lorenzo de Zavala, a hero of Texas's struggle for independence and the first vice president of the Republic of Texas. The library is open 8:00 A.M. to 5:00 P.M. Monday through Friday although the Genealogy Collection is closed on Monday.

Millet Opera House
110 East Ninth Street

Now the private Austin Club, tourists can enjoy this edifice from the outside only. But it's definitely worth a walk by when you're visiting downtown. Built in 1878, the opera house became a cultural center for the city. Its auditorium boasted 800 movable seats. The building, made of Texas limestone, was listed on the National Register of Historic Places in 1978.

Moonlight Towers
Corner of Ninth and Guadalupe Streets

At this location, which features a historical marker, visitors will find just one of the 17 Moonlight Towers that remain in Austin from 1895, when the towers provided the city's first public electric lights. Austin is the only city in the world to preserve its earliest electric street lamps. And they still work. At 165 feet, they're the city's tallest street lights and a truly unique attraction. The City of Austin contracted the Fort Wayne Electric Company to install 31 towers with carbon arc lamps, believing they would be easier to maintain than many small street lamps throughout the city. Some residents of Hyde Park, however, weren't so sure. They feared that the lights, sometimes called Austin moonlight, would trick the vegetables in their gardens into growing day and night. The 17 towers that remain, now with mercury vapor lights, can be found around downtown, in Hyde Park, and in Clarksville. The Moonlight Tower in Zilker Park, moved to the park from Congress Avenue in the 1960s, is used every Christmas to support the 3,500 multicolored lights on the Zilker Park Christmas Tree (see our chapter on Annual Events).

O. Henry Museum
409 East Fifth Street
(512) 472-1903
www.ci.austin.tx.us/parks/ohenry.htm

William Sydney Porter, who earned international fame as a short-story writer under his pen name, O. Henry, lived in this simple Queen Anne–style cottage for 3 of his nearly 11 years in Austin. Simply Will Porter when he arrived as a bachelor in 1884, Porter would see some of his greatest personal triumphs and his most devastating public humiliation during his era in Austin. It was here where Porter married, had his daughter, sold his first short story to a national publication—and was convicted of embezzlement and sentenced to prison. (A mock court trial conducted at the UT School of Law in 1998, the 100th anniversary of the original trial, exonerated him.) Porter, who lived the dapper bachelor life, singing at parties and serenading girls, worked a variety of odd jobs before he married Austinite Athol Estes when he was 24.

His most stable career before writing took over his life was at the Texas General Land Office, where he worked drawing maps for four years. The Land Office was later to appear in two of O. Henry's short stories. (See our listing on the Capitol Complex Visitor Center.)

When his politically appointed job ended, Porter was finally able to find another job handling accounts at the First National Bank of Austin. During this time, Porter also launched his weekly newspaper, *The Rolling Stone,* which revealed the beginnings of a great talent but lasted only one year. Porter was fired from the bank when the bank discovered shortages in his accounts. He was indicted several months later, fled to Honduras, and later returned—due largely to the failing health of his wife in Austin—to face the music. He was sentenced to five years in federal prison in Columbus, Ohio, and never returned to Texas. Porter spent the last eight years of his life drinking, gambling, living the extravagant life, and publishing 381 short stories. He died at age 47 in New York of cirrhosis of the liver, an enlarged heart, and complications of diabetes.

The cottage is much as it was during Porter's three years in it, from 1893 to 1895. Once slated for demolition, the home was moved twice in the 1930s from its original location at 308 East Fourth Street. Here visitors will find many furnishings and personal possessions belonging to Porter, his wife, and daughter, Margaret. Here also are first editions of O. Henry books, magazines featuring his stories, copies of *The Rolling Stone* newspaper, and family photographs. The museum conducts the O. Henry Writing Clubs for Austin school children and hosts several annual programs, including the O. Henry Pun-Off World Championship, a lively and popular event held every May since 1977.

The museum is open from noon to 5:00 P.M. Wednesday through Sunday. Admission and parking are free. Guests are asked to wear flat, soft-soled shoes to prevent damage to the original Bastrop pine floors.

The Old Bakery and Emporium
1006 Congress Avenue
(512) 477-5961

When Swedish immigrant Charles Lundberg opened his bakery in 1876, Austinites gathered to buy such delicacies as ladyfingers, sponge cake, and glazed kisses. Used as a bakery until 1936, the building then housed a number of different businesses, including a nightclub. By 1963 the Old Bakery, vacant and deteriorating, was scheduled for demolition. That's when the Austin Heritage Society and the Junior League stepped in to save it, through hard work and donations. Today the Old Bakery is registered as a national landmark. Owned and operated by the Austin Parks and Recreation Department, the bakery features a sandwich shop where you can still buy cookies but no ladyfingers or sponge cake. Most interesting, however, is the gift shop. Here visitors will find scores of handicrafts

made by Austin's most experienced artists, those age 50 and older. Custom orders are accepted, too. The Old Bakery also has a hospitality desk that provides information and brochures about Austin attractions. Just a half block down Congress from the State Capitol, the Old Bakery is a great place to stop on your tour of Austin. It's open Monday through Friday 9:00 A.M. to 4:00 P.M. but closed on weekends and holidays.

Paramount Theatre
713 Congress Avenue
(512) 472-2901
www.austintheatrealliance.org

An Austin jewel, the Paramount Theatre opened in 1915 under the name Majestic Theater. Now, beautifully restored to the most minute detail, the neoclassic structure is one of the nation's classic theaters. Today it hosts Broadway shows, local productions, musical events, and classic movies. Katharine Hepburn performed here, as did Sara Bernhardt, Helen Hayes, and Cab Calloway. The Paramount series for kids is a summer extravaganza. Unfortunately, the Paramount does not offer tours, so the only way to see the theater from the inside now is to buy a ticket to an event, although virtual tours are offered on the Web site. (See our chapter on The Arts.)

Scholz Garten
1607 San Jacinto Boulevard
(512) 474-1958

Built in 1866 by German immigrant August Scholz, the Scholz Garten has been serving up beer and German food ever since. This building is listed as a National Historic Site and as a Texas Landmark. General Armstrong Custer, who was stationed 2 blocks away during Reconstruction, reportedly ate here, and the University of Texas football team celebrated its first undefeated season here in 1893. Photographs from days of old adorn the walls. For more information see our chapters on Restaurants and Politics and Perspectives.

Sixth Street
Downtown between Congress Avenue and I-35

If you haven't spent an evening on Sixth Street, you haven't really experienced Austin. These few blocks, filled with live music venues, DJ clubs, and restaurants, continue to make up *the* entertainment district for Austin in many people's minds, even though downtown now offers several other hip areas. Within walking distance of many hotels, Sixth Street is one of Austin's top tourist draws. This street really comes alive after five. (See our Music Scene chapter for a listing of some of the clubs, and see the Close-up about Sixth Street in the Nightlife chapter.)

Symphony Square
1101 Red River Street
(512) 476-6064
www.austinsymphony.com/about/square

Four historic limestone buildings and a wonderful 350-seat outdoor amphitheater still used for live performances make up this complex, which serves as the offices of the Austin Symphony Orchestra and the Women's Symphony League and houses Cafe Serranos, a popular Mexican restaurant (see our Restaurants chapter). Located on the banks of historic Waller Creek since the 1970s, Symphony Square represents the efforts of a group of leading citizens, the City of Austin, the Urban Renewal League, and the Symphony itself to save and restore these 19th-century buildings. The provocative triangular shaped building at the corner of 11th and Red River Streets is believed to be one of just three stone triangular buildings remaining in Texas today. Built in 1871 by Jeremiah Hamilton, one of nine African-American legislators who served in the Texas Legislature, the building today bears his name and is used as the symphony's main office. Symphony Square also contains the Michael Doyle House, considered one of the few remaining examples of a simple, one-story stone cottage in Austin. The Hardeman House, also of native lime-stone, was moved from its original location to the square and is home to Cafe Serranos, which features a lovely outdoor patio overlooking the amphitheater. During the summer months, Serranos presents outdoor concerts on this stage, to the delight of all. Serranos caters private parties in the fourth building in this complex, the New Orleans Club Mercantile, a beautifully restored 19th-century building. On Wednesday mornings in June and July, the Austin Symphony Orchestra hosts Children's Day activities in the square. For information on that and for other children's activities sponsored by the symphony, see our chapter on Kidstuff. Also see our chapter on The Arts for more about the Symphony and its seasonal performances at the Bass Concert Hall.

Texas State Capitol
1100 Congress Avenue
(512) 463-0063
www.tspb.state.tx.us

"Here glitters a structure that shall stand as a sentinel of eternity to gaze upon the ages."

Now, more than a century since those words were spoken, visitors from all over the world come to gaze upon this magnificent monument to Texas. Temple Houston, the youngest son of Texas hero Sam Houston, dedicated Texas's new State Capitol, our "sentinel of eternity," on May 16, 1888. This Renaissance Revival–style structure, made of Texas pink granite and native limestone, now stands as gracious and grand as Texas itself on the hilltop overlooking Austin's historic Congress Avenue. Perched atop the soaring Rotunda, which at 311 feet is taller than our nation's Capitol, is the 15½-foot statue called the *Goddess of Liberty,* a 1986 aluminum replica of the original zinc goddess. Marble statues of Stephen F. Austin and Sam Houston carved by German-born sculptor Elisabet Ney grace the south foyer as does a portrait of Davy Crockett, martyr of the Alamo, holding his famous coonskin cap. The painting of the

While you're traveling around Austin, see if you can find our official state symbols. Our state bird is the mockingbird. Our flower is the bluebonnet. The pecan is our state tree, and our state fruit is the Texas red grapefruit. The monarch butterfly is Texas's official insect. This may come as no surprise, but our official state dish is chili. We even have a state pepper: the jalapeño. Oh yes, our state name comes from the Native American word Tejas, meaning friendly. That's why our state motto is "Friendship." And, of course, our state nickname is the Lone Star State.

Surrender of Santa Anna depicts a watershed event in Texas history, while other meaningful works of art can be found throughout the building.

More than a monument, more than a museum, the State Capitol is the seat of Texas government. In this building, among the pioneers of Texas's past, work the leaders of Texas's future. Among many other state government headquarters, the offices of the governor and secretary of state are here, along with the magnificent Senate and House chambers, occupied during the legislative sessions held every two years.

No trip to the capitol is complete unless you've stood on the Rotunda floor and looked up at the Texas star and the two-foot letters spelling out T-E-X-A-S on the ceiling. From below, they look about 3 inches tall. After you've gazed up, be sure to look down. Here are the seals of the six nations whose flags have flown over Texas: France, Spain, Mexico, the United States, the Confederate States of America, and, of course, the Republic of Texas. On the Rotunda's circular walls you will find the portraits of every president and governor of Texas beginning with the current chief executive. That means that each time a new governor is elected, every portrait in the Rotunda must be moved back one space.

Visitors can choose to walk through the capitol themselves or take a free regularly scheduled guided tour. We suggest the tour. Not only are the guides interesting and informative, they also will point out details you might miss and can also take you into areas otherwise locked, such as the Senate and House chambers. And these are definitely worth a look. When the Legislature is in session—every other year on odd years—visitors can watch our lawmakers in action from the third-floor public gallery, open on a first-come, first-served basis. Guided tours are also available of the capitol grounds. The massive grounds, with their many statues, sculptures, and beautiful old trees, are a sight unto themselves. When you're visiting the capitol, take a moment to enjoy this Austin treasure also. And don't forget to visit the Capitol Complex Visitor Center nearby. (See our previous listing in this chapter.)

A 1983 fire in the capitol set off such an alarm over the future integrity of the overcrowded, deteriorating building that plans were made to renovate and enlarge the capitol complex, which sits on 26 acres. By 1997 the massive restoration project, construction of an impressive underground extension, and restitution of the vast capitol grounds were complete. The project restored our legacy for future generations and the building that Temple Houston had said "fires the heart" was radiant once again.

The capitol is open 7:00 A.M. to 10:00 P.M. weekdays, 9:00 A.M. to 8:00 P.M. on weekends and holidays. Tours are offered on weekdays from 8:30 A.M. to 4:30 P.M., Saturday 9:30 A.M. to 3:30 P.M., and Sunday noon to 3:30 P.M.

THE UNIVERSITY OF TEXAS

The University of Texas at Austin, founded in 1883 on 40 acres, has grown to 357 acres, and that's just the main campus. Its historical significance, size, and allure as one of Texas' most beloved universities make UT a major tourist attraction. The university is roughly bounded by 26th Street on the north, Martin Luther King Boulevard on the south, I-35 on the east, and Guadalupe Street on the west.

Getting information about UT and its many small and large treasures is much easier these days, thanks largely to user-friendly improvements to the university's Web site. For a campus overview, go to the main site at www.utexas.edu. For more specific information about tours, go to www.utexas.edu/tours. We highly recommend spending some time navigating the tours section of this site before you arrive on campus, as it will provide you with some good basic information about what to see. Plus, it offers some interesting virtual tours, including "The University of Texas Virtual Campus," which provides photographs and details about the 40 acres. Here's where you go to find out about student-led campus walking tours, the after-dark tour called the Moonlight Prowl, and tours of the UT Tower Observation Deck. The self-guided tours listed on this site, however, are mainly for geology buffs. A good general-interest self-guided tour has yet to make its appearance on the Internet. UT does have hard copies of *The Perip: A Self-guided Walking Tour,* which is perhaps the best information available on campus sites, but they're hard to find. There's a recorded message about tours at (512) 475-6636 or (877) 475-6633 and a small Visitor Information Center in the Texas Union just off Guadalupe Street. Frankly, though, the Web stuff is much better.

Those interested in visiting the UT campus should be aware that streets inside the campus are closed to normal traffic (cars must bear an authorized sticker to enter) during school hours. It's okay to enter after 4:00 P.M. daily. The university recommends that visitors use one of the seven public parking garages scat-tered around campus, although these, too, can fill up. For information and maps about UT parking, go to www.utexas.edu/parking/parking/visitor. If you happen to find a parking space near UT on The Drag, don't buy a lottery ticket for awhile, as you've just used up your luck for the foreseeable future.

Information on the university's most noteworthy attractions follows.

Battle Oaks
Near 24th Street and Whitis Avenue
In an interesting twist of words, the historic Battle Oaks, three live oak trees at the northwest corner of the campus, are named in honor of the man who saved them, not the battle he waged to do so or the other trees in the grove that were destroyed earlier to build a fortress to protect the capital. The trees are named for Dr. W. J. Battle. His efforts to save the trees, slated for the ax to make room for a new biology building, have now taken on mythic grandeur. Some stories have him perching with a shotgun on one of the largest branches; others say he was on the ground with the shotgun to keep the tree choppers away. Neither version is probably true, but the story is fun anyway.

Of course, way before Battle, and perhaps one of the reasons he saved the trees—the site for the biology building was later moved—was a UT legend about this grouping of trees. According to the story, the largest of the three trees, which existed when Austin was home to Native Americans, learned to speak the native tongue. This tree brought eternal happiness to a young man when it whispered the name of the woman who loved him. When the new settlers came, the trees learned the ways of these people and provided shelter for them beneath their branches. When the only son of an old man was killed in battle, the oaks brought comfort. And when Northern troops were descending on Austin during the Civil War, all the trees in this grove, but the three remaining, gave their lives for the fortress.

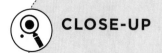

Lady Bird Johnson:
A National Treasure

One of the first display cases visitors encounter at the Lyndon Baines Johnson Library and Museum contains mementos of the whirlwind courtship between the future president of the United States and the woman who would be his bride, Lady Bird Taylor. Among the documents is a handwritten letter from the 21-year-old recent University of Texas graduate to her suitor.

"Lyndon, please tell me as soon as you can what the deal is," the letter reads. "I am afraid it's politics—Oh, I know I haven't any business—not any 'propri-etary interest'—but I would hate for you to go into politics . . ."

The year was 1934. Mrs. Johnson spent more than six decades in the public eye. During those years she evolved from the shy, nervous girl who deliberately dropped her grade point average in high school to avoid making the speech required of the class valedictorian to become one of the great First Ladies in American history. She will forever remain an American treasure, a Texas icon, and Austin's most beloved citizen. Each spring, Central Texas residents need only look to the roadside to see Lady Bird Johnson's reflection: There wildflowers abound, planted by both Mother Nature and the state highway department as a tribute to her advocacy.

On November 22, 1963, an assassin's bullet thrust Mrs. Johnson into the role of First Lady of the United States. Asked later what image she hoped to project to the nation, Mrs. Johnson replied, "My image will emerge in actions, not words."

Indeed. A genteel Southern woman whom fate would place at the very center of the turbulent 1960s, Mrs. Johnson's vigorous campaign in the Bible Belt helped the JFK-LBJ ticket take Texas and win the 1960 national election. In 1964, when it was her husband's turn to seek the presidency in his own right, Mrs. Johnson embarked on a massive whistle-stop tour through eight Southern states, often facing hostile crowds because of Johnson's support for civil rights. As First Lady she traveled to some of America's poorest regions to address the crisis of poverty in the country.

The United States had a lot on its mind in 1965. The Vietnam War was begin-ning to polarize the nation as Johnson's buildup of American troops expanded to 150,000. Mounting racial tension erupted in a five-day riot in the black section of Los Angeles known as Watts. Dr. Martin Luther King Jr. led marchers from Selma, Alabama, to a rally of more than 25,000 people in Montgomery, and more victims fell along the way. In 1965 President John-son signed the Medicare Social Security Bill into law and announced the creation of a "Great Society," his plan to help the politically and economically impoverished. Johnson's War on Poverty was in its sec-ond year in 1965. Congress passed a bill that year that called for limits on the emission of toxic pollutants in new vehicles. Poet Allen Ginsberg coined the phrase "Flower Power" at an antiwar rally in Berkeley, California, in 1965.

In Washington, the First Lady of the United States was wielding her own brand of flower power. Only old photographs and movies offer proof today of the blitz of billboards that once defiled America's roadsides. Mrs. Johnson changed all that, and became the first First Lady to actively campaign to get a bill made into law. In 1965, despite strong opposition, her noble vision for America paid off with the passage of the Highway Beautification Act, which sought to eliminate billboards and other eyesores from America's highways.

Her environmental campaign, in those days called "beautification," took her from Washington, where she saw to it that trees and more than a million tulips and daffodils were planted along the Potomac River, to spots across the United States, where she was among the first well-known leaders to champion environmental protection.

She's been honored so many times that the list of her awards fills an entire single-spaced page. In 1977 President Gerald Ford gave her the nation's highest civilian honor, the Presidential Medal of Freedom. President Ronald Reagan added the Congressional Gold Medal in 1988. "She claimed her own place in the hearts and history of the American people. In councils of power or in homes of the poor, she made government human with her unique compassion and her grace, warmth, and wisdom. Her leadership transformed the American landscape

and preserved its natural beauty as a national treasure," reads her Medal of Freedom certificate, on display along with the medal at the LBJ Library.

As a child growing up in the small East Texas town of Karnack, the girl born Claudia Alta Taylor on December 22, 1912, came to cherish the native flowers that flourished around her home. The daughter of Thomas Jefferson "T.J." Taylor, the wealthy owner of the town's general store, and Minnie Pattillo Taylor, Claudia was just 5 years old when her mother died after falling down a flight of stairs. The role of mothering was left to her maiden Aunt Effie Pattillo, a well-educated, cultured woman who came from Alabama to help raise Claudia and her two older brothers. It was a nursemaid who gave Claudia the name that would remain with her for life, saying she was just "as purty as a lady bird."

Lady Bird was 17 years old when she entered the University of Texas at Austin in 1930. Four years later she graduated with honors with degrees in journalism and history as well as with a teaching certificate. In Austin she met Lyndon Baines Johnson, the up-and-coming assistant to a Washington congressman. Within one day of their meeting, Johnson proposed and within two months they were married in San Antonio. He had literally swept her off her feet.

Much more than a Washington political wife, Mrs. Johnson was at her husband's side, providing advice and support, and promoting her own causes, throughout the more than three decades the couple spent in national politics. Johnson's election to Congress in 1937 was just the beginning.

In 1949 Texas voters sent him to the Senate where he remained, election after election, despite a near-fatal heart attack in 1955. In 1961 he became vice president of the United States. Less than two years later, Lady Bird was at his side when he took the oath of office aboard Air Force One following the assassination of President Kennedy.

Mrs. Johnson blossomed during her decades in Washington. She took a public-speaking course to overcome the fear that had kept her from making the high school valedictory speech. After World War II broke out and LBJ joined the service, Lady Bird ran his congressional office for the half a year Johnson was away. In 1943 the Johnsons, with Lady Bird at the helm, bought a small Austin radio station, KTBC. Mrs. Johnson, who did everything from paint the station walls to sign the checks, proved she was an astute businesswoman. On Thanksgiving Day 1952, KTBC became Central Texas' first television station, and the cornerstone of the family's multimillion-dollar fortune.

Her two daughters, Lynda Bird and Luci Baines, were born during the Washington years, and both were married in the White House. Mrs. Johnson, despite all her misgivings about a life in politics, had been the one to urge her husband to seek the offices of vice president and president, although LBJ's attempts to steer the country through the tumultuous '60s were harshly criticized. It was Lady Bird who finally convinced her husband not to seek reelection in 1968, going so far as to strengthen his famous withdrawal speech in which he said, "I will not seek and will not accept the nomination of my party for another term as your president." The Johnsons returned home to their beloved ranch west of Austin in January 1969. Lyndon Baines Johnson died there on January 22, 1973.

Following President Johnson's death, Mrs. Johnson divided her time between Austin and the family ranch in Stonewall, which the Johnsons donated to the American people as a national historic site. Through all these years she remained at the forefront of the American environmental movement, not as a figurehead but actively involved in the effort to preserve and protect the nation's natural beauty. In Austin she chaired the Town Lake Beautification Project, a community effort that resulted in the creation of the city's magnificent Town Lake Hike and Bike Trail (see our Parks and Recreation chapter). The city wanted to name Town Lake for Lady Bird, but she demurred. In 1982, on her 70th birthday, Mrs. Johnson founded Austin's National Wildflower Research Center. On a glorious spring day in 1998, the acclaimed center (see the listing in this chapter) was officially renamed the Lady Bird Johnson Wildflower Center in honor of this remarkable woman, whom First Lady Laura Bush called "the conductor of the symphony of wildflowers that bloom across Texas."

Mrs. Johnson, wearing a sunflower-bright yellow suit and her trademark radiant smile, received a warm standing ovation as she stood to unveil the new name on the center's logo. "I had great fun campaigning with Lyndon and falling in love with the natural beauty and diversity of this country," she told the audience, speaking in the soft East Texas drawl that has charmed even her staunchest opponents throughout her lifetime.

The Drag
Guadalupe Street
from Martin Luther King Boulevard to
26th Street

The University of Texas meets Austin on this lively strip filled with restaurants, coffeehouses, bookstores, shops, and the outdoor Renaissance Market (see our Shopping chapter), where you can buy tie-dyed clothes and jewelry made by Austin artisans. This is a great place to select UT T-shirts and other memorabilia or just take a break from sight-seeing on the UT campus. There are a couple of inviting coffeehouses along this strip, providing a perfect place for a rest—and a snack. Check out the University Co-op for books and gifts. Nomadic Notions is a top-notch shop for finding unique beads, jewelry-making items, and gifts. The Dobie Mall is here, too, along with the Dobie Theater, which runs popular movies as well as some great offbeat films (see our Nightlife chapter). The Drag, once made up of mostly locally owned shops, is starting to see more and more national chains move in. You'll find a Gap clothing store, Barnes & Noble Booksellers, a huge Tower Records, Sunglass Hut, and Einstein Brothers Bagels.

Jack S. Blanton Museum of Art
23rd and San Jacinto Streets
(512) 471-7324
www.blantonmuseum.org

UT's fine arts museum is one of the most-visited galleries in Austin. It features a wonderful permanent collection as well as changing temporary exhibits. For more on this gallery see our chapter on The Arts.

The Lyndon Baines Johnson Library
and Museum
2313 Red River Street
(512) 721-0200
www.lbjlib.utexas.edu/

While Americans have not gone in for a lot of fanfare about our former presidents, other than the Washington memorials, we do make an exception when it comes to our presidential libraries. And one of the greatest expressions of this American political tradition is the library and museum dedicated to President Lyndon Baines Johnson. Nowhere on earth can visitors see, hear, and learn as much about this compelling figure in American history and about the official politics of the turbulent 1960s as in the LBJ Library. This facility is the largest and most-visited presidential library in the country. But one doesn't just visit the LBJ Library; one *experiences* it. The Vietnam War, the Civil Rights Movement, the War on Poverty, and the Great Society all are represented, as well as some aspects of the '60s cultural scene. Here visitors will learn about Johnson's long and colorful political career, view mementos of the lives of President Johnson and First Lady Lady Bird Johnson, and visit the replica of the Oval Office as it was during Johnson's time (note especially the number of television sets and the news wires here. Johnson was a real newshound).

There also are two short video presentations of LBJ himself. A five-minute tape shows how he worked, and a seven-minute presentation gives great insight into the humor and personality of this charismatic Texan who was the nation's 36th president. For even better perspective, start your tour by watching the 20-minute movie that traces Johnson's life from his childhood on the banks of the Pedernales River west of Austin (see our Day Trips chapter) to the nation's highest office. The library houses 40 million pages of historical documents. The permanent exhibits are exceptional, and so are the temporary exhibits, a number of which the museum hosts each year. The museum and gift shop are open from 9:00 A.M. to 5:00 P.M. every day of the year except Christmas. And, because Johnson did not want people to have to pay to see his museum, it's the only presidential library that does not charge an entrance fee. Parking is free, too, in the lot on Red River Street.

Ahhhhh, Austin in springtime. The weather is perfect, and the fields and roadsides are filled with miles of bluebonnets. It's an annual tradition to find a field of bluebonnets and take your loved ones' pictures against this stunning backdrop. The Lady Bird Johnson Wildflower Center has tons of bluebonnets, but there are plenty all around the city.

Littlefield Building
At the northwest corner of
24th Street and Whitis Avenue

Built in 1894, this ornate red stone-and-brick Victorian mansion belonged to Major George W. Littlefield, an important UT benefactor and member of the Board of Regents. Standing on the edge of the original 40 acres, the mansion was bequeathed to the university in 1939. It was first used as practice rooms for UT music students and in World War II as headquarters for Naval Reserve Officers Training Corps, who set up a firing range in the attic. The first floor, restored to its original splendor, is open for visitors Monday through Friday from 8:00 A.M. to 5:00 P.M. Visitors are asked to enter the mansion through the east door.

Littlefield Memorial Fountain
21st Street and Whitis Avenue

Visit this fabulous fountain to enjoy its beauty and to mingle with the college students who come here to sit, have lunch, and socialize. Dedicated on March 26, 1933, the fountain has become a prominent landmark on the UT campus. Designed by Italian-born sculptor Pompeo Coppini, the fountain is meant to symbolize the revival of American patriotism during World War I, a spirit that Coppini felt had been lost during the Civil War. The large fountain consists of three-tiered pools with water jets spraying the larger-than-life bronze goddess standing on the prow of the battleship Columbia as it rushes to aid democracy abroad. The goddess Columbia holds in one hand the torch of freedom and in the other the palm of peace. The bronze figures of three horses rearing out of the water represent the surging ocean. On the left side of the grouping stands a young lad representing the army. Over the years this fountain has attracted all kinds of mischief. Soap bubbles and detergent have turned the normally still waters into a foaming spectacle, while an interesting array of reptiles, including alligators, have turned up in the fountain. The memorial, which includes the nearby statues of Texas and national notables, is dedicated both to "the men and women of the Confederacy who fought with valor and suffered with fortitude that states' rights be maintained . . ." and to the "sons and daughters of the University of Texas" who died in World War I.

The fountain is about half a block east of Guadalupe Street at 21st Street.

The Mustangs Sculpture
San Jacinto Street
at the base of the Texas Memorial Museum

Dedicated to the "spirited horses that carried the men who made Texas," this gorgeous statue of seven plunging mustangs is a landmark at the University of Texas. Unveiled in 1948, the statue is the work of Phimister Proctor, a famous sculptor of Western subjects. Proctor reportedly spent almost a year observing and measuring the anatomical details of a herd of painstakingly chosen *puros españoles*, Spanish mustangs. (FYI: It was the Spanish who introduced these powerful and wonderful horses to Texas.) The results are marvelous. Proctor created a band of horses that, since 1948, appears as if it could come to life at any moment.

Arno Nowotny Building
709 East Martin Luther King Boulevard

It's a shame UT did away with the visitor center in this pre–Civil War structure, which is listed on the National Register of Historic Places. Now visitors no longer have a good excuse to tour the home where General George Armstrong Custer (of Little Big Horn fame) lived briefly during Reconstruction. Designed by Abner Cook, Austin's leading antebellum builder who also did the Governor's Mansion, the Custer House was constructed in 1859 of 2-foot-thick rubble limestone with pine floors. (Today it's beautifully trimmed in burnt orange, UT's school color.) Acquired by the university in 1925 and restored in 1978, it is UT's oldest building and one of the few pre–Civil War buildings remaining in Austin. This structure is listed on the Civil War Discovery Trail.

Built as an asylum for the blind, which closed during the Civil War, the building was empty until Custer arrived with his wife, brother, father, and 4,000 volunteers in December 1865. He departed a few months later, and in August 1966 the building was reestablished as an institute for the blind. It was used as a training center for the U.S. military in both world wars. The building now houses UT's Urban Issues Program. It still contains some displays from its days as a visitor center, and the employees there are very friendly and helpful. This building is on UT's Heman Sweatt Campus (named for UT's first black law student) at the corner of Martin Luther King Boulevard, just off I-35.

Harry Ransom Center
Near Guadalupe and 21st Streets
(512) 471-8944
www.hrc.utexas.edu

Among the Ransom Center's exceptional properties are a rare Gutenberg Bible and the world's first photograph. The center is much more inviting to the general public since a major renovation was completed in 2003. See The Arts chapter for more about the center's world-class collections.

Santa Rita Oil Rig
At the corner of Trinity Street and Martin Luther King Boulevard

History buffs will want to search out this rig while touring the University of Texas campus. This little piece of machinery

stands as a powerful symbol of the riches UT gained from the legendary Santa Rita oil well in West Texas. On the morning of May 28, 1923, oil gushed forth from the well in Big Lake Oil Field on UT lands. For 19 years this oil rig worked to draw the black gold to the surface and help catapult the struggling university to fame as a first-class institution. (UT became one of Austin's economic pillars along the way.) For just short of 67 years, the Santa Rita oil well pumped money into the UT system. The Santa Rita also stands as a symbol of the entire system of oil and gas leases for state-owned land and in state ocean waters. The state bids out the leases to oil and gas companies, which pump the resource and then pay the state a royalty on the production, pumping literally millions into state coffers for public schools and higher education. The Santa Rita, by the way, got its name from a group of Catholic investors from New York. Apparently struggling with the decision over whether to invest in this unproven field, the investors went to their priest, who suggested they call on the aid of Santa Rita, Patron Saint of the Impossible. Hmmmm!

Texas Memorial Museum
2400 Trinity Street
(512) 471-1604
www.tmm.utexas.org

Opened in 1939 as a permanent memorial of the Texas Centennial celebrations, the Texas Memorial Museum is a showcase for the natural and social sciences. Here, among the bones, rocks, fossils, and dinosaur tracks, visitors will discover the distant—and not so distant—past. This museum is a must for anyone interested in the fields of geology, paleontology, zoology, botany, ecology, anthropology, or natural history. Life-size dioramas of Texas wildlife, habitat groups of native Texas birds, and displays of Texas's poisonous and harmless reptiles are just some of the treasures awaiting visitors in this museum.

Among the museum's many special attractions is the original 16-foot statue of the Goddess of Liberty that stood atop the State Capitol for nearly 100 years until she was replaced with a replica in 1986. The star she holds in her hand, however, is not the original. That can be viewed in the Capitol Complex Visitor Center. There's also the Onion Creek mosasaur, which serves as the centerpiece of the Hall of Geological History. The museum has an outstanding collection of fossil vertebrates. Here ancient amphibians and reptiles mingle with some of the giant Ice Age mammals, including saber-toothed cats and mastodons. There are also fascinating examples of dinosaur troikas. Tracks found in a 105-million-year-old limestone bed near Glen Rose, Texas, record forever the passage of several kinds of dinosaurs.

The Texas Memorial Museum, dedicated to the study and interpretation of the natural and social sciences, also contains internationally known research collections and laboratories. Although the museum focuses on Texas, there's also much to be seen about the Southwest and Latin America. The building itself is a work of art and a true attraction. The museum is open from 9:00 A.M. to 5:00 P.M. Monday through Friday, 10:00 A.M. to 5:00 P.M. Saturday, and 1:00 to 5:00 P.M. on Sunday. There's no entrance fee, but contributions are encouraged. Supporters may wish to consider joining the museum's membership organization.

THE TOWER

Just look up when you're on the UT campus and you'll find this 307-foot landmark, the most recognizable symbol of the university, which stands at the very heart of the original 40-acre campus. The Tower of the Main Building was completed in 1937 on the site of the university's first academic building, Old Main. The 27-story tower features a clock whose four faces are 14 feet, 8 inches, in diameter and the Knicker Carillon with its 56 bells that chime on the quarter hour and hour and are played at other times by the university's carillonneur.

The tower once shared the Austin skies with only one other soaring rival, the State Capitol. Its construction drew the ire of some Austin citizens back then, most notably Austin's master storyteller and UT professor J. Frank Dobie, who suggested the tower be laid on its side. Why, he complained aloud, with all the space in Texas, did a building here have to look like one in New York.

The soaring observation deck, however, afforded an excellent view of the city and quickly became a popular tourist attraction. But a tragic mass murder committed from the tower (see our History chapter) as well as a rash of suicides caused university officials to close the tower to the public in 1975. After being closed for nearly 25 years, the tower underwent a renovation and is once again open to the public for guided tours on weekends and on selected evenings during the summer only. Tickets for the nearly hourlong tour, including about 35 minutes on the observation deck, cost $5.00. Advance reservations are strongly recommended, as the tours fill up early. Call (512) 475-6633 or (877) 475-6633 to reserve.

The Spanish Renaissance–style structure, designed by Paul Cret of Philadelphia and built of Bedford Indiana limestone, is lighted to commemorate achievements in athletics and academics. There are so many different lighting schemes, each with its own significance, that the university once issued a guide to Tower lighting.

UMLAUF SCULPTURES

Around campus visitors will find 10 sculptures, most of them outdoors, created by Austin artist Charles Umlauf. (See our write-up on the Umlauf Sculpture Garden & Museum in this chapter.) Outside the Jack S. Blanton Museum of Art at the corner of San Jacinto and 23rd Streets is the bronze *Seated Bather II*. Outside the Alumni Center at 2110 San Jacinto is *Mother and Child*. In Centennial Park at Red River Street near 15th Street, across from the Frank Erwin Center, is *Three Muses.* And in front of the Business-Economics Building at West 24th Street is *The Family,* a 15-foot-tall bronze done in 1962. At the Harry Ransom Center near Guadalupe and 21st Streets, visitors will find two busts. There's a bronze portrait bust of Dr. Ransom in the entrance lobby and a portrait bust of Dr. Merton M. Minter. At the Peter Flawn Academic Center, on the main mall in front of the building, is Umlauf's 1962 bronze sculpture, *Torchbearers,* which is 12 feet high. The Law School Building at 727 East Dean Keeton Street features a portrait bust of General Ernest O. Thompson, done in 1953. The University Catholic Center, located at 2010 University, has Umlauf's Pieta done in bronze inside the Newman Chapel.

CENTRAL

The Neill-Cochran House Museum
2310 San Gabriel Street
(512) 478-2335

Austin's master builder Abner Cook designed and built this stately home in 1855 following a design plan that is similar to the Governor's Mansion, which Cook also built. Now operated as a museum by the Colonial Dames of America in the State of Texas, the home is a glorious example of Greek Revival architecture. Classic furnishings from the late 18th and early 19th centuries can be viewed throughout this beautifully kept home. The National Trust for Historic Preservation has called this house a "jewel and perfect example of the Texas version of the Greek Revival in the South." The home, originally built for Washington L. Hill, was purchased in 1876 by Colonel Andrew Neill. Judge T. B. Cochran bought the house in 1895 and made additions. The museum is open from 2:00 to 5:00 P.M. from Wednesday through Sunday. General admission is $2.00.

Elisabet Ney Museum
304 East 44th Street
(512) 458-2255
www.ci.austin.tx.us/elisabetney

This museum, once the Hyde Park home and studio of celebrated artist Elisabet Ney, features an array of about 50 portrait busts and full-figure statues of European notables, Texas heroes, and other figures. An entire section of the museum is dedicated to the life of this amazing sculptor who helped to establish Austin's artistic traditions. This is one museum that should not be missed on any tour of the arts in Austin. For more information about the museum and the home Ney built in the late 1800s, called Formosa, see our chapter on The Arts. The museum is open Wednesday through Saturday from 10:00 A.M. to 5:00 P.M. and Sunday from noon to 5:00 P.M. Admission is free.

Treaty Oak
Baylor Street, between West Fifth and West Sixth Streets

The poignant tale of Austin's beautiful and historic Treaty Oak will tug at your heart strings. Estimated to be between 500 and 600 years old, the Treaty Oak once stood more than three stories high and its branches covered more than half an acre. In the Hall of Fame of Forestry, the tree was described as "the most perfect specimen of a tree in North America." Legend has it that the Father of Texas, Stephen F. Austin, and leaders of local Indian tribes signed a treaty under the mighty oak, supposedly dividing the city between them. Although there is no historic evidence that this meeting ever took place, the legend persevered and people came from all over the country just to look at this incredible specimen.

Poisoned in 1989 by a man who was later caught and sentenced to nine years in prison, the majestic Treaty Oak is now about a third its original size, but still definitely worth a visit. Austin's heroic effort to save the Treaty Oak is another chapter in the tree's rich history. Specialists were brought in, sunscreens were erected, and people from all over the country prayed and sent letters along with more than $100,000 in donations to help save the tree. Since then, acorns and cuttings from the tree have been planted in Austin and the Treaty Oak was cloned so that identical copies of it are growing in Texas and other parts of the country. It's a story of survival. It's a story of Austin.

AROUND AUSTIN
South Central

Austin Nature and Science Center
301 Nature Center Drive
(512) 327-8181
www.ci.austin.tx.us/nature-science
A perfect place to enjoy Austin's great outdoors, the Austin Nature and Science Center in the Zilker Park Nature Preserve features 2 miles of trails with cliffs and a scenic outlook (see our Parks and Recreation chapter). But the facilities here go far beyond trails. Here, in the Visitor Pavilion, guests will learn about the two ecosystems—Hill Country and Caves, and Grasslands—that meet right smack in the middle of Austin. Displays also provide information on two minor ecosystems found throughout Central Texas: Ponds and Creeks, and Woodlands. Wildlife exhibits and a birds of prey exhibit are just a couple of the attractions found at this wonderful spot. (Be sure to see our Kidstuff chapter for more information on the Austin Nature and Science Center.) The center is open from 9:00 A.M. to 5:00 P.M. Monday through Saturday and from noon to 5:00 P.M. on Sunday throughout the year. Admission is free.

Philosophers' Rock Sculpture
Entrance to Barton Springs Pool
This exquisite bronze sculpture by artist Glenna Goodacre depicts three of Austin's illustrious figures engaged in

animated conversation—just as they were accustomed to doing in life. Life-size images of historian Walter Prescott Webb, naturalist Roy Bedichek, and J. Frank Dobie, humorist and folklorist, are presented in this large work, installed November 21, 1994. Webb stands fully clothed next to the rock (he never swam), while Dobie and Bedichek are seated, wearing swimming trunks. As you view this lively sculpture, it's difficult not to wonder what these three great "philosophers" are discussing.

Stevie Ray Vaughan Memorial
Auditorium Shores,
South side of Town Lake
near Riverside Drive and First Street
This larger-than-life bronze statue of the late blues/rock legend stands near the site where Vaughan played his last Austin concert on Auditorium Shores. The sculpture by artist Ralph Helmick depicts Vaughan in a relaxed pose wearing his trademark black hat and holding his guitar like a walking stick in his left hand. A long bronze shadow trails behind. When it was dedicated on November 21, 1993, Vaughan fans gathered in tribute to the Austin-based music man who died in a helicopter crash in 1990. The piece continues to draw admirers of both the artist it depicts and the artist who created it. (For more on Stevie Ray Vaughan, see the Close-up in our chapter on The Music Scene.)

Umlauf Sculpture Garden & Museum
605 Robert E. Lee Road
(512) 445-5582
www.umlaufsculpture.org
The outdoor setting of this wonderful sculpture garden combines Austin's love for the outdoors and for the arts. Acclaimed artist Charles Umlauf, whose works are on display in museums and public collections across the country, lived in Austin from 1941 until his death and was a University of Texas professor until 1981. The garden is the perfect outdoor setting for 62 of Umlauf's bronze and cast-stone

pieces. (For more on this inspiring Austin museum, see our chapter on The Arts.) The museum is open Wednesday through Friday from 10:00 A.M. to 4:30 P.M. and on Saturday and Sunday from 1:00 to 4:30 P.M. Nominal admission charge.

Zilker Botanical Garden
2220 Barton Springs Road
(512) 477–8672
www.zilkergarden.org

The eight theme gardens in this lovely spot are just some of the attractions at this lovely botanical garden, managed jointly by the Austin Area Garden Council and the City of Austin Parks and Recreation Department. Here visitors stroll among the 31 acres of displays and gardens to learn about different species of plants, get ideas for their own gardens, or just appreciate the beauty of nature. The Rose Garden features over 800 bushes. The Butterfly Garden and trail has been filled with flowers and plants that attract many species of Texas butterflies. The Green Garden is a showcase of water-tolerant plants and the principles of xeriscaping. The Prehistoric Garden re-creates a dinosaur habitat, in tribute to the dinosaur tracks and bones discovered here in 1992. The habitat includes a water-fall, pond, bog, and stream. In the Oriental Garden visitors will discover a series of waterfalls, lotus ponds, and an authentic teahouse. There is also a Cactus Garden and an Herb and Fragrance Garden. The Garden Council also sponsors a number of educational and cultural programs on-site as well as several popular annual events, including the Zilker Garden Festival in the spring. This is the place to come for anyone interested in gardening, as the Garden Center has information on all its member Austin garden clubs.

Here, too, visitors will find Pioneer Village, which includes two original log structures from the 1800s, a blacksmith shop, and an organic garden. The Swedish Log Cabin, built about 1838 on the "Govalle" Ranch—meaning "good grazing land"

Xeriscaping is environmentally friendly landscaping that requires about 40 percent less water than traditional land-scaping and often less chemical fertilizers and pesticides. In pro-environmental Austin a xeriscaped lawn is a wise choice—and can be beautiful and colorful to boot.

in Swedish—and moved to the botanical garden in 1966 is fully furnished with such 19th-century necessities as a spinning wheel, loom, and baby cradle. The small cabin was built by S. M. Swenson, a settler who encouraged migration of other Swedes to Texas and opened the cabin as a social center for the Swedish community. (Most of the activities must have taken place outdoors, however, as not too many people could have moved about here comfortably.) Right next to the cabin is the Esperanza School Building. Built in 1866, the log building was one of the earliest one-room rural school houses in Travis County. The interior of this school also is furnished as school children would have occupied it in the 19th century.

The Botanical Garden is open from 7:00 A.M. to sunset daily except on Thanksgiving, Christmas, and New Year's Day. Admission is free. There is a parking charge on weekends from March through November.

North

The Republic of Texas Museum
510 East Anderson Lane
(512) 339–1997

This fascinating space, which is meticu-lously run and cared for by the Daughters of the Republic of Texas, is packed with Texas history. Here visitors will learn about the men and women who fought for Texas independence and led the Republic of Texas from 1836 to 1846. The museum fea-tures award-winning permanent exhibits and a variety of touring shows. One outstanding section is called Great Grandma's Backyard, where visitors get to see and touch the household implements used by families in the mid-19th century. The museum also features an excellent collection of guns from that period, portraits and statues of Texas leaders, and much, much more. (See also our chapter on Kidstuff.)

South

St. Edward's University
3001 South Congress Avenue
(512) 448-8400
www.stedwards.edu

Don't miss the beautiful Gothic Revival-style Main Building and the other great attributes of this 180-acre campus. The Main Building is one of Austin's most stunning landmarks—a grand structure in the Southwest when it was built in 1889 and just as grand today. (For more information on this historic university, see our Higher Education chapter.)

Southwest

Austin Zoo
10807 Rawhide Trail
(512) 288-1490, (800) 291-1490
www.austinzoo.com

Located on the edge of Hill Country about 20 minutes from downtown Austin, the Austin Zoo is a great escape from the hustle and bustle of the city. Here visitors get a close-up view of domestic and exotic animals as well as a relaxing, enjoyable experience in a natural setting. (For more on Austin's zoo, see our Kidstuff chapter.)

Lady Bird Johnson Wildflower Center
4801 La Crosse Avenue
(512) 292-4100
www.wildflower.org

Established in 1982 as the National Wildlife Research Center, this delightful center was renamed in March of 1998 in honor of its founder, Austin's own Lady Bird Johnson. (See our profile of the former First Lady of the United States in this chapter.) This 42-acre Hill Country gem overflows with a brilliant variety of native plants and flowers and has become one of Austin's most visited spots. Here visitors will see and learn about our own state flower, the bluebonnet, as well as the glorious Indian paintbrush, which is as splendid as its name, and more than 500 other species of native plants. The center's 23 lovely perennial and seasonal gardens display in living color the bounty of Texas' botanical beauties. Much more than a showcase for the magnificent plant life of Texas, however, the center is an ecological sanctuary dedicated to the preservation and reestablishment of native plants—wildflowers, grasses, shrubs, and trees. It's the only national nonprofit organization fulfilling that mission and has become the leading national authority on native American plant life. Researchers, staff, and volunteers are committed to reversing the threat of extinction to about 3,000 endangered native plant species in North America, nearly 25 percent of the continent's natural plant life. This loss contributes to ecological havoc that goes way beyond vanished beauty. Accolades for the center's original conservation and ecological techniques have come from such prestigious organizations as the Smithsonian Institution and the National Wildlife Federation.

The center, which opened its impressive new facilities in 1995, features stone buildings designed in German Mission and ranch-style architecture to reflect the region's cultural diversity. There's also a wonderful observation tower offering an excellent view of the surrounding Hill Country, and a central courtyard and stone fountain, a nature trail, ponds, and picnic spots. The Wildflower Cafe is a great spot to have a sandwich or refreshment. The gift shop has a good selection of arts, crafts, posters, and books.

The center also features North America's largest rooftop rainwater collection system, which provides water for all the gardens. The place to begin the tour of this unique center, however, is at the Visitor Gallery. Here visitors are introduced to the Wildflower Center and can view interesting displays on the region's plant life. Young children especially will delight in hearing Ralph, the talking lawn mower, just one of the many features designed to appeal to children. Those interested in finding out more about specific plants can browse the research library. Education remains the center's primary goal. To that end, the center sponsors a number of conferences, lectures, and workshops on a variety of topics, many in the center's 232-seat auditorium. It also operates a clearinghouse so that people from across the country can obtain information about plants native to their region. *The Wildflower Handbook,* a source book on wildflowers and native plant landscaping, with nursery and information directories for all 50 states, is published by the Wildflower Center.

The grounds are open Tuesday through Sunday from 9:00 A.M. to 5:30 P.M. The Visitors Gallery is open Tuesday through Saturday from 9:00 A.M. to 4:00 P.M., and from 1:00 to 4:00 P.M. on Sunday. Admission is $5.00, with reduced rates for children and seniors. Regular visitors and supporters of the environment may wish to become members—or volunteers.

East

French Legation Museum
802 San Marcos Street
(512) 472-8180
www.frenchlegationmuseum.org
After King Louis Philippe of France officially recognized the fledgling Republic of Texas in 1839, he named Alphonse Dubois de Saligny as charge d'affaires and sent him to Austin. De Saligny, a flamboyant character, bought 22 acres of land on a beautiful Austin hilltop and began construction on his luxurious residence and carriage house, which are considered modest by today's standards. De Saligny, who insisted he be called Count, was anything but noble and more like a no-account scoundrel, leaving a trail of debts and angry citizens during his short stay here. While he awaited completion of his residence, de Saligny lived in downtown Austin, where he launched the infamous Pig War. Complaining that his neighbor's pigs were destroying his garden, de Saligny ordered his servant to shoot any pig that even looked as though it was going after the garden. The neighbor, Richard Bullock, retaliated by whacking the servant and threatening to come after de Saligny himself. That was about all de Saligny could take of Texas, and vice versa. He headed back to Louisiana and never occupied the home. The home was purchased by Dr. Joseph Robertson in 1848, and it remained in the family's hands for a century. In 1948 the state of Texas bought the property and placed it in custody of the Daughters of the Republic of Texas. They restored the home and opened it to the public in 1956. Today visitors will find many of the Robertson family furnishings as well as other period pieces. Guided tours include a visit to the original house and the reconstructed French Creole kitchen, which is fully equipped and contains many unique items. The replica of the carriage house contains an 1828 carriage, other exhibits, and a gift shop. Tours are conducted Tuesday through Sunday 1:00 to 4:30 P.M. The French Legation is also a popular spot for weddings. Nominal admission fee.

The French equivalent of our Independence Day, Bastille Day, July 14, is celebrated here with French song, food, and dance, and the legation also hosts a popular Christmas event when Pere Noel arrives to celebrate the season with a Gallic flair (see the listing in our Annual Events chapter).

George Washington Carver Museum
1165 Angelina Street
(512) 472-4809
www.ci.austin.tx.us/carver

This museum is distinguished for being the first African-American neighborhood museum in the state of Texas. The building that houses the museum was built in 1926 as Austin's first public library downtown. After a new library was built in 1933, this wood-frame structure was moved to East Austin and served as the city's first branch library. The George Washington Carver Museum opened October 24, 1980, and in the years since has evolved into a center of community involvement, enrichment, and education. Today the museum houses a permanent collection of photographs of and memorabilia associated with its namesake, the African American who was born the son of a slave and died a famous scientist. The museum, however, is most known for the constantly changing exhibits that pertain to the history and culture of Austin's African-American community. Its numerous education programs for adults and children include the annual A Smile on My Face workshop, which teaches children from all over the Austin area how to use a camera and darkroom equipment. It's open 10:00 A.M. to 6:00 P.M. Tuesday through Thursday and noon to 5:00 P.M. Friday and Saturday.

Huston-Tillotson College
900 Chicon Street
(512) 505-3025
www.htc.edu

While the campus has modernized over the past 125 years, two of Huston-Tillotson's historic buildings remain as splendid examples of turn-of-the-20th-century architecture. The Evans Industrial Building, built in 1911-12, was completely renovated in 1984 and designated as a Texas Historical Site. The Old Administration Building, constructed in 1913-14, is one of the few remaining examples of the Modified Prairie Style popularized by Frank Lloyd Wright. This building was entered in the National Register of Historic Places in 1993 and is slowly being restored. (For more on this historic African-American college, see our chapter on Higher Education.)

Oakwood Cemetery
16th and Navasota Streets

Austin's oldest cemetery is a scene of tranquility and beauty. Created in 1839, the cemetery is the final resting place for many Austin pioneers, prominent Austin families, and community leaders from the past and present. Athol Estes Porter, wife of short-story writer O. Henry, is interred here, as are former Texas Governor James Hogg and his daughter Ima. Mary Baylor, a driving force in the preservation of the Clarksville neighborhood, was buried here in 1997. The cemetery is chock-full of towering trees that provide wonderful shade in summer. The cemetery was added to the National Register of Historic Places in 1988.

Parque Zaragoza
Recreation Center Murals
2608 Gonzales Street
(512) 472-7142

Austin artist Fidencio Duran has captured the essence of the center's Hispanic neighborhood in a series of three immense—and immensely moving—narrative paintings that relate the story of the Hispanic experience in Austin to sweeping historical events in Mexico. *Cinco de Mayo* and *Diez y Seis* are the two 25-foot-tall murals in vivid color and detail that line the sides of the main entrance hall. Both begin with two infamous dates in Mexican history. *Cinco de Mayo*, or May fifth, depicts the Mexican battle at Puebla that resulted in the defeat of French invaders in 1862; *Diez y Seis* marks the event on September 16, 1810, when Father Miguel Hidalgo y Costilla uttered the famous Grito de Dolores, or cry, for independence from Spanish rule. These two epic paintings include homages to the 1929 Diez y Seis de Septiembre celebration in Austin, the neighborhood's first independence day festival. Residents will discover several East Austin landmarks within these works. Another stunning Duran mural, *Comite Patriota* is in the conference room. This series of murals, which visitors saw for the first time when the long-awaited recreation center opened in May 1996, highlight Austin's Hispanic culture and should not be missed. The center is open from 10:00 A.M. to 10:00 P.M. Monday through Thursday, 10:00 A.M. to 8:00 P.M. Friday, and 10:00 A.M. to 5:00 P.M. on Saturday.

Texas State Cemetery
901 Navasota Street
(512) 463-0605
www.cemetery.state.tx.us/
A must-see for anyone who wants to comprehend the scope of Texas history, the 18-acre Texas State Cemetery manages to be both tranquil and exhilarating at the same time. Visitors who walk among the tombs of many of Texas's most noted heroes and legends can't help envisioning the drama of the lives and times of these leaders. Stephen F. Austin, the Father of Texas, is buried here under a bronze statue that shows him standing with his right hand raised and holding a manuscript in his left hand inscribed with the words "Texas 1836." Confederate General Albert Sidney Johnson lies under the recumbent statue of him carved by Elisabet Ney, the German-born sculptor who made Austin her home. Among the other Texas leaders interred here is Barbara Jordan. A beloved scholar, teacher, and politician, Jordan was the first African American from Texas elected to the U.S. House of Representatives. Three-term Texas Governor John B. Connally is buried here along with the bullet fragments left in his body from when he was wounded during the Kennedy assassination. Lt. Governor Bob Bullock, the force behind the Texas State History Museum (see earlier in this chapter), is also interred here. And there are many more, including 10 other Texas governors, many famous writers and historians, and about 2,200 white marble

When planning outdoor activities, remember that Austin does have four seasons: November, December, January, and Summer. Or, as some like to say, Almost Summer, Summer, Like Summer, and Christmas.

headstones for veterans of the Confederate Army. Among the graves is that of General Edward Burleson, a vice president of the Republic of Texas and the first person to be buried in the cemetery after its creation in 1851.

A $4.7 million renovation and restoration project at the cemetery was completed in 1997. The project included construction of the visitor center made of Texas limestone and inspired by the long barracks of the Alamo. The visitor center serves as the main entrance to the cemetery and houses a permanent exhibit on Texas cemeteries. The landscaped grounds, stone recycling pond, and the lovely Plaza de los Recuerdos (Plaza of Memories) all contribute to the sense of serenity created at this very Texas location, often called the Arlington National Cemetery of Texas. The cemetery is open from 8:00 A.M. to 5:00 P.M. every day. The visitor center is closed Sunday, however. Guests can call ahead to arrange for guided tours, or they can do a self-guided tour with the help of information packets available at the visitor center.

West

Laguna Gloria Art Museum
3809 West 35th Street
(512) 458-8191
One of two facilities of the Austin Museum of Art, Laguna Gloria is important as much for its facilities as for the artworks it exhibits. Constructed in 1915–16 as a private residence, the Mediterranean-style villa covers more than 6,000 square feet. The outdoor amphitheater hosts a variety

of performance artists throughout the year. It's also a great place just to sit by the lake and have a picnic. The sculpture garden is wonderful. (For more information on Laguna Gloria, see our chapter on The Arts.)

Mount Bonnell
At the top of Mount Bonnell Road
off West 35th Street

This scenic spot overlooking Lake Austin has been attracting nature lovers—and romantic ones—for more than 150 years. At 785 feet above sea level, Mount Bonnell is one of the highest points in the Austin area and offers a view to end all views. Choose your partner wisely to make that first climb up the steps. According to local lore, two people who make their first climb together will fall in love. Some say Mount Bonnell was named after George W. Bonnell, a newspaperman and mercenary. Others claim it was named for Golden Nell and her "beau"—beau-nell— who leapt off the summit to their deaths in order to avoid capture by Native Americans. Visitors can also reach Mount Bonnell off Farm-to-Market Road 2222 (Bull Creek). (For more information on Mount Bonnell, see our chapter on Parks and Recreation.)

Lake Travis

The Oasis
6550 Comanche Trail
(512) 266-2442
www.oasis-austin.com

Consistently named one of the Top 10 Austin Area Attractions by the Austin Convention and Visitors Bureau, the Oasis offers one of the most stunning views in this entire area. From a vantage point of 450 feet above Lake Travis, the multitudes of outdoor decks (43 at last count!) and the indoor dining rooms look out across the lake and the Texas Hill Country. This is one of the best places to drink a margarita or two while watching a fabulous Austin sunset. The Oasis hosts live bands Thursday through Sunday nights. This establishment is also a full-service restaurant leaning heavily on Tex-Mex cuisine. Unfortunately it has a reputation for inconsistent quality, although the management is now committed to upgrading the food and has hired a new chef.

NATIONAL REGISTER DISTRICTS

While Austin has numerous residences and commercial buildings listed on the National Register of Historic Places, many of which we've mentioned in this chapter, the city also boasts a number of entire districts listed on this important National Register for historic preservation. Those who don't want to miss one stop on their tour of historic Austin should consider taking a walking tour of some of these uniquely Austin locations. See our listing under Austin Tours in this chapter if you're interested in a guided walking tour of some of the following neighborhoods, or pick up copies of the free "Historic Walking Tours" series at the Austin Visitor Center at 209 East Sixth Street (512–478–0098 or 800–866–GOAUSTIN). The National Park Service also has information on its Web site, www.cr.nps.gov/nr. They have brochures for Hyde Park, the Bremond District, and Congress Avenue and East Sixth Street. These brochures describe each building in more detail and give some interesting tidbits about the buildings' former owners. There's also a brochure available on Camp Mabry.

BARTON SPRINGS ARCHAEOLOGICAL AND HISTORIC DISTRICT

This district within Zilker Park in South Central Austin includes our favorite swimming spot and a most endangered treasure, Barton Springs Swimming Pool. Named to the National Register in 1985, this place is Austin through and through and should not be missed on any tour of Austin, prehistoric, historic, or otherwise. Barton Springs, comprising four principal springs, is the fifth-largest group of springs in the state of Texas. One of the many reasons this site is listed on the National Register of Historic Places is that human habitation has been traced back to approximately 6000 B.C. Archaeologists have found chipped-stone arrowheads, bone fragments, and prehistoric ceramics while digging in this area.

The springs are named for one of Austin's earliest modern settlers, William Barton, who moved to the springs in 1837 and built a home. While nothing remains of his homestead, there is evidence (a cistern) of the home built on the property in 1867 by the Rabb family, who came to Texas as part of Stephen F. Austin's first colony of Anglo settlers (see our History chapter). More modern structures that contributed to the springs' selection for the National Register include the concrete Zilker Amphitheater, built around one of the springs by Austin civic leader and philanthropist Andrew Jackson Zilker in the first decade of the 20th century. And then there's the famous Bath House. Built in 1946, this cool structure has been a source of pride for Austin for more than half a century. During a period when Texas architecture was largely ignored by the national press, the Bath House was the subject of a long article in *Architectural Digest* magazine. The article praised architect Dan Driscoll's ingenuity in designing an imaginative structure that was entirely appropriate for its site. The Bath House, still in use today next to the pool, is practically unchanged from the day it was built. (For more information on this 1,000-foot-long spring-fed pool, see our chapter on Parks and Recreation.) The pool itself is located at 2201 Barton Springs Road, but the register district is bounded on the north by Barton Springs Road, on the east by Robert E. Lee Road, and on the west by Barton Creek and is situated on both banks of the creek.

BREMOND NATIONAL REGISTER DISTRICT

For a glimpse into the lifestyles of the rich and prominent from a century ago, include the Bremond Block on your tour of downtown Austin. Here are some of the most elegant and elaborate 19th-century homes still found in the city. Italianate, Greek Revival, Colonial Revival, Queen Anne, and Second Empire are just some of the architectural styles borrowed for this collection of 14 homes built between 1854 and 1910. Many of these fabulous homes are historic landmarks. Three of the homes—the Walter Bremond House, the Pierre Bremond House, and the stunning John Bremond Jr. House—were built by Austin builder George Fiegel, who is notable for having planned, constructed, or remodeled many of the buildings on historic Congress Avenue.

The histories of those who built and occupied these dwellings are as interesting as the structures themselves. Eugene Bremond and his siblings grew up just a couple of blocks away as the children of wealthy merchant John Bremond Sr. As it happened, the Bremond homestead was catty-cornered from the homestead of another Austin merchant, John Robinson Sr. The warm friendship between the patriarchs of these two families must have cast a spell over both houses, because Eugene and two of his sisters married Robinsons. Eugene, who parlayed his father's wealth into a fortune first as a lender—it's said he charged 18 percent interest on loans made to early settlers—and then as a banker, bought the north half of the block in 1866 that was to bear his family's name. Over the years, as the families' children grew and married, the block became the Bremond family compound, just as Eugene had envisioned. Not all the homes in this district were owned by the Bremond line, however. Other wealthy Austinites also lived in this compound, including the Harvey North family, the Henry Hirshfelds, and William Phillips, one of Austin's first doctors. The district is between Seventh and

Eighth Streets and Guadalupe and San Antonio Streets.

CAMP MABRY NATIONAL REGISTER DISTRICT

Established in 1892 as a permanent training ground for the Texas Volunteer Guard, Camp Mabry is the third-oldest active military post in Texas. Today the West Austin camp is headquarters to the Texas Army National Guard, Texas Air National Guard, the Texas State Guard, and the Reserves. Among the many historic buildings on these huge grounds is the Texas Military Forces Museum, built in 1918 as the mess hall for the School of Automobile Mechanics. The mess hall accommodated 4,000 men and had the largest kitchen of its kind in Texas, covering 45,000 square feet. Today, the museum stands alone in presenting the history of the Texas military from the Texas Revolution to the present. Another special attraction on the grounds is the pond and picnic area that has been attracting Austinites for more than 100 years. Here visitors will find a rustic limestone dam, built in 1892 to create a bathing pool for the Texas Volunteer Guard. The Volunteer Guard, by the way, became the National Guard in 1903. The remaining buildings and grounds have been open to the public for self-guided walking tours, and there's a great cinder track and workout trail that Austinites have used for exercise. There are some vintage aircraft on display near the track. Security concerns in the fall of 2001 caused some areas of the camp to be closed, and future public access may continue to be limited.

Take special note of the many facilities here that were built by the Works Progress Administration (WPA), the federal program that put people to work during the Depression and wound up providing some of the country's best infrastructure. WPA projects at Camp Mabry include the stone wall and guard post that visitors pass upon entering the camp, the stone arch bridges near the picnic area, and a number of workshops and warehouses. The WPA also replaced the dam's original brick with limestone in 1938. Some of these WPA projects were built in the so-called CCC-rustic style, named after the Civilian Conservation Corps. One of the unique structures at Camp Mabry is the multicolored totem pole, presented to the camp in 1949 by the Royal Canadian Air Force in honor of the Texans who joined the RCAF to fight in World War II. The totem pole represents the Thunderbird family and the figures, from top to bottom, are the son, who makes thunder and wind; the daughter, keeper of hail storms; the mother, maker of lightning, thunder, and rain; and Chief Thunderbird, who attempts to subdue a dragon and make huge storms at the same time. The dragon is at the bottom of the totem pole. Camp Mabry was named in honor of Adjutant General Woodford Mabry of the Texas Volunteer Guard, among the first to see the need for a permanent training ground for the Texas military.

The museum is open Wednesday through Sunday from 10:00 A.M. to 4:00 P.M. The grounds are open from 6:00 A.M. to 10:00 P.M. The camp, listed on the National Register in 1996, is at 2200 West 35th Street. For more information call the camp at (512) 465–5001.

CLARKSVILLE NATIONAL REGISTER DISTRICT

Clarksville is one of four Austin communities founded by African Americans in the years following the end of slavery, on June

When you're looking for downtown attractions or lodging, remember that an address that includes the word "south" means south of Town Lake. Also know that Town Lake is that river-looking body of water downtown. It's a lake only because the river is dammed.

19, 1865. Named for Charles Clark, the name taken by freed slave Charles Griffin, the neighborhood started when Clark purchased two acres of wilderness land on what was then just west of the Austin city limits. In 1977 Clarksville became the first African-American neighborhood in Texas to be listed on the National Register of Historic Places. Many of the homes in this neighborhood were built between the 1870s and the 1930s (see our Relocation chapter). Today visitors can find the 1930s basilica-style building that houses the Sweet Home Missionary Baptist Church at 1725 West 11th Street (see our Worship chapter). The church was founded in the 1880s by the freed men and women who built new lives in this district. The neighborhood is in Central Austin and is bounded by MoPac on the west, 10th Street on the south, Waterston Avenue on the north, and West Lynn Street on the east. And don't miss Mary Baylor Clarksville Park at 1811 West 11th Street. This park was named in 1997 in honor of Mary Baylor, who passed away earlier that year. This dynamic community leader, the great-granddaughter of original Clarksville residents, spent a lifetime fighting to preserve Clarksville's unique character. The annual Clarksville Jazz Festival is held in June just outside this neighborhood in nearby Pease Park and other area venues. Look for more information in our Relocation chapter.

CONGRESS AVENUE NATIONAL REGISTER DISTRICT

With our grand Texas State Capitol as its crowning glory, Congress Avenue is a showcase for some of the city's finest late-19th-century commercial architecture. As you walk this 10-block district from the capitol south to Cesar Chavez Street, keep in mind that this street was once Austin's main thoroughfare and the nerve center for the capital of a fledgling frontier state. We've introduced you to several of this district's most important structures under

the individual listings above, including the State Capitol, the Governor's Mansion, the Old Bakery, and the Paramount Theater. We'll point out a few others here. The first is not a structure at all, but a small, unassuming park located at 11th Street and Congress Avenue. This easy-to-miss parklet actually has significant historical value. There was once a building here, built in 1881, that served as our State Capitol while the grander one you see just across the street was under construction. The University of Texas also held its first classes here in the fall of 1884. But as with an amazing number of Austin's old buildings, this one burned down in 1899. You can still see its foundation and cistern.

Also of note on this street is the Johns-Hamilton Building at 716 Congress Avenue. Built in 1870 with an elegant Gothic Revival storefront, the facade has been reconstructed. Just a few doors down are the Walter Tips and Edward Tips Buildings at 708–712 Congress Avenue. These two German-born brothers emigrated to the United States about 1850. Older brother Edward opened his hardware business at 708 Congress Avenue in 1865 and gave his brother a job as clerk. Not to be outdone, Walter built a much more elaborate structure for his business next door, which dealt in heavy machinery. The Walter Tips Building is a three-story structure that features Corinthian architecture on the first floor and Venetian Gothic architecture on the top two floors. Interior columns and girders in this building are made of recast exploded Confederate shells.

At the corner of Sixth Street and Congress Avenue is the Littlefield Building, which we mentioned in our chronicle of the Sixth Street Historic District. Down the block, at 512–520 Congress, is the Littlefield's rival, the Scarbrough Building, which housed the preeminent department store in Texas until the early 1980s. Built in 1909 in the Chicago style, the building's exterior was changed to an Art Deco style in 1931. Next to Scarbrough's, at number 504, is the Robinson-Rosner Building. Built in the mid-1850s, this is the oldest known building on Congress Avenue. We must also point out one of Abner Cook's buildings on this avenue. Cook was Austin's master builder during this era and is responsible for some of the city's most historic landmarks, including the Governor's Mansion and the Neill-Cochran House (see the listings in this chapter). He also built the Sampson-Henricks Building at 620 Congress Avenue in 1859. This, too, is one of Congress's oldest buildings and is distinguished for its Italianate style and excellent craftsmanship.

HYDE PARK NATIONAL REGISTER DISTRICT

Hyde Park represents the vision of Monroe Martin Shipe, an entrepreneur who came to Austin from Abilene, Kansas, in 1889. As president of the Missouri, Kansas, and Texas Land and Town Company, Shipe had resources as big as his dream. He bought the tract of land that was then in far North Austin, named it Hyde Park, for the distinguished London address, and spent the rest of his life living in and promoting his beloved neighborhood. Elisabet Ney, the sculptor famous for carving the marble statues of heroic Texans found in Austin, was among the first to build her home and studio in this 207-acre suburb, now listed as a National Register District. (See more about Elisabet Ney in this chapter.)

The site of the State Fair of Texas from 1875 to 1884, the area back in Shipe's day still had a prominent horse racing track and those who raced horses there would walk their horses up and down one of the main streets, which became known as The Speedway because of it. Speedway is still one of the major avenues in this Central Austin area.

One of Shipe's first actions to promote development of this suburb was to connect it to the city via his own electric streetcar system. Then he turned the

southwest section into a resort that included a dance pavilion and tree-lined walking paths. The middle-class homes, built mostly of wood between 1892 and 1925, reflect a variety of architectural styles and tastes (see our Relocation chapter). The first of Austin's historic Moonlight Towers was built in this neighborhood, and it still works. You'll find it at 41st Street and Speedway (see the previous listing in this chapter). A lovely park and playground, now called Shipe Park, was added in 1928 and remains a popular spot for neighborhood families today. The homes are privately owned and not available for tours. The Woodburn House, however, is a bed-and-breakfast establishment (see our Bed-and-Breakfasts chapter). Do take a moment to stop in at the Avenue B. Grocery at 4403 Avenue B. This small neighborhood store will take you back in time. This district is in Central Austin between 39th and 44th Streets and Avenue B to Avenue H.

MOORE'S CROSSING NATIONAL REGISTER DISTRICT

This community just south of the new Austin-Bergstrom International Airport in Southeast Austin was added to the National Register of Historic Places in 1996. The community dates to before the turn of the century and reached its peak of prosperity between 1880 and 1920. More than a dozen structures and sites contribute to this historic place, including homes, a henhouse, a barn, an abandoned metal-truss bridge, and, most significantly, a small country store, known as the Berry & Moore Bros. Store, which dates back to between 1900 and 1914. The store is particularly impressive and important to our historic preservation because these examples of country stores, which were the economic nucleus of rural communities, are becoming harder and harder to find. Moore's Crossing is in the area roughly bounded by Farm-to-Market Road 973, Old Burleson Road, and Onion Creek.

RAINEY STREET NATIONAL REGISTER DISTRICT

Located downtown near the Austin Convention Center between Driskill and River Streets, the Rainey Street district includes 21 Victorian cottages as well as 1930s bungalows and other historic structures. This was a working-class neighborhood during the late 19th and early 20th centuries. None of the structures is open to the public.

SHADOW LAWN NATIONAL REGISTER DISTRICT

This district includes a couple of blocks of residences within the Hyde Park neighborhood in Central Austin. The Depression-era homes are mostly one-story brick structures, many with Tudor Revival–style touches. The Shadow Lawn district is on Avenue G and Avenue H and includes part of the 3800 block of Duval Street.

SIXTH STREET NATIONAL REGISTER DISTRICT

By night, this strip defends its reputation as Austin's most-visited strip when tourists and residents out for a good time pack its lively, music-filled clubs and restaurants. (Don't miss our chapter on The Music Scene for the story of Sixth Street after dark.) By day, Sixth Street takes a breather. That's the time to stroll along the uncluttered sidewalks and take in the sites of one of Austin's most historic streets. This section is about East Sixth Street by day, when the sun illuminates the past. Known as Pecan Street in Austin's early days, this district is filled with more than two dozen fascinating examples of Victorian commercial architecture. Many of the buildings here were constructed during the building boom of the 1870s. Others followed in the 1880s and 1890s. Of course, these structures don't disappear at night. They're just a little harder to appreciate. The district encompasses a 9-block street from Lavaca Street on the west to I-35 on the east.

Start your tour at the corner of Sixth and Brazos streets at the famous Driskill Hotel, built in 1886. (See our chapter on Hotels and Motels for more on this landmark.) As you walk east on the north side of Sixth Street, you'll discover many more examples of Victorian architecture. Among the noteworthy structures on Old Pecan Street is the Hannig Building. Built in 1875 at 206 East Sixth Street, this Renaissance Revival–style structure is considered one of Austin's finest late-19th-century, Victorian commercial buildings. The Padgitt-Warmoth Building, built in 1885, is next at number 208. Once a saddlery and leather business, this is one of Old Pecan Street's most interesting buildings, with its fleur-de-lis cutouts and a Star of David cap.

In the next block is the Platt-Simpson Building at 310 East Sixth Street. This structure, built in 1871, was a livery stable and later a hardware store. St. Charles House, at number 316, was built in 1871 and once was a hotel and restaurant. Among the historic structures in the 400 block is the beautifully restored Dos Banderas at 410 East Sixth Street. Once a saloon and bawdy house, the building was closed in 1961 for housing "nefarious activities." Next door is the Quast Building, built in 1881 as a residence and later operated as a grocery store. This is one of the oldest stone buildings on the strip. The Risher-Nicholas Building at 422–424 East Sixth Street is another of the building-boom structures. Built in 1873, it became a drugstore in the early 1900s. Owner J. J. Jennings, a black physician, was once lauded for his work at building up "a trade that would do justice to any drugstore owned by any other race." The *Austin Watchman*, an early African-American newspaper, was published here in the early 1900s.

On the south side of Sixth Street, at 421 East Sixth Street, is the two-story stone and masonry Paggi Carriage Shop, constructed around 1875. Owner Michael Paggi is said to have been the first to bring an ice-making machine from France to Texas. Also on this block, visitors will find two 1875 structures, the J. L. Buass Building at number 407 and the Driskill-Day-Ford Building at number 403. The Cotton Exchange Building next door at 401 East Sixth also was built about this time. Across the street, at 325 East Sixth Street, is the Smith-Hage Building. Built in 1873, this building is a good example of commercial Victorian architecture during this time period, with its three arched windows on the second floor and topped by an elaborate metal cornice. One of Austin's few remaining cast iron–front buildings can be found at 209 East Sixth Street. This is the Morely-Grove Drug Store, originally built as a two-story structure in 1874. The third floor and a Queen Anne bay window were added about 20 years later. At the corner of Sixth and Congress is the Littlefield Building. Completed in 1912 and built for Major George Washington Littlefield (whose opulent home and the fountain named for him are on the UT campus), this elegant structure once was the tallest building between New Orleans and San Francisco. The building originally had eight floors, but Littlefield added another floor when the rival Scarbrough Building matched the Littlefield's height.

SWEDISH HILL NATIONAL REGISTER DISTRICT

This district is close to the Oakwood Cemetery just east of I-35 in East Austin. Visitors who walk along East 14th Street, East 15th Street, Olander Street, and Waller Street will discover 10 architecturally significant residences built from about 1880 to 1938, none open to the public. The neighborhood, now only partially intact, got its name from the area's Swedish immigrants.

WILLOW-SPENCE STREETS NATIONAL REGISTER DISTRICT

This district is in East Austin. Willow Street is a block south of First Street, just east of I-35. Spence Street is another block south of Willow. Along these two streets, visitors will find 38 historically noteworthy buildings constructed from about 1900 to the 1930s. None is open to the public.

ZILKER PARK NATIONAL REGISTER DISTRICT

This great Austin Park, which includes many historic structures and buildings, including a limestone Boy Scout hut, built in 1934, and a Girl Scout lodge built the same year, was added to the National Register of Historic Places in 1997. (For more on Austin's favorite community park, see our chapter on Parks and Recreation.)

TOURING GREATER AUSTIN . . .

. . . On Foot and On Wheel

Austin Astronomical Society Tours
Wild Basin Wilderness Preserve
805 North Loop 360 (Capital of Texas Highway)
(512) 327-7622
www.austinastro.org/wbtours.html
A bit off the beaten path but well worth the time are the monthly Stargazing and Moonlighting tours offered at Wild Basin Wilderness Preserve by members of the Austin Astronomical Society and Wild Basin volunteers. Although the tours can be canceled if the sky is overcast, these events are extremely popular and do fill up, so reservations are highly recommended. The operators suggest that visitors bring a flashlight, binoculars, drinking water, and a cushion or small folding chair. The preserve entrance is about 1 mile north of Bee Caves Road on the east side of Loop 360.

Austin Convention and Visitors Bureau
(512) 478-0098, (800) 866-GOAUSTIN
www.austintexas.org
The visitors bureau offers free guided

walking tours from March through November of the capitol grounds, historic Congress Avenue and Sixth Street, and the Bremond District. Tours of the capitol grounds are conducted on Saturdays at 2:00 P.M. and Sundays at 9:00 A.M., while the walking tour of Congress Avenue begins at 9:00 A.M. sharp Thursday through Saturday and at 2:00 P.M. on Sunday. The Bremond Historical District tour begins on Saturday and Sunday at 2:00 P.M. These tours leave from the south steps of the capitol building. While the visitors bureau does not run the tours of the State Capitol, it does provide information about the tours.

Austin Ghost Tours
(512) 443-3688
www.austinghosttours.com
Boo! For those looking for the decidedly unusual, the well-established Austin Ghost Tours offers a variety of adventures unlike any other tour company. Jeanine Plumer serves as both historian and storyteller as she takes visitors through Austin's haunted haunts. The Ghosts of Austin Tour conjures up the spirit world in a 90-minute walking tour that includes stops at the capitol, the Governor's Mansion, and the Driskill Hotel. The Graveyard Tour, beginning at the witching hour of midnight, is an hourlong cemetery tour to visit the perhaps-not-so-final resting places of some fascinating Texans, like Alamo survivor Susannah Dickinson and a man named Maurice Moore, the first Travis County sheriff to be killed in the line of duty. Then there's the Haunted Pub Crawl for those ages 21 and over who want to drink their spirits and have them too. Jeanine relates the true stories and legends of downtown's dearly departed while visiting some Sixth Street taverns. During Austin's Own Jack the Ripper Tour, visitors learn the story of the so-called Servant Girl Annihilator, who terrorized our city in the 1880s. Tours begin at the Hideout Coffee House at 617 Congress Avenue.

Group tours just not your trip? For independent-minded sightseers, there's Hit the Road Austin, *a CD or cassette complete with map that guides visitors on a lively, well-narrated driving tour of the city. They're for sale at the visitor center and at local bookstores.*

In addition to her regularly scheduled tours, Jeanine also offers private tours on other not-so-other-wordly subjects, such as the history of Austin and more. Call Jeanine for information. (Ghost Tours was previously called Austin Promenade Tours.)

Austin Overtures
(512) 659-9478
www.austinovertures.com
From the vantage point of a comfortable bright-fuchsia van, Austin Overtures offers 90-minute narrated tours of Austin that include 30 of Austin's major historical and cultural attractions on a 30-mile tour route. Experienced tour operators Dow and Mary Davidson launched this company in 2003, offering interesting, fun-and-fact-filled introductions to many of the places and people that make Austin what it is, such as *Austin City Limits,* the LBJ Library, Barton Springs, and the Congress Avenue bat colony. The tours are narrated by Dow, a Texas history buff whose great-great-grandfather founded the Texas town of Leakey. There are three daily scheduled departures from the Austin Convention and Vistors Bureau, at 9:30 A.M., 11:30 A.M., and 1:30 P.M. Special group tours can also be arranged.

Texpert Tours
(512) 383-TXTX (8989)
www.texperttours.com
Known locally as "the Texas Back Roads Scholar," Howie Richey offers entertaining, insightful tours of Austin and the Texas Hill Country based on his excellent knowl-

edge of and love for this region. His
enlightening tours of downtown Austin
provide much more than a look at buildings and scenery. He's got the scoop on
the history, geography, and quirky qualities of our fair city and exudes a hearty
respect for the region's natural wonders.
You'll think you've got your very own university professor in the vehicle with you.
Howie is a longtime Austinite and Univer-
siy of Texas grad (twice!), who also hosts
shows on Austin public radio. While the
Austin Downtown Tour is probably his
most popular, Howie can tailor an outing
to satisfy any group's interests. His Austin
tours are three hours long; the Hill Country trips run about four hours. He offers
departures at 9:00 A.M., 2:00 P.M., and 7:00
P.M. most days. It's important to reserve in
advance, as he customizes the trip for
each group and provides refreshments,
maps, souvenirs, and printed schedules.
He offers door-to-door service, meaning
he'll pick you up at your hotel or home.
Ask him also about canoe and raft trips,
hiking, and campouts.

. . . On Hoof

Austin Carriage Service
Tours starting and ending at several
downtown locations
(512) 243-0044
www.austincarriage.com

With Austin's weather so beautiful most of
the year, one great way to see the sites of
historic downtown and enjoy the outdoors
in style is to hop on a Vis-A-Vis. That's
French for face to face. Indeed. These
white horse-drawn carriages operated by
the Austin Carriage Service have seating
for up to six people, facing one another,
and each features a top that can be raised
in case of light rain or harsh sunlight. The
carriages, reproductions of a servant-
driven carriage from the 18th century, are
drawn by draft horses that stand about 6
feet tall and weigh 1,800 to 2,200 pounds.
Austin Carriage Service offers a variety of
regular tours that take in the sights on
Congress Avenue, Sixth Street, the State
Capitol and Governor's Mansion, Town
Lake, and more. Tours depart from several
downtown restaurants and hotels, including The Driskill, the Four Seasons, the
Hyatt Regency, Embassy Suites, and DoubleTree Guest Suites. The service offers
day, evening, and late-night rides. Call for
their schedule. In most cases, there's no
need to make a reservation. Just walk up
and enjoy the ride. A carriage can also be
dispatched to a specific location by making arrangements in advance. Drivers are
friendly and also serve as guides on your
historic tour. Fees vary according to the
length of the tour, which ranges from
about 20 minutes to 80 minutes.

Die Gelbe Rose Carriage
(512) 477-8824
From its base of operations near the
Radisson Hotel & Suites at East Cesar
Chavez Street and Congress Avenue, this
carriage company offers horse-drawn carriage tours around downtown's most
comely sights. Starting around sunset
daily, you can hail a carriage to the State
Capitol, head around to the Governor's
Mansion, or design your own tour. Call
ahead if you prefer to have a carriage
waiting at a certain time to whisk you
away. Magnificent Clydesdales are the
most common horses used for this task.

. . . On Rail

Austin Steam Train
(512) 477-8468
www.austinsteamtrain.org.
All aboard! Like the carriage rides above and the boat rides that follow, the mode of transportation for these tours is a big part of the fun. Take one—or all—of a number of rides on this popular train that runs on weekends year-round. Choices, depending on the season, include a day-long trip through the Texas Hill Country, a half-day Hill Country tour, a two-hour ride through East Austin, and specialty evening excursions, such as the Storybook Special for families with young children and the Murder Mystery Special and the New Year's Eve Special, both adult oriented. The Hill Country trains, which depart from Cedar Park in north Austin, run on the same tracks built in 1881 for the Austin & Northwestern Railroad. The pink granite used to build our State Capitol was hauled over these tracks in the 1880s.

The main locomotive for these trips is a steam engine, Southern Pacific #786, built in 1916. However, the vintage locomotive was still undergoing a massive overhaul in 2004, and diesel-powered engines were temporarily called into action. Check out the Web site for a schedule, rate information, and news on when the steam train will be back in service. The trains are operated by the Austin Steam Train Association, a community-based nonprofit organization whose volunteers go out of their way to make these trips fun for all.

. . . On Water

Austin Duck Adventures
(512) 4-SPLASH (477-5274)
www.austinducks.com
What's that strange yellow truck with the big tires rolling down Congress Avenue? It is one of the Austin Duck Adventure trucks, a combo vehicle that can ride on roads and splash into Town Lake for a cruise along the river. Tickets can be purchased at the Austin Convention and Visitors Bureau, 209 East Sixth Street.

Capital Cruises
At the Hyatt Regency Hotel,
208 Barton Springs Road
(512) 480-9264
www.capitalcruises.com
For private or public cruises of Town Lake, Capital Cruises offers a variety of tour options. Public tours, held March through October, include weekend dinner cruises and sight-seeing tours as well as the popular nightly bat-watching excursions. Capital Cruises also offers private cruises by reservation year-round. These include private and group dinner cruises, party boat cruises, and company outings. This company also has canoes, kayaks, pedal boats, and pontoons for rent. Tickets are required.

Lake Austin Riverboats
On Lake Austin
(512) 345-5220
www.austinriverboats.com
These two stern-wheeler riverboats are for chartered cruises of Lake Austin, complete with food and beverage service if you like. *Commodore's Pup* is for groups of 50 to 100 people, while the riverboat *Commodore* is designed for 100 to 300 people. Entertainment can also be arranged for that special party. Call them for rates.

Lone Star Riverboat
On the south shore of Town Lake
between the Congress Avenue Bridge
and South First Street Bridge
(512) 327-1388
www.lonestarriverboat.com
A double-decked paddle-wheel riverboat takes visitors on a one-hour cruise of scenic Town Lake from March through October. *Lone Star* offers a variety of cruise times, including a sunset tour and a close-up view of the evening flight of the bats from the Congress Avenue Bridge (see

the previous listing in this chapter). There's also a moonlight cruise on Friday night during summer. Group and private charters are also available. The schedule changes according to the time of year. Call for current tours. No reservations are required. Fees vary according to the type of cruise.

KIDSTUFF

ne morning hundreds of years ago, an acorn fell and grew in the earth. And that was me."

So begins *The Tree That Would Not Die,* a wonderful, beautifully illustrated children's book by Ellen Levine and Ted Rand about Austin's legendary Treaty Oak.

It may seem odd to begin a section on children's activities by mentioning a book, or our remarkable tree for that matter. However, this short, poignant book, available in most area bookstores, offers an excellent introduction to Austin for both children and adults. Folklore, history, and a somber slice of contemporary life intermingle to deliver a unique perspective on this fascinating city. And don't forget to take your little acorns to visit the real Treaty Oak in Central Austin (see our Attractions chapter).

Did we say little acorns? It seems to us that Austin views its children—both residents and visitors—as if they were wee acorns: little pods of potential that, if nurtured, will grow upright, strong and resilient. So whether yours is a little sprout, a precocious sapling, or a young tree whose branches are reaching for the sky, Austin offers plenty of sunshine, water, and fertilizer for all.

From the new, wonderfully expanded site of the Austin Children's Museum to children's theater, the Austin Zoo, indoor skating rinks, and great outdoor activities, Austinites have put a great deal of energy into providing recreational, educational, cultural, and simply fun activities for youth of all ages. The Central Texas area provides even more diversion, including that guaranteed kid-pleaser, the giant amusement park. All the Kidstuff activities and attractions we've included in this chapter can be found within 90 minutes of Austin, but most are right here at home. A word on ticket prices: Generally speaking, public institutions, museums, science centers, etc.,

charge nominal, family-friendly admission prices. Some of the privately run attractions in central Texas, particularly those focused on the area's natural wonders, charge a little more. Admission for a family of four to these attractions can cost around $50. Commercial attractions, including the major theme parks, are more expensive, and tickets for a family of four can cost well over $100 for a daily admission.

When it comes to day camps, Austin is a child's delight. Perhaps because so many parents here work, or maybe because Austin just loves its kids, there's a day camp to tickle nearly every child's fancy. Whether you're looking for camps for the whole summer or just a few days around the holidays or spring break, Austin has a place that's just right for you.

If you want your sprouts to enjoy their trip to Austin, be sure to visit some of the places listed here. We've provided six categories designed to direct you to Central Texas's most appealing attractions for "growing" children.

Fertilize Well: While this list includes those attractions designed to stimulate the mind, there's plenty of fun to be found, too.

Just Add Water: What would Central Texas be without diversions designed to get you nice and wet?

Supply Sunshine: These are a few of Austin's outdoor delights that appeal to children.

Let 'em Grow Crazy: For when the kids just need to let loose and have fun.

A Garden of Delights: Check this out for relaxing and entertaining spots that are sure to please.

Don't Eat the Daisies: Sure, Austin has all the fast-food chains that appeal to children, but here are a few local favorites, both homegrown and outside imports. See our Restaurants chapter for even more places to feed yourself and the kids.

At the end of the chapter, you'll find our listings of day camps in Austin. If a camp is what you're after, be sure to check out the other listings in this chapter also, as several also offer summer camps. And don't miss our chapter on Parks and Recreation for information on many more activities that are practically guaranteed to delight kids of all ages. Our chapters on Attractions, Spectator Sports, and The Arts offer events and attractions for the young and young at heart. The Literary Scene chapter provides information about our libraries and bookstores, including those that host story times.

FERTILIZE WELL

Aquarena Center
921 Aquarena Springs Drive, San Marcos
(512) 245–7575, (800) 999–9767
www.continuing-ed.swt.edu/aquarena

Take a ride on a glass-bottom boat on Spring Lake to view the pristine waters and aquatic life of Aquarena Springs, one of Central Texas's natural wonders. The freshwater springs that created the San Marcos River were formed millions of years ago by a fracture in the earth's crust, known today as the Balcones Fault. The river is home to more than 100 varieties of aquatic life, including several endangered species found nowhere else on earth. Well-informed tour guides take you on a relaxing adventure as you witness, through the bottom of the boat, the springs bubbling up from the Edwards Aquifer. There are also the underwater remains of an archeology dig that unearthed 12,000 years of history, including mastodon bones, Spanish gold coins, and arrowheads left by the hunter-gatherers who once lived here. This is a perfect place to spend a couple of hours.

This former theme park was acquired in 1994 by Texas State University, which changed the focus here from amusement to preservation and education. Aquarena Center features a lovely park next to the lake, a historic village, a gift shop and snack bar as well as a fascinating endangered species exhibit where visitors learn about the Texas blind salamander, the San Marcos salamander, and other aquatic life. Admission to the park and exhibits is free, but a fee is charged for a variety of boat tours, including ones focusing on ecology, endangered species, archeology, and history. Family-friendly admission prices. The center has offered special kids programs in summer, but check to see if they're still running. Aquarena Center is generally open seven days a week from 9:30 A.M. to 5:30 P.M. during the school year and 9:30 A.M. to 6:30 P.M. during summer, but do confirm closing times if you're planning to arrive late. For those planning to stay awhile in San Marcos, the Historic Inn at Aquarena Center is right on the lake. To get to the springs, take I–35 south from Austin, exit 206 to Aquarena Springs Drive, and go about 1.5 miles west.

Austin Children's Museum
Dell Discovery Center, 201 Colorado Street
(512) 472–2499
www.austinkids.org

Fun AND educational. What better combination is there to please children and parents alike? The Austin Children's Museum at Dell Discovery Center, which opened in December 1997, is a 7,000-square-foot playscape filled with galleries and hands-on activities designed to entertain and educate even the youngest visitors. This two-story facility (three if you count the small third-level Time Tower that includes exhibits of Austin history and features a tube slide to the first floor) is just packed with permanent and temporary exhibits—all aimed at encouraging youngsters to explore and use their imaginations.

In the largest permanent exhibit, Global CityWorks, children can pretend they're in charge of the city by role-playing in a doctor's office, a grocery store, a diner, a theater, a "bat" bridge, and more. There also is a recording area, a multimedia center, a teen gathering area, and a large space stocked with plenty of recycled materials that children can use to make art. The museum is open Tuesday through Saturday 10:00 A.M. to 5:00 P.M. and Sunday noon to 5:00 P.M. Admission is free on Wednesdays from 5:00 to 8:00 P.M. and Sundays from 4:00 to 5:00 P.M. The museum also offers a wide range of summer camps and special activities for children throughout the year.

**Austin Museum of Art
at Laguna Gloria
3809 West 35th Street
(512) 458-8191
www.amoa.org**
Housed in a historic villa, this great West Austin museum also hosts the city's art school for children and adults alike. While small children may feel too restricted in the exhibition space, the museum sits on a 12-acre site, complete with sculpture garden, that gives kids plenty of room to move around while still enjoying works of art. The school is in a separate building on-site. The museum also hosts several family-friendly outdoor festivals each year. Regular operating hours are Tuesday through Saturday from 10:00 A.M. to 5:00 P.M., Thursday from 10:00 A.M. to 8:00 P.M., and Sunday noon to 5:00 P.M. (See The Arts chapter for more details about the villa and the art school.)

**Austin Nature and Science Center
301 Nature Center Drive
(512) 327-8181
www.ci.austin.tx.us/nature.science**
Children will get a kick out of helping Eco Ernie discover signs of Austin wildlife on the Eco Detective Trail, learn about plants and animals in the Discovery Lab, and work in a paleontological dig in the Dino

Many of Austin's annual events are centered around children or include kid-friendly activities. Be sure to check out our chapter on Annual Events if you're looking for a great family activity.

Pit at this great center in the Zilker Park Nature Preserve. Injured owls, hawks, and vultures are featured in the Birds of Prey exhibit, while the Small Wonders exhibit displays 20 of Austin's small animals. The Nature and Science Center is a perfect introduction to Austin's unique ecosystems and to the wonders of Austin nature. (For more on the center see our chapter on Attractions.) The center is open 9:00 A.M. to 5:00 P.M. Monday through Saturday and Sunday noon to 5:00 P.M. Admission is free. The Austin Nature and Science Center also offers several summer camps for children ages 3 to 13.

**The Bob Bullock Texas State History Museum
1800 North Congress Avenue
(512) 936-8746
www.thestoryoftexas.com**
This new downtown museum just north of the capitol is a must visit for visitors of all ages, but kids will love the colorful exhibits that include a rhinestone-studded Cadillac and a spacesuit from an Apollo mission, not to mention cannons, old baseball uniforms, a cowgirl's jacket, and a Texas flying machine that actually was flown one year before the Wright Brothers. How's that for Texas bragging! The museum also houses Austin's only IMAX theater. (For a complete description of the museum, see our Attractions chapter.)

**George Washington Carver Museum
1165 Angelina Street
(512) 472-4809
www.carvermuseum.org**
Distinguished for being the first African-American neighborhood museum in the

state of Texas, the George Washington Carver Museum hosts a variety of activities for children throughout the year, including the annual A Smile on My Face workshop that teaches children the art of photography. The museum is open 10:00 A.M. to 6:00 P.M. Tuesday through Thursday, noon to 5:00 P.M. Friday and Saturday. (See our Attractions chapter for more information on this museum.)

Inner Space Cavern
I-35, exit 259, Georgetown
(512) 931-CAVE
www.innerspace.com

People tend to think that attractions located right beside the interstate are just tourist traps designed to get your money. This one, however, is one of the best and most accessible attractions around for both children and their families. Estimated to be 100 million years old, Inner Space Cavern was discovered in 1963 by workers testing core samples for construction of the interstate. It seems everywhere they drilled they found air pockets. Now opened for all to appreciate, this living cavern—meaning it continues to grow and develop—features an excellent array of formations beyond the typical stalactites and stalagmites. Guides will lead you on a 75-minute tour and point out such fascinating shapes as the Flowing Stone of Time, the Lake of the Moon, and more, including the bones of prehistoric animals who died in here. At a temperature of 72 to 74 degrees, this is the perfect spot to escape both the sizzling summer heat and the winter chill. Outside, the family can pan for gems and minerals. The cavern has a large gift shop and snack bar. The cavern, located just 24 miles north of downtown Austin, is open 9:00 A.M. to 6:00 P.M. daily. Admission fee—check the Web site for coupons. Tours depart regularly throughout the day with the last one beginning at 5:50 P.M.

Natural Bridge Caverns
26495 Natural Bridge Cavern Road
Natural Bridge Caverns
(210) 651-6101
www.naturalbridgecaverns.com

Located just north of San Antonio and southwest of New Braunfels off I-35 exit 175, Natural Bridge Caverns boasts more than 10,000 formations, including such wonders as Sherwood Forest, the Castle of the White Giant, and the King's Throne. These living caverns, discovered in 1960, present many spectacular sights, including one underground room that's as big as a football field. The cool caverns (average temperature is 72 degrees) are nestled amid Texas Hill Country terrain and provide plenty of shaded space outside for picnicking or relaxing. There's also a gift shop. The 75-minute tours depart about every 30 minutes beginning at 9:00 A.M. daily and ending at 6:00 P.M., except Thanksgiving, Christmas, and New Year's Day. Closing time varies depending on the season. Admission fee.

Splash! into the Edwards Aquifer
2201 Barton Springs Road
(512) 481-1466
www.ci.austin.tx.us/parks/
bartonspring.htm

This new hands-on educational center, which opened in the fall of 1998 at Barton Springs Pool, is a 1,400-square-foot interactive exhibit on the Barton Springs Edwards Aquifer. Splash! features a continuously running four-minute video, *Carved in Stone,* which shows how the springs were formed. An interactive three-dimensional relief map that uses animated lights to show the movement of the water lets children push the buttons to make the water flow. There's also a fascinating aquascape model of the aquifer. Aquariums here house specimens of the aquifer's aquatic life. This is a great place to learn about the Barton Springs salamander, an endangered species found only in Austin. Splash! is part of the Beverly Sheffield Education Center run by the Austin Parks and Recreation Department. The various exhibits are designed for use by children in 4th grade and up. Splash! is free to the public, although there may be a charge for guided tours. Call for hours of operation. (For more about Barton Springs, see our Close-up in the Parks and Recreation chapter.)

Star Gazing
T. S. Painter Hall Observatory,
near 24th Street and Speedway
(512) 232-4265

No. We're not talking about the kind of stargazing you'll find in our Close-up on Austin's film industry in The Arts chapter. This is the old-fashioned, out-of-this-world kind. The University of Texas astronomy department offers free stargazing experiences on the UT campus every Saturday night for the general public (from 10:00 to 11:00 P.M. for UT students and faculty on Friday), weather permitting, during the school year. Families with children seem especially attracted to this kind of educational fun. Astronomy students lead visitors on a tour of the stars, using a cool 10-inch-diameter telescope built in 1932. The fun starts around 8:30 P.M., but call ahead to confirm. No reservations are required. Parking is easy at this time of night, except when big UT events, like a Longhorns football game, are scheduled. For further information on other celestial events and stargazing activities, call the UT Sky Watchers Report at (512) 471-5007.

Texas State Capitol
1100 Congress Avenue
(512) 463-0063
www.the.state.tx.us/travel/
statecapitol.html

There's just no better way to introduce your youngsters to the legends and lore of Texas history than taking them on a tour of the Texas State Capitol. We've found the guides to be especially kind and patient with children, making sure to answer all their questions. (For more on this monument to Texas, including hours of operation, see our Attractions chapter.)

The Republic of Texas Museum
510 East Anderson Lane
(512) 339-1997

Do you know where and when the Texas Declaration of Independence was signed? How about the year Santa Anna was elected president of Mexico or the reason washing clothes was dangerous for women in the 1800s? The answer to these questions, and many more, can be found in the Republic of Texas Museum, a compact but fun and educational space for the whole family. Children and adults are given a separate list of scavenger hunt questions, the answers to which can be found by touring the exhibits. The littlest ones get to answer questions such as where is the chair with the two ears located or find the three chickens in the museum and what are their names? This museum, run by the Daughters of the Republic of Texas, is dedicated to the era of the Texas Republic (1836–1846). Young children especially like Great Grandma's Backyard, a collection of hands-on household items and implements used by families in the mid-19th century. There's something of interest for people of all ages here. The museum is open 10:00 A.M. to 4:00 P.M. Monday through Friday. General admission is $2.00, $1.00 for kids.

Umlauf Sculpture Garden & Museum
605 Robert E. Lee Road
(512) 445-5582
www.umlaufsculpture.org

Ask for the treasure hunt map when you visit the Umlauf Sculpture Garden, and your child will be delighted to chase around looking for some of Charles Umlauf's magnificent sculptures. (The diversion will allow you more time to enjoy the sculptures, too.) Because most of the statues are outdoors, this is a great place to introduce children to a museum. They don't have to keep quiet, and they don't have to keep their hands to themselves. (Yes, they can touch the outdoor sculptures!) They'll love you for it. (To find out more about this outdoor garden and indoor museum, including the hours of operation, see our Attractions chapter.)

Wonder World Park
1000 Prospect Street, San Marcos
(512) 392-3760
www.wonderworldpark.com

Unlike other caves in Texas that were formed by rushing water, this fascinating underground fissure was formed by a massive earthquake millions of years ago. You can actually see where the earth split, leaving jigsaw puzzle–like sections of rock that would fit right into each other if pushed back together. And because it's not growing, kids get to put their hands anywhere they like. Wonder World, said to be the only earthquake-formed cave in the country open for tours, drops more than 160 feet beneath the earth's surface but is accessible for children of all ages. Kid-friendly guides takes visitors on a 45-minute tour of this Texas marvel, pointing out all the prehistoric treasures and naturally glowing rocks. Wonder World also has a 190-foot aboveground observation tower, a deer-petting zoo, and an antigravity house. Theme park prices and coupons are available on the Web site. Kids younger than age 4 are admitted free. Admission for just the cave is $11 for adults and $9.00 for children. The cave is by far the best feature here. Wonder World is open 8:00 A.M. to 8:00 P.M. year-round.

Take a float along with you when you go to Deep Eddy's Summer Movies—and watch the flick from the pool. That will keep you cool.

JUST ADD WATER

Barton Springs
Zilker Park, 2201 Barton Springs Road
(512) 476-9044
www.cityofaustin.org/parks/bartonsprings

There's nothing like a cool—and we mean cool—dip in Austin's treasured spring-fed swimming pool to chill out the kids on a hot summer day and make them feel like real Austin Insiders. The water in the pool remains a constant 68 degrees throughout the year. (For more on this historic spot and for Austin's other great swimming spots, see our Parks and Recreation chapter.)

Deep Eddy Pool's Summer Movies
401 Deep Eddy Avenue
(512) 472-8546
www.ci.austin.tx.us/parks

Leave it to Austinites to figure out a way to combine water fun and flicks. West Austin's Deep Eddy Pool, one of our favorite swimming spots, presents family movies right next to the pool on Saturday night throughout the summer, starting in late May. The schedule includes such winners as *Antz, 101 Dalmatians, George of the Jungle, Dr. Doolittle,* and *Creature from the Black Lagoon,* presented in 3D. Come around 8:00 P.M., and bring a picnic basket or buy pizza at the pool. The films begin at about 9:00 P.M. or so, just around sunset. A nominal admission fee is charged.

Schlitterbahn Waterpark Resort
305 West Austin Street,
New Braunfels
(830) 625-2351
www.schlitterbahn.com

Never mind that this waterpark is about 50 miles south of Austin in New Braunfels. Schlitterbahn is one place many Austin families visit at least once, if not several times, during summer. Located on the banks of the spring-fed Comal River, Schlitterbahn is 65 acres of high-tech water rides, slides, pools, inner tube floats, and kiddie parks. The park has plenty of hair-raising rides sure to please the stoutest thrill-seeker in your group. Schlitterbahn also claims the world's first uphill water coaster. Picnic baskets (no glass or alcohol, please) are welcome here, and there are plenty of shaded areas and tables. The park is open late April to late September, but on weekends only during the school year. The fun starts at 10:00 A.M. daily and goes until closing time, which varies from 6:00 to 8:00 P.M. Admission is $25 to $35, depending on age. Midday passes, tickets for the Comal River Rapids only, and season tickets also are available. Parking is free. Schlitterbahn also runs two riverside resort hotels (at the same phone number).

Sea World Adventure Park
10500 Sea World Drive, San Antonio
(210) 523-3611
www.seaworld.com

Promise your youngsters a trip to Sea World and you're sure to get at least a day or two of good behavior in exchange. While there are plenty of thrilling water rides, wet playscapes, cool amusement park adventures, and shows, kids can actually learn something here, too. But keep that part under your hat. This giant park features the only major display of hammerhead sharks in North America, dozens of penguins, sea lions, whales, and, of course, the great Shamu. Sea World says its the world's largest sea life adventure park. While not all the rides are designed to get you wet, there are plenty to keep you cool on a hot summer day. Be sure to pack the swimsuits. Sea World is open March through October, mostly on weekends until school gets out. But all summer long this exciting place is open 10:00 A.M. to 10:00 P.M. Admission is in the $32 to $42 range. Two-day passes and season tickets also are available. This is definitely worth a trip to San Antonio.

If you go to Schlitterbahn, most locals know to stake a claim on a picnic table early in the day. Put your coolers and towels there and make it your base of operations. Don't leave valuables, of course.

Tubing
City Park, near University and Bobcat Drives, San Marcos
(512) 396-LION

To many Texans, the Hill Country is synonymous with river tubing, in which you ride down the river on big inner tubes. This inexpensive, low-tech pastime is loads of fun, especially on hot summer days. While some tubing areas can be dominated by older kids and young adults, the Lions Club operates a family-oriented tubing, swimming, and snorkeling spot on the San Marcos River in nearby San Marcos. They provide rides back to the park once you've gone downriver. You can even rent an extra tube, tie it to your own, and cart a cooler downstream if you like. This is refreshing and exhilarating fun, and all proceeds go to charity. All-day rental prices are very reasonable. It's open daily late May to early September from 10:00 A.M. to 7:00 P.M. The Lions Club also rents life vests for the little ones and lockers. Take Interstate 35 south to Exit 206 and follow Aquarena Springs Drive to University Drive. Turn left onto Bobcat Drive and right just before the railroad tracks. The Lions Club stand is next to the Texas National Guard Armory.

Volente Beach Water Park
16107 F.M. 2769, Leander
(512) 258-5109
www.volentebeach.com

For those hot, hot, hot summer days in Austin, this compact water park on Lake Travis offers some cool options. It features four great water slides of varying thrill levels, as well as a pool for swimming or volleyball and other fun water activities. Sprouts can play in the shallow pool and climb on the pirate ship in the middle. The sandy beach on the lake is large, even if the swimming area is not. There are WaveRunners and other boats for rent. Volente Beach is Austin's only water park and is quite small in comparison to a sprawling Fiesta Texas or Splash Town water park, but that doesn't prevent it from being a popular spot for kids of all ages. The Sundowner Grill serves entrees, desserts, and beverages, and visitors may also bring ice chests with food and soft drinks. (No glass, of course.) The water park is open weekends in April, May, and September and daily June through August.

SUPPLY SUNSHINE

Austin's Park 'n Pizza Experience
16231 North I-35
(512) 670-9600
www.austinspark.com
Open 365 days a year, this 22-acre park offers fun activities for all the kids—and for the kid in all of us. The hardest part of the day is trying to choose from among the park's many attractions, which include miniature golf, bumper boats, laser tag, go-karts, batting cages, a driving range, an indoor climbing wall, a huge arcade, and a thrill ride: the Ejection Seat, which shoots passengers 150 feet into the air. Of course all this exercise is going to work up some huge appetites. For that, there's the reasonably priced all-you-can-eat pizza, pasta, salad, and dessert buffet. The nice thing about this park is that attractions are individually priced, so you don't have to spend the whole day to get your money's worth. Family packages are also available. The park, 15 miles north of downtown Austin at exit 248, is open Sunday through Thursday from 10:00 A.M. to 11:00 P.M., Friday and Saturday from 10:00 A.M. to 1:00 A.M.

Austin Zoo
10807 Rawhide Trail
(512) 288-1490, (800) 291-1490
www.austinzoo.com
This Hill Country escape about 20 minutes southwest of downtown Austin is a perfect place to bring young children for a close-up look at the animals, a picnic, a pony ride, or a train ride. Compared to the sprawling superzoos many cities boast, Austin's zoo is small, rustic, and very laid back. That makes it easy on young ones and their parents—you don't need to rush madly around the park to see everything. Here visitors will find Bengal tigers, wallabies, capybaras, African lions, antelope, potbellied pigs, and many more exotic and domestic animals. There's a petting corral where you can purchase food to feed the animals. The zoo features a wonderful tortoise barn in which children can get a close-up view of several species. The Austin Zoo is open 10:00 A.M. to 6:00 P.M. daily. It's closed on Thanksgiving and Christmas. Admission is $6.00 for adults ($4.00 for 55 and older), $4.00 for children ages 2 to 12, and free for children younger than 2. There are discounts for grandparents and groups. Train and pony rides cost $2.00.

Butler Pitch & Putt Golf Course
201 Lee Barton Drive
(512) 477-4430
Tiger Woods would have loved this place when he was just a toddler trying to master the game of golf. This specially designed, nine-hole course in South Central Austin features holes about a third as long as standard ones—61 to 118 yards long—and also rents short clubs for the kids. Of course, adults who want a quick game of golf enjoy this wonderful course, too, which includes all the fun and frustrations of a regular course, including water hazards and the rough. Run by the Austin Parks and Recreation Department, this golf course is sure to please. It's open year-round. Greens fees are family-friendly. Club rental is extra.

Children's Day Art Park
Symphony Square, 1101 Red River Street
(512) 476-6064
www.austinsymphony.org

Children are encouraged to bang the drums, blow the horns, and fiddle the strings at the instrument "petting zoo," just one exciting feature of the Austin Symphony Orchestra's summer art park for children. These delightful outdoor events, held every Wednesday morning in June and July at historic Symphony Square, feature performances by symphony ensembles and by a variety of children's performers, including salsa bands, folk singers, and ballet folklorico. There's also an annual Teddy Bear Picnic, in which children bring their bears from home to compete for prizes like the oldest and biggest while musicians perform songs about bears. Symphony musicians are on hand each week to demonstrate the use of various instruments and to provide guidance. When the musical performance ends, children follow the Pied Piper down Waller Creek for more hands-on activities and face painting under a big tent. The Austin Symphony, Austin's oldest performing group, has sponsored these art parks for kids for more than 20 years. They're designed for kids ages 3 to 8, but everyone is invited. Very small admission fee. Check out the art park from 9:30 to 11:30 A.M. (See our chapter on The Arts for more symphony events for the whole family.)

Peter Pan Mini-Golf
1207 Barton Springs Road
(512) 472-1033

If you've got a hankering to play miniature golf until midnight—at least on Saturday—this is the place for you. Peter Pan offers two 18-hole miniature golf courses and a whole lot of fun for the little ones. What is it about this game that attracts so many kids and adults? It must be the challenge of trying to get that little ball up the hill around the obstacle and into the hole without screaming! Peter Pan is open year-round. Admission is $5.00 for adults

If you're here in springtime, when the bluebonnets are in bloom, do what Austinites do and take your child's picture amidst the flowers. Professional photographers will do this for you, too.

and $3.00 for children 5 and younger. You can arrive 20 minutes before opening to get signed up.

Slaughter Creek Metropolitan Park
4103 Slaughter Lane

Do you have an in-line skating fanatic in the family? This is the outdoor place for those who just couldn't leave home without the skates. The park features a 3-mile veloway (it's nice and smooth) and is popular with skaters and bikers. There are a playground, nature trail, sports courts, and picnic facilities here, too. This Southwest Austin park is next to the Lady Bird Johnson Wildflower Center. (See our Parks and Recreation Chapter for more about indoor roller rinks.)

J&M Aviaries
8647 U.S. 290 West
(512) 288-2199

This aviary in Southwest Austin features over 60 species of exotic birds and offers a tropical bird show on the weekends at 2:00 and 4:00 P.M. on Saturday and 1:00 and 3:00 P.M. Sunday. Admission is $5.00 for adults, $4.00 for children 12 and under; children 2 and under are free.

Wild Basin Wilderness Preserve
805 North Loop 360 (Capital of Texas Highway)
(512) 327-7622
www.wildbasin.org

Open from sunup to sundown, this is a perfect place to educate the kids, and yourself, about Austin's beautiful Hill Country terrain. This 227-acre preserve in West Austin is also great for nature walks as it features a trail system that runs

> *The upscale Arboretum Shopping Center at 10000 Research Boulevard in Northwest Austin has a lovely park that features five life-size granite cows that kids like to climb on. An Amy's ice cream shop and picnic tables are right there.*

throughout the area. Admission is $3.00 for adults and $1.00 for children 5 to 12. The preserve gives school tours during the week, so tour guides know just how to talk to youngsters and are prepared for the guided tours for visitors on weekends. Or you can take a self-guided tour and explore this park yourself. For the budding astronomer in the family, the Austin Astronomical Society holds a family-oriented stargazing party here each month as well as many other kid-friendly events. Nominal admission fee. Call (512) 416–5700, ext. 3560, for details. (See our Parks and Recreation chapter for information about other parks and preserves in the area.)

Zilker Park
2100 Barton Springs Road
(512) 472–4914

If, as they say, Barton Springs is the crown jewel of Austin, then Zilker Park is the crown. This 400-acre park is the city's largest park and definitely one of its most popular. There's a great playscape for kids, miniature train rides, jogging trails, and plenty of space to just run, play soccer, throw a Frisbee, or toss a ball. Tuck your swimsuits in the trunk when you head for the park, as Barton Springs Pool is right here and you might be tempted. (See our Parks and Recreation chapter for more details.)

LET 'EM GROW CRAZY

Blazer Tag Adventure Center
1701 West Ben White Boulevard
(512) 462–0202
www.blazerlazer.com

Billing itself as the "largest laser tag arena in Texas," this giant complex is blaster Nirvana. Whether your kids need to release some pent-up energy after a week of school or a weekend of sight-seeing, Blazer Tag is the place to go. The three-story, 10,000-square-foot arena offers players of all ages plenty of space to track down and then blast away at their opponents. Games are 20 minutes long and start every 20 minutes. The center also has a video arcade, snack bar, and Austin's only revolving rock-climbing wall. It's also a popular spot for parties of all kinds. Blazer Tag is closed Tuesday and Wednesday for private functions.

Chaparral Ice Center
14200 North I-35
(512) 252–8500
www.chaparralice.com

Kids can come daily for skating on their own or sign up for Learn-to-Skate classes. These well-run, well-maintained skating rinks offer a wonderful variety of year-round activities for children and adults, so be bold and lace up some skates for yourself. Classes are for skaters age three to adult. There also are classes in ice dance and hockey as well as hockey leagues for children and adults. Chaparral does birthday parties and has a full summer of camps for children. The center usually opens for public skating in the afternoons. Call for the current schedule. Admission and skate rental fees are family friendly.

Chuck E Cheese's
8038 Burnet Road
(512) 451–0296
502 West Ben White Boulevard
(512) 441–9681

Ahhhh, the coveted token! There just never seem to be enough of those discs of gold to satisfy even the youngest of competitors. To match wits with a machine and win those esteemed tickets is, at that very moment, the most awesome adventure on the planet. Austin's two Chuck E Cheese's locations, in North and South Central Austin, are filled with interactive arcade games, playscapes and air hockey tables that are sure to please. The good news for parents is that the food is pretty darn good too. There is pizza and hot dogs, snacks and soft drinks, and even a salad bar. At the end of the day, your youngsters get to go home with the prizes they've won in exchange for the tickets. Chuck E Cheese's does birthday parties too. The stores are open Sunday through Thursday from 10:00 A.M. to 10:00 P.M., Friday and Saturday 10:00 A.M. to 11:00 A.M.

Gymboree
8015 Shoal Creek Boulevard
(512) 671–7529 (main office)
Lake Creek Shopping Center
(Northwest)
12129 R.R. 620
Skyridge Plaza Shopping Center
2000 South I-35, Round Rock
www.gymboreeaustin.citysearch.com
This national learn-as-you-play program helps infants and youngsters develop motor and cognitive skills while building confidence. Gymboree utilizes up to 18 pieces of equipment to provide sensory stimulation for the young. There are singing and storytelling, noncompetitive sports for older children, lots of parent-child interaction, and plenty of things to crawl through and climb on. Trained instructors supervise the 45-minute, age-appropriate classes. Classes for newborns to age 4 are ongoing, so children can be enrolled anytime for a one-month minimum commitment. A free introductory class is available.

LAN's Edge
2525 West Anderson Lane, Suite 440
Northcross Mall
(512) 275–0761
www.lansedge.com
If your kids are into computer games, they'll love this new gaming center. With more than 50 titles to choose from, and more added all the time, LAN's Edge is one hopping spot. Players can choose from Xbox games played on 50-inch screens or PC games displayed on 21-inch

T1s. If all this sounds like a foreign language to you, just ask your kids to translate. It's open daily, but hours vary. Players pay $5.00 an hour, although less expensive packages are available. A photo ID is needed to get signed up.

Laser Quest Austin
523 Highland Mall Boulevard, Suite 100
(512) 459–5400
Strap on a vest, arm yourself with a laser, and enter the 8,000-square-foot maze for a heart-pounding game of laser tag. This giant maze has two levels and three towers to make the game even more exciting as you search for "victims" to blast with your light. The more people you tag, the higher your score. That is, if you don't get tagged too often by others. Both boys and girls, young and old, like this game. Music, fog, and strobe lights help create the atmosphere here. This is a great location for birthday parties and corporate team-building gatherings. Yes, adults love to play laser tag, too, so challenge your kids.

Le Fun
2200 Guadalupe Street
(512) 478–3509
3407 Wells Branch Parkway
(512) 388–2985
Le Fun is le place for the kind of entertainment kids like best: arcade games. Both of these popular locally owned locations—on The Drag at the University of Texas and up north in The Market at Wells Branch strip mall—provide that unique heart-pounding excitement that comes when kids triumph over le electronic rival—and then race off to challenge the next one. Each spot has plenty of games to keep the young, and not-so-young, occupied for hours. So be sure to send plenty of le cash!

Six Flags Fiesta Texas
17000 I-10 West, San Antonio
(210) 697-5050, (800) 473-4378
www.sixflags.com
You'll need to drive down to San Antonio for this one, but our resident kid advisor

for this chapter insists you'll gain major points with your children by letting them know that, yes, Central Texas offers a fantastic amusement park. Fiesta Texas is a blast—and not just for the kiddies. Thrilling rides, including Superman, the only floorless coaster in the Southwest, and a huge wooden coaster called The Rattler, will have your heart in your throat in no time. There also are plenty of exciting rides sure to get you wet—and cool! This giant park offers rides for people of all ages, a special children's area, plenty of shops and restaurants, great shows and, to top it off, a wonderful waterpark—don't forget to bring your swimsuits. This immaculate facility is so fun and so huge that many people purchase two-day or season passes. Fiesta Texas is open 10:00 A.M. to 10:00 P.M. daily throughout the summer and on weekends with shorter hours in spring and fall. Call for a schedule. The park is closed November to March. Daily admission is around $40 for teenagers and adults and around $25 for children. Seniors are eligible for discounted adult tickets. While you're in San Antonio, you might also want to check out Sea World (see the listing in this chapter). (See our Day Trips and Weekend Getaways chapter for more on San Antonio.)

YMCA
1100 West Cesar Chavez Street
(512) 322-9622 (main office)
Locations throughout the area
www.ymca.com

With five Austin locations and more in Pflugerville and Round Rock, there's sure to be a YMCA somewhere near you. They all offer plenty of sporting facilities and equipment, classes, and just plain fun. The good news for Austin members is that your membership card at one "Y" allows you access to all Austin locations. There is an initiation fee, and membership is offered by the month.

A GARDEN OF DELIGHTS

Cafe Monet
4477 South Lamar Boulevard, Suite 560
(512) 892-3200
www.cafemonet.org

This paint-your-own pottery studio is tucked away in a small storefront near the Borders bookstore (see our chapter on The Literary Scene) and not far from the Central Market Cafe (see the next section in this chapter) in the Westgate Central Market Center in Southwest Austin. Patrons simply pick out the ceramic piece they want to decorate, choose their colors, paint, and leave the pottery to be fired, picking it up three days later. The cafe offers children's parties for a minimum of eight kids at family-friendly prices. The studio also can be rented for private parties for the young and creative at heart of all ages. On Friday the studio offers special prices for an all-evening session. You can bring along your own snacks and beverages.

Ceramics Bayou
3736 Bee Caves Road, Suite 9
(512) 328-1168
www.ceramicsbayou.com

This paint-it-yourself ceramics studio offers a wide range of items—everything from simple tiles and coffee mugs to plates, platters, and animals. Children will delight in using their creative powers to design and paint their own piece. At Ceramics Bayou you pay for the piece plus $6.00 per studio hour per person. Finished pieces are fired in the kiln and ready for pickup in a few days. Hint: These make excellent gifts for parents, friends, or Grandma or Grandpa on their birthday. Speaking of birthdays, Ceramics Bayou hosts those too, as well as private parties. The studio is open Monday, Tuesday, Wednesday, and Saturday from 10:00 A.M. to 6:00 P.M., Thursday and Friday from 10:00 A.M. to 9:00 P.M., and Sunday noon to 5:00 P.M.

Hidden Talent
2525 West Anderson Lane
(512) 323-2551
www.hiddentalpaint.com
This studio in Northcross Shopping Mall features walls and walls of cast plaster of paris statues and wall ornaments for you and your little ones to paint on the premises. There are plenty of long tables stocked with an assortment of water-based paints and brushes for you to use. When you're finished, the employees will spray on a lacquer coat—and add glitter to your work if you like. Children have a blast here. And you pay only the price of the item. There's no additional cost for the paints. Hidden Talent hosts birthday parties and offers classes, but no experience is really needed for youngsters to paint a treasure to take home. Hidden Talent is open daily.

Paramount Theatre Kids' Classics
713 Congress Avenue
(512) 472-5470
www.theparamount.org
Austin's historic Paramount Theatre (see our chapter on The Arts) presents six seasonal productions aimed specifically at children ages 4 through 8. The Paramount brings in some of the country's top children's performers and theater companies for an exciting season of plays, musicals, and performing arts. The October through January season has included such productions as *Jack and the Giant Beanstalk,* presented by the acclaimed Dallas Children's Theater, *Swiss Family Robinson,* by Theatreworks/USA, Scholastic's *Magic School Bus* on tour, and more. This is fun for the whole family, and a great way to introduce youngsters to live theater. Many people subscribe to the full season, which includes five main series events and one extra production.

The Bats
Congress Avenue Bridge at Town Lake
www.batcon.org/discover/congress
Children ogle in wonder when North America's largest urban bat colony sets

Austin toymakers Georgean and Paul Kyle have been in business nearly a quarter-century. Look for their shop, Rootin' Ridge (in our Shopping chapter), when you want that special something for your child. Austin also has custom-made piñatas—something you don't find everywhere. See the Toys section of our Shopping chapter.

off en masse on the evening flight for food during spring and summer. This is a spectacle the whole family can enjoy. (For more on these Mexican free-tails, see our Attractions chapter.)

Zilker Park Trail of Lights and Christmas Tree
Zilker Park, 2100 Barton Springs Road
(512) 472-4914
It only lasts a few weeks once a year, but this is one of THE places to take your kids if you're here around the Christmas holiday. The "tree" is formed using Zilker Park's 165-foot-tall Moonlight Tower as the trunk and strings of multicolored lights—3,500 of them—to form the tree's cone shape. Children love to stand inside the tree and whirl around until the lights blur. Austin's annual Yule Fest celebration, which features the Trail of Lights, is another tradition that children love. (See our December Annual Events for more on this and on the Lighting of the Zilker Park Christmas Tree.) Admission to the park is free.

DON'T EAT THE DAISIES

Central Market Cafe
4001 North Lamar Boulevard
(512) 206-1020
4477 South Lamar Boulevard
(512) 899-4300
www.centralmarket.com
The great outdoor patio filled with picnic tables and a playscape that's close enough

to keep your eye on the kids are among the attractions for families at North Lamar Central Market Cafe. This casual restaurant, an extension of Austin's gourmet grocery store, has an extensive menu for people of all ages: Burgers, pasta, salads, pizzas, gourmet fare, and much more, including great desserts. The second location on South Lamar has a patio, but not the wide green space of the original. You place your order at the counter and retrieve your meal when your beeper lights up. Both Central Market locations have also indoor dining for when it's just too hot outside to breathe. There's live music on the patio at both locations several evenings a week. It's a great way to introduce children to the Austin music scene and get them fed, too. (For more about Central Market see our Close-up in the Shopping chapter.)

Dave & Buster's
9333 Research Boulevard
(512) 346–8015
www.daveandbusters.com
Guests ages 18 and under must be accompanied by an adult at this establishment, but that doesn't prevent it from being one extremely popular spot with Austin kids. Why? Eat well, play games, win prizes! One side of the huge facility is filled with all sorts of arcade and interactive games, including table shuffleboard and pocket billiards. Yes, adults must come along here, too. The dining room, which is separated from the gaming room, is much more upscale than the typical fun center, one of the reasons this Dallas-based chain is growing. It offers plenty of kid-pleasing menu items, including burgers, pizza and pasta. For heartier appetites there are steaks, chicken, and ribs. D&B's is open daily from 11:30 A.M. Closing time varies.

Gattitown
7101 Highway 71, Suite B
(512) 301–7777
Pizza and play are the order of the day at this restaurant located in the Oak Hill Plaza shopping center. Since the restaurant serves no alcoholic beverages it is popular with church youth groups. Entertainment includes video games, carousels, and bumper cars. Open Sunday through Thursday 11:00 A.M. to 9:00 P.M., Friday and Saturday 11:00 A.M. to 10:00 P.M.

Güero's Taco Bar
1412 South Congress Avenue
(512) 447–7688
This Austin institution on funky South Congress Avenue is a popular family eatery. While Chelsea wasn't with former President Clinton when he ate here several years ago, we're sure she would have been satisfied with the Mexican fare. The kid's menu includes quesadillas, breakfast tacos, chicken breast tacos, and enchiladas. All entrees come with rice and beans. The salsa bar is serve-it-yourself, so the food isn't too spicy for the kids. You won't have to chide the kids for squirming here. It's just comfy Austin.

Kerbey Lane Cafe
3704 Kerbey Lane
(512) 451–1436
2606 Guadalupe
(512) 477–5717
12602 Research Boulevard
(512) 258–7757
2700 South Lamar Boulevard
(512) 445–4451
Children just seem to love the huge plate-dwarfing pancakes served round the clock at this popular Austin eatery. But there are many more delicacies sure to please. The children's menu includes enchiladas, tacos, hamburgers, peanut butter and jelly sandwiches, ham and cheese, and other guaranteed kid pleasers. Prices are very reasonable, and with four Austin locations Kerbey Lane is easy to find. All four are open 24 hours a day.

Magnolia Cafe
2304 Lake Austin Boulevard
(512) 478–8645
1920 South Congress Avenue
(512) 445–0000

Homegrown and down home, Magnolia Cafe serves an excellent assortment of meals for children, including some nutritious items, like steamed broccoli with cheese or a grilled chicken dinner. There are plenty of other kid pleasers as well, including a chicken black bean taco, kid burger with home fries, fish taco, kid French toast, and a kid breakfast that includes an egg, pancake, and sausage or bacon and is served all day. There's nothing fancy about Magnolia Cafe but the food. Adults will be happy, too, and there's a good selection of vegetarian dishes. Both Magnolia Cafes are open 24 hours a day.

Romano's Macaroni Grill
9828 Great Hills Trail
(512) 795-0460
701 Loop 360 (Capital of Texas Highway)
(512) 329-0000
2501 I-35, Round Rock
(512) 341-7979
When you're in the mood for a little more upscale restaurant but still want to take the kids, try the Macaroni Grill. This Italian restaurant has a children's menu that includes, you guessed it, macaroni and cheese as well as ravioli, grilled cheese sandwiches, corn dogs, chicken tenders, pizzas, and more. The tablecloths are covered with sheets of white butcher paper, and crayons are provided. Macaroni Grill's two Austin locations are in the Northwest and the West.

T.G.I. Friday's
111 East Cesar Chavez Street
(512) 478-2991
10000 Research Boulevard
(512) 345-6410
It's a chain, but it's still one of our kid advisor's favorite Austin hangouts. Perhaps those boldly striped red and white tablecloths catch their attention. Kids get a packet of crayons and an activity book to keep them occupied while they wait, and there are always balloons for the little ones. We've even been there to see a magician walk among the tables and do tricks. Kids can choose between hot dogs, fish sticks, chicken fingers, grilled cheese, spaghetti, macaroni and cheese, or Friday's own pizzadilla, a pizza-quesadilla combo. The downtown Friday's is in the Radisson Hotel, and the Northwest location is in the Arboretum Shopping Center.

DAY CAMPS

You'll never have to hear those dreaded words, "There's nothing to do," if you enroll your child in one, or several, of Austin's amazing day camps. Austin offers something for every child, from the traditional camps that include a little of everything throughout the day to specialized camps in education, the arts, dance and gymnastics, magic, and all kinds of sports. Tuition for a one-week, full-day program generally ranges from about $100 to several hundred dollars, although specialty camps and University of Texas camps can cost more. Some camps offer financial aid, and some offer discounts if several family members enroll. The *Austin American-Statesman* publishes an annual camp guide, also.

Educational

Girlstart
608 West 22nd Street
(512) 916-4775
www.girlstart.org
The goal of this homegrown organization is to encourage and empower girls in mathematics, science, technology, and engineering. Girlstart has classes and programs year-round but also offers several wonderful summer camp opportunities. The campers have a choice of programs, like Mission to Mars, where campers work a week on either a Mission Control team or the mission ship. Through this effort they learn more about astronomy, biology, and engineering. Other camp themes might

include solving a mystery, becoming a Web diva, or working as an archaeologist or anthropologist in a virtual ancient world. The organization also offers day camps.

iD Tech Camp
University of Texas Campus
(888) 709-TECH
www.internaldrive.com

This national organization supervises technology summer camps at many of the country's top universities, including the University of Texas. The camper-to-staff ratio is low, and all kids have a computer at their command where they can learn the latest skills. The program offers financial aid for low-income children and holds girls-specific weeks. Weeklong programs include digital movie and video production, programming and robotics, game creation, and Web design. There are advanced classes for students ages 14 to 17. All skill levels are addressed.

Futurekids of Austin
3818 Far West Boulevard
(512) 346-8020
www.fkaustin.com

Start your children off on the road to computer literacy at an early age by enrolling them in a computer camp run by the people who pioneered a method of teaching to the young. Children ages 4 to 14 are offered themed adventures in computer training, including space, robotics, business operation, drama, and more. We introduced a youngster to this summer program and discovered at the end of the week that she was hooked on computer technology. These weeklong, half-day camps are held Monday through Thursday throughout the summer for children ages 6 to 14 and end with an open house for parents. Children ages 4 and 5 attend two-hour camps, also with themes, three days a week. Classes are offered for both children and adults throughout the school year. Austin's Futurekids also is spearheading an excellent program that takes computer learning into the schools.

Recreational

Camp Doublecreek
P.O. Box 5261
Doublecreek Drive, Round Rock 78683
(512) 255-3661
www.campdoublecreek.com

Swimming, archery, arts and crafts, gymnastics, basic horseback riding, and more are packed into each week of your child's summer at Camp Doublecreek. This well-established camp for children ages 4 through 12 has been delighting campers for nearly 30 years. A special parents day program is presented every four weeks. Thirteen pickup points are set up around Austin, and the camp day begins with camp songs and storytelling just as soon as children board the full-size buses that take them to this large acreage. Counselors are standing by at 7:30 A.M. to receive your child and buses return at 5:00 P.M., although counselors remain until 5:30 P.M. Camp Doublecreek holds an open house every Sunday from 3:00 to 5:00 P.M. for tours. To get to this farm, take I-35 north from Austin to the F.M. 1325 exit and go east for 2 miles. Take a left on Doublecreek Drive near the water tower and follow the road for 1.25 miles until it dead-ends at the farm.

Splish-Splash Summer Camp
2517 Enfield Road
(512) 477-7178
www.kids-are-first.com

This camp has it all: sports, gardening, science, swimming, cooking, arts and crafts, nature hikes, and overnight field trips. Designed for boys and girls ages 5 through 12, Splish-Splash offers two- and four-week sessions during the summer months. This camp is operated by the well-established Kids Are First day care school. Camp activities revolve around a different theme each week. Overnight field trips have included visits to Sea World and Splash Town in San Antonio, the Texas Ranger Museum in Waco, and Bastrop State Park.

YMCA Summer Camps
1100 West Cesar Chavez Street
(512) 476-6705
www.austinymca.org
The YMCA offers an entire summer of an incredible range of activities for children ages 4 to 15. This excellent program, one of the most diverse in the city, includes one-week camps for children ages 5 to 12 at different sites throughout Austin. Camps include amazing artists, lawn sports, space odyssey, super swimmer, leather crafts, rollermania, mad scientist, free wheelin', trail blazers, and Olympic week. The "Y" also offers camps in softball, basketball, soccer, flag football, baseball, fishing, roller hockey, golf, and cheerleading. Most of these camps run from 7:30 A.M. to 6:00 P.M. For kids who want even more adventure, the Y offers the two-week Rainbow Ranch Outdoor Adventure day camp for kids ages 9 to 12. This camp, at the Rainbow Ranch in nearby Buda, includes hiking, swimming, team sports, swimming, fishing, gardening, and arts and crafts. It also includes an overnight camp-out. Transportation is provided daily from the Y's main Town Lake branch. For children ages 11 to 15, the Y offers two-week teen camps that include college tours, swimming, in-line skating, intramural sports, tubing, community service, and much more. The Y's new summer program for 4- and 5-year-olds is held in Southwest Austin only and includes a range of indoor and outdoor activities, including swimming, music, computers, dramatic play, and more. Enrollment for this program is limited. Many of the other camps do sell out, so sign up early. Call the above number for a complete brochure of summer camp fun.

Dance and Gymnastics

Alisa's Dance Academy
3267 Bee Caves Road, Suite 139
(512) 327-2150
www.alisasdanceacademy.com
Alisa's summer camps are fun-filled, one-week, full- and half-day sessions for begin-

The First Tee of Greater Austin, (512-439-7000, www.firstteeaustin.org) is a member of a national nonprofit organization that provides affordable golf access to anyone, especially kids, who otherwise might not have an opportunity to play. The program also teaches children about responsibility, trust, decision-making, and more. Former president George H. W. Bush is the national honorary chairman.

ning and intermediate dancers ages 3 to 13. Packed into each session are classes in tap, jazz, ballet, theater, voice, and choreography as well as in drill team. Students put on a great end-of-camp show for parents each week. Children ages 3 to 5 attend half-day sessions from 9:00 A.M. to 1:00 P.M. while older students attend from 9:00 A.M. to 5:00 P.M. The littlest tykes, ages 2 to 4, may wish to sign up for weekly summer combo classes. The academy, which also offers dance classes for children and adults throughout the year and has its own dance company, is in the Westwood Shopping Center in West Austin.

Capital Gymnastics
13900 I-35 North
(512) 251-2439
www.capgym.com
This well-established gymnastics program, recognized as a national team training center by the United States Association of Gymnastics, offers a full school year of gymnastics and cheerleading training at several Austin locations, as well as a series of wonderful two-week summer camps at the Super-Center location at the above address. Camp activities include gymnastics, swimming, arts and crafts, games, outside playtime, movies, and much more. Children ages 5 to 13 may enroll in full- or half-day camps that run from 8:00 A.M. to 5:00 P.M., with extended hours available. Four-year-olds attend just

half-day sessions. Throughout the school year, Capital Gymnastics, with three other Austin locations in North, Central, and Northwest Austin, offers a wide range of classes for school-age boys and girls, parents, tots, and preschoolers. There also are competitive teams for boys and girls, and much more. Call them for a complete brochure of classes and activities offered at each location. Capital Gymnastics also does birthday parties and has Spring Break camps, a Mom's Day Out program, and summer classes.

If you've just moved to Austin, it's a good idea to get on the mailing list of some of the places listed in this chapter. Many send out flyers advertising special events and camps.

Dancers Workshop
11150 Research Boulevard, Suite 107
(512) 349-7197
www.dancersworkshopaustin.com
Dancers Workshop offers a full summer of excellent camps for beginning to advanced dancers ages 3 to 13. Experienced professional dancers and drama teachers present a full day of tap, ballet, jazz, voice, and drama to 1st graders and older, while preschoolers attend just in the morning from 9:00 A.M. to 1:00 P.M. Early-morning and after-work hours are also available. The weeklong camps end in a Friday evening in-studio performance for parents and friends. You'll be amazed at the dance steps your child can learn in just five days. Dancers Workshop also offers a drill team camp. While it's true these camps are largely attended by girls, boys are welcome, too. Dancers Workshop also offers classes for both beginners and advanced dancers throughout the school year and has its own outstanding dance company. Call for details.

The Arts

Austin Chamber Music Center
4930 Burnet Road, Suite 203
(512) 454-7562
www.austinchambermusic.org
For intermediate-level musicians and better, the Austin Chamber Music Center offers intensive training and rehearsing in a two-week day camp. The center accepts musicians from age 8 to 18 who play strings, winds, and the piano. The center forms groups according to instrument, like string quartets, wind quintets, and piano duos but also mixes instruments. There are also recreation activities and a daily music presentation. This camp concentrates on providing excellent coaching as well as music theory and musicianship classes. Hours are 9:00 A.M. to 5:30 P.M. This camp usually is held in early June. The Austin Chamber Music Center also offers a music academy throughout the school year.

Dougherty Arts Center
1110 Barton Springs Road
(512) 397-1468
www.ciaustin.tx.us/dougherty
This fine, age-specific summer program introduces young children to the visual and performing arts while taking older students to new levels of understanding and appreciation of the arts. Dougherty offers five two-week day camp sessions for children ages 3 to 14. Children ages 3 to 5 attend half-day sessions either in the morning or afternoon, while older campers attend full-day sessions from 9:00 A.M. to 5:00 P.M., with early and late extended hours available. Preschoolers are introduced to drama, movement, music, and the visual arts through a variety of activities. The program for children ages 6 to 8 stresses both the performing and visual arts and focuses on learning the process of creating art, not so much on the product. Beginning at age 9, children may select from programs that specialize in just the visual arts or just the perform-

ing arts. There's a camp that teaches computer animation, including cartooning and claymation.

Parents of children starting school in September will be pleased to know that Dougherty also holds one-week camps in August for children ages 6 to 10. Classes in the visual and performing arts are offered throughout the school year for children and adults.

Kids Acting
The Acting Studio, 5811–B Burnet Road
(512) 458–5437
www.kidsactingstudio.com

One of Austin's most popular and well-established studios for young actors throughout the year, Kids Acting also offers a variety of full- and half-day summer camps for children ages 4 to 18. One of the main events here is the presentation of a full-scale musical production, which involves children ages 9 to 18. While the schedule may vary, Kids Acting most recently offered camps in variety show, in which children learn to sing, dance, act, and do improvisational comedy; screen acting, which teaches campers to perform for television, film, and commercials; play production, which focuses on learning to write, cast, costume, rehearse, and perform a play; and combo camp, which combines aspects of all the camps. Kids Acting, established in 1980, presents a variety of musical theatrical shows with casts of young people throughout the year.

Zachary Scott Theatre
1510 Toomey Road
(512) 476–0594
www.zachscott.com

One of Austin's finest professional theaters, Zachary Scott has been providing instruction to budding performers through its Performing Arts School since 1970. Zach's school offers a variety of summer and holiday camps for children ages 5 to 14. Youngsters ages 5 to 7 may enroll in half-day creative drama camps, which include singing, music, creative move-

ment, dance, and more. There's a full-day musical theater camp for kids ages 8 to 10 and 11 to 14 who love to sing and dance. Zach's also offers a Theatre Variety Camp, also split into age groups, that includes acting basics, singing and vocal expression, comedy and improvisation, as well as creative movement. And for those who yearn to do stand-up comedy, there's the comedy camp. This program teaches the ins and outs of modern improvisation. Camp hours are from 9:00 A.M. to 5:00 P.M. with optional extended hours available.

The Performing Arts School also offers acting, singing, and comedy classes throughout the school year for young performers and holds auditions in late September and late January for the school's performance troupes. Yes, parents, Zach also offers classes for adults. By the way, Zach's two adult theater companies present shows specifically for preschool and school-age children's groups.

Magic

The Magic Camp
7306 Scenic Brook Drive
(512) 288–1596
www.magiccamp.com

Professional magician Kent Cummins is the wizard behind this exciting day camp for children ages 5 to 18. Campers learn magic tricks, juggling, puppetry, and more as they follow a program designed to engage the imagination. Full-day camps are divided between children ages 7 through 9 and 10 through 12. Children ages 5 and 6 attend half-day sessions. There's also a Performer's Academy for those 5 to 18 in which campers are assisted in developing their own act. The Magic Camp maintains a teacher-to-camper ratio of 1 to 5 or better, which includes adult staff members, teenage counselors, and counselors in training. Guest performers and teachers are invited in to share their expertise throughout the sessions. Tuition includes all supplies.

The address listed above is the Magic Camp office. The camp itself is held elsewhere.

Cummins also has held weekend getaway Magic Camps for adults only.

Sports

Austin Yacht Club
Junior Sailing Camps
5906 Beacon Drive
(512) 266-1336
www.austinyachtclub.org

Designed for children 8 to 18, the Austin Yacht Club Junior Sailing Camp concentrates on teaching young sailors the basics of sailing on Sunfish and Optimists. Classes are divided for beginners to advanced so that each child gets the maximum benefit from the learning experience. The four-week camps, held on Lake Travis in June, last from 8:00 A.M. to 5:00 P.M., but extended hours for working parents are available. Call the Yacht Club by April or May to sign up as these camps are limited in size and can fill up. For you adults out there, the Yacht Club also offers a one-time summer learn-to-sail clinic. Call for details.

Bear Creek Stables
13017 Bob Johnson Road
(512) 282-0250
www.bearcreekstables.com

Bear Creek offers weekly horseback riding sessions all summer for children ages 7 to 16. Both boys and girls, beginners to advanced, are taught Western pleasure and English horseback styles of riding on this 20-acre facility in Southwest Austin. Instructors, who stress that the emphasis is on the rider, also teach the care, grooming, and feeding of horses. A covered arena is perfect for rainy days. There's a riding presentation for parents on the Friday of each session, and each Wednesday is trail day. Hours are 8:00 A.M. to 4:00 P.M., with extended hours available. Bear Creek also offers English and Western riding lessons.

Blue Star Riding Center
9513 South U.S. 183
(512) 243-2583
www.b-star.com

Intermediate-level riders get to test their brain power and their knowledge of horses with a murder-mystery trail ride offered during their two-week session. Students must figure out whodunit by riding around the 50-acre ranch to find clues and interview witnesses. Blue Star, in business since 1985, also offers two-week sessions for beginning and advanced riders ages 8 to 18. Students are introduced to both Western and English styles of riding and learn about the care and feeding of horses. The center also has a covered arena. Blue Star is in Southeast Austin, but campers are offered pickup and drop-off service in Northeast, Northwest, and Southeast Austin. The riding center is home to the Violet Crown Pony Club, where students learn to participate in Olympic-style riding and jumping events. Blue Star offers riding lessons throughout the year as well as winter holiday and Spring Break camps.

Wolfgang Suhnholz Soccer Academy
Southwestern University Georgetown
(512) 258-2277
www.suhnholzsoccer.com

This soccer academy, established in 1988, offers full- and half-day sessions for both beginning and advanced soccer players on the campus of Southwestern University in Georgetown. Kids 5 to 15 enroll in these camps directed by Suhnholz, former coach for the U.S. National Team, Under 20 Division, and technical director of both the Lone Stars professional soccer team and the Capital Soccer Club for youth. The program, which stresses the fundamentals of soccer play, is coached by Lone Stars players and Capital Soccer Club coaches. Students are divided by age group and by ability. There are three weeklong sessions offered during the summer as well as a Spring Break camp.

UT Sports Camps

At last count, The University of Texas offered 14 different summer sports camps for kids, representing every major sport. These intensive training programs, which have a stellar reputation in Austin, attract budding athletes from across the state. The camps vary in length and time, some as short as three days and others as long as seven days. Some of the biggest names in coaching today, namely UT's excellent professional coaches, design these programs and most often are on hand daily to provide instruction and inspiration to young athletes. Many times, campers are treated to appearances by their favorite UT sports stars. The camps can be attended either as a day camp or a supervised overnight camp in which players stay in a UT dormitory or residence hall. All camps except for golf are held at the appropriate sports facility on the UT campus, usually the ones used by the collegiate athletes themselves. Imagine the delight of a budding football player who gets to take the field at Darrell K Royal–Texas Memorial Stadium for the first time or the swimmer awed by the facilities at the Jamail Texas Swimming Center. Each camp is offered for only a short time during the summer, so it's best to sign up early; www.texassports.com.

Longhorn Baseball Camp
(512) 471-3309

Held at Disch-Falk Field, home to the UT baseball team, and directed by UT's baseball coaching staff, the camp is open to all boys and girls between ages 7 and 18. There's an instructional and developmental camp, a specialty camp that focuses on key areas of hitting, pitching, defensive and offensive play, and an advanced camp for players between 15 and 18. Instruction covers all areas of the game. With a 1-to-4 coach-to-camper ratio, campers receive individual instruction aimed at helping each student reach his or her full potential.

Boys Basketball Camp
(512) 471-5816

UT head basketball coach Rick Barnes, his staff, and some of the best high school and collegiate coaches from across the state provide instruction to campers on shooting, passing, defense, rebounding, ball handling, and teamwork. The week-long camps, for boys ages 8 to 18, feature individualized instruction, daily league games and tournaments, guest speakers, and a report card and discussion of the player's individual skills. Campers are grouped according to age and ability level. The camp is held in the newly renovated Gregory Gym on the UT campus, but there are also satellite camps held in other Central Texas locations.

Girls Basketball Camp
(512) 471-8822

Conducted by Coach Jody Conradt, the winningest coach in collegiate women's basketball history, these camps offer intense basketball instruction with an emphasis on the fundamentals of dribbling, passing, and shooting as well as offensive and defensive positions. The camp, for players age 10 through high school, groups players according to age and skill level. These are challenging, competitive camps filled with plenty of drills and competitions. There's also an elite varsity camp for varsity players who want to improve their games. Current and former Longhorn players and talented coaches from across the state contribute to the coaching staff of this superb camp. Sessions are held at Gregory Gym on the UT campus.

Longhorn Diving Camp
(512) 471-7794

Open to boys and girls ages 12 to 18 and held at the Jamail Texas Swimming Center, one of the finest swimming facilities in the United States, the summer diving camp draws athletes from around the country. Each seven-day camp offers excellent learning opportunities and a challenging training environment for divers of all abilities. Divers attend lectures about the mechanics of diving, movement, and mental focus. They also receive two diving training sessions and an extensive exercise/stretching/spotting session each day. Instruction is provided in all areas of competitive diving.

Longhorn Football Camp
(512) 232-5088

Longhorn head coach Mack Brown directs this program and makes sure each player gets individual attention from the large staff of UT coaches and excellent high school football coaches. Junior Camp is for players entering 4th through 8th grades and is especially designed for the younger players. For older players in grades 9 through 12, there is a skills camp and a lineman camp. Each camp includes lectures, videotape evaluations, daily film study, speed development, weight training instruction, flexibility instruction, and more. These camps are held for four very long days. Camp runs from 9:00 A.M. to 7:30 P.M.

Longhorn Golf Camp
(512) 471-6169

For boys and girls ages 11 to 18, the UT golf camp is held at Austin-area golf courses. The one- or two-week, full-day sessions have been held in June. Young golfers receive instruction in all the fundamentals of the game.

Soccer Academy
(512) 471-3624
www.texassoccer.com

Young athletes who are serious about playing competitive soccer would do well to check out UT's Soccer Academy. These one-week programs are designed for developing elite or highly competitive soccer players and teams. There's a day camp for boys and girls ages 6 and older in which campers choose between the three-hour morning or evening session. Older children ages 12 and older are

offered a one-week overnight-only camp filled with competitive soccer instruction. This camp is directed by Chris Petrucelli, UT head soccer coach.

Longhorn Softball Camp
(512) 232-2046

Held at UT's new McCombs Field, this softball camp is designed for girls age 9 and older and includes training in the fundamentals and strategy. The three camp sessions offered include the four-day all-skills camp that lasts from 9:30 A.M. to 8:00 P.M., the pitcher/catcher camp, which includes three days of all-day instruction, and the elite varsity camp for players in 10th through 12th grades. Connie Clark, UT head softball coach, directs this great program.

Longhorn Swimming Camp
(512) 475-8652
www.longhornswimcamp.com

Designed for male and female competitive swimmers age 8 and older, the Longhorn Swimming Camp focuses on intensive long-course conditioning, stroke instruction, and analysis. Campers are required to have competitive swimming experience and to be planning to continue competing. This camp is divided into four ability groups. Camp includes swimming-specific dryland exercises, strength training, and flexibility exercises. Depending on ability level, long-course training lasts from one to two hours daily. Daily training also includes two one-hour sessions on technique. This camp is held at UT's fabulous Jamail Texas Swimming Center. The six-day sessions go from 8:30 A.M. to 8:00 P.M. The camps are directed by Eddie Reese, UT men's swimming coach, and Jill Sterkel, women's head coach.

Longhorn Tennis Camp
(512) 471-4404
www.longhorntenniscamp.com

The Penick-Allison Tennis Center, one of the finest collegiate tennis facilities in the United States, is home to the annual

Longhorn Tennis Camp. This program for boys and girls ages 10 to 18 offers skills training as well as important motivational and psychological training tools. The sessions are directed by both UT men's and women's head tennis coaches and include an experienced staff of college coaches, high school coaches, and men and women collegiate players. The six-day all-day camp includes private instruction, supervised play, mental training, team competition, and more. There's also one session dedicated to elite players. This camp always fills up quickly.

Track and Field/Cross Country Camp
(512) 471-3931

Aimed at boys and girls ages 11 to 17, this camp allows athletes to choose from among several areas of specialization, including distance/cross country, sprints, high jump, pole vault, hurdles, long jump/triple jump, shot/discus, and middle-distance running. This camp aims to help junior high and high school athletes improve their athletic performance by increasing their knowledge of the sport and their fitness levels. It is taught by some of the best track and field/cross-country coaches in the nation. This four-day session is held from 8:00 A.M. to 5:00 P.M.

Texas Volleyball Camp
(512) 471-0804
www.texasvolleyball.com

For girls entering 5th through 12th grades, the Texas Volleyball Camp shows young players how it is that UT women win so many games. This camp, under the leadership of head coach Jim Moore, provides instruction in all areas of the game. Skills camps emphasize the fundamentals, and on-court instruction is provided in serving, serve receiving, forearm passing, setting, attacking, team defense, blocking, and more. These camps end in a tournament. The setter/hitter camps are for girls entering 7th through 12th grades. The elite camp is for varsity-level players. The Texas Volleyball Camp, held at the newly renovated Gregory Gym, offers several different sessions.

ANNUAL EVENTS AND FESTIVALS

eekends are the raison d'être for life in Austin, at least that is what the calendar might lead you to think. The weekday workdays are the equivalent of bench time, as far as many Austinites are concerned.

The generally benign climate affords residents and visitors the opportunity to live life outdoors, and perhaps that is why so many weekend activities are linked to appreciation of sun, sky, and landscape. It is significant to note that springtime is the most active of all seasons when it comes to outdoor fiestas and festivals. This, after all, is when the Hill Country blossoms, the sun shines, and the sky is generally blue. (It is also the time when hotels are full and few rental cars are available.)

It is impossible to list all the annual events and festivals that take place in Austin and the surrounding Central Texas area. We have chosen our favorites and those that are both widely popular and long-standing. Outdoor events tend to outnumber indoor happenings on this list, reflecting not only the climate but also the local fondness for outdoor celebration. That is not to say there is a lack of indoor weekend activities—theater, music, books, and film are drawing cards for a number of well-established annual events.

Another characteristic of this list is the number of annual events that celebrate local culture, ethnic traditions, and historic events. Texans, nonnatives and newcomers will note, are eager to explore their past and have a strong sense of their state's history and culture. Many of the local festivals celebrate that sentiment.

Other events are just sheer expressions of what could be called Texas joy, an embracing of local life and folkways. Whether it is a Woodstock-style romp or

an old-fashioned church picnic, the operative word is celebration. So go forth and celebrate!

One note before you do: Admission prices, times, and even dates may vary from those listed. Many events are sponsored by nonprofit groups that face the vagaries of economic needs and demands. It is a good idea to check the local media and make a call for additional information before you go; however, should you strike out, don't worry, there is sure to be a weekend event going on somewhere in Central Texas on any given Saturday or Sunday.

JANUARY

Austin Boat & Fishing Show
Austin Convention Center,
500 East Cesar Chavez Boulevard
(512) 494-1128
www.austinboatshow.com
In a city where water recreation is a major pastime for many residents, this annual show is a popular winter event. The shows runs for four days, usually from noon to 10:00 P.M. on Thursday and Friday, 10:00 A.M. to 10:00 P.M. on Saturday, and 10:00 A.M. to 6:00 P.M. on Sunday. Admission fee.

Citywide Garage Sale and Antique Show
Palmer Events Center
900 Barton Springs Road
(512) 441-2828
www.cwgs.com
This is the first of usually once-a-month sales at the downtown Coliseum, which is located on the southern banks of Town Lake, just west of Palmer Auditorium. Most are scheduled in midmonth and are widely advertised. The merchandise varies

from kitschy items to genuine finds. (See the Citywide Garage Sale listing in our Shopping chapter.) Admission fee.

FronteraFest
Hyde Park Theatre, 511 West 43rd Street
(512) 479-PLAY
www.hydeparktheatre.com

Local theater critic Michael Barnes has called this "the most exciting fringe festival in the Southwest" and described it as "a Quaker meeting for Austin theater." The annual performance festival runs for five weeks beginning in late January and includes more than 50 productions put on under the auspices of Frontera @ Hyde Park Theatre, the theater company in one of the most popular neighborhoods in Central Austin (see Hyde Park in our Relocation chapter and Frontera Theatre in our Arts chapter). The events afford theater artists an opportunity to explore new territory and, as Barnes says, push the limits. Ticket prices vary and usually begin at around $3.00. Discount passes are available.

Red Eye Regatta
Lake Travis
(512) 266-1336
www.austinyachtclub.org

Sail into the new year with the Austin Yacht Club. On New Year's Day the club holds sailboat races on Lake Travis. Landlubbers can watch from the hills surrounding the lake, one of the parks along the shore (see our Parks and Recreation chapter), or from the deck of one of the restaurants with a view on the lake, including The Oasis and the Iguana Grill (see our Restaurants chapter).

FEBRUARY

Black History Month
(800) 926-2282
www.austintexas.org

Throughout February there are numerous celebrations and events relating to African-American history. In the very early

The Austin Convention Center maintains a calendar hot line, (512) 404-4404, for events at three major city facilities: the convention center, Palmer Auditorium, and the coliseum. www.austintexas.org

days of the city, almost a quarter of the city's residents were African Americans, some 155 out of 856 people living in the city. The Austin Convention & Visitors Bureau (telephone and Web site listed above) produces the *Austin African-American Visitors Guide* listing historic sites, cultural facilities, clubs, churches, and a guide to Austin's historic African-American neighborhoods. The guide can be picked up at the visitors center at 209 East Sixth Street.

Carnaval Brasileiro
Palmer Events Center, 900 Barton
Springs Road
(512) 452-6832
www.carnavalaustin.com

For more than 20 years, Austin has danced to the Brazilian beat of samba in a pre-Lenten festival of conga lines, costumes, and cacophony. A couple of thousand or more revelers gather, usually the Saturday before Lent, which can fall in February or March, to emulate Rio's famous Carnival. The costumes are hilarious and sometimes minimalist, which makes this a decidedly grown-up affair. The live music features top names in samba, including some who have performed in Brazil. The music gets under way around 8:00 P.M. and doesn't stop until the early hours of the morning. Tickets are on sale at various popular record and bookstores in Austin.

Mardi Gras
East Sixth Street
(512) 441-9015
www.6street.com

Austinites never met a festival they didn't like, and so it is only natural that the locals dip into the diversity of cultures in the city to celebrate as many festival days as possible. The Web site above is a great resource for information on Sixth Street. This is Austin's version of the worldwide celebration known as Fat Tuesday in English. Just as they do on New Year's Eve and Halloween, celebrants take to East Sixth Street in downtown Austin to flaunt their costumes, drink, eat, and party. Depending on the church calendar, this festival falls in either February or March.

Motorola Marathon
(512) 478–4265
www.motorolamarathon.com
The first Motorola-sponsored marathon was run in 1991, but this relative newcomer is becoming more well known and has been described as the fastest-growing in the country. The number of participants in this popular race grew to around 9,000 in recent years. Organizers now have capped the number of entrants at 7,500, who can register on-line or by phone for a chance to win the $10,000 first-place prize. Running experts give the sponsors top marks for organization. The course runs from far Northwest Austin toward downtown, ending up on the shores of Town Lake. The race is usually held on Presidents Day weekend. Participation costs range from around $35 to $100, depending on whether participants are running the marathon course as individuals, or as a relay team in the 26-mile race. The organizer of the race is RunTex, the running store with two locations in Austin (see the running section in our Parks and Recreation chapter). Registration and prices, even the course, vary each year, so it's a good idea to stop by or call RunTex at (512) 472–3254.

Old Gruene Market Days
Gruene
(830) 832–1721
www.gruenemarketdays.com
Once a ghost town south of Austin and north of New Braunfels, this revived community is just west of I–35 and the north-

ern banks of the Guadalupe River. The historic community is now a popular home for artists and crafters. Beginning in February, vendors selling Texas crafts and foods gather here for market days, held on the third Saturday and Sunday of each month. In December the market is held on the first weekend of the month. (See our Day Ttrips chapter for more information on Gruene.)

MARCH

Riverfest
Along the Colorado River
(888) TEXAS FUN
www.lcra.org
This is a conglomeration of festivals that takes place along a 500-mile stretch of the Colorado River. The Lower Colorado River Authority (LCRA) has united all these various festivals that occur from March through early May under the Riverfest umbrella and coordinates information on them. A complete list can be requested by calling the toll-free telephone number. Events take place in small and large communities, including Austin, from San Saba and Lampasas Counties northwest of the city to the Gulf Coast. They include a spring craft fair in El Campo, the Lometa Diamondback Jubilee (diamondbacks, as in rattlesnakes) in late March, and the River Rendezvous in La Grange for canoeing enthusiasts in late April. There are also nature celebrations and birding events, wildflower festivals, and watersports.

Spring Festival and Texas Craft
Exhibition
Winedale, near Round Top
(979) 249–2085
www.roundtop.org
This tiny village near Round Top, some 90 miles east of Austin, has served as the center for study of Texas culture under the auspices of the University of Texas. The collection of historic buildings was preserved by Ima Hogg, daughter of a Texas governor, who donated the land and buildings to the

university. The Round Top area is now a center for cultural events and antiques shops and home to artists and crafters. There are several festivals and events throughout the year that are well worth attending. (See our Day Trips chapter for more information on this historic area.) The third weekend in March, Winedale holds its annual Spring Festival and Texas Crafts Exhibition. This area is an easy drive from Austin but worth an overnight stay at one of the country bed-and-breakfasts in the area.

Spamarama
Waterloo Park
Red River and 15th Streets
(512) 467-7848
www.spamarama.com
Spam sushi? Spam kebobs? Perhaps Spam Jell-O? This annual event, dubbed the "Pandemonious Party of Potted Pork," is a tribute to that World War II staple, Spam, the potted ham that was pulled out of GI knapsacks in the woods of Germany and on the islands of the South Pacific. Cooks, some of them serious professional chefs, compete for prizes, but for those who would rather play with their food there is a Spam Toss, a Spam Relay featuring a Spam baton, and, of course, a Spam Jam. The latter does not involve strumming a Spam slice, but it does feature some of Austin's live bands and popular musicians. In recent years Steve Fromholz and the Uranium Savages have been on the menu. The cooking contest judges include celebrities like musician-author Kinky Friedman. Usually held in late March, sometimes early April, the location has changed over the years, so check the entertainment listings in the local paper. Admission charge.

Star of Texas Fair and Rodeo
Travis County Exposition
and Heritage Center, 7311 Decker Lane
(512) 919-3000
www.staroftexas.org
For two weeks in mid-March, country music fans flock to the livestock and

rodeo show at the Expo Center in far East Austin. The stars include musicians like Merle Haggard, Kathy Mattea, and Rick Trevino. The live music begins after the rodeo performances each night. Rodeo begins at 7:30 P.M., and the music usually starts two hours later. In addition to the music, there are livestock shows, a carnival, barbecue and food booths, and children's activities. Rodeo tickets are in addition to grounds admission fees. There is extensive coverage of the event in the local media. *Note:* The show overlaps with the SXSW Festival (see our Close-up in this chapter), and hotel rooms and rental cars are at a premium in March. (See our Spectator Sports chapter for more information.)

Taylor Jaycees National Rattlesnake
Sacking Championship
Murphy Park, Lake Drive, Taylor
(512) 365-1988
www.taylorjaycees.org
Not for the faint of heart, this annual event takes place in the small community of Taylor, northeast of Austin. Despite the fast-encroaching suburbs of Round Rock and Georgetown, Taylor is a small town with a rich history and a tradition of spending the first weekend in March sacking snakes. Amateur teams compete for the prize; even young snake handlers test their skills. Professional snake handlers are on hand to show how it's done. Visitors can also answer that age-old question—does fried rattlesnake meat taste like chicken? Admission fee.

Zilker Garden Festival
Austin Garden Center
Zilker Botanical Gardens
(512) 477-8672
www.zilker-garden.org
To paraphrase the pitch for the popular local public television show *Central Texas Gardener,* what flourishes in gardens elsewhere can end up in the compost heap in Austin given the local climate—sometimes too much rain, too much drought, sudden frost, summer heat, year-round shade,

CLOSE-UP

South by Southwest

Since 1986 when the first SXSW Music and Media Conference (South by Southwest, for the uninitiated) was held, it has grown to significant proportions. There is so much energy, growth, and creativity associated with this annual festival that it literally takes over the city, as nightclubs, theaters, conference halls, restaurants, and hotels get in on the action. The economic impact on Austin is estimated in the millions, perhaps as much as $20 million, and the number of musicians and entertainment professionals is counted in the thousands.

In addition to the SXSW Music festival, there is now a SXSW Film Festival and Conference and a SXSW Interactive Festival. The essence of the festival is to produce a creative critical mass that spills out and energizes all who come into contact with it. Hence, the city of Austin is awash in musicians, filmmakers, and high-tech multimedia types for the last two weeks of March. (A word of warning to anyone planning to come to Austin during the festival—make your

hotel, air, and car rental reservations well in advance.)

In the beginning, the conference was seen as a vehicle to focus attention on the Texas music scene, the so-called Third Coast. The festival is still kicked off at the Austin Music Hall with the Austin Music Awards, a decidedly funky version of the Grammys in which winners are chosen by the public at large—and top names in Austin music perform. The local alternative newspaper, the *Austin Chronicle,* organized the first festival (and remains a primary host), but the conference quickly grew and has expanded at record rates every year. The number of bands participating is approaching the 1,000 mark, performing at more than 50 venues in Austin. The acts include national and international headliners such as Asleep at the Wheel, Arlo Guthrie, Doug Sahm, Soul Asylum, Leon Rausch, Johnny Gimble, the Derailers, Kacy Crowley, Trish Murphy, Ana Egee, Lucinda Williams—and the list goes on. So extensive is the performance list that SXSW

year-round sun, and occasional high wind. Do not expect to transplant your gardening habits from Vermont or Georgia or Minnesota. That is not to say gardening cannot be rewarding in Austin; it simply means newcomers have to learn the rules. Garden enthusiasts can find many of the

answers at this annual event. Sponsored by 40 local garden clubs and plant societies, the festival attracts large crowds and offers plants for sale, advice, brochures, books, and gardening tools and equipment. There is a small admission fee.

press releases tend to look like the contract you sign to buy a refrigerator at Sears: yards and yards of tiny print. Reading that list of band names can be amusing—17 Hippies, a 47-piece band from Berlin, Germany, kicked off the 1998 keynote address.

Everyone is on alert during the festival to seek out the next wave. The panelists at the conference count among their numbers major record producers and influential music and film professionals who have come to view SXSW, according to festival sponsors, as "one of the most influential musical events in the world."

While conference participants sign up for the whole shebang of seminars and panel discussions ("Parenting in the Music Business" and "So IS Paul Dead?"), music enthusiasts opt to pay for a wristband that allows them to roam the nightclub scene and hear as many of the bands as possible. Conference fees cost several hundred dollars, but wristbands have been described as affordable. However, grumbling has been heard in recent years as wristband prices approached $100.

Availability and cost of wristbands have caused rumors of rebellion in the Austin ranks, but that has not detracted from the success of SXSW.

The creators of SXSW also launched a SXSW Film Festival, which has been described as "early Sundance," since entrants must be chosen by a panel in order to show their films. The four-day festival includes panels, workshops, meetings, mentor sessions, demo reel sessions, and the presentation of more than 150 films at various locations in Austin. Major agents, directors, and up-and-coming film producers attend.

Another spin-off festival held in conjunction with the film and music conferences is the SXSW Interactive Festival, dedicated to discussions and explorations of new media technology. Again, there are panel discussions, star speakers, and a trade show featuring local and national high-tech companies. The entertainment events include such things as cyberoperas and intercontinental Internet concerts.

The best way to absorb all the SXSW possibilities is to visit www.sxsw.com or get on the mailing list. Write to SXSW, P.O. Box 4999, Austin, TX 78765, call (512) 467-7979, or fax (512) 451-0754.

(To learn more about music in Austin, read The Music Scene chapter.)

Zilker Kite Festival
Zilker Park, 2100 Barton Springs Road
(512) 647-7888
www.zilkerkitefestival.com
March winds help more than 200 handmade kites take flight in one of the city's most popular free outdoor events. Usually held on the second Sunday of the month in the city's large downtown park, the festival is sometimes postponed because of spring rains. Anyone can come fly a kite, but there is also an organized competition. Categories include the smallest kite, the strongest-pulling kite,

the highest, and the most creative kite, but everyone's favorite is the largest kite. The event begins at 11:00 A.M. and is free. Given Austin's growth, parking at Zilker Park events can be a headache. In addition to parking in the park, additional space is available under the MoPac overpass to the west.

APRIL

The Annual Austin Rugby Tournament
Zilker Park, 2100 Barton Springs Road
www.austinrugby.com
Since 1968 this rugby tournament has attracted enthusiasts from across the region. Organizers tout it as the oldest and largest rugby tournament in the Southwest. There are several divisions of play in the two-day tournament and, true to rugby tradition, a post-tournament party on Sixth Street. The tournament's Web site lists telephone numbers for team contacts. (See the Rugby section in our Parks and Recreation chapter for more information on the local rugby scene.)

Annual Bluebonnet Festival
Historic Square, Burnet
(512) 756-4297
www.burnetchamber.org
This is one of several Hill Country events celebrating the wildflower season. Burnet is northwest of Austin on U.S. 281. In addition to an arts and crafts show, children's activities, a parade, and 5K and 10K runs, the festival also features a golf tournament, a classic car show, and special appearances by the Confederate Air Force, an association of vintage airplane owners. The events are scheduled over two weekends in mid-April. The festival is held in conjunction with the Highland Lakes Bluebonnet Trail, a scenic route through the Hill Country where many of the best stands of wildflowers can be viewed. Maps and stories about the best bluebonnet spots are frequently printed in the Austin newspaper.

Austin Auto Show
Austin Convention Center,
500 East Cesar Chavez Street
(512) 404-4404
This four-day spring show held late in the month features the latest cars, trucks, and vans. Hours are Thursday from noon to 10:00 P.M., Friday and Saturday from 10:00 A.M. to 10:00 P.M., and Sunday from 10:00 A.M. to 6:00 P.M. Admission fee; children younger than 12 are admitted free.

Austin Fine Arts Festival
Republic Square, Fifth and Guadalupe
Streets
(512) 458-6073
www.austinfineartsfestival.org
Formerly known as Laguna Gloria Fiesta in honor of Laguna Gloria Museum (see our Arts chapter), this festival has moved downtown near the site of the proposed Austin Museum of Art. This juried art show has featured the works of over 200 nationally recognized artists. To make the event festive there is music and children's activities. The festival is sponsored by the Austin Museum of Art Guild, and both the exhibitions and the creations of craftsmen that are offered for sale are top quality. Admission fee.

Austin International Poetry Festival
Various venues
(512) 502-8294
www.aipf.org
Usually held in mid-April, this citywide festival celebrates poetry in a variety of forms. Readings are held in bookstores, coffee shops, and pubs, as well as public places and feature published poets and inspired amateurs. The festival also includes several workshops and films.

The Bob Marley Festival
Auditorium Shores,
Riverside Drive and South First Street
(512) 773-5177
www.austinmarleyfest.com
This laid-back music concert celebrates the life of reggae singer Bob Marley.

There's no admission charge, but attendees are asked to bring a donation for the food bank. The event has collected more than 100,000 pounds of food for the needy. The all-day festival features both local and national reggae favorites.

The Capitol 10,000
Downtown, shores of Town Lake
(512) 445-3596
www.austin360.com

This 10K race is listed among the top 100 road races in the country by *Runner's World* magazine. First held in 1978, it has become a very popular event and attracts approximately 15,000 competitors and hundreds of spectators. The runners—and walkers—include famous Texans (President George W. Bush has run), the not so famous, the young, and the old. There are many wheelchair athletes also. The course changes every year but always ends on the shores of Town Lake. Entry fees vary. Participants are given a free T-shirt by the major race sponsor, the *Austin American-Statesman*. The shirt features the work of Pulitzer Prize–winning cartoonist Ben Sargent.

Earth Day
Auditorium Shores
(512) 477-1566
www.parkfest.org

Ecology Action sponsors this downtown fair and musical event. The aim of the celebration is to make being green fun. Here you'll find local vendors and nonprofit groups offering advice and information, tips on recycling, arts and crafts using recycled materials, and exhibits of the latest green technologies. The day's festivities also feature children's activities, live music all day, gourmet vegetarian food, and a farmers' market.

Easter Fires Pageant
Gillespie County Fairgrounds,
Highway 16, Fredericksburg
(830) 997-2359
www.gillespiefair.com/easterfires

More than 100 years ago, the story goes, settlers around Fredericksburg met with Native Americans at Eastertime for peace talks. The campfires could be seen burning in the night as talks went on. A pioneer mother and her children looked out over the hills, saw the fires, and the mother attempted to calm the children's fears by telling them a tale: The Easter Rabbit had started the fires to boil the eggs for Easter Sunday. And that's why every year on the Saturday before Easter, hundreds of people dressed in bunny suits and others dressed as Native Americans and settlers celebrate with a nighttime pageant in this Hill Country town, west of Austin. (See our Day Trips chapter for more on Fredericksburg.) This event blends local folklore with history and religion, and the sight of hundreds of people in bunny suits is not to be missed. Box seats and reserved seating are available, plus general admission.

Easter Pageant
Sunken Garden, San Gabriel Park,
Georgetown
(512) 930-4649

This popular outdoor pageant is held Easter weekend in a natural setting in Georgetown's major city park, just north of Round Rock and a short ride north up I-35 from Austin. The pageant, which features a large cast and a variety of live animals, is a musical drama telling the life of Jesus Christ. There are about 300 seats set up at the site, but the crowds are often larger, so many attendees bring lawn chairs and blankets. There are three free performances, Saturday at 4:00 P.M. and Sunday at 7:00 A.M. and 4:00 P.M. *Note:* Since the date of Easter is subject to the religious calendar, performance times are subject to change, depending on whether daylight saving time has gone into effect.

Eeyore's Birthday Party
Pease Park, Parkway Street off West
12th Street
(512) 448-5160
www.sexton.com/eeyores/

There is an old line about Austin being an elephant's graveyard for hippies, the place where all the old hippies come to die. Of course, many of them never left, judging from the number of old Hondas and VWs on the road. Some even had new little hippies to add to the population. But you don't have to be a full-time flower child to enjoy Eeyore's Birthday; however, it helps if you have a touch of Woodstock in your heart. (That makes it easier to understand the Summer of Love drumbeat.) Both old and young free spirits meet on the final Saturday of the month at Pease Park in Central Austin to listen to music, dress up (costumes with a pun are favored), paint their faces, dance, watch the jugglers—all for free from midmorning to sunset. Despite the Winnie the Pooh connection, Eeyore's Birthday Party might not be suitable for children. Area residents have complained about parking problems and the behavior of a few of the celebrants at this annual event, prompting calls for the party to be moved. So far, those lobbying for a move have been unsuccessful.

Emma Lee Turney's Round Top Antiques Fair
Round Top
(281) 493-5501
www.roundtopantiquesfair.com

Round Top is a wonderful, culture-rich community located in Fayette County, about 65 miles east of Austin. This small town is packed with historical homes, cozy bed-and-breakfasts, antiques and crafts shops, and restaurants. It is also home to a world-renowned music foundation (see Festival Institute under the June listings) and now two of the most renowned antiques fairs in the United States, one in the spring, the other in October. *Country Home* magazine has named this fair "one of the ten best antique fairs in the country," and dealers come from all over the United States and even the world to sell, shop, and mingle. Dubbed "the great American Country Show," the fair features furniture and home furnishings from all regions of the country, plus British and European works. (For more information on Round Top, see our Day Trips chapter.) In addition to the two big fairs, there are other antiques sales events and crafts shows, as well as theater presentations and music concerts throughout the year, so check out the small town's Web site: www. roundtop.org.

Johnson City Market Days
U.S. 290, Johnson City
(830) 868-7684
www.johnsoncity-texas.com

This two-day weekend festival in mid-April takes advantage of the usually glorious spring weather and wildflower scenes in the Hill Country west of Austin. The festival features artists' demonstrations, arts and crafts sales, food, and live music. President Lyndon B. Johnson's boyhood home (see our Day Trips chapter) at the nearby Johnson Settlement is the scene for cowboy songs and poetry readings that celebrate the Texas frontier life. There is a small admission to some events.

Liberty Hill Festival
Downtown Liberty Hill
(512) 515-5075

A small community, located in western Williamson County off Highway 29, Liberty Hill is feeling the hot breath of urban growth on its neck, but that has not taken the fun out of the town festival. In fact, it has just made it more popular. This old-fashioned celebration, usually held on the last Saturday of the month, features a pet parade, a cute-baby contest, horseshoe and washers tournament, arts and crafts stalls, a carnival, and a barbecue at the VFW Hall. On Sunday afternoon there is a gospel sing and covered-dish dinner at Foundation Park. Admission varies for events.

Market Days
Wimberley Lions Field, Wimberley
(512) 847-2201
www.visitwimberley.com/marketdays

On the first Saturday of every month from April to December, more than 400 vendors gather in Wimberley, southwest of Austin, to sell an assortment of arts, crafts, antiques, collectibles, and kitsch. This is one of the most popular flea markets in Central Texas. (See our Shopping chapter for more information.)

Old Settler's Music Festival
Salt Lick Pavilion
Camp Ben McCullough Road, Driftwood
(512) 370-4630
www.oldsettlersmusicfest.org

This folk music festival originated in Old Settler's Park in Round Rock, north of Austin, hence its name. But as it grew, the celebrants sought a larger site and moved south to Driftwood, a tiny community about 12 miles south of U.S. 290 on FM 1826, southwest of Austin. The two-day celebration of acoustic, bluegrass, jazz, and folk music is usually held on the first weekend of the month, drawing crowds that make a weekend of the event by camping out on-site. Adding to the atmosphere is the smell of barbecue cooking at the nearby Salt Lick barbecue restaurant (see our Restaurant chapter). A two-day ticket costs about $50, but call ahead. One-day tickets are also available.

Paddlefest
Town Lake
(512) 473-2644, (888) TEXAS FUN
www.lcra.org

This annual event, usually held the third Saturday in April, is part of the Lower Colorado River Authority's Riverfest celebration (see the general listing in March). The downtown Austin event features canoe and kayak racing for all ages and levels of expertise. One popular event is the 25K course that calls for kayak professionals to get out of the water and carry their boats for a stretch of the shoreline—called a portage. These competitors are canoe and kayak professionals who are competing for spots on the national team. Free brochures about Riverfest and Paddlefest can be requested by calling the toll-free number above.

The Real Antique Show
The Gillespie County Fairgrounds, Highway 16, Fredericksburg
(830) 995-2884
www.gillespiefair.com

This annual show, usually held on the third weekend in April, is dubbed the biggest antiques show in the Hill Country. Given the popularity of weekend getaways in Fredericksburg and the large number of antiques shops and historic homes in the town, this show is extremely popular. Less than a two-hour drive from Austin, it is an easy day trip (see our Day Trips chapter), but there is so much to see and do in Fredericksburg that many visitors go for a weekend. Make plans for overnight stays ahead of time. Admission charge.

Ride for the Roses
Various sites in the city
(512) 236-8820
www.laf.org

One of Austin's most beloved residents is legendary bicyclist Lance Armstrong. Armstrong, who is a cancer survivor, has broken records winning the Tour de France or, as Austinites call it, the Tour de Lance. According to the Lance Armstrong Foundation, Lance's cycling buddies first organized a race to show support for Lance's battle with cancer in 1997. The original race paralleled the training ride Lance and the group made through the hills west of Austin. Today the event has multiple features and spans a weekend. Some 7,000 participants enter bicycling events, plus there is a gala, silent auction, a 5K fun run, a health and sports expo, a Kids CARE ride at Auditorium Shores, and a Rock for the Roses outdoor concert featuring local and national bands. In 2001 Ride for the Roses Weekend raised over $1.5 million for the Lance Armstrong Foundation's cancer survivorship programs and services.

Safari
Austin Nature Center, West Zilker Park
(512) 451-3003
www.ci.austin.tx.us/nature-science/

This annual family festival on the last weekend of the month is a celebration of nature and a great event for a family outing. There are wildlife and environmental exhibits, games, entertainment, food, hands-on crafts activities, and rides. It is learning disguised as fun and a great way for children to become familiar with both their natural surroundings and the resources the nature center offers year-round (see our Kidstuff chapter). Admission fee. The fun begins at 10:00 A.M. and ends at 6:00 P.M. Saturday and Sunday. Check the newspaper for special parking and shuttle bus arrangements.

Spring Fling
Travis County Farmers' Market,
6701 Burnet Road
(512) 454-1002
The market kicks off the growing season with a celebration of local produce, including herbs, vegetables, flowers, and fruits. Since this is Austin, the live music capital of the world, there is music to serenade the springtime. Usually held on a Saturday early in the month, the Fling is just one of several annual events at the market, which is located in North Austin. The facility has outdoor stalls, specialty shops, and restaurants. (See our Shopping and Restaurants chapters for more information on the market.) Admission is free.

One of the charms of life in the Hill Country is the identity many small communities have maintained despite growth and change. These small towns hold annual festivals that offer a glimpse of Texas's past. We've listed several of them, but one local writer, Richard Zelade, has devised driving tours of the Hill Country that include a lot of background information about these Texas towns. His book, **Texas Monthly Guidebook to the Hill Country,** *is published by Gulf Publishing.*

Spring Herb Festival
Fredericksburg Herb Farm,
402 Whitney Street, Fredericksburg
(800) 259-4372
www.fredericksburgherbfarm.com
Everything you always wanted to know about herbs, from growing them to cooking with them and using them for health, home, and body, can be learned at this Hill Country herb farm festival. The Fredericksburg Herb Farm is a working farm that also operates as a spa, restaurant, bed-and-breakfast, and tearoom. The farm is a favorite shopping and overnight stay spot in Fredericksburg (see our Day Trips chapter) and a very popular destination during the spring wildflower season. Headquarters for the 14-acre farm is a restored historic limestone building 6 blocks south of Main Street off Milam Street. The farm's owners also operate a shop at 241 East Main Street. The spring fair, held in mid-April on Friday evening, Saturday, and Sunday, features plant sales, demonstrations, tours, food, and music. Admission charge.

The Texas Hill Country
Wine & Food Festival
Various locations
(512) 542-WINE
www.texaswineandfood.org
Texas chefs, vintners, cheesemakers, herb growers, and gourmets gather in Austin on the first weekend in April to celebrate Texas wine and foods. The first festival was held in 1985 and was the brainchild of several nationally and internationally recognized chefs, including Dean Fearing, executive chef of Dallas's Mansion on Turtle Creek, and Robert Del Grande, executive chef of Houston's Cafe Annie. The festival is headquartered at Austin's downtown Four Seasons Hotel, but events also take place at restaurants, posh and funky, throughout the city and locations outside the city. Experts in cuisine, wine, cigars, famous chefs and culinary authors from across the country

conduct seminars and tastings, create special menus, and host field trips. Admission to events varies from triple digits for a ticket for a celebration dinner to an affordable amount for a Taste of Texas sampler, featuring Texas foods, wine, and beer at a country barbecue. Chocolate cigars might be the dessert at a dinner, while bock beer–battered quail is likely to be on the menu at the outdoor tasting. For a brochure and information write to the festival at 1006 MoPac Circle, Suite 102, Austin, TX 78746.

The Texas Relays
The University of Texas Memorial Stadium, San Jacinto Street at Manor Road
(512) 471-3333, (800) 982-BEVO
www.texassports.com
The relays have been run at UT for more than 70 years and feature top high school and collegiate track and field competitors from across the nation. Usually scheduled for the first weekend in April, sessions begin on Friday morning and end Saturday afternoon. The preliminaries are held on Wednesday and Thursday and are free. Tickets available for one day or entire event. An all-session ticket costs $10. Call the toll-free number for additional information and advanced ticket purchase.

Theater Week
Various locations in Austin
(512) 416-5700
www.acotonline.org
This weeklong event, usually held the second week in April, is designed to introduce newcomers and people unfamiliar with the city's theatrical community to the Austin theater scene. The events include special performances and ticket offers, plus behind-the-scenes tours. The offerings run the gamut from musicals, classics, comedies, and locally written productions. The Austin Circle of Theaters organizes the event, and information on tickets and performance times are avail-

able from the theater hot line number above.

The University of Texas Press Book Sale
2100 Comal Street
(512) 471-7233
www.utexas.edu/utpress/index
Usually held in late April or early May, this annual sale is a great place to find book bargains, especially books on subjects like Texana, Latin-American studies, archaeology, Texas and Western history, plus titles that represent doctoral dissertations on subjects of all sorts. The sale is advertised in the local media. Early birds get the best selection.

Wildflower Day in the Spring
Lyndon Baines Johnson State Park,
U.S. 290, Stonewall
(830) 644-2252
When you stroll through the meadows of President Lyndon B. Johnson's ranch, it is so easy to understand the love of Texas wildflowers that inspired Lady Bird Johnson to embark on a lifetime of work to beautify America. Any spring weekend will afford visitors wonderful views and an opportunity to enhance their understanding of the Johnson family's love for this countryside; however, the park sets aside the third weekend of the month to hold special events celebrating the wildflowers. (For more information on the LBJ State Park, see our Day Trips chapter.)

Wildflowers Days Festival
Lady Bird Johnson National Wildflower Research Center, 4801 La Crosse Avenue
(512) 292-4100
www.wildflower.org
The research center celebrates the Hill Country spring wildflower season with a daylong festival featuring native plant experts and authors, an arts and crafts exhibit, and live music. Admission is $3.50 for adults, $2.00 for students and seniors, and $1.00 for children 5 and younger.

Yesterfest and the Salinas Art Festival
Bastrop City Park and Main Street,
Bastrop
(512) 321-6283
www.bastroptexas.com
Bastrop, the historic small community just east of Austin on Highway 71, is a town that has worked hard at maintaining its ties to the past. Several historic buildings line Main Street, where the art festival takes place on the third Saturday of the month. Out at the city park, the locals celebrate their pioneer past with historical exhibits, reenactments, craft demonstrations, music, and food. Native American dancers perform, cloggers and banjo players entertain, pipe and drum corps members join in Civil War reenactments, Scottish dancers make note of the town's ties to the Old Country, and it all winds up in a Main Street dance at night and a campfire stew dinner. Admission charge to the park. Parking is available at the Bastrop High School, and shuttles run to the park. Yesterfest begins at 10:00 A.M. and closes at 5:00 P.M.

MAY

Annual Sweet Peach Festival
Travis County Farmers' Market,
6701 Burnet Road
(512) 454-1002
This is a celebration of Hill Country peaches. Peaches are for sale, of course, plus there is peach mania at the market, with offerings of peach cobbler, peach ice cream, and peach preserves and jams. Admission is free.

Catholic Church Spring Picnic
American Legion Park, Shiner
(512) 594-3836
www.shinertx.com
Shiner is a small Central Texas town southeast of Austin well known as the home of Shiner beer. The town retains much of its German-American flavor, and one of the best ways to experience that is to visit the annual Catholic church picnic.

The event, which dates back to 1897 and is one of the biggest church picnics in the area, is free and features a country store, food, games like horseshoes, and dancing all day to polka bands. The fun continues into the evening with more dancing and a church dinner, featuring Shiner Picnic Stew, sausage, fried chicken, and all the fixin's. The event is held the Sunday before Memorial Day.

Chisholm Trail Roundup
City Park, Lockhart
(512) 398-2818
www.lockhart_tx.org
Back in 1840, Lockhart residents fought their way into the history books by defeating the Comanches at the Battle of Plum Creek. Later this small town southeast of Austin became a staging center for cattle being driven north on the Chisholm Trail to Abilene, Kansas. Lockhart had a reputation as a wild town, famous for its shoot-outs and feuds. The town history is celebrated with a reenactment of the battle, city tours, and a chili cook-off. The weekend-long festival in late May also includes dances, arts and crafts shows, and live music. Admission for events varies. If you are visiting, don't leave town without dropping in on a Texas landmark, Kreuz Market. This is where some of the world's most delicious barbecue is served up in simple style, slapped onto butcher paper, not plates, with a side order of white bread or crackers. Some enjoy their barbecue with a bottle of Big Red soda. The restaurant is at 208 South Commerce and is open daily except Sunday from 7:00 A.M. to 6:00 P.M.

Cinco de Mayo
Fiesta Gardens, 2101 Bergman Street
(512) 867-1999
www.austin-cincodemayo.com
On May 5, 1862, Mexican General Ignacio Zaragoza (who was born in Texas) defeated the army of French Emperor Louis Napoleon at Puebla, east of Mexico City. That blow against European imperialism is now a special holiday celebrated in

song and dance both in Mexico and Texas. In addition to celebrations at Fiesta Gardens in East Austin, folkloric dancers and mariachi bands often perform at the State Capitol in the rotunda. Most Cinco de Mayo events are free, but some of the evening celebrations at Fiesta Gardens may charge an entrance fee.

Historic Homes Tour
Various locations in Austin
(512) 474-5198
www.heritagesocietyaustin.org

On Mother's Day weekend, the Heritage Society of Austin offers history buffs an opportunity to tour some of the city's most historic homes. Each year, the tour has a different theme. One recent tour was dubbed "A Century of Style" and featured homes from the 1850s to the 1950s. The society has played an important role in saving Austin buildings. One of its first projects was to rescue the Driskill Hotel on Sixth Street back in the 1970s. Tickets are available in advance or at the homes on the tour.

Kerrville Folk Festival
Quiet Valley Ranch, Kerrville
(210) 257-3600,
(800) 435-8429, tickets only
www.kerrville-music.com

This legendary 10-day folk festival is held on a beautiful Hill Country ranch, southwest of Austin near Kerrville. There is a wide variety of bands—reggae, folk, country, etc. The festival usually begins the Thursday before Memorial Day. Quiet Valley Ranch has scenic campgrounds for those who want to stay for several days. Admission fees and campsite prices vary. Call for information. The ranch is 9 miles south of Kerrville on Highway 16. Among the popular performers are Butch Hancock, the Austin Lounge Lizards, Bill and Bonnie Hearne, Lyle Lovett, and Russia's Limpopo (the Kit Kat commercial jingle "Gimme a Break" band). The fans, particularly those who camp out for the festival, are known as "Kerrverts." Tom Pittman, a member of the Austin Lounge Lizards,

told an *Austin American–Statesman* writer: "The typical Kerrvert is a builder, a cellular phone salesman or something like that . . . they just want to get away from ringing telephones for two weeks." Some camp out primitive style; others pack up the fancy RV and head to the hills. The festival is also noted for its campfire gatherings and nightly revelry.

Mayfair, Artwalk and the Georgetown Fly-in
Various locations in Georgetown
(512) 930-3535
www.visitgeorgetown.org

Georgetown, just north of Round Rock, was a quiet small town that celebrated a May festival on the courthouse lawn for years. But these days the fast-growing community, just off I-35, expects 30,000 people or more to celebrate Mayfair on the first weekend of the month. Three events attract visitors: Mayfair, a large arts and crafts fair and carnival in the city's San Gabriel Park; Artwalk, an art show and performance festival on the town's historic downtown square; and the Georgetown Fly-in and Airshow featuring exhibits of vintage planes and battle re-enactments. Mayfair opens Friday evening at 5:00 P.M. and closes at midnight. Weekend hours are 10:00 A.M. to midnight on Saturday and noon to 6:00 P.M. on Sunday. Admission charge for adults, free for children 12 and younger. Artwalk is free and open from 10:00 A.M. to 6:00 P.M. Saturday and noon to 6:00 P.M. Sunday. The air show is at the Georgetown Airport and open from 10:00 A.M. to 6:00 P.M. Saturday and Sunday. Admission charge.

The O. Henry World Championship Pun-Off
O. Henry Museum,
Fourth Street at Neches in Brush Park
(512) 397-1465
www.ci.austin.tx.us/parks/ohenry

If you are a pun-lover, and apparently there are hundreds of them in Austin, this is the event for you. Each year, on the first

Sunday in May, up to 2,000 people gather at the O. Henry Museum (see our Attractions chapter) to watch and participate in the pun-off. The famous short-story writer William Sydney Porter, who wrote under the nom de plume of O. Henry, was a master punster. The event is free. To join the pun-off, simply show up.

Old Pecan Street Spring Arts Festival
Sixth Street, between Congress Avenue and I-35
(512) 441-9015
www.roadstarproductions.com

In Austin's early days, many of the downtown east-west streets were named for Texas trees, just as the north-south streets were and still are, for the most part, named for Texas rivers. Many of Austin's famous nightclubs are on Sixth Street, once called Pecan Street. The old name is revived for the spring and fall arts and crafts festivals held there. Several blocks of the street are blocked to vehicular traffic and turned into an outdoor art gallery and live music venue. Food booths sell a variety of carnival fare, including fajitas, cotton candy, hot dogs, and funnel cakes. The spring festival is usually held on the first weekend in May.

The Summer Concert Series
Waterloo Park
Red River and 15th Streets
downtown Austin
(512) 442-BAND
www.ci.austin.tx.us/parks/
summerconcerts

Organized by the Austin Federation of Musicians, this series of free outdoor summer concerts is held every Wednesday in May at 7:00 P.M. on Auditorium Shores, the south shore of Town Lake, just west of South Congress Avenue. Concerts also are held on Sunday afternoon at the Zilker Hillside Theater at 3:00 P.M. The concert series features a variety of bands and music, including rhythm and blues, Tejano, samba, and jazz. Bring a blanket or a lawn chair. Some refresh-

ments are sold at concession stands, but many music lovers bring along a picnic.

JUNE

Austin Chamber Music Festival
Various locations
(512) 454-0026
www.austinchambermusic.org

Imagine a chamber ensemble performing in the Victorian ballroom of the Driskill Hotel, or a music workshop for kids at the Austin Children's Museum. This three-week festival celebrating chamber music utilizes a variety of locations around the city, including churches, public spaces indoors and out, and evocative settings like the Driskill's ballroom.

Cedar Chopper Festival
Leander MHMR State Park, Leander
(512) 258-8007
www.cedarparkchamber.org

Cedar Park once was a tiny town settled by cedar choppers, men who made a living chopping down the Hill Country juniper trees called "cedars" and shipping them to be made into fence posts and lumber. These days, Cedar Park is a suburban community on the northwest fringes of the greater Austin area, but the new folks enjoy celebrating its past. On the second weekend in June, there is a community parade, lots of music, a chili cook-off, smoked turkey drumsticks for sale, arts and crafts (including some cedar items), and a street dance. The festival takes place in the state park, just off U.S. 183, 2 miles north of R.M. 620. Admission fee.

Clarksville-West End Jazz & Arts Festival
Various locations
(512) 443-3638

This concert salutes jazz greats with a series of club dates around Austin and a free concert in Pease Park, near the old Central Austin where the festival originated. The event is held on the second weekend in June.

Festival Institute at Festival Hill
Round Top
(409) 249-3129
www.festivalhill.org

In the early 1970s, classical pianist James Dick founded the festival at Round Top, the small German settlement east of Austin in Fayette County. Round Top has come to represent the best of the Texas cultural scene, combining great music, historical settings, and a bucolic atmosphere. There are concerts once a month throughout the year at the institute site, but a special midyear series dubbed Summerfest takes place on each weekend in June and the first two weekends of July. Concerts range from the strictly classical to the popular—for example, a concert of George Gershwin favorites. In addition to the concerts, the area offers much to see and do, including historic homes, antiques shops, gardens, and herb shops. (See our Day Trips chapter for more on Round Top.) Admission fee for the concerts, and performances are given Friday at 8:00 P.M. and Saturday at 3:00 and 8:00 P.M. For a concert schedule write to Festival Institute, P.O. Box 89, Round Top, TX 78954.

Juneteenth
Various locations

Juneteenth is an original Texas celebration and marks the day that Texas slaves learned of the Emancipation Proclamation. On June 19, 1865, Union commander Major General Gordon Granger took Galveston and announced to Texas slaves that they had been freed two years earlier. The day is now marked by festivals of music, barbecues, parades, celebrations of African-American culture, and gospel sings. Check the *Austin American-Statesman* and community newspapers for details of this yearly event. Juneteenth is now a state holiday.

Luling Watermelon Thump
Luling
(830) 875-3214
www.watermelonthump.com

Watermelons and natural gas are the two major "crops" in Luling, a small town southeast of Austin. The last weekend in June is set aside to honor the watermelon. There is a parade, a crowning of the Watermelon Queen, food, and music. The highlight of the weekend is the Watermelon Spitting Contest. Children, adults, and teams enter in separate categories. The record for spitting a seed is 68 feet, 9.125 inches according to the *Guinness Book of World Records*. Most of the events are free, but tickets to some events are necessary. The town is also home to the Central Texas Oil Patch Museum.

If you go, be sure to drive around the downtown area and take note of the small rocker wells, pumping natural gas from right under the city streets. Each well is decorated like a giant whirligig, one like Uncle Sam, another like a watermelon, of course.

JULY

A Night in Old Fredericksburg
Various locations in Fredericksburg
(830) 997-6523
www.fredericksburg-texas.com

This Hill Country town west of Austin has preserved its historic buildings, many of which capture the spirit of the German-American pioneers who settled here (see our Day Trips chapter). It is easy to spot the German influence in this town at any time of the year, but on the third weekend in July, the town celebrates with a citywide celebration of its German heritage. In recent years, cultural happenings with a Mexican-American flavor have been added to the festival of food, dance, music, and horse racing. Admission charge.

Austin Symphony Orchestra
July Fourth Concert and Fireworks
Auditorium Shores,
Riverside Drive and South First Street
(512) 476-6064
www.austinsymphony.org

As Austin grows, the size of the crowd gathering on the shores of Town Lake to watch the July Fourth concert gets larger and larger. The orchestra sets up on the southern shore of Town Lake on Auditorium Shores. The crowds spill over along both banks of the river, and some spectators enjoy the music from small canoes on the lake or on the rooftops of downtown office buildings. No powerboats are allowed on Town Lake. The grand finale is, of course, Tchaikovsky's "1812 Overture," complete with cannon and fireworks. The music begins at 8:30 P.M., but many families come down earlier and enjoy a family picnic. The fireworks usually start around 9:30 P.M. Parking is a major headache, and after the concert the city's major thoroughfares out of the downtown area are jammed, making the trip home a slow one. The concert is free. Tip: If you simply want to enjoy the fireworks, the view from Barton Creek Mall on Loop 360 (Capital of Texas Highway) southwest of downtown is an excellent one.

Barton Springs Diving Championships
Barton Springs Pool,
2201 Barton Springs Road
(512) 476–4521
www.ci.austin.tx.us/bartonsprings
Elvis is alive and diving at Barton Springs. At least he was in 1997, when he won the "Most Original" prize in this annual contest. The contest includes best splash, best dive, and most-original dive categories. Participants range in age, and their entry fees help fund environmental exhibits. Local musical groups also perform before and after the diving competition, which takes place on the third Sunday of the month. Flyers advertising the event and containing registration forms are widely distributed at Austin's pools, local grocery stores, and other outlets. Spectators pay an admission charge. Participants pay a registration fee. You can save a few dollars by preregistering.

Bastille Day
The French Legation,
802 San Marcos Street
(512) 472–8180
www.frenchlegationmuseum.org
The legation was the home and office of Comte Alphonse Dubois de Saligny,

charge d'affaires to the Republic of Texas. Francophiles and homesick French citizens gather on the Sunday closest to July 14 to celebrate the French equivalent of our July Fourth. The food is French, of course, and very good since it is concocted by local chefs and includes quiche, pâté, brioche, sorbet, pastries, and wine. The music is French, and the dancers, jugglers, and mimes celebrate traditional French culture. Admission fee.

Fourth of July Festival
San Gabriel Park, Georgetown
(512) 930–3545
www.georgetownchamber.org
Residents of Round Rock, Pflugerville, and other communities and neighborhoods in far North Austin find it more convenient to drive to the Williamson County seat, Georgetown, just north of Round Rock on I–35, for July Fourth celebrations. The day-long festival at the park begins at 10:00 A.M. and ends at 10:00 P.M. with fireworks. The day's activities are free and include a children's carnival, petting zoo, games, live music, and a barbecue cook-off.

Lakeway's Fabulous Fourth
Various locations in Lakeway,
Lake Travis
The idea here is to emulate the small-town celebrations many of us remember from the past. The parade begins at 8:30 A.M. at the Live Oak Clubhouse on Lakeway Drive in the Lakeway area on Lake Travis. From 11:00 A.M. to 4:00 P.M. there is a Picnic in the Park at City Park on Hurst Creek Road. Vendors sell watermelon, fajitas, hot dogs, corn on the cob—all the July Fourth fixin's. There are games for kids and live entertainment. Look for details on shuttle buses in the *Austin American–Statesman*'s roundup of Fourth of July activities. Admission is free.

Shakespeare at Winedale
Winedale Historic Center, near
Round Top
(409) 278–3530
www.shakespeare-winedale.org

Each summer, University of Texas English literature students gather at historic Winedale (see April events and our Day Trips chapter) to study and perform Shakespeare's plays. The students perform three plays in the theater barn in the historic settlement, beginning the last week of July and continuing through mid-August. Performances are Thursday and Friday at 7:30 P.M. and Saturday at 2:00 and 7:30 P.M. Admission fee. Winedale is about a 90-minute drive east of Austin.

United Confederate Veterans Reunion
Camp Ben McCullough, F.M. 1826
Descendants of Confederate veterans gather for eight days in July on the banks of Onion Creek, southwest of the Oak Hill area of Austin, just off F.M. 1826 near Driftwood. This extended family gathering has been held every year since 1904. The camp is named for the Texas general who was killed at the Battle of Pea Ridge in Arkansas on March 7, 1862. Visitors are welcome to attend the event and watch a variety of historical programs, including reenactments of Civil War life, dancing, and, of course, barbecues. Admission is free.

Western Days
Various locations in Elgin
(512) 281-4515
www.elgintx.com/westerndays
There is hardly a town within Central Texas that does not celebrate its founding or history, or simply its survival, with one festival or another. In Elgin, east of Austin, residents and visitors gather on the third weekend in July for dances, rodeos, arts and crafts exhibitions, and food. And it would not be Elgin without generous servings of Elgin sausage. Admission is charged at the dances and rodeos, but most events are free, and many take place in the city's Memorial Park. The festival is held on the fourth weekend of the month.

Willie Nelson's July Fourth Picnic
Waylon and Willie made Luckenbach a household name, and this tiny town, located on F.M. 1376 off U.S. 290 West, 13 miles from Fredericksburg, was home for several years to Willie's legendary Fourth of July Picnic. Nelson is renowned for his concerts, and no one gets shortchanged when he takes to the stage. Over the years, the picnic has changed locations, so it is wise to keep an eye on local music coverage in the media for prices, admission, and ticket numbers. It is an event that is popular, and concertgoers from all over Texas come to hear Willie sing, so book tickets in advance.

Zilker Summer Musical
Zilker Hillside Theater, Zilker Park
(512) 479-9491
www.zilker.org
Each summer, for more than 40 years, talented Austin musicians and actors have put on a popular Broadway musical in the open-air hillside "arena" adjacent to Barton Springs in the city's major downtown park. The musical is free and performances are at 8:30 P.M. Thursday through Sunday from mid-July through August.

AUGUST

Austin Bamboo Festival
Zilker Botanical Gardens
2220 Barton Springs Road
(512) 477-8672
Throughout the year there is a variety of events at the gardens, but this is one of the most popular. Bamboo in every shape and form is featured at this combination garden and crafts show. There are also demonstrations on how to grow various kinds of bamboo and how to use the canes in a variety of arts and crafts.

The *Austin Chronicle* Hot Sauce Festival
Waterloo Park, Red River and 15th Streets
(512) 454-5766
www.austinchronicle.com
Salsa has surpassed tomato ketchup as the national condiment, and Austinites are doing their share to continue that trend. A multitude of vendors set up

shop at the park for this daylong festival, offering free samples. There are food booths and a salsa contest for those hoping to hit the big time with their own salsa concoction.

Austin Gay and Lesbian International Film Festival
Various venues
(512) 302-9889
www.agliff.org

In keeping with Austin's building reputation as a film center, this two-week festival brings a variety of films to Austin theaters around the city.

Austin Latino Comedy Fiesta
713 Congress Avenue
(512) 472-5470
www.teatrohumanidad.com

The historic Paramount Theatre is home to this annual comedy festival that celebrates Austin's Latino culture. Stand-up comics and sketch artists perform at the weekend festival.

Fall Creek Grape Stomp
Fall Creek Vineyards, Llano County
(915) 379-5361
www.fcv.com

This Hill Country vineyard has established a national reputation for the quality of its wines. Located on the shores of Lake Buchanan, about 70 miles northwest of Austin, Fall Creek is a popular place to visit while touring the Hill Country. But for two days in August, the second and third Saturdays of the month, it is the quality of the fun that counts. The peace and quiet of the winery is broken by the cheers and hollers of barefooted kids and grown-ups stomping the grapes. The winery opens its doors from 11:00 A.M. to 5:00 P.M. so that visitors can roll up their jeans, strip off their socks, and jump into vats of red grapes. The experience is free.

(See our Close-up on Texas foods in the Restaurants chapter for more about Texas wine and wineries.)

Gillespie County Fair
Fairgrounds, Highway 16, Fredericksburg
(830) 997-6523
www.gillespiefair.com

This is the oldest county fair in the state and is well worth a visit for a glimpse of a time when the county fair was an important date on the local calendar. The fair includes a traditional livestock show, handicrafts and home-baked goods, horse races, a carnival, and dances in the evening. The fair takes place on the last weekend of September. Fairground admission is $5.00, free for children. Additional admission charges may be in place for other events.

Taylor International Barbeque Cookoff and Rodeo
Murphy Park, Taylor
(512) 352-1988
www.taylorjaycees.org

They take their barbecue very seriously in Taylor, even sleeping with their rigs on the Friday night before the contest on the third weekend of the month. There are several types of meat cooked at the event, not just beef, and cooks begin to prepare Friday evening. On Saturday the judging begins as contestants compete not for money but for much-coveted trophies. The winner is designated a Master Cook, while the runner-up is Reserve Master. The whole event is accompanied by live music, and there is also a well-respected rodeo in conjunction with the barbecue. The event is a fund-raiser for the local Jaycees, and admission charges vary for each event from approximately $5.00 to $10.00.

Texas Folklife Festival
Institute of Texan Cultures, HemisFair Park, San Antonio
(210) 458-2390
www.texancultures.utsa.edu

In case you had not noticed, Texans are very proud of their heritage and enjoy not only celebrating their own roots but also dipping into the ethnic melting pot to create truly Texas traditions. To sample the great variety of ethnic folkways that helped form modern Texas, the institute celebrates with this annual festival. The exhibits, demonstrations, music, and food are authentic and widen the horizons of both newcomers and visitors to the Lone Star State. The festival usually runs for several days and starts August 1. (See our Day Trips chapter for more information on San Antonio.) This event is well worth the drive to San Antonio, since it offers a colorful tapestry of Texas food, traditions, crafts, and music without the modern, commercial trappings that spoil so many country fairs. Not only does the festival bring together all the diverse ethnic groups in Texas, it is cross-generational as older Texans demonstrate traditional crafts and skills to the younger folks. This is a great family outing.

Zilker Park Jazz Festival
Zilker Park Amphitheatre, Zilker Park
(512) 440-1414
www.ci.austin.tx.us/zilker

There is no better way to spend a warm summer night than listening to the cool sounds of jazz float across Zilker Park, the city's favorite gathering spot throughout the seasons. (See our Parks and Recreation chapter.) Bring a blanket and something cold to drink, and enjoy the free summer festival.

SEPTEMBER

Annual Shakespeare Festival
Zilker Park, 2201 Barton Springs Road
(512) 454-BARD (2273)
www.austinshakespeare.org

The Sheffield Zilker Hillside Theater is the outdoor site of this late September, early October dramatic festival. Usually, one of the Bard of Avon's comedies is presented along with a drama on alternate nights. Bring along a blanket, a picnic, and perhaps a sweater if cooler weather has arrived.

Austin City Limits Festival
Zilker Park
2100 Barton Springs Road
www.aclfest.com

The same folks who brought America the legendary *Austin City Limits* television show on PBS sponsor this three day festival of music, food, arts, and crafts in the city's most famous park (see our Parks and Recreation chapter). There are multiple stages across 15 acres of parkland, plus an "Austin Food Court" and an art show. Capital Metro provides transportation to the site. The festival runs a very detailed Web site, where lists of bands, schedules, and information can be found and tickets may be purchased. Daily or three-day tickets are offered.

Austin Herbfest
2220 Barton Springs Road
(512) 477-8672
www.zilker-garden.org

Gardeners know that one thing we can raise in Austin gardens are herbs, particularly those Mediterranean plants like rosemary and basil that love our summer climate. Everything herbal, including books, plants, soaps, and perfumes, can be found at this garden festival held in early October at the Zilker Botanical Gardens. There are also demonstrations, lectures, and food booths.

Diez y Seis de Septiembre
Various locations

This is a major fiesta both north and south of the border, celebrating Mexico's demand for independence from Spain. On September 15, 1810, Padre Miguel Hidalgo y Costilla, a Mexican priest now hailed as the Father of Mexico, rang the parish church bells in the town of Dolores Hidalgo and summoned the Mexicans to support his call for freedom. That cry, or *grito*, is now a key element in every Diez y Seis fiesta as participants cry out "Mexico por los Mexicanos"—"Mexico for the Mexicans." But like the U.S. July Fourth celebration, serious history and fun are combined on Diez y Seis. Mariachi bands perform, folkloric dancers celebrate their heritage, and everyone eats really well. Austin's celebrations center on Fiesta Gardens, on the shores of Town Lake in East Austin. Nearby Elgin also holds its Chili Pepper Fest, with celebrations of the Mexican fiesta. There are ceremonies in Austin on the actual day of the holiday, but the fiesta is usually carried over to the weekend closest to the 16th, with events on several consecutive days. Check the local newspaper for details.

Fresh Chile Pepper Festival
6701 Burnet Road
(512) 454-1002
The arrival of the pepper harvest is hailed at the farmers' market with a weekend of all things peppery—recipes, samples, fresh, dried, and roasted chiles, plus dishes served at the market's restaurant. Pepper season is also celebrated at both Central Market locations (see our Shopping chapter Close-up) and at Chuy's restaurant (see our Restaurants chapter).

Kerrville Wine & Music Festival
Quiet Valley Ranch, Kerrville
(210) 257-3600
www.kerrville-music.com
This Labor Day weekend event is a shorter version of the famous spring Kerrville Folk Festival (see our listing in the May section). The events also include wine tastings and a crafts exhibit. The ranch has camping facilities. Admission varies with daily or weekend tickets, plus camping fees.

LBJ State Historical Park
Wildflower Day
Lyndon B. Johnson State Historical Park, Stonewall
(830) 644-2252
www.tpwd.state.tx.us/park.lbj
While spring is the season most noted for wildflowers, fall also offers a palette of flora that can be just as spectacular. One of the best places to enjoy the fall show is at LBJ Park. (See our Day Trips chapter for more information.)

Lone Star Weekend Aloft
Harris Branch, 10603 Harris Branch Parkway
(800) 788-6642
www.ballooning.net
This annual gathering of hot air balloonists is held on park land surrounding Harris Branch, a suburban development in Northeast Austin, just off U.S. 290 East. In years past, more than 100 balloonists have gathered for the two-day event, which includes balloon races and a balloon glow (the inflated balloons are illuminated at dusk). All the events are very photogenic. Admission fee; children 12 and younger are admitted free.

Oatmeal Festival
Bertram
(512) 335-2197
www.bertramchamber.org
This tongue-in-cheek Labor Day weekend festival has helped to revive a small community northwest of Round Rock on F.M. 243. The festivities include an oatmeal cook-off and eat-off, an oatmeal sculpture contest, and the Miss Bag of Oats (you have to be 55-plus) pageant. For the kids, there is a grasshopper parade where children can parade their pet insects. Most events are free.

Old Pecan Street Fall Arts Festival
Sixth Street, between Congress Avenue and I-35
(512) 441-9015
www.roadstarproductions.com

This weekend arts and crafts show mirrors the spring festival, which is detailed in our listing in May.

Salsa Music Festival
Waterloo Park, Red River and 15th Streets
(512) 899-8585
www.austinsalsa.com

This downtown park (Austin's first name was Waterloo—see our History Chapter) is the site of the above-mentioned *Austin Chronicle* hot sauce festival in August, but in late September or early October one type of salsa gives way to another as salsa the musical kind takes over. In addition to the music, there are food booths and kid's activities.

Teddy Bear Picnic
Northwest Recreation Center, 2913 Northland Drive
(512) 472-1305

Toddlers and baby boomers alike can be seen clutching their teddies as they make their way to the annual Teddy Bear Picnic sponsored by the Austin Junior Forum. They are all hoping their bear will win one of the contests at the event—best dressed, silliest, most lovingly worn— which is held on the second weekend of the month. The picnic is a fund-raiser for the Forum, which buys teddy bears for children who are in crisis. Emergency personnel carry the bears for the victims of abuse, accidents, or trauma. In addition to contests, there are children's activities, a petting zoo, and a teddy bear market. The picnic takes place from 10:00 A.M. to 4:00 P.M. on Saturday and Sunday. Admission fee. Capital Metro runs free shuttle buses to the picnic from the Texas Department of Transportation building at 35th Street and Jackson Avenue in Central Austin.

Texas Wildlife Exposition
4200 Smith School Road
(512) 389-4472
www.tpwd.state.tx.us/expo/

This large, free two-day fair in late September, early October is a favorite among outdoors enthusiasts. Exhibits focus on fishing and hunting skills, equipment and skill improvement. There are field dog trials, target shooting and archery contests, plus a variety of activities for children. The exposition is held in the Southeast Austin headquarters of the Texas Parks and Wildlife Department. (See our Parks and Recreation chapter for more information on hunting and fishing.)

OCTOBER

Austin Film Screenwriters Conference and Austin Film Festival
Various locations in the city
(512) 478-4795
www.austinfilmfestival.com

This fall festival, usually held at the beginning of the month, is fast becoming recognized as a significant film and cultural event. The conference offers screenwriters the opportunity to listen to panel discussions by top screenwriters, directors, and studio executives. Participants have included director Oliver Stone, actor Dennis Hopper, Mike Judge (creator of *King of the Hill* television show), screenwriters Eric Roth (*Forrest Gump*), Randall Wallace (*Braveheart*), Al Reinart (*Apollo 13*), Buck Henry (*The Graduate*), and many more. The accompanying film festival features either movies scheduled for release or movies that are making the festival circuit. The two festivals vary in admission prices. Tickets to individual films are available on show day. Passes to panel discussions and films also can be purchased for around $200, and full registration is approximately double that. The festival also includes a juried competition for screenwriters, and some of the winners have seen their work make it to the big silver screen as a result of the exposure here.

Emma Lee Turney's Round Top Antiques Fair
Round Top
(281) 493-5501
www.roundtopantiquesfair.com

Twice a year the cognoscenti of the antiques world flock to this small Texas town (see the fair listing in April for details). The fall event also celebrates Oktoberfest, a salute to the German heritage of many of the founders of Texas small towns and rural areas.

Fredericksburg Food & Wine Festival
(830) 997-8515
www.fbgfoodandwinefest.com
www.fredericksburgtexas.net
To celebrate the burgeoning Texas specialty food business and a growing number of wineries, the picturesque German town of Fredericksburg turns Market Square into a nosher's paradise. There are both food and wine tastings, an auction, and live music.

Frontier Days
Old Settlers Park, Round Rock
(512) 255-5805
www.ci.round.rock.tx.us
The only shoot-outs these days in Round Rock involve high school basketball tournaments. The only masks being worn are those donned by high-tech workers. But Round Rock, now a booming suburban community, was a typical frontier town back in 1878 when the streets were the setting for one of the most famous of Texas shoot-outs between the law and outlaw Sam Bass. "Texas's Beloved Bandit," as Bass was dubbed, rode into town intent on robbing the bank, but he ended the day buried in the local cemetery. Bass likely was dubbed "Beloved" because, in the

October is Texas Archaeology Month, celebrated statewide with hands-on exhibits, demonstrations, workshops, and opportunities to explore the rich Texas past. The Texas Historical Commission posts a events calendar on its Web site, www.thc.state.tx.us, or archaeology buffs can call (512) 463-6096 for more information.

grand Texas tradition of Bonnie and Clyde, bank robbers are somehow elevated to folk hero status. On the second weekend of the month the community celebrates Frontier Days, complete with a reenactment of the shoot-out, which is the headline event of the two-day festival. There is also a frog-jumping contest and hands-on demonstrations of butter-churning, whittling, soap making, and other pioneer skills. Children can try their hand at some of the skills. The grown-ups can eat fajitas and enjoy the live music, and the whole family can pose for old-style photos complete with a Longhorn steer in the picture. The event is open from 6:00 P.M. to midnight on Friday and from 10:00 A.M. to 1:00 A.M. on Saturday. Admission fee.

Gonzales Come and Take It Days
Town Square, Gonzales
(512) 672-6532
www.gonzalestexas.com
This weekend festival, held on the weekend closest to October 1, commemorates a famous event in the Texas Revolution. Gonzales, a settlement southeast of Austin, was home to a cannon the Texans felt would be targeted by the Mexican Army. In one of the revolution's early skirmishes, they prepared to confront the Army by making a famous revolutionary flag emblazoned with an image of the cannon and the words "Come and Take It." Gonzales also is noted as the only Texan settlement to respond to a request by Colonel Travis at the Alamo for reinforcements. The town has a rich history, and one of the local tales involves the antics of outlaw John Wesley Hardin, who lived around Gonzales for a while. The festival celebrates all this and more with historical reenactments, a historic homes tour, rodeo, and street dances. Admission is charged for some events.

Halloween at Jourdan-Bachman Pioneer Farm
11418 Sprinkle Cut-Off Road
(512) 837-1215
www.pioneerfarm.org

This is a popular place for children's outings (see our Kidstuff chapter), and a week before Halloween the farm offers kids a chance to learn the finer points of pumpkin carving. Other activities include traditional pioneer activities and hands-on exhibits. Admission charge.

Halloween on Sixth Street
Sixth Street, between Congress Avenue and I-35

Wholesale Halloween madness is one way to describe this event. As many as 60,000 costumed revelers have gathered on the street for the celebration. Several blocks are roped off to vehicular traffic, and participants are urged to walk in a vast oval pattern to avoid gridlock. Since the street is famous for its music clubs and bars, the noise level is high, and some partygoers do become a little rowdy. This is strictly a grown-up celebration and not recommended for children.

Hogeye Festival
Elgin
(512) 285-5721
www.elgintx.com/hogeye

Famed for its sausage, Elgin is a small town 19 miles east of Austin on U.S. 290 East. This typical Texas small town festival features cow patty bingo, a sausage cook-off (of course), a hog calling contest, music, arts and crafts, and a street dance.

The Mediterranean Festival
St. Alias Orthodox Church, 408 East 11th Street
(512) 476-2314

This downtown church holds its annual festival usually on a weekend in mid- or late October. The congregation is made up of families of Lebanese, Greek, Syrian, and Mediterranean descent. They celebrate their culture with food, song, and exhibits. Many Austin residents mark their calendars so that they can buy some of the delicious foods, particularly the pastries, sold at the festival. The church has a beautiful interior graced with traditional icons. Admission fee to the fund-raising activities.

Mesquite Art Festival
Marktplatz, Fredericksburg
(830) 997-8515
www.texasmesquiteassn.org

Texas ranchers regard it as a big, pesky weed that sucks up valuable groundwater; barbecue chefs love to soak it and toss it on the smoker; but for a band of talented craftsmen, mesquite wood from that gnarly, prickly tree with the feathery leaves is a wonderful material. In fall, members of the Texas Mesquite Association hold a crafts show in the downtown Marktplatz in the German-flavored Hill Country town of Fredericksburg, west of Austin (see our Day Trips chapter). Artists, woodcarvers, and furniture makers put an unbelievable variety of items on show, from rocking chairs to wonderful turned wooden bowls. The festival attracts thousands, but it is a wonderful way to view a native Texas art and enjoy a day trip to Fredericksburg.

Oktoberfest
Market Square, Fredericksburg
(830) 997-4810
www.oktoberfestinfbg.com

Fredericksburg has a strong German heritage; in fact, some of the older residents still speak in a form of German heard in 19th-century Europe. The traditional community festival features beer hall singing, waltz contests, and lots of sausage. Admission fee; free for those 6 and younger.

NOVEMBER

Austin Celtic Festival
406 West 17th Street
(512) 498-4908
www.austincelts.org

The Dog and Duck Pub touts itself as an authentic British pub, complete with dart boards and Scotch eggs (see our Nightlife chapter), and so it is appropriate that it serves as the headquarters for this Celtic music festival. Bands from both Austin and far away perform in this three-day event.

Austin Junior League Christmas Affair
Palmer Events Center, 900 Barton
Springs Road
(512) 467-8982
www.jlaustin.org
A sure sign that Christmas is just around the corner is the transformation of Palmer Auditorium into a shopping wonderland. More than 200 specialty merchants offer a variety of Christmas gift ideas, some easily affordable, others high-priced—for those who have been especially good. Not everyone shops at the affair, although the league raises hundreds of thousands of dollars for its community projects at the event, some just stroll, sip some Christmas spiced wine, and window-shop or gather decorating ideas for their own holiday celebrations. The affair is held the third weekend in November. The four-day event begins on Thursday and winds up on Sunday. Daily admission fee.

Chuy's
Children Giving to Children Parade
Congress Avenue
(888) 439-2489
www.chuysparade.com
This is a great way to teach children to give thanks on Thanksgiving weekend. Fast becoming a holiday tradition, this Saturday parade down Austin's main street celebrates two holidays in one. Organizers tout the parade as the Austin equivalent of New York's famous Macy's Thanksgiving Day parade. Balloons, some up to 80 feet high, depicting popular children's characters lead the parade, followed by marching bands, floats, dancers, clowns, and trucks filled with toys donated by children along the route. The donations go to the Austin Police Department's Operation Blue Santa, which gives toys to needy kids at Christmas. The parade is sponsored by Chuy's, the popular local restaurant—popular with kids because of the lively decor and popular with Mom and Dad because the staff tolerates 2-year-olds (see our Restaurants chapter).

Dia de los Muertos
Mexic-Arte Museum,
Fifth Street and Congress Avenue
(512) 480-9373
www.mexic-artemuseum.org
It means "Day of the Dead," and this quintessentially Mexican fiesta is celebrated on All Souls Day, November 1. In Mexico, families take food to the local cemetery on that day for a two-day celebration in honor of their ancestors. Families set up altars at the gravesite offering food and drink. Day of the Dead folk art is highly collectible, and much of it is humorous, mocking human foibles. Mexic-Arte Museum (see the Arts chapter) sponsors several Day of the Dead events, including the construction of a variety of ofrendas by local artists at its downtown museum site. Admission fee. There is also a parade down East Sixth Street onto Congress Avenue in celebration of Mexican and Chicano culture. Spectators are urged to wear typical Day of the Dead costumes, angels or skeletons, and watch low riders, dancers, and musicians parade on the avenue. Check the local paper for additional Dia de los Muertos events.

International Children's Festival
Austin Children's Museum
201 Colorado Street
(512) 472-2499
www.austinkids.org
The children's museum hosts this celebration of Austin's growing diversity. Arts and crafts by Austin children representing over 30 cultures from around the world are on display during this one-day art festival.

Texas Book Festival
Texas Capitol and various locations
(512) 477-4055
www.texasbookfestival.org
A recently conceived, but very successful, celebration of Texas literature (thanks in great part to First Lady Laura Bush), this festival includes book signings, seminars, discussions, and celebrations of literary

history. Every year a "class" photo of the participants is taken in the capitol rotunda, offering a picture of the diversity and extent of Texas literature. Among the panelists in recent years have been Jim Lehrer, Kinky Friedman, and Larry McMurtry. The participants also include literary luminaries with cultural or educational ties to Texas; for example, famous Mexican author and scholar Carlos Fuentes has participated. Admission to most events is free, but two fund-raising events are held, including a ball and a meet-the-authors reception. (See The Literary Scene chapter for more on this event.)

Powwow and American Indian Heritage Festival
Toney Burger Center, 3200 Jones Road
(512) 414-0159
www.austinpowwow.org
In 1991 the Austin Independent School District and local Native Americans joined to offer this free one-day, insightful festival to Austin residents. The goal was to share Native American culture with neighbors in Central Texas. Attendance has grown to more than 20,000 for the powwow, which usually is held on the first Saturday of November. From 10:00 A.M. to 10:00 P.M., area residents can sample Native American food, listen to storytellers, stroll through the craft booths and exhibits, and listen to American Indian music. The highlight of this free event is a dance competition, which features hundreds of dancers from dozens of tribes. Toney Burger Center is in Southwest Austin near the intersection of U.S. 290 West and Loop 360 (Capital of Texas Highway).

Wurstfest
Wurstfest Grounds, Land Park,
New Braunfels
(830) 625-9167, (800) 221-4369
www.wurstfest.com
New Braunfels was founded by Prince Carl von Solms-Braunfels in the 1840s. He was one of several German princes who set out to relieve German overpopulation by organizing immigration settlements in the New World. His settlement flourished, and now New Braunfels, roughly halfway between Austin and San Antonio, just off I-35, is a popular tourist spot (see our Day Trips chapter). Wurstfest is the city's version of Oktoberfest and attracts tens of thousands of visitors, who eat sausage, drink beer, sing songs, and spend money. Admission fee. Children 12 and younger are free.

DECEMBER

Armadillo Christmas Bazaar
Austin Music Hall, 208 Nueces Street
(512) 447-1605
www.armadillobazaar.com
This annual arts and crafts fair was originally held at the legendary Armadillo World Headquarters (see The Music Scene chapter) but now is housed in the Austin Music Hall in South Austin. The 'Dillo is long gone, but the spirit of the bazaar lives on as a showplace for local artists and craftspeople, some of them creating fanciful jewelry and whimsical toys. Local musicians also perform nightly at the two-week event, which begins in mid-December and ends Christmas Eve. It is open from 11:00 A.M. to 11:00 P.M. daily. Admission fee. Children younger than 12 are admitted free.

Candlelight Homes Tour
Fredericksburg
(830) 997-3600
www.fredericksburgtexas.com
The Historical Society hosts this annual tour on the second Saturday in December. Fredericksburg, west of Austin, is rich in historic landmarks and restored homes, and most of them are decorated for the season. Tickets are on sale at the Pioneer Museum, 309 West Main, and at Vereins Kirche, 100 West Main. Ticket prices vary. (See our Day Trips chapter for information on Fredericksburg.)

Christmas at the French Legation
French Legation, 802 San Marcos Street
(512) 472–8180
www.frenchlegationmuseum.org
The Daughters of the Texas Republic offer a glimpse of Christmas past as it might have been celebrated in the mid-19th century. The legation was built for Comte Alphonse Dubois de Saligny, France's charge d'affaires to the Republic of Texas. In addition to Christmas displays, choirs perform Christmas carols and holiday refreshments are offered. Pére Noel, the French Santa Claus, is on hand. The celebration takes place on the first Sunday of the month from 1:00 to 5:00 P.M. Admission fee. Proceeds benefit the legation museum. (See our Attractions chapter.)

Christmas Music and Theater
Various locations
With its rich and talented arts community, Austin offers a large variety of Christmas musical events. There are the long-standing traditions of the holiday, like the annual performances by the Austin Civic Ballet of *The Nutcracker* at Bass Concert Hall, (512) 469–SHOW. Handel's Messiah is performed by several musical entities, plus there is the annual "Sing It Yourself Messiah" at St. Matthews Episcopal Church, where the audience can join in with the Austin Civic Chorus. Call (512) 454–TIXS for information and tickets. Local theater and comedy troupes offer a variety of performances. Check the listings in the *Austin American–Statesman.*

Christmas Open House
Winedale Historic Center, near
Round Top
(409) 278–3530
www.roundtop.org
Christmas at Winedale is celebrated each year in a different historic home in this wonderful old settlement in Fayette County, east of Austin (see our Day Trips chapter). Usually held the Sunday before Christmas, the celebration features seasonal music and food. The many antiques shops offer one-of-a-kind Christmas gifts. Call for hours. There is a small admission charge.

Family Christmas Night
Downtown Round Rock
(512) 255–5805
On the first Saturday of the month, the City of Round Rock closes the downtown streets for a family celebration. At the heart of the event is the town's historic town square where Santa appears to assure Round Rock kids that he knows who has been naughty and who has been nice. The festivities begin at 7:00 P.M., and admission is free.

Feliz Navidad!
Various locations
There are a variety of Christmas events with a Mexican flavor held in Austin during the holidays. Plays depicting the nativity, folk music concerts, and folk art are popular at this time of year. La Pastorela, the traditional Latino nativity play, is performed by several groups. But one of the most interesting and authentic traditions takes place in mid-December as members of Our Lady of Guadalupe Church, 1209 East Ninth Street, enact La Posada. This is a tradition both in Mexico and Texas as the faithful reenact Joseph and Mary's search for a place to stay in Bethlehem. The faithful follow members, who are dressed as the Holy Family, as they go from door to door, asking for shelter. When the parade reaches the church there is a mass followed by Christmas treats, tamales, and Mexican hot chocolate. Check the arts and events listings in the *Austin American–Statesman* and local community newspapers.

Kwanzaa
Various locations
The Swahili word means "fruits of the harvest," and Kwanzaa, created in 1966, has proved fruitful as millions of African Americans embrace the celebration's principles. From December 26 to January 1, the seven days of Kwanzaa are dedicated to seven principles. In recent years,

African-American leaders in Austin have taken Kwanzaa from a family event to a community celebration. During the festival there are a variety of public events. Check the *Austin American–Statesman* and local community newspapers for details.

The Lighting of the Zilker Park Christmas Tree
Zilker Park, 2100 Barton Springs Road

This annual event on the first Sunday of the month is a true sign that Christmas is nigh. One the city's moonlight towers (see our Attractions chapter) was moved to the park and serves as the main "trunk" of the tree. Thousands of colored Christmas lights are strung from the top of the 165-foot tower to resemble a Christmas tree shape. Tradition calls for children to stand inside the pyramid and whirl around, making the lights blur. Young children are whisked around in their parents' arms. It is one of those simple holiday traditions that children never forget. Admission to the park is free.

Lights of the Blacklands
Small towns east of Austin
(512) 285–5721
www.elgintx.com

The holidays can be stressful, but one of the most relaxing ways to enjoy the season is to take a leisurely evening drive through some of the area's small towns and view the Christmas decorations. The towns east of Austin in what are called the Blacklands, a reference to the rich blackland prairie soil, suggest a tour beginning in Elgin on U.S. 290 and then on through Coupland, Thrall, Bartlett, and LaGrange. The route is featured on the Elgin City Web site.

New Year's Celebration on Sixth Street
Sixth Street, between Congress Avenue and I-35
(512) 441–9015

New Year's Eve in Austin's club scene is wild. Many clubs and downtown restaurants have special performances or menus in celebration. Check the local entertainment press for the particulars. Local tele-vision and radio stations camp out on Sixth Street rooftops to watch Austin's version of the "big ball" fall. The big ball falls at midnight, but that doesn't end the craziness as the party goes in clubs and on the street itself until the wee hours.

Pioneer Farm
Christmas Candlelight Tour
Jourdan-Bachman Pioneer Farm, 11418 Sprinkle Cut-Off Road
(512) 837–1215
www.pioneerfarm.org

Traditional Christmas activities reflecting the pioneer lifestyle are celebrated each weekend leading up to Christmas, many of them conducted by candlelight just as they would have been done in frontier days. Admission is $6.00. (See our Kid-stuff chapter for information on the farm.)

Texas Hill Country Regional Christmas Lighting Trail
Various locations
(860) 997–8515
www.fredericksburgtexas.com

Some of the most picturesque Christmas light shows can be seen in the small towns around the Austin area. Most of the lights are put up in early December and taken down after New Year's Day. Below are a few locations well worth visiting. The phone numbers are for the local chambers of commerce and visitor bureaus. Check the chamber Web sites, also.

Bastrop, to the east, decorates its historic downtown and Old Iron Bridge, (512) 321–2419.

Blanco, southwest of Austin, decorates the old courthouse with thousands of lights, (210) 438–2914.

Johnson City, west of Austin, is ablaze as the local residents cover homes, businesses, and the Blanco County Courthouse with lights, (830) 868–7684.

Llano, northwest of Austin, decorates the historic town square and the old courthouse with 10 miles of lights, (915) 556–5172.

Marble Falls, northwest of Austin, boasts it uses one million lights to decorate its Walkway of Lights, (800) 759-8178.

In Austin, the local television meteorologists often highlight spectacular Austin neighborhood decorations. One of the best is 37th Street, east of Guadalupe Street in Central Austin. Walking through this neighborhood is recommended, rather than driving.

In Round Rock the downtown historic district is decorated for the holidays, and in Cedar Park the Hill Country Flyer (see our Attractions chapter) departs from the train station in midafternoon for Burnet, then returns in the evening so that passengers can view the Hill Country homes decorated with lights. Call (512) 477-8468 for information.

Yule Fest
Zilker Park, 2100 Barton Springs Road
(512) 478-6875
www.ci.austin.tx.us/tol
For the last two weeks of December, the southern banks of Town Lake in Zilker Park are the site of Yule Fest and the Trail of Lights. This nighttime Christmas pageant features lighted set pieces decorated according to various Christmas themes. It is a popular family event that has seen lines grow longer and longer, prompting the city in 1998 to eliminate the special nights set aside for drive-through spectators and confine the trail to pedestrian traffic, bicycles, and special trams for the disabled. Capital Metro provides shuttle service to the park.

THE ARTS

What do 20-something slackers, a zany town named Tuna, a statewide high school competition, a giant university, and a celebrated European sculptor have in common? They all have added a few broad brush strokes to the colorful canvas of Austin arts.

Austin attracts artists. While that phenomenon dates back to the 1800s, Austin's status as a hub for artists has developed largely since the 1970s, when enough musicians, actors, writers, and painters had gathered to form an arts scene. Over the past few decades, more and more talented artists have found inspiration in Austin's artistic communities, and many of those have helped Austin earn a reputation for both appreciating and producing high-quality art. In his 2002 book, *The Rise of the Creative Class,* economist and author Richard Florida lists Austin as the No. 2 Creative Hot Spot in the nation. Read about the dynamic people and places in this chapter as well as in The Music Scene, The Literary Scene, Nightlife, and Attractions to discover many of the reasons Austin always gets such high praise. In this chapter we'll tell you about the visual artists and theater troupes, the dancers and filmmakers, the classical performers, and the choirs that make Austin sing.

Elisabet Ney, who had sculpted some of the great figures of Europe, was nearly 60 when she moved to Austin in the late 1800s. Back then, Austin had more gambling dens and brothels than galleries and theaters. Ney's celebrity status attracted influential men and women, many who believed, as did she, that art, music, and dance rank up there near water and air in importance to life. As Ney's hands transformed crude blocks of marble into glorious statues of Texas heroes, her spirit and her passion shaped a culture that prized the arts. Along the way, she became a pioneer of artistic development in the state of Texas. Her ability to inspire others during a time when the arts weren't exactly on the top of the Texas agenda led to the creation of the Texas Fine Arts Association (now called Arthouse) and later the Texas Commission on the Arts and the University of Texas art department.

The University of Texas gets major billing among the stars of Austin's cultural scene. The university's highly respected film and fine arts schools have turned out some of the most well-prepared graduates in the country. It's impossible to estimate the number of UT alumni, and professors, who are making significant contributions in Austin and around the country in the fields of dance, film, visual art, theater, literature, and music. UT's Performing Art Center is a world-class venue for world-class performers. The University Interscholastic League (UIL), a program started in 1910 to encourage educational development in Texas high schools through competition, began as a sports program. Since the 1920s the UIL has included an annual theater competition in which high schoolers from across the state vie for top honors. This Texas theater tradition, which produced Broadway's Tommy Tune and others, gets students hooked on theater at an early age.

Speaking of addictions, Austin—and most of the country, it seems—has developed a taste for Tuna. The crazy-quilt of characters that inhabit Tuna, Texas's third-smallest town, come to comic life on stage through actors Joe Sears and Jaston Williams, the Austinites who co-wrote (with Ed Howard) *Greater Tuna* and its two spin-offs. *Greater Tuna,* an Off-Broadway hit in the early 1980s, was followed by *A Tuna Christmas,* which garnered rave reviews on Broadway and earned Sears a Tony nomination. When the latest installment, *Red, White and Tuna,* debuted in

Austin in 1998, audience members shot out of their seats to give the pair a standing ovation. Quick-change artists Sears and Williams perform the parts of more than two dozen characters—male and female—in their fictional town of Smut Snatchers and hanging judges. Tuna fanatics know Aunt Pearl Burras and her sister Bertha Bumiller, Didi Snavely, Petey Fisk, and Vera Carp as well as they know their own families. *Greater Tuna,* presented in touring versions around the country, in an HBO production, in command performances at the White House, and in community theater all over the United States, has placed Austin on the national theatrical map.

What Tuna is to theater, *Slacker* is to film. This 1991 low-budget film by Austinite Richard Linklater made a bundle when it was released nationally and proved to the country that Austin has what it takes to make movies. A year later, Austin's Robert Rodriguez hit it big with *El Mariachi.* Since those films debuted, Austin filmmaking has jelled into an industry. (See our Close-up on Austin's film culture in this chapter.) Austin's large and small theater companies, visual artists, cutting-edge dancers, and performance artists are doing their parts to shake up the arts world, not just locally.

One of the most interesting aspects of Austin's modern-day arts scene is the evaporation of boundaries between the arts. When Austin's own Willie Nelson shows up on screen as an actor in movies, local filmgoers hold their collective breath in homage. Musician Joe Ely is doing well-respected multimedia art. Visual artists who sing, singers who paint, dancers who act, actors who write. It's a reflection on contemporary culture in general. The symbiosis of Austin's artistic scenes also offers Austin audiences incredible choices in venues. You'll find art exhibitions in theaters, dancers at museums, singers at art galleries, and film in the clubs.

Austin's rapid artistic development has not come without speed bumps. Today there isn't always enough space for many of Austin's performing and visual artists. While small warehouse-type theaters/galleries are popping up all over, Austin still cries out for larger state-of-the art venues. In response, a dedicated team of arts patrons is mounting a $72 million private fund-raising campaign to convert Palmer Auditorium on the south shores of Town Lake into a world-class facility. To be renamed the Joe R. Long and Teresa Lozano Long Center for the Performing Arts—the Long Center for short—it will open in the next few years. A new art museum is also envisioned for downtown, plus a Mexican-American Cultural Center and a new 500-seat Zachary Scott Theatre.

This chapter presents the Austin art scene on center stage—and the curtain is rising.

PERFORMING ARTS
Theater

When William Shakespeare wrote that "all the world's a stage," he might have been looking into the future at Austin. With more than 250 different shows a year produced by both national touring companies and the dozens of local troupes that perform at varying intervals, it often seems as though the whole city had been bitten by the bug. Check our local theater listings if you're in doubt. Many times, theater patrons have the luxury of choosing from as many as two dozen productions—at once.

Austin does theater in a variety of ways: big Broadway shows like 2004's *The Phantom of the Opera* at the University of Texas Performing Arts Center; sold-out performances by the wacky *Tuna* guys at the Paramount; the ambitiousness of a locally done *Angels in America* at Zachary Scott Theatre; lots of experimental shows staged in small converted warehouses; delightful productions geared toward kids; bilingual comedies and dramas; and performances celebrating the Bard himself on an outdoor stage.

Austin also is becoming increasingly known as an incubator of playwrights. In fact, in 2003 nine Austin playwrights qualified as finalists for the Actors Theatre of Louisville's Heideman Award, a prize given for the best play submitted to ATL's National Ten-Minute Play Contest. The year before, the prize was won by an Austinite. Of the more than 1,500 playwrights who submit plays for the contest, fewer than 100 reach the finals, which makes Austin's showing quite astounding. Each of these writers came out of the dynamic local organization, Austin Script Works (www.scriptworks.org), which offers services to playwrights at every stage of project development.

While theater can pop up in just about any nook and cranny around the city, we've identified Austin's main performance stages and theater troupes here. The stages are divided into three categories: The Main Stages are the city's larger, cushier, most formal theaters. The Outdoor Stage presents Austin's natural amphitheater; and The Warehouses highlight vintage buildings and warehouses that are increasingly being converted into small theaters by or for Austin's up-and-coming theater troupes. Additionally, we have a category called The Gypsies, which includes our favorite young theater troupes that perform anywhere they can find a space. Keep in mind that theater is very fluid here in Austin, so those troupes we've associated with a particular stage may perform in other locations as well.

This list will direct you to some of the best and most interesting theater Austin offers. For even more theater, check out the lineup at Austin's colleges and universities. The Austin Circle of Theaters (see the Arts Organizations in this chapter) calculates there are about 80 theater companies in our city. Some present works occasionally, while others, as you'll see here, are busy all the time.

We may all be actors on the stage of life, as Shakespeare suggested, but those who choose the theater as their life make it so much more interesting for the rest of us—as we like it.

The Main Stages

One World Theatre
7701 Bee Caves Road
(512) 330-9500,
(512) 32-WORLD (96753) for tickets
www.oneworldtheater.org

It was originally intended to be a large, even huge, home in West Austin, but it took a man who was dubbed "a California dreamer" by the *Austin American-Statesman* to turn it into a wonderful performing arts center. Hartt Stearns has created what theater critic Michael Barnes has dubbed "a wonder." Stearns, who studied samba under Brazilian master Mayuto Corea, runs the theater for a nonprofit group, Barton Creek Arts Center Limited. In addition to his commitment to bringing world-class artists to Austin, he also helped found a mission to help schoolchildren enjoy cultural offerings from around the world. The One World program is one of the most popular in Austin schools.

One World Theatre is a modern, Italianate structure that is an eye-grabber along Bee Caves Road. From its verandas visitors can look out over the Hill Country and the burgeoning high-priced neighborhoods in the area. Inside, the 300-seat auditorium wraps around the stage, offering the audience close-up, intimate views of the performers.

Half-price tickets to select Austin performances are available through AUSTIX Thursday through Saturday 11:00 A.M. to 5:00 P.M. at the visitor center, 209 East Sixth Street, and at BookPeople on Thursday from 4:00 to 7:00 P.M. Full-price tickets also are available Tuesday through Saturday at the visitor center. This service of the Austin Circle of Theaters also provides an "Austin Insiders' List" that is sent by e-mail and lists half-price shows for the coming weekend. Check the Web site at www.austix.com, or call (512) 474-8497 for information.

The eclectic offerings in past seasons have included Russian ballet stars, Tibetan monks, world-famous classical guitarists, the top names in chamber music, popular contemporary music stars, rock groups, and jazz legends.

Paramount Theatre for the Performing Arts
713 Congress Avenue
(512) 472-5470,
(512) 469-SHOW (7469) (Star Tickets)
www.austintheatrealliance.org

On a stage once graced by the Ziegfeld Follies, Helen Hayes, George M. Cohan, John Philip Sousa, the Marx Brothers, and more of history's great performers, the Paramount Theatre presents top artists from Austin and around the country. Built in 1915 as the Majestic Theatre, a vaudeville house that presented variety acts, this elegantly restored venue was designed by one of the most respected theater architects in the United States, John Eberson of Chicago. This is one of the few theaters left in the country that showed the movie *Casablanca* when it was originally released more than half a century ago.

Now listed on the National Register of Historic Places, the Paramount itself is one of the city's main attractions. And the attractions on stage are just as important. This major performing arts venue, which seats nearly 1,300 persons, is active almost 300 nights of the year, bringing live theater, dance, music, and classic movies to persons of all ages. This is where Austin's own blockbuster comedy *Greater Tuna* (www.greatertuna.com) got its start and where the two *Tuna* sequels, including 1998's *Red, White and Tuna,* packed the house. *The Foreigner,* another highlight of the Paramount's past, starred *Tuna* creators Jaston Williams and Joe Sears and was co-produced by Austinite Charles Duggan, who also produces Broadway shows in New York.

Excellent touring shows, blockbuster revues like *Beehive* and *Rockin' Christmas Party* produced by Austin's Zachary Scott Theatre, and the success of a homegrown musical theater company have combined to make the Paramount a must-stop for people all over Central Texas. Today, more than 180,000 people attend events at the theater each year.

This theater also presents *Kids' Classics,* a wonderful series of theatrical events for children, and the Summer Classic Film Series, classic movies from the Golden Age of Hollywood. The annual *Broadway Series,* presented October through May, includes productions by Broadway Texas as well as touring shows like *Damn Yankees* and *Kiss of the Spiderwoman,* some of which are duplicates of the original Broadway productions. The Paramount also presents *Extras,* which have included Debbie Reynolds, Maureen McGovern, Spalding Gray, and the nationally acclaimed percussion dance troupe Stomp. The theater also presents numerous dance performances by Austin-based, national, and international companies.

In 2000 the Paramount joined with its neighbor, the State Theater, to create the Austin Theatre Alliance, which offers season packages that include productions at both. Tickets may be purchased in person at the Paramount box office or over the phone with a credit card through Star Tickets. Tickets may also be purchased at Star Tickets centers in Albertson's grocery stores around town, at Waterloo Records, and at other outlets.

Riverbend Centre
4214 North Loop 360 (Capital of Texas Highway)
(512) 327-9416,
(512) 469-SHOW (Star Tickets)
www.riverbendcentre.com

Musical and theatrical stars performing in a house of prayer? Well, yes. This elegant 2,300-seat venue in one of Austin's most picturesque settings opened for public events in 2002 and has drawn acts like bluegrass singer Alison Krauss, pop star Kenny Loggins, and the Austin Symphony Orchestra. An 80-piece orchestra worked on the soundtrack of Austinite Robert Rodriguez's *Spy Kids 2* movie here. Built in

1998 as the Riverbend (Baptist) Church's "Home for Hope," this imposing hall, now one of Austin's largest performing arts venues, books musical groups, and public speakers and aims to also host theatrical productions. Constructed in a classical style (the interior layout resembles a Greek amphitheater), the limestone-and-wood facility has won a number of design awards.

**The State Theater
719 Congress Avenue
(512) 472-5143,
(512) 469-SHOW (4769) (Star Tickets)
www.austintheatrealliance.org**

This performing arts center presents shows of all kinds throughout the year but is home to the State Theater Company, an outstanding professional company operating in Austin since 1982. The State Theater Company presents an eclectic array of productions during its five-play mainstage season that runs from September through June. Productions include musicals, comedies, dramas, and at least one world premiere each season. The theater's commitment to developing and producing new and award-winning works has led to the staging of outstanding productions, including *The Dead Presidents' Club* and *The Night Hank Williams Died* by well-known Texas native Larry L. King. Included in the 2004 lineup was the world premiere of *Nightswim,* by Steve Moore. This unique play, set in Austin in 1959, is an homage to Austin icons Roy Bedichek, J. Frank Dobie, and Walter Prescott Webb (see The Literary Scene chapter).

After leading a somewhat nomadic life for many years, performing in different theaters around town, the company (formerly known as Live Oak) moved into the State Theater on historic Congress Avenue in 1995. An extensive renovation of the old movie house and the adjacent building resulted in another major performing arts center in downtown Austin. The State, located next door to Austin's classic Paramount Theatre, joined the Paramount in 2000 to create the Austin Theatre Alliance,

so now it's possible to get a season package that includes productions at both. The renovated State Theater, which includes two theaters of 400 and 100 seats each, rehearsal halls, scene and costume shops, and offices made its debut in 1999. The expanded facility allowed the company to double the size of its School of Acting, which provides professional training to children, teens, and adults. The theater also produces the annual Harvest Festival of New American Plays, a three-day event that awards cash prizes to playwrights and includes readings of new plays.

**University of Texas Performing
Arts Center
23rd Street and East Campus Drive
(512) 471-1444,
(512) 477-6060 (Texas Box Office)
www.utpac.org**

We've said it before, and we'll say it again. Having one of the country's largest universities in our own backyard has its advantages. The UT Performing Arts Center (PAC) is one of the biggies. This huge network of theaters, studios, rehearsal halls, and classrooms spreads to several campus locations. At the heart of the PAC system is the complex at 23rd and East Campus Drive.

This immense $44 million structure, which houses two theaters as well as rehearsal halls, offices, and massive support facilities, is one of the finest performing arts centers in the United States. Bass Concert Hall, UT's flagship theater, is a 3,000-seat auditorium with an atrium lobby and an orchestra pit that can accommodate even the largest musical group. The Austin Symphony Orchestra, Austin Lyric Opera, and Ballet Austin all present main stage productions here. Some of the finest touring artists and companies in the country also perform at Bass Concert Hall. Big Broadway touring shows in the recent past have included *Cats* and *The Graduate,* starring Jerry Hall. (Bass is scheduled to close in the spring of 2006 for an 18-month renovation, which may cause more than a few venue crises). Also in this complex is the McCollough Theatre, which seats 400 people and is used by both professional and student performers.

Many people, including local residents, tend to think of the Performing Arts Center as the Bass complex alone. In fact, there's much more. The Performing Arts Center also includes Bates Recital Hall in the Music Building adjacent to Bass. The recital hall is a 700-seat theater designed for acoustic excellence and equipped with a three-story pipe organ. This theater hosts musical performances by some of the best virtuoso performers of the day, as well as leading names in jazz, chamber and organ music, and more.

Other theaters around campus that contribute to the Performing Arts Center are the B. Iden Payne Theatre, a 500-seat facility used for both professional events and student theatrical productions, and Hogg Auditorium, a recently reintroduced theater that's almost as large as the Paramount and is also used for both professional and student events. A few smaller theaters and a dance studio complete the Performing Arts Center.

While the PAC is perhaps most known to the public at large for the world-class events it presents, we can't fail to mention the quality and range of many student productions offered at some of these theaters throughout the school year. UT students of theater, dance, film, and music present shows that are definitely worthwhile for any fan of the performing arts. Texas Box Office, with locations in H.E.B. grocery stores all over the area, is an easy way to buy tickets to PAC events. Tickets are also on sale directly at the PAC box office and other locations in town.

Zachary Scott Theatre Center
1510 Toomey Road
(512) 476-0541
www.zachscott.com
One of Austin's most exciting and innovative professional theater companies, Zachary Scott has been wowing Austin audiences for years with its broad spectrum of plays and musicals, including many

performed for the first time by a regional theater in the United States. Additionally, Zach (as it's known locally) has given Austin audiences wildly popular revues such as *Beehive* as well as *Shear Madness,* the longest-running play in Austin history.

Zach, Central Texas's oldest resident theater, began in 1933 when it was incorporated as the Austin Civic Theatre. The theater took a major leap forward in 1972 with construction of its first 240-seat theater at the present location. The theater was renamed that year in honor of Zachary Scott, an Austin-raised actor who went on to a successful Hollywood film career. A second 130-seat theater, and costume shop, classroom, rehearsal studio, and administrative offices were added later, during the time Zach was moving from community theater to become one of Austin's premier professional theaters. Several of Zach's shows have been so popular that the company has needed to rent Austin's larger Paramount Theatre to accommodate all audiences. A new 500-seat auditorium at South Lamar Boulevard and Riverside Drive is in the early planning stage.

Zach presents 8 to 10 productions during its yearlong season that runs from September through August on both stages, the main Kleberg Stage and the Whisenhunt Arena Stage. The Zachary Scott Theatre Center also operates a hugely popular Performing Arts School that draws thousands of children, teens, and adults each year. Zach's Project Inter-Act, a professional company of adult actors, performs children's shows for school students throughout the Southwest, including some outstanding original productions. Theater buffs should include a visit to Zach Scott on any tour of Austin.

The Outdoor Stage

Zilker Hillside Theater
2206 William Barton Drive
(512) 477-5335
www.ci.austin.tx.us/zilker/hillside.htm

Casual outdoor free arts! What better tribute to Austin than this great venue on a natural grassy amphitheater that hosts some of our city's most anticipated free shows. Start with the annual Zilker Summer Musical, an Austin tradition for nearly 50 years. This big, splashy show draws more than 2,000 persons a night to Zilker Park for some of the best outdoor performances Austin offers.

Another outstanding Austin event, Shakespeare Under the Stars (see the Austin Shakespeare Festival in The Gypsies listing), held each fall for more than 20 years, draws upward of 15,000 persons to the Hillside for a four-week engagement of an excitingly staged and costumed Shakespeare play. Past performances have included *Macbeth* and *Twelfth Night,* produced in association with the National Shakespeare Company. Officially named the Beverly S. Sheffield Zilker Hillside Theater, this spot also is home to the annual Trail of Lights Festival in December, the event that kicks off Zilker Park's wonderful Trail of Lights. You don't have to wait for an annual event to experience this great Austin theater, however. Bring a blanket and a picnic basket and enjoy the outdoors while watching any number of dance, musical, or theatrical events held in this comfy spot near Barton Springs Pool that has room for more than 2,500 persons. All events are free, but parking costs $2.00.

The Warehouse Stages

Arts on Real
2826 Real Street
(512) 472-2787
www.artsonreal.com
"Yelavich . . . is almost single-handedly responsible for the most exciting, most incredible, most downright stupendous theatre miracle that's hit Austin in many a year." That's what the *Austin Chronicle* had to say in 2003 about the grand opening of Blake Yelavich's East Austin space, Arts on Real. This former meat plant and

ice factory has been converted into a 120-seat theater, complete with a bar and gallery and including rehearsal space and a scene shop. This is now home to Yelavich's Naughty Austin Productions, which, as its name implies, has produced risqué shows as well as gay-themed plays. In fact, it was Naughty Austin's hit production of *Making Porn* in 2002 that helped finance this new facility. Naughty Austin, which has since branched out into more traditional theater, first gained prominence around here by producing musical parodies of local theater productions, a la Forbidden Broadway. Yelavich, a director, producer, writer, and actor, is now executive director of the nonprofit Arts Entertainment Group Inc. that operates the new space. When Arts on Real opened, rental dates were immediately snatched up by other groups around the city, so check the Web site for a listing of upcoming shows.

Auditorium on Waller Creek
710 East 41st Street
(512) 467–7756
Started in 1980, Different Stages (www.main.org/diffstages) is a nonprofit community theater company that produces works by playwrights that are defining forces in theater: Moliére, Shakespeare, Shaw, and O'Neill, to name a few. The company also has been the first to introduce Austin to new playwrights and has produced original works by Austin playwrights Ann Ciccolella and Tom White. Under the artistic directorship of Norman Blumensaadt, the company has presented more than 80 plays, including romantic, neoclassic, realistic, and surrealistic. Different Stages presents a full season of performances from the beginning of November to July, both here and at other Austin locations. Also presenting shows at this venue is the Onstage Theatre Company, (512-445-9866, www.onstagetheatreco.org), which was founded as a showcase for vintage comedies and dramas. Its goal is to present quality presentations of classic theater to

audiences in landmark theatres and opera houses throughout Texas. Its list of past productions includes *Educating Rita, Barefoot in the Park, The Gin Game,* and *The Mousetrap.*

Austin Playhouse
3601 South Congress Avenue, Building C
(512) 476-0084
www.austinplayhouse.com
Home to the Austin Playhouse theater troupe, this facility is located in the sensitively redeveloped Penn Field complex off South Congress Avenue. Built in 1914 at a flight training center for the Army Air Corps, the building reopened as a 150-seat theater in 2002. It also has a bar, coffee shop, and gallery. Austin Playhouse, which says it "is dedicated to providing opportunities for Austin artists and audiences to celebrate the human experience," is a professional company that presents four shows during its September-to-June season. The lineup has included original plays, including *Travesties* by Austin playwright Tom Stoppard, as well as such perennial favorites as *Kiss Me Kate* and *Private Lives.*

R-E or E-R? Austin can't seem to collectively decide whether to call its performing arts companies and venues "theaters," the American spelling, or "theatres," the British version. Some venues use both. If you're trying to find one of these spots on the Internet, check which comes first: the "E" or the "R." There's also "teatro," the Spanish way.

Blue Theater
916 Springdale Road
(512) 927-1118
www.bluetheater.org
A former truck shop built in the 1950s, this 100-seat theater presents productions by many young Austin troupes,

including Refraction Arts Project (www.refractionarts.org), the Rubber Repertory, the Dirigo Group, and a chick and a dude productions (see The Gypsies listing that follows). Located in a warehouse complex in East Austin, it opened as an arts venue in 2002 to offer theatrical productions, visual art, dance, music, and film.

Dougherty Arts Center
1110 Barton Springs Road
(512) 397-1471,
(512) 454-TIXS (box office)
www.ci.austin.tx.us/dougherty/theaterhome.htm
Built in the 1940s as a Naval and Marine Reserve Center, this wonderful facility was taken over by the Austin Parks and Recreation Department in 1978 and turned into one of the busiest arts venues in town. The Dougherty Arts Center (DAC) has it all: a comfortable 150-seat theater that's always hosting one show or another, an 1,800-square-foot art gallery, classrooms, and plenty of studio-lab spaces. It's impossible to list all the arts-related activities that go on at this center.

Teatro Humanidad has performed here, as has Austin's Ballet East Dance Theater. Teatro DAC also has hosted some shows for the Big Stinkin' International Improv and Sketch Festival, an annual event that draws comics from around the world to Austin. The Julia C. Butridge Gallery at DAC hosts art shows of all kinds by Austin-area artists and arts organizations. Exhibitions have been organized by Women Printmakers of Austin, the Texas Music Museum, Austin Community College, and La Peña, a nonprofit organization dedicated to promoting Latino art and artists. La Peña's annual Serie Print Project, presented here in the spring, is a great way to see up-and-coming artists.

Austin's only city-run arts complex, DAC provides arts enrichment to citizens of all ages and economic levels. Admission prices to DAC performing arts events are often very reasonable, while gallery admission is always free. Many of Austin's other excellent arts programs are operated out of the Dougherty Arts Center, including Art in Public Places, which commissions artworks for placement in city facilities for all to see and enjoy. (Be sure to see our chapter on Attractions for information on some of Austin's easily accessible artworks.) DAC runs a wide variety of programs for adults and students, including the nationally recognized Totally Cool, Totally Art program, in which professional artists work with teenagers at local recreation centers. DAC sponsors art classes in many genres and runs a wonderful summer camp program.

Esther's Follies
525 East Sixth Street
(512) 320-0553
www.esthersfollies.com

We'll tell you more about this laugh-a-minute riot of a comedy troupe in our chapter on Nightlife. They call themselves Texas's premier musical comedy revue, and we can't argue with that. We've taken more than one out-of-town guest to see Esther's Follies' great show, which combines some classic routines with constantly updated political satire. The follies can be found in a converted 1800s-era building on Austin's historic and hip East Sixth Street.

The Hideout
617 Congress Avenue
(512) 443-3688
www.thehideout.org

Near downtown's Paramount and State theaters, this inviting coffeehouse/bar also includes performance space for 150 souls on two stages and offers comedy, theater, music, and local film screenings. One of its unique offerings has been No Shame Theater, an open-mic night every other Friday for scriptwriters and others who want to test their material before a live audience. Opened as The Hideout in 1999, it's in a 1846 building (see the Nightlife chapter).

Hyde Park Theatre
511 West 43rd Street
(512) 479-7530,
(512) 479-7529 (box office)
www.hydeparktheatre.com

Since its founding in 1992, Hyde Park Theatre has grown into one of Austin's most well-respected and popular small troupes, presenting bold alternative works by both Austin artists and others from around the country, including several world premiere events each season.

Hyde Park also runs the largest and most intriguing performance festival in the Southwest: Fronterafest. This annual five-week fringe festival, held in January and February, provides a venue for hundreds of high-caliber local, regional and national artists who present nearly 100 separate acts (see our Annual Events and Festivals chapter). Fronterafest is produced in collaboration with Austin Script Works, a group dedicated to supporting emerging playwrights and developing new dramatic works. In addition to producing its own shows, Hyde Park Theatre also serves as performance home to other Austin gypsy troupes and fringe artists.

The Off Center
2211-A Hidalgo Street
(512) 474-7866

This 93-seat theater in a converted feed store presents shows by two of our city's most "Austin-tacious" theater troupes: Rude Mechanicals and Salvage Vanguard Theater. Founded in 1995, Rude Mechanicals (512-476-7833, www.rudemechs.com) has become one of Austin's most renowned and original companies and is known for its enormously creative—and brave—theatrical vision. The company received national attention and acclaim for its stage adaptation of *Lipstick Traces,* which played in New York in 2001 and other American cities in 2002. This ensemble-based company has been named the city's Best Theater Company four years in a row by the *Austin Chronicle*'s Readers' Poll. It also manages The

Off Center theater. Salvage Vanguard Theater (512-474-7886, www.salvagevanguard.org), is an exciting experimental company that has earned a reputation for presenting hot new writers to Austin in shows that, in recent seasons, were paired with a local band—so music fans no longer have to miss out on an interesting theater experience. Catering to Austin's hip crowd, Salvage Vanguard is known for performances that rock the ceiling. The nonprofit company presents several main stage shows, some of them world premieres, between March and December. Over the winter holidays SVT also presents its annual five-minute new-play festival and singalong. It's a blast.

Santa Cruz Center for Culture
1805 East Seventh Street
(512) 478-9717

This established cultural center is home to Austin's well-respected Aztlan Dance Company (see the Dance listing in this chapter), as well as the ProArts Collective and Proyecto Teatro. The theater, which opened in 1988 in a converted WWI-era warehouse, seats 120 persons and has become a center for both well-established and up-and-coming Latino arts projects on the East Side.

Tillery Street Theater
701 Tillery Street
(512) 472-2001

Tillery Street Theater opened in 2002, giving second rise to a former bakery and becoming one more addition to East Austin's growing cultural scene. With 200 seats and plenty of parking, Tillery Street is one of the largest warehouse theaters around town and has real potential to become a great performing arts space. In fact, Teatro Humanidad (512-389-0892, www.teatrohumanidad.com) is now staging several important productions here. Now under the artistic directorship of Roxanne Schroeder-Arce, Austin's bilingual theater company is a strong force in Latino theater. From 1994's *I Don't Have to Show You No Stinkin' Badges!* to the

acclaimed production of *Petra's Pecado* by Austinite Rupert Reyes that highlighted the company's first full season in 1997-98 and up to the present, Teatro Humanidad continues to impress Austin audiences. This theater company also performs at some of Austin's most well-known venues, including the Paramount Theatre and the Dougherty Arts Center. Don't worry if English is the only language you speak. This troupe goes out of its way to reach all members of its audience. The company presents several main stage productions each year, as well as works by the Latino Comedy Project it sponsors. LCP (www.lcp.org) is an award-winning showcase for Latino comedy writers, directors, and performers. Teatro Humanidad also has a Youth Theatre division that includes a Children's Play tour that performs across Texas.

The Velveeta Room
521 East Sixth Street
(512) 320-0198

Like its neighbor, Esther's Follies, the Velveeta Room is a beloved comedy spot on hip Sixth Street (see our listing in the Nightlife chapter).

The Vortex
2307 Manor Road
(512) 478-5282,
(512) 454-TIXS box office
www.vortexrep.org

Home to Austin's Vortex Repertory Company since 1994, the Vortex has become the place to go to see original cutting-edge performances that have included *Wisdom of the Crone,* conceived and directed by producing artistic director and Vortex founder Bonnie Cullum. Among the leaders of Austin's alternative theater scene, Vortex has produced scores of successful works since it was founded in 1988. World premieres, new plays, Texas premieres, and vibrant works by Shakespeare have all been presented on the Vortex stage. Vortex Productions is also very well known for its other incarnation, Ethos, an electronic music and multimedia performance troupe. Among the troupe's original works are the award-winning cybernetic opera *The X & Y Trilogy* and *Elytra,* the story of four female insect-angels who awaken in Heaven and find it in need of repair. Audiences love the extraordinary spectacle of these shows.

This East Austin theater, a once-abandoned warehouse that has been converted to an intimate 90-seat venue with comfortable theater seats, is used by other individual performers and theatrical companies for shows of all kinds. Vortex presents several major productions a year as well as a number of smaller performances that showcase this company's talents. Vortex also has earned a reputation in Austin for presenting shows by nationally known performance artists. Whether it's a simple one-person show with only a chair on stage or a full-scale production with elaborate scenery, lighting, and sound, the Vortex has done it all. The theater also sponsors Summer Youth Theater, which brings teenagers from around Austin to the theater to create, produce, and perform a theatrical show. Other Austin theater companies also perform here.

The Gypsies

Austin Shakespeare Festival
P.O. Box 683, Austin 78767
(512) 454-BARD (2273)
www.austinshakespeare.org

Mention Austin Shakespeare Festival around these parts and folks will immediately think of the wonderful free outdoor Shakespeare Under the Stars plays produced annually for the past two decades at the Zilker Hillside Theatre. These days, however, the name implies much, much more. Austin Shakespeare Festival now offers a year-round season of plays, both indoors and out. Additionally, while the primary focus is on Shakespeare, the company's productions are not limited to works by the Bard. Guy Roberts has led this professional company in delightful

new directions since his first season as artistic director in 2002–03. The results are impressive. In 2003 ASF received 20 nominations for local theater awards—more nominations than in all ASF's history combined—and Robert's production of *Henry V* received the year's B. Iden Payne Award as Outstanding Drama of the year, ASF's first-ever Outstanding Drama award. Roberts, an actor, director, and educator who has served in many capacities on the Austin theater scene over the years, now brings entertaining, stimulating and, most important, extremely accessible Shakespeare to our city. ASF most often performs at Zilker and at Austin Playhouse.

a chick & a dude productions
2200 Willow Creek Drive, #811
(512) 444-6920

Austin American–Statesman art critic Michael Barnes called them "the cool new rookies of Austin theatre." With good reason, too. This "chick," Melissa Livingston, and "dude," Shanon Weaver, took this town by storm with a hit show that garnered three of the city's most prestigious theater awards in 2003. These two long-time actors and playwrights formed a chick & a dude productions (yes, all lowercase) in 2002 when they decided to branch out. The title of their play, *HIT,* turned out to be prophetic, as indeed it was! Written by Weaver and directed by Livingston, the play won B. Iden Payne awards for Outstanding Original Script, Outstanding Director of a Drama, and Outstanding Cast Performance—beating out some much more established companies. Livingston and Weaver say their main goal is to be storytellers, creating "simple stories, told simply." Since its stellar beginning, the company also has done *Virginia,* rooted in the classic editorial "Yes, Virginia, There is a Santa Claus," and *Did You Say Love?* The two share writing responsibilities and mount productions at Hyde Park Theatre, the Blue Theater, or wherever they can find a space.

The Bedlam Faction
P.O. Box 4992, Austin 78765-4992
(512) 589-2332
www.bedlamfaction.com
Witty, playful theater. Those are the words
that come to mind when describing this
young theater collective formed in 2000
by a group of UT-trained Shakespearean
actors. The Bedlam Faction stages shows
the cast obviously enjoys doing—and the
joy spills right off the stage to the audience. The *Austin American–Statesman* said
this about one of Bedlam's most popular
shows: "*Reefer Madness* offers a night of
chuckles without requiring the audience be
in an altered state. Be careful, though,
because after just one show you just might
find yourself addicted to the always sur-
prising Bedlam Faction." Bedlam is an
ensemble-based group, meaning that no
one person heads the company and the
cast is responsible for directing itself. "This
allows the cast to be more involved and
invested in the process and the product of
the play," says John Botti, one of Bedlam's
many co-artistic directors. The up-and-
coming collective has already been nominated for several Austin theater awards
You can catch their shows most often at
Hyde Park Theatre or the Off Center.

The Dirigo Group
2501 Wickersham Lane, Suite 1932
(512) 440-9063
www.thedirigogroup.com
The Dirigo Group can always be counted
on to offer an imaginative approach to
both its adaptations and its original
shows. In fact, this troupe won the 2003
Austin Chronicle Critics' Award for Best
Theatre for a Fresh Look. "The dirigites'
inventiveness, commitment, and bravery
guaranty that the world will look a little
different after you leave their show," the
Chronicle lauded. Formed in 1999, this
troupe has been honored with many of
the Austin Circle of Theater's B. Iden
Payne awards as well. Led by co-artistic
directors Judson Jones, Christa Kimlicko
Jones, Lowell Bartholomee, and Ellie
McBride, Dirigo staged Bartholomee's first

full-length play, *The Middle of the Night*, in
2003. The company presents one of its
own original plays each year, one adaptation (or "reconsideration") of a classic, and
a new play by a known playwright, such
as its 2004 production of *The Mercy Seat*
by Neil LaBute. Dirigo works out of the
Blue Theater and others.

Tongue and Groove Theatre
1400 West 51st Street
(512) 502-0649
www.tongueandgroovetheatre.com
Founded in 1995 by four veterans of Fort
Worth's innovative Hip Pocket Theatre,
Tongue and Groove Theatre produces fun,
farcical, family-friendly plays that often
feature live bands and are reminiscent of
vaudeville, slapstick, or *commedia del-
l'arte*. Whether Tongue and Groove is producing its own original plays or works by
other playwrights, the company always
aims to integrate acting, dance, mime and
music. From its first production of *The
Billy-Club Puppets* by Federico Garcia-
Lorca in 1995, to the more recent *Seven
Wonders of the World (Plus One)*, Tongue
and Groove has managed to find that
magic formula that delights audiences
and critics alike. David Yeakle, Art Davis,
Cynthia Griffin-Davis, and Ellen Reeder
Yeakle have created a company that the
Austin Chronicle says "produces dreams,
full of larger-than-life spectacle, odd fantasy, and ribald humor. . . ." Tongue and
Groove often performs at the Vortex or
the Blue Theatre.

DANCE AND MUSIC

More and more Austin audiences are getting the "pointe" about Austin's rich dance
scene, which includes a number of established companies and even more individual dancers and choreographers who
bring their unique styles to stages all over
the city. In addition to the dance companies we've listed here, be sure to look for
special performances by troupes formed
for a specific production. Austin dancers

offer a wonderful cross section of styles, including classical ballet, tap, modern, postmodern, and folklorico. The leader among Austin dancer/choreographers is Deborah Hay, nationally recognized as one of the pioneers of postmodern New Dance. If you love dance, be sure to look for occasional performances by the Deborah Hay Dance Company (www.deborah hay.com). Andrea Ariel and Toni Bravo are other Austin dancers of note. Austin's main dance organization, Dance Umbrella, also sponsors dance and performance-art shows throughout the year by Austin talent as well as nationally and internationally known performers (see the Arts Organizations listing in this chapter)

Whether you like a toe-tapping good time, the skirt-swirling grandeur of a Mexican folk dance, the awesome power and grace of a dancer on pointe, or the stylized foot- and bodywork of modern dance, you'll be inspired by Austin's dance performances.

While Texas's mecca for classical music artists is about 70 miles east of Austin in Round Top (see our Day Trips chapter), you'll be pleased to know that you don't have to travel to hear exciting ensembles. In fact, in 2003 Austin's classical music scene took a giant leap forward when the University of Texas snagged highly coveted string ensemble, the Miro' Quartet (www.miroquartet.com) as its resident quartet. This internationally renowned foursome performs for the public at large. Additionally, Austin claims about two dozen classical music groups, about half choral, half instrumental. The two mentioned here are among Austin's leaders, but look, too, for outstanding performances by the Austin Choral Union, the Austin Vocal Arts Ensemble, River City Pops, the Austin Lyric Opera Chorus, and the Texas Chamber Consort. Those interested in performing will discover that these and many other musical groups, including barbershop and gospel choruses, accept new members by audition. Austin also claims several groups for children.

The classical guitar scene is also alive and well in Austin and has attracted enough outstanding guitarists to maintain the Austin Classical Guitar Society. The only nationally syndicated classical guitar program is produced right here in Austin and airs out of radio station KMFA. The crème de la crème of Austin's classical guitarists is world-class player and recording artist Adam Holzman (www.adamholz man.com). This virtuoso, who plays recital halls throughout the world, including Carnegie Hall, has won many prestigious international guitar competitions and has created UT's classical guitar program. In a music city dominated by singer/songwriters and rock 'n' rollers blasting chords through amplifiers, Holzman is the artist the *Austin American–Statesman* has called "the best guitar player in Austin you've never heard of."

Dance

Aztlan Dance Company
Santa Cruz Center
1805 East Seventh Street
(512) 478-9717
www.aztlandance.com
Both the critics and the public are raving about this dance company, which combines original contemporary choreography with traditional Latino folk steps, often set to the music of popular Latino recording artists. Founded in 1974, this company for many years performed mainly the classic regional folk dances of Mexico. In the past few years, however, choreographer and general director Roen Salinas has introduced a modern format that reflects the *danza folklorico* heritage but addresses the Hispanic culture of today's Texas. Instead of the flamboyant costumes typical of some regional dances of Mexico, for example, Aztlan dancers have worn blue jeans and T-shirts while dancing to the music of Los Lobos. In 2003 the company explored further facets of Latino culture, including sounds from the Big Band era of the 1940s and

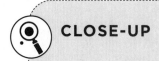

Lights! Camera! Austin!

One of the hottest tickets in Hollywood these days is a boarding pass to Austin. Filmmaking has come of age in Central Texas as many of Hollywood's brightest stars, directors, and producers discover what Austin-based movie moguls have known all along: These parts offer much more than just a great backdrop.

In just the past few years, Austin has become Texas's No. 1 moviemaking hub and has been listed among the top 10 filmmaking centers in the world by the independent trade magazine, *Moviemaker.* In 2003 Austin ranked No. 4 on *Moviemaker*'s list, behind Vancouver, Toronto, and New York. Feature films shot in and around Austin had combined budgets of more than $200 million in 2003 alone. That's a dramatic increase from the tallies of the mid-1980s, when Austin projects were budgeted at about $10 million a year.

Hollywood rolled out the red carpet—and much more—in 2003 when Austin director Robert Rodriguez staged the world premiere of *Spy Kids 3* at the Paramount Theatre. Two blocks of Congress Avenue, Austin's main downtown artery, were closed for a giant street party that included carnival rides, Texas barbecue, and live music. Director Richard Linklater (who *Chicago Sun-Times* film critic Roger Ebert called "the indie genius of Austin, Texas") also presented the regional premiere of his latest hit, *School of Rock,* here at home, while our city witnessed the rise of another local writer/director

when young Tim McCanlies opened *Secondhand Lions* in Austin.

Movie stars Sandra Bullock and Mary Steenburgen and producer Lynda Obst (*Sleepless in Seattle, Contact*) are just three of the Hollywood exiles who came here for the work and stayed for the freestyle kind of life Central Texas offers. Dennis Quaid appears to be next. Our local movie barons aren't the only ones bringing this region to a theater near you, however. If you've seen 2004's *Cheer Up,* starring Tommy Lee Jones, the latest version of *The Texas Chainsaw Massacre, The Life of David Gale* with Kevin Spacey, or *The Alamo,* starring Billy Bob Thornton, Dennis Quaid, and Jason Patric, you've seen movies made right around here. Of course you may not have known it, but that's the magic of the "Third Coast," as some like to call Austin. For *The Alamo,* set designers recreated the San Antonio of 1836 on 52 acres of private ranchland just outside Austin. (The set could open up for tours, we hear). The Chicago skyline that serves as the backdrop for the final scene in John Travolta's 1996 film *Michael* was shot on our own Sixth Street, while the mayor's office turned in a fine performance as the Pentagon in *Courage Under Fire,* and Symphony Square became a Moroccan market in *Secondhand Lions.*

In fact, the variety of movie locales in Central Texas is one big attraction for filmmakers. Want hills? Austin's got plenty of hills. How about a pine forest?

There's that nearby, too, as are prairies, lakes, and ranchland. Need a small town that time has forgotten? Austin is surrounded by towns that will fill that bill, complete with those old courthouses, town squares, and general stores that make all of us movie buffs willingly suspend our disbelief. Mild weather and sunny skies almost year-round add to Austin's appeal.

And there's more. The film term is "crew up." Anyone who sits through the credits that roll on and on at the end of a movie realizes the brain power that goes into making a film these days. Austin's film culture abounds with experts in almost every creative facet of filmmaking, from directors, screenwriters, and cinematographers to casting directors and film editors, makeup artists, and art directors, location managers and production managers, animators and special-effects magicians. Austin even has important entertainment lawyers and animal trainers. Then there's Harry Knowles, the young Austinite who turned his passion for movies into one of the hottest Web sites in the country for fellow denizens of dark theaters. Ain't It Cool News, at www.aint-it-cool-news.com, includes his own brand of movie reviews as well as the inside scoop on the filmmaking business around the country. Knowles is an industry unto himself and has been featured in major magazine articles around the country. (Now, we hear, he's writing a screenplay).

With so much creative talent packed into Austin, it's no wonder our city hosts two nationally known film festivals each year, as well as several other smaller fests that draw plenty a movie buff. The South by Southwest Film Festival and Conference (see our Close-up on SXSW in the Annual Events and Festivals chapter) and the Austin Film Festival, both more than a decade old now, draw many of the country's biggest films and filmmakers, as well as up-and-coming screenwriters.

Of all the major players in Austin today, Linklater is the guru of the city's vibrant film culture. Linklater, whose $23,000 independent film *Slacker,* set in Austin, grossed more than a million dollars in 1991, proved to Hollywood that Austin has what it takes to make lucrative films. Linklater has followed up with many more hits, including *Dazed and Confused,* starring University of Texas grads Matthew McConaughey and Renee Zellweger, *SubUrbia,* and *School of Rock.* He also established the Austin Film Center, complete with editing suites and a viewing room for dailies, a first for Austin. Before Linklater found major success, he helped establish the Austin Film Society in 1985.

The Film Society, one of the driving forces in Austin cinema today, has shown hundreds of free films, mostly experimental, repertory, and international films rarely seen in cities the size of Austin. In 1996 the Film Society created the Texas Filmmakers Production Fund, which has given tens of thousands of dollars in grants to budding filmmakers across Texas. The Film Society is credited with developing an audience appreciation for film that is unheard of in many other American cities.

The contributions of Rodriguez and Mike Judge to Austin film also are enormous. Rodriguez, whose 1992 flick *El Mariachi* skyrocketed him to the big time, followed up with the sequels *Desperado* and *Once Upon a Time in Mexico.* He also made the enormously popular *Spy Kids* trilogy, filmed in Austin of course. Judge, a filmmaker and the creator of the wildly successful animated television shows *Beavis and Butt-head* and *King of the Hill,* is another who has put his heart and talent behind Austin's film industry.

What does this movie mania mean to those of us who don't know a grip from a gaffer but are first in line to enjoy the finished product once it hits our local theaters? Plenty. In addition to the film festivals, movie buffs can find unique film fare at the Dobie Theatre next to the UT campus and the Alamo Drafthouse Theatres in North Austin and downtown (see our Nightlife chapter). Of course there's also always the chance of sighting a real movie star—or even getting a job as an extra in a film.

Some of the credit for Austin's rise to fame in the film industry of late goes to the City of Austin and the Austin Film Society, which respectively own and operate Austin Studios, a huge complex of sound stages and other filmmaking facilities in what were once airplane hangars at the old Robert Mueller airport. The University of Texas, whose film school has always provided local talent, announced in 2003 the creation of Burnt Orange Productions, a groundbreaking project to build its own independent movie studio in which students and Hollywood heavyweights make films together—for profit.

Musicians, artists, and writers have always found a haven in Austin. Some say it's Austin itself that brings out the creative side in people. But most agree that these creative communities feed off one another's enthusiasm, talent, and commitment to their work, which in turn inspires others. Austin is brimming with lone filmmakers working on little money and even less sleep to produce a film good enough to make it into a festival—and some do. In *Michael,* John Travolta's character tells his friend, "Remember, Sparky, no matter what they tell you, you can never have too much sugar." Filmmakers could say the same about Austin.

the pre-Columbian jungles of Veracruz. The company also added comedy dance dramas to its repertoire.

Aztlan still does Mexican folk dances, and does them extremely well, but this new choreography adds an exciting artistic dimension to the troupe. The company is based at East Austin's Santa Cruz Center but also performs at the Paramount and the Bass Concert Hall. Aztlan also has performed at venues all over the country and in Hong Kong and Great Britain. Academia Aztlan, which aims to promote a greater understanding of the Hispanic cultural arts, offers dance classes, workshops, lectures, art exhibits, and more at the Santa Cruz Center and elsewhere in Austin.

Ballet Austin
3002 Guadalupe Street
(512) 476-9051,
(512) 469-SHOW (7469) (Star Tickets)
www.balletaustin.com
Austin's premier classical ballet troupe has soared to new heights since 2000, when Stephen Mills stepped up as artistic director. Mills, who has been with the organization since 1987 as dancer, choreographer, and associate artistic director, received rave reviews and attention from across the country for his world-premiere production of *Hamlet* during his first year as director. In 2002 the company performed sold-out shows of *A Midsummer Night's Dream* at the Kennedy Center in Washington, D.C. Mills's national and international accomplishments as both a dancer and a choreographer are astounding. Under his leadership Ballet Austin is becoming one of the nation's finest developing ballet organizations.

Ballet Austin presents five seasonal ballets, including the much anticipated annual performances of *The Nutcracker* in December. Other Austin favorites have included performances of *Firebird, Ulysses,* and *Cinderella.* This accomplished company traces its roots to 1956, when it was chartered as the Austin Ballet Society. Over the years, the ballet evolved from a civic, all-volunteer organization to become a professional organization.

One major aspect of this company is the Ballet Austin Academy, also established in 1956, which offers classical ballet training as well as jazz, modern dance, and fitness classes to dancers from age 3 to adult. Ballet Austin II, an apprentice program, provides professional development for the 10-member second company.

Ballet Austin's performances are held at the Bass Concert Hall on the University of Texas campus. The company also offers full-length and mixed-repertoire performances throughout Texas. This community-based company goes all out to educate school students and adults alike.

One of Ballet Austin's most popular programs is the Fire House Focus. The public is invited to Ballet Austin's historic headquarters in an old firehouse to see part of a live rehearsal and have the opportunity to take part in an informal chat and discussion with Mills. Another program, Footlights, invites matineegoers to a half-hour preperformance discussion at the concert hall. For season tickets call the Ballet Austin box office at (512) 476-2163. The season runs from October to May.

Ballet East
At Dougherty Arts Center
(512) 385-2838,
(512) 454-TIXS (8497) (tickets)
www.balleteast.org
Founded by Rodolfo Mendez in 1982, Ballet East is a well-known community dance troupe made up of professional and emerging dancers and choreographers from many ethnic backgrounds. The company in residence in East Austin has a solid reputation for developing young dancers and for showcasing the talents of some of Austin's finest dancers and choreographers, including Toni Bravo, Andrea Ariel, and Melissa Villarreal. The company also works with guest choreographers from nationally known companies, including the Alvin Ailey American Dance School in New York and the Joyce Trisler Danscompany. Ballet East, which most often offers mixed repertoire programs, performs several times a year at various locations in Austin, most often at the Dougherty Arts Center.

Jacques Productions
www.jacquesproductions.org
Choreographer and performer Sally Jacques is the creative mastermind behind some of the most spellbinding and offbeat dance/performance art productions around these parts. She creates so-called site-specific performances, meaning that one production is developed for, say, a temporary construction scaffolding while another is developed for an airport hangar, and another for Barton Creek, and so on. A native of England,

Jacques has received many Austin awards as well as important grants in recognition of her work, including those from the National Endowment for the Arts, Art Matters of New York City, and the Texas Commission on the Arts. "As an artist I am always searching for ways to inspire and reveal a universal understanding of what it is to be alive in these times," she says on her Web site.

Kathy Dunn Hamrick Dance Company
P.O. Box 160432, Austin 78716
(512) 891-7703
www.kdhdance.com

This modern dance company has dazzled Austin audiences and critics since its first performance in 1999. *So Close,* performed with dancers moving behind, in front of, and through the audience, was named one of the Top Ten Dance Events of the year by the *Austin Chronicle.* It was no surprise, then, that by its second season the company had moved performances from a small studio to the larger State Theater to keep up with growing attendance. The company and its founder/ artistic director/dancer/choreographer Kathy Dunn Hamrick have won plenty more awards since then—and with good reason. Dunn Hamrick, a UT graduate, creates imaginative dances that often are accompanied by live musical ensembles.

Roy Lozano's Ballet Folklorico de Texas
1928-C Gaston Place Drive
(512) 928-1111
www.geocities.com/rlbftx

Be sure to check the dance listings for performances by Austin's own Ballet Folklorico de Texas, a company started in 1983 by the late Roy Lozano, a University of Texas alumnus who studied with the world-renowned Amalia Hernandez Ballet Folklorico de Mexico. Now under the artistic directorship of Jesus Chacon, this energetic company presents traditional Mexican folk dances from 19 regions of the country, each with its own dance style and stunning costumes. Ballet Folklorico is a professional troupe that per-

forms all over Texas and has also been asked to perform in Mexico. This company knows Mexican folk dance. The authentic, brightly colored costumes Ballet Folklorico is known for only add to the appeal of this fine dance troupe. Ballet Folklorico also operates a youth dance company and a dance school to train young dance talent in the many styles of traditional Mexican dance. Don't miss the company's annual show, *Fiesta,* at the Paramount in May.

Sharir+Bustamante Danceworks
P.O. Box 339, Austin 78767
(512) 232-5333
www.sbdanceworks.org

The top modern dance organization in Austin, if not the state of Texas, Sharir+Bustamante Danceworks is always on the forefront of new dance and is known for avant-garde choreography and performances. Founded in 1982 by choreographer Yacov Sharir, and later renamed to include the name of its longtime artistic codirector Jose Bustamante, this company is always on the cutting edge. In 2002, for example, S+B debuted *Honoria in Ciberspazio,* which it called "the first Internet opera."

Among S+B's most innovative projects over the years have been performances that juxtapose live dancers against computer-generated images, just one result of Sharir's experimentation with technology. The company presents a full season of performances in Austin and regularly tours regionally and nationally. The company also has been selected for international festivals in France, Spain, Israel, Canada, the Netherlands, and Portugal.

As the professional company-in-residence at the University of Texas College of Fine Arts for more than two decades, Sharir+Bustamante has collaborated with many internationally renowned companies, including Merce Cunningham. Sharir performs on UT Performing Arts Center stages as well as in other locations around Austin from November to April or May.

Tapestry Dance Company
507-B Pressler Street
(512) 474-9846
www.tapestry.org
Founded in 1989 by rhythm tap dancer
Acia Gray and ballet/jazz artist Deirdre
Strand, Tapestry is an acclaimed multiform
dance company that has delighted audiences all over Austin and in other parts of
the country during the company's national
performance tours. This professional, nonprofit company presents seasonal multiform concerts from October to June at
the Paramount and has thrilled Austin
audiences by hosting a number of international dance and musical artists. Tapestry's
annual Soul to Sole Tap Festival brings the
world's finest rhythm tap artists to Austin
for tap jams, concerts, film screenings,
and more. The company also operates a
preprofessional program and a downtown
dance academy that offers classes for
children and adults in rhythm tap, jazz,
and ballet. Tapestry is also known for
hosting numerous ethnic and cultural
events, including Irish step dancing, clog-
ging, and tango.

Music

Austin Civic Chorus
(512) 719-3300
www.chorusaustin.org
Founded in 1965 with just 32 singers,
Austin Civic Chorus today has 100 voices
ranging from high school students to senior citizens. This excellent chorus performs
two or three major choral/orchestral masterpieces a year for huge audiences from
all over Central Texas and is often a featured chorus with the Austin Symphony
Orchestra. Past performances of Austin
Civic Chorus have included *Songs of the
American People,* a concert of spirituals
and other American music that featured a
guest gospel choir and the singing voice
of Austin's accomplished Judy Arnold.
The Civic Chorus also has performed *The
Passion According to St. John* by Bach
and works from many other masters.

Other highlights of the year include
the annual Sing-It-Yourself *Messiah* in
December, a holiday tradition for hundreds of Austin families. Austin Civic Chorus also produces and performs the
annual *Summer Musical for Children,* a
fully costumed and choreographed show
presented free in eight performances
attended by more than 2,000 people. The
group works in cooperation with the
Austin Vocal Arts Ensemble to present a
choral education program in all of Austin
Independent School District's middle
schools. The Austin Civic Chorus performs
mainly in churches around Austin, most
often Northwest Hills United Methodist
Church.

Austin Lyric Opera
901 Barton Springs Road
(512) 472-5927, (512) 472-5992 (tickets)
www.austinlyricopera.org
Since its founding in 1986, Austin Lyric
Opera has grown dramatically to a seasonal attendance of nearly 35,000 persons
and has expanded its season to include 12
performances of three operas, most of
them sold-out events. That's an outstanding attendance record for a city the size of
Austin, and much of the credit goes to
Joseph McClain, the opera's cofounder and
general manager until 2003.

The company, now led by internationally renowned conductor Richard Buckley,
is known for presenting both the most
popular of the operatic repertoire as well
as works that explore the boundaries of
opera, including *The Ballad of Baby Doe,*
the company's first American work. Central Texas's only professional opera company brings major international and
American artists to Austin each season,
and the results have included many world-
class performances. *The Barber of Seville,*
Andrea Chenier, and *La Bohème* are just a
few of the performances that have highlighted past seasons.

The season features an opera every
other month from November through
March and has included a free outdoor
performance at the Zilker Hillside Theater

each October. All main stage performances are held at the Bass Concert Hall on
the University of Texas campus. Opera
attendance is on the rise nationwide, and
one of the reasons is the use of superti-
tles, the simultaneous translation into
English of the opera on a small screen
above the stage. Patrons of Austin Lyric
Opera and of operas throughout the
country no longer have to speak a foreign
language to understand the story. Austin
Lyric Opera has its own 65-member
orchestra and a 60-member semiprofes-
sional chorus.

Austin Lyric Opera has opened a new
facility, the Armstrong Community Music
School at Barton Springs Road, a modern
facility that houses a recital hall, a multimedia lab, classrooms, and teaching studios.

Austin Symphony Orchestra
1101 Red River Street
(512) 476-6064, (888) 4-MAESTRO
www.austinsymphony.org

Austin's oldest performing arts group, the
Austin Symphony Orchestra was founded
in 1911. In 1998 American Peter Bay arrived
in Austin as the symphony's conductor
and music director, following a two-year
search for the perfect conductor to lead
the orchestra to new artistic challenges
and to expand its audience even further in
Austin. Bay, especially known for his skill
at conducting large contemporary scores
and complex pieces, has introduced more
works of American composers and the-
matic programs, including music from film
scores, to the orchestra's extensive repertoire of classical music. In 2003 the symphony performed with famous singing
group the 5th Dimension. The orchestra
also presented concerts commemorating
President John F. Kennedy on the 40th
anniversary of his assassination. The performance of "JFK: The Voice of Peace" (a
work by local composer Dan Welcher)
was narrated by ABC News's Hugh Downs
and accompanied by the symphony.

The Austin Symphony Orchestra,
which performs its September-through-
May concert series at Bass Concert Hall
on the University of Texas campus, also
presents festive Holiday and Promenade
Pops Concerts at Palmer Auditorium, in
which the audience brings their own picnic dinners and sits at tables for an
evening of lighthearted music. The orchestra offers an assortment of nationally recognized youth programs, including the
Young People's Concerts in the spring,
which bring more than 28,000 elementary
students to Bass Concert Hall for live performances, and the Halloween Children's
Concert at the Paramount Theatre.

The symphony also conducts free
family concerts throughout the year and is
especially known for its popular July
Fourth concert and fireworks show on the
shores of Town Lake, which draws more
than 60,000 persons a year. (See our
Attractions chapter to learn more about
Symphony Square, the complex of historical buildings that houses symphony
offices and features an outdoor amphitheater and restaurant.)

Conspirare
(512) 476-5775
www.conspirare.org

Since its founding in 1991, Conspirare has
developed into a world-class ensemble
known for its entertaining, innovative, and
varied vocal music concerts. This professional chorus and orchestra specializes in
music for the human voice. Conspirare has
never been known to limit itself to just
one genre. Choral, classical, jazz, ethnic,
experimental, Broadway, old masterworks,
and contemporary compositions are all
presented by this company of 30 singers
from Austin and across the United States.
Founded as New Texas Fesitval by
renowned conductor Craig Hella Johnson,
Conspirare started out as an annual weeklong series of vocal music performances.
Now the choir performs additional concerts throughout the year, including the
annual "Christmas at the Carillon" show
performed in a historic chapel in West
Austin.

THE VISUAL ARTS

We can think of few better ways to spend an afternoon or a whole day than by visiting some of Austin's exceptional art museums and galleries. Access to the master artists of the past and present, including celebrated Austin and Texas artists, couldn't be easier. Austin offers two significant museums dedicated to the works of eminent sculptors Elisabet Ney and Charles Umlauf, who both lived and worked in Austin until their death. The gallery scene offers an excellent opportunity to view works by both established and emerging artists. There's always a chance you'll come face to face with the artists themselves, either working or simply enjoying the company of people like yourself who've come for the experience. You may return home with an art treasure that will delight you for years to come, or perhaps turn out to be a shrewd investment. At the very least, we guarantee you'll be enlightened. Austin seems dominated by so many "alternative" galleries that the term has lost its meaning to a certain extent. Alternative to what? we might ask. Prepare yourself for the unusual.

Austin still has not achieved the status of Dallas and Houston as a major hub for art buyers, but what it lacks in patrons is more than made up by a dynamic artistic community. There are several artists whose work is recognized, and coveted, far beyond our state's borders. What better way to become acquainted with these talented visionaries, as well as our city's many emerging artists, than by seeing exhibits of their work on their home turf. You'll be astounded by the range of styles and the diverse mediums on display by the painters, sculptors, photographers, and fine crafters working in Austin today.

Austin also is distinguished for producing fine arts prints. Master printmaker Sam Coronado, Flatbed Press, and Slugfest are leading the way in that arena. Austin's galleries are not limited to our

own artists, however. Among the galleries we've listed below you'll find work by some of the most interesting and well-known artists in the country today.

Don't let the idea of visiting a museum or gallery intimidate you, even if you're not an art expert. Austin's showrooms are staffed by knowledgeable, accessible experts, sometimes artists themselves, who are more than willing to offer on-the-spot advice, tips, and information about the artists and their works. Those of you who want to extend your study of the visual arts even further may want to check out some of the true art colonies that circle Austin in small towns like Salado, Wimberly, and Fredericksburg.

For more information on local museums and galleries, visit the Austin Museum Partnership's Web site at www.austin museums.org and the In the Galleries Austin site at www.inthegalleriesaustin.org.

Art Museums

Austin Museum of Art—Downtown
823 Congress Avenue
(512) 495-9224
www.amoa.org

After the Austin Museum of Art (AMOA) outgrew its location at Laguna Gloria, the institution, a public/private partnership between the City of Austin and the Austin Museum of Art, opened this additional 12,000-square-foot space in November 1996. The downtown space focuses on presenting temporary exhibits of significant 20th-century American visual art. Works by artists from the United States, Mexico, and the Caribbean are presented, including a strong showing of artists from Austin and around Texas.

The museum hosts 10 to 12 exhibitions annually, including those organized in-house and by other museums around the country. Past exhibitions have included an important retrospective in 2003 of the work of American pop art icon Andy Warhol. The museum also organized the show Michael Ray Charles: An American Artist's Work, 1989–1997, the first major retrospective of the well-known Austin artist whose work satirizes and critiques traditional and contemporary African-American stereotypes. Pieces by Austin's illustrious neo-Expressionist, Peter Saul, were featured in another show.

The Austin Museum of Art has announced plans to build a new 145,000-square-foot facility designed by Gluckman Mayner Architects of New York, whose principal architect, Richard Gluckman, has designed such buildings as the Georgia O'Keeffe Museum in Santa Fe, the Andy Warhol Museum in Pittsburgh, and the Deutsche Guggenheim in Berlin. The new design is described by AMOA as expressing "a cultivated modernism, combining functional and formal clarity with a sensuous approach towards materials and light that establishes a complementary relationship between the architectural quality of the building and the exhibition of contemporary art." Fund-raising for the new museum continues with no firm opening date set. The AMOA's current headquarters will remain open during construction.

The museum is open Tuesday through Saturday from 10:00 A.M. to 6:00 P.M. (until 8:00 P.M. on Thursday) and Sunday from noon to 5:00 P.M. Nominal admission fee. Reduced parking rates are available at the 823 Parking Garage on Ninth Street, or you can try to find a spot at the meters on the street.

Austin Museum of Art at Laguna Gloria
3809 West 35th Street
(512) 458-8191
www.amoa.org

One of Austin's most cherished treasures, Laguna Gloria reopened in 2003 following an extensive three-year restoration. And what a sight it is! This stucco-finished Italian-style villa, a National Historic site, is a great place to visit even if you're not a regular museumgoer. Built in 1916 and designed with meticulous care by its owner, Clara Driscoll, the five-story, 15-room villa sits on 12 acres beside Lake Austin. The gardens surrounding the estate, including a sculpture garden, also were restored to reflect Driscoll's vision. The grand lady herself ensured that her home would one day become a museum, deeding it in 1943 to the Texas Fine Arts Association (known as Arthouse today). The museum presents small-scale, long-term exhibitions and special events and is home to the museum's educational programs. This West Austin site was the only city art museum until the larger downtown facility opened in 1996. The site, a popular wedding venue, is once again available for rental. Members receive free admission to the museum, invitations to special events, subscriptions to museum publications and more. The museum is open Tuesday through Saturday from 10:00 A.M. to 5:00 P.M., Thursday from 10:00 A.M. to 8:00 P.M., and Sunday noon to 5:00 P.M. The Art School at Laguna Gloria, in a separate facility on the grounds, offers both children's classes and instruction for adults in painting, sculpture, graphic arts and more. The school can be reached at (512) 323-6380.

Jack S. Blanton Museum of Art
23rd and San Jacinto Streets
(512) 471-7324
www.blantonmuseum.org

The University of Texas fine arts museum, one of the leading university art museums in the country, is a key component of Austin's cultural scene as well as an important center of learning and culture for the entire state of Texas. Formerly known as the Archer M. Huntington Art Gallery, the name was changed in 1998 in anticipation of the new 150,000-square-foot state-of-the-art museum that is scheduled to open in the fall of 2005 at the northeast corner of Martin Luther King Jr. Boulevard and Congress Avenue.

The Blanton Museum's outstanding permanent collections are the most expansive in Central Texas, especially in the areas of American and contemporary art, Latin American art, and prints and drawings from all periods. Especially noteworthy is the museum's celebrated Suida-Manning Collection of Renaissance and Baroque paintings, drawings, and sculptures, as well as the James and Mari Michener Collection of 20th-century American paintings (see our Close-up of Michener in The Literary Scene chapter). In all, the collection includes more than 17,000 works of art spanning the history of Western civilization from antiquity to the present.

The Blanton, named for former chairman of the UT Board of Regents and arts advocate Jack Blanton, offers a constantly changing array of temporary exhibits of works by internationally known artists, major Texas artists, and University of Texas fine arts graduate students. The museum, a strong research-oriented teaching institution, also hosts an ongoing series of public lectures by museum curators, artists, and art historians from UT and around the country. This location houses the Department of Prints and Drawings, the largest and most historically balanced collection in the American South and Southwest. This collection, comprising 12,000 etchings, drawings, engravings, and more, includes both university-owned material and objects on long-term loan.

The museum is open from 9:00 A.M. to 5:00 P.M. Monday, Tuesday, Wednesday, and Friday; from 9:00 A.M. to 9:00 P.M. on Thursday; and 1:00 to 5:00 P.M. on Saturday and Sunday. It's closed on university holidays. Admission is free. If you've come by car,

park nearby in the garage at 24th and San Jacinto Streets. There is a parking fee.

Mexic-Arte Museum
419 Congress Avenue
(512) 480-9373
www.mexic-artemuseum.org

Since its founding in 1984 Mexic-Arte Museum has become Austin's leading organization for presenting and promoting art created by both local and internationally known Mexican and Latino artists. The museum features three galleries that exhibit works from Mexic-Arte's permanent collection as well as from touring and self-curated shows.

Among the more memorable shows in recent years, and there have been many, are The Nearest Edge of the World: Art and Cuba Now, which featured the work of contemporary young Cuban artists, and Mario Orozco Rivera, which featured work by Mexico's master painter. The annual Young Latino Artists Exhibition showcases the work of artists under age 35. Mexic-Arte works with the Mexican Consulate in Austin to bring exhibitions and programs from throughout Mexico.

This museum was founded by Sylvia Orozco, Pio Pulido, and Sam Coronado, three Austin artists who painted a mural at the former Arts Warehouse in Austin in exchange for exhibit space back in 1983. In its present location since 1988, the museum also presents musical, theatrical, and performing arts events. The museum also houses a gift shop. It's open 10:00 A.M. to 6:00 P.M. Monday through Thursday and 10:00 A.M. to 5:00 P.M. Friday and Saturday. Nominal admission fee.

Elisabet Ney Museum
304 East 44th Street
(512) 458-2255
www.ci.austin.tx.us/elisabetney

Celebrated sculptor Elisabet Ney put her artistic career back on track when she moved to Austin's Hyde Park in the late 1800s and built Formosa, now an extraordinary museum dedicated to the life and works of this sophisticated woman. Here visitors will discover a provocative array of about 50 portrait busts and full-figure statues of Texas heroes and of the European notables Ney sculpted as a young artist in Europe. Also here are the glorious sculptures of *Lady Macbeth, Prometheus Bound,* and *Sursum* (a Latin word meaning "to uplift your heart"), a delightful sculpture of two young nude boys.

The building itself, which Ney designed as her home and studio, also glorifies Ney's artistic sensibilities. Built in two phases and named Formosa, meaning beautiful in Portuguese, the studio lives up to its name. The first studio section, reminiscent of a Greek temple, was built in 1892, when Ney was 59 years old. Living quarters, which included a Gothic tower study for her husband, philosopher/scientist Edmund Montgomery, were added 10 years later. Today Formosa is listed on the National Register of Historic Places as well as both the Austin and Texas Registers.

The museum includes a wonderful section on the life of Ney herself. Here visitors will find many of the artist's tools as well as a hat, watch, teacup, glasses, and many other items used by the artist. Excellent written accounts of her life are on display here also. Visitors will learn that this great talent came to Texas from Europe with the idea of forsaking her career for, as she put it, the "more important art of molding flesh and blood"—in other words, to raise her two boys. Tragically, one son died at age 2. Twenty years later Ney accepted a commission to sculpt the figures of Sam Houston and Stephen F. Austin that stand in the Texas State Capitol today. Her career had resumed.

The museum stands as a monument to Ney's influence on the arts in Texas. Her ability to inspire others during a time when Texas slighted the arts led to the creation of the Texas Fine Arts Association (or Arthouse, as it is known today) and later the Texas Commission on the Arts and the University of Texas art department. The Elisabet Ney Museum,

one of the oldest museums in Texas, was founded after her death in 1907 by those Ney inspired during her lifetime. Ney's work can also be seen at the Texas State Cemetery, at UT, at the Smithsonian Institution in Washington, D.C., and in other museums in the United States and Europe.

The museum is open Wednesday through Saturday 10:00 A.M. to 5:00 P.M. and Sunday from noon to 5:00 P.M. Admission is free, as is parking on the residential streets around the building.

Harry Ransom Center
Near Guadalupe and 21st Streets
(512) 471-8944
www.hrc.utexas.edu

Officially named the Harry Ransom Humanities Research Center, the emphasis here has always been on providing researchers with access to the once-stodgy building's world-class collections of art, literary manuscripts, photography, music, and more. However, a 20-month, $14.5 million renovation completed in 2003 lets the light shine in on this Austin gem. The new glass walls and open spaces invite visitors to come in and stay awhile, while the arrangement of the collections makes it much easier for the general public to enjoy. There certainly are plenty of reasons to spend some time here. Among the center's exceptional properties are a 1455 Gutenberg Bible, one of just five existing complete copies of the first book printed with movable type, as well as the world's first photograph, taken by Frenchman Joseph Nicephore Niepce in 1826. There are important paintings by Mexican artists Diego Rivera, Frida Kahlo, and Rufino Tamayo, as well as artworks done by some literary greats, including D. H. Lawrence and Tennessee Williams. Literary manuscripts include works by Ernest Hemingway, William Faulkner, and Samuel Beckett.

In all, the Ransom Center houses 30 million literary manuscripts, 1 million rare books, 5 million photographs, and more than 100,000 works of art. Obviously it's impossible to display all these treasures at once, so the Center presents numerous exhibitions and events showcasing its collections. The galleries are open from 10:00 A.M. to 5:00 P.M. Tuesday, Wednesday, and Friday; from 10:00 A.M. to 7:00 P.M. Thursday, and from noon to 5:00 P.M. on weekends. Admission is free.

Umlauf Sculpture Garden & Museum
**605 Robert E. Lee Road
(512) 445–5582
www.umlaufsculpture.org**
Directors of the Umlauf Sculpture Garden & Museum like to say this garden epitomizes Austin: It's outdoors, casual, and lovely. And they have a great point. Here, in a totally Austin xeriscape garden and pond next to Zilker Park, visitors are treated to the fabulous sculptures of acclaimed artist Charles Umlauf, who came to Austin in 1941 and remained for the rest of his life.

The garden, terrace, and surrounding land provide a perfect outdoor setting for 62 of Umlauf's bronze and cast-stone sculptures. The pieces, which range from the realistic to the abstract, represent a wide range of subject matter, including children, family groupings, mythological and religious figures, refugees, small animals, and sensuous nudes. There are many more smaller sculptures made of exotic woods, marbles, and terra-cotta inside the glass-enclosed museum. The museum building got a beautiful new makeover in 2003 thanks to a movie that was filmed on-site.

Umlauf, who taught in the University of Texas art department for 40 years and retired in 1981 as professor emeritus, won nearly every professional award offered, including a Guggenheim Fellowship and a Ford Foundation Grant. His works can be seen in museums and public collections across the country, including the Smithsonian Institution in Washington, D.C., and the Metropolitan Museum of Art in New York. Umlauf's pieces can also be found on the UT campus and at a dozen sites around town, including the grounds of the

October is Austin's Visual Arts Month. The celebration includes important art exhibits, juried shows, and sales of area artists' work throughout the city, including the State Capitol and UT's Jack S. Blanton Museum of Art. Programs are available at the visitor center, 209 East Sixth Street.

Laguna Gloria Art Museum and the Texas State Cemetery (see our listings in this chapter).

In 1985 Umlauf and his wife, Angeline, donated their longtime home and studio and more than 200 pieces of his work to the City of Austin. The museum, built with private funds, opened in 1991. This is a wonderful place to visit and is also popular for weddings and other outdoor events. The museum is wheelchair-accessible and offers special programs for the visually and hearing impaired. It also hosts workshops for both children and adults and is a great place to bring children (see our Kidstuff chapter). The museum is open Wednesday through Friday from 10:00 A.M. to 4:30 P.M. and 1:00 to 4:30 P.M. on Saturday and Sunday. Nominal admission fee.

Galleries

Art on 5th
**1501 West Fifth Street
(512) 481-1111
www.arton5th.com**
One of Austin's largest and most diverse art galleries, Art on 5th features work by famous artists such as Miro, Picasso, and Dr. Seuss as well as exceptional undiscovered artists from around the world working in many genres. This well-designed, visitor-friendly gallery is owned by Joe Sigel, who owned galleries in Santa Fe and California for many years. It's open Monday through Saturday 10:00 A.M. to 6:00 P.M. and Sunday noon to 6:00 P.M.

Austin Galleries
1219 West Sixth Street
(512) 495–9363
www.austingalleries.com
After a tour of Austin and the surrounding Hill Country, you might be tempted to search out paintings that capture the stunning beauty of our hills. Among the more than 2,000 original works of art offered at Austin Galleries is as huge selection of Texas landscape paintings, as well as Impressionist, abstract, and classical paintings and original prints signed by Andy Warhol, Picasso, Jasper Johns, and others. And that's just the beginning.

Austin Spirit Gallery
1206 South Congress Avenue
(512) 444–8500
www.austinspiritgallery.com
Featuring the work of acclaimed Austin artist Fidencio Duran and other local artists, this inviting space on funky South Congress is perking up some ears. Duran, whose work includes the giant murals that greet passengers checking in at the airport and several other important murals around town, is an important local artist whose work is well worth seeing. The gallery also hosts temporary exhibits of other artists' work. It's currently open 11:00 A.M. to 7:00 P.M. Thursday through Saturday.

Clarksville Pottery & Galleries
4001 North Lamar Boulevard
(512) 454–9079
9828 Great Hills Trail, Suite 110
(512) 794–8580
330 Bee Caves Road
(512) 732–2821
www.clarksvillepottery.com
Clarksville Pottery & Galleries has grown from a small, one-man pottery shop and studio back in the '70s into a major retailer of fine arts and crafts with three prominent Austin locations. The stores offer handmade pottery by local and nationally known potters as well as an impressive selection of jewelry, glass, wall art, fine woodcrafts, fountains, and more.

The stores do a brisk business because in addition to offering some of the finest crafts available in Austin today, the local owners stock a good supply of items that are affordable.

Started by former art professor Arnie Popinsky and his wife, Syd, in the Clarksville neighborhood of Austin, the business has been chosen by *Niche* magazine as a "Top 100 Retailer of American Crafts." Insiders love to take out-of-town guests to Clarksville Pottery & Galleries. The Lamar store in Austin's Central Market is open Monday through Saturday from 10:00 A.M. to 6:30 P.M. The Great Hills store in the Arboretum area is open Monday through Saturday from 10:00 A.M. to 6:00 P.M. Both stores are open shorter hours on Sunday. The smaller Bee Caves location offers an excellent selection also. It's open Monday through Saturday 10:00 A.M. to 6:00 P.M.

Flatbed Press and Gallery
2832 East Martin Luther King Jr. Boulevard
(512) 477–9328, (866) 477–9328
www.flatbedpress.com
Flatbed Press's master printmakers work with some of the finest artists of the day to create limited-editions of original etchings, lithographs, and woodcuts. This press has a national reputation for producing state-of-the-art work. Additionally, the gallery exhibits and sells original paintings as well as works on paper by leading contemporary artists, including Austin's Michael Ray Charles and Melissa Miller. Flatbed also offers about a dozen classes in printmaking and other techniques for novice to experienced artists.

Guadalupe Arts Center
1705 Guadalupe Street
(512) 473–3775
www.guadalupearts.com
This complex is home to several galleries as well as studios for more than three dozen of Austin's working artists. The 1,600-square-foot space on the main floor features ever-changing exhibits and will

introduce you to some of the artists working in our city today. Among the many offering here is Pro-Jex Gallery, perhaps the best known photo gallery in town. All kinds of interesting work is featured in this small space. The Web site provides links to most of the artists working in the center. The Guadalupe Arts Center is owned and operated by Kevin J. Barry, who has provided an affordable, creative environment for area artists. A visit to this complex will start you out well on any tour of the visual arts in Austin, and if you're lucky you may get to see artists at work in their studios.

Images of Austin and the Southwest
4612 Burnet Road
(512) 451-1229
www.imagesofaustin.com

Austin artist Mary Doerr runs this gallery in a small house in Central Austin that showcases Doerr's attractive illustrations and watercolors, often depicting Austin, as well as the work of a number of other selected artists. The gallery features Southwestern sculptures and wall hangings as well as pottery, gourds, jewelry, limited-edition prints, and paintings. The store also does custom framing. Images of Austin and the Southwest is open 10:00 A.M. to 6:00 P.M. Monday through Saturday.

The Jones Center for Contemporary Art
700 Congress Avenue
(512) 453-5312
www.arthousetexas.org

Arthouse operates this downtown gallery as part of its efforts to nurture artists, promote contemporary Austin and Texas artists, and improve public awareness and appreciation of the state's visual artists. Formerly called the Texas Fine Arts Association, Arthouse was established in 1911. It is the oldest statewide visual arts organization in Texas and the only one devoted solely to contemporary art. Arthouse hosts a variety of exhibitions throughout the year, as well as special programs devoted to contemporary art. It's open daily, but operating hours vary.

Slugfest Printmaking Workshop & Gallery
1906 Miriam Avenue
(512) 477-7204
www.slugfestprints.com

Slugfest is a stellar printmaking operation that produces limited-edition original prints for both novice and established artists. Opened in 1996 by Margaret Simpson and Tom Druecker, both MFAs in printmaking and teachers at Austin universities, this press has an excellent reputation for producing museum-quality prints. The gallery hosts an excellent variety of shows. Slugfest also offers introductory workshops in lithography, relief printing, monotype, collograph, book arts, and letterpress.

El Taller Gallery
2438 West Anderson Lane, Suite C-3
(512) 302-0100
www.eltallergallery.com

Established in 1980 and owned by Olga O. Piña, El Taller Gallery has for many years been Austin's leading gallery for Southwestern art. El Taller carries work by Michael Atkinson, Amado Peña, R. C. Gorman, Poteet Victory, Darryl Willison, and others. In recent years the gallery has expanded to include traditional landscapes, florals, and engravings by several Austin artists, including Rick Hodgins, Betty Rhodes, Earlayne Chance, and Sue Kemp.

It's open Tuesday through Saturday 10:00 A.M. to 6:00 P.M.

Wild About Music
721 Congress Avenue
(512) 708-1700
www.wildaboutmusic.com

What better combination for Austin than an art gallery and gift shop that celebrates music? Everything in the locally owned shop has a music or performing arts motif, including accessories, clothing, jewelry, glass, and stationery. Wild About Music (WAM) features exceptional work by more than 100 artists, including some nationally known Central Texas artists as well as others from around the country.

Acclaimed Austin musician Joe Ely is the most prominent of WAM's artists who also are bona fide musicians, but there are other musicians/visual artists as well as dozens of visual artists who are inspired by music.

This gallery also hosts a variety of special events, including art demonstrations, touring art shows, and, of course, live music performances. Wild About Music is open 11:00 A.M. to 7:00 P.M. Monday through Saturday. Located next to two performing arts centers, the State Theater and the Paramount Theatre, the store often stays open later on theater nights.

Women & Their Work
1710 Lavaca Street
(512) 477-1064
www.womenandtheirwork.org

This statewide nonprofit organization dedicated to promoting women in the arts celebrated its 25th anniversary in 2003. Make no mistake—this is much more than just an art gallery. Women & Their Work is the only organization of its kind in Texas that embraces all the arts. The organization promotes women artists in visual art, dance, music, theater, literature, and film and it is one of Austin's premier resources for the arts. There's also a nice gift shop here that, like the gallery, is open Monday through Saturday.

Gallery exhibitions featuring painting, sculpture, photography, fine crafts, and works on paper change regularly. Women & Their Work presents more than 50 diverse events each year, including juried and invitational exhibitions of Texas artists as well as solo and group exhibitions. The organization also produces dance, musical, and theatrical performances featuring local, regional, and national performing artists, often collaborative ventures with other groups. We especially like this organization's motto: "Women & Their Work is dedicated to the belief that women artists should be seen and heard. And paid."

Yard Dog Folk Art
1510 South Congress Avenue
(512) 912-1613
www.yarddog.com

Fascinating is the word that comes to mind to describe the work of the folk artists, many of them nationally known, represented here. Art dealer Randy Franklin opened this gallery in South Central Austin in 1995 and handles work by artists from the American South. Be sure to ask him about the various artists represented here; they have interesting stories. The outsider art of well-known Austin artist Ike Morgan, a mental patient who has lived many years in the Austin State Hospital, is for sale here as is the work of Sybil Gibson, the Rev. J. L. Hunter, and many more. This gallery is definitely worth a visit. It's open from 11:00 A.M. to 6:00 P.M. Wednesday through Saturday and noon to 5:00 P.M. on Sunday. This area of South Congress Avenue is a fun place to visit even if you're not a folk art buff. The strip is lined with other funky shops and restaurants that will satisfy any craving for the unusual.

Arts Organizations

Art in Public Places
1110 Barton Springs Road, Suite 201
(512) 397-1455
www.ci.austin.tx.us/aipp

Established in 1985, the City of Austin's Art in Public Places (AIPP) program was Texas's first municipal effort to purchase and place works of art in public areas. Since then, AIPP has installed artworks at the Austin-Bergstrom International Airport, the Austin Convention Center, libraries, parks, recreation centers and many more spots for everyone to enjoy. The program has involved talented artists of local and national renown, while the collection represents the broad range of mediums, styles, and cultural sensibilities. Check the AIPP Web site to view some of Austin's outstanding public art.

Austin Circle of Theaters
701 Tillery Street, Suite 9
(512) 247-2531
www.acotonline.org

Long before they sell a single ticket, take their first bows, or earn a rave review, many of Austin's theater companies first pass through the door at Austin Circle of Theaters (ACoT). This outstanding non-profit organization works to nurture and promote the city's performng arts community and attract new audiences to the arts. ACoT's annual B. Iden Payne Awards are the most prestigious performing arts awards in the city.

For the public at large, ACoT sponsors the excellent AUSTIX box office (see the Insiders' Tip in this chapter), which offers easy access to full- and half-price tickets for the city's performing arts events. It offers the ease of finding great local performances simply by flipping to the large ACoT advertisement on newspaper arts pages. For its more than 70 theater, music, and dance member groups, ACoT provides opportunities to help them develop survival strategies, and it helps start-ups by serving as an umbrella organization. ACoT is a strong voice of arts' advocacy in the community. In other words, this is one toasty art incubator for Austin. Anyone can reap the many benefits of becoming an ACoT member. Check the Web site for details.

Dance Umbrella
3710 Cedar Street, Suite 288
(512) 450-0456
www.danceumbrella.com

Whether it's bringing local and internationally renowned dance companies to the Austin stage or helping a young dance company find its legs, Dance Umbrella has been supporting the movement arts in our city since it was founded in 1977. This non-profit organization with about 100 artistic members also aims to promote dance and dance companies throughout the region with its many programs and services. After all, the organization is based on the philosophy "that the arts help describe, define, and deepen our experience of living." Membership is open to one and all and provides discounts on performances.

Included in the Austin Theatre Alliance's community outreach efforts is a program called Skinny's Gallery, which provides free admission to children who otherwise could not afford a ticket. It's named for former Austin theater owner Skinny Pryor, who is known for letting under-privileged children see a show for a glass of water and a smile.

Texas Folklife Resources
1317 S. Congress Avenue
(512) 441-Y'ALL (9255)
www.texasfolklife.org

Modern-day Texas culture is a rich blend of ethnic and regional traditions dating back hundreds of years. There's no better way to discover how well those traditions have survived than by attending events sponsored by Texas Folklife Resources (TFR). This dynamic nonprofit organization brings the best of those living, breathing cultures to the forefront of public awareness today through a comprehensive calendar of events in Austin and around the state.

TFR works with folk artists all over Texas to document living traditions and present them to the public in many forms, including exhibitions, concerts, radio programs, and demonstrations. Among TFR's many successful projects is Texas Folk Masters, which puts outstanding traditional Texas musicians on stage at the Paramount Theatre. The organization also offers photography exhibitions that showcase traditional Texas blues clubs and its honky-tonk culture. And there's more: gospel music, powwow craft traditions, works in wood by folk artists, and songs and ballads of the Texas-Mexico border.

TFR also operates the Apprenticeships in the Folk Arts program, which encourages master folk artists to pass their traditions on to qualified apprentices in their community. Check the Web site often to keep fully informed of TFR's extensive list of events. Better yet, join TFR and help present, preserve, and promote the folk arts and folklife of the Lone Star State.

VU/Austin
www.vuaustin.org

Visual Arts United of Austin, which goes by the shortened name VU/Austin, is a coalition of many of the area's visual arts organizations that, among other goals, aims to advance Austin's national image as a visual arts center. Among its many projects is sponsorship of the annual Visual Arts Month in October, a fascinating series of citywide art exhibits and other events that showcase the work of member artists. VU/Austin is working to help create a visual arts district or center for our city with the goal of attracting more artists and patrons. Among its many member organizations are the Austin Museum of Art, the Austin Visual Arts Association, UT's Jack S. Blanton Museum of Art, and Arthouse, the Texas fine arts association. Like with the other arts organizations, membership is open to the public.

THE LITERARY SCENE

The tempo of the earth-dwellers to whom I have been listening for many years is the tempo of growing grass, of a solitary buzzard sailing over a valley, of the wind from the south in April, of the lengthening of a tree's shadow on a summer afternoon, of the rise and fall of flames in a fireplace on a winter night. . . ."

With those words, J. Frank Dobie, Texas's first nationally known writer, introduced his book *Tales of Old-Time Texas*, published in 1928 and still available, along with many of his other two dozen collections, at bookstores today.

In this chapter we'll delve into Austin's rich literary history and describe our present status as a writers' mecca. But for those of you in a rush to explore the Austin of letters, we'll get right to the point: If you like books, you'll love Austin.

J. Frank Dobie is one of the reasons. Dobie, a University of Texas professor from 1914 to 1947, with occasional absences, was born in the Texas brush country and lived in and around Austin for most of his adult life—that is, when he was not off wandering around Mexico and the American Southwest in search of someone with a tale to tell.

"Frank Dobie became a hunter of legends and a gatherer of folk tales and the result was one of the most important bodies of literature produced by a Southwesterner," wrote Neil B. Carmony, who edited a collection of Dobie's stories for the book *Afield with J. Frank Dobie*, published in 1992, 28 years after the writer's death.

Names of other luminaries grace Austin's past, including historian Walter Prescott Webb and naturalist Roy Bedichek, who together with Dobie formed a triumvirate of intellectuals that electrified the city's literary ambience.

William Sydney Porter, who later was to gain international notoriety as the short-story writer O. Henry, published his first short fiction here in his literary magazine the *Rolling Stone*. A Porter story that appeared in the October 27, 1894, issue of the *Rolling Stone* gave Austin one of its most endearing nicknames: City of the Violet Crown. (See our chapter on Attractions for more about O. Henry.) Austinite and LBJ aide Billy Brammer is still known around these parts for his 1962 political novel, *The Gay Place*.

John Henry Faulk, for whom our central library is named, was a multitalented writer, actor, New York radio show host, and defender of the First Amendment. As vice president of the American Federation of Television and Radio Artists, Faulk insisted the union take a stand against McCarthy-era blacklistings of entertainers—and was himself blacklisted. Faulk fought back and as a result won the largest libel judgment awarded up to that time. He was one of Dobie's students.

Internationally celebrated short-story writer Katherine Anne Porter (1890–1980) grew up 20 miles down the road from Austin in the small town of Kyle. Her relationship with Texas, however, was a stormy one. It infuriated her, for example, that the Texas Institute of Letters chose to honor Dobie instead of her when it gave its 1939 award for the best book by a Texas writer. (Folklorist Sylvia Ann Grider has written that "Porter's emotional attachment to her home state fell victim to the cowboy mentality that has traditionally proclaimed Texas a fine place for men and horses, but hell on women and oxen.") Of course her fame eclipsed Dobie's, which probably brought her no small amount of satisfaction. While Porter lived most of her adult life outside Texas, she nevertheless wrote some of her finest fiction about her home state and chose to be buried in Texas.

Pioneering Texas journalist Bess Whitehead Scott, who broke gender barriers in 1915 as the first woman news reporter in Houston, was a beloved member of the Austin writers community until her death in 1997 at age 107. Noted folklorist and poet J. Mason Brewer, the first African American to become a member of the Texas Institute of Letters and the first African-American vice president of the American Folklore Society, found inspiration among members of his own family in their East Austin home. Dobie called Brewer's work "genuine and delightful." Pulitzer Prize–winning author James Michener is another illustrious writer who found inspiration in Austin—and inspired others. (Find out more about Michener's contributions to Austin's literary scene in our Close-up in this chapter.)

Some of these trailblazers not only established Austin's literary traditions but also helped this city earn a reputation as a haven for writers and free thinkers, a distinction that has endured. Austin's literary scene, in fact, is more vibrant today than ever before. Perhaps even Dobie would be amazed at the sheer number of Austin writers and at the contributions many of them have made to the nation's literary wealth. To read Austin writers is to take a joyride on the roller coaster of literary expression: novels, mysteries, science fiction, cyberpunk, suspense, history, poetry, travel, books for children and young adults, essays, memoirs, how-to books, cookbooks, political satires, biographies, screenplays, short stories. The list goes on. Our city claims best-selling and award-winning writers in a number of genres, as well as a host of successful poets, playwrights, and screenwriters. Fans of Molly Ivins, Louis Sachar, Christopher Reich, Lance Armstrong, Sarah Bird, and the others we list in our Reader's Primer below will be pleased to know these artists live right here in Austin.

It's impossible to pinpoint just one catalyst for Austin's literary explosion. We'd have to include Austin's own magnetism. Once experienced, Austin is hard to abandon. The superlative efforts of the Writers' League of Texas to promote and encourage the city's writers has had impressive results. The league, with 1,200 members, is one of the largest writers' organizations in the country.

Two Austin publications, *Texas Monthly* magazine and the *Texas Observer,* have long and rich traditions of attracting excellent writers to Austin, many of whom have gone on to achieve literary fame. The vibrant music scene and flourishing film industry, illuminated by excellent local songwriters and screenwriters, add further dimension to Austin's literary landscape. (See our chapter on The Music Scene and our Close-up on the film industry in The Arts chapter.) Of course, the presence of outstanding intellectuals at the University of Texas, St. Edward's University, and our other colleges and universities has added untold riches to Austin's writing legacy. Adding further dimension to the scene are the university presses and many small- and medium-size publishing houses that are willing to gamble that an author's work will be of interest to others.

The last decade of the 20th century roused an unprecedented flurry of interest in Austin's literary arts. Major bookstore chains Barnes & Noble and Borders Books, which opened here in the mid-1990s, joined Austin's esteemed superstore, Book People, so that now book lovers don't have far to go to find a giant bookstore. These stores host an astounding assortment of readings by national and local authors, as well as book signings and other literary events that bring the written word to life. Several of Austin's small- and medium-sized bookstores have long traditions of providing venues for local and national writers of poetry and prose, as do a number of other venues around town, including the Harry Ransom Center at the University of Texas and St. Edward's University in South Austin. The James Michener Center for Writers, appropriately housed in J. Frank Dobie's former home on Waller Creek, sponsors a wonderful series of readings by national and international writers.

Texas Writers Month, first organized in 1994, has become an outstanding statewide celebration of Texas's literary artists. The annual May festival, held in Austin and other major cities around the state, includes book panels, readings, children's events, literacy benefits, signings, musical events, and film. Texas Writers Month, originally conceived to convince booksellers to give local authors more prominence in their stores, has become a premier celebration of Texas writers.

The Texas Book Festival, started in 1996, is another major Austin event for writers and readers alike. Laura Bush was a driving force behind the festival when she was first lady of Texas. The November festival, which raises money for Texas public libraries, features readings and panel discussions by more than 100 authors who have been published the previous year. Texans, Texas natives, and those who've written about the Lone Star State are invited to participate. A giant book fair, musical events, children's activities, and more highlight this celebration of the state's literary heritage. The Austin International Poetry Festival, held in April since 1993, draws poets and poetry fans from around the globe to Austin. Other venues around town, including Ruta Maya Coffee House, Mexic-Arte Museum, and some of the bookstores listed in this chapter, feature poetry readings throughout the year.

A READER'S PRIMER OF AUSTIN

One of the pleasures of visiting or moving to a new town is the opportunity to discover the writers who contribute to the region's literary landscape. Austin is in no short supply when it comes to outstanding writers, as you'll see here. While there are just too many Austin authors to include all of them, we've introduced you to a selection of some of the best known and some of our favorites. We promise that you'll be thrilled with their diversity and inspired by their talent. Check with our local libraries and bookstores for more about our city's other literary stars. Of course it's just not possible to know Texas well unless you've at least read the works of John Graves, Larry McMurtry, and John L. King. While not Austinites, their intimate observations embody the heart and soul of Texas in its multitude of forms.

Some of the information we've provided about the authors comes to us from the Texas Book Festival and the Writers' League of Texas. They were most helpful.

Jeff Abbott: "It was really rude of Beta Harcher to argue with me right before she got killed." So begins Abbot's first novel, *Do Unto Others,* which won an Agatha Award for Best First Mystery. Since then he's written a series of fun mysteries set in the small town of Mirabeau, Texas. His hero is librarian Jordan Poteet. Look also for Abbott's books *The Only Good Yankee, Promises of Home,* and *Distant Blood.*

Lance Armstrong: Five time Tour de France winner and Austin's hometown hero, Armstrong has written, with contributor Sally Jenkins, two inspirational books about his life as a cancer survivor and international cycling champion. *It's Not About the Bike: My Journey Back to Life* and its sequel, *Every Second Counts,* published in 2003, were both hugely successful. He also cowrote the training guide, *The Lance Armstrong Performance Program: Seven Weeks to the Perfect Ride.*

(See our Spectator Sports chapter for a Close-up of Armstrong.)

Neal Barrett, Jr.: *Skinny Annie Blues* was the first in a series of popular Barrett mysteries featuring Wiley Moss. He also wrote *Dead Dog Blues* and *Pink Vodka Blues.* He is also known for his novel *The Hereafter Game,* which the *Washington Post* called "one of the great American novels."

Austin Bay: This nationally syndicated columnist on security issues and frequent commentator on NPR's *Morning Edition* is also a well-respected novelist. Bay's 2003 novel, *The Wrong Side of Brightness,* is a techno-thriller set in postwar Iraq. Look, too, for his other works: *Prism: A Novel* and *Target: Iraq.* Bay, a colonel in the U.S. Army Reserve and former Pentagon consultant, has been called "a true military insider and a powerful storyteller."

Sarah Bird: Bird's work has been called "nothing short of brilliant" and "falling off the chair hilarious" by prestigious publications around the country. This talented writer of such books as *Virgin of the Rodeo, The Mommy Club,* and *The Boyfriend School* is also a screenwriter, essayist, and magazine writer who has written for *Cosmopolitan, Ms.* magazine, the *New York Times Magazine,* and the *Texas Observer. Virgin of the Rodeo* received a starred review in *Publisher's Weekly,* which said, "The search for a delinquent father drives this waggish and wonderful novel about the Southwest rodeo circuit out of the chute and into the winner's circle." Her long-awaited, award-winning fourth novel, *The Yokota Officers Club,* was published in 2001.

Liz Carpenter: "Austin's answer to Irma Bombeck" is one way best-selling author Liz Carpenter has been described. This Austin treasure spent nearly 20 years as a newspaper correspondent in Washington before she became the first journalist to serve as a First Lady's press secretary, working for sister Texan Lady Bird Johnson. Her books include *Ruffles and Flourishes,* about her days in the Johnson White House; *Getting Better All the Time,* about aging and widowhood; and *Unplanned Parenthood: Confessions of a Seventy-Something Surrogate Mother,* her story of becoming the mother of three teenagers.

Gary Cartwright: A senior editor for *Texas Monthly* magazine, Cartwright is a multi-award-winning author and journalist. Cartwright's books include *Confessions of a Washed-up Sportswriter, Dirty Dealing,* and *Blood Will Tell.* His 1998 book *HeartWiseGuy: How to Live the Good Life After a Heart Attack* is a personal account of the author's own recovery after a heart attack and advice on how to care for an aging body. He has been the recipient of the Dobie-Paisano Fellowship and has won two prestigious Texas Institute of Letters awards. Cartwright also has cowritten and coproduced movies. *Blood Will Tell* was filmed by CBS as a four-hour miniseries. Don't miss *Texas Monthly* for outstanding articles by Cartwright.

The new book by wacky writer Kinky Friedman lists "Ten Things You Would Never Hear a Real Texan Say," like "I've got two cases of Perrier for the Super Bowl," and "Duct tape won't fix that." The book is **Kinky Friedman's Guide to Texas Etiquette: Or How to Get to Heaven or Hell Without Going Through Dallas-Fort Worth.**

Kinky Friedman: A UT graduate, Friedman made a name for himself back in the 1970s as songwriter and lead singer for the irreverent Kinky Friedman and the Texas Jewboys. Now living on a ranch in the Texas Hill Country, Friedman has turned to writing. And what a writer he is! Molly Ivins (read about her below) said Friedman "spreads more joy than Ross Perot's ears." His numerous books include *Road Kill,*

Armadillo & Old Lace, Elvis, Jesus & Coca-Cola, and *Blast from the Past.* These humorous quasi-autobiographical mysteries feature a Jewish Texan country-western music singer turned private detective named, you guessed it, Kinky Friedman. One of his latest books is *Kinky Friedman's Guide to Texas Etiquette: Or How to Get to Heaven or Hell without Going Through Dallas-Fort Worth.*

Spike Gillespie: With a name like Spike—coupled with no small amount of talent—this Austinite is destined for stardom. *Surrender (But Don't Give Yourself Away)* is a collection of 46 Gillespie essays that appeared in such publications as the *Washington Post,* the *Austin Chronicle,* the *Dallas Morning News, Bust,* and *Gargoyle.* "There are odes to my good days and bad, to trips I've taken—both real and metaphorical, to holiness found in unexpected places, to men I have not slept with, to learning to live sober. . .," Gillespie has said. Her other book is called *All the Wrong Men and One Perfect Boy: A Memoir.*

Stephen Harrigan: A contributing editor to *Texas Monthly* magazine, Harrigan is the multi-talented author of *Water and Light: A Diver's Journey to a Coral Reef, Aransas,* and the great collection of essays about Texas, *A Natural State,* which the *Washington Post* described as "recommended reading not just for Texans but for all who would explore their connections to the natural world." Harrigan also wrote *The Last of His Tribe,* a movie for HBO.

Jim Hightower: Brilliant, funny, and oh so opinionated, Austin's beloved/behated radio commentator, newspaper columnist, and muckraking journalist is a man of the people and for the people—even if, as he says, our government officials are not. In a series of caustically humorous books, Hightower takes issue with the powers that be. His latest, 2003's *Thieves in High Places: They've Stolen Our Country—and It's Time to Take It Back,* lambastes the Bush administration for creating a "Klep-

tocrat Nation," which he defines as "a body of people ruled by thieves. . . ." His other books, also written in his trademark down-home style, are *If the Gods Had Meant for Us to Vote, They'd Have Given Us Candidates,* and *There's Nothing in the Middle of the Road but Yellow Stripes and Dead Armadillos: A Work of Political Subversion.* Need we say more?

Molly Ivins: Syndicated columnist Molly Ivins has turned her sardonic wit on President George W. Bush of late in books titled *Bushwacked: Life in George W. Bush's America* and *Shrub: The Short but Happy Political Life of George W. Bush,* both written with Lou Dubose. Her earlier book, *Molly Ivins Can't Say That, Can She?,* spent more than a year on the *New York Times* best-seller list. Another book, *You Got to Dance with Them What Brung You,* features such astute Ivins observations as, "There's nothing you can do about being born liberal—fish gotta swim and hearts gotta bleed." She also has written *Nothing but Good Times Ahead.* This nationally syndicated columnist for the *Fort Worth Star-Telegram,* who can also be read in the *Austin American-Statesman,* writes with humor and insight about Texas politics and other happenings. Ivins, a former writer for the *Texas Observer,* has won a number of journalism awards and has been a finalist for the Pulitzer Prize three times.

David Lindsey: Mystery lovers adore Lindsey's works, which include *An Absence of Light, Mercy, A Cold Mind,* and *Requiem for a Glass Heart,* which was purchased by Universal Studios. He is a best-selling author in Britain and is known for his meticulous research, which has included working with the FBI and detectives in the Houston Police Department. *Publishers Weekly* called *Mercy,* set in Houston, "a lean, gripping, psychological thriller. Written with masterly skill."

Angela Shelf Medearis: *The Ghost of Sifty-Sifty Sam* is just one of the books

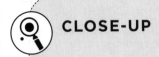

James Michener:
A Memorable Character

Pulitzer Prize–winning author James Michener, whose 1991 memoir is titled *The World Is My Home,* chose Austin as his home for many of the last, always prolific, years of his life. Over the course of the Michener Age here, Austin was to become a richer city, not merely because of the millions in art and monetary endowments he gave to the University of Texas but also because of Michener's generosity of spirit.

Here was a man whose own life was one of America's great rags-to-riches tales; a man whose appetite for adventure and unquenchable thirst for knowledge were matched only by a gift—he called it a passion—for telling a story; a man who spent his life, and most of his fortune, giving back to the people and communities that had embraced him.

Michener was no stranger to the Capital City when he arrived in 1982 to begin work on his sweeping saga of the Lone Star State. He had known the Austin of the 1940s, when he came as an editor following publication of his first book, and he'd known the Austin of the 1960s, when he returned to donate his huge 20th-century American Art collection to the University of Texas. By the time the 1980s rolled around, Michener had been decorated with America's highest civilian honor, the Presidential Medal of Freedom. His reputation as America's Storyteller was as solid as his hefty novels—and so was his fame as one of the country's most generous writers. At the time of his death, it was estimated that Michener had given $117 million to museums, libraries, individ-

uals, and universities around the country. The largest beneficiary of Michener's generosity was the University of Texas at Austin, which received $44.2 million from the late-in-life Austinite.

Michener's first novel, *Tales of the South Pacific,* published in 1947 when the author was 40 years old, had earned him a Pulitzer Prize. The bestsellers that followed, including *The Fires of Spring, The Bridges at Toko-ri, Sayonara, Caravans, The Source, Iberia, Centennial, The Drifters,* and *The Covenant,* earned him millions of loyal readers who found his fictionalized version of history more exciting, more moving, and even more educational than anything they'd read in nonfiction. It warranted not even a pause when critics called his work too preachy, his characters too one-dimensional, or his dialogue too contrived. Readers made Michener famous as they stampeded to the bookstores to get their hands on his latest epic. Perhaps it was his ability to create characters with whom readers could identify that won him such a loyal following.

"I have endeavored to center my writing upon ordinary but memorable characters whose lives shed a kind of radiance, whose behavior, good or bad, illuminated what I was striving to impart, and whose noble, craven, godlike or hellish deportment stood surrogate for the behavior of human beings the reader has known," he wrote in his memoir.

Bill Clements, then governor of Texas, invited Michener to Austin in 1981 to work on a book about Texas for the sesquicentennial. Published in 1985, when Michener

James Michener founded the Texas Center for Writers, now named in his honor, at the University of Texas. PETER A. SILVA

cover photograph of the author sitting atop Austin's breathtaking Mount Bonnell (see our Attractions chapter).

Born of unknown parents on February 3, 1907, in New York City, Michener was taken as an orphan to a poorhouse in Doylestown, Pennsylvania. Mabel Michener, a Quaker, gave him a name, food, and shelter when her finances allowed and, most important, a love for learning. "We were very poor," Michener told the Statesman on the occasion of his 89th birthday. "As a child I had nothing. I never had a sled. I never had a bicycle. I never had a baseball glove. I never had anything. But I did have people who loved me and looked after my education."

He spent much of his childhood reading books in the public library, excelled in school and sports, and earned a basketball scholarship to Pennsylvania's Swarthmore College, where he went on to graduate with highest honors in 1929. He taught at a prep school for two years and then won a two-year scholarship for study and travel in Europe, where he took classes at St. Andrew's University in Scotland. According to published reports, Michener studied art in London and Italy, spent a winter in the Outer Hebrides, where he collected folk songs and stories, worked on a Mediterranean cargo vessel, and toured northern Spain with a group of bullfighters. Following his return to the United States, Michener earned a master's degree in education from the University of Northern Colorado and then taught at UNC and at Harvard University's School of Education. He was working on a doctorate in education at Harvard when he enlisted in the service in World War II. During his tour of duty with the Navy, Michener served on about 49 different South Pacific islands. The result was *Tales*

was 78, the 1,096-page epic turned out to be his longest work. Like *Hawaii, Space,* and *Chesapeake* before it, and *Poland, Alaska,* and *Mexico* that followed, *Texas* required no dramatic title. The image the title conjured in people's imaginations, and the bold name of the author below it, was enough to turn Texas into a million-copy blockbuster.

Michener and his wife, Mari, found a home in Austin during the years the author spent researching and writing his Texas saga. According to the *Austin American–Statesman,* Michener once told a friend as they walked down the West Austin street where he lived, "You know, I think I'm happier living on this street than any street I've lived on in my life." That statement said a great deal about the man who considered the world his home. His memoir features a of the South Pacific. At 41, James Michener turned to writing full time.

Michener followed up his first novel with *The Fires of Spring*, which his closest friends in Austin say reveals more about the author than his official memoir. The book tells the story of a poor Pennsylvania boy who becomes a writer. The books that followed championed universal ideals: racial and religious tolerance, self-reliance, hard work, and human understanding. His belief in the brotherhood of humanity was perhaps one of the strongest undercurrents in his books. A self-described fiery liberal, Michener said in a 1972 interview, "I've never felt in a position to reject anybody. I could be Jewish, part Negro, probably not Oriental, but almost anything else. This has loomed large in my thoughts."

His works represent decades of cultural immersion around the globe. He traveled from Japan to Korea and Hungary, a long stay in Hawaii and then on to Afghanistan and Spain, South Africa, Colorado and Israel, Chesapeake Bay, and Poland. Texas was Michener's next stop and still the septuagenarian didn't slow down. He was 80 when he published *Alaska* in 1987 and there were 16 books to follow, including *Caribbean* and *Six Days in Havana,* a book he wrote with his Austin friend and associate John Kings. Texas was too big a theme for just one

book, albeit his longest, however. *The Eagle and the Raven,* his story of Mexican General Antonio Lopez de Santa Anna and Texas independence hero Sam Houston, was published in 1990. Seven more books followed before Michener published *Recessional* in 1994, which dealt with the right to die with dignity. Mari, his wife of nearly 40 years, died that same year of cancer and is buried next to her husband in Austin. (Michener's two previous marriages had ended in divorce. He never had children.) His last book, *A Century of Sonnets,* was published in 1997.

In his half century of work, Michener wrote nearly 50 books of nonfiction and fiction, many of them as thick as bricks. Along the way, Michener found time to establish the Texas Center for Writers—renamed the James Michener Center for Writers following his death in 1997—to enlighten writers for generations to come. Center director Jim Magnuson recalled in a *Texas Monthly* tribute following the author's death that Michener's involvement with UT writing students started informally. Michener asked to sit in on Magnuson's graduate fiction workshop as a teaching assistant. "The students were in awe of him, and he took their work seriously," Magnuson wrote. "He was like a Dutch uncle—encouraging, but concerned that no one got too big for his britches."

written by this distinguished Austin writer of multicultural children's books and cookbooks. *Dancing with the Indians, The Singing Man,* and *Rum Tum Tum* are among her books for children. Her cookbooks include *A Kwanzaa Celebration* and *Ideas for Entertaining.*

Michael Moorcock: Moorcock, who lives in nearby Bastrop, is a multi-award-winning author of adventure and fantasy novels. He has written more than 100 books, including *Tales from the Texas Woods, The War Amongst the Angels, Fabulous Harbors,* and the *Elric* series,

The university announced in 1988 that Michener was donating $1 million to create an interdisciplinary master of fine arts degree. Under Michener's plan, the program would train students in poetry, prose, screenwriting, and playwriting. It would go a step further, however, by requiring students to work in more than one genre. Another $3 million Michener gift to the program came in 1990. Two years later, Michener gave a whopping $15 million to the program. "I was stunned—it was far and away the largest gift ever made to support creative writing anywhere," Magnuson wrote in his article for the December 1997 issue of *Texas Monthly,* which featured Michener on the cover under the headline, "The Most-Generous Texans."

In the fall of 1993, the Texas Center for Writers admitted the first class of students into its MFA program. Michener, according to Magnuson, offered to read and critique the students' work and was well known for his involvement with them. Each fall he would invite the new class to his home and was a regular guest at the center's annual barbecue, where he would greet each student. Today the Michener Center for Writers is among the nation's most selective writing programs, admitting just 10 new students each fall and awarding them a $12,000-a-year stipend. Some of the finest writers in the world come to Austin to teach and give seminars at the center. More important, graduates of the young program have gone on to find success in a number of writing fields. The public at large also benefits from the center. An impressive series of world-renowned authors have come to Austin, courtesy of the center, to offer readings and host discussions of their work.

Marla Akin, program coordinator for the Michener Center for Writers, says Michener's life is an inspiration to students and to the center itself. "The money that fuels this program is something he worked to earn," she says. "He had such a work ethic and such a strong philosophy about sharing the bounty. He gave away 90 percent of what he made, and a good portion of that he gave to help other people find their voices as writers."

James Michener died of kidney failure on October 16, 1997, within two weeks of voluntarily terminating dialysis. He was 90. In a 1988 interview on *Good Morning America,* Michener talked about his craft. "I think I have a passion for telling a story and then working on it until I think it's coherent," he said. "I'm proud of my profession. I'm a writer. I never say I'm an author, that's somebody else. I'm a real good writer."

He was also a real good human being.

Blood, Gloriana, and *Mother London.* Michael also edits anthologies and writes short stories, rock songs, screenplays, and essays.

Laurence Parent: Parent produces stunningly beautiful books of photographs about the Lone Star State, including *Texas, The Texas Hill Country: A Postcard Book, Scenic Driving Texas,* and *Hiking Big Bend National Park.* He gave up a career in engineering to become a freelance photographer and writer. His 2004 *Texas Nature* calendar is breathtaking.

Turk Pipkin: Pipkin, a contributing editor to *Texas Monthly* magazine, switches easily from TV to books to journalism. *Fast Greens, Born of the River, Be a Clown!* and *The Winner's Guide to the Texas Lottery* are among his excellent books. He coedited *Barton Springs Eternal: The Soul of a City* and has written and produced a number of television programs.

Christopher Reich: Reich's debut thriller, *Numbered Account,* hit the bookstores with a bang in 1998 and became a *New York Times* best-seller along the way. Reich, born in Tokyo, drew on his experiences working in a major Swiss bank for three years to provide the basis for this gripping story. His follow-up books are *The First Billion* and *The Devil's Banker,* published in 2003.

Trevor Romain: Romain has written and illustrated more than a dozen books for children, including *Bullies Are a Pain in the Brain* and *How to Do Homework without Throwing Up.* He is a board member of the Candlelighter's Childhood Cancer Foundation and says his work with sick children has inspired his writing.

Louis Sachar: *Holes,* Sachar's novel about a boy wrongly accused of a crime and sent to a camp for juvenile delinquents in a dried-out Texas lake, won the 1998 National Book Award and the 1999 Newbery Medal—and made a star of Austinite Sachar. Legions of middle-graders across the country, however, were big Sachar fans way before *Holes* came along. Young readers get a kick out of books like *Dogs Don't Tell Jokes, There's a Boy in the Girls' Bathroom,* and *The Boy Who Lost His Face.* Sachar, who gave up a career in law to become a writer, titled his first book *Sideways Stories from Wayside School.* The book features a character called Louis the Yard Teacher—the nickname schoolchildren had given Sachar when he supervised kids on the playground. *Holes* was made into a major motion picture in 2003. Sachar wrote the screenplay.

Steven Saylor: Saylor has written an excellent series of books—nine so far—set in ancient Rome. Called the *Roma Sub Rosa* series, the books combine historical fiction with a good dose of mystery. This University of Texas graduate in history has appeared on the History Channel as an expert on Roman life and politics. The latest book in the series is *A Mist of Prophecies.*

Edwin "Bud" Shrake: Shrake was a sportswriter who worked for the *Dallas Morning News* and the *Dallas Times Herald* before becoming a staff writer for *Sports Illustrated.* His 15 books include *Strange Peaches* and *Blood Reckoning* as well as celebrity autobiographies of Willie Nelson and Barry Switzer. Shrake also has written more than a half dozen screenplays. He cowrote Harvey Penick's *Little Red Book,* the best-selling sports book ever (see our Golf chapter). The University of Texas Press reissued Shrake's classic *Blessed McGill* in 1997.

William Browning Spencer: This science fiction and horror writer's first novel, *Maybe I'll Call Anna,* won a New American Writings Award. *Resume with Monsters,* a satirical novel, won the 1995 Best Novel Award from the International Horror Critics Guild. He also has written *Zod Wallop.* Spencer writes both novels and short stories.

Bruce Sterling: A science fiction novelist, short-story writer, and magazine columnist, Sterling is one of the country's leading voices in science fiction and cyberpunk. His work includes the science fiction novels *The Artificial Kid* and *Heavy Weather.* His nonfiction book *The Hacker Crackdown: Law and Disorder on the Electronic Frontier* deals with computer crimes and civil liberties.

Jesse Sublett: For hard-boiled, set-in-Austin mysteries, Sublett's work is unparalleled. Look for his Texas music mysteries, *Rock Critic Murders* as well as *Tough Baby* and *Boiled in Concrete.* Sublett's work also includes more than 25 documentaries, and he has written for television and multimedia.

Mary Willis Walker: *All the Dead Lie Down* is the latest novel from this multi-award-winning Austin mystery writer. Walker's first novel, *Zero at the Bone,* won both the Agatha and Macavity Awards. *Red Scream,* her second book, won both an Edgar Award from the Mystery Writers of America and a Violet Crown Award from the Writers' League of Texas. *Under the Beetle's Cellar* won the Hammett Award from the International Association of Crime Writers. Her set-in-Austin mysteries are wonderful.

Lawrence Wright: "*Remembering Satan* catapults Wright to the front rank of American journalists." That's what *Newsweek* said in 1994 about Wright's tragic story of recovered memory. Wright, a staff writer for the *New Yorker,* also has written for *Texas Monthly, Rolling Stone,* and the *New York Times Magazine.* His wonderful books also include *City Children, Country Summer, In the New World* (subtitled *Growing up in America from the Sixties to the Eighties*), *Saints and Sinners,* about religion in America, and *Twins,* published in 1997.

Five Texans

John Erickson: Erickson has written a series of books for children that have reached near-classic status and are wonderful for new or visiting pint-size Texans. Hank the Cowdog, who has been described as a "canine Don Knotts," is always solving one mystery or another as he fulfills his duties as Head of Ranch Security. Hank has been featured in more than 30 books by Erickson since the author started writing more than 30 years ago while working as a full-time cowboy, farm hand, and ranch manager. Erickson, a UT graduate, now lives on a ranch along the Oklahoma border in Perryton, Texas.

> The Austin Jewish Book Fair is a local literary tradition. Started in 1983, the fair features nationally known speakers, programs for the whole family, and books, tapes, and CDs for sale. The fair is held in November at the Dell Jewish Community Center. Most events are free. Call (512) 735–8058 or visit www.jcaaonline.org for information.

John Graves: One doesn't read John Graves so much as listen while he relates his personal, often poignant, accounts of life and death in Texas. It takes a page, perhaps two, to quiet the modern-day hubbub in your head that anxiously wonders how long he's going to take to describe the fish running in the Brazos River before you realize that you ARE on the river, or sitting around a campfire immersed in the voice of a superlative storyteller. Graves, one of Texas's preeminent authors, has earned a horde of loyal fans who reside far beyond our state's borders. His classic *Goodbye to a River,* published in 1960, is one reason. *Hard Scrabble* and *From a Limestone Ledge* are others. A wonderful anthology of Graves's writing, *A John Graves Reader,* published in 1996 by the University of Texas Press, includes selections from these three books as well as stories first published elsewhere. This collection is a perfect introduction to Graves's work. Don't pass by the introduction to *Reader.* It's written by Edwin "Bud" Shrake (see the previous listing). Graves, who lives in Glen Rose, Texas, also has written for such magazines as *Atlantic Monthly* and *Texas Monthly.*

Larry L. King: You can take Larry L. King out of Texas, but you can't take the Texan out of Larry L. King. This East Texas–born playwright, screenwriter, novelist, essayist, and short-story writer may be best known to the outside world as coauthor of *The Best Little Whorehouse in Texas,* his hit Broadway musical that was later made into a movie. King also conquered Broadway with *The Night Hank Williams Died*. His excellent political novel, *The One-Eyed Man*, was published in 1966. King's work has appeared in periodicals such as the *Texas Observer, Texas Monthly,* the *Washingtonian,* and *Parade*. He's won an Emmy Award, the Helen Hayes Award, and the Stanley Walker Journalism Award and has been nominated for a Tony and a National Book Award. In 1997 the University of Texas Press published King's *True Facts, Tall Tales, Pure Fiction,* a collection of 19 of King's outstanding essays and short stories. That volume, along with the 1984 collection *Warning: Writer at Work,* will have even you Yankees wishing you'd been born under the Lone Star. King now lives in Washington, D.C.

Larry McMurtry: *Lonesome Dove, Terms of Endearment, The Last Picture Show*. We probably don't need to say any more about this prolific Texan, but we will. A Pulitzer Prize–winner, McMurtry has published more than a score of novels and two collections of essays and has written more than 30 screenplays. It doesn't seem too much of a stretch to say most everyone knows of the adventures of Texas Rangers August McCrae and Woodrow F. Call, whose lives are depicted in the epic *Lonesome Dove* and its sequels and prequel, *Streets of Laredo, Dead Man's Walk,* and *Comanche Moon*. Moviegoers and miniseries watchers have seen McMurtry's stories come to life again and again. It's practically a rule in Texas: Read McMurtry before you get here.

Dan Jenkins: *Baja Oklahoma* is one of the most hilarious books about Texas we've ever read. At times profane and even sexist, *Baja* nonetheless will have you falling down with laughter as you follow the trials and tribulations of waitress and aspiring country-western songwriter Juanita (born under the sign of polyester) Hutchins and the other characters who frequent Herb's Cafe. Jenkins, a Fort Worth native who now lives in Manhattan, is a former senior writer for *Sports Illustrated* and a monthly columnist for *Playboy* magazine. He's written other acclaimed books, including *Semi-Tough* and *Dead Solid Perfect*.

BUY THE BOOK

As if in a scene by Kafka, you innocently walk through a door and suddenly you're transformed—into a worm, no less. As you look around you realize the room is crawling with all kinds of worms: big ones, baby ones, curly haired ones, bearded ones, coffee-drinking worms, worms wearing ties, worms taking notes. It's a community, a coterie, a coven of worms. Ahhhh.

You're right at home. Whether it's 10:00 in the morning or 10:00 at night, Austin's bookstores are teeming with those literate critters known as bookworms. Austin consistently ranks among the top 10 cities in per capita sales of books, according to nationwide studies done by the book industry. From small specialty stores to giant superstores, Austin's booksellers cater to the complex tastes of our readers. Readings and book signings by nationally known and local authors, comfy couches, and cafes are just a few of the features some bookstores offer to lure readers—and to add life to Austin's literary scene. For those of you who can't wait to savor the Austin bookstore experience, read below for a listing of some of our outstanding shops.

Throughout Greater Austin

Barnes & Noble Booksellers
Seven stores in Austin and Round Rock
(512) 328–3155
www.barnesandnoble.com
This large New York–based chain arrived in Austin in 1994 and has grown to include seven superstores around the city and in Round Rock. Barnes & Noble wasted no time in becoming part of, and promoting,

Austin's literary, musical, and artistic communities. Each store hosts a number of monthly book discussion groups on a variety of areas of interest, including fiction, nonfiction, science fiction, and Texana. The stores are a popular place to attend regular book readings and book signings by local, national, and international writers and screenwriters. Barnes & Noble has also sponsored a number of uniquely Austin events, including *Texas Monthly* magazine's 25th anniversary celebration in 1998. The stores also are extremely active in promoting and hosting events for the annual Texas Writer's Month celebration in May. There's so much going on at Barnes & Noble that each store publishes a monthly calendar of events. Several stores feature a large music section with headphones for sampling a variety of artists. The children's sections are wonderful, and so are the numerous story times the stores host each week. Barnes & Noble also works in conjunction with local and national organizations that promote literacy and is involved with the Austin Independent School District's Adopt-a-School program. In 1998 Barnes & Noble became cosponsor of the Writers' League of Texas's annual Violet Crown Awards program. The inviting aroma of coffee permeates these stores, thanks to the great cafe and pastry shop inside each one. In addition to the Barnes & Noble stores, this chain also owns Austin's Bookstop and the B. Dalton's bookstores.

The Web site gives the addresses of all B&N stores in the area.

Half Price Books
Five stores in Austin and Round Rock
(512) 454-3664
www.halfpricebooks.com

With four Austin locations and another in Round Rock, Half Price Books offers Central Texans easy access to its wide selection of used and new books, including rare and out-of-print titles and Texana and Americana titles not easily found elsewhere. The Dallas-based chain opened its first Austin store in 1975 and continues

to expand within the city. Half Price Books has a good selection of children's books as well as music in all formats, magazines, and videos. New books sell for half the current retail price or less. The store buys used books, magazines, videos, and music.

Central

Adventures in Crime & Space Books
609-A West Sixth Street
(512) 473-2665
www.crimeandspace.com

Locally owned and operated since 1994, Adventures in Crime & Space has captured a faithful Austin clientele. The store's 20,000 new and used titles include horror, mystery, and science fiction books as well as a number of rare titles and books on art. Art card collectors will find a wide assortment of decks devoted to different artists in the genre. Adventures in Crime & Space also buys used books.

Austin Books
5002 North Lamar Boulevard
(512) 454-4197
www.austinbooks.com

For a huge selection of comics and books that celebrate American pop culture, Austin Books is the place to go. This locally owned store, serving Austin since 1978, specializes in science fiction, fantasy, and mystery of the American potboiler type. The store stocks about 500 new titles of comic books as well as thousands more classics. The store also has a lot of collectible science fiction as well as out-of-print and hard-to-find titles. Want to know the names of all the crew members of Speed Buggy? These guys have the answer. Some good had to come of their youth spent in front of a television set. Austin Books also has movie posters, vintage toys, and sports cards.

Bevo's Bookstore
1202 West Avenue
(512) 477-2992
www.bevos.com

Located near Austin Community College's Rio Grande campus, Bevo's sells ACC textbooks, school supplies, study aides, gift items, and souvenirs. This store and its branch in North Austin at 11900 Metric Boulevard near the ACC Northridge campus stock thousands of titles of textbooks and also offer collegiate clothing. Originally located on The Drag across from the University of Texas, this locally owned business was once a shop for UT supplies, hence the name Bevo's. The Web site online store still offers UT clothing and such.

BookPeople
603 North Lamar Boulevard
(512) 472-5050
www.bookpeople.com

This Austin institution was the city's first book superstore and continues to be one of Austin's major literary venues. With more than 200,000 titles, BookPeople is one of the largest bookstores in Texas. It definitely is one of Austin's favorite spots to shop for books and to hear authors read from their works. Founded in 1970 by two University of Texas students, the store later became Grok, an alternative bookstore. BookPeople, still locally owned and operated, has grown to encompass a huge selection of books in all genres and is especially known for an excellent selection of books on alternative healing, computers, and cooking. The store features a wonderful children's section and great newsstand as well as books on tape, gift items, and computer software for children

and adults. BookPeople's contributions to the Austin literary scene through the years have been enormous. This store goes out of its way to sell books written by local authors, even going so far as to buy books that are self-published. The store features a section of books about Texas and another dedicated to Texas authors. BookPeople sponsors regular book discussion groups and hosts three weekly story times for children, including one for preschoolers. Check out their monthly calendar for upcoming events. BookPeople has announced plans to move to a new location across the street on Sixth Street.

Bookstop
4001 North Lamar Boulevard
(512) 452-9541
www.barnesandnoble.com

Started by Austin entrepreneur Gary Hoover, this discount bookstore chain scored an immediate hit with the Austin book-buying public, which delighted in the store's huge selection—and special prices. Owned since 1989 by Barnes & Noble Booksellers, Bookstop continues its discount tradition. Hoover's idea was for regular customers to buy a membership card, which then afforded them discounts on *New York Times* best-sellers, magazines, and other purchases. The idea has been adopted by major booksellers like Barnes & Noble. Other Bookstop stores have assumed the B&N name, but this popular store retains the Austin home-grown name.

Book Woman
918 West 12th Street
(512) 472-2785
www.ebookwoman.booksense.com

This Austin original will celebrate its 30th anniversary in 2005. Book Woman specializes in new books by and about girls and women, but that tells only part of the story. Since 1975 this shop has been a showcase for women writers and musicians. Book Woman, owned by Austinite Susan Post, sponsors a monthly book club for women and hosts readings and book signings by local and national writers. The regular music series held on the third Friday of each month features women singers and songwriters. In addition to its great fiction section, the shop stocks an impressive collection of books on such subjects as self-help, women's health and psychology, girls and teens, memoirs, biographies, spirituality, and feminism. It has a wonderful section dedicated to Latina and Chicana books and another section of lesbian fiction and nonfiction works. There's also a small used-book section. The store has a good-sized music section, and also sells pride jewelry, bumper stickers, buttons, and magnets. Book Woman also has a great selection of T-shirts that laud women artists and feminist politics. The community bulletin board, which displays information on events and services of interest to women, is a popular feature of this store. Book Woman is part of the feminist bookstores network and can do special orders from that catalog.

Funny Papers
2021 Guadalupe Street
(512) 478-9718
This is one of Austin's one-stop shops for fans of comic books, role-playing games, collectible card games, collectible figurines, and more. Funny Papers sells comic book–related collectibles and many types of players' handbooks that go along with role-playing games. This unique store, which opened in Dobie Mall near the UT campus in 1990, receives about 100 new comic book titles each week and also stocks a wide selection of back issues and trade paperbacks. Funny Papers has an assortment of collectible card games as well as magic cards and all the supplies needed for card collectors. Regular comic book subscribers receive a discount.

Hart of Austin Antiquarian Books
1009 West Sixth Street
(512) 477-7755
Locally owned and operated since 1992, this large antiquarian bookstore is located in the delightful Whit Hanks Antiques complex. Owner Pat Hart offers several thousand used and rare books in all genres. The store also buys book and offers appraisals.

University Co-op Bookstore
2244 Guadalupe Street
(512) 476-7211, (800) 255-1896
www.universitycoop.com
Founded in 1896, the University Co-op is owned by the students, faculty, and staff of the University of Texas at Austin. The bookstore offers UT and Austin Community College textbooks as well as books for UT Extension classes, correspondence courses, and informal classes. This is also a great place to shop for UT apparel, gifts, and souvenirs as well as greeting cards, art, and school supplies. The store has been on The Drag right across the street from the UT campus since 1919, although it moved one door down in 1998 to make room for a new Barnes & Noble. The Co-op East Bookstore at 2902 Medical Arts Street also has some souvenirs but mainly carries textbooks for the UT Law School, the nursing program, and other graduate programs. The co-op has expanded recently to include two other locations on Guadalupe Street: the Annex and the Co-op for Women. There also are locations at 605 West 13th Street and 2237 East Riverside Drive.

South Central

Resistencia Book Store
1801-A South First Street
(512) 416-8885
www.resistenciabooks.com
Owned by Austin poet raulrsalinas (that's his legal name), Resistencia adds an important dimension to the Austin literary scene. This specialty store, established in Austin in the early 1980s and located in South Central Austin since 1992, is well known for promoting the literary arts through its sponsorship of regular poetry readings, book signings, and book readings by local and national authors. The store specializes

in Native American, Chicano, Latino, African-American, and feminist literature, poetry, and history. Resistencia also features CDs and tapes by local and international musicians in its specialty areas. The store offers literary magazines, T-shirts, and posters and features a community bulletin board announcing literary events. On the the first and third Friday of each month, Resistencia hosts "Cafe Libero," a poetry reading and open-mic event for poets to try out their stuff. This is one store that Austin relies on for more than books.

Whole Life Books
1006 South Lamar Boulevard
(512) 443-6794

This nonprofit bookstore, music store, and gift shop specializes in books on alternative health, metaphysics, spirituality, meditation, and New Age topics. Whole Life Books, which opened in 1983, is the only store of its kind in Austin that does not exist for commercial purposes. Austinite Ted Lanier, former UT graduate student in psychology and the former owner of a "hippie bicycle shop," started the operation as a reading room so that people could investigate for themselves the possible approaches to discovering nonmaterial spiritual reality. His patrons, however, wanted to buy the books they discovered in the reading room—and a business was born. The store now stocks about 40,000 titles as well as a wide assortment of CDs and tapes. Candles, wind chimes, incense, and jewelry can also be found at Whole Life Books.

Southwest

Borders Books, Music and Cafe
4477 South Lamar Boulevard
(512) 891-8974
www.borders.com

There are always stacks of bargain books on the sidewalk outside this popular bookstore and cafe in the Westgate Central Market shopping center. Part of the national chain, the bookstore has an extensive stock, plus a large selection of magazines, periodicals, and newspapers, including international editions. See the listing in the Northwest section for more details on Borders' local activities.

North

Ark of Austin
2438 West Anderson Lane
(512) 451-7606

For Bibles as well as books, music, and gifts with a Christian theme, Ark of Austin is the place to go. Located in the West Anderson Plaza shopping center, Ark is an Austin-owned shop in business since 1979. The store offers thousands of new hardbacks and paperbacks as well as jewelry, calendars, stationery, cards, and blank books. Ark also has Christian CDs, tapes, and song books for the music lover.

B. Dalton Bookseller
Highland Mall, 6001 Airport Boulevard
(512) 452-5739

This national chain of mall bookstores now owned by Barnes & Noble has been serving Austin for nearly three decades. B. Dalton has two stores in North Austin malls that stock a full range of hardbacks, paperbacks, children's books, and books on tape as well as national and local magazines. The stores also sponsor occasional book signings and book readings.

Emmaus Catholic Books & Gifts Company
6001 Burnet Road
(512) 458-2479

Serving Austin since the early 1980s, Emmaus Catholic Books & Gifts offers a wide range of religious books in English and Spanish, as well as Bibles, rosaries, gifts, and cards. Emmaus also sells music tapes.

West

Over the Rainbow
2727 Exposition Boulevard, Suite 123
(512) 477-2954

Primarily a toy store, Over the Rainbow also stocks a large selection of books for children. This locally owned shop has been in the same spot since 1975. Parents will find chapter books, early reading, and picture books, as well as art books and lots of educational games and toys.

Northwest

Booksource
13729 Research Boulevard
(512) 258-1313

Booksource carries about 20,000 titles of new and used books and specializes in collectible first editions. The Austin-owned store, opened in 1987, also carries comic books and original comic book artwork. Booksource, in the Lake Creek Festival shopping center, has a wide selection of both hardbacks and paperbacks, fiction, and some nonfiction.

Borders Books, Music and Cafe
10225 Research Boulevard
(512) 795-9553
www.borders.com

This superstore, which opened in 1995, has earned a great reputation for its support of the Austin literary and music communities. Readers, writers, music lovers, and musicians have found a place in this wonderful store. Borders hosts five book discussion groups each month, including one for young adults. Local and national authors regularly appear at Borders for book readings and/or signings, book discussion panels, and other events of interest to the literary community. Borders also is active in sponsoring events for the annual Texas Writers Month celebration in May.

The children's department is always buzzing with activity, and the store hosts two regular story times for children each week. This store has an outstanding selection of computer books and a great Texana section, as well as many other well-stocked specialty areas. Borders has a fantastic music department, which includes many headphones for sampling music selections.

It also features live music performances on Friday and Saturday. Borders hosts regular events to coincide with new record releases by well-known musicians. The Austin store, one of the Ann Arbor, Michigan–based chain's more than 180 stores nationwide, is a member of the Austin School District's Adopt-a-School program and is active in other community organizations, including the Austin Writers' League. The inviting coffee shop serves a wide range of gourmet coffees as well as pastries and sandwiches. Don't miss the monthly calendar of events to stay abreast of the latest happenings at Borders.

Sue's Book Exchange
13450 Research Boulevard
(512) 250-0175
1205 Round Rock Avenue, Round Rock
(512) 244-9193

This locally owned store and its branch in Round Rock feature new and used books of all kinds. And Sue's accepts trade-ins for discounts on books—a very popular aspect of this bookstore. About half the Austin store is dedicated to romance books and includes both best-sellers and series romances. Romance fans will also find the trade magazine *Romantic Times*. The stores also stock a number of fiction and nonfiction books of all types. Sue's offers up to a 20 percent discount on new books and sells used paperbacks for half the cover price. With the trade-in of a comparable book, clients can buy used paperbacks for a quarter of the cover price.

Waldenbooks/Waldenkids
Lakeline Mall, 11200 Lakeline Mall Drive
(512) 257-1950
www.waldenbooks.com

The largest mall book retailer in the country, Waldenbooks has been in Austin for more than 15 years and at its present location since the Lakeline Mall opened in 1996. This Austin location is one of the chain's large-format stores; it features a larger title selection than most and has a special area with a separate entrance for children's books, called Waldenkids. The

The Austin Public Library operates a Youth Services Events Hotline at (512) 974-7302 that provides information about kid-oriented activities at city libraries, including author visits, story times, musical events, and more. Also learn about the library's Wired for Youth programs, which give young people access to computer technology, at www.wiredforyouth.com.

store is part of the Borders Group Inc. national chain that includes Borders Books in Austin and Brentanos in other cities in Texas. The store also sells magazines and books on tape. Waldenbooks offers a discount program, which includes all Waldenbooks and Brentano's nationwide. For an annual fee, customers can join the Preferred Reader Program, which offers a discount on all purchases except magazines and gift certificates.

BORROW THE BOOK

As centers of learning and for community outreach, Austin's public libraries are among our greatest public assets. Despite the bookstore boom of the 1990s, which brought hundreds of thousands of books to our community, more and more citizens are turning to the public libraries for their reading material. Of course there's no place like the library for doing research, getting on the Internet free of charge, or checking out that vintage recording. Those attractions, and the surge in Austin's population in recent years, have put a strain on our already limited library resources.

Authorities say the materials collection at the present Central Library is about a third the size it should be to meet Austin's needs. Despite limited resources, however, the library system has won a number of awards for its efforts to make reading and research materials available to everyone, to increase literacy in the city of Austin,

and to provide after-school tutoring. Our library was named Library of the Year in 1993 by *Library Journal* and Gale Research for its innovative and creative approach to programming in the face of funding shortages. Austin's existing Central Library, whose 363,000 volumes leave no room for additional books, will remain a substandard facility for at least several years to come (although city officials are on the lookout for a suitable downtown site for a new facility). Don't let the statistics prevent you from enjoying our public libraries, however. We couldn't get by a week without seeking out one or another of our libraries—and we always come home with an armload of books.

The Austin public library system is made up of 22 facilities that include the John Henry Faulk Central Library, the Austin History Center, and 20 branch libraries located all over the city. The library's collection includes 2.5 million items, including the History Center's vast collection. Austin's strong neighborhood associations have convinced the City of Austin to construct more and more branch libraries, and these same groups have successfully thwarted attempts to close smaller branches. As a result, Austin's branch library system provides easy access to books and to the Internet for citizens all over the city. Some branches are within a mile or two of each other. The hub of the interconnected system continues to be the Central Library, however, which is more than 10 times the size of some of our branches. While branch libraries do not always have the book you want, the library system allows for books to be sent from the Central Library or another branch, usually within a couple of days.

Due to cutbacks in the city budget, operating hours at branch libraries were reduced in 2003, and now only the Central Library is open seven days a week. The branch libraries listed below are generally open five days a week, although a couple open also for a few hours on Sunday. Weekday hours are usually 10:00 A.M. to

9:00 P.M. and Saturday 10:00 A.M. to 5:00 P.M. Call before you go to verify hours.

Central

John Henry Faulk Central Library
800 Guadalupe Street
(512) 499-7300
Named for revered Austinite John Henry Faulk (see the introduction to this chapter for more on Faulk), Austin's Central Library has more than 360,000 books, manuscripts, periodicals, artistic prints, and recordings. It also features 26 computers that connect to the Internet. In 2003 the library begin offering wireless Internet connections for those who wish to connect to the Web via their own laptops. The library is open Monday through Thursday from 10:00 A.M. to 9:00 P.M., Friday and Saturday from 10:00 A.M. to 6:00 P.M., and Sunday noon to 6:00 P.M.

Austin History Center
810 Guadalupe Street
(512) 499-7480
This building, which served as Austin's city library for nearly half a century, is now home to one of the leading local history collections in the state. The History Center houses more than one million items documenting the history of Austin to the present day. It's closed Thursday and Friday. (See our Attractions chapter for more about this wonderful facility.)

There is also one branch library in Central Austin:

Yarborough Branch
2200 Hancock Drive
(512) 454-7208
Closed Thursday and Sunday.

South Central

Twin Oaks Branch
2301 South Congress Avenue, #7
(512) 442-4664
Closed Thursday and Sunday.

North

Little Walnut Creek Branch
835 West Rundberg Lane
(512) 836-8975
Closed Friday and Sunday.

North Village Branch
2139 West Anderson Lane
(512) 458-2239
Closed Thursday and Sunday.

South

Manchaca Road Branch
5500 Manchaca Road
(512) 447-6651
Closed Friday.

Pleasant Hill Branch
211 East William Cannon Drive
(512) 441-7993
Closed Thursday and Sunday.

East

Carver Branch
1607 Pennsylvania Avenue (until October 2004)
1161 Angelina Street (after October 2004)
(512) 472-8954
Closed Thursday and Sunday.

Cepeda Branch
651 North Pleasant Valley Road
(512) 499-7372
Closed Thursday and Sunday.

Oak Springs Branch
3101 Oak Springs Drive
(512) 926-4453
Closed Friday and Sunday.

Terrazas Branch
1105 East Cesar Chavez Street
(512) 472-7312
Closed for remodeling until January 2005.

West

Howson Branch
2500 Exposition Boulevard
(512) 472-3584
Closed Friday and Sunday.

Northwest

Milwood Branch
12500 Amherst Drive
(512) 339-2355
Closed Friday and Sunday.

Old Quarry Branch
7051 Village Center Drive
(512) 345-4435
Closed Friday and Sunday.

Spicewood Springs Branch
8637 Spicewood Springs Road
(512) 258-9070
Closed Thursday and Sunday.

Northeast

Saint John Branch
7500 Blessing Avenue
(512) 974-7570
Closed Thursday and Sunday.

University Hills Branch
4721 Loyola Lane
(512) 929-0551
Closed Friday and Sunday.

Windsor Park Branch
5833 Westminster Drive
(512) 928-0333
Closed Friday and Sunday.

Southeast

Daniel E. Ruiz Branch
1600 Grove Boulevard
(512) 974-7500
Closed Friday and Sunday.

Southeast Austin Community Branch
5803 Nuckols Crossing Road
(512) 462-1452
Closed Friday and Sunday.

Southwest

Hampton Branch at Oak Hill
5125 Convict Hill Road
(512) 892-6680
Closed Thursday and Sunday.

University of Texas Libraries

It pays to have one of the largest universities in the country right in your own backyard, especially when that university has a great library system—the fifth-largest academic library in North America to be exact. The UT library system comprises 17 facilities, including 14 general libraries—all but the Marine Science Library located in Austin and most open to the public. Visitors who wish to use these UT libraries may acquire a Courtesy Borrower Card, available for a $40 annual fee or apply for a free TexShare card from the Austin Public Library. Call your branch library for details on how to apply for a TexShare card. Information is available at the Courtesy Borrower Desk at the main UT library, the Perry-Castañeda Library (512-495-4305). Brochures describing the libraries, their locations, and hours of operation, which vary, can also be obtained at the Borrower Desk. For general information call (512) 495-4350. On-site use of the other three system libraries—the Center for American History, the Harry Ransom Humanities Research Center, and the Tarlton Law Library—is free.

We've provided information about the main libraries here. For information about all UT libraries and their locations, visit the university's Web site at www.utexas.edu. Vehicular access to the main campus is restricted during normal school hours, so if you'd like to visit one of the UT libraries, it's best to park in one of the lots or parking garages located off campus nearby.

Perry-Castañeda Library
21st and Speedway Streets
(512) 495-4250
The main library of the UT system contains about three million volumes in all subject fields. The PCL, as it is known, emphasizes the humanities, the social sciences, business, and education. Subject strengths are American and British history, the South, 20th-century American literature, and modern German literature. The PCL also houses the Map Collection, the East Asian Program, South Asian Program, and the Middle Eastern Program. U.S. government and United Nations documents can also be found here, along with other collections. Most of the books available for loan are found on levels 3 to 6.

Undergraduate Library
Flawn Academic Center
Near 24th and Guadalupe Streets
(512) 495-4444
The materials in the Undergraduate Library (UGL) are particularly useful to lower-division undergraduates and include a media collection to support classroom instruction and individual research. The Student Microcomputer Facility in the UGL has several hundred workstations and is the largest microcomputer facility on campus but is exclusively for student use. There's also an Audiovisual Library that contains films, musical recordings, and spoken recordings. This facility is just west of the UT Tower.

The Nettie Lee Benson
Latin American Collection
Sid Richardson Hall, Manor Road
Between Red River Street and East
Campus Drive
(512) 495-4520
Adjacent to the LBJ Library on campus, the Nettie Lee Benson Latin American

If you have a TexShare card from the public library in Austin, you can borrow materials from the University of Texas, Austin Community College, and public libraries outside the city without having to pay a membership fee. Ask your local library for details.

Collection is an internationally renowned collection of books and many more materials on subjects relating to Latin America and writings by Latin Americans. The collection includes the Mexican American Library Program, which collects materials relating to all aspects of Spanish-speaking people in the United States, especially Mexican Americans.

Fine Arts Library
Fine Arts Library and Administration Building
Near 23rd and Trinity Streets
(512) 495-4480
The library includes materials on art, the performing arts, and music, including plenty about Austin's modern music scene. The art collection emphasizes 19th- and 20th-century art of the Americas but includes materials on all art movements and schools, the philosophy of art, art education, and aesthetics.

The music collection provides support for teaching and research in applied music, music education, musicology, and more. The performing arts collection is designed to support studies in drama history, performance, play production, playwriting, drama education, and dance. The library also houses the Historic Music Recordings Collection, with facilities to play selections.

Special UT Libraries

These libraries are not part of UT's Borrower Card network, but on-site use is free.

Center for American History
Sid Richardson Hall
(512) 495-4532

More than half the people who use the Center for American History are not associated with the University of Texas. This center, adjacent to the LBJ Library, offers free access to materials after patrons complete an application form and show a photo ID. No materials may be checked out.

The holdings of the Texas Collection Library, the Archives and Manuscripts Unit, the Fleming University Writings Collections, Natchez Trace Collection, Bexar Archives, Congressional History Collection, Sam Rayburn Library and Museum (Bonham, Texas), and the Texas Newspaper and Non-Textural Records Unit form the most extensive collection of Texana in existence and provide a major resource for the study of Southern, Western, and Southwestern history.

Harry Ransom Humanities Research Center
Near 21st and Guadalupe Streets
(512) 471-8944

Visitors may use the materials here free of charge by filling out an application and showing a photo ID. Materials may not be checked out. The center's collections include more than 1 million books, about 30 million manuscripts, 5 million photographs, and 40,000 pieces of literary iconography. The center offers extensive resources in 20th-century English and American literature and contain important resources for research in English literature from the 17th through 19th centuries. The center also hosts book readings.

Tarlton Law Library
Townes Hall, East Dean Keeton Street
Between San Jacinto Boulevard and East Campus Drive
(512) 471-7726

The sixth-largest academic law library in the United States and the largest in the Southwest, the Tarlton Law Library contains more than one million volumes of law and law-related materials. Access to the library is free, but users who wish to check out materials must obtain a borrower card for a fee. This is separate from the general libraries Borrower Card.

Texas State University Collection

Southwestern Writers Collection
Alkek Library, Seventh Floor,
Texas State University,
San Marcos
(512) 245-2313

It's well worth the trip to San Marcos, about 35 miles south of Austin, to explore Texas State University's great Southwestern Writers Collection. The collection, which began in 1986 with a major gift of J. Frank Dobie materials from Austinites Bill and Sally Wittliff, has grown into an important archive that records the literary and artistic spirit of the American Southwest. The collection includes books, manuscripts, personal papers, and artifacts of Southwestern writers. The Wittliff Gallery of Southwest & Mexican Photography, which opened in 1996, exhibits work of important photographers of the region, included the internationally renowned Texas photographer Keith Carter. Entrance to both collections is free and open to the public. Materials may not be checked out. Patrons must show a photo ID to enter.

Community Libraries

Cedar Park Public Library
550 Discovery Boulevard, Cedar Park
(512) 259-5353
www.ci.cedar-park.tx.us/library

Opened in 1981, the Cedar Park Public Library now holds about 70,000 book titles as well as videos, books on tape, music CDs, and more than 100 magazine and newspaper titles. The library also has Internet computers for public use. The library is free for Cedar Park residents. Others may obtain a card for $20 for six months or $35 per year. The library is open Monday through Thursday from 9:00 A.M. to 9:00 P.M., Friday and Saturday from 9:00 A.M. to 5:00 P.M., and Sunday 1:00 to 6:00 P.M.

Lake Travis Community Library
3322 R.R. 620 South
(512) 263-2885
www.ltlibrary.org
This library at Lake Travis High School serves Lake Travis community residents as well as all those summer visitors who flock to the lake. In addition to the fiction and nonfiction sections, the library features a good-size children's section, large print books, newspapers and magazines, audio and video cassettes, as well as Internet computers for public use. This library also features an ongoing bag-of-books sale to raise funds. For $5.00 visitors can buy duplicate books that have been donated to the library. Volunteers who staff this library in summer say this program is especially popular with out-of-town visitors. Operating hours vary according to season. Proof of Texas residency is the only ID required to check out books.

Pflugerville Community Library
102 Tenth Street, Pflugerville
(512) 251-9185
www.library.cityofpflugerville.com
Once housed in an old home in what was euphemistically called "downtown" Pflugerville, the library, like other city services, found itself overwhelmed by the growth of the once-quiet little town northwest of Austin. A bond program raised the funds for the new facility, which is located between the local high school and a middle school. There are now 38,500 volumes on the shelves, eight computers, plus three "kid-friendly" computer stations, a reference library, and a children's library, appropriate for a community where many of the residents are young families. There is no fee to belong to the library. Open Monday through Thursday 10:00 A.M. to 8:00 P.M., Friday 10:00 A.M. to 6:00 P.M., and Saturday from 10:00 A.M. to 4:00 P.M.

Robert G. and Helen Griffith Round Rock Public Library
216 East Main Street, Round Rock
(512) 218-7003
www.ci.round-rock.tx.us/library/library.html
The city's library, located in the heart of Round Rock's historic district, has expanded from 11,000 square feet to 42,000 square feet and has been renamed in honor of library patrons Robert G. and Helen Griffith. The library now boasts 140,000 items, including books, videos, CDs, and books on tape. There are 40 computer stations, including eight filtered computers for young patrons to use to access the Internet. Given the area's continued growth, more expansion is planned, perhaps into branch libraries. There is no fee for residents of Round Rock; patrons from outside the city limits pay $25 per year for an individual library card, $40 for a family. The library is open Monday through Thursday 9:00 A.M. to 9:00 P.M., Friday and Saturday 9:00 A.M. to 6:00 P.M., and Sunday 1:00 to 6:00 P.M.

WRITERS' ORGANIZATIONS

Writers, like other addicts, need support and there's no better comfort to be found than at the meetings of the groups listed here. We have yet to hear of one that has cured writing fever, however.

Writers' League of Texas
1501 West Fifth Street, Suite E-2
(512) 499-8914
www.writersleague.org
Established in 1981, the Writers' League of Texas has grown from a group of writers gathered in an Austin backyard to include more than 1,200 members, more than half living outside Central Texas. Formerly called the Austin Writers' League, the name was changed to reflect the membership base as well as the many programs the league offers to writers throughout the state. This fine organization, the largest in Texas, is highly involved

For offbeat encounters with Austin's literary scene, don't miss the annual O. Henry Pun-Off in May at the O. Henry Museum (see our chapter on Annual Events), or check newspaper listings for local Poetry Slam events.

in developing the Austin literary scene and providing support for its members. League members host many informal classes, workshops, and retreats for writers of many genres. The league also honors members with a number of annual awards and cash prizes. The Violet Crown Awards are given in three categories: fiction, nonfiction, and literary nonfiction. The Teddy Book Award goes to a writer of children's books. There's also a Manuscript Contest that recognizes high writing achievement in a number of categories. Additionally, the league awards writing fellowships totaling about $18,000 per year.

The nonprofit organization maintains a library and resource center that contains more than 1,500 volumes and includes books written by members that can be checked out. The league's monthly newsletter, the *Texas Writer,* provides a wealth of information for writers and book lovers. General meetings, open to the public, are held the third Thursday of each month and feature a speaker or panel of experts on topics of interest to writers. The league also has information about local writers' groups for specific genres. Regular membership is $50 a year.

Texas Institute of Letters
P.O. Box 298300, Fort Worth 76129
This honorary organization, established in 1936, recognizes practicing writers who have demonstrated substantial literary achievement, as well as others who have had a positive influence on the literary arts. Members, who are invited to join, must have a substantial connection to Texas. Most important for nonmembers, the TIL, as it is known, determines the winners of about $20,000 in annual writing prizes that are backed by foundations or individuals. The prizes include the prestigious $6,000 Jesse Jones Award for the best fiction book and the $5,000 Carr P. Collins Award for the best nonfiction book. Other awards are given for poetry, journalism, short stories, children's books, and book design. Additionally, the TIL and the University of Texas determine two annual winners of the Paisano Fellowship, which gives writers a six-month residence at J. Frank Dobie's Paisano ranch and a large stipend. The goals of the TIL are to stimulate interest in Texas letters, recognize distinctive achievement in the field, and promote fellowship among those interested in the literary and cultural development of the state.

PARKS AND RECREATION

No one who has stood on the edge of a Hill Country pasture in springtime could deny the beauty of Central Texas, but even long after the riot of colorful wildflowers is gone there is much to admire in the landscape of the Hill Country. Familiarity breeds admiration and learning about the particulars makes both residents and visitors appreciate the whole.

Central Texas is not only home to some of the world's intriguing and delicate fauna and flora but is also a land where residents enjoy a generally benign climate. This is a place where Christmas Day may be celebrated with a walk in the sun along Town Lake or a swim in Barton Springs Pool. Life, for much of the year, is lived outdoors in Austin.

Though Austin's nightlife and music scenes are touted, it is also the city's fondness for outdoor activities and an abundance of parks, greenbelts, and preserves that give Austin a reputation as a livable city. Pockets of greenery are fiercely defended against the pressures of urban sprawl. The Highland Lakes, which bring nature into the heart of the city via Town Lake, serve as a natural lifeline between the Hill Country and the city dweller.

The city also rises to the modern challenge to provide its citizens with something to do on the weekends other than mow the lawn. There are 5K runs, 10K runs, marathons, bicycle races, kite-flying contests, and rugby games. There are rocks to be climbed and Frisbees to be thrown.

This chapter offers a look at area parks and gives an overview of the many recreational activities popular in Central Texas. It is divided into three general sections: Parks, Recreation, and Watersports. The Parks section focuses on state, lake, county, and city parks. The Recreation section is divided into activities, and the Watersports section offers tips on how to enjoy Austin's lakes, rivers, and swimming facilities.

Please note: Wildlife, notably birds and deer, are abundant around Austin, but so are insects and snakes, so pack insect bite treatment and wear sturdy boots when hiking on nature trails. Snakes play a vital role in the ecosystem and are usually shy creatures that avoid human contact. Most snakebites can be treated successfully if aid is sought quickly. If you plan to be outdoors frequently in Austin, familiarize yourself with the snakes found in the Texas countryside; there are several good Texas wildlife guides available at local bookstores (see the Borrow the Book section of The Literary Scene chapter).

PARKS
State Parks

Forget packing up the family station wagon and driving for hours to reach a campsite or popular natural landmark a la *National Lampoon's Summer Vacation*. There are at least two dozen state parks within an easy two-hour drive of Austin. In total, there are 145 state parks under the management of the Texas Parks & Wildlife Department (800–792–1112, www.tpwd .state.tx.us). This is a first-class Web site with downloadable maps and PDF files that detail the state's parks, wildlife management areas (WMAs), and areas of interest, including biking, camping, driving tours, equestrian activities, fishing, hunting, and wildlife viewing. Visitors can make reservations on-line or by e-mail, plus fax and telephone numbers for campsites and cabins are listed. This is a great site to visit before planning a day trip, a weekend away, or a family vacation.

Among the 41 historical sites are several national landmarks, including the Admiral Nimitz Museum and Historical Center in Fredericksburg and Lyndon Johnson State Park in Stonewall, both to the west of Austin and easily accessible (see our Day Trips chapter).

Other state parks in Central Texas offer visitors an opportunity to experience Texas natural history. Most offer camping, water sports, nature trails for hiking, walking, or mountain biking, plus picnic facilities and perhaps equestrian trails. We have highlighted those near Austin that offer a variety of outdoor activities.

Admission to most state parks is between $1.00 and $5.00 per person. There is a 12-month passport that offers free admission for seniors, discounts or free admissions for veterans and disabled visitors, and discounted rates for Texas residents. These Gold Conservation Passports are available for an annual fee, currently $50, and are a real bargain. They entitle the bearer and the occupants of his or her vehicle to unlimited access to certain state areas and parks, depending on the color of the passport. These can be purchased at any state park, regional law enforcement office, or at the Austin Parks and Wildlife headquarters listed below. Passports also can be purchased on the Web site or by calling (800) 895–4248. There is a $5.00 charge for credit card purchases. A passport also includes one free tour of a Texas historical site, the quarterly *Texas Conservation Passport Journal,* and a reduced subscription to *Texas Parks and Wildlife* magazine.

Most state parks have camping facilities. Advance reservations are advised. Most parks are open for day visitors from 8:00 A.M. to 10:00 P.M., but call ahead for hours of operation, particularly on holidays. Parks that have certain natural attractions, greenbelts, nature trails, or swimming holes may have special hours and blackout dates.

Bastrop State Park
Highway 21,
1.5 miles east of Bastrop
(512) 321-2101

This 3,503 acre park 32 miles east of Austin is popular, perhaps because its landscape is so different from the surrounding countryside. The park is home to the "Lost Pines," a forest of pine trees (Texans call them "piney woods") that would seem to be more at home in East Texas. During the Depression, the Civilian Conservation Corps built several log cabins at the park, which are now popular for family getaways. There are 12 cabins accommodating from two to eight persons. Reservations and a deposit are required. All cabins have bathrooms, kitchen facilities, air-conditioning, and wood-burning fireplaces. Prices range from $65 to $110. For reservations call (512) 389–8900. No pets are allowed except for those aiding the physically challenged. Call the park number above for reservations and information.

The park also has camping facilities, a swimming pool open in the summertime, fishing on a 10-acre lake, hiking, golfing on a nine-hole course, and hiking trails. Park rangers offer guided nature tours, popular from January to March during the breeding season of the endangered Houston toad.

Scenic Park Road 1 connects with Buescher State Park, 15 miles east.

Buescher State Park
F.M. 153 off Highway 71, Smithville
(512) 237-2241

This 1,016-acre park, pronounced "Bisher" State Park, is a favorite spot for area fishermen. A 30-acre lake is stocked with trout, bass, and other fish. There are campsites, screened shelters, and picnic areas. Unlike nearby Bastrop State Park, oak trees and Blackland prairie dominate the landscape here. Popular activities at the park include biking, hiking, swimming, and boating.

Colorado Bend State Park
F.M. 580, west of Lampasas near Bend
(915) 628–3240
Take U.S. 183 to Lampasas, go west on F.M. 580 for about 24 miles, and then follow signs to the park. This 5,328-acre park offers primitive camping, hiking, fishing, swimming, mountain biking, birding, cave tours, and nature walks to the beautiful 60-foot-high Gorman Falls, particularly popular with bird-watchers.

Enchanted Rock State Natural Area
Rural R 965, north of Fredericksburg
(325) 247–3903
This popular and legendary park is 18 miles north of Fredericksburg (see our Day Trips chapter). The major feature of this 1,643-acre park is Enchanted Rock, a 640-acre granite outcropping, a vast stone dome that rises above the Hill Country landscape, similar to its geological cousins Uluru (Ayers Rock) in Australia and Stone Mountain in Georgia. (Enchanted Rock is second only to Stone Mountain in the U.S. rock outcropping category.) Hikers who are in good form can hike to the top (it's easier than Uluru) to enjoy an unparalleled view of Texas.

See our Day Trips chapter to learn more about the Native American origins of the "enchanted" part of the name. It is the "rock" part of the name that beckons the more down-to-earth types who are interested in rock climbing. In addition, there is camping, both tent and primitive, hiking, nature trails, and picnicking. Given its spectacular views and easy access from major population centers, the park reaches its visitor and parking limits early on weekends. Get an early start.

Inks Lake State Park
Highway 29 on Park Road 4, near Burnet
(512) 793–2223
This 1,201-acre Highland Lakes park 9 miles west of Burnet offers camping, recreational vehicle hookups, backpacking, hiking, golfing, boating, canoeing (canoes and paddleboats for rent), waterskiing, scuba diving, and fishing. It is a favorite for boaters and fishermen. The park offers nature trail walks and canoe tours in spring and fall. There is a sunset bat watch, and a grocery store is on-site. A nine-hole golf course is operated by Highland Lakes Golf Club, (512–793–2859), and the daily fee is $10 or less, depending on the day and time.

In 2001 the park added minicabin facilities that have four bunk beds with mattresses, renting for under $50 a night. The air-conditioned cabins also have table and chairs, a ceiling fan, an outdoor grill and fire ring, plus a water spigot.

The best time to call the state parks reservation number (512–389–8900) is midweek (Wednesday and Thursday), when call volumes are lighter. Monday and Tuesday and the week before major holidays are the busiest times. Before you go, visit the park you have chosen on-line at www.twpd.state.tx.us to download a detailed map in PDF format.

McKinney Falls State Park
5808 McKinney Falls Parkway, Austin
(512) 243–1643
Located just 13 miles southeast of downtown Austin off U.S. 183, this 744-acre park encompasses the lands around the confluence of Williamson and Onion Creeks, which flow across southern Hays and Travis Counties. The park is named for Texas pioneer Thomas McKinney, whose ruined home still stands near the confluence of the creeks. He was one of Stephen F. Austin's original 300 colonists.

The pool under the falls is a popular swimming spot, but it is limited to those days when park rangers deem it safe. On some days the bacteria count may be high due to pollution from upstream, nonpoint sources, so call ahead if you want to swim.

The park also has hiking, biking, fishing, picnicking, several screened shelters with bunk beds (no mattresses), and camping facilities. There are nature study areas, a dirt-bike trail, and group picnic facilities.

Pedernales Falls State Park
F.M. 3232, near Johnson City
(830) 868-7304
The park, 32 miles west of Austin, is reached by taking U.S. 290 West, then heading north for 8 miles on F.M. 3232. The spectacular falls are the highlight of this 5,211-acre park, formerly part of the Circle Bar Ranch. The falls are even more spectacular after a sudden spring rain, when the Pedernales River exhibits all the dangerous beauty of a Hill Country river in flash flood. Newcomers to Central Texas should be aware that even the driest creekbed can become a rushing torrent in literally minutes. The force and power of the water is deceptive, and powerful undertows can overturn large trucks and buses in seconds. Do not ignore warnings to keep to the high ground.

With its vast tumble of boulders and Hill Country plants and trees, the falls are beautiful, even on dry summer days. The park has fishing and nature study facilities, picnic sites, a hike and bike trail, swimming in the lower 3 miles of the river and an equestrian trail.

The Texas state parks system celebrated 75 years of stewardship in 1998. One handy guide to the state system is a map of Texas showing all the state park sites. Call (800) 786-8644. The cost is $3.11 to cover postage and handling.

The Lake Parks

The image of Texas as a land of deserts and vast, treeless wilderness owes a lot more to Hollywood than reality. That is especially true in Central Texas, where lakes abound. Most of them are not nature's work but owe their existence to people with gigantic imaginations who roamed the Texas political landscape in the first half of the 20th century.

Between 1843 and 1938 several devastating floods washed through the Hill Country along the path of the Colorado River. The horror of flooding was contrasted with the blight of drought. Texas leaders looked to the hills and dreamed of damming the river to stem the floods, defeat droughts, and harness the river's power to electrify the wilderness. With the help of engineers and laborers, they succeeded, and now the Highland Lakes climb 646 feet, stretch over 150 miles long, and encompass 56,000 acres of water and 700 miles of shoreline, making up the greatest concentration of fresh water in Texas.

In 1934 the Texas Legislature created the Lower Colorado River Authority (LCRA), a state agency that administers the chain of artificial lakes and dams created to harness the Colorado River. Today it is one of the most influential state agencies in terms of environmental policy. Though a major power generator, LCRA relies, for the most part, on Wyoming coal and Texas natural gas, not the dams, to light the homes of Texas Hill Country residents.

Hydroelectricity may be a very small part of the function of the Highland Lakes these days, but the lakes are still a vital force in the battle against floods and are a critical water supply for some communities in the area. They also provide water for rice farms downstream, a major Texas agricultural crop. Lake levels are susceptible to weather vagaries and downstream demand, so area residents, particularly those living lakeside, keep a close eye on local weather forecasts, which include lake information. Lake levels and water flows are of interest not only to lake residents; they are of vital importance to the recreation industry, which is now a major economic force in the Highland Lakes area.

There are three major links in the lake chain in the area around and in Austin.

The most urban link in the chain is Town Lake, 5 miles long from Tom Miller Dam in West Austin, near Redbud Trail, to Long-horn Dam in East Austin near Pleasant Valley Road.

Lake Austin is 20 miles long, stretch-ing from Mansfield Dam on Lake Travis to Tom Miller Dam. Lake Austin is the oldest of the Highland Lakes. In 1893 it cost a million dollars to build the dam that was later replaced by Tom Miller Dam. In 1900 water poured over the original dam, flood-ing downtown Austin and causing many drownings. Another million-dollar renova-tion was undertaken in 1912 but not com-pleted. Finally, with the creation of the LCRA, the work was completed in 1938. The dam, named for former Austin Mayor Tom Miller, has withstood many heavy rains since.

Lake Travis is 64 miles long and was formed by the construction of the 266-foot-high, 7,089-foot-long Mansfield Dam, which was built in 1941 and named for Texas Congressman J. J. Mansfield. Not only is the lake an increasingly popular recreational spot but its shores also are prized real estate.

With the booming growth, the High-land Lakes are just one focus of the debate among environmentalists and the development community. On the recre-ation front, there are increasing concerns about crowding on the lakes as personal watercraft, yachts, swimmers, scuba divers, water-skiers, windsurfers, and ciga-rette boats vie for space. Personal water-craft have been banned from the lakes during the three major summer holiday weekends: Memorial Day, Fourth of July, and Labor Day. Following verbal clashes and some accidents between motorized crafts and sailing vessels, there has been some discussion by the LCRA of "zoning" the lakes for various activities.

To the west of Lake Travis is Lake Buchanan, pronounced *Buck-ANN-un* by the locals (see our Texas Pronunciation guide in the Overview chapter). Created by the Buchanan Dam, the 31-mile-long lake is the highest in the chain and covers the largest surface area, although Lake Travis contains more water. The LCRA operates several parks on the lake as does Burnet County. The LCRA has set aside 16,000 acres for parks and reserves along the Colorado River—developed parks, envi-ronmental learning centers, recreational areas, and river access sites. The LCRA's Web site is a valuable resource and offers detailed guides and downloadable maps, which can be very handy when trying to locate remote areas and boating docks. These parks typically feature little artificial landscaping—hills have not been leveled, and large green spaces are usually Hill Country meadows rather than planted lawns. Picnic and campsites are shaded by oak trees and trails lined with juniper trees.

For more information about all the Highland Lakes, see our Day Trips chapter.

The Lower Colorado River Authority (LCRA)
(512) 473-3200, (800) 776-5272; ext. 3366
www.lcra.org
In addition to a wealth of information on water safety and quality, weather fore-casts, and utility, energy, and conservation issues, the agency also offers newcomers and visitors a park visitor's package, avail-able by calling the local number listed previously and requesting extension 4083. For detailed information on specific parks, detailed directions, and reservations where necessary, call extension 3366.

LCRA Primitive Areas

The river authority operates a primitive recreation system along the lake system. These campsites are in natural areas where the typical rugged Hill Country landscape has been minimally disrupted. Most of the sites are in out-of-the-way places, and visitors will need detailed directions or a good area map to find them. Call (512) 473-3200, ext. 4083 for directions and information. Some charge a nominal use fee, around $5.00.

Camp Creek Primitive Area
Lake Travis, off F.M. 1431
This 600-acre park, east of Marble Falls, 18 miles west of Lago Vista, has nature trails, boat ramps, boating, camping, and picnic facilities.

Gloster Bend Primitive Area
Lake Travis, off F.M. 1431
Approximately 6 miles west of Lago Vista, this lakeside site has camping and picnic facilities. Day use only is recommended, but the boat ramp is available 24 hours a day.

Grelle Primitive Area
Lake Travis,
off Highway 71 near Spicewood
Grelle is a 400-acre park with woods, trails, camping, and access to the lake. The hiking trails are challenging. Next door is the popular Krause Springs swimming hole (see the Swimming section of this chapter). Overnight camping is allowed.

Muleshoe Bend Primitive Area
Lake Travis,
off Highway 71 past Bee Cave
A 900-acre facility with trails, lake access, camping, and picnicking near the Ridge Harbor subdivision on Burnet County Road 414. This wilderness area is very popular with mountain bikers.

The Narrows Primitive Area
Lake Travis,
off Highway 71 near Spicewood
This rugged site has a boat ramp, picnic areas, and primitive campsites. This is one of the smallest parks in the system, encompassing only 250 acres. It is used primarily as a boat ramp facility (the only public ramp on the upper south side of the lake), since there are neither potable water nor rest rooms on-site.

Shaffer Bend Primitive Area
Lake Travis, off F.M. 1431
A 535-acre park with camping, picnicking, and lake access about 17 miles west of Lago Vista. The terrain is rough and

suitable to trucks and four-wheel-drive vehicles.

Turkey Bend (East) Primitive Area
Lake Travis, off F.M. 1431
A 400-acre park with great views of the lake and surrounding countryside. The park has camping and picnic facilities and lake access. The park is about 10 miles west of Lago Vista.

Travis County Parks

Travis County, home to the capital city, operates 20 parks under its Travis National Resources department (TNR) throughout the county, many of them on the banks of Lake Travis and Lake Austin, and other small, urban parks in suburban areas beyond municipal limits. Generally the Lake Austin parks charge no fees, but those on Lake Travis may have vehicle charges and individual entrance fees, generally around $5.00 per day for each vehicle, $2.00 for bicyclists, and around $10.00 per day for primitive camping. You can reach Travis County Parks Visitor Information and Reservations at (512) 473-9437, www.co.travis.tx.us/tnr/parks.

Arkansas Bend
Sylvester Ford Road, off R.M. 1431
This 195-acre LCRA park on the shores of Lake Travis is not as primitive as some other LCRA parks and is operated by the county. The Hill Country landscape is a backdrop to picnic areas equipped with barbecue pits. The park has hiking trails, swimming facilities, a boat ramp, and campsites.

Ben Fisher
F.M. 973 off U.S. 290 East
This park is in eastern Travis County and has picnic and barbecue facilities, hiking trails, and sports courts. The landscape east of Austin is called Blackland Prairie, and much of it is fertile farmland. Parks in this area have undulating hills, meadows covered with wildflowers, both spring and

fall, and large pecan trees. Pecan harvesting is a favorite fall pastime.

Bob Wentz Park at Windy Point
On Lake Travis,
access from Comanche Trail
This 21-acre LCRA lakeside park has barbecue pits, picnic sites, hiking trails, playgrounds, a swimming area, showers, and a boat ramp for sailboats. It is popular among windsurfers and scuba divers.

Cypress Creek
On Lake Travis,
Anderson Mill Road at R.M. 2769
The landscape in this LCRA park on Lake Travis retains its wild character, but there have been some additions, including barbecue pits and picnic areas. The park offers access to the lake for swimming and primitive camping.

Dink Pearson Park
On Lake Travis near Lago Vista
Dink Pearson is a lakeside park with picnic and barbecue facilities, access to the lake for swimmers, and a boat ramp.

Fritz Hughes
Lake Austin, near Mansfield Dam
This is a good spot for family picnics but is not suitable for swimming. The park has picnic and barbecue facilities plus a playscape.

Hippie Hollow
Lake Travis,
near Comanche Trail off R.M. 620
This is an Austin landmark. (Its formal name is MacGregor Park, but nobody calls it that.) This clothing-optional LCRA park is open to individuals age 18 and older and is particularly popular among gay sun seekers. You can swim in the lake, sunbathe on the park's beach and rocks, or hike on the trails (shoes recommended).

Little Webberville
On the Colorado River near F.M. 969
This Colorado River park 20 miles east of Austin, near the community of Webberville, has both picnic and barbecue areas. The park also has playscapes and a boat ramp. It is a popular entry point on the river for kayakers and canoeists.

Mansfield Dam
Rural Route 620
On Lake Travis, just west of Mansfield Dam, this county park offers picnic and barbecue facilities, swimming, a boat ramp, and overnight camping facilities. It is a short walk to the dam, which offers a close-up view of engineering feats in Central Texas. The dam is also a favorite place for hawks and other birds of prey to ride the thermal wind currents, which rise off the cliffs and the tall dam. Dive groups often camp overnight here, but no individual camping is allowed.

Pace Bend
2701 F.M. 2322,
4.6 miles off Highway 71
(512) 264-1482
This 1,000-acre-plus park (sometimes called Paleface Park) has equestrian facilities, trails, campsites, picnic and barbecue facilities, plus swimming in the lake.

Richard Moya
Burleson Road, 2.6 miles from the
intersection of U.S. 183 and Burleson
Road in eastern Travis County
Named after a popular former county commissioner, this park is a favorite spot for family picnics, particularly on Mexican-American holidays and birthdays, when the smell of fajitas cooking and the sound of piñatas being whacked fill the air. Portions of the original downtown Congress Avenue Bridge, c. 1884, now span Onion Creek in the park. This day-use park is only 20 minutes from downtown and is a popular location for baseball and softball tournaments.

Sandy Creek
On Lake Travis off Lime Creek Road
Another rugged hillside park on Lake Travis, this park has hiking trails, offers access to the lake for swimmers and boaters, and has primitive camping facilities.

Selma Hughes Park
Lake Austin off Quinlan Park Road

This is the site of a popular boat ramp on busy Lake Austin. There are picnic facilities with barbecue pits.

Tom Hughes Park
Lake Travis on Tom Hughes Park Road, off Rural Route 620

Swimming is the popular attraction in this small county park, which is open in daylight hours only.

Webberville
F.M. 969

This large and popular county park is 3 miles east of Webberville in eastern Travis County on the banks of the Colorado River at the Travis/Bastrop county line. There are picnic and barbecue facilities, hiking trails, playscapes, a boat ramp, ballfields, sports courts, and equestrian facilities. The large picnic pavilions can be reserved for gatherings by calling the Travis County parks reservations number at (512) 473-9437.

Windmill Run
U.S. 290 West and Highway 71

Windmill Run is a neighborhood park near the Windmill Run subdivision in Oak Hill, with picnic and barbecue facilities, hiking trails, and ballfields.

Austin City Parks

The city boasts nearly 208 city parks, 25 hike and bike trails and greenbelts, plus 11 nature preserves (see our Nature Preserves section in this chapter), all encompassing more than 16,076 acres of urban retreats. The parks are in all areas of the city and vary in size and character. Some are small, urban oases of peace and quiet where the neighborhood kids can toss a ball, couples can walk the dog, or an office worker can pause for a moment or two of lunchtime bird-watching or newspaper-reading. Others are popular gathering spots for annual events—rugby tournaments, summer theater, a Mexican Independence Day celebration, or a whimsical festival in honor of Eeyore, Winnie the Pooh's sidekick.

Given the large number of city parks, we have picked out several of particularly interesting character and detailed them below. The city offers detailed information about all city parks in several brochures, available on request from the Parks and Recreation Department (PARD) and on the city's Web site, both listed below. The parks are listed alphabetically, ending with Zilker Park, the city's major park in the heart of the city and home to Barton Springs Pool, an icon that is perhaps the ultimate natural symbol of Austin life (see our Close-up in this chapter).

Austin has more than 20 miles of surfaced scenic paths in the city's natural greenbelts, plus untold miles of wooded tracks. Bicycles are permitted, but motorized vehicles are not. Pets on leashes are allowed. The city's parks department has been building separate trails for hikers, joggers, walkers, and bikers, but there are several popular trails, notably around Town Lake, where the groups must coexist. Rock climbers on the Barton Creek greenbelt also have been at odds with mountain bikers. Peaceful coexistence is encouraged.

The curfew on all trails is 10:00 P.M. They reopen at 5:00 A.M. To access a greenbelt, head for the address listed with each park. Parking is limited at some greenbelt locations, and space is at a premium on weekends, particularly when the weather sends much of Austin outdoors.

**Austin Parks and
Recreation Department (PARD)
200 South Lamar Boulevard
(512) 974-6700
www.ci.austin.tx.us/parks**

Residents and visitors alike should stop by the main office of PARD, as it is called, and pick up a wealth of material on Austin recreational activities and facilities. The office is just south of Town Lake. The city's Web site also has extensive information and downloadable maps.

Barton Creek Greenbelt
3755-B Loop 360 (Capital of Texas Highway)

This is one of the city's most popular, and most crowded, greenbelts, particularly on lazy summer days. The trail follows Barton Creek through the canyon that cuts across Southwest Austin and offers a retreat to the Hill Country without leaving the city limits.

Barton Creek has six official access points, called trailheads, and one very popular unofficial entry. The designated trailheads are at Zilker Park, west of Barton Springs Pool; the intersection of Spyglass Drive and Barton Skyway; 2010 Homedale Drive, behind Barton Hills Elementary School; the Gus Fruh Access at 2642 Barton Hills Drive; the Brodie Oaks office complex, off Loop 360 west of Lamar Boulevard; and the intersection of Camp Craft Road and Scottish Woods Trail. The Gus Fruh and Brodie Oaks access points are wheelchair-accessible.

The unofficial access point is easily spotted on a balmy weekend afternoon. The shoulder of the access road leading from Loop 360 (Capital of Texas Highway) onto MoPac south is lined with cars. Just a few yards away, a wide stretch of the creek creates a swimming hole that attracts large crowds on warm days.

Boggy Creek Greenbelt
1114 Nile Street

This East Austin trail runs 3 miles from Rosewood Park to Zaragosa Park. Trails in the eastern half of the city, roughly defined as east of I–35, have different flora from those in the western half. The eastern half of the city is built over Blackland Prairie—rich, black soil, compared with the rocky, limestone landscape in the west. The creeks and greenbelts in the east are often shaded by pecan trees and have woodland plants along their banks.

Bull Creek Park and Greenbelt
6701 Lakewood Drive

This park and greenbelt is a popular spot, particularly in spring when the rains fill the creek, attracting swimmers and waders. In summer the creek is usually very low or dry. There are picnic facilities and hike and bike trails. The 120-acre greenbelt attracts hikers and mountain bikers. The park is off Loop 360 (Capital of Texas Highway) and south of Spicewood Springs Road.

Emma Long Metropolitan Park (City Park)
1600 City Park Road
(512) 346–1831

This large 1,147-acre park with 3 miles of Lake Austin shoreline has boat ramps and picnic sites. It is the oldest city park and is more traditional, showing the human hand in its landscaping and facilities.

Johnson Creek
2100 Enfield Road

This mile-long urban trail runs from Town Lake to Enfield Road, paralleling MoPac. Trail-users can access the greenbelt from the Austin High School parking lot.

Lake Walter E. Long Metropolitan Park
6614 Blue Bluff Road
(512) 926–5230

In Northeast Travis County, this 1,300-acre lake is well known for its fishing and water activities. There are campsites, hike and bike trails, plus park roads that are popular with bicyclists and runners.

Mary Moore Searight Metropolitan Park
907 Slaughter Lane

This is a new park in far South Austin. The 344 acres contain an 18-hole disc (Frisbee) golf course, a 2-mile hike and bike trail, a 2½-mile equestrian trail, and a fishing pier over Slaughter Creek. There are basketball, tennis, and volleyball courts, plus baseball and soccer facilities, barbecue pits, and a picnic gazebo for large parties.

Mount Bonnell Park
3800 Mount Bonnell Road, off Scenic Road

For 140 years tourists have been coming to Mount Bonnell and climbing the 99 steps

(785 feet) to the peak for a great view of the city. No mountain, but a sturdy climb.

Several local legends purport to account for the mount's name. One claims it is named in honor of George W. Bonnell, a New Yorker who came to Texas to fight in the War of Independence against Mexico. He fought the Native Americans and was a sometime newspaper editor. He met his death on December 26, 1842, when he was captured and shot by Mexican troops.

Others say the name is a corruption of the names Beau and Nell, two lovers who were married on the peak minutes before a Native American attack. After their first kiss, they leapt to their death. Other legends are variations on this theme, involving Native American princesses and beautiful Spanish senoritas, all forced to take a dive. On a serious note, visitors should be careful at the peak, since an unfortunate few have slipped and fallen down the hillside.

Mount Bonnell is the stuff of romance and a popular spot for young couples who want to watch the stars come out over Austin—a particularly romantic spot for University of Texas students, who can get a clear view of the UT Tower, aglow in orange light when the university's athletic teams win. It is also a great spot for a picnic with a view. The park opens at 5:00 A.M. for sunrise viewing and closes at 10:00 P.M.

Pease Park
1100 Kingsbury Street

Along Shoal Creek between 12th and 24th streets, this Central Austin park is popular among lunchtime picnickers and joggers. The land was donated by former Governor Elisha M. Pease, hence the name. During the Civil War General George Armstrong Custer camped on this site and buried 35 of his men here. There are legends of buried treasure here involving a lost cache of money supposedly stolen by a paymaster in the Mexican Army. Digging, of course, is forbidden.

These days it is known for happier occasions, including Eeyore's Birthday, an annual free-spirit celebration—sort of a mini Woodstock-meets-Mardi Gras event—that includes both the whimsical and the outrageous (see our Annual Events chapter). Street parking on Kingsbury Street and neighboring roads is permitted but quickly fills up during Eeyore's Birthday. The popularity of this park, particularly the Eeyore's Birthday event, has created tension between park users and the neighborhood. So far, efforts to force the celebration to another location have proved unsuccessful.

Shoal Creek Hike and Bike Trail
Lamar Boulevard, from 38th Street to Town Lake

This wide, 3-mile-long greenbelt along the urban pathway of Shoal Creek, roughly paralleling Lamar Boulevard, winds through the heart of Central Austin and can be accessed at many points along the way. This popular trail was heavily damaged by flash floods in 1981. Repairs and flood-control devices have restored the trail, which is always alive with runners, walkers, kids, and dogs. Like other urban Austin creekbeds, Shoal Creek has an early warning system in place to alert residents and emergency workers of flash floods. These high-tech devices can be seen near bridges and low crossings on city creeks. They look like large traffic signal boxes and are equipped with solar panels and antennas. The warning system does not sound off but sends alerts to a central point so that emergency workers can monitor rising waters.

Slaughter Creek Metropolitan Park
507 West Slaughter Lane

Adjacent to the Lady Bird Johnson Wildflower Center in Southwest Austin, this park is at its best in spring, when the Hill Country wildflowers bloom throughout the park. That's not to say the park is not worth a visit during the other seasons. The prime attraction is the 3-mile veloway, which attracts bicyclists and in-line skaters. The park also has a nature trail, picnic facilities, playground, soccer fields, volleyball, and basketball courts.

Town Lake Metropolitan Park

Along the Colorado River from Tom Miller Dam in West Austin to the U.S. 183 bridge in East Austin, this park graces the Colorado River as it winds through the heart of downtown Austin. There have been suggestions in the past that this stretch of river should be renamed in honor of former First Lady Lady Bird Johnson, who led the beautification effort, but, typically, she has declined the honor.

No other Austin city park, with the exception of nearby Zilker Park, so captures the Austin spirit. From dawn to beyond dusk, the Hike and Bike Trail is filled with joggers, walkers, bicyclists, nature lovers, and dog walkers enjoying the riverside pathways. Spring is an especially beautiful time for a stroll along Town Lake as flowering cherry trees, some of them gifts from Japan, bloom alongside native redbud trees. The parks department also periodically offers the public the opportunity to plant a tree in the park and dedicate it to a loved one.

The southern shore of Town Lake, just west of South First Street, is known as Auditorium Shores and is the site for outdoor concerts, including the annual July Fourth Pops Concert (see our Annual Events chapter) and various festivals.

In quieter moments, wildlife, particularly turtles, ducks, and swans, can be seen swimming and feeding along the banks of Town Lake. Only nonmotorized craft are allowed on this stretch of the lake, such as canoes, kayaks, and paddleboats, which can be rented in nearby Zilker Park (see our Boating section in this chapter). The Austin Rowing Club has its clubhouse on the north shore near the Four Seasons Hotel, and lone rowers can be seen sculling in the early morning through the light fog rising from the lake. No swimming is allowed in the lake.

On the northern bank of Town Lake and east of I–35 is Fiesta Gardens, a popular community concert and celebration spot. Two notable Mexican-American holidays are celebrated here, Cinco de Mayo and Diez y Seis de Septiembre (see our Annual Events chapter).

Woolridge Square is a little gem of a park in downtown Austin—squeezed between the Travis County Courthouse and the Austin History Center, 9th and 10th Streets on Guadalupe. The park's Victorian bandstand sits in the center of a natural amphitheater and has been the site of weddings, political rallies, small concerts, and one murder (according to legend).

Waller Creek Greenbelt
403 East 15th Street

Stretching from 15th Street to Town Lake, the Waller Street greenbelt is a mixture of urban greenbelt and urban blight. The northern stretch is quite pleasant. City voters recently approved a bond election to improve the southern end of the trail. Supporters touted creating an urban riverwalk, similar to San Antonio's famous riverside trail.

Waterloo Park
403 East 15th Street

This central city park lies just east of the capitol and is a quiet retreat in the heart of the city. It is also a popular spot for several gatherings during the year, including a Renaissance Festival where participants evoke the spirit of the Middle Ages with jousts and minstrels, country fair–style booths, and crafters' stalls (see our Annual Events chapter).

Zilker Botanical Gardens
2200 Barton Springs Road
(512) 477-8672

Just north of Zilker Park (see the subsequent listing) and part of the Zilker experience, the gardens are also home to the Austin Garden Center. There are several gardens within the grounds, including a rose garden (a popular site for weddings), a cactus and succulent garden, fragrance and butterfly gardens, and woodland trails. There is also a xeriscape garden, where native plants are shown off to great

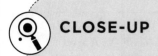

Austin's Beloved Waterin' Hole

Barton Springs Pool has been called the soul of Austin, and that is really not an exaggeration. This treasured, spring-fed pool stands both as a symbol of Austin's lifestyle, a measure of its commitment to the environment, a political rallying point, and even a place of spiritual and psychological renewal. This 1,000-by-125-foot unchlorinated swimming pool, fed by natural spring waters, stands at the heart of Zilker Park and serves as a touchstone for all that was and is Austin.

Its symbolic value cannot be underestimated, while its value as a recreational asset is just as highly rated.

The pool is fed by spring waters that bubble up at the rate of 35 million gallons a day through the 354-square-mile Edwards Aquifer, an underground limestone formation that stretches from downtown Austin west through the Hill Country. Rains that fall on the hills west of the city filter down through the limestone and emerge at temperatures between 67 and 70 degrees Fahrenheit.

For hundreds of years, before European explorers ventured onto Texas soil, Native Americans gathered around the springs, according to archaeologists. Later, Spanish explorers paused to rest here. In the 19th century among the settlers who came to Austin was William "Uncle Billy" Barton. He set up a homestead near the springs in 1837 and eventually gave his name to both the springs and the creek. City records show that on December 16, 1839, Barton agreed to "give possession of the stream of water from my big spring" for a sawmill. For the next 70 years, the land passed through several owners, eventually being sold to Colonel A. J. Zilker in 1907.

During those years, more and more Austinites began to use the pool. At first just male residents swam there, but in 1880 a ladies swimming club was formed. While some ethnic minorities swam there in the latter years of the 19th century, by the 1950s the overwhelming majority of African Americans and Mexican Americans did not swim at the pool. That changed with the Civil Rights Movement, and now the city pool is a gathering place for all Austinites and visitors.

In 1917 Zilker deeded the springs and the surrounding 35 acres to the city, and Zilker and his gift are now memorialized in the name of the city park where Barton Springs Pool stands. An additional 330 acres were added to the park in 1932 when Zilker gave the land to Austin schools, which then, as part of the agreement, sold the acreage to the city for $200,000. The bathhouse that now stands at the entrance to the pool was built in 1947 and replaced the original bathhouse erected in 1922 by the chamber of commerce and the Lions Club. For a time there was talk of making the springs a city municipal water source, but contamination from fecal coliform was found in some samples and that idea was discouraged. Contamination is still occasionally found in samples, particularly after heavy rains.

The concrete sides of the pool, which mark the current length and breadth, were built in 1929. The pool was by then an Austin fixture. Former Texas Congressman Bob Eckhardt, a well-known environmentalist, remembers swimming there as a 5-year-old boy in 1918. His father, a doctor, would come home from the office and pack the family off for an afternoon swim. In honor of his support for the pool, Eckhardt, who still swims there daily when the air temperature is above 80, was granted a lifetime swimming pass in the summer of 1998 by the Austin City Council. (When it is too cool to swim, he rides his bike, just as he did as a Congress member in Washington.)

Eckhardt's support for Barton Springs had special meaning in 1998; that was the year he and many others engaged in the Great Salamander Debate. An examination of this confrontation offers a lesson in what Barton Springs is all about:

Since the late '60s, Austin environmentalists, let's dub them the "Greens," have faced off against the "Developers" (see our History and Politics and Perspectives chapters). Barton Springs became a symbol of that fight when the Save Our Springs Alliance (SOS) was formed in the 1980s to do battle against development over the Edwards Aquifer, the watershed that feeds the springs. Armed with federal conservation legislation, laws such as the Endangered Species Act (ESA), the Greens lobbied federal regulators and took cases to federal court to fight development.

The Greens saw an opportunity to add another arrow to their quiver in the fight when it was discovered in the early 1990s that the tiny salamander that had been swimming underfoot for years was in fact a rare species found only in the waters of the spring and pool. The inch-long salamander has a pale yellow-cream body, flat snout, long limbs, four toes on its front legs, five on the back, and a short, finned tail marked with a narrow orange-yellow stripe and is unique to the springs. In the early '90s the Greens pressed for the salamander to be listed as an endangered species.

In 1994 the Clinton Administration announced that the salamander would be listed. Then Interior Secretary Bruce Babbitt changed his mind about listing it. Federal and state officials announced a water conservation agreement instead that was touted as a way to protect the aquifer, the springs, and the pool waters. The Greens were very critical of the compromise and went to federal court to force the listing of the salamander. U.S. District Judge Lucius Bunton of Midland, Texas, agreed with them and ordered the administration to review its decision. In spring 1997, the Barton Springs salamander was placed on the ESA list.

In January 1998 an attorney who had, in the past, represented landowners and developers, filed suit on behalf of two scientists against the city, charging that the City of Austin was violating the ESA by killing salamanders during routine pool cleanings, when the water level was lowered and the pool bottom scrubbed. The Greens said the lawsuit was aimed at shutting down the pool and claimed that mean-spirited developers were behind the action, but the attorney and his clients insisted they only wanted the city to follow the federal laws and protect the salamander. The local media was filled with supporters and detractors, and some observers said the Greens had been hoisted on their own petard.

The Greens cried foul and questioned the motives of the plaintiffs. After a great deal of legal maneuvering, U.S. District Judge Sam Sparks of Austin refused to stop the pool cleanings, issuing his ruling in a poem:

> Barton Springs is a true Austin shrine,
> A hundred years of swimming sublime.
> Now the plaintiffs say swimmers must go
> 'Cause of "stress" to critters, 50 or so.
> They want no cleaning 'cause of these bottom feeders,
> Saying it's the law from our Congressional leaders.
> But really nothing has changed in all these years
> Despite federal laws and these plaintiff's fears
> Both salamander and swimmer enjoy the springs that are cool.
> And cleaning is necessary for both species in the pool.
> The City is doing its best with full federal support,
> So no temporary injunction shall issue from this Court.
> Therefore, today, Austin's citizens get away with a rhyme;
> But, the truth is they might not be so lucky the next time.
> The Endangered Species Act in its extreme makes no sense.
> Only Congress can change it to make this problem past tense.

The city set about developing new cleaning methods with the blessings of the federal regulators. During all this legal wrangling, Barton Springs Pool had been shut down for extended periods for time-consuming cleanings that involved sending biologists to search the pool bottom and scoop up any stranded salamanders and return them to the spring while city workers carefully scrubbed the pool bottom. By late summer 1998, the city was holding hearings hoping to devise an acceptable cleaning program, plus make some modifications to the pool so that salamanders and swimmers could peacefully coexist.

The salamanders have now become a popular feature on T-shirts and in paintings that decorate the pool bathhouse. They also have joined the pantheon of Austin-area endangered species, which includes golden-cheeked warblers and black-capped vireos, both songbirds.

Few swimmers claim to have actually seen a Barton Springs salamander, but for those who regard Barton Springs Pool as more than a place to swim, the knowledge that the little creatures also enjoy the waters just adds to the beauty and wonder of the place.

For information about pool hours and admission, see our listing under Swimming in this chapter.

advantage. Admission to the garden center is free except for certain weekends (see our Annual Events chapter) when garden shows are held on the grounds.

The most beautiful part of the garden center is the Taniguchi Oriental Garden, created by the late Isamu Taniguchi, a native of Osaka, Japan. Taniguchi moved to the United States as a young man, worked as a farmer in California and the Rio Grande Valley, and then retired to Austin in the 1960s. Taniguchi, whose son was a noted Austin architect, spent 18 months creating the garden along the hillside site. He worked for free with his own plans and no oversight or interference from city planners. His creation is a symbol of peace, just as Taniguchi wished. He died in 1992 at age 94. The best time to visit the garden is on a quiet weekday, since it is a popular attraction on weekends. Many Austin families like to take family portraits in one of the many artfully designed little rooms that are so typical of Japanese garden design.

Zilker Park
2100 Barton Springs Road
(512) 472-4914
This 400-acre downtown park, just south of Town Lake and east of MoPac, is the city's most well-known park and one of its most popular. It became a city park in 1917 when Colonel A. J. Zilker donated the land to the city. The most famous and revered attraction in the park is Barton Springs Pool (see our Close-up in this chapter), but it is also a place of pilgrimage for other reasons. At Christmas one of the city's so-called moonlight towers (see our Attractions chapter) serves as the trunk of the Zilker Park Christmas Tree (see our Annual Events chapter), visible from miles around. The "tree" is created by Christmas lights strung in maypole fashion from the tower to the ground. Tradition calls for children to stand inside the tree and spin around until the lights are blurred and the kids are dizzy. Small children are spun around in a grown-up's arms, making both kid and grown-up enjoy the dizzy spell.

Inside the City of Austin, dogs must be leashed, but even Fido can enjoy the city's famous free-spirit lifestyle in certain designated parks (www.ci.austin.tx.us/parks/dogparks). One of the most popular spots is in Zilker Park in an area bounded by Stratford Drive, Barton Springs Road, and Lou Neff Drive. For a complete list of places to let Fido feel the wind in his hair, free and unfettered, call the parks department at (512) 974-6700.

Zilker is home to a miniature train, playscape, picnic grounds, a "folf" course, rugby and soccer fields, and a canoe and kayak concession (see our Boating section in this chapter). A grass-covered hillside serves as a natural amphitheater for summer musicals (see our Annual Events and The Arts chapters for more information).

The park is open daily from 6:00 A.M. to 10:00 P.M. and is free. There is a small parking fee on weekends when the park is very busy.

Round Rock

The city's parks department operates about 30 parks in the city limits, most of them small, neighborhood parks that serve as play areas for neighborhood children and places to relax, perhaps jog, play tennis, or shoot a few baskets for teens and adults. Parks with hike and bike trails, swimming pools, or tennis courts are listed in the Recreation and Watersports sections of this chapter under those specific categories. The city's three major parks are described below.

Round Rock Parks and Recreation Department (PARD)
605 Palm Valley Boulevard
(512) 218-5540
www.ci.round-rock.tx.us
The city's PARD publishes a program brochure and guides to the city's parks

that are available on request. In addition to athletic programs, PARD offers country and ballroom dance classes, Jazzercise, programs for toddlers and seniors, pre-school and youth programs, plus Cool Kids Camp, an afternoon recreation program for elementary kids.

Lake Creek Park
800 Deerfoot Drive
Home to the municipal swimming pool, this 15-acre park also has a playscape area and a pavilion, which can be used for community events. The municipal pool opens a few weeks before Memorial Day and closes around Labor Day. For the first few weeks in May, the pool is open only on the weekends and then is open daily after Memorial Day.

Old Settlers Park
2800 Palm Valley Boulevard
This large, 439-acre park has soccer and softball fields, hike and bike trails, playscapes, a folf course, and picnic areas. It is also the site of Old Settler Week (see our Annual Events chapter), when Williamson County celebrates its pioneer roots with music, food, and carnivals, plus a reenactment of the shootout between outlaw Sam Bass and the law. There is a large pavilion at the park, which is a focal point during community celebrations.

Round Rock Memorial Park
I-35 and R.M. 620
The city's other major park is home to the Legion Field softball complex. In addition to the softball fields, the park features a hike and bike trail, playscape, and picnic areas.

Pflugerville

Pflugerville Parks and Recreation Department (PARD)
700 Railroad Avenue
(512) 251-5082
www.cityofpflugerville.com

The city of Pflugerville boasts that the city's parks are a "hometown kind of place, where you and your friends and coworkers can celebrate without a lot of big-city fuss and bother." The city's PARD has developed a master plan aimed at helping the city make the transition from a tiny, rural town to a growing suburban community. The city's parks are connected by an integrated trail system, connecting many of the neighborhoods in the city.

PARD also provides swimming, gymnastics, aerobics, soccer, volleyball, and basketball programs. There is the Summer Pfun Camp and PARD-organized events such as 5K Pfun Run and Walk, Pfall Pfest, and the Pumpkin Pflyer bicycle tour.

Gilleland Creek Park
700 Railroad Avenue
The anchor for the city's integrated trail system, Gilleland also boasts a community swimming pool, picnic areas, and volleyball courts.

Pfluger Park
City Park Road
This large city park is home to soccer and softball fields, sand volleyball facilities, and basketball courts. The park's picnic area has barbecue pits and a playscape, and there are several nature trails running through the park.

Cedar Park

Cedar Park Parks and Recreation (PARD)
600 North Bell Boulevard
(512) 258-4121, ext. 6830
www.ci.cedar-park.tx.us
As Cedar Park grows, the number of city parks increases as the city attempts to keep up with the area's booming population. There are 11 neighborhood parks, most of them with picnic facilities and playscapes. Many also have tennis and basketball courts, and some have sand volleyball facilities. The city's parks and

recreation department offers information on all city parks and recreation programs. A proposed parks master plan is posted on the city's Web site.

Elizabeth M. Milburn
Community Park
1901 Sun Chase Boulevard

This is the crown jewel of the Cedar Park park system. At the heart of the recently completed park facility is an eight-lane, 25-meter lap pool, with an adjoining recreational pool with a water playscape and a 117-foot water slide. The new park has several soccer fields, plus a large pavilion with picnic tables for reunions and special events. There are also three large gazebos in the park. Scattered throughout the park are picnic tables and barbecue grills, plus tennis courts, a basketball court, a sand volleyball area, playscapes, and a hiking path circling the park.

NATURE PRESERVES

Within the Austin city limits are several nature preserves that offer visitors a glimpse of the wild beauty of both the Hill Country and the prairie to the east of Austin. In addition to city preserves, Travis County and the LCRA are also guardians to several nature areas.

Austin Nature Preserves

The city operates 11 nature preserves and a nature center. There are strict rules of behavior within the preserves, designed to protect the ecosystems. Access to some of the preserves is by prearrangement only, and group tours are available. For information call (512) 327-7723. The preserves' pages on the city's PARD Web site offer downloadable maps and brochures.

Motorized vehicles, bicycles, pets, firearms, and hunting are prohibited in the nature preserves. Visitors are required to keep noise levels low and stay on trails and may not remove plants or animals from the area.

Austin Nature Center
303 Nature Center Drive
(512) 327-8181

The center's central exhibit is "The Nature of Austin," illustrating four habitats found in the area—ponds, grasslands, woodlands, and a Hill Country cave. The live exhibits feature Texas wildlife—animals that have been rescued and because of permanent injury or extensive human contact cannot be returned to their habitat. The center also has a discovery lab and is surrounded by 80 acres of nature preserve with 2 miles of trails. The "dino pit" exhibit features fossils and bones found at a Congress Avenue building site.

Barrow Preserve
7715 Long Point Drive

This 10-acre preserve is on the upper reaches of Bull Creek in Northwest Austin. It has spring-fed canyons and hiking trails.

Blunn Creek Preserve
1200 St. Edwards Drive

This preserve near the St. Edward's University campus in South Austin boasts two lookout points that offer great views of the city, one of which is atop a 100-million-year-old coral reef. This area of Central Texas once was an inland sea, and now it is surrounded by urban neighborhoods. Within its confines can be seen the remains of volcanic ash deposits spewed out by a dozen active volcanoes that rumbled in this area some 80 million years ago.

The preserve contains three distinct zones, each with its own distinct flora. The riparian woodland, along the creek, has cottonwood, pecan, and native black willows, while the rolling prairie has grasses, wildflowers, cactus, and redbud trees. The third zone, the uplands, has the distinctive live oaks seen throughout the city and

Austin Metropolitan Trails Council is a coalition of public, private, and non-profit organizations, neighborhood associations, and individuals working to "promote a comprehensive system of greenways and trails in the greater Austin area." You can contact the council through the Austin Parks and Recreation Department at (512) 499-6700.

delicate Texas persimmon trees that grow underneath the canopies of the large oaks.

Colorado River Preserve
U.S. 183 at the Montopolis Bridge, 5827 Levander Loop
On the banks of the Colorado River, west of the Montopolis Bridge in East Austin, this 43-acre preserve offers views of river life, including turtles, herons, and cranes along the sandy banks of the river.

Indiangrass Wildlife Sanctuary
Walter E. Long Metropolitan Park, 6614 Blue Bluff Road, off U.S. 290 East
The sanctuary is in a 200-acre section of Walter E. Long Park in Northeast Austin. The sanctuary is designed to protect Blackland Prairie habitat for a variety of flora and fauna, notably a variety of prairie grasses. The wetlands along Lake Long are home to an abundance of wildlife. Access is limited to guided tours only.

Karst Preserve
3900 Deer Lane
This interesting preserve is off Brodie Lane in Southwest Austin and adjacent to the Maple Run subdivision. Karst is the name scientists have given to the type of honeycombed limestone formations found in several areas of the world, including the Texas Hill Country. This eight-acre site, and this part of Austin, is riddled with sink-holes, caves, and honeycombed limestone. Walking over a large expanse of grass, say a soccer field, it is possible to feel the temperature change around your ankles as you pass over trapped pockets of cool air. Some of the caves are off-limits, and visitors may want to think twice before stepping off the trail to explore sinkholes, since they are home to scorpions, spiders, and snakes.

Mayfield Preserve
3505 West 35th Street
This is a small city enclave that reflects 19th-century Austin. The 22-acre preserve in Central Austin embraces five lily ponds, palm trees, woodlands, and several old cottages, including one from the late 19th century. A cross between a preserve and a park, this quiet spot is very popular with children, who can approach the peacocks (watch out, they have tempers!) and tame deer for close-up viewing. The preserve is next door to Laguna Gloria Art Museum (see our The Arts chapter) in West Austin.

Onion Creek Preserve
7001 Onion Creek Road
This secluded preserve is north of Highway 71 along Onion Creek and is open to guided tours by reservation only.

Vireo Preserve
1107 North Capital of Texas Highway
East of the 100 and 200 blocks of Loop 360 North (Capital of Texas Highway), this rugged section of Hill Country is home to the rare black-capped vireo, one of several bird species threatened by development in Central Texas. The preserve is open for guided tours only.

Zilker Nature Preserve
This is a 60-acre preserve at the western end of the park (see the listing under Austin Parks in this chapter), which includes 2 miles of trails along cliff edges on the banks of Barton Creek.

Balcones Canyonlands

The Austin growth boom has led to a great loss of natural habitat, particularly west of Austin in the rugged Hill Country, a land whose outward appearance belies its sensitivity. Following a grand political tug-of-war between pro-development forces and environmentalists (see our Politics and Perspectives chapter), city leaders, environmentalists, developers, and concerned landowners sat down and forged an agreement for a unique preservation effort, dubbed the Balcones Canyonlands Conservation Plan (BCCP).

What has emerged is one of the most significant preservation efforts in Texas. The BCCP embraces over 30,000 acres west of Austin, and more acreage is being sought to add to this vast area just west of the city. Part of the BCCP is the Balcones Canyonlands National Wildlife Refuge, an area run by the U.S. Fish and Wildlife Service. The City of Austin, Travis County, the LCRA, and several private landowners also are part of the BCCP effort. The Austin BCCP office is located at 10711 Burnet Road, Suite 201, (512) 339–9432. All the agencies involved have information about the BCCP on their respective web sites, but one way to get a wealth of information and find links to all the agencies and environmental groups involved in the effort is to visit www.friendsofbalcones.org.

Balcones Canyonlands National Wildlife Refuge

The public areas of the refuge are located near the community of Lago Vista, northwest of Austin. Detailed maps of the rural access points are on the refuge Web site, accessible through a link at www.friendsofbalcones.org, or by calling the BCCP Austin office (see above). The refuge gets its name from the Spanish explorers who, when they saw the terraced hills west of what is now Austin, dubbed the land "Balcones." From afar, the land looks dry and scrubby, but numerous creeks run through, over, and under the terrain, and wildflowers, grasses, trees, and plants abound. This is home to the endangered golden-cheeked warbler and black-capped vireo, two little birds whose

songs can still be heard thanks to efforts like the BCCP.

The refuge has two public areas: Warbler Vista Trail, just outside Lago Vista on F.M. 1431, and Doeskin Ranch, located on F.M. 1174. Warbler Vista has two trails through the limestone terraces—Cactus Rocks Trail is a 0.6-mile one-way trail and is an easy to moderate hike. This trail winds through golden-cheeked warbler habitat of juniper and hardwood trees. The warblers arrive from Mexico and Latin America in mid-March and leave in July. Pick up a guide pamphlet at the parking lot kiosk. Keep in mind this is a delicate ecosystem dedicated to the birds, so no pets or rowdy activity. The Vista Knoll Trail is 1.2 miles round-trip and is a moderate hike. This trail offers great views of Lake Travis and Lago Vista. The Shin Oak Observation Deck is set in the middle of black-capped vireo habitat. The deck is closed for a short period in spring just as the vireos arrive to minimize the disturbance to the birds. Check the refuge Web site for the specific dates the deck is closed each year. Once the birds settle into nesting activities, the observation deck is reopened to visitors. The refuge is open from sunrise to sunset, but some areas may be closed for public hunts or bird nesting activities.

The Texas Ornithological Society and the Travis Audubon Society conduct field trips to the refuge, and several annual events throughout the year offer information and tours. One of the most popular events is the Annual Texas Songbird Festival hosted by the Lago Vista community in late April or early May. Master naturalists lead area birding expeditions, some to the refuge and others to backyard habitats. There are workshops and seminars on bird photography, butterfly gardening, landscaping fort wildlife, etc. Local craftspeople also show their wares. Contact the Lago Vista Chamber of Commerce at (512) 267–7952, (888) 328–5246, or visit: songbirdfestival.homestead.com/.

LCRA Preserves

The Lower Colorado River Authority (LCRA) operates two preserves near Austin—McKinney Roughs and Westcave Preserve, listed below—and Canyon of the Eagles, detailed in our Day Trips chapter. The authority has embarked on an aggressive expansion program and plans to have additional environmental learning centers in place by 2004 along its territory, which reaches from the Hill Country lakes to the Gulf of Mexico.

McKinney Roughs Preserve
North Bastrop, Highway 71
(512) 303-5073,
(800) 776-5272; ext. 3512
www.lcra.org
Located a little over 13 miles east of the Austin-Bergstrom International Airport on U.S. 71, this 1,100-acre preserve includes rolling canyons, wildflower meadows, and meandering river bends illustrating four unique ecosystems This pristine property was to have been a housing development, but the LCRA stepped in and purchased the land. The preserve is open to canoeists, hikers, horseback riders, birders, and picnickers who simply want to enjoy the pastoral scenes. The Mark Rose Environmental Learning Center hosts educational programs and activities for students, teachers, and the general public. The center has a 128-room dormitory and is home to the Academy in the Roughs, an overnight environmental learning program for children. There is small entrance fee, reduced for seniors and children; horseback riders pay a larger fee and provide their own horses.

Westcave Preserve
Hamilton Pool Road, R.M. 3238
(830) 825-3442
www.westcave.org
Not far from Hamilton Pool Preserve (see above) is an almost mystical place, a natural collapsed grotto that was formed 150,000 years ago, effectively creating a giant terrarium covered by towering cypress trees. The sheltered environment creates a unique ecosystem where orchids and other semitropical plants flourish. Temperature differences between the grotto floor and the surrounding countryside above can be as much as 25 degrees—a wonderful place for a summer escape. Westcave's 30 acres also are home to several endangered species, including the golden-cheeked warbler. The preserve is operated by the LCRA and the private Westcave Preservation Corporation and is open only on weekends or for special visits. Access is limited to guided tours at 10:00 A.M., noon, and 2:00 and 4:00 P.M. Tours also are limited to 30 persons at a time. In March 2003 a new study center designed by well-known Texas architect Robert Jackson opened on the site, and this sensitively designed building now operates as a study and education center. There is a nominal entrance fee.

Travis County Preserves

Hamilton Pool Preserve
Hamilton Pool Road, R.M. 3238
(512) 264-2740
www.co.travis.tx.us/tnr/parks
Hamilton Pool Preserve is part of the Balcones Canyonlands (see the listing above), and it offers visitors a wonderful look at the beauties of the Hill Country. At the heart of the preserve is the pool, a natural pool fed by a waterfall along Hamilton Creek, a branch of the Pedernales River. The waters spills out over limestone outcroppings and create a 50-foot waterfall into the box canyon. The flora of the canyon and the surrounding grasslands vary in color and texture with the seasons. In addition to endangered and rare birds, there are several rare plant species in the preserve. Because of the sensitive, fragile nature of the land, visitors are limited to 75 a day; and because of the beautiful swimming, the parking lot fills up fast. Call ahead, or perhaps plan a weekday visit. Visitors may picnic, hike, or engage in group nature walks and study

groups. There is no overnight camping, and pets are not allowed. Guided tours are available every Sunday at 10:00 A.M. or by appointment. Sturdy shoes and lots of drinking water are recommended. During dry weather the waterfall may slow to a trickle, but the pool remains filled; however, the pool is closed to swimming when the bacteria count climbs. In heavy rains the park may be closed because of typical Hill Country flooding. The preserve has no concessions.

Wild Basin Wilderness Preserve
805 North Loop 360 (Capital of Texas Highway)
(512) 327-7622
www.wildbasin.org
The traffic whizzes by on Loop 360, but just a few steps off the roadway is a 227-acre wilderness literally within minutes of downtown Austin. Travis County operates this preserve, but it exists because of the efforts in the 1970s of seven extraordinary women who were dubbed the "Now or Never" group. Their goal was to establish the natural area as an outdoor lab for children's science education and teacher training, and the seven women took the task on as a Bicentennial Project. For more on how they won the day, visit www.wildbasin.org, the home page of the volunteers who still help maintain and fund the project. There are 2.5 miles of hiking trails that pass through woodland, grassland, and stream-side habitats that are home to threatened and endangered species and hundreds of native plants, animals, and birds. Wild Basin's nature education programs are funded by special events, memberships, corporate donations, and grants. The entrance to Wild Basin is on the east side of Loop 360 at 805 North Capital of Texas Highway, 1.5 miles north of Bee Caves Road, or 3.25 miles south of the Loop 360 bridge over Lake Austin. The preserve is open from sunrise to sunset, and while there are no entrance fees, donations are accepted. There is a small gift shop at the site.

RECREATION OPPORTUNITIES

Looking to play rugby? Climb a rock wall? Join a soccer club? Find the best place to go in-line skating, or view the sunrise from a hot-air balloon? This Recreation section offers a play-by-play breakdown on sports activities in Austin. First, some general information:

Austin Parks and Recreation Department (PARD)
200 South Lamar Boulevard
(512) 974-6700
www.ci.austin.tx.us/parks
The City of Austin Parks and Recreation Department (PARD) operates 17 recreation centers throughout the city, which offer a wide variety of activities, day camps, youth programs, lessons in sports activities, and league supervision. PARD is a good place to begin when researching availability of facilities, lessons, and league activity.

Cedar Park Parks and Recreation (PARD)
600 North Bell Boulevard
(512) 258-4121, ext. 6830
www.ci.cedar-park.tx.us
Cedar Park's parks and recreation department is developing a variety of programs to meet the town's growing population, including league sports, swimming, aerobics, and water safety classes.

Pflugerville Parks and Recreation Department (PARD)
700 Railroad Avenue
(512) 251-5082
www.cityofpflugerville.com
Pflugerville PARD offers swimming, gymnastics, aerobics, soccer, volleyball, and basketball programs. Since Pfun is part of the Pflugerville lifestyle, the PARD also organizes a Summer Pfun Camp and events such as 5K Pfun Run and Walk, Pfall Pfest, and the Pumpkin Pflyer bicycle tour.

Round Rock Parks and Recreation Department (PARD)
301 West Bagdad Street
(512) 218-5540
www.ci.round-rock.tx.us

The Round Rock PARD organizes several adult sports leagues, including flag football, basketball, and softball and offers a wide variety of adult programs—country dance, ballroom dance, and Jazzercise classes—for all age groups. Youth programs include gymnastics, karate, dance, and tennis classes. The Cool Kids Camp is an after-noon recreation program designed for elementary-age children. Program schedules and information are available on request.

University of Texas Recreational Sports Outdoor Program
(512) 471-3116
www.utrecsports.com

The university offers noncredit courses in outdoor sports, including canoeing, rock climbing, windsurfing, cycling, hiking, fitness and personal training, massage, and health education. Classes are open to UT staff, students, faculty, and members of the community. They are very popular, so sign up early.

YMCA

There are six YWCA branches in the greater Austin area. A branch in Round Rock area and another in Cedar Park are both under the auspices of the Williamson County YMCA. As the area grows, additional facilities are planned.

Metro YMCA Office
(512) 322-9622
www.austinymca.org

This office offers information on programs and facilities at all Y branches in the area. The Web site has detailed descriptions of each branch, plus downloadable maps and information on child care, summer camps, and special events.

Townlake Branch (downtown)
100 West Cesar Chavez Boulevard
(512) 542-9622

Northwest Family Branch
5807 McNeil Drive
(512) 335-9622
North Park Family Branch
9616 North Lamar Boulevard, Suite 130
(512) 973-9622
Pflugerville Center
15803 Windermere Drive
(512) 928-9622
East Communities Branch
5315 Ed Bluestein Boulevard
(512) 933-9622
Southwest Family Branch
6219 Oakclaire Drive
(512) 891-9622

YMCA of Greater Williamson County
200 Buttercup Creek Boulevard
Cedar Park
(512) 250-9622
1812 North Mays Street
Round Rock
(512) 246-9622
www.ymcawilliamsonco.org

The Y is always a good place to seek out other athletes with similar interests. The downtown location is just north of the Town Lake Hike and Bike Trail, which makes it a popular fitness club for downtown workers. The Southwest location is in "downtown" Oak Hill in a former privately owned fitness club that was acquired by the Y. The clubs are popular and have up-to-date fitness equipment, whirlpools, saunas, swimming pools, steam rooms, gyms, indoor running tracks, etc. The Oak Hill branch has a rock-climbing wall and racquetball courts. The newest addition to the YMCA's facilities in Austin is in East Austin, an area that has lacked top flight recreational facilities. The new Y is built on 125 acres donated by IBM along Walnut Creek. Other corporate citizens came together to build a first-class facility with a fitness center, swimming pool with water slides, lap pool, and even a computer lab. The fees for families have been reduced in East Austin, also, so that many of the city's less fortunate families can enjoy membership.

Bicycling

Bicycling has taken off in the Hill Country, where both road-racing and mountain-biking enthusiasts face some rugged challenges, given the terrain. One of Austin's most famous residents is international racing champion Lance Armstrong, who has raced in several charity events here and who did some of his training in the hills around Austin—one favorite bicycling route for road racers is Loop 360, also known as Capital of Texas Highway. (See the Close-up profile of Armstrong in our Spectator Sports chapter.)

The 3-mile Veloway in Slaughter Creek Metropolitan Park (see the Austin Parks section of this chapter) is another popular spot for cyclists. Local mountain bikers also enjoy riding the trail in the Barton Creek Greenbelt. Check the Parks section of this chapter for other area venues for road and off-road cycling.

The Bull Creek Greenbelt in Northwest Austin (see our Parks listings above for more details on all these sites) has a hilly bike path in unspoiled, natural surroundings. The Shoal Creek Hike and Bike Trail wends through the center of the city in a more urban parklike setting, while the 2-mile trail in Southwest Austin at the Mary Moore Seabright Metropolitan Park flows through the rolling, wooded hills, typical of the natural landscape in this area.

Another popular route is along the 10-mile Town Lake Hike and Bike Trail, but the popularity and accessibility of this facility has led to some squabbles between joggers and cyclists. There also has been some concern expressed by nature lovers over the impact of mountain bikes on the delicate ecosystem in the area's nature preserves.

Several area parks have extensive mountain trails and park roads that are popular with cyclists. Local cycle shops sell maps of the area showing popular trails. Among the most popular are Colorado Bend State Park (again, see our Parks listings above) and McKinney Falls

State Park. The latter has a 3.5-mile trail characterized by woodlands and gently rolling hills. Since McKinney is just 13 miles southeast of Austin, this is easily accessible to local riders.

One popular road route among cyclists is Park Road 1C between Buescher and Bastrop State Parks, about a 40-minute drive east of Austin. This is a very challenging ride, as the 13 miles of paved road climbs through steep hills.

The emergence of cycling as a popular sport has brought road racing events to Austin (see our Annual Events and Festivals chapter). Bicyclists are respected in Austin—the city even has a bicycle coordinator on its planning staff (see our Getting Here, Getting Around chapter).

The 3-mile veloway in the Slaughter Creek Metropolitan Park was designed for cyclists, but in-line skaters also find this winding paved trail through the park a wonderful place to roll. No joggers are allowed on the veloway. The park is located at 4103 Slaughter Lane in Southwest Austin and is open seven days a week from sunrise to sunset.

Austin Cycling Association
(512) 282-7413
www.ccsi.com/~aca
The group publishes a monthly newsletter that previews upcoming events, describes the best places to test your skills, and keeps track of the bicycle scene, including recreational and transportation issues.

Austin Flyers
www.austinflyers.com
This club touts itself as "everybody's cycling club," and its Web site offers extensive listings about area activities for cycling enthusiasts, be they actively involved or simply passive spectators. The club offers a calendar of events, riding lessons, safety tips, and message boards.

The LCRA's excellent Web site (www.lcra.org) offers several "adventures" pages, which give tips to mountain bikers and equestrians, among others. The site also has links to parks and preserves that are wheelchair-friendly.

Austin Ridge Riders
www.austinridgeriders.com
Dedicated to the Austin mountain biking community, the Ridge Riders organize fun rides and races and offer information on popular trails in Central Texas.

Bicycle Sport Shop
1426 Toomey Road
(512) 477-3472
10947 Research Boulevard
(512) 345-7460
www.bicyclesportshop.com
Just west of Lamar Boulevard and River-side Drive, this local shop offers sales, rentals, and information on the local scene. A second location is on Research Boulevard (U.S. 183) in Northwest Austin.

University Cyclery
2901 North Lamar Boulevard
(512) 474-6696
www.universitycycle.com
This University of Texas area store offers rentals, sales, repairs, and information on the Austin cycling scene.

Bird-watching

Texas is the center lane of the migratory pathway of many North American birds, making the state a popular spot for bird-watching. Local environmentalists are working hard to raise the consciousness of newcomers about endangered species in the area, and several nature preserves are dedicated to protecting these species. For more information, see the Preserves section of this chapter.

Travis County Audubon Society
(512) 926-8751
www.travisaudubon.org
There are more than 2,500 members of this local chapter of the society, which meets every month and usually holds at least one field trip a month. From backyard birding to treks into the Hill Country in search of elusive and endangered species such as the golden-cheeked warbler, the society offers practical advice to both members and non-members who are eager to protect and conserve the ecosystems so vital to bird life in Central Texas. Every December the group holds a Christmas bird count, its contribution to the national count. The telephone number above offers information on the group's activities and also serves as a birding hot line, informing callers about recent sightings and migratory patterns.

Vanishing Texas River Cruise
Lake Buchanan
(512) 756-6986
www.vtrc.com
In addition to offering wildflower cruises in spring, this company also offers winter river cruises up the Colorado River Canyon to view the largest colony of American bald eagles in the state.

Bowling

There are several Austin area bowling facilities. Austin also has hosted professional bowling tournaments, and most lanes offer facilities for disabled bowlers plus party planning for large groups. The latest craze to hit local lanes is Electric Bowling, known in other parts of the country as Extreme Bowling or Glow-in-the-Dark Bowling. By pumping up the music and bringing down the lights, the bowling facility owners hope to attract a younger crowd and boost interest in the sport.

Two area associations are a good place to obtain information about local bowling activity and league play: the Austin Bowling Association located at 8820 Business Park Drive (512-670-9315, www.austin.bowling.org), and the Austin Women's Bowling Association, located at 5700 Grover Avenue (512-453-8714).

Highland Lanes
8909 Burnet Road
(512) 458-1215

This North Austin bowling facility is home to Electric Bowling three times a week, on Friday and Saturday from 11:00 P.M. to 1:00 A.M. and Tuesday evenings from 8:00 to 10:00 P.M. The lights in the 40-lane facility are dimmed, and special lighting effects kick in with the music. Highland Lanes also offers bumper bowling for kids, eliminating gutter balls and ensuring that kids hit at least some of the pins. There are leagues on-site for teens, women, men, and seniors. The lanes are open from 9:30 A.M. to midnight Sunday through Thursday and 9:30 A.M. to 1:00 A.M. Friday and Saturday.

Showplace Lanes
9504 North I-35
(512) 834-7733

A large 52-lane facility in North Austin, Showplace is open 24 hours a day. There is a sports bar on-site, plus two video game rooms and a nursery. A dart league also holds its events here.

Westgate Lanes
2701 William Cannon Drive
(512) 443-6864

Home to several popular summer youth leagues, Westgate has 40 lanes and is located in South Austin. The bowling alley is open daily from 10:00 A.M. to midnight Sunday through Thursday and 10:00 A.M. to 2:00 A.M. on Friday and Saturday.

Camping

Camping is not just a recreational activity in Central Texas, it is a way of life for some residents who have chosen to make their homes in the area's private facilities. Perhaps the most famous "campsite" for motor homes is the Shady Grove RV Park

smack in the middle of town in an old pecan grove and a few blocks from Zilker Park. Campsites catering to short-term visitors can be found along the I-35 corridor and on the shores of the Highland Lakes.

The Parks section lists area parks with camping facilities, and we have included some of the most popular here in this section, along with privately operated facilities. The Lower Colorado River Authority operates several parks with primitive camping areas (see the LCRA Primitive Areas section). Two guides that are very useful for campers visiting Central Texas are *The Texas State Travel Guide,* published by the Texas Department of Transportation (800-452-9292); and the *Lower Colorado River Authority (LCRA) Visitors Package* (800-776-5272; ext. 4083, or 512-473-4083).

In addition to the Web sites for the state, county, city, and LCRA (see above), other good resources include:

Texas Association of Campground Owners
6900 Oak Leaf Drive, Orange
(512) 459-8226, (409) 886-4082
www.gocampingamerica.com/texas

Texas KOA Kampgrounds Owners Association
602 Gembler Road, San Antonio
(210) 547-5201

Texas Parks & Wildlife Department
4200 Smith School Road
(512) 389-4800, (800) 792-1112
www.twpd.state.tx.us

Austin Convention & Visitors Bureau
209 East Sixth Street
(512) 478-0098, (800) 866-GOAUSTIN
www.austincvb.com

Texas Travel Information Center
Old General Land Office Building
Capitol Grounds
112 East 11th Street
(512) 463-8586, (800) 452-9292

Austin Lone Star RV Resort
7009 South I-35
(512) 444-6322
www.austinlonestar.com

There are 159 RV sites, eight cabins, and camping facilities at this South Austin campground. Campsites rent and cabins are available for under $50 a night. Access to the site is controlled, and there are facilities for handicapped visitors. The main lodge has a fireplace, a full kitchen, color television, jukebox, and swimming pool. There is a small grocery store and laundry facilities on site. Telephone hookups, compatible with modems, and television hookups also are available.

Austin RV Park North
4001 Prairie Lane
(512) 244-0610

The 25 spaces at this North Austin park, near the intersection of I-35 and F.M. 1325, may be rented on a daily basis for around $20 a night, a little over $100 a week, and around $400 a month. The sites all have electricity, water, and sewage hookups. There is a pool at the park.

Armadillo RV
4913 Hudson Bend Road
(512) 266-9012

This Lake Travis–area RV park has 38 large shaded lots, all with a view of Lake Travis, that rent for around $20 a day, or approximately $250 to $275 a month. Cable tele-

vision and telephone hookups are extra. There is an on-site laundry facility, a grocery store nearby, and three marinas within a half mile of the facility. Children and pets are welcome.

Buescher State Park
F.M. 153, off Highway 71, Smithville
(512) 237-2241

A popular spot for fishermen, Buescher (pronounced "Bisher") State Park has 34 campsites (20 for tents or pop-ups and 14 for RVs) and four screened shelters. Showers and rest rooms are available for campers. Admission to the park is $3.00 and free for those 13 and younger. Tent campsites are $7.00 a night; RV sites with water and electricity are $10.00 a night.

Camp Chautauqua at Lake Travis
R.M. 2322, off Highway 71
(512) 264-1752

The LCRA operates this park on the shores of Lake Travis on behalf of the Adopt-the-Colorado-River Foundation. The site is host to chautauquas on the environment—the Native American name that came to signify summer educational programs popular in the late 19th century—and is open to the public for camping. Cabins at the camp cost $25 a night, RV hookups $15, tents $7.00 to $10.00. Admission to the park is $4.00, $3.00 for seniors, and free for children 13 and younger.

Emma Long Metropolitan Park
(City Park)
1600 City Park Road
(512) 346-1831

This large 1,147-acre Austin park with 3 miles of Lake Austin shoreline is a popular weekend camping spot (see the Austin City Parks section of this chapter). There are 20 sites with water and electricity, plus 50 tent sites. Campers may stay for up to two weeks. The entry fee to the park is $3.00 during the week and $5.00 on weekends. Tent sites are $6.00 per night and $10.00 for sites with utilities. The campsites are on an alluvial plain, adjacent to Lake Austin with the hilly park

Many Texas landowners, farmers, and ranchers have turned to ecotourism to help them survive difficult financial times in rural America. Others simply want to share the wonders of Texas with visitors. The state agency charged with boosting Texas tourism, the Texas Department of Economic Development (TDED), has developed a Web site where visitors can find ecotourist opportunities, including birding, trail riding, wilderness camping, and fishing—check out traveltex.com.

in the background. This is a very popular site, so reservations should be made early.

Enchanted Rock State Natural Area
R.R. 965, north of Fredericksburg
(915) 247-3903
This popular and legendary state park, detailed above under State Parks, is 18 miles north of Fredericksburg (see our Day Trips chapter). Only walk-in campers and backpackers may pitch their tents in this carefully protected natural area. There are no facilities for RVs or pop-up campers. Campers must call the state's camping reservations number at (512) 389-8900. Walk-in campers pay the park admission fee of $5.00 for those 13 and older, plus $9.00 a day camping fee with a maximum of eight people at a walk-in site. Backpackers pay the entrance fee, plus $7.00 daily camping rate with a maximum of four people at each campsite.

Hudson Bend RV Park
5003 Hudson Bend Road
(512) 266-8300
www.hbrv.com
Sites are available at this Lake Travis–area facility by the day ($20), week ($80), or month ($250), and all are served with water, electricity, and free cable television. There are 29 pads at this shady site and also six storage sheds available for rent to extended-stay campers.

McKinney Falls State Park
5808 McKinney Falls Parkway
(512) 243-1643
Its location, just 13 miles southeast of downtown Austin off U.S. 183, ensures that this 640-acre state park is usually filled with campers on holidays and weekends. (See our State Parks section for a full description of the park.) There are 84 sites in the park for tents, pop-ups, or RVs, and these cost $12 a night, including water and electricity. There are eight walk-in primitive sites for hikers, costing $7.00 a night. The park entrance fee is $2.00 per person, free for those 13 and younger. McKinney also rents three screened shelters for $20 a

night. The two-room shelters are furnished with eight bunk beds, a cold-water sink, picnic table, and barbecue grill.

Pace Bend Park
2701 F.M. 2322,
4.5 miles off Highway 71
(512) 264-1482
This 1,000-plus-acre Travis County park (sometimes called Paleface Park) is likely to be packed with campers on weekends and during summer holidays. The park, described in our Travis County Parks section above, has more than 400 sites for tents, pop-ups, and RVs. There are also primitive tent sites. Admission to the park is $5.00 per vehicle, $10 for overnight stays. Sites with water and electricity cost $15 a night. The park has a strict quiet time in effect from 10:00 P.M. to 7:00 A.M., and dogs can be allowed to run free if their owners are in control of them. Reservations are critical at this park, since it fills up very quickly on major holiday weekends.

Recreation Plantation
County Road 198, Dripping Springs
(512) 894-0567
If you're looking to camp with a crowd, then consider renting this self-described "event facility." For $750 a weekend, the minimum rate, you can rent this 40-acre campsite with its own creek frontage and swimming hole. The facility also has a two-bedroom cabin on the property and a stage. There are tent sites and RV hookups, also, making this a great place for family reunions and corporate getaways.

Shady Grove RV Park
1600 Barton Springs Road
(512) 499-8432
Shady Grove is just that—a grove of old pecan trees that offers shade and comfort to the 27 sites on this downtown campers' haven east of Zilker Park on Barton Springs Road. Shady Grove has a '50s small-town feel to it, which is probably why rental sites are hard to come by here. The park has many permanent residents

who enjoy a laid-back lifestyle in the "shady grove." The park is tucked in between several popular restaurants, including a '50s-style hamburger joint with the same name as the RV park (see our Restaurants chapter). Monthly rental rates are $350 and include electricity, basic cable service, water and sewer, plus trash pickup. There is an on-site laundry facility.

City Leagues

Austin is a team player kind of town. Take a weekend tour of the city's parks and recreation areas and you are likely to see a wide variety of sports teams at play. One of the best resources for information on local team sports is the city's parks and recreation department or PARD offices. See the full listing of PARD offices in the previous Recreation introduction.

Another good resource for information on team sports is the YMCA. The Y has six locations in Austin, offering basketball, volleyball, soccer, basketball, and T-ball. Listings for the facilities are also listed in the previous section.

Baseball, basketball, soccer, and softball are popular team sports in Austin. The area has an abundance of baseball leagues for all ages. Check with the area PARD for Little League, Optimist, and Kiwanis league teams. The Austin PARD

League officers change with the seasons, and with the advent of the Internet many city sports leagues are relying on their Web site to reach out to fellow sport fans—abandoning the answering machine in favor of e-mail. Consequently, some listings in this chapter show only a Web site. If you have no access to the Internet, call the city PARD office at (512) 974-6700; they will put you in contact with the appropriate league official.

supervises several basketball leagues, and the Y offers league and pickup games.

Central Texas is home to soccer moms and dads by the thousands, but the sport also attracts Gen-Xers and even older "footballers" from the expatriate crowd in Austin. There are numerous soccer leagues; the vast majority fall under the auspices of two organizations.

The Capital Area Youth Soccer Association at 1029 Reinli Street, Suite 6 (512-302-4580, www.caysa.org), has more than 15,000 members. It is an umbrella group that oversees youth league and tournament play in the Central Texas area. The association also offers coaching and referee training sessions and hosts two annual invitational tournaments.

The Austin Municipal Soccer Association (512-288-5133, www.amsapremier .com) is also an umbrella association that organizes men's, women's, and coed league and tournament play in Austin. The Web site offers soccer news from around the world.

One of the best ways to keep track of league play at all levels is to visit one of the Austin area soccer stores. Soccer World has four locations: 5446 U.S. 290 West (Southwest area), (512) 899-1135; 221 South Lamar Boulevard (Central), (512) 320-8447; 13376 Research Boulevard (Northwest), (512) 257-8560; and Soccer World Indoor Center, 1404 Royston Lane, (512) 990-3100.

Another center of soccer activity in the Round Rock-Pflugerville area is the Longhorn Soccer Club, run by Laszlo Marton, a former Hungarian and Austrian professional soccer player. The club offers top-quality coaching and training for soccer players of all ages and summer camps. Contact the camp at 1235 Blackthorn Drive, Round Rock (512-990-1234, www.longhornsoccerclub.org).

Softball is an extremely popular sport year-round in Austin. The Austin PARD serves as the major clearinghouse for schedules, league, and fee information. Call the PARD Athletics Office at (512) 480-3015. Many of the teams play at the

Pleasant Valley Sports Complex, 1225 South Pleasant Valley Road, (512) 445-7595. For softball league information in Round Rock, call (512) 218-5540.

Disc Golf (Folf)

Pitching a Frisbee at a target is a popular sport in Austin, and many of the area's neighborhood parks feature either 9- or 18-hole folf courses. The discs can be found at local sporting goods stores (see our Shopping chapter). On the Web, www.discrevolution.com rates courses around the United States—Austin's rank from three to four stars, with five being tops.

Austin Recreation Center
1301 Shoal Creek Boulevard
(512) 476-5662
The center offers classes to would-be folf masters.

Bartholomew Park
5201 Berkman Drive
(512) 974-6700
This 18-hole course is in Northeast Austin.

Mary Moore Searight Park
907 Slaughter Lane
This 18-hole course is part of a fairly new park in Austin's growing southern suburbs.

Old Settlers Park
3300 Palm Valley Road, Round Rock
This course is in Round Rock's major city park and claims to be the longest folf course in America (see our Parks section above).

Pease Park
1100 Kingsbury Street
This course is very popular among University of Texas students who live in the neighborhood.

Slaughter Creek Metropolitan Park
5507 Slaughter Lane
This pleasant, relatively new Southwest Austin park boasts a new nine-hole folf course and gets four stars from discrevolution.com.

Wells Branch Greenbelt
Wells Branch Parkway at Wells Port Drive
(512) 251-9814
A new nine-hole course in the Wells Branch subdivision of North Austin, this facility is open to Wells Branch residents only.

Zilker Park
2100 Barton Springs Road
You"ll find this nine-hole course at the western edge of the city's premier park. It's a popular weekend course, also ranked at four stars.

Fishing

Texans have a reputation for telling tall tales, but when it comes to fishing they have lots to boast about. The state has more than 5,175 square miles of inland fresh water, including lakes, rivers, and creeks, plus 624 miles of shoreline. There is a wide variety of fish available for the taking, provided the fish are biting. Native fish include black bass, crappie, bluegill, and catfish. Freshwater fishing areas also have been stocked with nonnative species, including Florida bass, walleye, and rainbow trout, and saltwater species, including redfish and striped bass. The Texas Parks & Wildlife Department reports that several Texas lakes are producing striped bass weighing over 30 pounds—some Texas tale!

Texas residents can buy an annual combination fishing-hunting license for $25. Fishing licenses vary in cost and can be purchased on an annual or two-week basis by residents. Nonresident fishermen over the age of 17 must purchase a license, and these can cost $30 for an annual license or $20 for a five-day license. There are additional charges for stamps for certain fish.

Licenses are sold at sporting goods and tackle stores, some county courthouses,

Parks & Wildlife offices, and by some local game wardens. The Texas Parks & Wildlife Department also produces several excellent guides to Texas fishing. The department's magazine (see our Media chapter) is also an excellent resource.

Texas Parks & Wildlife Department
4200 Smith School Road
(512) 389-4800, (800) 792-1112
www.tpwd.state.tx.us
The Highland Lakes are popular among anglers (see our Parks listings in this chapter for access and location). Lake Austin record catches include a 43-pound striped bass. Bass fishing is popular in the quieter areas of Lake Austin and Lake Buchanan. Fishing is permitted on Town Lake in Central Austin, and after years of concern about urban runoff, the city has lifted its warning about consuming your catch. In fact, the river has been stocked with trout.

Bastrop State Park, Bastrop
Highway 21, 1.5 miles east of Bastrop
(512) 321-2101
Lake Bastrop boasts a lighted pier. The record catch here is a 43.5-pound catfish. See our State Parks section of this chapter for a description of facilities here.

Buescher State Park, Smithville
F.M. 153, off Highway 71
(512) 237-2241
This state park is considered a fisherman's paradise by some. The park's 30-acre lake is stocked with catfish, bass, crappie, perch, and rainbow trout.

Fishing Gear

Austin Angler
312½ Congress Avenue
(512) 472-4553
www.austinangler.com
This downtown store is so renowned as an angler's shopping paradise it was featured in a national credit card TV ad. This is the place to go for tips, equipment, and even a license.

Git Bit
(512) 280-2861
www.gitbitfishing.com
This fishing guide service, run by Mike Hastings, a national tournament fisherman and commentator, offers half-day and full-day bass fishing trips on Lake Travis, a noted hot spot for summertime bass fishing.

Fitness Centers

Fitness centers, gyms, aerobics classes, tai chi sessions, health clubs—Austin has them all. Some offer activities priced per session, while others offer membership. There is a wide range of services and amenities, from the basic nuts-and-bolts weight rooms to highly personalized training programs. Several national chains are present in Austin, including Gold's Gym.

Crenshaw Athletic Club
5000 Fairview Drive
(512) 453-5551
www.crenshaws.com
This is an old Austin favorite, home for more than 50 years to generations of Austin's families. Located in Central Austin, Crenshaw is noted for its family facilities and popular children's gym. The club has an indoor pool and track, plus weight rooms and cardio training equipment.

Gregory Gymnasium
2101 Speedway on the UT campus
(512) 471-6370
www.utrecsports.org
Under the auspices of its RecSports program (see the Recreation Opportunities listing earlier in this chapter), students, ex-students, faculty, staff, and community members can enjoy the extensive facilities at the UT gym. The facilities are vast and include basketball and volleyball courts, indoor jogging, squash courts, weight rooms, climbing walls, even a big screen TV and a coffee shop.

The Hills Fitness Center
4615 Bee Caves Road
(512) 327-4881
www.thehillsfitness.com
If Kevin's Cityview is the South Austin gym, this is the West Austin fitness club. Located on a beautiful 12-acre wooded campus, the center features both indoor and outdoor pools; racquetball, squash, and basketball courts; a child-care center and a cafe, among other amenities.

Hyde Park Gym
4125 Guadalupe Street
(512) 459-9174
www.hydepark.com
"No chrome. No contracts." is the advertising motto of this university-area gym in one of Austin's favorite and most colorful neighborhoods, Hyde Park. The owners describe the place as down-to-earth, and it is, with cement floors, free weights, and no fancy contracts to sign. Personal trainers are available.

Kevin's Cityview Athletic Club
1126 South Lamar Boulevard
(512) 445-2348
A South Austin institution and, consistent with that neighborhood's image, the real thing with real sweat. A favorite among some of Austin's longtime residents, including writers Bud Shrake and Gary Cartwright (see our chapter on The Literary Scene), who turned to former owner Big Steve (now a consultant) for advice. Big Steve also advises clients of all ages and recently developed a program for an 81-year-old health-seeker. You may spot one of the city's cultural or musical well-knowns working out here after a hard day's night in this self-described "old Austin" gym. The basics are practiced here, plus the staff includes a martial arts expert and a boxing coach.

Premiere Lady and Spa
7028 Wood Hollow Drive
(512) 418-9399
6800 Westgate Boulevard 78745
(512) 707-7700

A very popular fitness center in Northwest Austin, this facility caters to women only. In addition to fitness equipment, the center also has a pool, whirlpools, and steam and sauna rooms. There are aerobics and fitness classes, plus clients can avail themselves of personal care services, such as a hair and nail treatment, facials, massage therapy, and tanning. The club has in-house child care available.

St. David's Health and Fitness Center
900 East 30th Street
(512) 397-4263
www.sdhcp.com
Month-to-month memberships are available at this Central Austin health club, which is affiliated with the St. David's Medical Center. The club has rowing machines, step machines, Cybex weight machines, ski machines, treadmills, and stationary bikes. Aerobics classes and individual exercise programs are offered.

YMCA
See a list of YMCA branches under Recreation Opportunities, earlier in this chapter.
There are six YMCA facilities in the Austin area and two additional branches under the auspices of the Williamson County YMCA. All offer summer programs, workout facilities, classes in a variety of sports, and recreational league play. All also offer free weights, treadmills, step machines, NordicTracks, rowing machines, stationary bikes, aerobics classes, cardiotheater, and whirlpools. The Southwest has a Nautilus circuit, Town Lake has a Cybex circuit, and the North Park branch has a Magnum circuit. Family and individual memberships are available, and guests receive one free visit a year and must be accompanied by a Y member. Out-of-town visitors with a Y membership in another city are welcome—bring along your Y membership card.

24 Fitness Super Sport
10616 Research Boulevard
(512) 794-9151
www.24hourfitness.com

This large Northwest Austin branch of the fitness club chain is packed with fitness equipment, including circuit training, gear, treadmills, and step machines. The club offers members a variety of classes—cardio-combo, step aerobics, and water exercises, including an arthritis warm-water exercise program. In addition to the swimming pool, there is an indoor track and facilities for massage and sauna. Members pay a monthly fee and are given a preliminary fitness test with a personal trainer to help them develop an exercise program.

Flying

See our Getting Here, Getting Around chapter for information on flying lessons and sight-seeing tours.

Hiking

Austin's greenbelts, hike and bike trails in Cedar Park, Pflugerville, and Round Rock (see our Parks section above), and hundreds of miles of trails in nearby state parks offer a great variety of terrain, levels of difficulty, and scenic views for hiking enthusiasts.

Some of the easiest trails to access are within the Austin Greenbelt network. For more information and brochures showing trails and access points, call Austin PARD at (512) 499-6700. One

good way to get started is to join the Sierra Club for its city hikes (www.sierra club.org/austin). The Lone Star Chapter is headquartered at 54 Chicon Street in Austin, (512) 477-1729.

Popular scenic hikes include the trails at McKinney Falls State Park in Southeast Austin and Wolf Mountain Trail in Pedernales Park and Hamilton Pool Park, both west of Austin (see our Parks section in this chapter). A good resource for hikers is the Hill Country Information Service (512-478-1337, www.txinfo.com), which offers U.S. Geological Survey maps and other illustrated guides to Hill Country. Other good resources are outfitters listed in our Shopping chapter.

The Colorado River Walkers of Austin (512-495-6294, www.onr.com/user/dbar ber/crw) organizes scenic hikes. Another Hill Country group that carries on a German tradition of hiking is Volkssporting in Fredericksburg. Call (800) 830-WALK for information on Texas and national activities. If you need to learn more about backpacking and hiking, consider taking a course at the University of Texas Recreational Sports Division, (512) 471-1093.

Horseback Riding

True to its Texas character, there are several major rodeo and equestrian events in Austin each year. (See our Annual Events chapter for details.) Several area ranches offer horseback riding—be sure the owner/ operator has a Texas Department of Health certificate posted.

Bear Creek Stables
13017 Bob Johnson Road
(512) 282-0250
This 25-acre private trail riding facility is located in the area Austin residents call Manchaca, a small South Austin community that has been swallowed up by the growing metropolis. The horses are well behaved and the scenery bucolic, making it a great place for a family outing. Children under 7 years of age may not ride.

ℹ️ *Looking for the ultimate city slicker experience? How about a few days at a Central Texas dude ranch? The Hill Country town of Bandera, about 120 miles southwest of Austin, is home to several well-known dude ranches that offer horseback adventures, evenings on the front porch, and chuck wagon food; some find it quite high class. Check out www.duderanches.com/Texas.*

Cameron Equestrian Center
13404 Cameron Road
(512) 272–4301
This Northeast Austin stable and training center offers English- and Western-style lessons and riding opportunities.

White Fences Equestrian Center
8601 Bluff Springs Road
(512) 282–6248
The trail ride here is along a greenbelt owned by Travis County where riders are likely to see a variety of Texas fauna and flora in quiet, serene surroundings. Family rides are available, and the little guys can rent ponies for the trek.

Hot Air Ballooning

The skies over Austin are filled with balloons each September during the annual Lone Star Weekend Aloft (see our Annual Events chapter). During the rest of the year, the following companies offer quiet rides in the sky. Before floating away, check the pilot's FAA certification. Most flights begin in the early morning, and prices per person can range from $150 to $350.

Central Texas Ballooning Association
(512) 479–9421
www.main.org/ctba
This group maintains a list of members who hold commercial hot air balloon certificates.

Hunting

Deer hunting is a popular pastime in the Texas Hill Country, where more white-tailed deer live than in any other part of the country. So dense is the population that suburban Austin residents often find their gardens have become a favorite noshing place for small herds of deer. Driving in the Hill Country at night also can be a challenge, since the abundant deer love to graze on the roadside grasses—usually the grass on the other side of the road.

The Hill Country also is home to several exotic game ranches where, for a hefty fee, hunters can track and hunt wild Corsican rams, African aoudad sheep, Indian blackbuck antelope, and axis and sika deer. (Axis deer is a popular item on some area restaurant menus, notably Hudson's-on-the-Bend, one of Austin's leading restaurants. Read about it in our Restaurants chapter.)

Much of the hunting in Texas takes place on private lands where landowners rent out leases or allow hunters to come onto their land for a fee during peak season. The Texas Parks & Wildlife Department 4200 Smith School Road, Austin, (512) 389–4800 or (800) 792–1112, offers several free comprehensive guides to Texas hunting, including *The Guide to Texas Hunting*. The Web site (www.tpwd.state.tx.us/hunt) is a vast source of information on where hunters may apply on-line for permits.

Ice Sports

Ice sports are becoming more and more popular in Austin, perhaps because of the influx of new residents from colder climates. Youth ice hockey leagues are growing fast.

Chaparral Ice Center
14200 North I-35
(512) 252–8500
www.chaparralice.com
Public skating, classes, hockey leagues, birthday parties, and broom ball are all offered at these facilities in North Austin. They also offer a pro shop and locker facilities. Round Rock PARD offers ice-skating classes at the I-35 location. The I-35 rink is open Monday through Friday from 12:15 to 5:00 P.M., on Tuesday and Thursday from 8:15 to 10:15 P.M., Friday from 6:30 to 11:00 P.M., Saturday from 1:15 to 11:00 P.M., and Sunday from 1:15 to 4:00 P.M. Skating admission is $5.00, and skates rent for $3.00 a pair. Chaparral recently purchased the Anderson Lane facility. Call for hours and admission charges.

Rock Climbing

This is a fast-growing recreational activity in Austin. Central Texas Mountaineers Association (www.texasclimber.com) keeps track of area activities. A favorite outing for local rock climbers is to Enchanted Rock Park near Fredericksburg, about 90 miles west of Austin (see above under State Parks).

Aspire Adventures
110 Brown Street, Hutto
(512) 759-2088
www.climbtexas.com
Hutto, just a stone's throw from Austin, is now regarded as part of the greater Austin metro area. Aspire is a guide service for rock climbers and also offers classes at facilities around Austin. The company's Web site lists numerous links to rock-climbing clubs and facilities around the state and beyond.

Austin Rock Gym
4401 Friedrich Lane, Suite 300
8300 North Lamar Boulevard
(512) 416-9299
www.austinrockgym.com
This Austin gym with two locations, one south, the other north, has a 30-foot rock wall and offers classes for both kids and adults. There is a pro shop, plus patrons can rent equipment. Austin Rock also offers guide services for climbs around Central Texas.

University of Texas
Recreational Sports
(512) 471-3116
www.utrecsports.org
Information about the classes is detailed in the Recreation section previously in this chapter. Rock climbing classes are included in the curriculum.

YMCA Southwest
6219 Oakclaire Drive,
off U.S. 290 West
(512) 891-9622
The Southwest branch of the Y has a rock-climbing wall and offers classes.

Membership is required to enjoy the Y's facilities; however, guests may pay for one annual visit if they are accompanied by a member.

Roller-skating

These roller-skating facilities are generally open in the evenings until 11:00 P.M. Some offer afternoon sessions, particularly on weekends; however, be forewarned the rinks do close for private parties, so it is wise to call ahead. Admission prices are generally $4.00 and under; in-line skates cost a couple of dollars more. They also offer a variety of party packages ranging in price from around $5.00 to $9.00 per person, depending on whether party favors and snacks are included.

Playland Skating Center
8822 McCann Drive
(512) 452-1901
The Northeast Austin center offers rollerskating, in-line skating, and special adults nights.

Skateworld
9514 Anderson Mill Road
(512) 258-8886
Skating lessons and hockey leagues are featured at this Northwest Austin skating rink.

Round Rock Roller Rink
2120 North Mays Street
(512) 218-0103
This center touts its family activities, including skating for families and Christian music on Monday.

Rugby

Rugby can be an exciting game to watch, even if you don't understand the rules—or apparent lack of them. Spectators should remember rugby is a tough sport that often encompasses certain off-pitch lifestyle habits; i.e., revelry. There are two rugby clubs in Austin; several of their players hail from foreign countries where rugby is popular. Both teams have won titles, gone on tour, and hosted visits from foreign teams.

The Austin Rugby Football Club
P.O. Box 12932, Austin 78711
(512) 419-4784 hot line
(512) 926-9017 clubhouse
www.austinrugby.com

The Austin Rugby Football Club was founded in the spring of 1967 and was the first club in the Southwestern United States. In 1978 the club became the first rugby club in the United States to purchase its own grounds, and in 1985 the team built a clubhouse—it is one of only two rugby clubs in the United States with its own clubhouse and grounds. Call the clubhouse for directions to the club in East Austin, which can be difficult to find without detailed directions.

The Austin Huns
(512) 459-HUNS
ww.hunsrugby.org

The Austin Huns RFC Pitch is in Zilker Park, and games are usually played on Saturday afternoon. After the game the Huns head for Nasty's, "Homeland of the Huns," a neighborhood bar at 606 Maiden Lane in Central Austin. The Austin Huns Rugby Football Club was founded in 1972 when the second side of the Austin Rugby Football Club broke away to form their own team.

Austin Valkyries
www.austinvalkyries.com

The Austin Valkyries Women's Rugby Football organization is eager for new members. Ranked No. 2 in the Western United States, the Valkyries train Tuesday and Thursday at Burr Field, a facility the club owns in Northeast Austin. The site is hard to find, and the dirt road into the pitch is muddy in rainy weather. The Valkyries suggest using a four-wheel-drive vehicle on wet days. Check the Web site for directions.

Running/Walking

There are 5K, 10K, and marathon events throughout the year in Austin (see our Annual Events chapter). RunTex, the running equipment stores, are a good source of calendar events (www.runtex.com). There are four in Austin: 422 West Riverside Drive, (512) 472-3254; 9901 North Capital of Texas Highway, (512) 343-1164; 4001 North Lamar Boulevard, Suite 510 in Central Park, (512) 454-9255; and 2201 Lake Austin Boulevard, (512) 477-9464. The Austin Runner's Club serves as a clearinghouse of information; call (512) 436-1919, or visit www.austinrunners.org.

In addition to the Town Lake Hike and Bike Trail, a popular walking spot is Camp Mabry, headquarters of the Texas Army and Air National Guard, at 35th Street and MoPac in West Austin. The headquarters belies its name and is, in fact, a bucolic park with trees, grass expanses with only the occasional vintage fighter plane on view. There is an oval cinder track for die-hard runners and walkers. Following the events of September 11, 2001, Camp Mabry was closed to the public, but Austinites are hopeful the facility will be reopened.

See the Austin Parks listings in this chapter for hike and bike trails in the city.

Tennis

In addition to private facilities at some of the area's top resorts (see our Resorts Close-up in the Hotels and Motels chapter) and country clubs, there are 28 first-come, first-served municipal tennis court facilities, some with two courts, others four, located in all sectors of Austin. Tennis players also have access to several school courts during the summer months. For a complete list contact PARD at (512) 480-3020 (www.ci.austin.tx.us). Courts are concrete, asphalt, or laykold and are available free of charge. A wonderful resource for tennis players of all ages is www.austin-tennis-resource.com. This Web site has maps of tennis court locations, retail support for tennis players in the city, special events and tournaments, league stats, even some national and international tennis news.

Reservations are necessary and fees are charged to play on the courts at the city's four municipal tennis center facilities, which are larger and have lighting. All courts are laykold and lighted. Fees are $3.00 for adults and $2.50 for children in prime time, which is Monday through Thursday after 6:00 P.M. and Saturday and Sunday before 6:00 P.M. Fees are lower at other times.

The Capital Area Tennis Association at 3625 Manchaca Road, (512) 443-8384, www.austintennis.org, is an excellent resource for tennis players. Organized in 1974 and dedicated to promoting amateur tennis competition, the association keeps its members informed of tennis activities in the greater Austin area; conducts educational tennis clinics and seminars; organizes competitive events to fund youth programs and new court construction; and offers consulting services to public officials about the development of tennis facilities. Membership fees are less than $15 a year for adults.

Caswell
24th Street and Lamar Boulevard
(512) 478-6268

This Central Austin tennis center has nine courts and is open from 8:00 A.M. to 10:00 P.M. Monday through Thursday, Friday 8:00 A.M. to 9:00 P.M., and Saturday and Sunday from 8:00 A.M. to 6:00 P.M. A summer tennis league is headquartered here, and lessons are offered.

Pharr
Wilshire Boulevard at Airport Boulevard
(512) 477-7773

This tennis center in North Austin has eight full courts and is open daily from 8:30 A.M. to 10:30 P.M. Monday through Thursday and until 7:00 P.M. Friday, Saturday, and Sunday.

Austin High
1715 West Street
(512) 477-7802

This tennis facility is in Central Austin, just east of MoPac at Austin High School. There are eight courts available after school is out during the school year and daily during the summer months.

South Austin
South Fifth Street and Cumberland Road
(512) 442-1466

The city's South Austin facility has 10 courts and is open Monday through Friday from 9:00 A.M. to 10:00 P.M. and Saturday and Sunday from 9:00 A.M. to 6:00 P.M. In the summer, beginning in June, the center opens 30 minutes earlier.

Wells Branch Community Center
2106 Klattenhoff Drive
(512) 251-9814

The two lighted courts here are open to Wells Branch residents in this North Austin neighborhood.

ROUND ROCK

Several of the city's parks have free courts, including Frontier Park, 1502 Frontier Trail; Greenslopes Park, 1600 Gattis School Road; McNeil Park, 3701 North I-35; Round Rock West Park, 500 Round Rock West; Stark Park, 1409 Provident Lane; and Stella Park, 803 Nancy Drive. Call Round Rock PARD at (512) 218-5540 for information.

CEDAR PARK

The city's newest park, Elizabeth M. Milburn Community Park, 1901 Sun Chase Boulevard, has tennis facilities. Call the Cedar Park PARD at (512) 258-4121 for information.

Volleyball

SAND VOLLEYBALL

There are several sand volleyball courts in the city's parks, plus a few commercial locations where volleyball enthusiasts gather. Check out www.austin volleyball.com.

Austin Park facilities
Austin PARD
(512) 974-6700
There are four public sand volleyball courts with nets in Zilker Park in a green space area north of Barton Springs Road. The three courts at Pease Park lack nets, but you can rent them from PARD.

Aussie's Bar and Grill
306 Barton Springs Road
(512) 480-0952
(512) 474-2255 (volleyball hot line)
This is a haven for local sand court players. The restaurant operates league play throughout the summer.

Carlos 'N Charlie's
5981 Hiline Road
(512) 266-1683
www.cncaustin.com
Cousin to those wacky Mexican restaurants south of the border, made popular by spring breakers in Cancun, this Emerald Point restaurant has a well-regarded sand volleyball complex. The restaurant rents out the volleyball court and party room for $200 a day for private parties.

Volente Beach
16107 Wharf Cove
(512) 258-5109
www.volentebeach.com
Volente Beach is a private lakeside park that offers volleyball, windsurfing, swimming, and other beach/lake activities. It opens at 11:00 A.M. daily, closing at 10:00 P.M. during the week and 11:00 P.M. on weekends. There are three lighted sand volleyball courts on site. Admission is $4.00.

INDOOR VOLLEYBALL

The Austin PARD operates two indoor volleyball leagues: one located at the Austin Recreation Center, 1301 Shoal Creek Boulevard, (512) 476-5662, and one located at the Northwest Recreation Center, 2913 Northland Drive, (512) 458-4107. League play is year-round and includes men's, women's, and coed teams.

There is a popular new sport on the Austin scene—cricket! Given the influx of immigrants from countries formerly colonized by the Brits, many of whom work in the high-tech industry, the sport has taken hold in Texas. There are four clubs in the area—the Round Rock Cricket Club, the Hill Country Cricket Association, the Austin Cricket Club, and the University Cricket Club. Schedules, contacts, league results, and special events are listed at www.centraltxcricket.org.

WATER SPORTS

Newcomers to the Texas Hill Country often are taken aback by the abundance of lakes, rivers, and creeks in the area. Don't judge Texas by the movies—too often those Hollywood Westerns were filmed in Mexico, Utah, or someplace the director thought looked like Texas. Thanks to Mother Nature and Texas politicians, the Austin area abounds in lakes that, in addition to providing electricity for millions of Texans and irrigation for farmers and ranchers, offer opportunities for a wide variety of water sports.

The Highland Lakes, formed by damming the Colorado River, are the major water attraction in the area. However, Central Texas also has rivers, creeks, natural swimming holes, and, of course, the waterhole some have called the "soul of Austin," Barton Springs Pool (see our Close-up in this chapter). This section is divided into several categories encompassing boating (canoeing, rowing, and sailing), scuba diving, swimming, water-skiing, and windsurfing.

There are several invaluable resources for the water sports enthusiast:

Texas Parks & Wildlife Department
4200 Smith School Road
(512) 389-8900
www.tpwd.state.tx.us
This state agency is not only charged with maintaining the state's parks but also enforcing water safety laws (see our Boating Safety information in this chapter). Copies of the rules and guidelines on water safety can be obtained from the agency, in addition to information about state facilities, including boat ramps, on Texas lakes and rivers.

The Lower Colorado River Authority
(LCRA)
(512) 473-3200
www.lcra.org
Much of the Highland Lakes area falls under the auspices of the LCRA, a state-promulgated agency that is charged with running the utility and overseeing the recreational facilities that are a by-product of the electricity-generating side of the business. In addition to operating parks along the lakes, the LCRA also offers boating safety classes. There are several public boat ramps in the LCRA parks and primitive areas (see our Lake Parks section previously in this chapter).

Travis County Parks
(512) 473-9437
www.co.travis.tx.us/tnr/parks
In addition to state parks and wildlife and LCRA wardens, the Travis County Sheriff's Office also has deputies aboard patrol boats on some areas of the lakes. Many

of the county parks (see our Travis County Parks section above) include boat ramps.

The Austin Parks and Recreation
Department (PARD)
(512) 974-6700
www.ci.austin.tx.us.parks
Austin's penchant for the outdoor life means a major focus for PARD in assisting and serving water sports enthusiasts. In addition to operating a network of municipal and neighborhood pools (see our subsequent Swimming section), PARD offers classes in canoeing, kayaking, and sailing. The department also operates Emma Long Metropolitan Park (see our Austin City Parks section above), the closest boat ramp to downtown Austin and the only city-run ramp on Lake Austin—Walsh Landing, 1 block north of the western end of Enfield Drive.

Boating

SAFETY

Alarmed by the rising numbers of accidents on Texas waterways, the state legislature passed tougher boating laws in 1997. The highlights include:

- Teenagers 13 to 15 must take a boating education course before they can legally operate a boat of 15 HP or more without adult supervision. Since 2001 all 13- to 17-year-olds must complete water safety courses before they can operate a boat or watercraft without adult supervision.
- Children younger than 13 must be accompanied by an adult when operating boats of 10 HP or more or a sailboat longer than 14 feet.
- Jet Skis and other personal watercraft cannot be operated except at slow speed within 50 feet of other personal watercraft, stationary objects, the shoreline, or other boats.
- Of course, driving a boat or personal watercraft while intoxicated is against the law.

There are several sports programs for disabled children in Austin. The Austin Parks and Recreation Department offers therapeutic recreation programs, and the YMCA has several programs for special-needs children and adults.

BOAT RENTALS AND MARINAS

Literally dozens of companies rent boats, sailboats, canoes, pontoon boats, and even large party boats in the Austin area. Most also rent personal watercraft. Several of the larger marinas and rental companies are listed below. It is wise to check the Yellow Pages, then call around to check prices and availability. For busy holiday weekends, rentals should be made far in advance.

Be aware that there is strict enforcement of state and local boating laws, particularly drunken sailing laws, on area waterways. That enforcement is beefed on the Highland Lakes during holiday weekends. Boat rental agents will brief renters on the laws and local sailing "highway" rules and courtesies, and they will stress safety. Most require a deposit in the form of a credit card, and renters will be held liable for any damage to the craft.

Marinas offer both storage slips for sail and power boats, plus full service for gasoline and marine supplies. Many also rent boats, houseboats, and personal watercraft.

AquaVentures
(512) 327-2200
www.austinaquaventures.com
This Austin boat rental company delivers ski boats, personal watercraft, and pontoons to marinas on Lake Travis and the Highland Lakes.

Austin Aqua Fun
(512) 459-4FUN
This company rents boats on both Lake Austin and Lake Travis. Their stable includes pontoons, personal watercraft, and ski boats. The company also offers ski instruction. Pickups are arranged at various locations on the lakes.

Beach Front Boat Rentals
Volente Beach, 16120 Wharf Cove
(512) 258-8400
The marina at this private lakeside park at the northern end of Lake Travis off R.M. 2769 rents personal watercraft and ski boats.

Emerald Point Marina
5973 Hiline Road
(512) 266-1535
The marina is next door to the popular Carlos 'N Charlie's Bar & Grill on Lake Travis (see our Nightlife chapter). In addition to being a full-service marina with store and gas station, the facility rents houseboats, ski boats, and personal watercraft.

Just For Fun Watercraft Rental
5973 Hiline Road
(512) 266-9710
Hurst Harbor Marina
16405 Marina Point
www.jff.net
This boat rental on Lake Travis Emerald Point Marina and Hurst Harbor offers a variety of craft, including pontoon boats and party craft for groups up to 150 people.

Lakeway Marina
Lakeway on Lake Travis
(512) 261-7511
www.lakewaymarina.com
One of the larger marinas on the lake, this business offers boat rentals, lessons, fishing guides, and sunset cruises.

Canoeing and Kayaking

Austin Canoe & Kayak
9705 Burnet Road
(512) 719-4386
www.austinkayak.com
This North Austin store boasts the largest selection of kayaks and canoes for sale in Central Texas. In addition to sales of several major brands, the shop also offers rentals.

Austin Outdoor Gear
3411 North I-35
(512) 473-2644
www.kayaktexas.com
Novices and experienced outdoorsmen are encouraged to check out this north Austin store where both new and consignment outdoor equipment can be found.

The store offers classes in outdoor skills and also rents camping equipment.

Austin Paddling Club
www.austinpaddling.org

The club is dedicated to promoting canoeing, kayaking, and rafting and meets monthly at the LCRA Hancock Building, 3701 Lake Austin Boulevard.

Capital Cruises
Hyatt Hotel Town Lake
(512) 480-9264
www.capitalcruises.com

Looking for a unique way to view the evening bat flight at the Congress Avenue Bridge? Consider renting a canoe, kayak, or electric pedal boat from this Town Lake–based boat company.

Zilker Park Canoe Rentals
2000 Barton Springs Road
(512) 478-3852
www.fastair.com/zilker

Since no motorized craft is allowed on Town Lake, one of the best ways to enjoy it is in a canoe or kayak, which can be rented at this concession in Zilker Park from 11:00 A.M. to dusk daily, March through Labor Day. If you are unfamiliar with the joys of canoeing, try your hand at Paddlefest, the annual April celebration, when a section of Town Lake is roped off and canoes are rented for short trips across the lake (see our Annual Events chapter).

Cruises

Austin Party Cruises
2215 Westlake Drive
Lake Austin
(512) 328-9887
Lake Travis
(512) 266-3788
www.austinpartycruises.com

Party boats can be rented for sunset cruises, birthday parties, scenic cruises of both lakes, and corporate events. The company also offers catering services.

Capital Cruises
Hyatt Hotel Town Lake
(512) 480-9264
www.capitalcruises.com

In addition to renting electric boats and canoes (see previous listing), Capital also offers dinner cruises on Town Lake, bat-watching parties, and sight-seeing trips up and down the downtown lake.

Riverboats
6917 Greenshores Drive
(512) 345-5220
www.austinriverboats.com

The company's two riverboats, *Commodore Riverboat* and *Commodore's Pup*, can accommodate 50 to 500 people as they cruise Lake Austin. The boats can be rented for parties, receptions, and corporate outings. Full food and beverage service is available on both boats.

Vanishing Texas River Cruise
Lake Buchanan
(512) 756-6986
www.vtrc.com

In addition to eagle-watching cruises (see Bird-watching above in this chapter), Vanishing River offers fall foliage cruises, summer sunset dinner cruises, trips to admire the wildflowers in spring, and even tours of Fall Creek Vineyards (see the Close-up on Texas foods in the Restaurants chapter).

Rowing

Austin Rowing Club
223-B East Cesar Chavez Boulevard
(512) 472-0726
www.austinrowing.org

The advent of rowing on Town Lake has given Austinites the opportunity to view one of the most picturesque of early-morning city sights: a lone rower skimming the waters of Town Lake in the morning mist. The rowing club is on the northern bank of Town Lake, near the Four Seasons Hotel. The club serves as headquarters for collegiate team events on Town Lake and serves noncollegiate members of the rowing club. Classes are offered for beginners.

Sailing

The Austin Yacht Club
5906 Beacon Drive
(512) 266-1336
www.austinyachtclub.com
The club sponsors races every Sunday out on Lake Travis and hosts several regattas and races throughout the year. The club is a good source of information on local sailing opportunities and practices, resources, and classes (see our chapters on Spectator Sports and Kidstuff).

Commander's Point Yacht Basin
Lake Travis
(512) 266-2333
One of the few marinas on the lake that rents sailboats and offers training for beginners, Commander's Point is home to a large sailing fleet. The marina also rents captained boats for visitors who want to enjoy a sail on Lake Travis but do not know the ropes.

Sail Aweigh
(512) 250-8141
www.ccsi.com/~sailaweigh
Sailing lessons with a U.S. Coast Guard–licensed master are offered by this Austin business. The company also offers chartered, captained cruises on Lake Travis.

Texas Sailing Academy
101 Lakeway Drive, Lake Travis
(512) 261-6193
www.texassailing.com
The academy has been offering sailing lessons on the lake since 1965. Day and weekly charters, captained cruises, and sailboat rentals are also available.

Scuba Diving

Aquatic Adventures
12129 Rural Route 620
(512) 219-1220

Saturday-morning dives in nearby Lake Travis are a specialty here. The facility also has an on-site swimming pool for lessons and is home to a scuba club.

Pisces Scuba
11401 F.M. 2222
(512) 258-6646
This scuba school and rental outlet touts the wonders of freshwater diving in Lake Travis, plus organizes trips to other national and international locations. Pisces offers classes and rents and services equipment.

Tom's Dive & Ski
5909 Burnet Road
(512) 451-3425
www.tomsscuba.com
Offering classes at all levels from beginners to advanced, plus specialties such as underwater archeology, this North Austin diving facility has a 3,000-square-foot, 10-foot-deep pool. The school organizes local fun dives, outings to the Gulf of Mexico, and international dive trips to such places as Cozumel in the Yucatan.

Swimming

The Central Texas climate can make swimming a joy or, on a hot day, a necessity. Even on the coldest days of the year, enthusiasts will head for the constant 68 degrees of Barton Springs Pool (see our Close-up in this chapter), which, unlike many municipal and neighborhood pools, is open year-round. Of course, the area's lakes and creeks are open throughout the year, but there are dangers there. Diving into creek or riverbeds can be dangerous, as water depths can vary with the seasons and rocky bottoms pose hidden dangers. The lakes are really water-filled valleys; rocks, buried tree limbs, and duckweed can pose dangers. No swimming is allowed in Town Lake, and it is unlikely you would want to swim there anyway given urban runoff problems.

Instead, head for one of the many neighborhood pools, natural-fed pools, or favorite water holes in the area.

Swimming Lessons

American Red Cross
(512) 928-4271
www.redcrossaustin.org

The Red Cross offers a variety of swimming classes for students of all ages and varying degrees of proficiency.

Capital Area Rehabilitation Center
919 West 28½ Street
(512) 478-2581

The center offers classes for adults, children, and handicapped students. There are also sessions for persons suffering from chronic disorders such as arthritis.

Crenshaw Athletic Club
5000 Fairview Drive
(512) 453-5551
www.crenshaws.com

Fitness and water aerobic classes for swimmers with chronic disabilities, or those embarking on a health regimen, are offered at this Central Austin fitness center.

YMCA

All Y facilities listed in our Fitness section earlier in this chapter have indoor pools and a full schedule of swimming classes for all ages and ability levels.

Austin City Pools

There are two categories of city-run outdoor pools in Austin: municipal pools and neighborhood pools. Municipal pools are large, deep pools and charge small fees for daily use. Multivisit passes are available from the PARD. All municipal pools have wading areas, lap lanes, diving boards, concessions, and sunbathing areas. There are picnic sites adjacent to the pools. Generally neighborhood pools are free, open during summer months, and no deeper than 5 feet. All pools have lifeguards, and all may be rented before and after regular operating hours.

There are 27 neighborhood pools throughout the city. Call the Aquatics office below for a list and a map. The neighborhood pools usually open in May and operate on a weekend-only schedule until Memorial Day, when they go into daily operation. In mid-August they resume weekend-only operation and then close before Labor Day. Admission and hours of operation vary at each location.

Austin Aquatics Office
400 Deep Eddy Avenue
(512) 974-9333
www.ci.austin.tx.us/parks/aquatics

This city PARD hot line lists class schedules, fee information, and status of city pools.

Bartholomew Pool
1800 East 51st Street
(512) 928-0014

This municipal pool serves Northeast Austin. Specific times are set aside for recreational swims, lap swimming, and lessons.

Barton Springs
Zilker Park, 2201 Barton Springs Road
(512) 476-9044

Revered as an icon, the "soul of Austin," this hallowed swimming pool is featured in our Close-up in this chapter.

The pool is open daily, and even during the coldest days of winter you'll see swimmers enjoying the 68-degree water. It is open in spring and fall, from mid-March to Memorial Day, Labor Day to October 31, from 5:00 A.M. to 10:00 P.M. There are no lifeguards on duty from 5:00 to 9:00 A.M. and from 8:00 to 10:00 P.M. The pool closes on Monday and Thursday at 7:30 P.M.

From Memorial Day to Labor Day, the pool is open from 5:00 A.M. to 10:00 P.M. There are no lifeguards from 5:00 to 9:00 A.M. and from 9:00 to 10:00 P.M. The pool closes at 7:30 P.M. Monday and Thursday.

From October 31 to mid-March, hours are 5:00 A.M. to 10:00 P.M., and there are no lifeguards on duty from 5:00 to 9:00 A.M. and dusk to 10:00 P.M.

There are no entrance fees during the winter season. Admission during the rest of the year is $2.50 for adults, Monday through Friday, $2.75 on the weekends; $.50 for juniors (12 to 17); and $.25 for children 11 and younger.

Call to make sure the pool is open—cleanings and occasional heavy rains do close the pool. There is a gift shop and information booth at the bathhouse, plus a snack bar.

Deep Eddy
401 Deep Eddy Avenue
(512) 472-8546
This West Austin pool is fed by an artesian well, and its fresh water is a major attraction, especially for families who let the little ones wade in the large, shallow end of the pool. Eilers Park at the intersection of MoPac and Lake Austin Boulevard is home to the pool. The early morning hours are set aside for lap swimmers.

Garrison
6001 Manchaca Road
(512) 442-4048
Serving South Austin, Garrison opens in early May and closes in mid-August. Lap swimmers have the pool to themselves during early morning and late evening on weekdays. Recreational swimming and swim lessons also have designated hours on weekdays and weekends.

Mabel Davis
3427 Parker Lane
(512) 441-5247
This Southeast Austin pool opens in mid-May and closes in August. Lap swimmers have the pool to themselves on weekdays from 9:00 to 10:00 A.M. Swim lessons are also offered here during the week.

Northwest Austin Pool
7000 Ardath Street
(512) 453-0194
This Northwest Austin municipal pool opens a little earlier (late April) and closes a little later (mid-September) than some of the other city pools. Lap swimmers enjoy early-morning and late-evening weekday hours here.

Wells Branch Pool
2106 Klattenhoff Drive
(512) 251-9932
This facility, in the Wells Branch Municipal District in far North Austin, is dedicated for the use of Wells Branch residents.

Round Rock City Pools

There are two municipal pools in Round Rock. Call the city's Parks Department at (512) 218-5540 for operating hours and information about swimming lessons and summer fun activities at the pools.

Micki Krebsbach Memorial Pool
301 Deepwood Drive
(512) 218-7090
This city pool opens in early May and operates on a weekends-only schedule until Memorial Day. The pool is open daily through the summer, then shifts to a weekend schedule from mid-August to the end of September. Daily admission to both city pools is $1.25 for those 18 and older and 75 cents for children 17 and younger. Swim passes are available for multiple visits.

Lake Creek Swimming Pool
Lake Creek Park, 800 Deerfoot Drive
(512) 218-7030
The pool opens in mid-May on weekends only and then shifts to a daily schedule on Memorial Day for the summer, shutting down in mid-August.

Pflugerville City Pool

Gilleland Creek Park Pool
700 Railroad Avenue
(512) 990-4392
The community pool is located in the city's major park that serves as the focal point of a citywide trail system. Picnic sites are adjacent to the pool, which is open daily throughout the summer. The city's PARD offers swimming and aquatics lessons here.

Cedar Park Pools

Buttercup Creek Pool
407 Twin Oak Trail
(512) 250-9578

The pool opens in early May and operates much of the month on a weekend-only schedule, then switches to a daily schedule following Memorial Day, closing down in mid-August. The pool has a lap swimming area and 1-meter and 3-meter diving boards. The city's PARD offers swimming lessons, water aerobics, and family nights at the pool.

Elizabeth M. Milburn Aquatic Facility
1901 Sun Chase Boulevard
(512) 331-9317

This swimming complex includes an eight-lane, 25-meter lap pool and an adjoining recreational pool with a water playscape and a 117-foot water slide. The pool's bathhouse has showers, a concession area, an arcade, and an aquatics office. The lap pool is heated and remains open year-round.

Swimming Holes

There are three natural swimming holes within a 90-minute drive of Austin. Not all are open year-round, and some may be closed when high water proves dangerous or park operators limit human traffic to protect delicate ecosystems. It cannot be overemphasized that swimmers must exercise caution when swimming in natural locations. Underwater hazards can prove deadly, and not a summer goes by without area residents mourning the loss of someone killed from diving into a natural hole.

Blue Hole
County Road 173, Wimberley
(512) 847-9127

Several years ago there were negotiations by Hays County government to purchase Blue Hole and turn it into a county park, but the talks broke off and Blue Hole remains privately owned. *Texas Monthly* magazine named this swimming hole (featured in several movies) as one of the top 10 in Texas. It is along Cypress Creek, near Wimberley, and operates as a club. Members pay by the day, week, or month, plus pay a seasonal entrance fee.

Hamilton Pool
Hamilton Pool Road,
F.M. 3238, off Highway 71
(512) 264-2740
www.co.travis.tx.us/tnr/parks/hamilton

The pool and the grotto that serve as the crown jewel of this 232-acre park (see our Travis County Parks section above) were formed when the dome of an underground river collapsed thousands of years ago. The grotto is now a unique ecosystem. The emphasis is on the environment here, so access to the pool for swimmers is limited. Calling ahead is vital. Once the 100-car parking lot is full, the park closes.

Krause Springs
Spur 191, off Highway 71
(830) 693-4181

Devotees of swimming holes tout this natural pool as a great place to take the family, since the waters are clear and shallow. The pool, which is listed on the National Register of Historic Places, is about 7 miles west of the point where the Pedernales River meets Highway 71. Turn north on Spur 191 and follow the signs. The pool is on privately owned land that is shaded by large cypress trees. There are picnic and camping facilities at the pool. Daily admission is $2.50 for adults and $2.00 for children ages 4 to 11. There are additional fees for overnight stays.

Windsurfing

Windsurfing is a popular pastime on the Highland Lakes. There are two areas of Lake Travis where windsurfers tend to gather—Mansfield Dam and Windy Point, both near Travis County Parks. Mansfield Dam Park is on R.M. 620 and Windy Point is off Bob Wentz Park (see our Travis County Park section).

Austin Windsurfer Club
www.geocities.com/austinwindsurf/
The club has adopted Bob Wentz Park as its club project, working to keep the park clean and litter free. In addition to serving as a clearinghouse for windsurfers, the club also meets socially every month, usually at a Lake Travis–area restaurant.

Volente Beach
16107 Wharf Cove
(512) 258-5109
www.volentebeach.com
This private lakeside park at the northern end of Lake Travis off R.M. 2769 rents windsurfers. There is a $4.00 admission to the park.

Water-skiing

There are two area ski clubs that offer information on classes, tournaments, and tips about good ski locations.

Austin Ski Club
(512) 327-1115
The club sponsors two major tournaments each year—the Texas State Championships in mid-July and the Austin Ski Club Novice Slalom in late August.

Capital Area Water Ski Club
P.O. Box 180875, Austin 78718
www.waterskiaustin.com
The club offers several tournaments throughout the year and touts itself as a "competitive ski club" where members can test their skills against members with similar skill levels. Coaching and clinics are also part of the club's activities.

GOLF

Austin is the home of the famous *Little Red Book*.

"Aha!" some might say—at last, proof that Austin politics is decidedly more left-footed than the rest of Texas. But we are not talking about Chairman Mao's little book here, but Harvey's.

Harvey Penick was the revered golfing pro and teacher who is credited by some of the best players, both amateur and pro, with helping them better their game and reach inner golfing peace. Penick, who lived from 1904 to 1995, is more than an Austin legend. Long known in U.S. golfing circles, Penick became a worldwide legend in the final three years of his life when his small, succinct, plain-talking books of golf wisdom became international bestsellers. In 1992 Austin writer and screenwriter Bud Shrake teamed up with Penick to write the *Little Red Book*. When it became a runaway hit, they followed with a second little book, *And If You Play, You're My Friend*, followed by a third, *For All Who Love the Game*. They were working on a fourth when the much-loved Penick died.

Two weeks before he died in an Austin hospital, Penick was visited by one of his longtime students, pro golfer Ben Crenshaw, who was having trouble with his putting game. Penick gave him the advice he needed. Also, just days before he died, Penick saw another of his star pupils score a major breakthrough. Davis Love Jr. won the Freeport McMoran Classic in New Orleans and made the cut for the Masters. Penick died before the Masters ended, but Crenshaw and Love battled it out that year—Crenshaw winning, Love coming in second. Crenshaw said he felt Penick was the 15th club in his bag. Penick's "simple philosophies about golf and life" had helped him win.

Harvey Penick's life spanned almost a century of golf in Austin. He began as a caddy in 1913 and after high school took a job as the pro at the Austin Country Club (ACC). He taught Crenshaw and Tom Kite at the old ACC, now the Riverside Golf Club (see our listing in this chapter), and passed on his quiet knowledge of the game to several generations of golfers. A bronze statue of Penick, shown passing on tips to Tom Kite, stands near the ninth green of the ACC course in the hills of West Austin.

Penick, a religious man, mixed his love of golf with a wonder and praise of nature—easy to do on some of Austin's attractive golf courses. In addition to having some of the most beautiful and challenging golf courses in the country, Austin is also an egalitarian place. The city maintains several excellent municipal courses that can be played at very reasonable rates.

This chapter is divided into four parts—Austin Municipal Courses, Daily-Fee Courses, Private Courses, and Driving Ranges. For greens fees and cart rental prices, use the chart below.

And for the ultimate pampered golf experience, we've listed several golf resorts.

PRICE CODE

$	under $25 for greens fees or cart rental
$$	$25 to $50
$$$	$51 to $100
$$$$	$101 and up

AUSTIN MUNICIPAL COURSES

There are six municipal golf courses in the Austin area. Each course offers public league and tournament play, and lessons are available at each course. The city also hosts the Austin Junior Golf Academy for children ages 8 to 18. Call either the Austin Parks and Recreation Department's golf office at (512) 480–3020 (www.ci.austin.tx.us/parks/golf), or the office at each course listed below.

Annual cards allow you to play weekdays at any municipal course and seven days a week at the Hancock course. You also pay a small surcharge of around $2.00 per round for seniors and juniors and a little more per round for adults. (Fees, of course, may change as government budgets are scrutinized every year.) Seniors and juniors also get a considerable discount on daily greens fees, which top out at around $25 on prime weekend play days.

Approximate prices for the annual cards are:

- Individual: $750
- Senior: $380
- College Golf Team Member: $280
- Junior: $240
- Summer Junior: $70

Bergstrom Golf Course $
10330 Golf Course Road off U.S. 71
(512) 530–4653

This 18-hole golf course used to serve the former Bergstrom USAF base, now home to the city's international airport. The city has assumed ownership of the course and describes it this way: "Measuring 6,576 yards from the Blue Tees, the difficult par threes and long par fives require well thought shot-making. There are very few water hazards, but the small greens require a good tee shot for the best angle." Weekday tee times can be made seven days in advance; weekend tee times can be reserved beginning Tuesday at 7:00 A.M. Like all other city courses, the fees are very reasonable, around $10.

Jimmy Clay Golf Club $
5400 Jimmy Clay Drive
(512) 444–0999

There are two courses at this municipal golf club located in Southeast Austin:

The 6,749-yard Roy Kizer Course is 18 holes, par 71, and has a driving range. The course is described as a "thinking man's golf course" because of its carefully laid

out design. The 57 acres of lakes and marshes surrounding the course add to its natural beauty. Tee times for weekdays are taken three days in advance; Friday, Saturday, and Sunday tee times are taken on Tuesday beginning at 7:00 A.M.

Greens fees depend on the day of the week and time of day.

The 6,857-yard Jimmy Clay course has 18 holes, par 72. Tee times for weekdays are taken one day in advance; weekend tee times are taken Friday beginning at 7:00 A.M.

Hancock Golf Course $
811 East 41st Street
(512) 453–0276

Built in 1899, this is the oldest golf course in the state of Texas. Located in Central Austin, not far from the popular old Hyde Park neighborhood (see our Relocation chapter), this is a pretty course with rolling hills and a small creek that meanders through its heart. The nine-hole course is 2,633 yards, par 35.

Reservations are not required, but groups of four or more can make a reservation one day in advance. Sunday group reservations must be made Friday.

Seniors and juniors pay reduced fees, and there are lower fees for evening and sunset play.

Lions Municipal Golf Course $
2910 Enfield Road
(512) 477–6963

In West Austin, south of Enfield and west of MoPac, this is the oldest municipal course in Austin, but nevertheless very popular. This is a 6,001-yard course, par 71. There is an irons-only driving range, also.

Tee times for weekdays are taken one day in advance; weekend tee times are taken Friday beginning at 7:00 A.M.

Morris-Williams Golf Course $
4300 Manor Road
(512) 926-1298

This 18-hole municipal course is in East Austin, southeast of the old Robert Mueller Municipal Airport. When the airport site is developed, this golf course is likely to be a prime selling point for the residences that will be part of the new neighborhood. The 6,636-yard, par 72, course is built on an undulating landscape and has a driving range.

Tee times for weekdays are taken one day in advance, weekend tee times are taken Friday beginning at 7:00 A.M.

Greens fees depend on the age of the golfer, the time of day, and day of the week.

Round Rock

Forest Creek Golf Club $$-$$$
99 Twin Ridge Parkway
(512) 388-2874
www.forestcreek.com

This municipal golf course has gained a great reputation not only for its challenging design but also for the quality of the pros who have worked at the club. J. L. Lewis, who went on to the PGA, was the club's first pro. The club is open daily. The par 72 course has 18 holes in 7,154 yards.

The club has a golf shop, driving range, putting green, dining facilities, and even a stocked fishing lake.

DAILY-FEE COURSES

Bluebonnet Hill Golf Course $-$$
9100 Decker Lane
(512) 272-4228

Located in northeast Travis County near Manor, this public course was built to attract beginning golfers and has become very popular. It takes its name from the rolling Hill Country landscape, particularly beautiful in spring when the bluebonnets bloom. Bluebonnet is rated one of the top 25 public courses in Texas according to the *Dallas Morning News*.

The 6,503-yard course is 18 holes, par 72. Facilities include a driving range, snack bar, putting green, and chipping green.

Butler Park Pitch and Putt
Golf Course $
1201 West Riverside Drive
(512) 477-9025

For almost 50 years Winston Kinser operated this tiny private, very inexpensive course on city-owned land just south of Town Lake in the heart of Austin. Kinser died in 2000, but his dream lives on. The par 27, 805-yard course is tucked away just east of Lamar Boulevard and south of Riverside Drive. Each of the nine holes is par 3, and the longest hole is No. 8, 118 yards. This is a great place to find out if golf is for you. You can rent clubs (you won't need a cart). The course opens at 8:30 A.M. and closes at dusk.

Circle C Golf Cub $$$
7401 Highway 45
(512) 288-4297
www.circlecranch.com

This club was designed to give patrons of a daily-fee course a country-club feel. Near the southern end of MoPac in Southwest Austin in the Circle C subdivision, the course apparently succeeded. It was named one of the best new clubs in Texas in 1992 and has remained popular. The course was designed by Jay Morrish to attract new golfers and is regarded as a fun place to play. Circle C is next door to the Lady Bird Johnson National Wildflower Research Center, and the same rugged beauty preserved at the center is apparent around the golf course.

The 18-hole course is 6,859 yards, par 72. Players can avail themselves of the driving range, putting green, dining room, meeting rooms, and the 24-hour/10-day advance tee hot line. There is also shuttle service from area hotels.

Riverside Golf Course $$
1020 Grove Boulevard
(512) 386-7077

This course is a part of golf history. Now a public course in Southeast Austin, this was the home of the Austin Country Club and the place where Harvey Penick taught golf luminaries like Ben Crenshaw and Tom Kite. Penick was the club pro when Austin Community College moved here in 1950. The course is lined with old oak and pecan trees that once stood witness as some of Austin's wealthiest citizens and future national golf champions played. Now it is owned by Austin Community College and open at very low fees to all comers.

The 6,500-yard course is 18 holes, par 71. There is a snack bar and picnic area on site, plus a putting green, golf shop, and chipping green.

Pflugerville

Blackhawk Golf Club $$
2714 Kelly Lane
(512) 251-9000
www.blackhawkgolf.com

Build it, and they will come! This is true of the Blackhawk Golf Club, which was built in the early '90s by John and Martha Leach in what was then the small country town of Pflugerville, northeast of Austin. These days the club is surrounded by the suburban boomtown of Pflugerville. John Leach turned to his sister-in-law for the design of the course—she is Hollis Stacy, three-time U.S. Women's Open Champion, who decided to enter the male-dominated profession of golf course architecture.

Working with local architect Charles Howard, they turned a dairy farm into a highly praised public golf course with abundant water and trees. The 6,636-yard course is 18 holes, par 72. Facilities include a driving range, golf shop, and snack bar.

Greens fees include a cart. There are reduced fees for twilight play and for seniors during the week.

PRIVATE COURSES

Austin Country Club $$$
4408 Long Champ Drive
(512) 328-0090
www.austincountryclub.com

This is the spiritual home of Harvey Penick, who was the club's first pro. A bronze statue of the revered teacher stands near the ninth green. He is shown giving tips to former student Tom Kite, the international golf champion who holds the course record, 64.

This is the third home for the club, which was chartered in 1898, one of the two oldest in the state. The current course in West Austin was designed by Pete Dye, one of the world's top golf course designers. Experts rate this course as one of the toughest in the Central Texas area.

The 6,822-yard course is on the shores of Lake Austin—18 holes, par 72.

Balcones Country Club $$
Balcones Course
8600 Balcones Club Drive
(512) 258-2775
Spicewood Course
11210 Spicewood Club Drive
(512) 258-6763
www.balconescountryclub.com

There are two courses at this Northwest Austin club south of U.S. 183, near Spicewood. Each course has its own club and pros, plus members enjoy an additional central clubhouse. The club is one of the largest in the Austin area and has given special emphasis to its junior program.

The rolling hills of the Balcones course are favored by walkers. The 6,649-yard course is 18 holes, par 70. The 6,706-yard Spicewood course is 18 holes, par 72. Spicewood has greater elevation changes, plus more water elements. Twilight rates, after 4:00 P.M., are half price.

i

Avid golfers sometimes build a vacation trip around a visit to Austin's Golfsmith megastore, located in North Austin at 11000 North I-35, (512) 837-1245, toll-free (800) 815-3873 (www.golfsmith.com). The complex is home to the Harvey Penick Golfing Academy, created with the blessing of the legendary Austin teacher whose legacy is noted in the introduction to this chapter.

Great Hills Golf Club $$
5914 Lost Horizon Drive
(512) 345-0505
www.greathillscc.com

This club is known for its wonderful, authentic Hill Country landscape with rolling hills, cliffs, and canyons. It is in West Austin but priced in a much more affordable range than its nearby neighbors—Barton Creek Resort and Austin Country Club. Great Hills is regarded as a great bargain and a challenging course.

The 6,599-yard course is 18 holes, par 72. The clubhouse has both casual and formal dining rooms, a swimming pool, and tennis courts.

Hills of Lakeway Golf Course $$$
26 Club Estates Parkway
(512) 261-7272
www.thehillscc.com

This Hill Country course west of R.M. 620 near Lake Travis has been ranked among the top five in Texas. It was designed by Jack Nicklaus, one of his first courses in Texas. The course follows a creek and offers wonderful vistas of the surrounding rugged hills.

This 6,954-yard, 18-hole, par 72 course has a marina, tennis courts, swimming pool, driving range, and putting green on-site.

Lost Creek Country Club $$$
2612 Lost Creek Boulevard
(512) 892-2032
www.lostcreekclub.com

Located just west of Loop 360 (Capital of Texas Highway) in an area of rugged canyonland, this club is not far from Austin's most noted golf resort, Barton Creek. The land around the Lost Creek fairways and greens is rugged, and the precipitous drops along the edges of the course make control even more important than usual. The natural rise and fall of the land, plus the hazards, make the course challenging.

This 18-hole course is 6,522 yards, par 72. The clubhouse offers both golf and tennis pro shops, a swimming pool, and formal and casual dining areas. There is a driving range, practice bunker, and putting green on site. Closed on Monday.

Onion Creek Country Club $$$
2510 Onion Creek Parkway
(512) 282-2162
www.onioncreekclub.com

This course was designed by Masters Champion Jimmy Demaret in collaboration with George Fazio. It has been described as a classic golf course, and for many years it was the home of the original Legends of Golf tournament on the Senior PGA Tour. The Legends was played here for 12 years, and it proved to be a major building block for the seniors' tour.

Located in far South Austin, the course is the anchor for a country club–style residential development. The clubhouse has all the amenities. The 18-hole course is 6,367 yards, par 70.

River Place Golf Club $$
4207 River Place Boulevard
(512) 346-6784
www.riverplaceclub.com

On the shores of Lake Austin, west of the city, this course has been a symbol of the economic roller-coaster ride of the past 20 years. Originally planned to be part of an upscale Hill Country development on the shores of Lake Austin, it was caught up in the development versus antigrowth wars, then the real estate downturn of the 1980s. Finally, in 1991 it was placed on the auction block by the Resolution Trust Corporation.

Now, after a redesign by professional golfer Tom Kite, the course is described as attractive and sometimes challenging. The 18-hole course is 6,611 yards, par 71. Facilities include a driving range, snack bar, and putting green.

Greens fees include carts. Twilight fees go into effect after 2:00 P.M.

GOLF RESORTS

**Barton Creek Conference Resort
and Country Club** $$$$
8212 Barton Club Drive
(512) 329-4000, (800) 336-6157
www.bartoncreek.com

This resort with its four highly praised golf courses and beautiful 4,000-acre site is built on one of the most sought after and fought over pieces of land in Austin. Located just a dozen miles from downtown, the resort was created along the banks of Barton Creek, which winds through the hills before feeding the underground spring that, in turn, feeds Barton Springs. Some of Austin's most vocal environmentalists protested its construction, but others have praised the development for its ecological sensitivity—the golf courses are maintained without many of the traditional fertilizers typically used on golf courses, and efforts have been made to embrace the local flora into the resort design. The greens and fairways are planted with drought-resistant grasses to cut down on water usage.

The club has four courses, described below, all designed by leading names in golf course architecture.

Given the resort's popularity as both a country club and conference center, not all four courses are available every day to resort play, with the exception of the Lakeside course. The resort also offers several golf packages.

While golf is a great reason to visit the Barton Creek club, the resort also offers other recreational facilities, including skeet shooting, tennis, and "supersports" for groups—volleyball, tug-of-war, and obstacle courses. Jogging, swimming, boating, fishing, horseback riding, sight-seeing, even factory outlet mall tours are available.

The resort has several dining facilities, including one of the few restaurants in Austin where a jacket is required. On-site there is a fitness center and a spa where you can have everything from facials to salt rubs, marine fango massages to aromatic loofah scrubs.

There are 147 guest rooms at the resort with views of the golf course and the surrounding Hill Country. An additional 158 rooms were added to the resort in 2000. Room rates are offered on both the American Plan (three meals included) and the European Plan (no meals). Prices begin at $230 and range up to $1,100 for the Presidential Suite.

The Crenshaw & Coore Course
This was designed by Austinite Ben Crenshaw and his partner, Bill Coore. True to Crenshaw's philosophy, the course is traditional and follows the terrain with broad, rolling fairways. This 18-hole course is 6,678 yards, par 71.

The Fazio Foothills Course
This is dubbed the resort's signature course, and its dramatic design shows the distinctive signature of Tom Fazio. There are cliff-lined fairways, waterfalls, and even caves. *Golf Digest* has rated this Fazio course one of the Best Resort Courses in America, second in Texas and 60th in the ranking of the 100 greatest golf courses in America. The course also has won the USGA's National Environmental Steward Award.

The Fazio Canyons Course
A second Fazio course has been added to the resort, and this one features more of the stunning Hill Country features Fazio incorporated into the first course, including hilltop views, meandering creeks, and small canyons where the native flora has been maintained.

The Arnold Palmer–Lakeside Course
Arnold Palmer designed this course, which opened in 1986 as the Hidden Hills Country Club. Barton Creek now owns and operates the course about 25 miles from the resort on the shores of Lake Travis. The course has been named among the most beautiful in Texas by the *Dallas Morning News*. Golfers enjoy great views from the clubhouse overlooking the lake. The 6,956-yard course is 18 holes, par 72.

Lakeway Inn   **$$$$**
101 Lakeway Drive
(512) 261-6600, (800) LAKEWAY
www.lakewayinn.com
This resort hotel on Lake Travis, west of the city, offers golfers and tennis players opportunities to pursue their sports while enjoying the other recreational activities available at the Highland Lakes. The hotel underwent a major restoration in 2000 and reopened with refurbished rooms, facilities, and restaurants. There are two golf courses made available to Lakeway Inn guests, and tennis players can enjoy the World of Tennis with its 26 indoor and outdoor courts. There is also a fitness center, outdoor jogging trails, two swimming pools, and a marina.

Live Oak Golf Course was created in 1964 by designer Leon Howard. Development restrictions were not in place back then, and Howard was given permission to dredge soil from the lake bottom to spread on the course. Twelve years later, Howard built the Yaupon Course at the resort. Both offer dramatic views of the lake—two holes on Live Oak are adjacent to the marina.

Live Oak is 18 holes, 6,643 yards, par 72. Yaupon is 18 holes, 6,565 yards, par 72. The resort offers a variety of packages, and greens fees are included in the price of packages.

DRIVING RANGES

Ben White Golf Center
714 East Ben White Boulevard
(512) 462-2104
This facility in South Austin has 50 lighted grass tees, a nine-hole putting green, and offers chipping green lessons.

Eaglequest
10515 North MoPac
(512) 345-2013
Located in North Austin near Braker Lane, this facility has a driving range, putting green, an indoor learning center, and pro shop and offers lessons.

Golfsmith Practice Facility
11000 North I-35
(512) 837-1810
Located next door to the Golfsmith Factory Outlet, the driving range has 70 lighted tees. Golfsmith offers custom golf clubs, clinics, practice greens, computerized swing analysis, factory tours, snack bar, and Harvey Penick irons and woods.

Mister Tee
13910 North R.M. 620
(512) 335-4444
There are 25 lighted tees at this Northwest Austin driving range.

Oak Hill Driving Range
5243 U.S. 290 West
(512) 892-5634
This Southwest Austin driving range has 65 lighted tees.

SPECTATOR SPORTS

Let's face it. When it comes to professional sports, Austin isn't exactly in the big leagues. While the thousands of Austinites who enjoy major league sports find themselves sitting in left field, so to speak, there is still much to celebrate when it comes to sports in Austin. What our city lacks in major league sports is more than made up by Austin's passion for University of Texas sports teams. While UT didn't coin the phrase "Winning isn't everything, it's the only thing," it has lived by that sentiment for more than a century of athletic achievement and has produced national championship teams in a wide range of sports time and time again. UT's nationally recognized Hook 'em Horns hand signal wasn't voted the best in the country by *Sports Illustrated* magazine in 1997 for nothing.

Austin also is home to the Ice Bats, a minor league professional ice hockey team that draws die-hard fans from all over the region, and a new arena football team, the Austin Wranglers. Our neighbors in Round Rock claim a very popular minor league baseball team, the Round Rock Express.

Sports spectators will discover that Austin boasts an important annual rodeo, a horse track, hugely popular marathons, and several spectacular boat races each year. Bicyclists and cycling fans will be pleased to note that not only is Austin home to five-time Tour de France winner Lance Armstrong but our city also hosts his foundation's annual Ride for the Roses. (See the Close-up of our hometown hero in this chapter.)

Another plus for sports fans is Austin's unique location between San Antonio, Dallas, and Houston, all within a three-hour drive of our city—and an even shorter flight. San Antonio is 80 miles south on I-35. This quirk of logistical fate affords Austinites incredible choices among major league sports teams in both men's and women's basketball, baseball, soccer, ice hockey, and, of course, football—the national pastime of Texas. In fact, one of the best spectator sports to be seen in this part of the world is the weekly high school football game, usually held on Thursday or Friday during the season, particularly those in some of the small towns where the game is the social event of the week. Check the sports pages of the *Austin American–Statesman* for schedules, and take in a game on a cool fall evening.

Whether your competitive spirit is most roused by a whistle, a buzzer, a starter's pistol, or those simple words, "batter up," you're sure to find a Texas sport to call your own.

MINOR LEAGUE SPORTS
Baseball

Round Rock Express
Dell Diamond, 3.5 miles east of I-35 on Highway 79, Round Rock
(512) 255–BALL (2255)
(512) 469–7469 (Star Tickets)
www.roundrockexpress.com
It took several major league players to bring minor league baseball to Round Rock, but when former Texas Ranger Hall of Famer Nolan Ryan and heavyweight techie Michael Dell are on the team, success is assured. Naming the Double-A team was easy, given Ryan's nickname as "The Ryan Express" for his awesome fastball during his playing days. The Round Rock Express rolled into the spanking-new Dell Diamond in 1999. The team was so succcessful, both in performance and in fan attendance, that owners felt confident enough to move on up, announcing the purchase of the Triple-A Edmonton Trappers of Canada, who will begin play as the

Express in 2005.

The current Round Rock team will move to Corpus Christi and will still be owned by Ryan and his family.

In preparation for the new team, more luxury suites have been added to the 10,000-seat Dell Diamond, named to honor the Round Rock computer giant's efforts to bring minor league ball to Central Texas. The stadium is designed with families and comfort in mind, and even the cheapest seats have chairbacks and cupholders. There's also a swimming pool complex and a children's fun center, which includes a climbing wall. General admission prices are family friendly, but make your reservations well ahead of time. The season runs from April to September.

Ice Hockey

Austin Ice Bats
7311 Decker Lane
(512) 927-PUCK,
(512) 469-SHOW (Star Tickets
box office)
www.icebats.com
The perfect place in Austin for those with a "bat attitude" is in the Travis County Exposition Center on Ice Bats game night. The Expo Center, fondly known as the Bat Cave, has been home to minor league ice hockey since the team was formed in 1996. This exciting team quickly earned a large and loyal following. In its first season the team led the newly formed Western Professional Hockey League in total attendance, drawing more than 6,200 people per game. The team, now a member of the Central Hockey League, has consistently drawn rabid (we can't resist) fans

If you select upper arena seats for Ice Bats games at the Travis County Exposition Center, be sure to take along a cushion or blanket to sit on. The metal benches are hard and cold!

and has finished in the top rankings since its first season.

Training camp starts around the first of October, and hockey fans are always invited to watch the team practice. Call them for a schedule. The Ice Bats train at the Expo Center in Southeast Austin. The Expo Center, home to the annual Austin/Travis County Livestock Show & Rodeo, wasn't exactly designed for ice hockey but has served the team well. Just try to avoid getting seats off in the corners, where the visibility isn't great.

Tickets range in price from $10 to $30. Season tickets and packages also are available. You can purchase tickets at the Ice Bats Box Office at the Expo Center and at Star Tickets outlets around town, or charge by phone through Star Tickets. Texas's only NHL team is the Dallas Stars. For information about the Stars call (817) 273-5100. The Ice Bats are affiliated with the Houston Aeros of the International Hockey League.

MAJOR LEAGUES AROUND TEXAS
NFL Football

Dallas Cowboys
Texas Stadium, 2401 East Airport
Freeway, Irving
(972) 785-5000
www.dallascowboys.com
The Dallas Cowboys have competed in the Super Bowl a record eight times and have taken home the trophy in five of those games to tie with San Francisco as the winningest team in Super Bowl history. In recent years the star has faded, but that has not stopped fans from flocking to Texas Stadium, in the Dallas suburb of Irving. Touted as "America's Team," the Cowboys draw fans from across the state during football season. (The Cowboys also are popular in Mexico, where they often play a preseason game, and their regular season schedule is featured on television.) Even when the Cowboys fall on hard times,

66,000 fans fill the stands at Texas Stadium. Most die-hard fans purchase season tickets, which range in price from several hundred dollars to quite a few thousand for seats on the 50-yard line right behind the Cowboys' bench. But those seats can be hard to come by, as season ticket holders don't like to give them up. Individual tickets sell for about $35 and are usually available only in the upper and lower end zones because season-ticket holders dominate the stadium.

Houston Texans
Reliant Stadium, 2 Reliant Park, Houston
(866) GO–TEXANS
www.houstontexans.com

In 2002 the Houston Texans became the first NFL team in 41 years to win its expansion debut when the team stunned intrastate rival the Dallas Cowboys 19–10 in the Texans' brand-new stadium. Major league football, which had disappeared from Houston with the departure of the Oilers, was back. While the Texans went on to win just four games their first season, Houston fans are solidly behind this team. Season tickets for the 2003–2004 season sold out months before the preseason kickoff. Reliant Stadium, a 69,500-seat state-of-the-art facility, got the nod to host Super Bowl XXXVIII on February 1, 2004. Among its many attributes, Reliant is the world's first retractable-roof football stadium, which makes sense in a city whose perennial weather forecast is partly cloudy with a chance of rain. Individual tickets start at $35.

NBA Basketball

San Antonio Spurs
Alamodome, 100 Montana Street, San Antonio
(210) 554–SPUR (7787),
(210) 224–9600 (Ticketmaster)
www.nba.com/spurs

Austin's closest major league sports venue is about 80 miles down I–35 in San Antonio. This is a popular team for basketball

> *The hottest new football stadium in Central Texas is the $20.5 million high school facility in Round Rock. The stadium seats 11,000 fans and features a 20-by-20-foot replay screen. After all, Texas is the place "where finishing second in football is kinda like taking your sister to the prom," says Austin American–Statesman columnist John Kelso.*

fans throughout Central Texas, and the Spurs make a special effort to promote the team in Austin by making appearances at schools and in shopping malls. An average 18,000 people attend Spurs home games. The Spurs joined the National Basketball Association in 1976 along with the New York Nets, Denver Nuggets, and Indiana Pacers when the former American Basketball Association merged with the NBA. The team has played in San Antonio's Alamodome since the $186-million facility opened in 1993. The Alamodome, which is used for many sporting, concert, and other events, holds about 20,550 people for normal Spurs games and upwards of 34,000 for special Spurs games. Tickets range in price from around $20 to triple digits for regular season games, although tickets can go lower when upper level seats are opened up. Tickets can be purchased at the Alamodome box office on the southwest corner of the facility or by calling the Spurs box office or Ticketmaster. The regular season runs October through April.

Houston Rockets
Toyota Center, 1510 Polk Street, Houston
(866) 446–8849
www.nba.com/rockets

Two-time National Basketball Association champions, the Houston Rockets joined the NBA in 1967 as the San Diego Rockets. The team moved to Houston four seasons later and rewarded supporters with NBA titles in 1994 and 1995. After 28 years in the same complex, the Rockets moved downtown to the brand-new Toyota Center for the 2003–2004 season. The center, which seats 18,300, is a welcome change for Rockets fans, who had to fight for tickets at the too-small Compaq Center. The season runs from October through April. Individual tickets range in price from $10 to $200.

Dallas Mavericks
American Airlines Center
2500 Victory Avenue, Dallas
(877) 316–3553
www.nba.com/mavericks

Dallas was home to the Chaparrals of the American Basketball Association from 1967 to 1973 but lost its professional basketball team when the Chaparrals moved to San Antonio as the Spurs in 1973. Seven years later pro basketball returned to Big D at the 18,042-seat Reunion Arena when the Dallas Mavericks became an expansion team of the NBA. Three years later the Mavs recorded their first winning season and followed that up with five more winning years that included half a dozen trips to the NBA playoffs. Although Dallas didn't fare as well in the 1990s. Maverick fans have remained loyal. Individual tickets range in price from very reasonable to midrange double digits. and can be purchased with a credit card by phone or at the American Airlines Arena box office or Dillard's department stores in the Dallas area.

WNBA Basketball

Houston Comets
Toyota Center, 1510 Polk Street, Houston
(713) 627–9622
www.wnba.com/comets

The Houston Comets dominated the Women's National Basketball Association for the first four years of its existence, winning the championship in 1997, 1998, 1999, and 2000. By the end of the 2003 season, the Comets had appeared in postseason play for seven straight years. The WNBA has grown dramatically since its eight-member inaugural season and now totals 14 teams across the country. Like their "brothers" in the NBA, the Comets moved to Houston's new Toyota Center for the 2004 season, which runs from May to September.

Major League Baseball

Houston Astros
Minute Maid Park. 501 Crawford Street, Houston
(877) 9-ASTROS
www.mlb.com

Established in 1962 as the Houston Colt .45s, the team became the Astros in 1965 and moved into the then-new Houston Astrodome, a huge complex that seated more than 54,000 baseball fans. The Astros have won several Central Division pennants, including in 1997 and 1998, but haven't yet made it to the World Series. In 2000 the team moved to a new state-of-the-art facility in downtown Houston. The new park, which is located near the George Brown Convention Center and next door to Union Station, is a tribute to old ballparks revered by lovers of the game. One unique feature is the retractable roof that can move into place within 12 minutes if inclement weather threatens. The new ballpark opened to rave reviews, even if the team didn't live up to the ballpark's excellence. The Astros also renovated Union Station, a classic railroad station built in 1911 and designed by the same architect who designed Grand Central Station in New York. The team has its executive offices in the building, plus a cafe and shops for the fans. In recognition of the historic location, the Astros had a replica of a 1860s steam engine made; it runs on an 800-foot track inside the stadium whenever the Astros score a home run. Tickets at the new park are very affordable, ranging from $5.00 to $29.00, and kids can watch the game for $1.00 from the outfield deck. The regular season runs April through September.

Texas Rangers
The Ballpark at Arlington,
1000 Ballpark Way, Arlington
(817) 273-5100
www.mlb.com

Formerly the Washington Senators, the team came to Dallas in 1972 as the Texas Rangers. The Rangers, managed by Buck Showalter, have had a large and loyal following over the years and in 1996, 1998, and 1999 treated fans to an American League West division championship. The Rangers also hosted the 1995 All-Star Game. Playing since 1994 in a $191 million state-of-the-art complex, the Rangers claim one of the top stadiums in the country. Even if you're not a baseball fan, the Ballpark is a sight to behold. In addition to the 49,166 seats and boxes, the Ballpark features the Legends of the Game Baseball Museum, which contains some 1,000 baseball artifacts from the 1800s to the present, including some items on loan from the National Baseball Hall of Fame. The complex also features a children's learning center with a 12-acre lake, interactive exhibits, and a youth ballpark. The Ballpark was built under the direction of George W. Bush when he served as the Rangers managing partner. An ardent baseball fan, Bush has been heard to say that baseball should be played on grass, with wooden bats, and outdoors—the Ballpark is living proof of his belief.

Tickets can be charged by phone through the number listed above. Individual ticket prices range from $4.00 to $30.00. While tickets are sold at the door, it's best to order your tickets early; these games can and do sell out.

National Hockey League

Dallas Stars
American Airlines Center
2500 Victory Drive, Dallas
(214) GO-STARS (467-8277)
www.dallasstars.com

Texas law allows ticket brokers to resell tickets at higher than the face value—sometimes much higher. So if you're absolutely dying to see a game that is announced as sold out, or if you just want to get a great seat and are willing to pay the price, check the Yellow Pages under Tickets for any number of local ticket brokers.

Mention "big league sports" and "Dallas" to many sports fans and they will likely think football and the Dallas Cowboys. But despite the Sunbelt climate, ice hockey has a long history and loyal following in Big D. The city's first professional ice hockey team played in Fair Park Ice Arena in 1941. At the time, the local paper carried ads touting the game as "the most dangerous game in the world" and "murder on ice." No one was killed on the ice when the Texans debuted, but some in the audience may have wondered why fans were greeted by girls in Chinese costumes handing out candles and cookies. The reason? Owner Clarence E. Linz, a proud patriot, had decided to donate half the evening's proceeds to the United China Relief Fund. The evening was a big success, with almost 5,000 fans paying 80 cents for a reserved seat and $2.25 for a box seat. The original Texans, members of the American Hockey Association, played the 1941 season before World War II called a halt to play. The team reunited in 1945 and the fans came back, staying loyal to the team until its demise in 1949.

From 1967 to 1982, the Chicago Blackhawks ran a minor league affiliate called the Dallas Blackhawks. Then in 1993, the major league Dallas Stars walked onto the ice. In 2001, the team began the season in the brand-new state-of-the-art American Airlines Center. The arena was erected on a cleared industrial site in the northwest section of downtown and can be seen by motorists travelling through downtown on I-35East. (Take the Continental Drive exit to get a closer view of the new arena.) The $325 million arena "sits on a buried super-highway of fiber-optic cable," enabling the fans to enjoy high-tech replay boards, state-of-the-art public address systems, even Internet access in the suites and conference rooms. The popularity of NHL hockey in Dallas is evident to anyone who visits the new arena. Season tickets for the NHL Dallas Stars have been sold out since 1998, and a single-night ticket, if you can find one, will cost you around $100. To check out ticket availability, call the number above, or go to www.tickets.com.

Arena Football

The Austin Wranglers
Frank Erwin Center, 1701 Red River
Street
(877) 289–6235 (tickets)
www.austinwranglers.com
A professional football team finally took the "field" in Austin in 2004 after the Arena Football League (AFL) awarded a franchise to the new Austin Wranglers. General Manager Greg Feste heads the Austin ownership group that includes several former NFL players. Arena football, one of today's fastest-growing professional sports, is a fast-paced game in which big nets guard the end zone instead of goal posts and foam boards surround the field

---

While UT football is often just as exciting as any professional game, remember that this is a college game. No smoking is allowed and no alcoholic beverages are sold or allowed in the stadium. The Texas Ex-Student's Association, fondly known as the Texas Exes, hosts a lively outdoor pregame celebration just across the street from the stadium on San Jacinto Street. They sell food, beer, and soft drinks—and will tell you how to join the organization. The event is open to the public.

---

of play. The Wranglers are one new addition to the rapidly expanding AFL, which also includes the Dallas Desperados, owned by the Cowboys' Jerry Jones, and a team in Philadelphia partially owned by singer Jon Bon Jovi. NBC televises these games, which average more than 11,000 fans per game. The Wranglers play indoors at the 16,000-seat Erwin Center from February through May.

UNIVERSITY OF TEXAS SPORTS

Longhorns Football
Darrell K Royal-Memorial Stadium,
23rd Street and Campus Drive
(512) 477–6060 (Texas box office)
www.texassports.com
www.texasboxoffice.com
No sporting event in Austin comes close to Texas football for the sheer number of burnt orange–clad fans that turn out to support this team. An average of 74,000 Longhorns fans—students, Texas Exes, and just plain football buffs—unite as one big family in Darrell K Royal-Memorial Stadium when the Longhorns play at home. In fact, Texas football is so popular here that many times over the years fans have stood to watch hotly contested games, jamming the stadium to way over capacity.

To attend a UT football game is to become part of a Texas tradition that dates back more than a century. Established in 1893, the Longhorns have left an impressive mark on national collegiate football. Over the years, Longhorn loyalists have been rewarded with a number of national and conference titles and more than three dozen NCAA postseason bowl games. They have been treated to performances by Heisman Trophy–winner and future NFL Hall-of-Famer Earl Campbell (1974–1977), now an Austin resident, as well as by dozens of All Americans, future NFL players, and other trophy winners. In 1996 the Longhorns defeated Nebraska to win the first-ever Big 12 Conference championship. In 1998 senior halfback Ricky

Williams broke conference and national collegiate records, culminating his UT career with a Heisman Trophy. The list of accolades for this team goes on and on. Mack Brown, former head coach of the North Carolina Tar Heels, became Texas's 28th head football coach in 1998, succeeding John Mackovic, who, despite the 1996 Big 12 championship, presided over a rare losing season for the Longhorns the following season.

Known simply as Memorial Stadium since it was inaugurated in 1924, UT added legendary head football coach Darrell K Royal's name to the stadium in 1996. Royal had led the Longhorns to three national championships and 11 Southwest Conference titles in his 20 seasons at UT (1957–1976). A major renovation and enlargement of the stadium in 1998 raised the seating capacity to 80,106 and included the addition of a 16-row upper deck on the east side of the stadium and 1,600 field-level seats as well as construction of 52 stadium suites and a club room designed for 1,200 people. The five or six seasonal home games are usually played on Saturday afternoon during the fall football season, which runs from September through November. It's best to get your tickets early, as these games can sell out, even in the bigger stadium.

Longhorns Baseball
Disch-Falk Field,
I-35 and Martin Luther King Drive
(512) 471-3333, (800) 982–BEVO

UT baseball fans from across Austin share the blissful moment of striding past the turnstile, ticket in hand, through the stadium tunnel and into the arena that is widely recognized as the best collegiate baseball facility in the country. This team, founded in 1895, has won an impressive five national championships, the latest in 2002.

Disch-Falk Field, built in 1975 at a cost of $2.5 million and named for two former Longhorn coaches, holds 5,000 baseball fans in the main chairback area and can be expanded to hold more. As many as 8,000 fans have packed this facility for

> *Bevo, the live Longhorn steer that serves as the UT mascot, made his first appearance at a UT football game on Thanksgiving Day 1916. Bevo, by the way, was the name of a Budweiser near-beer product that was popular around campus during that period.*

important, hotly contested collegiate games. However, this is one UT sporting event for which tickets can most often be purchased at the gate.

The Longhorns play an average 30 home games a year during the January through May season.

Longhorns Softball
McCombs Field
Martin Luther King Drive and Comal Street
(512) 471-3333, (800) 982–BEVO
www.texasboxoffice.com

Just a home run's distance from home plate at Disch-Falk Field is McCombs Field, a $4.5 million softball complex that's arguably one of the best in the country. Of course the team that plays on it is also top notch. A varsity team since just the late 1990s, the Longhorns have won three Big 12 Conference Tournament titles and two Big 12 regular-season titles and have appeared twice in the College World Series, most recently in 2003. The team has included noted pitchers Christa Williams, a 1996 and 2000 Olympic gold medalist on the U.S. Women's Softball Team, and Cat Osterman, the 2003 USA Softball National Player of the Year and member of the U.S. National Softball Team.

Coach Connie Clark, a former collegiate All-American pitcher and 1987 Broderick National Softball Player of the Year, has earned high praise for her leadership of this team since it ascended to varsity status. The Longhorns play about 15 home games, mostly double-headers, during the regular season, which runs February through April. These games can and do sell out, so get

CLOSE-UP

Lance Armstrong— Austin's Hometown Hero

"He's from Austin, you know."

Who among Lance Armstrong's hometown fans—and there are so many of us—has never heard those words drop impulsively from our lips? It's not just that Lance is a champion cyclist who has won the Tour de France a stunning *five* consecutive times already, although that's part of it. And it's not only because he first had to triumph over an advanced case of cancer, or because he formed a cancer foundation to help others even before he knew whether he'd survive the disease himself, although those are part of it, too. We're mostly proud of our hometown hero because he's lived his life—on and off the bike—with such style, such dignity, such humanity, such heart. So when we casually mention that Lance Armstrong is one of us, or when we call the world's most famous bicycle race the Tour de Lance, we pay tribute to the neighbor we've come to admire these past years. He has reminded us just how high the human spirit can soar.

Each October, cyclists, cancer survivors, and supporters from around the world converge on our city to participate in the Lance Armstrong Foundation (LAF)'s Ride for the Roses Weekend (see the Annual Events chapter). Founded in 1997, the LAF has raised more than $26 million to fund cancer survivorship programs and research. Not bad for an organization that Lance has said "started on a paper napkin in a Mexican restaurant in Austin, Texas." The foundation, however, is just one of the many ways Lance has reached out to others. In 1995, before he became a household name, he created the Junior Olympic Race Series to promote cycling among America's youth. He has co-written two best-selling memoirs that address in candid detail his struggle to survive cancer and get back to the business of living (see The Literary Scene chapter). And when he's not out there training for or winning races, Lance travels the globe on behalf of his foundation and others to raise cancer awareness and help strengthen the resolve of those stricken with the disease.

Born September 18, 1971, in the Dallas suburb of Plano, Lance gained fame in 1991

your tickets early. The team also has an exhibition-game schedule in the fall.

Longhorns Basketball
Frank Erwin Center, 1701 Red River Street
(512) 471-3333,
(512) 477-6060 (Texas box office)
Few teams on the UT campus have cap-tured the attention and admiration of Austin sports fans like our women's basketball team. Over the past 20 years, the team has attracted the most fans in women's basketball history with a total attendance of well over 1.4 million. Success on the court is the reason. Led by Coach Jody Conradt since 1976, the Longhorns have

Five-time Tour de France winner Lance Armstrong calls Austin home. COURTESY OF CAPITAL SPORTS & ENTERTAINMENT

the number one–ranked cyclist in the world. Later that year he was diagnosed with testicular cancer, which had spread to his lungs and brain. Given less than a 50/50 chance of survival, Lance underwent two operations and a debilitating treatment program. While still battling the disease, he created the LAF. By 1998 he was cancer free—and ready to ride into history.

His stunning comeback victory in the 1999 Tour de France is now legendary, and the four Tour wins that followed are nothing short of miraculous. In 2002 *Sports Illustrated* named Lance its Sportsman of the Year, calling him "more than a bicyclist now, more than an athlete. He's become a kind of hope machine."

Wherever he goes from here, one thing is certain: Coasting is not in Lance Armstrong's nature.

by winning the U.S. Amateur Cyclng Championship. In 1993, after picking himself up from a humbling last-place finish in his professional debut, Lance secured his spot in U.S. cycling history with his victory in the million-dollar Triple Crown. By 1996 he was

won a stunning 80 percent of their games.

During the 14-year history of the Southwest Conference, the Longhorns took 10 regular-season titles and won nine tournaments. In 1986 the Longhorns became the first women's basketball team in the history of the National Collegiate Athletic Association to record a perfect

season with a 34–0 record. The Longhorns, who moved to the Big 12 conference for the 1996–97 season, draw an average of more than 5,000 fans to the Frank Erwin Center for the approximately 16 home games played during the regular season, which runs November through February.

The University of Texas Longhorn Band, "the Showband of the Southwest," performs at UT football games and also makes appearances at important events around the country. The band owns the largest bass drum in the world, nicknamed "Big Bertha."

Runnin' Horns

Frank Erwin Center, 1701 Red River Street
(512) 471-3333,
(512) 477-6060 (Texas box office)

With crowds averaging 13,000 fans for each home game, UT's Runnin' Horns men's basketball team is one of the biggest draws in town—and in college basketball anywhere. Founded in 1906, the Horns were members of the Southwest Conference (SWC) from 1915 to 1996. During that time the Horns racked up an impressive 22 SWC titles (12 outright) and a 648-449 total record. In 1997 the Horns along with Southwest Conference members Baylor, Texas A&M, and Texas Tech merged with Big Eight teams to form the Big 12. The Runnin' Horns hold court for regular season games at the Erwin Center November through February.

THE BEST OF THE REST
Car Racing

Thunder Hill Raceway, 24601 I-35, Kyle
(512) 262-1352
www.thunderhillraceway.com

Located just off I-35 exit 210, about 25 miles south of Austin, Thunder Hill Raceway presents exciting racing events every Saturday evening from March through September. This is not a sport to watch, it's a sport to experience as the cars speed around a ³/₈-mile oval asphalt track, sometimes faster than 120 miles per hour. Thunder Hill, Central Texas's newest and most modern track, opened in 1998 and features a 3,600-seat open-air stadium. The raceway presents hobby stock cars, superstocks, and limited late models regularly and each week also

adds a special feature race, such as Texas pro sedans, super late models, and American race trucks.

Thunder Hill also sponsors RV shows, car shows, and fairs as well as an ongoing live music concert series. Gates open at 5:30 P.M. Racing starts at 7:00 P.M. Tickets are on sale at the door. Admission is $10.00 for adults, $7.50 for children ages 6 through 12. Children younger than 6 are admitted free.

Running

Austin Convention and Visitors Bureau
201 East Second Street
(512) 478-0098
www.austintexas.org

Two Austin footraces draw lots of spectators each year. The Motorola Marathon (www.motorolamarathon.com) usually held the second Sunday of February, draws more than 10,000 participants. Runners start in far Northwest Austin and wind up, hopefully, 26 kilometers later on the shores of Town Lake downtown. The prize money purse totals $100,000, with $10,000 awarded to both the overall male and overall female winners. In April Austin hosts the Statesman Capitol 10,000, among the top 100 road races in the country. This 10K event draws about 15,000 competitors as well as crowds of spectators. (See our Parks and Recreation chapter for more information on running events and venues.)

Rodeos

Austin/Travis County Exposition and Heritage Center, 7311 Decker Lane
(512) 467-9811,
(512) 477-6060 (Texas box office)
www.staroftexas.org

Yee haw!! There's nothing like a great rodeo to let you know you've arrived in Texas. Austin's big event is the annual Austin/Travis County Livestock Show & Rodeo held in mid-March. This huge competition, on the official Professional Rodeo

Cowboys Association (PRCA) circuit, draws thousands and thousands of people from all over the state for 11 fun-filled days and nights of bull riding, calf roping, team roping, steer wrestling, barrel racing, saddle bronc riding, bareback riding, and much, much more.

Rodeo events aren't the only highlight of this celebration. The livestock show and auction culminates in the award for the Grand Champion Steer, which in 1997 sold for a record $50,000. This is also the Travis County Fair and offers fun for people of all ages. There's even a Kid's Town, which features a barnyard and petting zoo, children's shows, and many contests, including the biggest bubble contest, the jump rope contest, the whistling contest, and the cow-chip toss. To top it all off, the rodeo features a major concert performance each evening. Brooks & Dunn, Merle Haggard, the Mavericks, and many more outstanding musical performers have appeared at this wildly popular event.

There's more to the rodeo than meets the eye, however. Run by a nonprofit organization, the rodeo is also the largest nonprofit fund-raiser for educational programs in Travis County, raising millions of dollars for educational programs and academic scholarships.

Of course the largest and most well-known PRCA rodeo in Texas (and one of the largest in the country) is the Houston Livestock Show and Rodeo held in late February or early March in Reliant Stadium. Like the Austin event, the Houston rodeo offers live music entertainment every night as well as other events for the whole family. Waco, just 90 miles up I-35, holds the annual Dodge Texas Circuit Finals Rodeo. This event, held around the New Year, features the top 15 finalists in all seven rodeo events for the state of Texas. San Antonio, 80 miles south of Austin on I-35, also hosts one of the state's biggest rodeos in early February, while the prestigious Fort Worth rodeo is held in the latter part of January.

Once you've attended the Austin/Travis County Rodeo or any of our state's other outstanding rodeos, you may be hooked on cowboy culture for life. Two publications will keep you up to date on professional and amateur rodeo events around Texas and around the country. The first is the PRCA's official publication, *Prorodeo Sports News*. This magazine contains a calendar of events as well as articles pertaining to the circuit. Call (800) RODEO-4U to subscribe. Also of interest is *Cowboy Sports News*. Published in Sealy, Texas, this is the official publication of the Cowboys Professional Rodeo Association (CPRA). The CPRA, while it contains the term "professional" in its title, is an amateur organization. *Cowboy Sports News* lists literally hundreds of events of interest to amateur rodeo fans around Texas and is distributed free at feed and Western stores in Texas and other states. For information on paid subscriptions call (409) 885-1127.

Sailboat Racing

**Austin Yacht Club, 5906 Beacon Drive
(512) 266-1336
www.austinyachtclub.org**
Austin wouldn't be Austin if it didn't have a spectator sport that took advantage of our great waterways. The Austin Yacht Club sponsors three major annual sailboat regattas as well as a number of other races throughout the year. The kickoff event for the summer season is the Turnback Canyon Regatta held over Memorial Day weekend. Lake Travis's oldest and most spectacular sailboat race, the Turnback Canyon event is held over 25 miles of winding river from Mansfield Dam to Lago Vista. This regatta, which began in the 1950s as the Bluebonnet Regatta, offers sailors a choice between competing in the two-day, 50-mile race or taking the same course in a more relaxed "cruising" mode. Nearly 100 boats compete in this great annual spectacle.

The Governor's Cup Regatta, held over the Fourth of July and the weekend before, also draws a huge number of sailboats. This race, in which boats follow a course laid out by buoys, is held in the main basin at Lake Travis, the area just below Mansfield Dam. Centerboard boats race one weekend while the larger keel boats race the next.

The Fall Regatta features two races over two days. Racers sail from the Yacht Club to Lakeway and back the first day. A buoy race is held in the main basin on the second day.

Sailors may call the Yacht Club for information on how to participate in these events, while those with sailing experience may post information about themselves on the club's bulletin board if they would like to crew these boats.

Spectators will find that the Turnback is best viewed from the Iguana Grill restaurant or Lakeway Inn. The Governor's Cup can best be seen from the Oasis Restaurant on Lake Travis, from Windy Point, an LCRA Lake on Comanche Trail, or from atop Mansfield Dam. The first day of the Fall Regatta is best viewed from the Iguana Grill or Lakeway Inn near the finish line. Always bring your binoculars for these events.

The Austin Yacht Club, founded in 1952, aims to promote the sport of sailboat racing. The club sponsors a summer sailing class for adults and camps for children.

Horse Racing

Manor Downs
U.S. 290 East and Manor Downs Road, Manor
(512) 272-5581
www.manordowns.com
Established in 1974 as a quarterhorse racetrack for racing enthusiasts, Manor Downs became a pari-mutuel betting track in 1990 after Texas legalized that form of gambling. The Downs, now offering Thoroughbred racing, too, features live horse racing on weekends starting about 1:30 P.M. during the spring season (from about February to around the end of May). Manor Downs also offers simulcast racing from tracks around the country on screens at other times during the spring meet and

throughout the year. While not the fanciest racetrack in Central Texas, Manor Downs is the closest Austinites can get to live horse racing. It's also a wonderful gathering place for the state's horsemen and women who come in from all over to take part in this age-old Texas tradition. The track features covered stadium-type wood seating as well as good old-fashioned picnic tables at track level—all the better for enjoying the barbecue, fajitas, and grilled sandwiches served daily. There's also an air-conditioned Turf Club where, for an extra $5.00, you can sit at the more comfortable tables and chairs while watching the races on TV screens. Admission ranges from $2.00 to $5.00, seniors pay just $1.00. This track, just northeast of Austin, is easy to find. Just follow U.S. 290 East from the I-35 junction for about 10 minutes. You can't miss the huge signs pointing the way to the track. Call the number listed for a recorded message of the racing schedule and the simulcast events of the day.

Retama Park
1 Retama Parkway, Selma
(210) 651-7000
www.retamapark.com
This ultramodern horse racing park features Thoroughbred and quarterhorse racing May through June and Thoroughbred racing late July to mid-October. Retama also offers simulcast racing year-round from top tracks across the country, including the Kentucky Derby, Preakness, Belmont, and the Breeders Cup. Retama has a spectacular indoor grandstand and clubhouse as well as a sports bar and terrace dining. Live racing May to June begins at 6:30 P.M. Thursday through Saturday and 5:00 P.M. on Sunday. Races for the Thoroughbred meet begin at 6:30 P.M. Wednesday through Saturday. General admission is $2.50. Simulcast admission is $2.00. Retama charges $3.00 extra for a reserved seat in the clubhouse. Selma is about 65 miles south of Austin on I-35. Take the 174-A exit and follow the signs. Retama is just west of the interstate.

DAY TRIPS AND
WEEKEND GETAWAYS

Covering 267,339 square miles and boasting hundreds of miles of seashore, soaring mountains, plunging valleys, vast plains and prairies, pine forests, deserts, islands, lakes of all sizes and shapes, giant metroplexes, small towns, and wide open spaces galore, Texas is much more than a state—"It's a Whole Other Country,"as our boosters like to say. At the very heart of it all, in spirit if not precise geographic center, lies Austin.

It's no wonder, then, that when Central Texans plan a vacation we often look no farther than our own great big bountiful backyard. In fact, for the day trips and weekend getaways we cover in this chapter, we can't even include all the fascinating sights Texas has to offer. Some are just too far away to make even a weekend trip feasible.

We've limited this section to those regions within a three-hour drive of Austin. That decision has forced us to leave out the Gulf of Mexico seashores at Padre Island, Galveston, Port Aransas, and Corpus Christi. We had to bypass the Davis and Guadalupe Mountains and the breathtaking canyonlands of Big Bend National Park. (However, if you want to tour that area look for the *Insiders' Guide to Corpus Christi.*) We're missing the Tex-Mex border cities of El Paso, Laredo, and Brownsville. We had to skip the Big Thicket, pass over the Little River, shun East Texas, and ignore West Texas.

"Could there possibly be anything left?" the uninitiated among you may ask. You'll soon find out. In this chapter we'll take you on a brief tour of three of America's 10 largest cities: Dallas, Houston, and San Antonio, all within a three-hour drive of Austin and each distinct in its own way. For the history buffs among you, we've included an entire section on San Antonio's famous missions, starting of course with the Alamo.

Another historic journey, though of more modern times, takes you to Johnson City, boyhood home of our country's 36th president. We'll also introduce you to LBJ's beloved ranch, the "Texas White House" during the Johnson Administration, and the place where the elder statesman came home to retire following a lifetime of public service. Both of these areas make up the LBJ National Historic Park.

Not to overlook Texas's other U.S. presidents, we'll introduce you to Bryan/College Station, home of the George Bush Presidential Library and Museum, site of sprawling Texas A&M University, and domicile of UT's archrivals, the A&M Aggies. Of course #41, as the Bush family calls former President George H. W. Bush, has a library, while #43, President George W. Bush, just has a ranch for now. Located in Crawford, a tiny unincorporated community southwest of Waco, Prairie Church Ranch is well hidden from public view, but visitors to town can drop by the local coffee shop and pick up a Crawford souvenir. It is an easy side trip on the way to or from Dallas.

We'll tell you about Gruene, a former ghost town that emerged from ruin to become a thriving city, especially on weekends when the chicken-fried steak disappears faster than the time it takes to pronounce the city's name correctly. This is one place Austinites visit regularly to shop for antiques or to crowd into the historic Gruene Hall for an evening of first-class live music.

We had to include Round Top and Winedale, two communities east of Austin renowned as meccas of classical music and theater. One of the state's oldest communities, Round Top is home to the International Festival Institute, founded by a concert pianist. Winedale hosts the annual Shakespeare at Winedale festival. Austinites flock to these cities throughout the year to partake of their great annual events and to step back in time.

The little town of Salado, just a stone's throw from Austin, could have been a contender. An up-and-coming town in the 1880s, Salado was bypassed when the railroad finally came to Central Texas. While railroad towns thrived, Salado slipped into obscurity. Discovered by artists in the second half of the 20th century, Salado is now back on track, so to speak, and a popular day trip or weekend getaway from Austin.

Of course, we couldn't forget Fredericksburg, one of Austin's favorite weekend getaways and a prime example of Hill Country living. This quaint town, founded by German immigrants in 1846, boasts a Main Street that has earned a spot on the National Register of Historic Places. Main Street shops offering antiques, apparel, and arts and crafts do a bustling business on weekends as visitors pour in from all over the region. This is one great place to spot a movie star or two, or perhaps just enjoy an authentic German meal.

Considering the important German influences on the culture and development of Central Texas over the past 150 years, it wouldn't do to mention just one German-infused town. New Braunfels, too, retains much of its German flavor, literally. From the great German restaurants to the annual Wurstfest sausage festival, New Braunfels is a delight for the taste buds. We'll give you two other reasons this town attracts Central Texans year-round.

Appropriately, the Highland Lakes come last. After you've spent even a little time trying to see all the sights Central Texas has to offer, you may need to just get away from it all and relax for a while on a boat or on a beach. Any one of the four lakes we describe in this section will do the trick.

Before you head out, check our Annual Events and Festivals chapter for events in these day trip destinations. Also have a look at our Texas Pronunciation Guide in the Area Overview chapter so that you'll sound like an Insider when you get there.

A note about ticket prices: In general, museums and art galleries in Texas either charge no entrance fee or a minimal amount, making them affordable for most visitors. Tickets to entertainment facilities—Seaworld, Six Flags, etc.—are in the double digits, approaching $50 in some cases for adults. Generally, professional sports tickets range from the affordable at major league baseball games to the stratospheric at basketball or football games, particularly when the teams are winning. Check before you go, since prices at these entertainment and sports facilities frequently change.

Whether you decide to head north, south, east, or west to major cities, small towns, or a place of quiet solitude, you're sure to find a spot that is Texas through and through.

UP NORTH
Salado

The Village of Salado, 55 miles north of Austin on I-35, is just that—a village, and a charming one, that owes its existence now to the fact that history passed it by. Founded in 1859 at a low-water crossing of Salado Creek, it looked like Salado was destined to become a growing community, especially with the founding of Salado College in 1859. By 1884 the community was on its way to being a town with seven churches, 14 stores, two hotels, two blacksmiths, and three cotton gins. But when the railroads were built to the north and east, Salado slipped back to being a village.

Salado's population dwindled from 900 in 1882 to 400 by 1914 and only slightly over 200 in 1950, according to the community's publications. But then artists and artisans began to settle in the area, buying up the old buildings and opening art galleries and antiques shops. Now the village has more than 130 businesses and attracts weekend visitors who come here to relax, browse the stores, and soak up the area's history. A great resource is the Salado Web site (www.salado.com), which offers information on lodging, shops, dining, events, and recreation in this historical community.

One of the best ways to learn about the area is to request a copy of the Driving Tour Tape prepared by the Bell County Historical Commission. Visitors can write to the Bell County Historical Commission, Bell County Courthouse, Belton, TX 76513, or ask at one of Salado's landmarks, like the Stagecoach Inn, 1 Main Street, on the east side of I-35, (254) 947-5111, www.inn-at-salado.com.

The modern 82-room Stagecoach Inn stands adjacent to what remains of the Shady Villa Hotel, where Sam Houston was said to have slept in 1850. Other famous guests include General George Armstrong Custer and cattlemen Charles Goodnight and Shanghai Pierce, who stopped at this historic spot along the Chisholm Trail.

What remains of the old hotel is part of the inn's restaurant, which also includes an open-air atrium built around a 500-year-old burr oak. Newer dining rooms adjoining the original two-story clapboard building serve guests at lunch and dinner, but in keeping with tradition the waitresses always recite the menu by heart—prime rib, plate-size steaks, fried chicken, baked ham and lamb, plus desserts such as homemade pie and cobbler.

Salado abounds with historical connections. In the 1830s Sterling C. Robertson, himself of Scottish descent, established a colony here; many of the settlers were Scots. In November Salado hosts the Annual Gathering of the Clans on the Village Green near the Stagecoach Inn. Hundreds of Texans and Americans of Scottish descent descend on Salado for the weekend festival. Call (254) 947-5232

Traveling around Texas by car will eventually lead you to a two-lane state highway. When these highways have wide shoulders, it's customary for slower vehicles to drive on the shoulder briefly to allow faster cars to pass. Frankly, we don't know if that's legal, but it's the Texas way.

for information. Another famous Salado native, with Scottish ties of her own, is Liz Carpenter, former press secretary to Lady Bird Johnson and now an Austin writer.

Visitors also flock to Salado for the annual Salado Christmas Stroll & Holiday Home Tour, usually held on the first two weekends of December. Salado is a favorite choice of Central Texans for Christmas shopping and celebrating the season, so the village's hotels and guest houses are booked in advance. There is also a large July Fourth picnic, a summer art fair in August, and a December village artists' sale. Call the Salado Chamber of Commerce, (254) 947-5040, for information on these events or check the calendar at www.salado.com. At the Table Rock Amphitheater, (254) 947-9205, an outdoor dinner theater in the community, the Tablerock Theatre group puts on annual performances of a historical pageant, *Salado Legends,* during the summer and dramatizations of Dickens's *A Christmas Carol* in December.

More than 130 buildings in Salado are listed on the National Register of Historic Places, and several of them serve as guest houses and bed-and-breakfast inns. Some are small cottages with cozy fireplaces, while others are large Victorian homes. Some are located in rural settings, others are just a few steps from the shopping district. Duffers may want to ask about the Mill Creek Country Club & Guest Houses (254) 947-5141, www.mill creekgolfresort.com, which has a Robert Trent Jones II 18-hole golf course as well as swimming and tennis facilities.

The old homes also offer romantic and charming backdrops for dining in Salado. Several serve lunch and afternoon tea, including Browning's Courtyard Cafe on Salado Square, (254) 947-8666; Cathy's Boardwalk Cafe, (254) 947-8162; and the Pink Rose Tea Room on Main Street, (254) 947-9110. Gourmet dinners are served on weekends at the Inn on the Creek, (254) 947-5554, a Victorian bed-and-breakfast on Center Circle. Reservations are required. Pietro's Italian Restaurant & Pizzeria, 302 North Main Street, (254) 947-0559, offers a change of pace for lunch and dinner. The Range at the Barton House, Main Street (254) 947-3828, offers American cuisine with French and Mediterranean touches for lunch and dinner Wednesday through Sunday. No Texas village would be complete without Mexican food, which can be enjoyed at the Salado Mansion, Main Street, (254) 947-5157. Mexican food served in an 1857 mansion—no place but Salado.

Sustenance is necessary in Salado since the village has so many shops it is impossible to list them all here. There are herbalists, antiques dealers, custom furniture stores—Barnhill-Britt sells hand-crafted furniture constructed of antique longleaf pine taken from 19th-century Texas buildings; Benton's has custom-order iron beds—Amish quilts, children's fashions, Oriental rugs, Christmas ornaments, folk art, bride's gifts, rare books, top women's fashion (Grace Jones, One Royal Street, occupies a building that was the Salado bank and attracts customers from all over the country), native plants, tribal art, gourmet foods, jewelry and rabbits everywhere (Wigglesworth Place, Rock Creek at Main, a Salado Christmas favorite), paintings and sculpture (the Windberg Gallery, Main Street, features the work of famed Texas artist Dalhart Windberg), and on and on.

Salado is an unincorporated village, but the chamber of commerce estimates the population of permanent residents is about 1,500—which means there is a shop for about every 10 residents in the area.

Most of the shops are open daily, although some do close on Sunday. Most are in the immediate area of Main Street.

From Salado you could return to Austin or continue up I-35 to the fast-paced world of the Dallas/Fort Worth Metroplex.

Dallas/Fort Worth

While many audacious Austinites make the 400-mile round-trip drive or half-hour flights to and from this sprawling metroplex in one day, there are just too many things to see and do for us to suggest you do the same. This is definitely a weekend getaway destination. The big dilemma if you're driving up is deciding which way to go once you pass Hillsboro, where I-35 divides. West will take you to Fort Worth, known fondly as Cowtown. This city proudly proclaims itself as the place "where the West begins." Don't be fooled by the lingo, though; this city is a cultural wonderland. East will take you to sophisticated Dallas, the Big D to those who realize its size translates into grandeur. Both offer an astonishing assortment of things to do, places to go, people to see. We'll point out some of the highlights.

This is an exciting area, encompassing many cities in addition to Fort Worth and Dallas. Arlington and Irving are just two of the larger suburbs. Whatever you choose to visit, you'll find that the metroplex is user-friendly and sure to please. Note, also, that this region has perfected a light rail system that Austin has only dreamed about. If you don't want to hassle with parking or trying to find your way around town, check the schedule and routes for the area's DART light rail system, (214) 979-1111. You'll be amazed at how efficiently it operates and how many places it serves.

Home to the annual Texas State Fair in September and October, Dallas's Fair Park attracts tourists throughout the year. This area has been home to Texas state fairs for more than 100 years. New facilities were built here to house the Texas Centennial

Exposition of 1936. Now a National Historic Landmark because of its collection of Art Deco buildings from the period, Fair Park is a 277-acre city park that includes museums, sports venues, entertainment complexes, an aquarium, and more. Call the Fair Park administrative offices (214) 565-9931, www.fairparkdallas.com, to find out about the following venues. Located east of downtown Dallas and bounded by Cullum Boulevard and Fitzhugh, Parry, and Washington Avenues, Fair Park is a must-see. Of course, the Cotton Bowl Stadium is always a big draw. Besides the annual New Year's Day game, the stadium also hosts the annual "Red River War" football game between UT and the University of Oklahoma in the fall as well as a variety of other football games and sporting events. The Coca Cola Starplex Amphitheater, (214) 712-7518, is a 20,000-seat entertainment venue hosting more than three dozen major concerts each year. The Music Hall seats 3,420 people and hosts theater, music, and opera events throughout the year. The Coliseum is a great place to see sporting events, including rodeos, polo matches, and horse shows.

Fair Park also is home to the African American Museum, (214) 565-9026, at 3536 Grand Avenue. This is the most complete facility in the Southwest dedicated to African-American art, history, and culture. The museum also sponsors regular free jazz concerts and other events. It's closed Monday only, but hours vary. Admission is free. Nearby is the Dallas Museum of Natural History, (214) 421-3466, www.dallasdino.com. The Hall of Prehistoric Texas, which includes the nation's largest prehistoric sea turtle, is just one of the many attractions of this facility. Also here is a hands-on discovery center for children, called City Safari. It's open daily, except for major holidays. Admission prices are family-friendly. Children of all ages will love the Dallas World Aquarium, (214) 670-8443. Located at First Street and Martin Luther King Boulevard, the aquarium is easy to spot. It's right in front of Fair Park's giant Ferris

wheel. Open daily, the aquarium is home to almost 4,000 sea creatures. Ask about regular times for shark and piranha feedings, which are preceded by a short talk. Admission charge. The Age of Steam Railroad Museum, (214) 428-0101, at 1105 Washington Street, features more than four dozen pieces of historic railroad equipment, including actual railroad cars dating to the early 1900s. The museum is open Thursday through Sunday only. General admission is very reasonable. The Science Place and TI Founders IMAX Theater, 1318 Second Avenue, (214) 428-5555, is open seven days a week. This hands-on science center is literally packed with exhibits to delight children of all ages. And don't miss out on the opportunity to see an IMAX movie on the giant screen or attend a sky show in the planetarium. Admission charge. IMAX shows cost extra.

The Dallas Museum of Art, 1717 North Harwood Street, (214) 922-1200, in the Arts District is among the city's major attractions. The DMA owns a significant collection of art dating from prehistoric to modern times. The museum also hosts regular traveling exhibitions. General admission is free, although there could be a charge for special exhibits. Another highlight of this district is the Morton H. Meyerson Symphony Center, (214) 629-0203, at 2301 Flora Street. Designed by renowned architect I. M. Pei, the center is home to the Dallas Symphony Orchestra. Call about performances or for tours of this elegant center.

One perennial favorite of visitors from around the world is Dealey Plaza, where President John F. Kennedy was assassinated while passing through in a motorcade on November 22, 1963. Now a National Historic Landmark District, the plaza features a lovely park with a JFK memorial plaque. Of course, the controversial "grassy knoll" is here, too. Dealey Plaza is in downtown Dallas near the West End District. Nearby is the Sixth Floor Museum, (214) 747-6660, www.jfk.org, at 411 Elm Street. Alleged JFK assassin Lee Harvey Oswald is said to have fired the fatal shots from an open window on the sixth floor of what was then the Texas School Book Depository (now the Dallas County Administration Building). While both the Kennedy family and the city of Dallas resisted efforts to memorialize this site, public interest remained so intense through the years that a museum was finally opened. Among the many fascinating exhibits here are hundreds of photographs, documentary films, and a large-scale model of Dealey Plaza prepared by the Warren Commission, which investigated the assassination. The museum is open daily. Admission fee, children under age 6 free.

If you're one of those Americans who reject the Warren Commission findings that Lee Harvey Oswald was the lone gunman who killed JFK, you might want to check out the Conspiracy Museum, (214) 741-3040, at 110 South Market Street. In addition to displays furthering the debate over who actually killed Kennedy, visitors will find exhibits dedicated to theories on the assassinations of Robert Kennedy, Martin Luther King, President Lincoln, and others. The museum is open daily 10:00 A.M. to 6:00 P.M. Admission charge.

While Austin isn't a paradise of major league sporting events, Dallas is close enough to provide adequate stimulation for sports fans of every variety. The ever-popular Dallas Cowboys, (972) 785-5000, play at Texas Stadium in nearby Irving at 2401 East Airport Freeway. The Texas

Rangers, (817) 273-5100, major league baseball team play at the Ballpark at Arlington, 1000 Ballpark Way. The Ballpark itself is a great tourist destination, featuring the Legends of the Game Baseball Museum, a children's learning center with interactive exhibits, a youth ballpark, and a 12-acre lake. The NBA Dallas Mavericks, (214) 748-1808, play at the American Airlines Center at 2500 Victory Boulevard.

Another exciting place to visit is Deep Ellum, a revitalized district filled with theaters, restaurants, nightclubs, shops, and galleries (www.deepellumtx.com). Centered around Elm Street east of downtown, this district got its name because locals thought of the area as the deep end of Elm Street, and shortened it to Deep Ellum. During its heyday in the 1930s and 1940s, Deep Ellum was the principal cultural district of Dallas's African-American community. Clubs here drew some of the most renowned local acts of the time, including Leadbelly and Blind Lemon Jefferson, who went on to national fame. The area deteriorated after World War II, but in recent years it has made a big comeback. While you won't lack for food in this area, you might try one of the nicer, more upscale restaurants, the Green Room, (214) 748-7666, at 2715 Elm Street. It always seems to be crowded—perhaps it's the eclectic menu. It's open daily for dinner.

The sparkling downtown Dallas skyline can best be viewed from the 50-story Reunion Tower at the Hyatt Regency Dallas Hotel, (214) 651-1234 or (800) 233-1234, at 300 Reunion Boulevard. And you don't have to be a guest of this upscale hotel, a downtown landmark, to enjoy the view. The tower, topped by a geodesic dome, features three levels. The Lookout is an indoor-outdoor observation deck that offers a 360-degree view of the city. The next level up is the Antares Restaurant, (214) 712-7145, which slowly rotates to provide a bird's-eye view of the city while you're dining. It's open for lunch, dinner, and Sunday brunch. At the very top is The Dome, which also rotates. This is the hotel's cocktail lounge and the perfect place to enjoy a drink before—or after—a night on the town.

The renowned Dallas Zoo, (214) 670–8626, www.dallaszoo.com, at 650 South R. L. Thorton Freeway, was 116 years old in 2004. This 100-acre park, about 3 miles south of downtown, features more than 2,000 animals. Zoo North allows visitors a close-up view of red pandas, ocelots, wallabies, and more and includes the Bird and Reptile Building and the Rainforest Aviary. The 25-acre Wilds of Africa section of the park has been named the best African zoo exhibit in the country. It's open daily. Admission fee.

Stargazers will want to take a tour of the National Museum of Communications and the Movie Studios at Las Colinas, (972) 869–3456, at 6301 North O'Connor Road, Building One, in Irving. One of the only working movie studios between the two coasts, the Movie Studios at Las Colinas offer visitors a chance to see inside, though not while movies are shooting. The museum includes a massive collection of communications equipment and movie memorabilia. Admission fee.

Who needs to go to Paris or New York to shop when Dallas is right up the road? Dallas, of course, is home to the original Neiman Marcus store, which opened in 1907 and quickly put this city on the national fashion map. Today Dallas is a retail giant, filled with hundreds of shops offering everything from designer fashions to discount goods. Start your tour of the Dallas shopping scene at the original Neiman Marcus store, (214) 573–5800, at 1618 Main Street. Now the chain's flagship store, it features a fifth floor exhibit on its history as well as plenty of upscale items to purchase. The Galleria, (214) 702–7100, at I–635 and Dallas Parkway North is another Dallas shopping experience. This four-level mall, which includes an ice skating rink, features more than 200 stores. Saks Fifth Avenue, Macy's, Marshall Field's, and many other shops are here, as are plenty of restaurants. Northpark Center, (214) 363–7441, at Northwest Highway and

North Central Expressway is another popular upscale mall. It has a major Neiman Marcus store as well as a Lord & Taylor, Barneys New York, and many other department stores and specialty shops. For a unique shopping experience, try the Crescent, (214) 871–8500, at 200 Cedar Springs. This crescent-shaped complex includes a small but well-selected collection of antiques and specialty shops, art galleries, and restaurants. Those looking for high-fashion Western wear should check out Henry Jackalope, (214) 692–8928, at 6731 Snider Plaza. This shop features clothing by top designers. The Dallas Farmers' Market, (214) 939–2808, is one of the largest in the country. Open daily year-round, the market is filled with stalls offering fresh produce, herbs, flowers, and more. The market, at 1010 South Pearl, spreads over 4 city blocks.

If you have children along who've grown tired of the shops and the museums, give them a break at Six Flags Over Texas, (817) 640–8900, www.sixflags.com/parks/overtexas, in Arlington at I–30 and Highway 360. This giant amusement park, featuring more than 100 attractions, brings in visitors from around the world. Hours vary according to the season. Admission charges are in the mid-double digits for adults, less for children and senior citizens. Across I–30 is Six Flags Hurricane Harbor, (817) 265–3356, said to be America's largest water park. It's open May through September. Hours vary.

If you are planning to spend the night in Dallas, your choices are virtually limitless. While you can usually expect to spend about $20 a night more than you would in Austin for a good quality chain motel, the varieties and locations will put you close to about anywhere you want to be in town. Of course if you're looking for that truly special weekend getaway, and have the money to spend, the Mansion on Turtle Creek, (214) 559–2100 or (800) 527–5432, www.mansiononturtlecreek.com, at 2821 Turtle Creek Boulevard is considered one of the best hotels in the United States. This nine-story Italian

Renaissance–style mansion was built in the 1920s by a cattle baron. You'll feel as if you've reached nirvana. The restaurant here is also top of the line. Another historic, and upscale, choice in lodging is the Adolphus Hotel, (214) 742-8200 or (800) 221-9083, at 1321 Commerce Street downtown (www.hoteladolphus.com). Built by brewery magnate Adolphus Busch in 1912, this hotel is the only one to survive Dallas's downtown grand hotel era. It's a perfect place from which to explore the downtown historic district and pamper yourself at the same time.

Dining can be anything from a quick and casual home-style meal to a full-blown elegant multicourse affair, like you'd find at the Mansion on Turtle Creek. One of Dallas's favorite steakhouses is Del Frisco's, (972) 490-9000, at 5251 Spring Valley. It's expensive, but the beef is out of sight. For a real down home and inexpensive restaurant, try Celebration, (214) 351-5681, at 4503 West Lovers Lane out near Love Field. It features such items as pot roast, fried catfish, meat loaf—you get the picture. Another nearby casual restaurant is Kathleen's Art Cafe, (214) 691-2355, at 4424 Lovers Lane. This cafe focuses on New American cuisine. For good and inexpensive Italian food, we suggest Campisi's Egyptian Inn, (214) 827-0355, at 5610 Mockingbird Lane, about 4 miles north of downtown. It's open for lunch and dinner daily.

The Dallas Convention & Visitors Bureau, (214) 746-2677 or (800) C-DAL-LAS, www.dallascvb.com, is at 1201 Elm Street, Suite 2000. Check with the bureau for more information about this city or to request an information packet by mail.

If you've decided to take that left branch of I-35 and head toward Fort Worth, you'll find many exciting weekend activities designed to enlighten or entertain.

Among our favorite Fort Worth gems is the Kimbell Art Museum, (817) 332-8451, www.kimbellart.org, at 333 Camp Bowie Boulevard in what is known as the Cultural District west of downtown. This area is bounded by Camp Bowie Boulevard, University Drive, and Montgomery Street. The museums we've listed in this district are open Tuesday through Sunday with varying hours. Admission is free, except where noted. The Kimbell maintains a huge permanent collection, including works by Picasso, Monet, Rembrandt, and many other masters, and offers excellent touring shows throughout the year. There is an admission charge for special exhibits only. If you're too immersed in the art to leave for lunch, the buffet here offers some interesting choices.

Art and architecture lovers won't want to miss the Modern Art Museum of Fort Worth, (817) 738-9215, themodern.org, at 3200 Darnell Street in the cultural district. The Modern, as it's called, is the oldest museum in Texas and one of the oldest in the western United States. The building that houses its huge collection, however, is anything but old. A brand-new Modern opened to the public in December 2002, and it is a sight to behold! Designed by Japanese architect Tadao Ando, the building comprises five flat-roofed pavilions sitting on a 1.5-acre pond. The museum's permanent collection consists of about 2,600 works of post–WW II art, including paintings, sculpture, drawings, prints, and photographs.

Also in this district is the Amon Carter Museum, (817) 738-1933, www.cartermuseum.org, at 3501 Camp Bowie Boulevard, which focuses on American art. Carter, who founded the *Fort Worth Star-Telegram,* bequeathed his collection of Western art to the city along with a foundation to establish a museum. The museum resembles an American Indian lodge. The museum reopened in 2001 after a $39-million renovation and expansion.

The Fort Worth Museum of Science and History, (817) 255-9300, www.fortworthmuseum.org, at 1501 Montgomery Street is a delightful place to take children because of the many hands-on exhibits. This huge museum includes nine permanent galleries that cover science and history from prehistoric to modern times.

There's also a planetarium and OMNI theater. It's open daily. Admission fee. Admission to the planetarium and the theater is extra. The sprawling Fort Worth Botanic Garden, (817) 871–7689, also is here at 3220 Botanic Garden Drive. This delightful center is chock-full of specialty gardens and features more than 150,000 plants. It's open daily. General admission is free, although there is a small charge to enter the Japanese Garden and the Conservatory. The Will Rogers Memorial Center, (817) 871–8150, is at Amon Carter Square in this district. The center hosts the annual Southwestern Exposition and Livestock Show as well as equestrian events of all kinds. Named for noted cowboy humorist Will Rogers, the center features a statue of Rogers on horseback.

Another area that attracts oodles of tourists is the Stockyards National Historic District north of downtown. This district, along North Main Street from 23rd to 28th Streets, encompasses the old stockyards that were once the second largest in the country. The cattle pens here once spread out as far as the eye could see, holding livestock for slaughter by the on-site meat packing plants. Only a fraction of the pens remain today, but they are still put to good use, both as a reminder of days gone by and as useful holding pens for the livestock auctions held here. The Stockyards Collection and Museum, (817) 625–5087, www.fortworth stockyards.org, in the Stockyards Livestock Exchange Building at 131 East Exchange Avenue is a few rooms dedicated to the glory days of the stockyards, the meat-packing industry, and the railroads that made it all happen.

You'll also find boutiques, gift shops, and saloons in this district as well as many other attractions. Stop in at the Stockyards Visitor Center, (817) 624–4741, at 130 East Exchange Avenue to pick up information about Stockyards attractions and about attractions and lodgings around the city. The center is open daily. A guided walking tour of this district also starts here. You can also board the Tarantula Steam Train,

(817) 654–0898, here to experience the thrill of passenger train travel. One of the major attractions in this area is Billy Bob's Texas, (817) 624–7117, at 2520 Rodeo Plaza, www.billybobstexas.com, the world's largest honky-tonk. Seeing is believing. This club features 40 bar stations and two dance floors and still has room for a rodeo arena where, on weekends, you can watch rodeo cowboys ride the bulls. Of course live music is a major attraction, presented nightly. Admission fees vary from the minimal to the affordable.

One of our favorite Fort Worth Tex-Mex restaurants is near the stockyards at 2201 North Commerce Street. Joe T. Garcia's, (817) 626–4356, www.joe-ts.com, has been called one of America's best grassroots restaurants by the James Beard Foundation. Still, prices are moderate and the food is excellent. It's open for lunch and dinner daily. Last we heard, the restaurant still didn't accept credit cards. On the other hand, while you're at the Stockyards you might want a sample of what made this district famous—steak. Cattlemen's Steakhouse, (817) 624–3945, has been serving up great steaks from its location at 2458 North Main Street for more than half a century. And the prices are very reasonable. Cattlemen's is open daily for lunch and dinner. Of course the menu includes nonsteak items. too.

Don't miss out on Sundance Square district in the beautifully restored area of historic downtown, bounded by Throckmorton, Calhoun, Second, and Fifth Streets. The Ashton Hotel, 610 Main Street, (817) 332–0100, was built in 1916. Renovated and reopened in 2001, the Ashton is a member of the Small Luxury Hotels of the World group, www.slh.com, and the hotel is a comfortable base for a tour of Fort Worth's attractions. The Fort Worth Convention and Visitors Bureau, (817) 336–8791 or (800) 433–5747, www.fort worth.com, is at 415 Throckmorton Street. This is a good place to stock up on free maps and pamphlets describing fun things to do throughout Fort Worth. The entertainment district, named for the famous Western outlaw the Sundance Kid, is now filled with specialty shops, art galleries, nightclubs, restaurants, theaters, and more. One of our favorite restaurants is in this district. Reata, (817) 336–1009, at 500 Throckmorton Street on the 35th floor offers a fantastic view of the city along with modern Tex-Mex and Texas fare. And it's moderately priced. Reata is open daily for lunch and dinner.

Whether you're heading to Dallas/ Fort Worth or plan to spend several days exploring the entire metroplex, be sure to check in with the visitor centers or read the local newspapers for a listing of special events. In addition to some wonderful annual events and festivals in the area, you also might happen upon performances by the many outstanding classical performance companies—ballet, opera, symphony, for example—that add to the allure of this region. Of course there are also plenty of live musical performers around town.

DOWN SOUTH
San Antonio

A perfect day trip and an even better weekend getaway, the home of the venerable Alamo is one of Texas's largest and most exciting cities—and one of the top tourist destinations in the state. Just 80 miles south of Austin on I-35, this Mexican-American–flavored city pulsates with activity day and night and is a second home to many Austinites, who regularly make the trip for professional sporting events, rock concerts, amusement parks, and shopping and to see the sights again and again.

Start off your visit downtown at the Alamo, (210) 225–1391, www.thealamo.org, Texas's most famous shrine. Read about the colorful history of this building in our subsequent section on the San Antonio Missions. The Alamo and museum featuring Alamo relics and more are open Monday through Saturday 9:00 A.M. to 6:30 P.M. and

Sunday 10:00 A.M. to 6:30 P.M. during the summer, until 5:30 P.M. the rest of the year. Donations are suggested as admission.

Directly across from the Alamo at 329 Alamo Plaza are the new Guinness World Records Museum and Ripley's Haunted Adventure, (210) 226–2828, www.haunted adventure.com. The Guinness Museum, opened in 2003, offers an interactive experience that brings the famous book to life. Brought to you by those famous wax-museum folks at Ripley's, the Haunted Adventure is indeed a bone-chilling haunted house, full of special effects and live actors to really get your blood running. The two can be visited separately, although a great deal is offered for a combined ticket.

Just 2 blocks from the Alamo is the Buckhorn Saloon & Museum at 318 East Houston Street, (210) 247–4000. Voted "2002 Best Attraction" by San Antonio's Downtown Alliance, it features the one-of-a-kind Wax Museum of Texas History as well as two stories of exotic collections, including cowboy memorabilia and a two-headed calf. There's also a shooting gallery, arcade, and a curio shop for Texas collectibles. The Alamo Plaza is also the place to buy tickets and board classic, early-20th-century-style trolleys for the Lone Star Trolley Tours, (210) 224–9299. These one-hour narrated tours are designed to introduce visitors to historic downtown San Antonio.

Within walking distance from the Alamo is San Antonio's famous River Walk. Visitors flock here from around the country to stroll along the San Antonio River's Paseo del Rio. The lovely tree-lined River Walk, a level below the bustling streets of downtown, goes on for several miles and is packed with restaurants featuring outdoor patios, cafes, shops, upscale hotels, and clubs. The River Walk boasts a Hard Rock Cafe for those who want the ultimate in hip as well as a number of homegrown favorites; open daily and offering a variety of cuisines. Don't feel like walking the whole distance? Take a half-hour scenic riverboat cruise and let the tour guide point out all the sights. There are several access points to the riverboat cruises along the walk. Nearby is La Villita, the little village. Narrow streets, patios, and authentic adobe houses hearken back to an earlier time in this restored Mexican village that features restaurants and shops. The General Cos House in La Villita is a historic structure as well as an excellent example of early San Antonio homes. Market Square or El Mercado, (210) 207-8600, is nearby at 514 West Commerce Street. This is a Mexican-style shopping district that features fresh produce and lots of local and imported Mexican handicrafts.

One entrance to San Antonio's huge downtown shopping center, the Rivercenter Mall, (210) 225-0000, is right on the River Walk. This giant, modern complex features shops and restaurants. Here visitors can find the IMAX Theater to view *Alamo: The Price of Freedom,* a 45-minute docudrama that relates the story of the Alamo martyrs.

While you're downtown, don't miss HemisFair Park, site of the 1968 Texas World's Fair. The 750-foot needlelike Tower of the Americas that dominates this park features two dining levels as well as an observation deck offering a panoramic view of the city. The Institute of Texas Cultures, (210) 458-2300, and the Mexican Cultural Institute, (210) 227-0123, can both be found at HemisFair Park. The Institute features a wide variety of exhibits dedicated to Texas's rich ethnic and cultural history as well as a multimedia show presented four times daily in the central dome. The Mexican Cultural Institute is a great place to see works by contemporary Mexican artists. The institute also hosts the annual Texas Folklife Festival in August (see our Annual Events and Festivals chapter).

The Alamodome, (210) 207-3663, www.sanantonio.gov/dome, at 100 Montana Street, is accessible from the River Walk. It is home to the San Antonio Spurs NBA basketball team and hosts an impressive variety of professional and college sporting events, major concerts, and more throughout the year.

Boasting more than a million residents, San Antonio is a large sprawling city with wonderful sights scattered all around. If art museums are your fancy, San Antonio offers the McNay Art Museum, (210) 824-5368, www.mcnay art.org, at 6000 New Braunfels Street. This former mansion of Marion Koogler McNay features outstanding works by 19th- and 20th-century painters, including Cezanne, Van Gogh, Gauguin, Diego Rivera, and Winslow Homer, to name a few. The San Antonio Museum of Art, (210) 978-8169, www.sa-museum.org, at 200 West Jones Avenue is in a historic brewery and includes six buildings housing artwork from pre-Columbian to modern times. If you want to learn about Texas's natural history, visit the Witte Museum of History and Science, (210) 357-1990, www.wittemuseum.org, at 3801 Broadway. This popular tourist spot features numerous exhibits as well as dioramas of Texas wildlife and flora. Four early Texas houses and a furnished log cabin have been rebuilt on the grounds here. The Witte's hours are the same as the museum of art.

To further enjoy Texas flora, visit the Botanical Gardens, (210) 207-3250, at 555 Funston Street. This 33-acre site includes a massive glass-enclosed, belowground conservatory as well as sprawling outdoor

Annual family membership to the Austin Children's Museum at the "Inventor" or "Benefactor" levels, beginning at $125, allows your family free admission to more than 250 museums and science and technology centers in Texas and around the country. Among those participating are the Houston Space Center, the Children's Museum of Houston, the Dallas Natural History Museum, and the Witte Museum in San Antonio. Be sure to carry your card when you travel.

gardens of all kinds. Here visitors will find the Formal Gardens, Biblical Garden, Garden for the Blind, Japanese Garden, and Children's Garden, as well as gardens that celebrate native Texas plants.

Built in 1929 and listed on the National Register of Historic Places, the magnificently restored Majestic Theater is home to the San Antonio Symphony and Broadway in San Antonio, which presents world-class theater and musical performances and also some great comedians. The Majestic, at 224 East Houston Street, (210) 226-3333, www.majesticempire.com, is a fabulously ornate building whose merits alone are worth a trip to San Antonio.

For another glimpse of San Antonio's architectural history, tour the elegant King William District, which is lined with homes built in the 19th century by wealthy German merchants. Although most of the restored homes in this 25-block district are private, daily tours are offered at the Edward Steves Homestead at 509 King William Street, (210) 225-5924. You can pick up a pamphlet for a walking tour at the Conservation Society office at 107 King William Street, or visit www.sa conservation.org. There are several B&Bs in this area.

If you're traveling with children, San Antonio is a perfect getaway. This city features the biggest and best amusement park in Central Texas, Six Flags Fiesta Texas, (210) 697-5050 or (800) 473-4378, www.sixflags.com/parks/fiestatexas, as well as the wonderful Sea World Adventure Park, (210) 523-3611, www.seaworld.com /seaworld.tx. (See our Kidstuff chapter for more information.) And there's more: Splashtown, (210) 227-1100, www.splash townsa.com, is another great water park for children of all ages. The 15-acre park is loaded with children's activities and features water slides, a sandy beach, and the world's largest surf-tech pool. It's open April to September. The San Antonio Zoo, (210) 734-7183, boasts the third-largest collection of animals in North America, with more than 3,000 animals. Special exhibits

include animals from Australia and Africa as well as huge aquariums housing a variety of marine life. It's open year-round near downtown at 3903 North St. Mary's Street. No city seems complete these days unless it has a children's museum. The San Antonio Children's Museum, located at 305 East Houston Street, (210) 212-4453, is packed with hands-on activities for kids. This site is within walking distance of the Alamo.

If you're planning to spend the weekend in San Antonio, be aware that while the downtown hotels offer the easiest access to the Alamo, the River Walk, and all the other downtown tourist destinations, they also are more expensive than those in outlying areas. If you want to splurge, stay at the historic La Mansion del Rio Hotel, (210) 518-1000 or (800) 292-7300, www.lamansion.com. This 337-room luxury hotel, built in 1852 as a private boys' school, is right on the River Walk. Nearby is another historic lodging, the Menger Hotel, (210) 223-4361 or (800) 345-9285, www.historicmenger.com. This elegantly restored hotel, built in 1859, has 350 rooms. Even if you don't opt to stay here, drop into the hotel bar, since this is where Teddy Roosevelt rallied and recruited his Roughriders prior to embarking for Cuba in the Spanish-American War. For less expensive accommodations downtown, try the Days Inn Alamo River Walk, (210) 227-6233 or (800) DAYS-INN.

Many people like to enjoy at least one meal on the trendy River Walk—it's part of the San Antonio experience. But if you're the kind who likes to get out to explore the city and mingle with the locals, try some of our favorites around town. El Mirador, (210) 225-9444, at 722 South St. Mary's Street in the King William District serves traditional Mexican food as well as contemporary Mexican recipes. It's moderately priced and usually crowded, but the excellent food is worth the wait. Another spot for Mexican fare is Rosario's, (210) 223-1806, at 1014 South Alamo Street. This casual spot, in an up-and-coming district south of downtown called Southtown, offers a full menu of great south-of-the-border cuisine. It, too, can get quite crowded, because this is one place San Antonio comes for Mexican food. In an area known as the St. Mary's District, there's an old two-story building that tilts. This is the Liberty Bar, (210) 227–1187, at 328 East Josephine Street. The building, now a chic restaurant, survived a San Antonio flood in 1921, which is why it leans a bit. The menu is eclectic.

Check with the San Antonio Visitor Center, (210) 270–8748 or (800) 447–3372, www.sanantoniocvb.com, for more information about the Alamo City. It's at 317 Alamo Plaza, just across from the Alamo.

San Antonio Missions

They have been compared to a pearl necklace strung along the banks of the San Antonio River, and it is an apt metaphor for the five Spanish missions that stand inside the city limits of this bustling modern city whose Spanish name is a daily reminder of the diverse cultural history of Texas.

The San Antonio River has been tamed now and channeled off to wind around cafes and bars, shopping centers, and convention halls. The fields that surrounded the Spanish missions are now filled, for the most part, with shops, movie theaters, homes, and highways. But within the garden walls of these old Spanish buildings, the past has survived the centuries, providing visitors a glimpse of life in 18th-century Texas. However, they are not just symbols of the past but also a vibrant part of present-day city life—four of the five original missions are parish churches where neighbors can stop for a daily prayer or congregate on feast days for music and celebration.

Touring the five missions, particularly the four that are now part of San Antonio National Missions Park, is a wonderful way for newcomers, visitors, and even long-time Texas residents to acquaint themselves with a vital part of Texas history. But a tour of the missions is more than a history lesson. It also offers visitors an opportunity to view some of the most beautiful buildings in Texas, plus experience the ambience of San Antonio's old neighborhoods and feel the kinship many residents have to their parish churches. It is a great family outing—new interactive media exhibits help bring the Texas frontier to life for young and old alike. Take along a picnic, since the grounds and gardens of the missions are ideal for an outdoor meal.

The U.S. National Parks Service has a comprehensive Web site with maps and brochures at www.nps.gov/saan/.

The most famous of the five missions is the Alamo, the monument to Texas independence that is situated just a short walk from the River Walk (see our San Antonio day trip mentioned previously). The Alamo is no longer a church but is maintained literally as a shrine to the fallen heroes by the Daughters of the Republic of Texas (www.thealamo.org). Given its location in the heart of San Antonio, it is the starting point for our mission tour. The 5.5-mile Mission Trail is clearly marked by brown signs posted around the city. Drivers can pick up the first sign on South Alamo Street at Market Street. The San Antonio Visitor Center, (210) 270–8748 or (800) 447–3372, at 317 Alamo Street, across from the famous landmark, has information about the missions, plus transportation maps and information. In addition, Bus No. 40 of San Antonio's excellent bus system connects the missions along Mission Trail.

The Alamo was the first Spanish mission built in what is now the city of San Antonio. Named Mission San Antonio de Valero, it was founded in 1718 and then moved to the current site in 1724. The name "Alamo" is believed to have been derived from the Spanish word for cottonwood tree, the species of tree that often grows along riverbanks in the Southwest. Jack Harmon, author of *Texas Missions and Landmarks,* published by the Institute of Texas Cultures (an invaluable resource in researching this day trip), states that the Alamo was "ill-omened from the beginning." In 1728 an epidemic killed almost all the baptized Native Americans who were living around the mission. It was not the first epidemic to hit the mission, which had other troubles—the first church on the site collapsed; the second was never finished.

By 1793 the mission had been secularized as the brothers focused their religious efforts elsewhere in the area. By 1807 it was being used as a military base, and it continued in that capacity until the famous siege. The Alamo became the "Cradle of Texas Liberty" when a band of 189 Texas volunteers attempted to hold off an invading Mexican army of thousands led by General Santa Anna. The siege lasted 13 days, from February 23 to March 6, 1836, and resulted in the total annihilation of the Alamo defenders, including James Bowie, Davy Crockett, and Colonel William Barret Travis. Rallying around the battle cry "Remember the Alamo," a Texas battalion led by Sam Houston defeated the Mexicans and captured Santa Anna a month later at the Battle of San Jacinto near Houston. Texas had gained its independence!

Today the exterior of the Alamo and the gardens that are contained within its walls are most evocative of a Spanish mission. The interior is quiet and devoid of the ornaments and everyday items that would have filled a Spanish mission in the 18th century. The paintings on the walls, the display cases showing artifacts from the battle, the cold flagstone floors, and dim lighting underscore the fact that this was a place where men died in battle.

The bleak history of the Alamo stands in stark contrast to the other four missions within the San Antonio city limits—the only city in the country that can claim five missions within its boundaries. Unlike the Alamo, the four other missions in the city remain under the direction of the Archdiocese of San Antonio, which is responsible for the spiritual functions of the missions while the National Park Service maintains and runs the sites. The federal government took the missions into the federal park system in the early 1990s, collectively dubbing them the San Antonio Missions Historical Park, (210) 229–5701. Admission to the missions is free, although donations are accepted and encouraged. The park facilities and visitor information centers are open daily from 9:00 A.M. to 5:00 P.M. They are closed Christmas and New Year's Day, but the churches remain open.

There are four missions in the park, all south of downtown in proximity to the San Antonio River. In their early days, the missions occupied some of the best farmland along the river, thanks to the generosity of the Spanish Crown. According to Harmon, the missions served three purposes for the Spanish government: to convert the Native Americans, to discourage French expansion from Louisiana, and to prepare the region for further colonization. Given these goals, the missions were designed to serve both military and religious objectives, hence the compound design concept.

The first of the missions on the trail is Mission Nuestra Senora de la Purisma Concepcion (Mission of Our Lady of the Immaculate Conception), usually referred to simply as Mission Concepcion. The mission is at the edge of downtown San Antonio at 807 Mission Road, (210) 229–5732. It is the oldest unrestored church structure in the United States and was dedicated in December 1755. Like the other missions, Concepcion occupied other sites until the current one was chosen in 1731. The ruined walls of the mission compound can be traced from the church to the riverbank.

The church walls are 4 feet thick, and the outer walls were originally decorated in vivid colors, patterns, and flower designs. This kind of stucco decoration would have been familiar to Native Americans throughout the Americas, who also covered their pyramids with colorful designs. The stucco has faded and fallen off the limestone walls now, but inside, visitors can see some original faded designs in the bell tower. Over the years the walls have been marred by graffiti, some dating back into the mid-19th century.

Concepcion was secularized and then abandoned in 1824. It was the site of a battle in the Texas War of Independence, but in 1855 the Brothers of Mary returned and restored the church to the parish.

Mission San José y Miguel de Aguayo has been dubbed the best pearl in the strand of missions, the so-called "Queen of the Missions." Mission San José, 5539 San José Street, (210) 229–4770, is the largest, the most informative, and some say the most beautiful of the missions. (The second half of its name is in honor of the Spanish Marquis Miguel de Aguayo, who consolidated Spain's control of Texas.) If you only have time for one mission, this should be it. In 1996 the Park Service opened an extensive, interactive information center here in the old granaries that offers a comprehensive look at mission life.

Mission San José was founded by Father Antonio Margil de Jesus, a famous Franciscan, in 1720. It was designed to be a large compound, surrounded by tall walls and four huge gates. Inside were the small homes of the Native Americans—up to 200 lived here in 1749, and by 1786 it was reported that 350 people lived here, including 110 Native American warriors converted from various tribes, who helped beat back attacks by Comanches and Apaches. The Native Americans also worked the fields, and at its economic peak, according to Harmon, the San José ranch ran 1,500 cattle and 5,000 sheep and produced 4,000 bushels of corn.

The church itself at Mission San José is famous for one particular architectural element, the Rose Window. Carved by Spanish master mason Pedro Huizar, who was sent by the king to teach the Native Americans his art, the window has been hailed as one of the most beautiful examples of Spanish Colonial architecture in the United States. There are various legends associated with the window, includ-

ing one that it is Huizar's tribute to a lost love who drowned on her way from Spain to marry him. Huizar's other handiwork can be seen in various images of the saints that appear in the chapel. A small cemetery nearby contains the bodies of Huizar and some of the early friars who worked at San José.

Every Sunday at noon there is a mariachi mass featuring the lyrical music of Mexico inside the church—come early in order to find a seat. In early December the parishioners perform Los Pastores, a miracle play with Spanish origins. Beyond the mission walls are a major highway, businesses, and movie theaters, but inside, the 18th century seems alive.

San Juan Capistrano, 9102 Graf Street, (210) 229–5734, is the third mission on the trail. Small, simple, and peaceful, San Juan is set in natural surroundings that help the visitor get in touch with the past. Originally located in East Texas, the mission was moved to San Antonio in 1731. The chapel, which now serves as a parish church, was built in 1756. The figures of Christ and the Virgin inside are made of cornstalk pith, a lost art that was practiced by the Native Americans. There is an interpretative trail at the mission, which takes visitors along a third of a mile walk to the riverbank.

San Francisco de la Espada is the most southern of the missions and, although surrounded by the city, it retains a pastoral air, perhaps because some of the fields surrounding the mission are still worked and are still irrigated by the Espada Aqueduct. The Espada Acequia, the water system, was built in the 1730s and continues to work.

There is something of a mystery about the name of this mission. St. Francis of the Sword is the literal translation and the peace-loving saint, usually depicted with birds and animals, was originally depicted here bearing a sword. Some historians suggest it is likely "espada" was in honor of a notable person with this name; others suggest it was a gesture of strength, an image the missions were supposed to project.

There is a sense of peace about the place. Inside, the chapel is simple and devoid of a lot of decoration. The Stations of the Cross are simply marked in numerals on the walls. Sitting inside the small chapel is a peaceful way to end a visit to the Mission Trail.

Two other Spanish Colonial sites are well worth adding to a tour of old San Antonio. Both are downtown. The Spanish Governor's Palace, located at 105 Military Plaza, (210) 224-0601, was completed in 1749 and was the home of the captain of the presidio, not the governor, although that name has stuck. Officially called the Commandancia, it is typical of a high-ranking official's home in colonial Spain. Above the doorway is the imperial double eagle, symbol of the Hapsburg emperors and part of the coat-of-arms of Philip V, who was both a Hapsburg and a Bourbon by birth.

The "palace" is far from palatial, but it is a wonderful example of colonial architecture and the 3-foot-thick walls ensure that even on the hottest days the interior is cool. It stands across the street from San Antonio's current City Hall. Open daily from 9:00 A.M. (10:00 A.M. on Sunday) until 5:00 P.M., there is a nominal admission charge.

Another noted landmark in the center of the city is San Fernando Cathedral, 115 Main Plaza, (210) 227-1297. The church was begun in 1738 by the original Canary Islanders who settled San Antonio. Completed in 1749, it went on to become famous as the place where Jim Bowie married and allegedly where some of the heroes of the Alamo are buried—but there is much dispute about that. The sanctuary is the oldest part of the building and was part of the original structure, making it the oldest cathedral sanctuary in the United States. The rest of the church was constructed around the sanctuary in 1868 and is Gothic Revival style. There are frequent mariachi masses here; the schedule is posted at the cathedral.

If your visit to San Antonio's missions has you hooked on Spanish Colonial history in Texas, consider visiting the El Paso region, where several beautiful missions also stand, or take a weekend getaway from Austin to Goliad, about a three-hour drive southeast of Austin, to visit the Presidio de la Bahia, a Spanish fort and church that stands in one of the most historic regions of Texas. Spring is a great time to visit Goliad, since wildflowers blanket the La Bahia grounds. Fiesta Zaragoza is held on the weekend closest to May 5, Cinco de Mayo, because native son General Ignacio de la Zaragoza, a Mexican hero, defeated the French at the Battle of Puebla on that date in 1862. For more information about Goliad, call the chamber of commerce at (361) 645-3563, www.goliadcc.org.

New Braunfels

Only an hour's drive from Austin, or right on your way if you're returning to Austin from San Antonio, New Braunfels attracts visitors for two primary reasons—antiques shopping and water sports. The latter draws thousands of visitors, especially in summer, to a variety of artificial and natural waterways to tube, raft, swim, paddle, and plop in the cool, wet stuff.

The two sides of New Braunfels have led to a growth boom, and Comal County has been cited as the fastest growing county in Texas in recent years. Many of the visitors come to enjoy swimming in Landa Park, (830) 608-2165, the downtown home of the state's largest spring-fed pool and also home to a stretch of the Comal River. Another popular destination is Schlitterbahn, the state's biggest water park, which is detailed in our Kidstuff chapter.

Given all the activities available in the area, crowds flock to New Braunfels on weekends in the peak summer season, but thanks to its old German roots the town has maintained its charm. The town is named after Prince Carl of Solms-Braunfels, a member of the Mainzer Adelsverein, or League of Nobles, who encouraged German emigration in the 1840s as an escape from economic hard times in Germany. The young Republic of Texas offered land grants to the nobles as an inducement for European settlers. Prince Carl brought over a large contingent in 1844, many of whom died on the coast of Texas due to an epidemic. The survivors settled in New Braunfels in 1844, and by 1855 the town was the fourth largest in Texas. Meanwhile, Prince Carl had gone home since his fiancée refused to come to Texas.

There are several invocations of the Prince's name in and around the town, including Prince Solms Park, where tubers pay a small admission fee to tube in the Comal River, and the Prince Solms Inn, 295 East San Antonio Street, (830) 625-9169, www.princesolmsinn.com, an upscale bed-and-breakfast in a restored Victorian home. Advance reservations are a must at this popular guest house and at the on-site cellar restaurant, Wolfgang's Kellar, where elegant German and European cuisine is served. Another hotel with great character is the Faust Hotel, 240 South Seguin Street, (830) 625-7791, www.fausthotel.com, just 1 block south of the town plaza. The Faust, now a National Landmark Hotel, was built in 1928 and has been restored to reflect that period. The rooms here all have character and are decorated individually.

New Braunfels is of great interest to architecture buffs, particularly for the tiny Sunday houses built by German farmers in the 19th century as weekend town cottages. Many have been restored, but others stand waiting for the deep pockets and eager hands of would-be restorers. Many of the town's antiques shops are housed in old German homes. The New Braunfels Chamber of Commerce, 390 South Seguin Street, (830) 625-2385, www.nbcham.org, offers an "antique crawl" map.

The chamber also provides a historic walking tour map to guide visitors through the vibrant downtown area, where there are more than 30 historic buildings. The heart of the community is the plaza, where the traffic is slowed by a roundabout, and the restored buildings reflect the prosperity enjoyed by the town's forefathers.

Early life in New Braunfels is depicted at the Sophienburg Museum, 401 West Coll Street, (830) 629-1572. Named for Prince Carl's fiancée, who declined to head for the frontier, the museum is built on a small hill where the prince had planned to build his honeymoon castle. The building housed his administrative offices and now has several exhibits showing life on the Texas frontier. The museum is open daily from 10:00 A.M. to 5:00 P.M. except Sunday, when it is open from 1:00 to 5:00 P.M. There is a small admission fee.

Another New Braunfels museum is one of those little gems often tucked away in small towns that receive little attention in these days of theme parks. The Museum of Texas Handmade Furniture, 1370 Church Hill Drive, (830) 629-6504, features more than 75 examples of handcrafted furniture made by German cabinetmakers working in the mid-19th century on the Texas frontier. Housed in the Breustadt House, c. 1858, and listed in the National Register of Historic Places, the museum is open to the public daily during the summer and on weekends the rest of the year.

Nearby, at 1300 Church Hill Drive, the city's Conservation Society has relocated a number of historic buildings in Conservation Plaza. They include several homes, a one-room schoolhouse, a music studio, a barn, and a general store. Some have been completely restored; others are awaiting restoration. The society holds a folklife festival here in early May, (830) 625-8766, and the buildings are open at irregular hours during the rest of the year (www.nbconservation.org).

Another good way to capture the spirit of 19th-century New Braunfels is to eat at one of the town's German-style restaurants. Krause's Cafe, 148 Castell Street, (830) 625-7581, has been serving German dishes, barbecue, and just plain, old-fashioned American cooking since 1938. This is where the courthouse crowd and the business leaders come for breakfast and lunch. The cafe also serves dinner, including chili (William Gebhardt perfected his chili powder formula in downtown New Braunfels a century ago), steaks, and burgers. Leave room for pie—Krause's has a wide selection. The cafe is open for breakfast, lunch, and dinner daily; closed Sunday and for three weeks in September. No credit cards are taken here.

True to its German roots, New Braunfels is noted for its sausage. The New Braunfels Smokehouse, (830) 625-2416, www.nbsmokehouse.com (they ship!), at the intersection of I-35 and Highway 46 began life as a smokehouse for local farmers and ranchers more than 50 years ago. Now it is a restaurant featuring several varieties of sausage and barbecue, plus smoked hams and turkeys. The restaurant is open for breakfast, lunch, and dinner daily, and there is a gift shop and mail-order business on the premises.

Sausage is celebrated with relish (and onions) at Wurstfest, the annual 10-day festival that attracts tens of thousands of visitors to New Braunfels every November. The festival centers on sausage-eating, beer drinking, and polka dancing (see our Annual Events and Festivals chapter).

Gruene

It is pronounced "Green," and for the savvy developers who revived this ghost town north of New Braunfels, the name proved propitious. These days, old Gruene (www.gruene.net) is anything but a ghost town, particularly on weekends when visitors stroll the narrow streets looking for antiques bargains, visiting craft shops and studios, kicking up a storm at the local dance hall, or digging into a chicken-fried steak.

Ernest Gruene originally settled in New Braunfels and then moved his family to this area, about 5 miles north of New Braunfels, in 1872. His son Henry D. Gruene became very influential, and so the town was named after him.

After Henry died in 1920, Gruene suffered two fatal blows—the boll weevil killed the cotton crop and the Depression hit. The city turned into a ghost town, and the old buildings lay empty for years. When investors discovered the community, it looked as if time had stopped back in the '30s. Now this community on F.M. 306 just north of New Braunfels and about an hour's drive south of Austin on I-35 is listed on the National Register of Historic Places. There is only one intersection in Gruene, and most businesses lie either on Gruene Road or Hunter Road, making a tour of the town easy on the legs.

You will want to save some energy if you plan to spend the evening at Texas's oldest dance hall, Gruene Hall, (830) 606-1281, where some of the top names in country music have played, including Garth Brooks. The first dance was in 1878, and now the bar-cum-dance hall opens daily around midday so visitors can enjoy a longneck or two. The old hall has remained stuck in the years between the two world wars. The posters on the walls are advertisements from the era; there is no air-conditioning—the windows and doors are opened wide to catch the breeze—and there are burlap bags hanging from the ceiling. Cover charges for evening performances vary.

During the week, Gruene is quiet unless a popular band is playing, but on the weekends the little town fills up. Tubers are attracted to the Guadalupe River in summertime (Gruene is on the north bank of the river), while antiques hunters and shoppers come to the village to stroll the stores and galleries.

There is an abundance of bed-and-breakfast accommodations in town and the upscale Gruene Mansion Inn, located at 1275 Gruene Road, (830) 629-2641, where guests stay in restored 1870 cottages with views of the Guadalupe River. The hotel also operates the Restaurant at Gruene Mansion Inn, (830) 620-0760, which serves lunch and dinner daily inside or out on the deck overlooking the river. The menu features a variety of cuisines, including Cajun, German, and continental.

The Gruene Homestead Inn sits on eight acres of farmland, and several of the old farm buildings have been renovated and converted to unique bedrooms. Cottages and old homes from the area also have been relocated on the farm and restored. The rooms at the inn are all individually decorated and have sitting areas or porches for relaxing after a day of activities on the river or among the shops nearby. The inn is located at 832 Gruene Road, (800) 238-5534 or (830) 606-0216, www.greunehomesteadinn.com.

Also overlooking the river is the Grist Mill Restaurant, (830) 625-0684, 1287 Gruene Road, housed not in a gristmill but in a converted 100-year-old cotton gin. Lunch and dinner are served daily, and the menu features typical all-American fare—burgers, sandwiches, salads, steaks—plus some Tex-Mex and barbecue dishes.

Most of the businesses in Gruene offer free brochures illustrating walking tours of the community. One popular stop on the tour is the Guadalupe Valley Winery, also housed in an old cotton gin, at 1720 Hunter Road, (830) 629-2351.

Hunter Road has several antiques stores and the old Gruene General Store, built in 1878, that now sells Texana, including cookbooks, cookies, and kitchen equipment, and offers sodas from the old-style soda fountain. Several artisans, including potters and ironworkers, have studios along Hunter Road, and the Greune Antique Mall is home to several dealers.

Gruene is popular year-round, but visitors mark their calendars for the monthly Market Days, held the third weekend of the months February through November, when more than 100 arts and crafts vendors gather in Gruene (see our Annual Events and Festivals chapter).

For more information on Gruene, call the Gruene Information Center at (830) 629-5077.

OUT EAST

Round Top and Winedale

These two tiny communities in Fayette County, about 90 miles east of Austin, have become world-renowned for their cultural events, their celebrations of music and theater that take place in several beautifully restored 19th-century Texas buildings set in landscaped grounds, and two nationally renowned antiques fairs. But even when there are no events scheduled at Round Top or Winedale, a day trip to the area can be an opportunity for city dwellers to catch a glimpse of small-town Texas.

Round Top is one of the state's oldest communities—the first Fourth of July in Texas was celebrated here in 1828, long before Texas was a republic or a state in the Union. In the mid-19th century several German and Swedish families settled here, but the community never grew beyond a mere handful of homes. Then in the 1960s, artists and wealthy Texans began to be attracted to the area's natural beauty, buying up the old homes and restoring them.

In 1971 concert pianist James Dick chose Round Top as the home for his music institute, designed to offer students an opportunity to study with leading musicians. Dick established the International Festival Institute in historic Round Top. During its first five years, the Festival Institute leased facilities, but a master plan for development of a 200-acre campus was adopted. The first major facility, the Mary Moody Northern Pavilion, was acquired in 1973. It was the largest transportable stage in the world and was used for open-air concerts until 1983. Later it was housed in the 1,200-seat Festival Concert Hall, on which construction began in 1980, until the permanent stage was completed in the Concert Hall in 1993. An abandoned school building and six acres of land east of Round Top were acquired in 1973 for the campus, now named Festival Hill. The grounds are open to the public, and they make a great setting for a spring picnic.

Several historic buildings were moved to the festival site. The first historic structure moved to Festival Hill came from nearby LaGrange and was named the William Lockhart Clayton House in honor of the man who created the Marshall Plan. Built in 1885, it was renovated in 1976 for faculty offices, teaching facilities, and indoor concerts. The Menke House, built in 1902, was moved to Festival Hill from Hempstead and renovated as a faculty residence and conference center in 1979. Its Gothic Revival ceilings, woodwork, and staircases make it a showcase of Texas carpentry.

The historic sanctuary of the former Travis Street United Methodist Church of LaGrange, built in 1883, was moved to Festival Hill in 1994 for restoration as a center for chamber music, organ recitals, lectures, and seminars. It was renamed the Edythe Bates Old Chapel to honor one of the great Texan patronesses of the fine arts and houses an 1835 Henry Erben pipe organ. The Festival Institute Museum and Library exhibits art collections in the Festival Concert Hall and the historic house restorations.

There are now 17 musical programs during June and July each year. The August-to-April Concerts Series, the Early Music Festival, and other programs bring the total number of year-round concerts to more than 50. These include orchestral, chamber music, choral, vocal, brass, woodwinds, and solo performances. The repertoire extends from ancient to contemporary music.

The campus is also used for conferences, meetings, and retreats by businesses and professional organizations. A series of distinguished museum lectures is presented at Festival Hill each year. The campus, famed for its gardens, rare trees, herb collections, cascades, fountains, and unusual landscaping is a destination for visitors from all over the world; the grounds are open daily.

Tickets may be purchased at the Concert Hall beginning one hour prior to each concert, and season tickets are available. For information on the musical season or individual concerts, call (979) 249–3129, www.festivalhill.org.

Nearby Winedale has been a center for ethnic studies since Ima Hogg, daughter of a former Texas governor, donated the grounds and several historic buildings to the University of Texas in 1967. Winedale is also home to the Shakespeare at Winedale festival where UT students perform several of Shakespeare's plays in an 1894 barn-turned-theater at various times during the year (www.shakespeare-winedale.org).

Like Round Top, the grounds are open to the public, and there is a small admission charge. Winedale is open May through October on Saturday from 10:00 A.M. to 6:00 P.M., Sunday from noon to 6:00 P.M., and November through April from 9:00 A.M. to 5:00 P.M. on Saturday and noon to 5:00 P.M. on Sunday. Tours of the on-site historic buildings can be arranged, (979) 278–3530, and there is a marked nature trail. There are several annual events that bring visitors to Winedale, including a Christmas Open House featuring seasonal music and food, a spring festival and Texas Craft Exhibition, and a German Oktoberfest, all detailed in our Annual Events and Festivals chapter.

There are numerous bed-and-breakfast and guest house accommodations in the Round Top/Winedale area, and many are listed on the roundtop.org Web site. Some Austin residents prefer to stay overnight in the area after a concert or play, turning a night outing into a weekend getaway. Accommodations range in price. If you plan an overnight stay, book well in advance during those times when concerts and theater presentations are scheduled.

Several restaurants in the area feature country cooking, including Klump's restaurant, (979) 249–5696, in Round Top. It's open Wednesday through Saturday for breakfast, lunch, and dinner and Sunday and Tuesday for breakfast and lunch. Closed Monday.

The area also has become popular among antiques collectors. In addition to shops in the communities of Round Top, Winedale, Shelby, Warrenton, and Carmine, antiques dealers come from across the country for the first weekend in April and October to the Antiques Fair (see our Annual Events chapter).

To reach Round Top or Winedale, take U.S. 290 east toward Houston from Austin. Just beyond Giddings look for Highway 237; head south and follow the signs to Round Top. Winedale is just east of Round Top on F.M. 2714. Many of the merchants in the area have tourist maps showing the locations of the various small communities and lists of accommodations and area attractions, and there is a visitor center on the square in Round Top. Another good place to gather information about local happenings is the Round Top Mercantile Company, on Highway 237, (979) 249-3117, www.roundtopmercantile.com, which is open seven days a week. Look for the store's Texaco pumps on the west side of the highway as you drive into Round Top.

Houston

If you've been around Austin long enough to start complaining about the traffic jams and the high-speed lifestyle that are beginning to replace Austin's good ol' laid-back days, it's time to visit Houston, the fourth largest city in the United States. Houston is in every way the giant metropolis that Austin is not—not yet, at least. This racially diverse, multicultural mecca is filled with so many excellent cultural destinations, shopping adventures, institutions of higher education, sporting events, family activities, and dining delights that the traffic seems a small price to pay. Nearby is the Johnson Space Center, NASA mission control. A little farther down the road is the beach at Galveston on the Gulf of Mexico.

The local newspapers in Houston, Dallas/Fort Worth, and San Antonio publish weekly sections devoted to news, reviews, and listings of cultural and entertainment events. These cities also have weekly freebie publications highlighting happenings around their cities. Look for the Houston Chronicle's *weekend section on Thursday. The* Dallas Morning News, Fort Worth Star-Telegram, *and* San Antonio Express-News *publish their entertainment pullouts on Friday. On other days of the week, look for these free weeklies: the* Dallas Observer *and the* Met *in Dallas/Fort Worth, the* San Antonio Current *and the* Houston Press.

Texas independence hero Sam Houston tried hard to make his namesake city the capital of Texas (read all about it in our History chapter), but Austin won out. Instead, Houston has become the industrial and financial capital for much of Texas. Located 165 miles southwest of Austin, Houston rests on the Coastal Plains of Texas—so be prepared for humidity. Houstonians, in fact, joke that the weather forecast is always the same: partly cloudy with a chance of rain.

You can't go wrong by starting your tour of Houston in beautiful Hermann Park, just a few miles southwest of downtown. This large urban park has a golf course, a lake, and plenty of room to just stroll or picnic. The Houston Zoo is inside the park at 1513 North Macgregor Drive, (713) 533-6500, wild.houstonzoo.org. Here you'll find hundreds of exotic animals as well as a tropical birdhouse and aquariums. The Touch Tank allows visitors to touch sea creatures. Also in Hermann Park is the Miller Outdoor Theater. Now this is a find! The amphitheater presents free outdoor performances, including symphony, opera, contemporary musicals, and all kinds of dance beginning in April each season. For an even better view, the theater reserves some paid seats up front.

One of the most fascinating aspects of this city is its ever-growing Museum District (www.houston-guide.com/guide/arts) near Hermann Park. It would take visitors at least a couple of days to appreciate all the wonders in this sprawling district. The Museum of Natural Science, (713) 639–4600, at 1 Hermann Circle Drive is a huge complex that includes the Cockrell Butterfly Center, the Burke Baker Planetarium, the Wortham IMAX Theater, and much more. This outstanding facility is definitely worth a visit. Check out the Energy Hall, which guides visitors through the complete process of oil exploration. For a region that refines 50 percent of all U.S. petrochemicals, this exhibit is perfectly located. There also are interactive physical science exhibits and a hall dedicated to archaeology of the western hemisphere. The museum is open Monday through Saturday 9:00 A.M. to 6:00 P.M. and Sunday 11:00 A.M. to 6:00 P.M. General admission is $4.00 for the main exhibits, but expect to pay more for entrance to the other facilities.

Near the natural science museum is the new Museum of Health & Medical Science, (713) 521–1515, at 1515 Hermann Drive. This new facility boasts a "Texas-size view of the human body" and includes models of giant organs as well as many hands-on exhibits. It's open Tuesday through Saturday 9:00 A.M. to 5:00 P.M. and Sunday noon to 5:00 P.M. General admission is $4.00. Two other special interest museums also are in walking distance. The Children's Museum of Houston, (713) 522–1138, is at 1500 Binz Street. This large, delightful space offers a changing assortment of hands-on exhibits for children of all ages. It's open Tuesday through Saturday 9:00 A.M. to 5:00 P.M. and Sunday noon to 5:00 P.M. General admission is $5.00. Check, however, for special discount nights and Monday openings. The Holocaust Museum Houston, (713) 942-8000, at 5401 Caroline Street is the first of its kind in the Southwest and

serves as an educational center and memorial to the millions of victims of Nazi death camps. The institution, opened in 1996, features a multimedia exhibition space with constantly changing shows as well as a library and a theater where visitors can see a video about Holocaust survivors now living in Houston. The museum is open Monday through Friday 9:00 A.M. to 5:00 P.M. and Saturday and Sunday noon to 5:00 P.M. Admission is free.

If art is your passion, the vast Museum District will keep you enthralled for hours and hours. The Contemporary Art Museum, or CAM, (713) 284-8250, at 5216 Montrose Boulevard is filled with works by a variety of local, national, and international contemporary artists. CAM is open Tuesday through Saturday 10:00 A.M. to 5:00 P.M., till 9:00 P.M. on Thursday, and Sunday noon to 5:00 P.M. Admission is free. The Museum of Fine Arts, (713) 639-7300, is across the street at 1001 Bissonnet Street. This Houston treasure possesses a collection of more than 35,000 works from around the world and hosts regular special exhibits. The museum is open Tuesday through Saturday 10:00 A.M. to 5:00 P.M., until 9:00 P.M. on Thursday, and Sunday 12:15 to 6:00 P.M. General admission is $3.00. Head north on Bissonnet Street a couple of blocks to the Glassel School, where you can see the work of the school's art students on display for free Monday through Friday.

If you're looking for a truly unique place to stay in Houston and prefer to be in the Museum District, check out the upscale Park Plaza Warwick Hotel, (713) 526-1991, at 5701 Main Street. Built in 1926 and retaining all the classic elegance of a bygone era, the Warwick is a historic treasure. Even if you're not a guest, the Warwick has an excellent Sunday brunch on its top floor. Windows on all sides offer an excellent view of this area of Houston. Call ahead and request a table by the window. If you're traveling with children, or just don't like to wait to be served, try Butera's Restaurant, (713) 523-0722, near the Museum District at 4621 Montrose Street.

Casual is the theme here as patrons serve themselves cafeteria style. You'll find a great assortment of deli-style foods, hot and cold sandwiches, hot pastas, desserts, and more. Butera's opens daily at 11:00 A.M. and serves lunch and dinner.

You'll want to drive from this area to another collection of museums in the northwest corner of the Museum District. Here art lovers will find a cluster of four impressive facilities. Start at the Menil Collection, (713) 525–9404, at 1515 Sul Ross Street. This museum was established in 1987 to exhibit the significant private collection of Houstonians John and Dominique de Menil and includes more than 15,000 pieces from antiquity to the 20th century. Admission is free. Nearby at 1519 Branard Street is the Menil's Cy Twombly Gallery, (713) 525–9450, which features about 35 paintings, sculptures, and works on paper by the American artist. Also nearby is the Rothko Chapel, (713) 524–9839, at 3900 Yupon Street. Called a chapel because of its meditative environment, the Rothko Chapel houses works by the late abstract painter. The Byzantine Chapel Museum, (713) 521–3990, dedicated to Byzantine art, is nearby.

The Houston arts scene wouldn't be complete without the exceptional performing arts for which this city is known. The Theater District in downtown Houston near Texas and Louisiana Streets includes performance spaces for many of the city's finest. Call (800) 828–ARTS or visit www.houstontheaterdistrict.org for a schedule of performances by the city's outstanding classical companies, the Houston Ballet, the Houston Grand Opera, and the Houston Symphony. The Alley Theater, (800) 259–ALLE, established in 1947, is one of the oldest resident professional theater companies in the country. This city also claims several multicultural arts centers, including Talento Bilingue de Houston, (713) 222–1213, and Kuumba House, (713) 524–1079.

If sporting events are your style, you're in for a treat. Houston has opened three brand spanking new sports arenas since the start of the century: Minute Maid Park, Reliant Stadium, and the Toyota Center. Each facility is home to at least one of Houston's major league teams (see our chapter on Spectator Sports for listings). Minute Maid Park, opened in 2000, is the Houston Astros' home turf and a tourist attraction all on its own. Reliant Stadium opened in 2001 for the city's new NFL team, the Houston Texans, and also hosts the annual Houston Livestock Show and Rodeo in late February or early March. The Toyota Center had its grand opening in the fall of 2003. It's home court for the Houston Rockets NBA team and the Houston Comets WNBA team and also hosts a variety of other entertainment and sporting events.

Minute Maid Park, at 501 Crawford Street, (713) 259–TOUR, is a fun place to see a game—or not. Walk-up, behind-the-scenes tours of this impressive facility are offered year-round every day but Sunday at 10:00 A.M., noon, and 2:00 P.M., unless there's a game scheduled. Call ahead to confirm. Tickets are sold at the Shed, the Astros' retail store in newly restored Union Station at the corner of Crawford Street and Texas Avenue downtown. The park was designed to reflect Houston's historical ties with the railroads—and is a tribute to ballparks from the good old days. A full-size vintage locomotive runs on 800 feet of track on the left-field wall. Another unique attribute of this facility is the retractable roof that is closed in inclement weather.

Don't forget the kids when you plan your Houston outing. SplashTown Waterpark, (281) 355–3300, just a few minutes north of downtown Houston at 21300 North I-45 in neighboring Spring is another premier attraction for families. This exciting park, part of the Six Flags chain features more than 40 rides on 50 shaded acres. It's open April through September, with varying hours of operation. Six Flags Astro-World and Six Flags WaterWorld, (713) 799–8234, www.sixflags.com, are at the 610 South Loop, Fannin Street exit. This complex, part of Texas's premier amusement park system, features all the

> *When traveling to Houston, choose a hotel or motel closest to your main tourist destinations. It will save you time and prevent the mental anguish that comes from being stuck in traffic. Planning to visit sights all over town? Avoid the main highways at rush hour if you can.*

thrill rides you could possibly pack into one day as well as water rides, shows, restaurants, and more.

If you're planning to spend the night in the Six Flags area and don't want to spend an arm and a leg, we recommend the Residence Inn by Marriott, (713) 660-7993, at 7710 South Main Street or the Holiday Inn Astrodome, (713) 790-1900, at 8111 Kirby Drive. Both are within minutes of The Galleria (read on to find out why you want to be near The Galleria) and the Museum District.

Those with higher education on their minds might want to tour the campus of Rice University near Hermann Park. Call the Office of Admissions at (713) 527-4036 for information about guided walking tours of the campus that are offered Monday through Friday at 11:00 A.M. and 3:00 P.M. during the school year. You can also check with the office about its summer schedule. Or just stroll around this shady 285-acre campus by yourself, taking in the sights of the elegant Mediterranean-style buildings.

Houston is also a shopper's paradise. People come from all over to shop at The Galleria, (713) 621-1907, Houston's elegant and upscale mall. Located at 5075 Westheimer at Post Oak Road, The Galleria is the focal point of the Uptown Galleria Area. The Galleria features more than 300 world-class stores, including Neiman Marcus, Saks Fifth Avenue, Lord & Taylor, Gianni Versace, and Tiffany & Co. There's also a large ice-skating rink here, plenty of informal restaurants, and the posh Westin Galleria Hotel, (800) WESTIN-1. Across

the street is the Centre at Post Oak, (713) 866-6905, with more than 25 specialty shops and restaurants, including the great children's toy store F.A.O. Schwarz. Drive north on Post Oak Road from The Galleria and you'll discover a number of other malls and shops, including the Post Oak Shopping Center. The luxury Houstonian Hotel, Club & Spa, (800) 231-2759, is also in the Galleria Area at 111 North Post Oak Lane. Of course you don't have to stay in a luxury hotel. For more reasonably priced accommodations, see those listed previously with the Astrodome, or check out La Quinta Inns in the area at (866) 725-1661, www.lq.com, or the Comfort Suites-Galleria at (713) 787-0004. Within this area is one of Houston's finest restaurants. If you're traveling to Houston for a special event—second honeymoon, birthday, big job promotion—and want to splurge on a gourmet meal, try Cafe Annie, (713) 840-1111, at 1728 Post Oak Boulevard. It's open for lunch and dinner weekdays and for dinner Saturday.

A good excuse to visit the Houston Ship Channel, one of this city's claims to fame, is to head out to Brady Island just a few miles east of downtown for an enormous buffet meal. Brady's Landing, (713) 928-9921, at 8505 Cypress Street and its next door neighbor Shanghai Red, (713) 926-6666, at 8501 Cypress Street feature similar menus, and both offer views of the ship channel. They have excellent Sunday brunch buffets for about $18.95 for adults as well as buffets at other times during the week. Brady's has a prime rib and seafood buffet on Friday and Saturday.

Many people visit Houston from across Texas and across the country specifically for this next attraction. The Johnson Space Center with Space Center Houston, (281) 244-2100 or (800) 972-0369, www. jsc.nasa.gov, is at 1601 NASA Road 1 off I-45 about midway between Houston and Galveston. When Apollo 13 astronaut Jim Lovell spoke those fateful words, "Houston, we have a problem," back in 1970, he was talking to Mission Control at the Space Center. This exciting and educational complex includes a tram tour of the sprawling NASA complex, featuring Mission Control, the Space Shuttle Training Facility, and the Space Environment Simulation Laboratory. Space Center Houston is the stimulating visitor center here and includes all kinds of hands-on activities as well as an IMAX theater offering thrilling space movies. It's open daily.

If you decide to go on to Galveston, check in at the visitor information centers in Moody Civic Center at Seawall Boulevard and 24th Street or in the Strand Historic District at 2215 Strand for a wealth of information about this great tourist destination. The visitor bureau Web site is www.galvestoncvb.com.

In Houston, stop in at the Visitor Information Center at 801 Congress Street to pick up the magazine *Official Guide to Houston* published by the Greater Houston Convention and Visitor Bureau for even more things to do and sites to see in this great American city. The center also has maps, brochures, and a schedule of upcoming events. Better still, plan ahead and request that literature be mailed to you or check www.houston-guide.com. The numbers are (713) 227-3100 and (800) 231-7799.

Bryan/College Station

Given the intense sports rivalry between the University of Texas and Texas A&M University, it's practically treason for an Austinite to tout the merits of College Station—home of the Aggies of A&M. This college town and neighboring Bryan (you can't tell where one begins and the other leaves off) offer all kinds of treats for the day-tripper or weekend visitor. College Station, 101 miles northeast of Austin, is an easy, stress-free drive along a route now designated as the "Presidential Corridor."

The corridor—U.S. 290 East and Highway 21—connects Texas's two presidential libraries, the Lyndon Baines Johnson Library in Austin and College Station's George Bush Presidential Library and

Museum, (979) 260-9552, www.bush library.tamu.edu, which opened at Texas A&M University in November 1997. It's worth the trip alone to visit this massive facility dedicated to the life and times of the 41st president of the United States. With more than 25,000 square feet of exhibition space, the museum chronicles Bush's life from his youth in Greenwich, Connecticut, to his service as a pilot in the U.S. Navy and through his bold move to the Texas oil fields in the mid-1940s.

In vivid detail, visitors learn about Bush's career as a congressman, ambassador to the United Nations, director of the C.I.A., then vice president and president of the United States. Here visitors will find the largest and most complete exhibit in the country dedicated to the 1991 Gulf War. There's also a huge slab of the Berlin Wall, graffiti and all. One section of the museum is dedicated to former First Lady Barbara Bush's efforts on behalf of literacy, volunteerism, and AIDS prevention. Of course the library is also a research institution and includes 38 million pages of President Bush's official and personal papers. The library, located on the A&M West Campus, is open Monday through Saturday 9:30 A.M. to 5:00 P.M. and Sunday noon to 5:00 P.M. There is a small admission fee, but children age 16 and younger are admitted free.

Just a short distance from the Bush library is the main campus of Texas A&M University, Texas's oldest public college. A&M, the state's land grant college, was founded in 1876 as an all-male military college. On August 23, 1963, the name of the Agricultural and Mechanical College was changed to Texas A&M University. Today A&M is among the 10 largest universities in the United States, with more than 41,000 students, and ranks among the top three institutions nationally in undergraduate enrollment in agriculture, business administration, and architecture.

A&M's nationally known Corps of Cadets program—now open to men and women—has produced more military officers than any other institution in the country except for the service academies. Start your tour of this sprawling campus with a visit to the Aggieland Visitor Center in Rudder Tower on the main campus, (979) 845-5851, www.tamu.edu. Some points of interest include the Academic Building, built in 1912 on the site of Old Main, the first building on campus; the Albritton Bell Tower, a 138-foot tower that contains a 49-bell carillon; the Memorial Student Center, opened in 1950 and dedicated to former students who died in World War II; the Student Recreation Center, the largest student rec center of its kind in the country, completed in 1995; the Cadet Quad, home to those world-famous cadets; and Kyle Field, the impressive 70,210-seat football stadium—home to UT's archrival.

Check, too, for a listing of events at A&M's Reed Arena, (979) 862-REED, reed.tamu.edu. Opened in 1998, the arena features sporting events, concerts, ice shows, circuses and much more. Also in College Station is Wolf Pen Creek Amphitheater, (979) 764-3408. This lovely outdoor arena hosts a wide range of music and entertainment, including some of Austin's finest musical performers.

Bryan is home to the Brazos Valley Museum of Natural History, (979) 776-2195. The museum features a collection of fossils found in the Brazos Valley as well as a constantly changing array of temporary exhibits. Youngsters will find plenty to do in the nature lab and discovery room. The museum is open Tuesday through Saturday 10:00 A.M. to 5:00 P.M. And be sure to take your children to the new Children's Museum of the Brazos Valley, (979) 779-5437. Opened in 1997, the museum features all kinds of hands-on learning activities and displays, including the inspiration gallery in which children can perform a puppet show, disassemble a VCR, or paint a Volkswagen Beetle. The museum is open Wednesday through Saturday 10:00 A.M. to 5:00 P.M. and Sunday 1:00 to 5:00 P.M.

One of our favorite spots in Bryan is the Messina Hof Winery at 4545 Old Reliance Road, (979) 778-9463, www.messinahof.com. Established with the release of its first vintage in 1983, Messina Hof boasts a 200-year heritage with the family traditions of winemaker Paul Bonarrigo going back six generations to Messina, Sicily. Winery tours and tastings, just $5.00 for adults, attract tourists from all over the region. Messina Hof, the most awarded premium winery in the state, produces a variety of red, white, and blush wines as well as ports and champagne. At the inviting guest center, visitors can purchase wines as well as a number of other gourmet foods made with the local product, including Riesling raspberry hazelnut fudge. Yum! Recently opened are the Vintage House Trattoria, serving international cuisine at lunchtime Tuesday through Saturday. For those planning a weekend trip to the area, the winery offers the Vinter's Loft bed-and-breakfast.

Of course this area offers dozens of hotels and motels—where else would all those Aggie parents and supporters stay? Families like the reasonably priced Vineyard Court Executive Suites, (979) 693-1220, at 216 Dominik Drive. The two-room suites include a small kitchen. For more luxury there's the College Station Hilton, (979) 693-7500, at 801 University Drive East.

There's no shortage of restaurants in this area either. From the diner-type college hangouts to more elegant surroundings, Bryan and College Station will not fail to provide sustenance. We've seen many Aggie parents and their college kids at the Oxford Street Restaurant & Pub, (979) 268-0792. Dark wood, low lighting, and a Sherlock Holmes motif lend Oxford Street its British flair. The menu includes a full selection of appetizers as well as steaks, chicken, seafood, and prime rib. The restaurant, at 1710 Briarcrest Drive in Bryan, is open daily beginning at 11:00 A.M. The Deluxe Diner, (979) 846-7466, at 203 University Drive in College Station, is a great place for a variety of home-style burgers and sandwiches, salads, chicken-fried steak, and fried chicken. The Deluxe is open daily for breakfast, lunch, and dinner starting at 6:00 A.M. Save some change for the jukebox.

While you're in the area, you might consider making the drive to Brenham to tour the cool business that put this town on the map. The Blue Bell Creamery, (800) 327–8135, offers tours and samples of its great ice cream Monday through Friday from 10:00 A.M. to 3:00 P.M. Reservations are recommended.

For more information about Bryan/College Station, call the Convention and Visitor Bureau at (800) 777–8292 or visit their Web site at www.bryan-collegestation.org.

OUT WEST

Johnson City/ LBJ Ranch

No, Johnson City was not named after the 36th president of the United States, Lyndon Baines, but one of his ancestors. The young LBJ was raised in the town bearing his family name. Johnson City, 50 miles southwest of Austin, and the LBJ Ranch in Stonewall, about 13 miles farther west, combine to make a perfect day trip from Austin. As you might expect, attractions in these two locations center around the life of the late President Johnson. The LBJ National Historic Park (www.nps.gov/lyjo/), in fact, includes both the ranch and LBJ's boyhood home as well as the nearby Johnson Settlement.

Start your visit in Johnson City with a tour of the visitor center, (830) 868–7128, www.lbjcountry.com, on Lady Bird Lane. Turn south off U.S. 290 (Main Street) at Avenue G and drive 2 blocks to Lady Bird Lane. Here you can pick up a map of the complex and a brochure on the park and also see the excellent exhibits, including scores of photographs, dedicated to LBJ's life and career. You can also listen to tape recordings of LBJ, Lady Bird Johnson, and other state and national leaders speaking on major issues of the 1960s, including

poverty, health, civil rights, and the environment. This modern, stone facility also includes a gift shop and bookstore. It's open daily, except major holidays, from 8:45 A.M. to 5:00 P.M.

Across the street is LBJ's Boyhood Home. This simple but comfortable Folk Victorian style house was LBJ's home from the age of 5 in 1913 until he married Lady Bird in 1934. It was here, on the front porch, that Johnson made his first public speech in 1937, announcing his candidacy for the U.S. House of Representatives. National Park Service guides provide a brief introduction about the restored home and the career of LBJ every half hour throughout the day beginning at 9:00 A.M. A few items inside the home are original, but many are period pieces. An interesting collection of Johnson family photographs adorn the walls. Admission is free.

From here walk about 4 blocks along a cinder path through bucolic Hill Country terrain (you cannot drive it) to the Johnson Settlement. This exhibit hall is filled with displays detailing the selection of Johnson City as the site for the town in 1879 and features all kinds of fascinating stories about frontier life, including the cowboys, the cattle drives, the trails, and farming. The pleasant covered porch of this stone building is adorned with rocking chairs and has drinking fountains and rest rooms. Another block down the path is the dogtrot cabin that once belonged to President Johnson's grandfather. The cabin, which has a shaded breezeway—through which a dog could easily trot—is typical of structures built during the 1800s.

This area also includes an authentic chuck wagon, used during cattle drives to haul food and supplies for the cowboys. There's also the James Polk Johnson Barn, built by the nephew of LBJ's grandfather in 1875, as well as a windmill, water tank, and cooler house. Across the field, in a penned enclosure, you might spy a herd of longhorn cattle grazing in the field.

If you're in the mood for a bite of lunch before leaving Johnson City, we recommend the Feed Mill Cafe, (830) 868–7771, just down the block off U.S. 290. This restaurant in a converted feed mill is decorated in kitschy beer-joint fashion and offers homestyle meals daily beginning at 6:30 A.M. The menu includes everything from eggs to burgers and salads to steaks, chicken, and seafood. The Feed Mill presents live music Friday and Saturday evenings as well as Sunday afternoon.

While you're in Johnson City, you might also want to check out two attractions not related to LBJ. Take F.M. 2766 about 8 miles to Pedernales Falls State Park. The 4,800-acre park features water falls, fishing, swimming, hiking, camping, and great places to picnic. Children will enjoy visiting the Exotic Resort Zoo, (830) 868-4357, on Highway 281, 4 miles north of Johnson City. The zoo's trams take visitors on one-hour guided tours of the 137-acre park that is filled with more than 500 exotic animals from around the world, many that will come right up and eat out of your hand. It's open daily beginning at 9:00 A.M. Closing times vary between 5:00 and 6:00 P.M. depending on the season. This is also a great place to bring a picnic lunch. Admission is $8.95 for adults, $6.95 for children 12 and younger.

Now, it's time to head for Stonewall and the LBJ Ranch, also known as the Texas White House. On your way to Stonewall, however, you might want to make a quick stop at the Hye Post Office, (830) 644-2465, which is right on U.S. 290 about halfway between Johnson City and Stonewall. The future president mailed his first letter here at the age of 4 and returned as president in 1965 to swear in Lawrence F. O'Brien as Postmaster General. This old post office and general store, built in 1904, is a Texas Historic Landmark.

Follow U.S. 290 west a few more miles until you see the large signs indicating the entrance to the Lyndon B. Johnson National Historic Park, (830) 868-7128, www.nps.gov/lyjo. A 75-minute guided bus tour of the LBJ Ranch District is offered from 10:00 A.M. to 4:00 P.M. daily. There is no set schedule, as buses depart depending on demand. National Park Service

guides will point out all the areas of interest in this historic spread, including LBJ's reconstructed birthplace, the site where Johnson was born August 27, 1908 (the house was rebuilt by President Johnson in 1964); the Johnson Family Cemetery where generations of Johnsons are buried, including the president; and the show barn, which is the center of present-day ranching operations. You are allowed to get off the bus and look around at these three sites. The bus tour also takes you past the Junction School, where the future president learned to read at age 4, and the Grandparent's Farmhouse, where Johnson's paternal grandparents lived out their lives. The Ranch House, also known as the Texas White House, is on the tour, but visitors cannot go in as this is still the home of Lady Bird Johnson. General admission is $3.00. Children ages 6 and younger are admitted free.

You can now retrace your path to Austin or head farther west to Fredericksburg.

Fredericksburg

This Hill Country town is so packed with things to do that it is easy to make a half dozen day trips or weekend getaways out of this destination. There is something here for history buffs, antiques lovers, foodies, outdoor enthusiasts, architectural historians, and military historians.

Fredericksburg, named for Prince Frederick of Prussia, is kin to New Braunfels (see our day trip under Down South), as both were founded by the Society for the Protection of German Immigrants— New Braunfels in 1845 and Fredericksburg in 1846. The settlers moved into the Comanche territory, and in 1847 their leader, Baron Ottfried Hans von Meusebach, negotiated a peace treaty with the Comanche that is commemorated every year with the Easter Fires Pageant, an event that involves hundreds of people in Easter Bunny suits, Comanches and pioneers, Easter eggs, and bonfires (read the details in our Annual Events and Festivals chapter).

Fredericksburg has retained its German character in its architecture and cultural traditions. Indeed, many old timers still speak what is called old High German and can be heard talking among themselves on the streets and in stores. Local churches also offer German services and songs. The Vereins Kirche Museum (the People's Church Museum) in Market Square, at the heart of the city, is a famous landmark. The octagonal building is now a museum of local history that is open Monday through Saturday from 10:00 A.M. to 2:00 P.M. There is a small admission charge.

The heart of the town is listed on the National Register of Historic Places. One very wide street cuts through the town, wide enough, it is said, for a team of oxen and a wagon to be turned around. Most of the sights are on Main Street or just a block or two off the thoroughfare. During the Gold Rush of 1849, Fredericksburg merchants made their fortunes as prospectors stocked up at the last Western outpost before embarking into the heart of Indian Territory. These days there is a similar feel to the town as tourists browse the antiques shops along Main Street, and the locals talk about the latest movie star who has bought a little piece of the picturesque Hill Country. Some Austinites own weekend homes in the town.

One of the first sights the visitor driving in from Austin sees is the Admiral Nimitz State Historical Park, 340 East Main Street, (830) 997-4379, www.tpwd.state.tx.us/park/nimitz. Chester Nimitz, who commanded the Pacific Fleet in World War II, grew up in landlocked Fredericksburg, and his grandfather once owned the Steamboat Hotel that now serves as the museum; the building looks remarkably nautical. The museum is open daily from 8:00 A.M. to 5:00 P.M. Admission is $3.00, $1.50 for students. Children age 6 and younger are admitted free.

A highlight of the museum is an exhibit featuring one of the tiny sub-

Early summer is peach season in the Texas Hill Country. If you're heading to Johnson City, Stonewall, or Fredericksburg, be sure to stop at any one of a number of businesses along U.S. 290 that sell fresh, ripe peaches, homegrown tomatoes, and other fruits. Some even have homemade peach ice cream!

marines used in the attack on Pearl Harbor. Other interactive and audiovisual exhibits illustrate the fierce battles in the Pacific. The George Bush Gallery of the Pacific War details the wartime experience of the 41st president, who was shot down in the Pacific. The Plaza of the Presidents consists of 10 monoliths detailing the wartime service of 10 presidents, beginning with President Franklin Roosevelt. In stark contrast to the exhibits, the museum is also home to a Japanese Garden of Peace, given by the people of Japan to the facility. There is a replica of the study and teahouse used by Admiral Togo, Nimitz's counterpart in the Imperial Japanese Navy.

Adding to the military flavor of the Fredericksburg area is the Hangar Hotel, a 2003 addition to the abundant lodging scene in town. This unique hotel, built in a hangar at the Gillespie County Airport, evokes a World War II Pacific Theater officer's club. The rooms are furnished with leather chairs and mahogany sleigh beds, and there is a Forties-era diner on-site. The hotel is located at 155 Airport Road, (830) 997-9990, www.hangarhotel.com.

Military buffs also may want to visit nearby Fort Martin Scott, 1606 East Main Street, (830) 997-9895, www.fortmartin scott.com, a c. 1848 frontier fort that is now being restored. The only original building is the guardhouse, but replicas of original buildings are being constructed. Historical reenactments are periodically held here, and there is ongoing archaeological work at the site. During the summer the fort is open Wednesday through

Saturday, and there is a small admission charge. After Labor Day and through March, the fort is open only on weekends.

Many visitors are drawn to Fredericksburg by the architecture and rich pioneer history. The Pioneer Museum, 309 West Main Street, is made up of several buildings, including a home and general store built in 1849, a barn and smokehouse, a firefighting museum, a pioneer log cabin, an 1855 church, and the Weber Sunday House. These tiny houses, sometimes just a single room, can be seen in both Fredericksburg and New Braunfels. They are called Sunday houses because they were built by farmers and ranchers as a place to bring the family on the weekend for Sunday church services. Many of them have been restored and are used as weekend homes by city dwellers. One of the best times of the year to see them is in spring when many of the tiny gardens are filled with wildflowers.

The Fredericksburg Chamber of Commerce, (830) 997-6523, www.fredericksburg-texas.com, provides walking tour maps and other pamphlets that give detailed information about the Sunday homes and other sights in the city. The maps and brochures also are available at many local businesses, including the German-style restaurants that dot Main Street. The Altdorf Restaurant, 301 West Main Street, has a beer garden and serves lunch and dinner daily, except Tuesday. The Old German Bakery and Restaurant, 225 West Main Street, (830) 997-9084, serves breakfast, lunch, and dinner and sells typical German baked goods, including rye bread, which often runs out early in the day. The bakery is closed on Tuesday and Wednesday.

The Fredericksburg Brewing Co., 245 East Main Street, (830) 997-1646, sells its own Pedernales Pilsner, a good choice after strolling through some of the 100 shops on Main Street, where many artisans and artists and collectors of antiques and Texana are located. Candle-making and glassblowing are just two of the crafts demonstrated here. One of the specialty shops is an outlet for Fredericksburg Herb Farms (see our Annual Events and Festivals chapter for a description of the local farm and its annual herb festival) where shoppers can buy oils and vinegars flavored with herbs grown in the Hill Country.

In addition to the Easter Fires and the herb festival, there are several other annual events that draw visitors throughout the year. In April there is a large antiques show; A Night in Old Fredericksburg is celebrated in July with food, dance, and song; the oldest county fair in Texas takes place in September with a traditional livestock show, horse races, a crafts and home-baked goods competition, plus evening dances; Oktoberfest celebrates the town's German heritage; and at Christmas there is the Candlelight Homes Tour, which offers wonderful views of some of the city's historical homes. All are detailed in our Annual Events and Festivals chapter.

Fredericksburg is 85 miles west of Austin on U.S. 290, so it is an easy day trip from the city and can be combined with a trip to the LBJ Ranch or Johnson City. (If you're traveling in June or July, be sure to stop along the way at one of the peach stands lining the highway.) But it is also a great weekend getaway location since the town has a wealth of bed-and-breakfast facilities and guest cottages. The latter are perfect for a romantic weekend since they are very private. Listings appear on the town's Web site, above.

Lovers of the outdoors also head for Fredericksburg to visit Enchanted Rock State Park, just 18 miles north of the city, where a granite dome rises some 325 feet from the earth and offers wide views of the area (see our Parks and Recreation chapter). There are also several vineyards in the countryside around Fredericksburg, including Bell Mountain Vineyards, (830) 685-3297, on Highway 16 about 14 miles north of town. Two other wineries are about 10 miles east of town on U.S. 290: Becker Vineyards, (830) 644-2681, www.beckervineyards.com, and Grape

Creek Vineyards, (830) 644–2710, www.grapecreek.com. All offer tastings and tours.

Given the wealth of things to see and do in Fredericksburg, it is an ideal destination for a spur-of-the-moment day trip.

The Highland Lakes

Perhaps you've already had the pleasure of making a trip out to Austin's beautiful Lake Travis, maybe even taken a swim in the refreshing waters or toured the lake from cove to inviting cove by boat. Possibly you've seen or boated up and down Lake Austin, that lovely stretch of Colorado River between West Austin's Tom Miller Dam and the Mansfield Dam. If so, you've seen two of Central Texas's six Highland Lakes. (Find out more about these two lakes in our chapter on Parks and Recreation.)

Make no mistake, however. Viewing Austin's two Highland Lakes definitely does not mean you've seen them all. Lake Buchanan, Inks Lake, Lake LBJ, and Lake Marble Falls all have their own distinct personality, and the only way to discover their wonders is to spend some time visiting them—one by one. Each lake is within 75 miles northwest of Austin, some closer, making visits to them either a perfect day trip or a wonderful weekend getaway.

The lakes, created by a series of six dams built on the Colorado River during the Depression of the 1930s and 1940s, vary immensely in size, shape, and degree of development. The dams were built and are managed by the Lower Colorado River Authority (LCRA), www.lcra.org, which aimed to control the flood-prone river while providing a dependable source of water and electricity for the Texas Hill Country. For information about the lakes, the dams, or any number of the parks and campsites operated by the LCRA, call (800) PRO-LCRA or phone the Park Information Hot Line at (512) 473–4083. The common denominator that unites all these lakes is the focus on water activities: swim-

ming, boating, and fishing. Camping, either in tents or RVs, is extremely popular around these lakes, although in most cases the campsites are either primitive or just a step above, meaning you'll find rest rooms in some but hardly ever showers. In most cases you'll enjoy the offerings much more by either taking along a boat, renting a pontoon or personal watercraft (PWC), or taking a guided cruise. We'll tell you where to find some of the best in each of those categories. While there are a few trails, the Highland Lakes are not renowned for attracting large numbers of hikers or bikers. If you're determined to hike, we'll point out a couple of good spots.

Before heading out on your excursion, you might want to pick up a copy of the map "Highland Lakes North" published by A.I.D. Associates, Inc., or any similar map of the lake area available at retail stores around Austin. Also check out www.high landlakes.com. Besides helping you chart your trip to the lake, these maps provide vital information on lake depths and water hazards and also point out landmarks, tourist destinations, places to gas up your boat, and accommodations.

Lake Buchanan

Let's start with the granddaddy of them all: Lake Buchanan. While it's the oldest, largest, and northernmost (farthest from Austin) of all the Highland Lakes, Lake Buchanan is also one of the most undeveloped, retaining the feel of a laid-back fishing haven. (Although more boating enthusiasts from the "big cities" are beginning to discover the lake.) The eastern shoreline stands out for its rugged, hilly terrain and towering cliffs. (Drivers should take special precaution here.) The western shore is closer to lake level and offers plenty of spots to just stop off and get your feet wet or take a swim.

This immense water basin, which covers 23,060 acres (36 square miles), was created with the completion of the 2.08-mile-long Buchanan Dam in 1937. While the basin itself is dotted by modest lakeside communities, simple bungalow rental units, camping areas, and RV parks, the breathtaking region upriver is banked by huge privately owned ranches. These landowners thus far have agreed to reject development of the area, choosing to lease some parts out only to hunters. So what you get is a view of the river much as it was in the distant past. This area is especially noted for its three scenic waterfalls—Fall Creek Falls, Deer Creek Falls, and Post Oak Falls—as well as for the gorgeous cliffs and rock formations that line the shores. Birds, deer, and other wildlife are common sights on this stretch. Only one or two houses can be seen all the way up to Colorado Bend State Park, (915) 628-3240, on the northernmost end of the lake. The park, filled with towering shade trees, is one of the nicest campsites on the lake. It has portable rest rooms but no shower facilities or electrical hookups. This campsite, on the western shore, is accessible from the towns of Lampasas or Cherokee by car or by boat. Hikers and mountain bikers will be pleased to know this park also offers excellent choices for both.

Very important to know about boating on Lake Buchanan: This is not a deep lake even in times of abundant rainfall, so be sure to use your map, or better yet talk to the locals, and steer clear of sandbars and other hazards. If you're planning to boat upriver, please note that the Alexander Boat Dock, (915) 379-2721, on the western side of the lake is the northernmost point to obtain gas. Once past this point, there is absolutely no more gas available, so you must carry plenty on board. Local experts warn that it is unsafe to try to boat upstream from Colorado Bend State Park, as you'll run into small but very rocky rapids. You'll find public boat ramps on both sides of the lake at the various parks, including Burnet County Park (Buchanan Dam), (512) 756-4297; Burnet County Park (White Bluff), same phone number, both on the eastern side of the lake; and Llano County Park, (915) 247-4352, on the southwestern shore; and the Cedar Point

Resource Area (LCRA Hotline) in the northwest. The various rental bungalows and cottages around the lake also feature boat ramps. You don't have to go way upstream to enjoy boating on the lake, however. The huge reservoir is perfect for sailing, speedboating, and bopping around on those ever-popular personal watercraft.

If you decide to rent a pontoon, fishing boat, or PWC, the following businesses can serve your needs: Lake Point Resort, (512) 793-2918, is just a couple miles west of the dam. The Indian Hills Stop & Go, (512) 793-6438, is on Highway 29 going west from the dam a few blocks before the intersection with State Road 1431. If you're staying in the northwest area of the lake, try Max Alexander's, (915) 379-2721. Each of these businesses offers different types of boats, and each has its own rates. Be aware that you will be asked to leave a deposit or credit card.

This lake also offers excellent scenic drives year-round but especially in springtime when the wildflowers are in bloom. Designated the "Bluebonnet Capital of Texas" by the state legislature, this area and neighboring Inks Lake attract scores of visitors to the Bluebonnet Trail each year during the spectacular wildflower season, which runs March through May depending on rainfall. The Lake Buchanan/Inks Lake Chamber of Commerce, (512) 793-2803, located at Buchanan Dam, offers an annual brochure and operates a hot line of the best viewing locations.

We suggest a stop off at the Buchanan Dam Museum and Visitor Center right off Highway 29 on the southeastern tip of the lake. It is open Monday through Friday 8:00 A.M. to 4:00 P.M. and 1:00 to 4:00 P.M. weekends and holidays. Here you'll find a fascinating pictorial history of the construction of the dam, comments from a few of the hundreds of workers who found highly coveted Depression-era jobs building the immense barrier, as well as information about the Kingsland Archeological Center on Lake

LBJ. The visitor center also features an 18-minute documentary about the dam itself. Also, this is where you'd come to take a free guided tour of the huge generating facility. Tours generally run from May to September. And don't miss out on the opportunity to take a stroll along the impressive pedestrian walkway that leads from the visitor center all the way out to the spillway. This is the best way to see for yourself what a huge undertaking this project was—and get a great view of Lake Buchanan at the same time. For those not interested in making the trek, there's an outdoor observation deck right off the parking lot.

From here you can choose to either head up the eastern side of the lake or follow the western shore. Both have their own attributes and attractions. Going up north on the eastern shoreline is the recreational development Canyon of the Eagles, (512) 756-8787 or (800) 977-0081, www.canyonoftheeagles.com. This 940-acre site includes a 64-room lodge, an RV park, camping facilities, a beach, general store, and, best of all, a nature preserve for wildlife such a the bald eagle and the golden-cheeked warbler. The Eagle Eye Observatory also is here, offering visitors a chance to peer through a 16-inch Ealing Cassegrain telescope and to chart the skies from a unique observing field. Stargazing parties are scheduled regularly. This is the place to catch the Vanishing Texas River Cruise on the *Texas Eagle II*, a 70-foot, 200-passenger boat with two observation decks.

Several tours are offered year round, including the popular 2½-hour guided scenic wilderness cruise up the Colorado River Canyon. Bring your own picnic; most people do. Tours held November through March are especially fascinating because they take visitors upriver to see the winter habitat of the largest colony of American bald eagles in the state. Wildflower tours, vineyard tours, and sunset dinner cruises also are offered. You don't have to be guest of the park to take a cruise. Call or check the Web site for a schedule and prices.

The western side of Lake Buchanan also has some great attractions, most notably the Fall Creek Vineyards and Winery, (915) 379-5351. This winery, 2.2 miles north of the community of Tow (pronounced *toe*) on the northwest shores of the lake, offers tours, wine tastings, and sales of its award-winning products. Read about this winery in our Close-up in the Restaurants chapter. To enter the winery, guests drive up a road adorned on both sides by the grapevines that produce some of this winery's product. While tours are held daily during the peak season (March through November) and every day but Sunday the rest of the year, we've found that more extensive tours are given on weekends. But if you just want a brief introduction to the operations and a short tour of the facilities, any time is a good time to visit Fall Creek. Of course if you happen to be in the area in late August, check with the winery for its annual grape stomp festivities.

Also on this side of the lake is the wonderfully primitive Cedar Point Resource Area (LCRA hot line) a few miles south of Tow on State Road 2241. This rugged 400-acre waterfront park is dotted with some lovely spots to pitch a tent right near the lake. There's not one modern amenity here, except a boat ramp, but Mother Nature has endowed it with lovely shade trees and plenty of secluded spots. There's no cost to camp here. Just pitch your tent and enjoy. If you enjoy hiking, this is a very good option.

Fishing is still a major attraction on Lake Buchanan. The Ken Milam Guide Service, (915) 379-2051, at the Alexander Boat Dock in Tow, offers year-round fishing excursions for striped bass on the lake and welcomes children and adults. Milam, who has been in business since 1982, offers several fishing packages, including full- and half-day excursions. Also on the lake is the Crawford Guide Service, (915) 388-9187, which also offers full- and half-day all-inclusive excursions on the lake in search of those coveted striped bass, called stripers by the locals. Jim Crawford, who runs this operation, grew up on the lake. For those who want to drop a pole in the water, the Hi-Line Lake Resort & RV Park, (915) 379-1065 or (888) 379-1065, on the western shore just south of the Tow community, features an excellent all-weather fishing marina. The enclosed and lighted marina, which also has an outdoor dock, is a perfect place to fish for crappie, white bass, largemouth bass, catfish, and striped bass. And you can fish here day and night. The Hi-Line also can arrange guided service.

If you choose to spend the night on the lake, remember that simple cottages and bungalows are the norm, usually with the added attraction of a kitchenette. Don't come to Lake Buchanan expecting luxury surroundings. The emphasis here is on getting out and enjoying the water. While there are several such locations scattered around the lake, among our favorite is the Hi-Line Lake Resort & RV Park (see telephone numbers listed previously). Jim and Charlotte DeGroat operate the Hi-Line, which features 16 air-conditioned cottages that have new kitchenettes with full-size refrigerators, microwaves, and cook tops—a perfect place to fry up that fish you caught. The RV park offers plenty of spacious sites featuring full hookups. This property also has a lovely sandy beach, perfect for swimming, as well as a boat ramp and outdoor grills. For dining on the water, check out the Rod & Reel Grille, (915) 379-1065, at Hi-Line Resort. This charming spot features an extensive menu that includes everything from burgers to steaks, chicken, and seafood. It's open for dinner Monday, Thursday, and Friday, and for lunch and dinner on the weekend. By the way, Jim is also extremely knowledgeable about the lake itself and is a great source of information.

Across the lake on the eastern shore is the well-established Silver Creek Lodge, (512) 756-4854. Silver Creek offers well-maintained air-conditioned cabins with kitchenettes, RV spaces, a swimming pool, a covered fishing dock, covered boat stalls, and a boat ramp. Silver Creek also

provides fishing guide services and has a pump to gas up your boat.

Inks Lake

Just a few miles west of the Buchanan Dam off Highway 29 is Inks Lake in what is known as the Central Texas Mineral Region. (Enter at Park Road 4 and travel south.) Only 4.2 miles long and just 0.6 mile at its widest points, Inks Lake is dwarfed by its gargantuan neighbor. Yet the lake is surrounded by such rugged natural beauty—highlighted by towering oak trees, wildflowers, scenic bluffs, and huge boulders of granite and pink gneiss—that it attracts nature lovers, campers, boaters, and fishing enthusiasts year-round. This lake was the second created on the Colorado River after the 1,548-foot Roy Inks Dam was completed in 1938.

Inks Lake features one of the most popular state parks in Texas. Inks Lake State Park, (512) 793-2223, is one of the most fully equipped parks in the region, offering both tent and RV sites, a few enclosed shelters, showers and rest rooms, picnicking, swimming, trails, a boat ramp, and even a public golf course. The 1,200-acre park extends along the entire eastern shoreline of the lake. Be sure to stop at the scenic overlook along Park Road 4 and check out the Devil's Water-hole, which has a beautiful waterfall. Teenagers just love to climb on the huge granite boulders that adorn this area.

Entrance to the park is $4.00 a person for those 13 and older. If you're planning to explore several state parks, however, do what most Texans do and buy a one-year vehicle pass for $50 that allows unlimited access to all state parks. You can purchase the passes at any park headquarters, at Wal-Mart stores, or any other place that sells hunting and fishing licenses.

From Inks Lake you might want to follow Park Road 4 south about 10 minutes to Longhorn Cavern State Park, (512) 756-4680. While not on a lake, this wonderful 637-acre state park is nevertheless a great place for picnicking and hiking. No overnight camping is permitted. Of course the major attraction here is the cavern itself. Located in Backbone Ridge, a huge piece of Ellenburge limestone formed by a shallow sea more than 450 million years ago, the cavern is open for daily tours year-round. The 1¼-mile round-trip walking tour takes about 85 minutes.

Lake LBJ

If Buchanan and Inks Lakes are the rugged members of the family, Lake LBJ is the refined cousin. The Colorado River meanders down from Inks Lake and branches out to skirt the town of Kingsland before it widens near the towns of Sunrise Beach on the western shore and Granite Shoals on the east. Once called Granite Shoals Lake, it was renamed in 1965 to recognize President Lyndon Johnson's efforts on behalf of the LCRA. At 6,200 acres, this gorgeous lake is the second largest of these four. Created by the Wirtz Dam, Lake LBJ offers plenty of wide open waters for speedboats, sailboats, and personal watercraft. Unlike Inks and Buchanan, however, Lake LBJ stands out for the upscale homes and large manicured lawns that surround the basin. This lake is becoming increasingly developed and includes the new resort community of Horseshoe Bay and others.

Because of its emphasis on residential development, this lake is not stocked with rental units, although there are a few. Our favorite is the secluded Sandyland Resort, (915) 388–4521, at 212 Skyline Drive in the community of Sunrise Beach. This charming two-story lodge features all lakefront rooms, some with kitchenettes, and suites with kitchens. Sandyland also has a lovely, lighted fishing dock, a swimming pool, a boat ramp, and a marina that offers both fuel and a small store. Here guests can rent personal watercraft and pontoon boats or request a guided tour of the lake. This is just a lovely location overlooking a nice wide section of the lake. While this

resort does not have a sandy beach, there are two nice beaches nearby. Ask owners Krista and Brad Foster for directions. You can also call ahead and request a brochure. Upriver in Kingsland is the River Oaks Lodge, (915) 388–4818, at Highway 1431 West. This lodge offers eight fully equipped cabins as well as an enclosed fishing house and boat ramps and stalls. The lodge also features a floating gazebo as well as a swimming, picnicking, and play areas. Granite Shoals also has a great vacation getaway. The Tropical Hideaway Beach Resort and Marina, (210) 598–9896 or (800) 662–4431, at 604 Highcrest Drive is a lovely condominium complex that offers daily rentals of its one- and two-bedroom suites. All rooms feature living areas, kitchens, and private balconies. The grounds here are highlighted by a truly unique Tiki Village that will have you feeling as if you're in the tropics. The outdoor restaurant and bar is shaded by beach-style thatched palapas. You'll also find a swimming pool, sandy beach, and tennis courts.

If you're heading south on Highway 1431 from Kingsland, be sure to take a few moments to stop at Lookout Mountain, just a few miles south of State Road 2342. This scenic overlook provides an excellent overall view of the Colorado River valley. A few minutes farther south off this highway is the Kingsland Archeological Site, (830) 598–5261, which is open by reservation only. The 10-acre site on the shores of Lake LBJ is a 5,000-year-old prehistoric campsite for hunter-gatherers along the Colorado River. Since it was discovered in 1988, archaeologists have uncovered more than 100,000 artifacts, including projectile points, grinding stones, and animal bone fragments. Photos of this site are on display at the Buchanan Dam Visitor Center.

Lake Marble Falls

Like Lake Austin, Lake Marble Falls is an inner-city lake that appears more like the river it is than a wide open lake.

Nevertheless, this 6-mile lake has grown so popular over the years that the community of Marble Falls and the huge Meadow Lake Country Club have grown up around it. The well-shaded 18-acre Johnson Park, (210) 693–3615, on the lake features a public boat ramp, a playscape for children, picnic area, overnight camping, and rest rooms. Nearby is Lakeside Park (same phone), which also has a boat ramp but is designated for day use only. Entrance to both parks is free. RV campers will want to check out the Riverview RV Park, (830) 693–3910, on the shores of Lake Marble Falls at 200 River Road. This site offers full hookups as well as rest rooms, showers,

and laundry facilities. There really isn't much in the way of lakeside dining in Marble Falls, but if you're ready for a good, inexpensive home-style meal, try the Blue Bonnet Cafe in town at 211 Highway 281 South, (512) 693–2344. You'll find everything from burgers to chicken-fried steak, pot roast, fried chicken livers, and fried catfish. The homemade biscuits melt in your mouth, as do the pies. The Blue Bonnet is open for breakfast, lunch, and dinner Monday through Saturday, and breakfast and lunch on Sunday.

Once you've toured all the Highland Lakes, you'll know for yourself why they are the pride of the Texas Hill Country.

RELOCATION 🏠

Growth is many things to Austin-area residents. For some it means opportunity, broader horizons, and wider dreams; but for others it has come to mean the struggle to maintain the city's identity and quality of life that have been Austin hallmarks. The spirit of Austin is treasured by both longtime residents and newcomers. One key to the preservation of the city's unique character is the vitality of its neighborhoods.

Even the word "neighborhood" is loaded with meaning in Austin. Some neighborhood organizations have wielded considerable political clout at City Hall (see our Politics and Perspectives chapter), while others have created unique identities that act as a draw to both visitors and residents. Even some of the newest neighborhoods have distinct personalities and have established strong internal bonds as a result of political fights or commitments to community activities.

In Austin, as in some of the smaller rural communities that have been absorbed by the city's growth, maintaining the neighborhood character, the particular sense of place, has been both a challenge and a goal. Many of the area's neighborhoods have succeeded; others have not. But with growth has come a dynamism that has revitalized some neighborhoods, created new ones, and, at a minimum, kept the quality-of-life issue on the front burner for every Central Texas resident.

The city has been leaping up the population list in record time in recent years. In January 1998, Austin surpassed Seattle as the 22nd-largest city in the United States, and landed in the top 20 by spring as the city annexed several suburban developments on its periphery. Beyond the city limits, the greater Austin metropolitan area has topped the million resident mark, and

demographers are predicting the area will surpass 2 million residents in the early years of this century.

There is a lot of hoopla about the growth in Austin population numbers, but don't be fooled by the numbers. There are approximately one million residents in the greater metropolitan area and about half that number within the city limits. While downtown maintains some of the flavor of a midsized city, there has been a boom in downtown development that promises to give the heart of the city more of the feel of a busy, urban area. Businesses, particularly high-tech companies, are eager to locate downtown, many of the older high-rises and warehouses are being converted to lofts, and the nightlife and restaurant scenes are even more vibrant. (See our Restaurants and Nightlife chapters.)

This booming growth has given both old and new area residents pause. Growth is leaving its mark on central Texas in many ways. On the plus side, growth has given the city a more cosmopolitan air. There is a greater diversity of restaurants, more shops and theaters, and the city's increasingly multicultural population celebrates ethnic traditions and cultural differences. The largest Hindu temple in North America is not far from one of the area's most popular country barbecue joints.

Growth means choice and numerous choices for homeowners in terms of location and price. But growth also means traffic jams. Rush-hour commutes are now a factor for homebuyers, in addition to access to city services—police, fire, EMS, libraries, even parks.

Several significant trends in Austin's growth offer insight into what makes Austin neighborhoods tick. We begin with a look at some of these trends, followed by a geographic tour of some of the city's neighborhoods.

NEW URBANISM

It's a phrase that is much discussed in planning circles and in architecture schools across the country. For the uninitiated, "new urbanism" might be simply summed up as a return to the old neighborhoods of fond memory. Advocates, such as Miami architect Andres Duany, considered the grandfather of the movement, see it as a way to create neighborhoods reminiscent of those communities where many Americans lived in the years before suburban sprawl became the norm. A place where residents could shop at the grocery store, drop in for a haircut, or pick up a fresh loaf of bread within just minutes of home.

Hal Box, former dean of the University of Texas architecture school, has adopted a litmus test for examples of the new urbanism—it is the "five minute Popsicle rule." Every child should be able to walk or ride a bike to the neighborhood store for a Popsicle and be home safely within five minutes. There are several "Popsicle rule" neighborhoods in Austin. Some of them are in upper-income neighborhoods, others in some of the city's older, working-class neighborhoods, but much attention is paid to how they function and what makes them livable by city planners and neighborhood activists.

Austin has hosted several important conferences on New Urbanism and in 1997 launched an effort to draft a building and planning code that would embrace the spirit of the movement. The goal is not to develop a cookie-cutter approach to neighborhood design but to allow each neighborhood to develop its own identity.

DOWNTOWN DISCOVERY

Another important trend in the growth of Austin has been the rediscovery of downtown as a place to live and to work. Several high-tech companies embarked on major downtown development projects in 2000, although a couple stalled in the dot.com bust. Thanks to the presence of the Texas Capitol and the city's vibrant music scene, downtown Austin is alive both day and night and has not suffered the sort of blight some of America's cities have experienced. However, living in the immediate downtown area was limited, until recently, to a couple of condominium towers within a few blocks of the capitol, occupied primarily by lobbyists and politicians during the legislature's biennial sessions, and a small number of apartment developments. Now, within blocks of the city's main street, Congress Avenue, apartments and lofts offer residents a downtown lifestyle, although not at bargain-basement prices. In the fall of 2003 there were an estimated 3,000 apartments and condos under construction in the downtown area.

Ten blocks to the west of Congress Avenue is the hub of another downtown center that has become a magnet and a model for inner-city growth. Once the corner of Lamar Boulevard and West Sixth Street was an area dominated by car lots and automobile showrooms. Now, at the heart of this hub are the headquarters of two quintessential Austin companies. These local legends—Whole Foods Market, headquarters of a NASDAQ-traded gourmet/health food grocery store chain, and GSD&M, an award-winning national advertising agency—were founded by Texas baby boomers.

Whole Foods and GSD&M's "Idea City" headquarters are at the heart of an urban neighborhood of bookstores, ice cream parlors, coffee shops, and bakeries, all within a stone's throw of several new loft and apartment developments. The price tags are not cheap—rentals are in the four-digit-a-month range, and condominium-lofts can cost anywhere from $150,000 to $500,000. This is one of those Austin neighborhoods that locals love to visit.

The Austin City Council has encouraged residential development downtown by offering tax abatements for developers. Some Austin residents are leery of this trend and fearful that they will be unable to afford their "new" neighborhoods. The Rainey Street neighborhood is a small area south of the downtown Austin Convention Center and just west of I-35. Many of the residents here live in small, wooden frame houses and rent, rather than own. Lots in the neighborhoods are now selling for as much as $100,000 and are snapped up by developers with an eye to building condominiums and town homes.

GENTRIFICATION

The downtown development trend is linked to two other Austin market characteristics: the gentrification of older, inner-city neighborhoods and what planners call "infilling." Eager to live closer to downtown, or in one of the city's colorful, older neighborhoods, buyers are looking for empty lots or rundown properties, and then either building or moving older homes onto the property.

The gentrification of older central city neighborhoods has been a trend in Austin for several years, but the market pressure to develop housing availability close to downtown has put the trend on the fast track. Homes west of downtown have enjoyed prestige and market value for several decades—a one bedroom bungalow in west Central Austin can cost $350,000. Now, that trend is beginning to occur south of Town Lake in older neighborhoods along South Congress Avenue, popularly called SoCo.

Many of the new residents are young, urban pioneers who are taking on the challenges of moving into older, rundown neighborhoods in areas north of the University of Texas campus and just west of I-35 around the Hancock Center shopping plaza. Generally, neighborhoods close to downtown and west of the capitol have been the first to ride the gentrification boom and are now firmly established as prestigious neighborhoods, where a relatively small home can cost $300,000.

The Austin Neighborhood Council serves as a clearinghouse for Austin's diverse neighborhoods (www.ancweb.org).

Of course, the other side of the gentrification trend is a growing lack of affordable housing. The Real Estate Center at Texas A&M University has named Austin the second-least affordable market in Texas. The center compares the median household income needed to qualify for a mortgage to the median-priced home in the area.

The picture is getting tougher for average families, and there has been a growing concern that working people, particularly those providing vital services—police, firefighters, teachers, and city workers—are being priced out of the market. Drawing on the expertise of scholars and policy leaders, the city has created several task forces to look not only at the question of affordable housing, but also wages. Despite the shortage of affordable housing for low-income residents, real estate agents do emphasize the diversity of the market in Austin.

The key to finding a bargain, particularly in an older neighborhood, is knowing which neighborhoods are being revived and which are suffering from the usual urban ills, including problems with crime and vandalism. That can be difficult for a newcomer, but Austin's active neighborhood association infrastructure can provide assistance. The City of Austin maintains a community registry, a reference guide to the approximately 300 active neighborhood associations in the city. It can be requested by contacting the planning department's neighborhood section at (512) 499-2648, www.ci.austin.tx.us/housing.

SUBURBAN EXPANSION

While some Austin residents are looking to the heart of the city for a home, others are looking to the hills. The major growth trend in the past two decades has been the expansion of the greater Austin area to the west. Back in the 1970s, the Austin City Council adopted a growth plan that called for expansion along the city's north-south corridor defined by I-35. The council was reflecting the concerns of environmentalists, who wanted to protect the vast underground Edwards Aquifer, the underground watershed that feeds Austin's icon and symbol of community environmental sensibilities, Barton Springs Pool in downtown Zilker Park (see our Close-up in the Parks and Recreation chapter).

But the lure of the Hill Country with its distinctive flora and scenic views proved more overwhelming. Much of the growth has occurred in the northwest, west, and southwest. In fact, the word "west" has something of a cachet in Austin real estate circles. The area's most prestigious neighborhoods are in West Austin; West Lake Hills, the incorporated community west of MoPac (Loop 1); and in western Travis County toward the Highland Lakes.

Austin is built on the border of two distinct geographic areas. I-35 roughly tracks the break between the Hill Country and the Blackland Prairie. To the west are rolling hills, live oak trees, and scrub dominated by so-called cedar trees (actually junipers) growing in the thin soil that barely dusts the limestone ridges. East of the interstate the land is flatter, covered with rich, black soil in which pecan trees flourish.

Both areas are picturesque, but the desire to live west may have more to do with age-old social patterns that have little to do with a modern, integrated Austin. Like so many other cities, the interstate highway also serves as a barrier between downtown and Austin's predominantly ethnic neighborhoods. Austin's neighborhoods are well integrated, particularly newer subdivisions, but like most American cities, Austin still has two distinct neighborhoods east of I-35 that historically have been primarily African-American and Hispanic. These neighborhoods have strong identities. Neighborhood groups there have fought both to preserve community identity and to improve city services in their communities.

The lure of living west has pushed development out beyond the Austin city limits, absorbing once small communities like Cedar Park, northwest of Austin in the next county. Just as the greater Austin area has pushed over the Travis County line into Williamson County in the northwest, in the southwest suburban developments have spilled over into Hays County. The small community of Dripping Springs, on U.S. 290 West about 15 miles from the Austin city limits, is feeling the growth boom as homeowners eager for a spacious home on perhaps an acre or two of land are locating there. The search for the Hill Country life is now spreading out even farther west. Communities 60 miles or more from Austin are seeing home developments spring up in their communities. The growth also has spread east to some of the wonderful small, rural towns in the rolling farmland around communities like Smithville and Bastrop.

THE HIGH PRICE BOOM

One of the hottest commodities in the Austin real estate market has been high-priced homes, those costing $1 million and up. Realtors attribute this trend to the impact of the city's growing high-tech sector. In 2000 the area had virtually full

Most taxpayers in Central Texas pay property taxes to three jurisdictions— the local school district, the city, and the county. An Austin city resident pays taxes to Austin Independent School District, the City of Austin, Travis County, and Austin Community College tax district. School taxes are about 60 percent of a property tax bill in Central Texas.

employment, as the experts define it, with the unemployment rate at 2 percent. December 2003 figures place the jobless rate at 4.8 percent. The high-tech industry had produced a group of entrepreneurs and a large number of employees with valuable stock options.

Leading the pack, of course, was Michael Dell, founder of Dell Computer, who built a new home in West Lake Hills that has been compared to Bill Gates's mansion in Seattle. Dell's home was appraised by tax authorities at $22.5 million—an appraisal he challenged—which was only half of what Gates's home allegedly cost. However, it did symbolize the high price boom in Austin. Dell's home is not the norm. By 1997 the number of million dollar homes sold in the area jumped some 15 percent, and that trend continued into the new century, stalling a little in 2002.

These high-priced homes are found in the city's most prestigious neighborhoods, some in close proximity to downtown, others out in the hills. An old ivy-clad mansion in the Enfield neighborhood close to downtown might sell for $2 million, while a sprawling lakeside home in the hills above Lake Austin might sell for $3 million. Some of the large homes in the hills reflect traditional Hill Country architecture with limestone walls, Mexican tile floors, and rustic timbers, while others are mock Tudor or French chateau–style.

The economic boom made some old Austin hands nervous. They remember the roller-coaster ride of the '80s. First, home prices escalated as the local economy boomed. But the boom was nurtured by a commercial real estate bubble that was being fed by high oil prices and easy loans. Then came the bust as oil prices plummeted and savings and loans closed. A person who bought a home in 1980 in Austin has seen it double in price, then fall by a third or more, then rise again to more than double its original value.

Most economists considered the current boom to be built on much more stable economic ground than the '80s boom.

But the increasing number of homes, the number of choices available, and the variety of neighborhoods have created a very complex market. The dot.com bust created a glut in some high-end developments. Two key factors are price and location. Traffic and commute times were a Houston or Dallas issue five years ago, but now Austin homebuyers must balance affordability with access.

Prices in most neighborhoods have continued to rise, but perhaps not as quickly, some dipping in 2002 and then beginning to rise again in late 2003. Realtors agree there is no single phrase that describes the Austin real estate market, except perhaps "complex."

We'll take a look at the city by geographic area.

NEIGHBORHOODS
Central

The geographic center of the City of Austin lies somewhere around Highland Mall at the intersection of I-35 and U.S. 290 East, several miles north of the capitol. But most Austin area residents consider the center of the city to be the downtown area, along the shores of Town Lake and around the Texas Capitol. Given the city's fast growth, old and new residents often have a different view of where Central Austin becomes North Austin, or where west gives way to northwest, but there is little doubt that the heart of Austin is the downtown area.

For the purposes of this book, we will define Central Austin as the area east of MoPac (Loop 1); south of R.M. 2222, known as Koenig Lane as it crosses the central section of the city; west of I-35; and north of Town Lake.

The central area embraces some of the city's most prestigious addresses and some of its more run-down, older neighborhoods. It also contains one of the most quintessential neighborhoods, Hyde Park, defined by advocates of new urbanism as a perfect "Popsicle rule" community.

Hyde Park was the city's first planned suburb. In 1889 Colonel Monroe Martin Shipe, a businessman from Abilene, Kansas, came to Austin and purchased a 206-acre plot of land in what was then far north Austin. The new suburb had its own electric streetcar system, dance pavilion, and walking paths. Shipe first built large Victorian homes for some of Austin's leading citizens. Later, smaller Craftsman-style bungalows were added to the neighborhood.

Today, Hyde Park is not only a much-sought-after address but also a popular spot for lunch or coffee with friends from across the city. Located north of the University of Texas campus and bounded by Guadalupe Street on the west and 38th Street on the south, the smallest condominium in the neighborhood may sell for close to $100,000, while larger homes are $250,000 and up. It is the ambience of Hyde Park that drives the prices. There are several small restaurants in the neighborhood, a gym, post office, and fire station, a couple of neighborhood grocery stores, and a bakery where the neighbors post notices on the bulletin board.

The Hancock Recreation Center is within Hyde Park, and the city-owned Hancock Golf Course lies along the eastern edge of the neighborhood. On the northern perimeter, off 45th Street, is the Elisabet Ney Museum, the former studio of the 19th-century sculptor whose work can be seen at the Texas Capitol.

Every year on Father's Day weekend, the neighborhood opens its doors for a historic homes tour. Visitors stroll the tree-shaded, wide sidewalks and visit some of the restored Victorian homes that give Hyde Park its charm. Hyde Park defines the much-touted Austin quality of life.

Several miles southwest of Hyde Park is the Enfield neighborhood, east of MoPac (Loop 1) and west of Shoal Creek, the creek that wends its way south through Central Austin to Town Lake, running alongside Lamar Boulevard for much of its course. As it crosses Shoal Creek, 15th Street becomes Enfield Road, running west through this affluent old neighborhood.

You can still find a few small apartments tucked away over old garages and in some of the smaller houses of the area, and even a small c. 1960s apartment complex or two along the major thoroughfare, Enfield Road. But the area is best known for its large homes with hefty price tags, set back on wooded lots lining the area's curving streets. Homes in Enfield can sell for up to $1.5 million or more. Even small, modest homes sell in the $250,000 range. After all, it's just a five-minute drive from the capitol, which can be clearly seen as residents cross over the creek onto 15th Street.

Another central neighborhood with a unique character is Clarksville, just south of Enfield Park. Sometimes described as part of West Austin (a reflection of the days when the city was much smaller), Clarksville is bordered on the west by MoPac, on the south by 10th Street, and north by Waterston Avenue. The property was originally owned by Texas Governor E. M. Pease, who gave the land to his former slaves in 1863 as an effort to keep them as workers on his plantation.

The neighborhood is named for Charles Griffin, who changed his last name to Clark after he was freed. Clark bought a two-acre plot on 10th Street in 1871. Some of the current residents are descendants of the founders, but the neighborhood has changed over the years. Originally, according to local historians, Clarksville was home to about 250 African Americans. That number has diminished as the demographics of the neighborhood have changed.

In 1997 one of the keepers of the Clarksville flame, Mary Baylor, died. Baylor's great-grandmother was an original Clarksville resident—the African-American community was then a half mile outside the city limits. Baylor lived her whole life on West 10th Street in the home of her ancestors and was very active as a community leader.

The *Austin American–Statesman* lauded her on the day of her funeral for her efforts to save Clarksville for the low- and middle-income families who had called it home for generations. She personally led the effort to have 18 low-income homes built in the neighborhood. Baylor's funeral was held at the Sweet Home Baptist Church, the church her ancestors built in 1882 in their small neighborhood.

Clarksville remains a mix of comfortable, modest homes and some gentrified houses priced in the $300,000 range. Within the neighborhood are several shops (see our Shopping chapter), bakeries, a pottery store, and restaurants, including one of Austin's top dining spots, Jeffrey's (see our Restaurants chapter). Like Hyde Park, Clarksville is a favorite place for city residents to visit. The neighborhood is also host to the annual Clarksville Jazz Festival (get more information in our Annual Events and Festivals chapter).

Central and South Austinites have an affection for changing the names of streets and rivers as their paths cross the city. In fact, rivers even become lakes— Town Lake, the portion of the Colorado River that runs through the heart of Austin, once represented a dividing line for some in the city. *Austin American–Statesman* humor columnist John Kelso helped engender the myth of North-South differences in the mid-'80s. North Austin, the mythology went, was land of the yuppies while south of the river was occupied by "bubbas," laid-back old hippies, and assorted free spirits. For several years, Kelso helped to hype an annual tug-of-war where North met South on the banks of the river.

Those distinctions have faded somewhat, but South Austin is still viewed by some as a haven for free spirits. The distinctions have faded, perhaps, because the older neighborhoods south of the river are being eyed as fertile territory for downtown living. Prices in neighborhoods south of the river have escalated. One of the most popular neighborhoods is Travis Heights, an area east of South Congress Avenue, south of Riverside Drive, and west of I-35.

Homes in Travis Heights vary from 50-year-old bungalows to newer models, restored or relocated in this quiet neighborhood of rolling hills and large oaks, just minutes from downtown. The smallest bungalow in Travis Heights can cost upwards of $250,000, larger homes $300,000 plus.

The popularity of the neighborhood has prompted gentrification and infilling on its southern borders, along streets like West Mary, where small homes now sell for $150,000. The South Congress Avenue corridor is undergoing rapid change. Once known for its X-rated movie theaters, streetwalkers, and even an old feed store, the wide avenue is now alive with restaurants, antiques shops, bakeries, boutiques, and a software store.

The changes have affected the Bouldin Creek neighborhood, located west of South Congress Avenue, north of Oltorf Street. Older homes in this area are being snapped up by buyers eager to live near downtown. The neighborhood remains a mix of rundown houses, fixer-uppers, and newly renovated homes. In the middle of this diverse neighborhood is one of Austin's most famous restaurants, Green Pastures, an upscale restaurant housed in what was once a Victorian-era family mansion. The southern portion of this area has a distinct Hispanic flavor, with popular Mexican bakeries and restaurants occupying the corner lots. (For more information on dining in this neighborhood, see our Restaurants chapter.)

The area south of Town Lake, west of Lamar Boulevard, and east of MoPac is one of Austin's most popular, older neighborhoods. Zilker Park wraps around the northern end of the area, while the Barton Creek Greenbelt winds around its western perimeter. Older homes in the Zilker neighborhood are much sought after, and prices begin at about $200,000 plus. Farther south is the Barton Hills neighborhood where homes built 30 years ago are selling for $200,000 plus. The area has two critically acclaimed elementary schools, Zilker and Barton Hills, and enjoys quick access to downtown.

South Austin has continued to march southward, and neighborhoods age much like tree rings as the visitor drives south along the area's three major north-south streets—South Congress Avenue, South First Street, and Manchaca Road.

Much of the area between Oltorf and U.S. 290 West is a mixture of older homes in working-class neighborhoods, some of them with a strong Hispanic flavor; others are home to free-spirit Austinites who frequent the area's ethnic restaurants.

South of U.S. 290 West, low- and middle-income homes, many of them built in the 1970s, give way to newer subdivisions. South of William Cannon Drive, neighborhoods like Cherry Creek, Southwest Oaks, Buckingham Estates, and Texas Oaks offer low- to midpriced homes, many of them dubbed "starter homes," that sell in the $125,000 plus range. These are traditional subdivisions with duplexes or apartments on the outer flanks of the neighborhood, single-family homes on the inner streets, and shopping facilities at nearby major intersections. Like most new homes in Austin, yards are enclosed with 6-foot privacy fencing, and most homes are constructed with at least the front wall faced in the local limestone or brick.

It is clear to anyone driving on I-35 south of the city that growth is pushing the Austin suburbs farther and farther south. Small communities like Buda are now the focus of new home developments, some aimed at offering a country lifestyle, others targeted at middle income families who are having a difficult time finding comfortable, larger homes at affordable prices.

Southwest

In 1980, the intersection of South Lamar Boulevard and U.S. 290 West was bordered by a sheep farm. Now it is home on all four sides to shopping centers, and a major highway construction project has created a whirligig of flyovers and underpasses to speed traffic in all directions. A Neiman-Marcus outlet store now stands where the sheep once grazed.

Southwest Austin, roughly defined as the area south of U.S. 290 West and west of Brodie Lane, is one of the fastest-growing areas of the city, despite efforts to slow growth through restrictive city planning ordinances (see our Politics and Perspectives chapter). Much of the area sits above the recharge zone for the southern portion of the Edwards Aquifer, in the Barton Creek watershed. But the area's pleasant topography and easy access to downtown via MoPac has proved too much of a lure.

The Austin city limits do encompass much of this area, but a tiny island of real estate called the City of Sunset Valley marks the entrance to Southwest Austin. This area has few homes but has fast become a shopping mecca for residents in this part of Austin. Two large farm homesteads occupied much of the small community for years but now have been sold to retail developers. Since Sunset Valley has a lower sales tax than the City of Austin, the shops here enjoy an advantage over other area merchants.

Brodie Lane flows through Sunset Valley. In 2000 evidence of the rising prices of land within a short driving distance to downtown became clear when a developer declared his plans to build homes in the $350,000 range just off Brodie Lane in Sunset Valley. Brodie Lane is lined with several large apartment complexes, then an area of smaller, lower priced homes before reaching Shady Hollow and the

Estates of Southland Oaks. These two far southwest neighborhoods feature new homes on large 1.5-acre lots that sell in the $250,000 range.

West of Sunset Valley, U.S. 290 West passes through a community called Oak Hill. This area was settled in the 1840s and has long been a part of Austin, but it has clung to its name and some of its identity as a small community in the escarpment above the city. It was known by a variety of names until the locals settled on Oak Hill around the turn of the last century. The name is appropriate since the land here rises above the city and is shaded by hundreds, if not thousands of live oaks.

The massive U.S. 290 West construction project has stripped the Oak Hill area of some its personality. One wag erected a sign when construction began asking "Will it still be Oak Hill when there are no oaks and no hill anymore?" The old highway was lined with a few small strip centers erected in pseudo Old West style that gave Oak Hill its country character. One symbol of the old Oak Hill remains, the Rock Store, now a pizza restaurant (see our Restaurants chapter), built by pioneer James Patton. It took Patton 19 years to build the store; he finished in 1898. The local elementary school is named in his honor.

Oak Hill is also the site of Convict Hill—a neighborhood is named in its honor. Here, from 1882 to 1886, convict labor was used to quarry limestone for the construction of the Texas Capitol. The stone was used in the capitol's basement. During the operation, eight convicts died and are buried somewhere in the neighborhood on the hill in unmarked graves. The hill stands above the highway just as it splits with U.S. 290 West heading toward Johnson City and Highway 71 heading northwest to the Highland Lakes. The split is called the "Y" by Austin residents.

Oak Hill is now surrounded by several new neighborhoods and a large Motorola plant close to the Y. The neighborhoods here are popular because of the proliferation of oak trees and the relatively easy commute into town. A non-rush-hour ride

from the Y to downtown is about 15 minutes, and even a rush hour commute is faster than a ride into the city from northwest suburbs.

Neighborhoods in this area include Westcreek, Maple Run, Legend Oaks, and The Village at Western Oaks. Homes range from $140,000 for a smaller 1,500-square-foot home to $250,000 plus.

Southwest of the Y and south of Slaughter Lane is the Circle C Ranch development, named for the ranch that once operated in this area. This development was built under the auspices of a Municipal Utility District, a MUD, a device created by the legislature and much used in the Houston area by developers who sold bonds to support the infrastructure in nonincorporated areas. In early 1998 Circle C was annexed into Austin, but not without protest from some of the homeowners.

Environmentalists had opposed the Circle C construction, but developers and residents boast of its attractive assets, including a large greenbelt, golf course, swim center, and community building. There are plans to add more amenities, including recreational and business centers. The developer, Gary Bradley, also donated Circle C land to house the nearby Lady Bird Johnson National Wildflower Research Center (see our Attractions chapter). Land also was donated for a veloway and nature trail for bicycle riders and walkers. Homes range from $160,000 to $400,000.

Development does not stop at the Austin southwest city limits. There are several rural neighborhoods along F.M. 1826, known as Camp Ben McCullough Road, which runs southwest off U.S. 290 West, just west of the Y. Other developments can be found farther along U.S. 290 West toward the Hays County line and Dripping Springs. Most of these homes are on larger lots, over an acre or two, and attract homebuyers who want a little rural atmosphere but a short commute into the city. Some of the homes are quite large, and prices range from $250,000 to much higher.

The push to the Southwest and West continues at a fast pace and rural ranchland, some of it quite beautiful with creeks, live oak stands, and wildflower pastures, is being subdivided, often into what some Texans dub "ranchettes"—1, 2, or 10 acre plots. Even once small, quiet communities like Johnson City, boyhood home of President Lyndon B. Johnson (see our Day Trips chapter), are being eyed by Austinites who work in the city but like the peace and quiet of the countryside. Those seeking a piece of the rural lifestyle can expect to pay for the pleasure with prices beginning in the $250,000 plus range.

West

As noted earlier, the area known as Clarksville, just east of MoPac (Loop 1), once was a half mile outside the city limits. Today the Austin city limits do not extend much beyond that, but the hills above the city are home to people who consider themselves Austinites. For our purposes, West Austin is the area west of MoPac and north of U.S. 290 West and south of Lake Austin and R.M. 2222.

Within the city limits, West Austin means two of the city's most prestigious neighborhoods. West of MoPac, between Enfield Road in the south and West 35th Street in the north are Tarrytown and Brykerwoods.

In the last century this part of Austin was home to several large estates. After World War II, the landowners began to subdivide the land. The neighborhoods have been built out over a period of 50 years by a variety of builders, and homes vary in size and personality. Price is consistent—it's high. The tiniest cottage in this area can cost $300,000, while large homes can sell for several million dollars. But the sheer variety of homes, the old trees, and beautifully landscaped gardens make this a favorite location.

The same amount of money can buy a whole lot more house in other parts of the city, but the Tarrytown or Brykerwoods address is still sought after. Many of the city's business and political leaders live in this area. Its proximity to downtown, the two highly rated elementary schools in the area, Casis and Brykerwood, plus the neighborhood's "village" atmosphere attracts homebuyers.

In addition to several small European-style shopping centers with cafes and shops, there are neighborhood churches, several parks, and the nearby Lions Municipal Golf Course. One of the city's popular swimming pools, Deep Eddy, is in this area.

Another of Austin's prestigious addresses is not in Austin at all. West Lake Hills is an incorporated city that overlooks downtown from the western hills, west of MoPac and east of Loop 360 (Capital of Texas Highway). A major attraction for homeowners in this area is the highly rated Eanes Independent School District, which encompasses West Lake Hills and much of the surrounding area. (See our Schools and Child Care chapter for more information.)

West Lake has its own city government, newspaper, the *West Lake Picayune,* and personality. Many of the homes are on steep, curved roads that have wonderful views of the downtown skyline. Homes in West Lake are varied in price, size, and style but generally are more expensive than most areas in Austin. Few "starter" homes are available in West Lake, and even small homes cost $250,000 plus. Prices generally begin in the $350,000 range.

Tucked in between the southeast corner of West Lake Hills and MoPac is the small incorporated community of Rollingwood. Home prices here are generally upscale and expensive, but some older homes can be found in the $250,000 range. Several large mansions line the cliffs above Town Lake in the Rollingwood area.

The major thoroughfare in West Lake Hills is R.M. 2244, popularly known as Bee Caves Road. This winding, hilly road is lined with several shopping centers that serve the West Lake community. Growth has been a hot issue for West Lake residents, also, particularly the proliferation of large retail centers at the intersection of Bee Caves Road and Loop 360 (Capital of Texas Highway).

The development along Loop 360 is an indication of the boom in the hills west of Austin. The highway was originally planned as a scenic loop with few traffic lights. It has maintained its scenic quality, but there are now several major intersections along the roadway, many leading to new subdivisions. The homebuyer who plans to spend $250,000 and wants more than a two-bedroom/one-bath Tarrytown cottage has a multitude of choices in the western environs of Travis County.

Just west of Loop 360 and south of Bee Caves Road is Lost Creek, a neighborhood of large family homes on generously sized lots carved out of the hillsides on the eastern edge of Barton Creek. The creek, which feeds Barton Springs Pool, runs through the Lost Creek Country Club. On the western banks of the creek is the Lost Creek Estates development, and a little farther north is The Estates of Barton Creek, home of the Barton Creek Country Club. The development of the Barton Creek club was hard fought by environmentalists, but the developers have won recognition for their environmentally sensitive golf course design and landscaping methods. Homes in this area begin around $250,000 and go up and up.

The hills south of Lake Austin and north and west of West Lake Hills are home to an ever-increasing number of developments of large, comfortable homes priced beginning at $200,000 and going up into the half-million-dollar-and-beyond range. Among them are Rob Roy, Davenport Ranch, West Rim, and The Preserve. They remain outside the Austin city limits, but some are likely to be targeted for annexation by the City of Austin.

City leaders have defended annexation plans, saying Austin must not become a city where suburban flight threatens the city's viability. Many of the area's higher priced homes are being built west of the city in the Hill Country. The hottest building areas are also outside Austin, and sales taxes show businesses also are moving to the new suburban areas. While West Lake Hills is beyond the city's reach, new subdivisions are not. Davenport Ranch has been placed on the city's annexation list.

East of Lake Austin and south of R.M. 2222 are high-priced developments along the riverbank and in the city limits, including Cat Mountain with homes starting at $300,000.

West of Austin, out toward Lake Travis, are several new developments and one well-known, longtime incorporated resort area called Lakeway. The latter offers a variety of homes and condominiums that vary in price from $150,000 to a half-million dollars. Popular as a retirement and weekend home area, Lakeway offers a golf course, boating and tennis facilities, even a small airfield. Newer developments "out at the lake," as Austinites call it, are the Steiner Ranch, with new homes from $210,000, and St. Andrews at Lakeway, courtyard homes from $130,000.

Northwest

On the north bank of Lake Austin, prices are not quite as steep as those developments west and south of the river. These new, comfortable family neighborhoods feature large homes with prices beginning in the $200,000 range. Shepherd Mountain features homes from $210,000, while Jester Estates has large homes from $240,000 to the $350,000 range.

The neighborhoods east of Loop 360 and west of MoPac feature a variety of homes, some enjoying stratospheric views and prices approaching $500,000. Generally, older homes in this area are closer to MoPac and are priced much lower. Homes in Highland Hills, south of Far West Boulevard and west of MoPac, are priced in the $150,000 range.

This pattern holds true for much of the northwest area. Older neighborhoods—old is relative in this part of Austin—dating from the early 1980s and on flatter sections of land inside the city limits are priced in $100,000 to $200,000 range. Newer developments, usually outside the city limits on the hillsides and canyons to the west, are more expensive.

Northwest Austin is particularly attractive to employees working for the major high-tech companies, many located along U.S. 183 North, dubbed Research Boulevard as it flows through Northwest Austin. Once a lonely highway that led out of the city, the boulevard is now a major urban roadway, lined with a multitude of shopping centers. Small communities that were once simply a gas station and a house or two along the road, places like Jollyville and Pond Springs, are now busy intersections where the shopping centers boast sushi bars and Korean take-out.

South of Research are several neighborhoods built around the private Balcones Country Club. Homes in this area are in the $200,000-plus range.

The northwest corridor has seen the area's most explosive growth, and Austin has spilled over the Travis County line and into Williamson County. Anderson Mill Estates, one of the first Northwest Austin subdivisions with midsized homes in the $150,000-plus range, is actually in Williamson County and has a different tax rate. Children living in this area attend schools in the Round Rock Independent School District. While Austin has annexed a corridor of land along Research Boulevard, into Williamson County and to the Cedar Park city limits, beyond that strip fire, police, and EMS services are the responsibility of Williamson County authorities.

The residential area to the east and west of Research beyond Anderson Mill Road has seen home prices become static as market diversity increased. The growth along the Research Boulevard corridor also has led to long commute times for residents who have jobs in other areas of the city, a factor that may have contributed to static home prices.

North

The area north of R.M. 2222, known as Koenig Lane between MoPac and I-35, is a mixture of older, middle-class neighborhoods and some rundown areas. There has been periodic talk of turning Koenig Lane into a major east-west boulevard—the debate over east-west traffic flow is a perennial political topic—but it remains a four-lane urban road (see our Politics and Perspectives chapter).

Generally to the west of Burnet Road, particularly in the Allandale neighborhood along Shoal Creek, there are many spacious 1960s-era, ranch-style homes that fetch prices in the $175,000-plus range. The advice of a knowledgeable Realtor is well advised in shopping North Austin. There are pockets of wonderful older homes that have survived the urban onslaught of strip shopping centers and suburban flight, but there are also rundown neighborhoods.

Just as in South Austin, the farther a visitor drives toward the city limits the newer the homes become. Many of the northern subdivisions are touted as ripe territory for "starter homes."

Adjacent to the northern city limits is a planned community, Wells Branch, developed as a Municipal Utility District

(MUD). Wells Branch has a variety of homes, apartments, and condominiums ranging in price from $100,000 up to $180,000. The MUD is well designed and landscaped. Shops and gas stations have inconspicuous signs that give the area a well-groomed look.

Northeast

Throughout the 1990s boom, the area east of I-35 and north of U.S. 290 East escaped much of the growth frenzy found in other parts of the city. But the location of a large Samsung facility in the area just outside the city, plus the relocation of several government office buildings to light industrial parks in the northeast, has prompted suburban development. The new developments are, for the most part, targeted at middle-income families, with prices beginning around $120,000. A few farther out toward the small town of Manor list at lower prices.

Meanwhile, the older neighborhoods within the northeast sector of the city are being eyed as gentrification targets, particularly since the old airport has closed. The older ranch-style homes built in the 1960s are attracting buyers who want to pay around $120,000, knowing they have a fixer-upper on their hands.

East

Roughly defined as east of I-35, south of U.S. 290 East, and north of Town Lake, this large area of Austin is destined for change. Just east of the interstate in the northwest quadrant of this section is the old Robert Mueller Municipal Airport.

The city has developed a community discussion process to decide what will be done with the facility. Since it adjoins a municipal golf course in the south, many community leaders have called for a mixed-use development of housing, shops, and recreational facilities. The airport closing already has had an impact on

prices of homes formerly in the flight path of the old facility.

Immediately to the north of the airport and to the southwest are two older neighborhoods that are beginning to attract the attention of homebuyers who want to live closer to the city center. Again, this is an area where the advice of a real estate agent is invaluable. It is also a good idea to talk to neighbors and check with city planners about the future of the area.

The interstate has served as a dividing line in the city, particularly separating the predominantly older African-American and Hispanic neighborhoods that lie south of the airport. Efforts have been under way, with some success, to bring affordable housing and home ownership to this area of the city.

Austin neighborhoods are integrated, but like most other large cities, there are neighborhoods where there is an ethnic concentration. Generally, the area south of Rosewood Avenue and north of Town Lake has a distinctive Hispanic cultural flavor. Many popular Mexican restaurants are located here, also ethnic groceries and tortilla factories. Neighborhood associations in East Austin have fought to maintain their communities' identity and have resisted powerful forces, including the expanding University of Texas, which forged a compromise with area residents over condemnation rights.

Southeast

Just as the northeast has not matched Northwest Austin in growth, so Southeast Austin has not seen the boom experienced by Southwest Austin. There are many apartment complexes east of I-35 along the East Oltorf Street corridor, and there have been several entry-level subdivisions built in far Southeast Austin. Homes in this area sell in the $100,000 range.

At the southernmost point of the Austin city limits, on the east side of I-35, is one of Austin's well-known golf communities. Onion Creek was, for many years, home to the Legends of Golf tournament. The secluded country club has a variety of homes and condominiums beginning at around $250,000 for a small home.

Round Rock

For many of their Austin neighbors, Round Rock is viewed as a booming bedroom community on their northern border, a place to avoid during rush hour if you are headed north on I–35 to Dallas. But for Round Rock residents their fast-growing town is home, and they are turning to historic preservation and neighborhood planning to keep it that way.

Round Rock gets its name from a round rock. The large rock is located in the middle of Brushy Creek, which flows through what is now a city. Brushy Creek was the name of the village that sprang up here in 1852. Many of the Victorian-era homes in the town center now enjoy protective historic status.

Sam Bass, the infamous Texas outlaw, is buried in the Old Round Rock Cemetery. Until 20 years ago, the shoot-out between Sam Bass and Texas Rangers, sheriff's deputies, and local citizens was the liveliest thing that had ever happened in Round Rock. But with the growth boom

in Central Texas, things have been humming in Round Rock for the past two decades. (Demographers predict the population of Williamson County could quadruple from 176,000 to 736,000 by 2030.)

Round Rock offers a variety of new homes, ranging from small homes suitable for a young family or empty-nest couple in the $100,000 range to large homes with five bedrooms and three living areas for $300,000 and up. Some of the area neighborhoods are west of the city limits—several are in the tree-shaded countryside near Brushy Creek. The city's historic homes also are prized.

Major employers, including Dell Computer, have located in Round Rock, but many residents do commute to nearby Austin, making rush-hour traffic on I–35 a headache. There are plans to build a second north-south toll road along the right-of-way owned by the Missouri Kansas Railroad, east of the interstate. It will be known as Texas Highway 130 or MoKan, just as the major north-south highway in Austin built along the Missouri-Pacific right-of-way is called MoPac by the locals.

Round Rock does have a reputation as a good place to raise a family. The community's conservative values are touted by city boosters, and comparisons are made with the much more liberal politics and lifestyles favored in Austin. These are clichéd images, of course, but voting patterns and jury decisions tend to reinforce the two communities' respective images.

Williamson County also touts its lower crime rates compared with the more urban Austin in Travis County.

Pflugerville

Ten years ago, about 4,000 people lived in Pflugerville, the small community southeast of Round Rock and northeast of Austin. In the last three months of 1997 the same number moved into the community. This small farming community is the latest home hot spot in central Texas,

One of the attractions of living in the hills west of Austin is the beauty of the natural surroundings. In addition to the flora—the wildflowers, the live oaks, redbud trees, and cactus flowers—there is the fauna. There are many species of birds, and in late summer the monarch butterflies pass through on their way to Mexico. And then there are the deer. Some Austinites feed the neighborhood deer; others complain about them. Nurseries sell deer-resistant plants, and neighbors swap stories of how to keep the deer out of their roses (human hair clippings).

particularly for homeowners who feel priced out of the Austin market.

A four-bedroom, two-bath, 2,000-square-foot home costs a little over $100,000 in Pflugerville, much less than a comparable home in Austin. Plus Pflugerville has maintained its small-town aura, locally run schools, and low crime rate.

The area is experiencing some growing pains, and the city council has been forced to raise taxes and annex new areas to support city services. But the city is also putting taxes into city facilities like a recreation center and town library, hoping to add to the city's attractiveness as a good place to find an affordable home in which to raise a family. The new north-south MoKan highway will pass through the area.

Cedar Park

The old-timers in Cedar Park remember how the community got its name. Cedar posts were the town's main business until a few years ago. The small community on U.S. 183, northwest of Austin, was home to several cedar yards where fence posts were stacked before being shipped to ranches all over the West.

Every June, the town's history is celebrated at the Annual Cedar Chopper Festival. Before 1990 most of the festival-goers came from out of town to enjoy the parade, sample the down-home cooking, and take a carnival ride. Now, many of the town's 13,000 new residents join in the community festival.

Cedar Park is trying to hold on to its history, but it is also attempting to attract high-tech companies and other businesses to help boost the local tax rolls and make Cedar Park something more than a bedroom community by developing a pedestrian-friendly downtown center. Homes in the area, which includes the neighboring community of Leander, offer homebuyers a variety of choices from affordable three-bedroom/two-bath homes in the $100,000 range to larger

homes for around $200,000. Developers are intent on creating neighborhoods, not just suburbs.

The area also features rural homes popularly known as "ranchettes," large country homes on three- or four-acre lots with enough room for a small horse stable or a kennel run.

APARTMENTS

As the millennium began, the good news was that Austin had been enjoying a three-year apartment-building boom, but the bad news was that rents and occupancy rates were high. A January 1998 study by M/PF Research Inc. found Austin was the third most expensive rental market in the South. That trend has continued, despite a burst of apartment building activity.

Limited availability drove the marketplace, according to researchers, making Austin the 15th most expensive nationally. In early 2000, 95 percent of the area's 81,400 apartments were filled, according to Capitol Market Research of Austin.

Rental prices rose, just as home prices did in Austin, and despite a good supply rents remain high. A one-bedroom apartment in one of the city's newest developments averages $850 a month. Finding affordable housing in the rental category also is a challenge in Austin.

The area's low unemployment rate is one factor in the expensive market, according to analysts. Another factor is the city's attraction to young college graduates, many of whom are attracted to Austin by the lifestyle and the high salaries paid by high-tech industries. One local marketing firm has reported that some young newcomers were coming to the area on spec, without job offers, and finding work readily available.

But the booming economy has put some working Austinites in crisis. The Austin Tenant's Council, (512) 474-1961, a nonprofit social service agency, tries to help apartment renters who cannot afford rent increases.

Those who can afford the rents and are able to find a vacancy enjoy a lot of amenities. Most new apartment complexes are gated and provide residents with increased security. Many have security cameras in each unit that offer residents a view of the main gate and allow them to buzz visitors through after verifying their identities. Garages are an added feature, plus whole home music systems. Most have recreational facilities, including work-out rooms, swimming pools, and tennis courts. Others offer business centers.

The extras offered by the newest apartment homes include gizmos like T1 lines for Internet access, cybercafes, and built-in computer desks. Want to get away from the high-tech world? Take a book to the "reading grotto," or stroll through the rose garden. One new development in Austin also offers a potting shed, an organic fruit orchard, and herb and flower-cutting gardens.

Many of the new developments are located along the MoPac corridor, Loop 360 (Capital of Texas Highway), and in Southwest and Northwest Austin, but there also has been some development along south Congress Avenue and north of the University in Central Austin.

Apartments for Rent is a monthly magazine that offers an overview of the area rental market, including some of the newest developments and older apart-ment facilities. The *TV Guide*–size maga-zine is available at many grocery stores and can be ordered at (512) 326-1133. The guide is published in 24 states and the District of Columbia. Out-of-town resi-dents can order a complimentary copy of the Austin magazine by calling (900) 420-0040. There is a $4.00 charge for the call.

REAL ESTATE RESOURCES

There are more than 4,000 real estate agents and Realtors in the greater Austin area, some operating as individuals, others as members of large, long-established firms. Most offer relocation and custom-building services. For a complete list of agencies, contact the Austin Board of Real-tors at (512) 454-7636 (www.abor.org), or consult the Yellow Pages.

The Austin Board of Realtors (512-454-7636, www.abor.org) lists over 5,500 area properties using a new com-puter system dubbed Stellar. This Multiple Listing Service gives potential homebuy-ers an opportunity to take a tour of cen-tral Texas and see what the home market is like in various parts of the area.

THE SENIOR SCENE

What can you say about a city where one of the leading senior citizens is Willie Nelson? The graying ponytail may be one symbol of Austin's senior scene; another may be a subtle shift in attention to senior issues as more and more boomers slip into their 50s.

Of course, not all Austin's seniors are aging musicians. Among the retired ranks, or semiretired, perhaps, are astronaut James Lovell, former First Lady Lady Bird Johnson (see our Close-up in the Attractions chapter), and a host of other notables in science, the arts, and public service. Not all are famous, of course, but like so many other aging Americans they have a wealth of lifetime experience and energy to offer. Austin's active lifestyle and activist attitudes offer many outlets for that energy and experience.

Austin's population is aging, but the percentage of people over the age of 65 in the Austin area is below the national average—7 percent in Travis and Williamson Counties, compared with 12 percent in the United States. When it comes to the number of residents 65 or older, among the 77 U.S. cities with populations of over 200,000, Austin ranks 71st.

The 1990 and 2000 U.S. censuses revealed some interesting information about demographic trends in Texas. The fastest-growing segment of the state population is persons ages 25 to 44, representing around 40 percent of the Texas population, compared with about 30 percent nationally. The average age of an Austin city resident is 28.9 years.

However, as a Sunbelt state, retirees do come to Texas. They go particularly to the Rio Grande Valley near the Mexican border, where many retired Midwesterners spend their winters; San Antonio, whose extensive military infrastructure makes it attractive to retired military personnel;

and the Hill Country to which many affluent retirees are attracted by the climate and lifestyle. In Central Texas the small communities of Wimberly, southwest of Austin; Fredericksburg, west of Austin; and San Marcos, particularly along the Guadalupe River south of Austin, are attracting retirees.

In the Austin area the older-than-65 population is spread out across many neighborhoods. Austin's older neighborhoods, such as Hyde Park, Allandale, and Travis Heights, have their longtime residents. Many newcomers are attracted to the Highland Lakes area, where the many recreational facilities (see our Parks and Recreation and Golf chapters) offer amenities many seek. Two areas noted for their concentration of senior citizens are Lakeway and Lago Vista, both on Lake Travis, but these communities are by no means restricted to senior citizens.

In Round Rock and the Williamson County area, the percentage of persons older than 65 matches Travis County, 7 percent, but the number of residents younger than 18 is higher—24 percent in Travis, 31 percent in Williamson County.

Developers of retirement homes are finding Williamson County attractive because of its low crime rate, its small-town feel combined with nearby big-city health services, and, perhaps for some, its more conservative lifestyle. One major development is Del Webb's Sun City Georgetown in northern Williamson County.

Sun City is the latest manifestation of a fairly recent trend in central Texas that has seen the development of housing alternatives for retirees. Compared with some other regions of the state and other Sunbelt communities, there is not an abundance of retirement communities in the area, but the numbers are growing. However, there already have been some tensions between retired residents and the local tax districts over increasing property taxes to support the booming public school systems in Williamson County.

SENIOR RESOURCES

In response to the aging of America, local businesses are beginning to recognize a market and, in true American fashion, responding to a need. One local Austin real estate company with longtime experience in the marketplace has created a new service to help people find a new, smaller house or a home in a retirement community.

Several agencies and organizations that offer information, advice, and research on community housing and nursing homes. These are a good starting point before embarking on tours or visits to facilities aimed at attracting and serving seniors. All the experts emphasize that research and careful consideration are vital before making a move to a new home, a residential facility, or a nursing home.

The attorney general offers two publications for consumers: the *Rights of the Elderly* and *Selecting a Nursing Home*. For copies write to the Texas Attorney General, Attn: Brochure Division, P.O. Box 12548, Austin, TX 78711, or call (512) 936-1300.

Amelia Bullock Relocation Services
8008 Spicewood Lane
(512) 345-7030, (800) 531-5029
www.ameliabullock.com
The company has been an Austin presence since 1969. In addition to its services for employees relocating to Austin, the company now offers Timely Solutions, a program to help seniors move to new homes, perhaps smaller homes or homes in communities geared to the senior lifestyle.

American Association of Retired Persons (AARP)
98 San Jacinto Boulevard
(512) 480-9797
www.aarp.org
This downtown office serves as the state headquarters of the influential national group for 50-plus Americans. Well-known for its advocacy, the AARP also offers information on a variety of topics of interest to seniors. Members receive travel discounts, access to a mail-order pharmacy service, and insurance coverage. Many local chapters hold their meetings at the city's senior activity centers.

Area Agency on Aging of the Capital Area
2512 West I-35, Suite 340
(512) 916-6062
TTY 916-6016, (888) 622-9111
www.aaacap.org
This is a clearinghouse and ombudsman service agency for the 10 counties of Central Texas. It is a good resource for information on nutrition, transportation, home help, health screening, and legal services. The agency's Web site also lists a variety of links to other agencies and programs including the following:

Texas Department of Human Services
Nursing home complaints
(800) 458-9858

Adult Protective Services, Adult Abuse and Financial Exploitation Hot Line
(800) 252-5400

Texas Department on Aging, Ombudsman Hot Line,
(800) 252-2412

Nursing Facility Information Helpline
(800) 252-8016

Home Health Agency Abuse Reporting Hot Line,
(800) 228-1570

Veterans Administration Benefits
Information and Assistance,
(800) 827-1000

Legal Hot Line for Older Texans
(800) 622-2520

Alzheimer Association,
(800) 272-3900

Texas Attorney General Consumer
Helpline (800) 621-0508

Medicaid Hot Line, (800) 772-1213

Medicare Hot Line, (800) MEDICARE
(633-4227)

Austin Groups for the Elderly (AGE)
3710 Cedar Street
(512) 451-4611
www.ageofaustin.org
Housed in a wonderful Central Austin historic building, c. 1902, AGE is an umbrella agency for more than a dozen nonprofit agencies. It is worth visiting the center both to enjoy the architecture and pick up information on a variety of services—adult day care, respite care, emergency residence for abused and neglected elders, family counseling, information, referral, mental health care, and adult education. Seniors here also will find a newspaper, the *Senior Advocate,* (512) 451-7433, aimed at what one national radio host calls "seasoned" citizens, and the Senior-Net Computer Learning Center, aimed at helping seniors become computer savvy, (512) 451-1932, www.seniornet.com.

CEACO Inc. (Central East Austin
Community Organization)
2326 East Cesar Chavez Street
(512) 236-8901
Located in East Austin, not far from downtown, this community-based organization offers a variety of services and programs aimed at fostering economic, social, and self-development. CEACO offers employ-

There are perks when you hit 55. Sylvia Spade-Kershaw has written Discounts & Good Deals for Seniors in Texas, *which wraps them up in one neat package. The book is available at local bookstores.*

ment and volunteer advice and assistance, wellness classes, including stress reduction, plus transportation for area residents.

Family Eldercare
2210 Hancock Drive
(512) 450-0844
www.familyeldercare.org
Located in Central Austin, this nonprofit organization offers a wide variety of services for seniors. Eldercare receives some funds from the United Way. Programs include The Gatekeeper, a training program for social service workers and volunteers, plus business owners and members of community groups who interact with the elderly. The program trains them to identify and assist seniors who are suffering from abuse or neglect or who are being exploited.

Another Eldercare program is In Home Care and Respite Services, (512) 467-6168, which provides care for home-bound adults. There is also an Alzheimer's program as part of this service.

Volunteers are trained in the guardianship and money management program, and then they are matched with seniors who need legal guardians, representative payees, or money managers.

Eldercare also publishes the *Travis County Guide to Services for Older Adults,* which lists services for seniors. The publication costs $25 and is available by calling (512) 451-0106.

The *Retirement Community and*
Apartment Guide
(512) 476-5335
This guide is produced by Goodwill Industries under the auspices of its Older

Worker Program. The information contained in the guide is supplied by the retirement communities and senior housing facilities.

Round Rock Senior Nutrition
(512) 255-4970
Seniors in Williamson County can call this number for information about a variety of recreational, nutritional, and assistance programs offered by both government and nonprofit groups in the area.

The *Senior Advocate*
3710 Cedar Street
(512) 451-7433
www.senioradvocatenews.com
The *Senior Advocate* has grown from a newsletter to a newspaper in the past 20 years and now has an on-line presence in addition to its paper format. The goal is to provide "interesting, accurate, and vital information on issues and resources important to seniors," according to its publishers, Dave and Dana Smith. The paper has won several awards for editorial excellence and community service. In 1999 the paper won the National Mature Media Awards, ahead of such publications as *Parade* and *Essence* magazines. The paper was also honored with an Outstanding Media Coverage award from the City of Austin in 1999 for publishing employment opportunities for seniors each month at no cost to the city. The job listings are a partnership effort between Austin's Senior Programs division and Experience Unlimited, a placement agency for individuals who are 50 years of age or older.

Austin Senior's Guide *is published annually and gives tips on senior living in the Austin area, plus information on discounts and products of interest to seniors,* (512) 257-7607, www.seniorsguide.net.

Senior health care centers/ private sector
Austin's two major health care providers run medical centers aimed specifically at the needs of seniors. St. David's Healthcare Partnership (www.sdhc.com) has two clinics, both in north Austin, one at 3300 West Anderson Lane, Suite 308, (512) 901-8250; the other at 5222 Burnet Road, Suite 200 (512) 420-9775. The Seton Healthcare Network (www.seton.net) operates a senior clinic in the Lakeway area in far West Austin at 1602 Lohman's Crossing Road, (512) 261-1758.

Texas Department on Aging
4900 North Lamar Boulevard
(512) 424-6840, (800) 444-2727
www.tdoa.state.tx.us
This is a state agency designed to assist seniors. The hot line, at the 800 number listed above, offers information and referrals on senior services.

Texas Attorney General
(512) 463-2100, (800) 252-8011
www.oag.state.tx.us
Consumers may request two detailed brochures from the Texas Attorney General, the state's chief law enforcement officer who is empowered to bring suit against offending facilities, including nursing homes and residential homes for the disabled and the mentally handicapped. Both the current and previous attorneys general have filed suit to close down offending facilities. However, some consumer and advocacy groups have criticized the state legislature for allowing the nursing home industry to influence regulation. In 1997 legislation was passed aimed at responding to those criticisms. Write to: Research and Legal Support Division, Office of the Attorney General, Attn: Brochure Division, P.O. Box 12548, Austin, TX 78711.

Texas Department of Human Services (TDHS)
(512) 438-3011, (800) 458-9858
www.dhs.state.tx.us
This state agency can provide consumers with the last two years of compliance history of any facility. The agency says consumers should expect to see some compliance failures on any report, since even the most minor are listed by state inspectors. TDHS can answer four questions: How many complaints have there been in the last year? How many quality-of-care violations have there been in the past two years? When was the last visit by TDHS and why? Has the owner had other facilities recommended for closure?

Texas Department of Insurance (TDI)
(512) 463-6169, (800) 578-4677
www.tdi.state.tx.us
The state agency charged with oversight of the insurance industry in Texas provides consumers free of charge and on request with *A Shopper's Guide to Long-term Care*. This brochure is published by the National Association of Insurance Commissioners. The agency also offers a great variety of insurance publications on all kinds of policies and state regulations, many of which are helpful to newcomers.

RESIDENTIAL OPTIONS

Making a move is a major step at any age, and certainly a step that is not be taken lightly. Experts recommend carefully weighing needs, both current and future; lifestyle habits and patterns; location; and, of course, cost. Another important part of the process is to visit the community and spend time there. Apply some of the same rules experts recommend in choosing a day care center for children—visit at different times; talk to the residents and the staff; compare notes with others (important for children helping their parents find a place to live); and read the fine print.

The number of retirement communities and facilities is increasing in Central Texas, and there also are attempts to build affordable housing in Austin, a growing need as housing prices soar. We've offered a sampling. The Area Agency on Aging of the Capital Area (above) offers an extensive list.

Buckner Villas
11110 Tom Adams Drive
(512) 836-1515
www.bucknervillas.citysearch.com
This is a North Austin nonprofit rental community offering a variety of residential options in a Christian environment. The facility offers the flexibility for residents to change their environment as needs change, from independent and assisted living to nursing home care. Apartments have two bedrooms and full kitchens. The facility also has an Alzheimer's program.

The Heritage at Gaines Ranch
4409 Gaines Ranch Loop
(512) 899-8400
This rental community in West Austin opened in early 1999. The community has both independent living apartments and an assisted-living program. There is an on-site health clinic, fitness and exercise programs, dining services and 24-hour concierge, housekeeping, and transportation services.

Holiday Corporation
The Clairmont, 12463 Los Indios Trail
(512) 331-7195
The Continental, 4604 South Lamar Boulevard
(512) 892-5995
Englewood Estates, 2603 Jones Road
(512) 892-7226
Renaissance-Austin,
11279 Taylor Draper Lane
(512) 338-0995
www.holidayretirementcorp.com
This national company operates four facilities in Austin. Each offers month-to-month rentals, catering of three meals a day, weekly housekeeping, paid utilities, planned activities, and on-site resident managers. Some have beauty shop and barber facilities and transportation services.

The Island on Lake Travis
3404 American Drive
(512) 267–7107, (800) 422–4753
www.retirenet.com/theisland
Literally on an island connected by causeway to the mainland, this independent living community is designed for active seniors. Rental apartments in this Lago Vista–area facility, northwest of Austin, have 24-hour security, indoor parking, an on-site restaurant, weekly housekeeping, and recreational facilities.

i

Every Generation's Concern, a 160-page publication of Gray Panthers of Austin, is a manual to help older adults and their families make choices regarding health and social services. It is available for a $6.00 donation plus postage and handling. Call (512) 458-3738.

The Summit at Westlake Hills
1034 Liberty Park Drive
(512) 328–3775
The Summit at Lakeway
1915 Lohmans Crossing Road
(512) 261–7146
The Summit at Northwest Hills
5715 Mesa Drive
(512) 454–5900
The three retirement communities at West Lake Hills west of Austin have been dubbed "retirement living for those who aren't the retiring type." The luxury rental communities have a variety of apartments, 24-hour security, transportation, catering, an on-site health care center, and recreational activities. The three are American Retirement Corporation facilities.

Westminster Manor
Retirement Community
4100 Jackson Avenue
(512) 454–4711

This facility in Central Austin, near Seton Medical Center, has what it calls a Life Care Program, which allows residents to buy their apartments and a care program. Up to 90 percent of the entrance fee is returned to the buyer's estate, and a portion of the fee is deductible as a prepaid medical expense.

ADVOCACY

Gray Panthers of Austin
3710 Cedar Street
(512) 458–3738
www.gp-austin.org
Located in Central Austin in the same facility as Eldercare, this senior citizen advocacy group has a national reputation for its organizational skills and education workshops. The group produces several handy publications, among them *A Caregivers Manual*.

Senior Strategist Group
(512) 458–2517
Senior Strategist Group is a nonprofit speakers bureau that addresses older adult audiences on senior-related topics such as consumer advocacy, legal and financial issues, care-giving, and protection from fraud.

TRANSPORTATION

Austin Capital Metro, (512) 389–7400, www.capmetro.austin.tx.us, the area public transportation service, has several programs designed for seniors. In a city some call an elephant's graveyard for hippies, the free bus pass for seniors is called an EasyRider. These passes are free to citizens 65 and older and can be obtained by showing your Medicare card, driver's license, or Capital Metro senior ID. An ID may be purchased for $3.00 at the downtown Metro office, 106 East Eighth Street, which is open from 7:30 A.M. to 5:30 P.M.

weekdays. It just takes a few minutes to process the ID.

Groups of 20 seniors or more can request free transportation from 10:00 A.M. to 2:00 P.M. weekdays, 6:00 A.M. to 10:00 P.M. on weekends. Advanced reservations are required; call (512) 389-7583.

Capital Metro also offers curb-to-curb service and connections to medical services in some areas of the city. There is also a special transit service for the disabled. (See our Getting Here, Getting Around chapter.)

For general schedule information, call (512) 474-1200. Many grocery stores also stock bus schedules at their customer service counters.

Medi Wheels
(512) 476-6325

This service offers rides to medical appointments to people 55 or older. Please call a week in advance of your appointment.

Support Services
(512) 480-3012
www.ci.asutin.tx.us/parks/seniors

This PARD program offers nonemergency medical transportation for seniors 60 and older. Reservations are required, with 24-hour notice. Reservations can be made for medical, personal, and group travel.

LIFETIME LEARNING

Austin Community College
5930 Middle Fiskville Road
(512) 223-7000
www.austin.cc.tx.us

The city's community college has several campuses around the area (see our Higher Education chapter). In addition to a full curriculum of credit courses, ACC offers a variety of enrichment programs, some of them aimed at topics of particular concern to the elderly, including family care-giving, retirement and recreation, and aging classes.

Elderhostel
The University of Texas
(512) 471-3500
www.elderhostel.org

The University of Texas offers five-day noncredit programs in the liberal arts at seven Elderhostel sites. They are at University of Texas in Austin, Big Bend National Park in far Southwest Texas, San Antonio, Galveston, El Paso, and Fort Worth. Art, music, and literature are the themes of the various programs. Lodging, meals, and field trips are included in the $365 tuition fee.

Lifetime Learning Institute
Concordia Lutheran College, 3400 I-35
(512) 452-7661
www.concordia.edu

In fall and spring, Concordia offers several eight-week courses for people 50 and older on a variety of topics such as art appreciation, foreign languages, Texas history, financial planning, and social and political history. Tuition is $15 per course, and classes are held at a variety of locations around the city.

Seniornet
www.seniornet.com

This Web-based site provides a wide variety of information for seniors, with links to local services. In conjunction with the site there is a computer training program in Austin located at Austin Groups for the Elderly (see earlier in this chapter).

Texas Elderhostel
(512) 471-2780
www.utexas.edu/cee/texaselderhostel/

This program is a clearinghouse for information on Elderhostel programs around the state at institutes of higher learning and cultural institutions (the University of Texas programs are listed previously in this chapter). Call for a catalog, which includes information about classes held in state parks, wildlife refuges, and research institutes.

University of Texas
Continuing Education
The Thompson Conference Center
26th and Red River Streets
(512) 471-4652
www.utexas.edu/cee
This facility is near the LBJ Presidential Library on the eastern edge of the campus. Two community outreach programs offer classes for seniors. There is an annual membership program, Learning Activities for Mature People, featuring a series lecture and classes in fall, winter, and spring for $125. Three six-week programs, titled Seminars for Adult Growth and Enrichment, are offered annually in fall, winter, and spring. The cost is $195.

COMMUNITY ACTIVITIES

A wide variety of recreational activities are aimed at area seniors, and many of them can be found at a network of senior activity centers. These community facilities offer a place to meet for recreation, networking, and nutrition. Most city-run centers offer a hot lunch for a nominal fee, around $1.00.

The centers are operated by the Senior Program, which has numerous brochures and newsletters detailing programs and locations.

Activities at the centers range from arts and crafts to health and fitness classes, line dancing, mah-jongg, poetry clubs and investment clubs, pool tournaments, stamp collectors' gatherings, and outings.

Austin

Senior Programs and Service Centers
Main Office,
3726 Manor Road
(512) 480-3000
www.ci.austin.tx.us/parks/sractivity.htm
There are senior activities at all the city's recreation centers and several smaller senior centers at various locations throughout the city. There are also three designated Senior Activity Centers in the city, listed below. All have extensive senior programs and support services, and all serve a hot lunch for a small charge. Transportation is provided on request.

Conley-Guerrero
Senior Activity Center
808 Nile Street
(512) 478-7695
The daily programs here are designed to enhance the quality of life for seniors in East Austin. Seniors gather at the senior center daily to exercise. Domino sessions are a popular pastime, as are the ceramics classes. The center also arranges out-of-town trips for shopping and recreation, and there are popular regular events like Blue Jean Day and Over the Rainbow Social Evenings.

Lamar Senior Activity Center
2874 Shoal Crest Avenue
(512) 474-5921
The seniors at this Central Austin center are avid tripsters, heading off on theater and museum outings to Houston and Dallas, and visiting historic Texas sites, including the new Bush Presidential Library in College Station. Ballroom dancing is a popular activity and dances are held usually three times a week. There is also an array of classes offered in games and arts and crafts. In addition, a driving safety class is offered that grants graduates a cut in their insurance premiums.

South Austin Senior Activity Center
3911 Manchaca Road
(512) 448-0787
Bridge, dominos, and mah-jongg are popular pastimes at this South Austin center. Students in the ceramics classes can fire their creations in the on-site kiln. Oil painting classes are also offered. The center also organizes day trips to country music concerts, shopping trips to the outlet malls, and visits to major art exhibits in Dallas and Houston.

Round Rock

Round Rock Senior Center
205 East Main Street
(512) 255-4970
www.ci.round-rock.tx.us/parks-rec/
seniors
This senior activity center is open from 8:00 A.M. to 3:00 P.M. daily and offers a wide variety of senior services and recreational pursuits. The center also serves meals.

Pflugerville

Austin/Travis
County Health and Human Services
15803 Windermere Drive
(512) 251-4168
This is a senior citizen activity center that offers opportunities for recreation and interaction, plus support services and meals.

NUTRITION

Maintaining a healthy diet can be difficult for some seniors, particularly those on a tight budget or those who find themselves suddenly alone or unable to cook and shop for groceries. The programs listed below can lend a helping hand.

Meals on Wheels and More
2222 Rosewood Avenue
(512) 476-6325
www.mealsonwheelsandmore.org
This network of volunteers delivers hot, nutritious meals to the homes of over 2,000 people who can no longer prepare food for themselves or leave their homes. The program also offers other services including:

- Groceries to Go—volunteers shop for participants who are unable to make a

The Texas Silver-Haired Legislature is a nonprofit, nonpartisan group that works with the state legislature on senior issues. Delegates serve two-year terms. For participation information, contact the Area Agency on Aging of the Capital Area at (512) 916-6062.

trip to the grocery store, and deliver vital groceries to their homes.
- Medi Wheels—volunteers provide transportation to and from medical appointments for over 400 older people.
- Care Calls—volunteers brighten someone's day with a friendly telephone call, giving lonely seniors a chance to hear a friendly voice and talk to someone who will listen.
- Handy Wheels—volunteers perform minor home safety repairs such as installing smoke alarms, bathroom safety bars, house numbers, and replacing light bulbs, to the residences of the homebound.

All of these programs welcome volunteers. If you want to make a donation, check out the Web site, where you can buy Stubb's Gospel CD, music from the city's legendary barbecue joint.

Senior Support Services
(512) 480-3004
This program provides lunches every weekday to senior citizens at 18 locations in Travis County, including the city's PARD Senior Activity Centers (see previous listing). To be eligible you must be 60 or the spouse of someone enrolled in the meals program. The cost of the hot lunch is minimal, as low as 50 cents, a little more in some locations. Additional activities include shopping, field trips, educational programs, and holiday events. Free transportation also is provided with 24 hours notice. Call (512) 480-3012.

Williamson-Burnet County Opportunities Inc.
(512) 930-9011
This two-county service nutrition program offers meals-on-wheels and other nutrition services for seniors in Williamson and Burnet Counties.

Caregivers
Far Northwest Caregivers
(512) 250-5021
Lakeway Service League
(512) 261-3514
North Central Caregivers
(512) 453-2273
Northeast Austin Caregivers
(512) 459-1122
South Austin Caregivers
(512) 445-5552
Southeast Austin Caregivers
(512) 472-0997
West Austin Caregivers
(512) 472-6339
Round Rock Caregivers
(512) 310-1060
This national program relies on local churches, synagogues, and mosques to set up their own grassroots organization to reach out to needy members of the community in a variety of ways. Caregivers is a network of volunteers who help those seniors who want to remain in their homes maintain their independence. Volunteers do small but meaningful tasks for the seniors, including driving them to appointments or grocery shopping for them.

Telephone Reassurance Program
United Austin for the Elderly
(512) 476-6325
This service offers a daily contact program for seniors who live alone. Volunteers also have Phone-A-Friend, a program aimed at contacting lonely seniors.

JOB OPPORTUNITIES

The high-tech field gets a lot of attention for its youthful workforce, but there are opportunities for talented, skilled workers of all ages in Austin. One good place to find information on job availability for seniors is at the Austin PARD Web site, www.ci.austin.tx.us/parks/seniors.

Austin Senior Aides
(512) 480-3006
This PARD program matches seniors with nonprofit agencies for part-time work. On-the-job training is offered. To participate, a person must be 55 or older and have a low income.

Experience Unlimited
(512) 480-3013
This PARD program encourages individuals 50 or older to register with the program's job referral bank. One of the program's innovative programs offered lifeguard jobs to seniors at the city's swimming pools.

Old Bakery and Emporium
1006 Congress Avenue
(512) 477-5961
A PARD program provides a showcase at the Old Bakery and Emporium for talented seniors to display and sell their crafts at this downtown attraction. (See our Attractions chapter.)

Older Worker Program
Goodwill Industries,
300 North Lamar Boulevard
(512) 476-5335
www.austingoodwill.org
This program for 55 and older residents offers employment counseling, job development training, and placement assistance. Goodwill also offers training in areas, including computer skills and nurse's aide classes.

Texas Workforce Commission
South Austin Office,
4175 Friedrich Lane, Suite 200
(512) 381-1695
North Austin Office,
825 East Rundberg Lane
(512) 719-4145

East Austin Office,
3401 Webberville Road
(512) 223-5400
Round Rock Office, 1609 Chisholm Trail
(512) 244-2207
www.twc.state.tx.us
Formerly known as the Texas Employment Commission, this state agency offers employment counseling and referrals to Texas residents. The department also has a Mature Worker Services program that conducts seminars to help workers hone their interview and resume-writing skills.

VOLUNTEER OPPORTUNITIES

Opportunities abound for those with a lifetime of skills to help others in the community. From local museums to the police department, rape-crisis centers to literacy programs, the possibilities for meaningful activity are enormous. We have listed several volunteer clearinghouse organizations and groups who seek out seniors. Each year, around Christmas, the *Austin American–Statesman* publishes a comprehensive wish list from various community groups seeking either volunteers or donations.

Volunteer Solutions
www.volunteersolutions.com
In 1997 a group of MIT students was searching for a way to make the Web work for America's needy. They came up with this Web site that tries to match volunteers with nonprofit agencies. The Web site has grown and now includes several cities across the United States, including an Austin site where over 200 local nonprofits are listed. A great resource for anyone searching for a way to serve the community.

Following is a list of groups that use volunteers.

American Red Cross
www.redcross.org
Central Texas Office,
2218 Pershing Drive
(512) 928-4271
Williamson County Office
1106 South Mays Street, Round Rock
(512) 255-9899

Care Calls, (512) 476-6325

Court Appointed Special Advocates (CASA)
(512) 443-2272
www.casatravis.org

Foster Grandparents, (512) 371-6098

Retired and Senior Volunteer Program (RSVP), (512) 854-RSVP (7787)
www.rsvpaustin.org

United Way, (512) 323-1899
www.uway-austin.org

HEALTH CARE AND WELLNESS

The first hint that Austin is a city that values wellness is the constant reminder over the airport public address system: Austin is a Clean Air City. Smoking is strictly verboten in most public places, although the rise of cigar bars suggests there is a backlash to political correctness among some Austinites. Perhaps that is an indication of another much-valued community trait—tolerance.

That tolerance combined with a willingness to try new approaches also means Austin is a place where alternative therapies and health care options are widely available. Even Austin pets get to choose between traditional and alternative medical care here; one of our pets has been treated with acupuncture and Chinese herbal therapy—at the suggestion, we might add, of our "regular" vet.

Health food stores, including the flagship store of the now national and publicly traded Whole Foods Market chain (see our Shopping chapter), are not only evidence of Austin's concerns about wellness but also serve as conduits for alternative therapy information. Even the mainstream stores stock organic foods, offer herbal supplements, and sometimes have on-site massage.

In addition to concerns about diet and health care, Austin residents place a great deal of emphasis on exercise. Running, jogging, walking, swimming, and bicycling are important activities, and visitors can see daily evidence of this around Town Lake and at Barton Springs Pool (see our Parks and Recreation chapter).

Austin is consistently included on top-10 lists of great places to live in the United States, and one of the criteria is the quality of health care available in a community. There is little doubt that Austin has a wide variety of health care options and an extensive support system that relies on both experts and grassroots networks.

There is also little doubt that the city's health care system has been evolving and will continue to expand and change in the years ahead. The U.S. health care system has been undergoing some radical and profound changes in the past few decades; this, combined with Austin's growth, has created a fluid picture of the Central Texas health care infrastructure.

In the past couple of years, consolidations, expansions, and new developments have changed the medical scene. These changes are particularly apparent when reviewing the hospital and clinic scene in Austin and surrounding areas. There are two major players in Austin—the Seton Good Health Network (www.goodhealth .com) and the St. David's Healthcare Partnership (www.sdhcp.com). A third player, Scott & White, a health care provider based in Temple, Texas, is making aggressive moves into Williamson County, notably in Round Rock and Cedar Park, with plans to build an ambulatory care center in Round Rock and clinics in both Round Rock and Cedar Park. Seton has expanded in Southwest Austin and is setting up clinic facilities in the Highland Lakes area. All three regularly make business page headlines with their latest plans.

A new hospital, Heart Hospital of Austin, opened in 2000 in the area where Seton's main hospital is located, a part of the city around 35th Street and North Lamar Boulevard, viewed as a medical center.

There are several health research facilities in Austin focused on drug and therapy trials. These research facilities frequently advertise in the local media for volunteers (sometimes with pay) to participate in drug trials.

FINDING A PHYSICIAN

This can be a difficult task for newcomers to any city. Both Seton and Columbia/St. David's operate physician referral services. Seton's Physician Referral number is (512) 324-4450. For information about the St. David's system, call (512) 482-4100; for physician referral call (512) 478-DOCS (3627). Scott & White's health plan information line is (800) 758-3012. The Scott & White Clinic in Round Rock can be reached at (512) 310-3000 or toll free at (888) 883-3676.

There are also several professional organizations that offer referrals to their members. They include the Austin Travis County Chiropractic Society Referral Service, (512) 263-3434; Capital Area Psychological Association, (512) 451-4983; Texas Chiropractic Association, (512) 477-9292; Texas Psychological Association, (512) 454-2449; and the Travis County Medical Society, (512) 458-1121.

HOSPITALS

Central

Brackenridge Hospital
601 East 15th Street
(512) 324-7000
www.seton.net

The city-owned hospital serves as the regional trauma center for the Central Texas area and is served by STARflight medical helicopter services. The hospital also has a children's emergency room facility that offers state-of-the-art crisis care. After grappling with deficits, the city turned operation of the downtown hospital over to the capable hands of the Daughters of Charity, who also run the Seton Healthcare Network, which includes other hospitals and clinics in the Austin

area. The 360-year-old Catholic order has gained a reputation for providing quality health care for both insured and needy patients while managing to retain profitability in a volatile marketplace.

Brackenridge is an acute-care hospital that in addition to the trauma center, provides maternity, critical care, surgery, orthopedics, and nephrology services.

Children's Hospital
601 East 15th Street
(512) 480-1818
www.seton.net

Next door to Brackenridge, this Seton Healthcare Network facility is dedicated to the care of children, offering treatment to heart and cancer patients, long-term care for chronically ill children, and a pediatric intensive care unit. Next door to the hospital is the Ronald MacDonald House, 403 East 15th Street, (512) 472-9844, which provides affordable accommodations for the families of children being treated at the hospital.

Heart Hospital of Austin
3801 North Lamar Boulevard
(512) 407-7000
www.hearthospitalofaustin.com

This newest entry on the Austin medical scene is situated at the southern end of a large swath of land sold by the state to private developers. The original Central Market sits on a portion of the land (see our Shopping chapter), and the hospital occupies a site to the south. Focused on heart health care, the facility also has a full-service emergency room.

St. David's Medical Center
919 East 32nd Street
(512) 476-7111
www.sdhcp.com

Part of the St. David's Healthcare Partnership, this downtown hospital is an acute-care facility. Medical services include a rehabilitation center, a psychiatric center for children, maternity and reproductive technology services, and cardiac and urodynamics programs.

Seton Medical Center
1201 West 38th Street
(512) 323-1000
www.seton.net
The home base for the Sisters of Charity network of medical facilities in Austin, Seton Medical Center offers a wide range of medical and surgical services. It is in a "medical arts" area of Austin, where many of the city's physicians and medical support services are located. Offerings include a 24-hour emergency room, a neonatal center, a maternity facility, and cancer care services. It is also the headquarters for Seton's Good Health program, which focuses on wellness issues. For the families of patients, the hospital operates a nearby accommodations facility, Seton League House at 3207 Wabash Avenue, (512) 323-1999. The Seton system also includes home care programs, senior health centers, and several clinics throughout the greater Austin area.

Seton Shoal Creek Hospital
3501 Mills Avenue
(512) 452-0361
www.seton.net
This private psychiatric hospital also managed by the Seton network serves patients of all ages and is situated along a pleasant stretch of Shoal Creek in the central medical arts area of the city around 35th Street.

South

South Austin Hospital
901 West Ben White Boulevard
(512) 447-2211
www.southaustinhospital.com
St. David's operates this acute-care facility in south Austin. The hospital has a 24-hour emergency room, a cardiovascular center, maternity services, and a neurological center. It also offers lithotripsy for noninvasive kidney stone removal.

Southwest

Seton Southwest Medical Center
7900 F.M. 1826
(512) 324-9000
www.goodhealth.com
In response to the fast-growing Southwest section of the city, the Seton network opened a new medical center and emergency room in 2000 on F. M. 1826, known to the locals as Camp Ben McCullough Road. The facility is at the corner of F.M. 1826 and U.S. 290 West.

Northwest

Seton Northwest Hospital
11113 Research Boulevard
(512) 324-6000
www.seton.net
This northwest branch of the Seton network has a minor emergency center, plus 24-hour emergency room, birthing units, and maternity services. Seton also offers Good Health School wellness programs on-site, and the facility houses the Seton Northwest Sports Medicine practice. A similar facility is planned for Southwest Austin.

North

Austin Diagnostic Medical Center
12221 MoPac Boulevard North
(512) 901-1000
www.sdhcp.com
Part of the St. David's Healthcare Partnership, this north Austin hospital has acute-care medical and surgical units, a 24-hour emergency room, an outpatient surgery center, maternity facilities, a women's center, rehabilitation services, and oncology programs. The facility also houses the Austin Travel Clinic, where would-be world wanderers can receive the necessary shots and health information for travel to any part of the world.

Round Rock

Round Rock Medical Center
2400 Round Rock Avenue
(512) 341-1000
www.sdhcp.com
Following a major $28 million expansion, this acute-care hospital serves the southern Williamson County area. Part of the St. David's Healthcare Partnership, the hospital has a 24-hour emergency room, family birthing center, medical-surgical unit, intensive-care unit, cardiopulmonary services center, plus an outpatient surgery facility.

PUBLIC HEALTH SERVICES

The Austin/Travis County Health and Human Services Department, (512) 972-5400, is a joint city and county tax supported service agency that oversees the operation of 13 community clinics in the city of Austin and the surrounding area. The agency also oversees immunization outreach programs that are held in local shopping malls. The clinics offer maternity care, well-child checkups, dental services at some locations, and tests and treatment for tuberculosis, sexually transmitted diseases, and HIV. The Women, Infant and Children's Nutrition program, commonly known as the WIC program, is also administered by the health department. Fees are charged according to the ability of the patient to pay, but the agency says no one is turned away. Call (512) 416-0366 in Austin for locations (www. ci.austin.tx.us/health).

Community Clinics
Volunteer Health Care Clinic
4215 Medical Parkway
(512) 459-6002
This clinic serves patients who are not eligible for city or county support, Medicare or Medicaid, and do not have their own insurance. The clinic treats only minor illness. Donations are welcome, but no one is turned away.

People's Community Clinic
2909 North I-35
(512) 478-8924
www.pcclinic.org
Payment is on a sliding scale at this community clinic. No one is refused treatment. The clinic offers adult outpatient and pediatric medical care, free immunizations, family-planning and prenatal services, treatment of sexually transmitted diseases, and women's health services. The clinic's Web site is an excellent resource to resources for the needy.

Seton McCarthy Community Health Center
2811 East Second Street
(512) 323-4930
www.seton.net
The Seton network provides medical |care and social services for residents in the East Austin area. No one is turned away, and fees are charged on a sliding scale. The center is named for the much-loved Bishop McCarthy, now retired.

Seton South Community Health Center
3706 South First Street
(512) 323-4940
www.seton.net
The center provides similar services to those at the network's East Austin location, listed previously, including medical care and social services on a sliding-fee scale. No one is turned away.

Round Rock

Round Rock Health Clinic
2000 North Mays Street, Suite 109
(512) 255-5120
www.roundrockhealthclinic.org
Medicaid and Medicare patients are accepted at this outpatient clinic that offers well-child checkups, prenatal care, and family medicine.

Williamson County and Cities
Health District Clinic
211 Commerce Street
(512) 248-3257, (800) 890-6296
www.publichealthwilliamson.org
Williamson County and cities in the area fund local public health clinics that provide medical services on a sliding-fee scale. Screenings for diabetes and blood pressure tests for seniors are among the services provided. The clinics also offer prenatal care, well-child checkups, and testing and counseling for tuberculosis, sexually transmitted diseases, and HIV.

Cedar Park

Williamson County and Cities Health
Care District Clinic
600 North Bell, Suite 200
(512) 918-1001
www.publichealthwilliamson.org
The clinic offers medical services on a sliding-fee scale, plus diabetes and blood pressure screenings for seniors and prenatal and well-child services. Counseling for those diagnosed with tuberculosis, sexually transmitted diseases, and HIV also is available.

Hospice Austin, (512) 342-4700, www.hospiceaustin.org, serves both Travis and Williamson Counties, covering the Austin and Round Rock metropolitan area. Hospice offers medical, spiritual, and bereavement care for terminally ill patients and their families on an outpatient basis. Payment is on an ability-to-pay basis.

AIDS SERVICES

The Austin area has an extensive network of services and programs to assist and support people with HIV and AIDS. For a complete listing of the services, call the AIDS information line, (512) 458-AIDS, or contact AIDS Services of Austin (www.asaustin.org).

AIDS Services of Austin
P.O. Box 4874, Austin 78765
(512) 458-AIDS
www.asaustin.org
A clearinghouse for AIDS information in Central Texas, this agency serves HIV-positive individuals and their families. The agency also provides information on AIDS network services like the Animal Companions program, a volunteer group that provides grooming, veterinary care, in-home care, and a food bank for the pets of AIDS patients.

Community AIDS
Resource & Education (CARE)
1633 East Second Street
(512) 473-2273
CARE provides legal referrals, counseling, transportation, screening, and other services for HIV-positive individuals.

Dental Clinic
3000 Medical Arts Street
(512) 479-6633
Dental care for HIV and AIDS patients is offered on a sliding scale by this Central Austin clinic.

HIV Wellness Center
4301 North I-35
(512) 467-0088
The wellness center offers a holistic approach to care for people with HIV and AIDS. Among the therapies are nutritional counseling, acupuncture, massage, and other alternative approaches aimed at boosting the immune system.

Informe SIDA
1715 East Sixth Street
(512) 472-2001
SIDA is the Spanish acronym for AIDS. This program offers bilingual HIV/AIDS outreach and education, plus support groups and emergency assistance.

Additional AIDS resources include the following:

- Austin/Travis County Health Department, HIV Services, (512) 708–3500
- Austin Area HIV Planning Council, (512) 499–2407
- David Powell Clinic (Austin–Travis County Health Department HIV clinic), (512) 380–4300
- HIV Study Group (experimental drug trials), (512) 450–1866
- Interfaith Care Alliance (AIDS care teams), (512) 477–3213
- National Aids Hot Line, (800) 342–AIDS
- People's Community Clinic (see above), (512) 478–8942
- Pediatric AIDS League, (512) 892–4776
- Project REACH (HIV education for people of color), (512) 476–4610
- Project Transitions (hospice, assisted living, and supportive housing), (512) 454–8646
- Texas Department of Health, HIV Division, (512) 490–2505
- Waterloo Counseling Center, (512) 444–9922

SUPPORT SERVICES

There is an extensive web of support groups in the Austin area for those with medical, psychological, or family problems. The Austin Area Mental Health Association, (512) 454–7463, operates a clearinghouse to connect individuals to support groups. The listings maintained by the association are not limited to mental health care groups; they include information on medical recovery support groups and substance-abuse groups.

Support group information is also available from local chapters of national associations like the Arthritis Foundation, the American Cancer Society, and Overeaters Anonymous. These groups can be found in the Yellow Pages.

MENTAL HEALTH SERVICES

The Austin area has a wide array of mental health agencies and support services. The Austin area office of the Mental Health Association, (512) 454–7463, offers information and referral services. Following is a sampling of the major agencies and service groups.

The Arc of the Capital Area
2818 San Gabriel Street
(512) 476–7044
www.arcofthecapitalarea.org
The Arc offers support services for families with a mentally retarded member. Those programs include the following: Pilot Parent, providing support groups and other assistance for families of children with disabilities such as spina bifida, autism, cerebral palsy, or mental retardation; Project Chance, working with developmentally disabled juveniles and adults who have been involved with the criminal justice program; Community Advocacy Services, matching volunteers one on one with mentally retarded or developmentally disabled adults living in the community or at Austin State School; and Community Living Assistance and Support Services, helping many individuals who might be forced by their disabilities to live in nursing homes or other institutional settings to live in group homes or even on their own.

Austin Child Guidance Center
810 West 45th Street
(512) 451–2242
www.austinchildguidance.org
Individual, family, and group therapy are offered at the center, which also provides counseling and testing services, child-abuse services, and parent classes. Fees are charged on a sliding-scale basis.

Austin Recovery Center Inc.
8402 Cross Park Drive
(512) 997-0101
www.austinrecovery.org
The center operates a detoxification unit, plus outpatient and inpatient care for chemically dependent adults and teens.

Austin State Hospital
4110 Guadalupe Street
(512) 452-0381
www.mhmr.state.tx.us
The hospital is under the auspices of the Texas Department of Mental Health and Mental Retardation system, which includes seven other state hospitals around Texas. The Austin facility serves the 37-county Central Texas area. Approximately 300 teens and adults receive care at the hospital.

Austin is a pet-friendly city, but accidents do happen to our treasured pets. Here are several important numbers to keep handy:

- *ASPCA Animal Poison Control Center, toll-free (888) 426-4435*

- *Austin Animal Cruelty, (512) 974-5750 or 311*

- *Animal Control or report abuse and roadside animal sales, (512) 972-6060*

- *24-hour animal emergency hospitals:*
  Animal Emergency Hospital of Austin
  4106 North Lamar Boulevard
  (512) 459-4336

  Emergency Animal Clinic of Northwest Austin
  12034 Research Boulevard
  (512) 331-6121

  Emergency Animal Clinic of Northwest Austin, Southwest Branch
  4544 South Lamar, Suite 760
  (512) 899-0955

Austin-Travis County Mental Health Mental Retardation Center
1430 Collier Street
(512) 447-4141
www.atcmhmr.com
The center operates a 24-hour hot line, (512) 472-HELP, in addition to emergency psychiatric services and programs for mental illness, mental retardation, and substance abuse. Other services include psychiatric case management, vocational and educational services, diagnosis and evaluation, infant-parent training, child abuse services, and homeless services. Fees are determined by the individual's ability to pay.

Austin Women's Addiction Referral and Education Center (AWARE)
1524 South I-35, Suite 315
(512) 326-1222
www.ywcaaustin.org
This YWCA program offers chemical-dependency counseling, assessment, education, information, and referral.

People's Community Clinic
2909 North I-35
(512) 478-8924
www.pcclinic.org
This community clinic (see above) also provides mental health services and links to other community services.

St. David's Pavilion
1025 East 32nd Street
(512) 867-5800
www.sdhcp.com
This clinic, part of the Columbia St. David's Healthcare Network, provides both in- and outpatient care for men, women, and children. The pavilion has a special program for those with eating disorders.

IMMEDIATE-CARE FACILITIES

In the trade they are sometimes called "doc-in-a-box," and immediate-care facilities are springing up in shopping centers and near busy intersections throughout the area. They provide nonemergency, outpatient care for weekend gardeners with battered green thumbs, Sunday jocks, and visitors who slip and fall while getting into the Austin spirit. Call ahead for hours and specific locations, and check your insurance before you check in.

South

Pro Med Medical Care Center
3801 South Lamar Boulevard
(512) 447-9661

St. David's Medicenter
1100 South I-35
(512) 443-5995

Southwest

St. David's Medicenter
6600 South MoPac, Suite 2180
(512) 891-0168

Northwest

Pro Med Medical Care Center
13831 North Highway 183
(512) 250-0424

North

Pro Med Medical Care Center
2000 West Anderson Lane
(512) 452-0361

St. David's Medicenter
810 West Braker Lane
(512) 339-8114

St. David's Medicenter
6611 U.S. 290 East
(512) 467-2052

Southeast

St. David's Medicenter
1100 South I-35
(512) 443-5995

Round Rock

St. David's Medicenter
117 Louis Hearne Road
(512) 244-2244

ALTERNATIVE MEDICINE

Austin is a hotbed of alternative therapies and wellness programs, and some practitioners of traditional medicine also include aspects of holistic healing in their own treatments. The area's hospitals offer wellness programs, plus several fitness centers (see our Parks and Recreation chapter) formulate wellness programs for clients. There are consultants who work with employers to develop wellness and exercise programs for employees or individuals. All manner of therapies are available, including Chinese, homeopathic, ayurvedic, and Taoist tai chi. Check the Yellow Pages for alternative therapies—the acupuncture listings also include herbal and nutritional therapies.

Another good resource are the bulletin boards at local health food stores. The large outdoor bulletin board at the Whole Foods Market, Sixth Street and Lamar Boulevard, features a variety of alternative therapy providers. (See our Shopping chapter for information.)

Mark Blumenthal runs a nonprofit organization, headquartered in Austin, called the American Botanical Council. The council produces a magazine, *Herbal-Gram,* that focuses on herbal research and federal regulation of supplements. The council can be contacted at P.O. Box 201660, Austin, TX 78720, or (512) 331-8868, www.herbalgram.org.

Emergency Numbers

Emergency police, fire, and EMS Services in the Austin area	911
Police, nonemergency	311
Poison Center	(800) POISON-1
Crisis Intervention/Suicide Hot Line	(512) 472-HELP (4357) or (512) 703-1395
Social Services Referral Hot Line operated by United Way	211 or (512) 973-9203, press 2
Travis County Sheriff's Mental Health Unit	(512) 703-1345
Alcoholics Anonymous	(512) 444-0071, (512) 441-3369 (Spanish)
Safe Place for victims of rape, sexual abuse, and domestic violence	(512) 267-SAFE
Williamson County Crisis Center	(800) 460-SAFE

A WORD ABOUT ALLERGIES

Allergies. Sooner or later you're gonna get 'em. At least that is what the experts predict for many newcomers to Austin. The abundance of flora has its downside for Central Texas residents. In the winter months—December, January, and February—the junipers in the Hill Country produce pollen that sets off the "cedar fever" season—the trees are colloquially known as cedars, but they are in fact junipers. Some opine that the purple haze produced by the pollen prompted Austin to be dubbed the City of the Violet Crown. Most sufferers are too busy sniffling and wiping their watery eyes to notice the violet glow.

In spring the live oak and elm pollens bring on misery for some, then in summer there are grasses and, of course, year-round attacks by mold spores and animal dander. Not everyone succumbs, but so many do that the local television stations broadcast allergy counts on their daily newscasts. In a classic case of market supply and demand, allergists do a booming business in Austin.

HIGHER EDUCATION

Back in the 1920s and 1930s, Austin's leaders billed our city as "The Athens of the West," both in tribute to, and promotion of, the element of culture bestowed by the area's colleges and universities. While we dropped that lofty title decades ago, Austin's distinction as an eminent educational center of the South remains. Our institutes of higher education add luster to the jewel that is Austin. For its sheer size and importance in the economic development of Austin, the University of Texas stands in a class by itself. But Austin's other fine colleges and universities are vitally linked to this city in countless ways as well. The symbiosis that exists between the Austin community and its various institutes of higher education is one of the defining characteristics of the region.

One need only walk through the campuses of our institutes to get a feel for Austin's educational traditions. The sprawling UT campus with its giant shade trees, sculptures, fountains, mammoth buildings, and the 27-story UT Tower, which has become as much an Austin landmark as a UT symbol, are enough to inspire a certain reverence. The Gothic Revival–style Main Building on the St. Edward's University campus stands as a stately landmark in South Austin, while Huston-Tillotson College's elevated site overlooking downtown from the east is a living legacy to Austin's education of African Americans during Reconstruction and ever since. Austin Community College's many modern campuses around the city serve as a reminder that there's always room for more centers of learning here. Texas State University south of us in San Marcos and Southwestern University north in Georgetown frame Austin with educational foundations dating back more than a century.

Austin is a thriving intellectual community today, and our area colleges and universities serve to nourish our citizens' appetites for more and more knowledge. About 35 percent of the city's adults have had four years of college or more, and another 27 percent have had some college. More than 113,000 students are enrolled in institutes of higher education in the greater Austin area, nearly half of those at the University of Texas alone. And that doesn't include the many thousands more lifelong learners who attend workshops, seminars, or other continuing education classes every year for the joy of learning and for the benefits advanced learning extend.

Our institutes of higher education are noted also for their involvement in the community. Among UT's many public outreach efforts are programs to encourage youth to stay in school, academic residency camps that attract minority students from across the state, a criminal defense clinic that provides legal advice for those unable to afford a lawyer, and a program to help small businesses become more efficient. Huston-Tillotson is an integral force in the enrichment of the East Austin community, while the various programs and services Austin's other schools provide are aimed at the betterment of the city as a whole.

For cultural enrichment, we Austinites often turn to our colleges and universities. Art exhibits, lectures, theater, festivals, fairs, sporting events, symphonies, and jazz performances are just some of the many offerings we can enjoy on a regular basis.

The contribution these institutes have made to Austin's bright prospects for the 21st century is enormous. Austin's highly educated population was one of the attributes that attracted the high-tech industry to this area in the 1970s and one of the reasons its numbers continue to grow today. UT's outstanding research facilities act as a huge magnet for these industries, while the city's academic programs, many now aimed at training high-tech workers, continue to turn out qualified graduates.

It's impossible to imagine what life would be like in Austin without our colleges and universities. The University of Texas is not only the flagship of the state university system, it's one of the economic and cultural pillars of Austin. For decades, Austin's economy—and its reputation as an educational and political center—rested on UT and on state government. While UT's burden may be lightened now as new enterprises help drive Austin's economy, its significance to Austin will endure.

Nature endowed Austin with natural beauty—rolling wooded hills and peaceful rivers. Lawmakers, churches, and private citizens from all walks of life endowed Austin with its institutes of higher education. The Austin leaders who once envisioned "a university of the first class" could never have foreseen this.

Here, listed by size, are the colleges and universities that enrich our city.

Texas Box Office, (512) 477–6060 (charge-by-phone), www.texas boxoffice.com, is the place to go if you want tickets to UT athletics, performing arts, or any upcoming event at UT's Erwin Center.

The University of Texas at Austin
24th and Guadalupe Streets
(512) 471-3434
www.utexas.edu

The 40 acres! This fond nickname for the University of Texas at Austin (UT) dates back to 1839, when city planners set aside a 40-acre plot called College Hill to be used for an institute of higher learning. UT didn't come along for another 44 years—and almost didn't come to Austin at all. The University officially opened on that 40-acre site on September 15, 1883. Today the University of Texas at Austin's main

campus alone sits on more than 350 acres, while the university operates major research facilities on 915 additional acres around the city. UT owns the Marine Science Institute at Port Aransas, the McDonald Observatory near Fort Davis, the Winedale Historical Center near Round Top, the Bee Cave Research Center west of Austin, and writer J. Frank Dobie's ranch in Paisano. To top it off, the University of Texas at Austin is the flagship of the UT System's 15 campuses spread throughout the state. It's the city's largest employer, with 20,000 workers. And, according to fall 2003 enrollment figures, UT is the nation's largest university, with more than 51,000 students, including full- and part-time scholars.

UT faculty members have won scores of prestigious awards, honors, and medals—Nobel Prizes, Pulitzer Prizes, the National Medal of Science, and the National Medal of Technology—and have been named to distinguished societies, institutes, and academies across the nation. Many alumni have gone on to leave their mark, both on Austin and on the world. Lady Bird Johnson, Walter Cronkite, Bill Moyers, Lloyd Bentsen, and First Lady Laura Bush are all UT alumni. UT's academic programs and professional schools often rank among the top programs and schools in the country. Seven UT doctoral programs rank in the top 10 in the nation, according to the National Research Council. Civil engineering, computer sciences, aerospace engineering, classics, astrophysics/astronomy, chemical engineering, and the ecology, evolution, and behavior program all made the top-10 list.

The university's academic programs, made up of 15 colleges and schools, the Graduate School, and the Division of Continuing Education, offer more than 100 undergraduate degree programs and 170 graduate programs. Exceptional facilities abound, including the fifth-largest academic library in North America, with nearly 8 million volumes (see our chapter on The Literary Scene), the Harry Ransom

Humanities Research Center, an internationally recognized rare book and manuscript library, as well as state-of-the-art computer facilities.

UT is one of the reasons why so many people around the country get dreamy-eyed just hearing the name Austin. Before the high-tech industry came along to rocket Austin's name into the stratosphere, before the music scene crystallized to give Austin such a hip reputation, before big business discovered us, before the legions of filmmakers and tourists arrived, there was UT. While UT can't take credit for all the excitement surrounding Austin today, its contributions are enormous. Along with state government, the University of Texas has provided the foundation for much of what Austin has become. UT is noted for graduating so many students who've fallen in love with Austin's natural beauty and tolerant atmosphere that they can't bear to leave.

It's no wonder UT students and the public at large get along so well. Not only do these scholars, some of the nation's brightest, bring a palpable energy to this city (and make valuable contributions to its social consciousness—and conscience), having one of the nation's largest universities at our doorstep gives Austinites incredible opportunities for cultural and educational enhancement, for cutting-edge knowledge in an extraordinary range of professional fields—and for just plain fun. A stroll down "The Drag," the part of Guadalupe Street that runs alongside UT, will have anyone feeling like a college student in minutes. This strip, with its bookstores, restaurants, coffeehouses, shops, and markets, is the melting pot of UT and the city.

At UT's helm is Larry Faulkner, who became the university's 27th president in 1998. Faulkner, who received his doctorate in chemistry from UT and then taught at the university, came to Austin from his post as provost and vice chancellor for academic affairs at the University of Illinois at Urbana-Champaign. Faulkner arrived in Austin just a few months after

O's Campus Cafe and Catering, with one sit-down restaurant and three kiosks around the UT campus, was featured on the Food Network's The Best of Campus Hot Spots. *This fresh-food operation by the people at Austin's chic Jeffrey's restaurant, serves popular standards like breakfast tacos, as well as gourmet dishes like blackened fish sandwiches and dulce de leche cheesecake. The main location is in the ACES building at 201 East 24th Street. The Web site is www.aces.utexas.edu/ocafe.*

the university launched its largest fund-raising campaign ever.

"We're Texas" is the slogan for UT-Austin created by UT grads at Austin's mega-advertising agency GSD&M. The slogan was used to kick off UT's $1 billion seven-year fund-raiser, aimed at compensating for dwindling state support of higher education. With the campaign, the university aims to ensure that UT remains the system's flagship university in every sense of the word.

Faulker also has been front and center in UT's drive to diversify its student population. In a 1996 ruling on the case *Hopwood v. Texas,* the Fifth Circuit Court of Appeals had effectively halted the use of affirmative action in admissions, forcing UT to devise new methods to attract minority students. A 1997 state law that guarantees a slot in the university for the top 10 percent of students from every Texas high school has aided in balancing student numbers. According to preliminary enrollment figures for fall 2003, 16.3 percent of UT freshmen were Hispanic and 4.1 percent were African American—in both cases an increase over the previous year, but not as high as pre-Hopwood levels. Schools like UT that believe strongly in affirmative action welcomed the 2003 U.S. Supreme Court decision upholding the

University of Michigan's affirmative action policy. Faulkner has announced that UT will resume considering race and ethnicity in its admissions procedures by 2005 at the latest.

Faulkner, meanwhile, continues to face the challenging issue of overcrowding at UT, especially now that the university has topped 50,000 students. Just the simple fact of moving students in and out of the downtown campus each day is a major concern, let along the struggle to ensure that students don't end up feeling like longhorns—the four-legged kind.

One place on campus notorious for overcrowding is Darrel K. Royal–Texas Memorial Stadium on a football Saturday. Texas Longhorns games are often the hottest ticket in town as the university and the city turn out to support their beloved team. (See our chapter on Spectator Sports.) Football isn't the only game in town, however. Many other Longhorns teams draw big crowds, including the UT women's basketball team. UT puts great emphasis on sports and goes all out to recruit some of the nation's top athletes. As a result, Longhorns teams have won more Southwest Conference championships in all sports than any other college or university. In accordance with tradition, the UT Tower glows orange many a night celebrating major UT athletic victories. In addition to intercollegiate sports, which involve less than 500 students, UT's recreational sports program attracts about 80 percent of the student body.

For both students and members of the general public interested in continuing education, culture, and entertainment, UT offers an enormous range of options. The Performing Arts Center's public performance spaces and backup facilities, including the Bass Concert Hall and the Bates Recital Hall, rank among the top five on any American campus. The Frank C. Erwin Jr. Special Events Center hosts more than 250 annual events. The Jack S. Blanton Museum of Art has an extensive permanent collection, and the Texas Memorial Museum holds extensive teaching and research collections and an exhibition space that includes the original Goddess of Liberty statue from atop the State Capitol. Of course UT also is home to the Lyndon Baines Johnson Library and Museum (see our chapters on Attractions and The Arts).

UT sponsors two popular programs for the continuing education of Austin's adult community and for other nontraditional students. The University Extension program allows students to get college credit on a more flexible schedule. This nondegree evening program is aimed at filling students' educational gaps and continuing educational needs. University Extension offers more than 200 courses from anthropology to zoology and awards extension credit that could be applied to a degree program. The extension program also allows students to work toward a Business Foundations Certificate, classes that provide solid basics in business concepts and practices. Students don't have to be accepted to UT to enroll in any of these classes.

Much more casual is UT's Informal Classes program. This efficiently run program provides an amazing variety of workshops, short courses, and certificate programs for anyone interested. Here students can take short classes—from a couple of hours to several sessions—in hundreds of subjects, including such things as country dance, money management, creative writing, computers, and how to buy a house. Students can sign up over the phone with a credit card, and the university will mail a receipt and information on where the class is located, most often on the UT campus. (Parking can be a challenge.) UT students, senior citizens, and members of the alumni association get discounts on most classes. There are

 UT's famous "Hook 'em Horns" hand signal was first introduced at a campus pep rally—in 1955!

about six sessions per year, and schedules are available at distribution points around the city.

Austin Community College
5930 Middle Fiskville Road
(512) 223-7000
www.austin.cc.tx.us

Austin Community College, which celebrated its 32nd birthday in 2004, is the baby in the neighborhood when it comes to Austin's institutions of higher learning, most of which were born in the 1800s. Perhaps that's why we call it "junior" college. In fact, this public two-year undergraduate college is far from junior in size and in importance to the Austin area. ACC's enrollment has grown to more than 29,000 students on seven campuses around Austin. Another 18,000 students take noncredit courses at ACC campuses and at various distance learning sites around the region.

The college is the second-largest institute of higher learning in the Austin area, after the University of Texas. That is certainly welcome news to those who fought to establish ACC back in the 1960s when, according to the prevailing conventional wisdom, Austin didn't need another college, what with UT and all the city's other fine colleges and universities. In fact, earlier efforts to establish a community college failed twice. At least some of ACC's success can be attributed to its achievement in taking higher education directly to the people it serves. The college's main campuses dot the Austin map from Oak Hill in the south to Cedar Park in the north, to the racially mixed, working class area of East Austin. Each of these campuses demonstrates a strong commitment to provide education to all of Austin's residents.

Today, ACC offers two-year associate degrees and one-year certificates in 176 concentrations: 72 in applied sciences, 16 in the arts, 12 in science, and 76 certificates in technical programs. Students who graduate with an associate of arts or associate of science degree are prepared to transfer to a four-year college or university. The two-year associate of applied science degree prepares students to enter the local job market or transfer to select universities. For students studying for one-year certificates, ACC is a technical or vocational school, offering courses in such subjects as building construction, automotive technology, financial management, office administration, child development, surgical technology, and electronic technology.

As Austin's demand for high-tech workers skyrockets, ACC has established itself as one of the major learning centers focused on filling those jobs. It has invested in both technical infrastructure and in designing programs and courses of study aimed at preparing students for high-tech positions. The semiconductor manufacturing technology program and strong emphasis on classes in the software programming language Java are two of ACC's efforts in this area.

ACC also is gaining a reputation for its role in serving the specific needs of the Austin business community. Two ACC liaisons work with businesses to determine the skills they require for new employees. Then, ACC offers courses to teach those skills. Additionally, the Center for Career and Business Development offers noncredit courses that teach new or updated skills needed by the existing employees of local businesses, industries, and governmental agencies. Each year more than 16,000 employees from 1,500 companies enroll in these specialized courses, some of them designed specifically for the company.

ACC's range of courses embraces wide segments of the Austin population. Students who've dropped out of high school can prepare for their General Educational Development (GED) exam at ACC, or they may study to earn a regular high school diploma. There also are courses for adults who want to improve basic skills in preparation for college and for students who want to learn English as a second language. From there, students may choose to pursue courses in job training, with on-the-job apprenticeships leading directly to employment. An important segment of ACC's population takes classes in a wide range of academic courses, including the basics in mathematics, sciences, and language arts, that can transfer to a four-year college or university. In that regard, ACC is a strong institution, with some 4,000 of its students co-enrolled each year at the University of Texas. For that segment of the population that just can't get enough schooling, ACC offers an enormous variety of classes to audit or for credit.

In all, the last decade has proved to be an interesting time for ACC. During that decade, the college moved ahead with the opening of new campuses, developed many new programs to better serve the community, invested in programs and infrastructure, and established a strong presence in this area.

Students at Texas State University in San Marcos like to rub their hands over the landmark statue of the fighting stallions to conjure up good luck on a test. The Fight of the Stallions, a 17-foot-high sculpture on the campus, depicts two stallions engaged in a fierce battle. A nude rider attempts to subdue one horse while another rider, also nude, cowers below. The sculpture was a 1951 gift from the artist, noted sculptor Anna Hyatt Huntington, and her husband, Archer Huntington, of South Carolina.

Texas State University–San Marcos
601 University Drive, San Marcos
(512) 245–2111
www.txstate.edu
This increasingly prestigious university about 35 miles south of Austin celebrated its centennial in 2003—with a name change! Southwest Texas State University is now Texas State University–San Marcos. It's the area's third-largest institution of higher education, with more than 26,000 students. More than half its students com-mute from outside San Marcos, including many from the Austin area.

Texas State—the alma mater of President Lyndon Johnson—gets national recognition in several areas: The Association of Teacher Educators calls it one of the top-three teacher education programs in the country, the Association of American Geographers consistently ranks its geography department the best in the nation. Some faculty members in geography, speech communication, business, mathematics, and mass communication have been recognized as national leaders in their fields. Texas State is also proud of its record in recruiting ethnic minorities, which now make up 25 percent of the student body. The university, in fact, is among the top 20 producers of Hispanic undergraduate degrees in the country. Additionally, the university receives accolades for its enormous fund-raising efforts and steady increases in endowments. Its first capital campaign, concluded in 1999, raised $74.6 million on a goal of $60 million. Since 1988 the endowment has grown from $15 million to $55 million.

Texas State's geography department was the first to offer a doctoral program in 1996 and today offers two Ph.D. programs. In addition to its well-respected teaching program, the university is known for its business school. The university offers 114 undergraduate majors in education, applied arts, business, fine arts and communication, health professions, liberal arts, and science. The school also offers 81 master's and six doctoral programs. Texas State is the lead institution operating the Round Rock Higher Education Center just north of Austin.

Among the university's collections is the Southwestern Writers Collection, which includes J. Frank Dobie properties (see our chapter on The Literary Scene) as well as an extensive archive of written material that captures the literary and artistic spirit of the American Southwest. The *Lonesome Dove* archives in this collection include props and memorabilia from the film set of Texan Larry

McMurtry's epic story about cattle driving.

Texas State first opened its doors in 1903 as a teacher training college called Southwest Texas State Normal School. Through the years it became a normal college, teachers college, and then college. TS became a university in 1969. Located on 427 acres and surrounded by magnificent cypress and pecan trees, the campus sits on the banks of the San Marcos River on the edge of the Texas Hill Country. The university offers a vast range of student activities, including more than 50 special-interest organizations, 36 honorary associations, and more than 30 professional groups in addition to 20 fraternities and 10 sororities. TS athletes compete at the NCAA Division I level in eight men's and seven women's sports. The university also offers a wide range of programs for talented students in dance, band, choir, jazz, symphony orchestra, music theater, and opera.

St. Edward's University
3001 South Congress Avenue
(512) 448–8400
www.stedwards.edu

A private Roman Catholic liberal arts university, St. Edward's offers undergraduate and graduate degrees to its 4,400 students from across the United States and abroad.

Located in South Austin on 180 acres of rolling hills, the university was founded in 1885 as a college but got its start 12 years earlier when it opened as a school with just three farm boys enrolled the first year. As the school grew and began boarding students, Austin residents started referring to St. Edward's as the Catholic Farm due to the fact that it fed its faculty and staff by raising beef, grain, vegetables, and fruit on its own land. The Main Building, the imposing Gothic Revival–style building made of Texas white limestone, was dedicated in 1889—a grand structure for sure in the early Southwest. Rebuilt after a fire destroyed it in 1903, the Main Building was designated a Texas Historic Landmark in 1973.

Today, St. Edward's confers undergraduate degrees in more than 50 areas, as well as seven master's degrees in business administration, business administration in entrepreneurship, counseling, human services, computer information sciences, liberal arts, and organizational leadership and ethics. The undergraduate curriculum has been recognized by the Carnegie Foundation as among the most rigorous in the nation.

In addition to awarding degrees, the university is recognized for its tradition of producing graduates with strong values, both through required course work in ethics, philosophy, or religious studies and through its community outreach programs. It also gets high marks for its adult education program and for its efforts on behalf of Hispanic students, who make up 26 percent of the student body. St. Edward's is home to the nation's longest continuously running College Assistant Migrant Program (CAMP), a nationally recognized program that celebrated its 30th anniversary in 2003. CAMP provides freshman scholarships and financial aid to the children of migrant farmworkers. Many of the students who have taken advantage of this program over the years are first-generation college students in their families. St. Edward's has been repeatedly listed among *Hispanic Magazine*'s "Best Schools for Hispanic Students." Additionally, the school has taken the lead role in the Austin ENLACE program, designed to improve higher education opportunities for Hispanic youth.

In the 1990s St. Edward's launched its first major fund-raising campaign, called Second Century. With income generated from the effort, the university built a $6.2 million campus center, a state-of-the art academic building, and a new residence hall, which opened in 2003. The campus master plan calls for the construction of several more buildings in the coming years. The university endowment, meanwhile, has grown from $4.8 million in 1985 to more than $38 million today.

Athletes at St. Edward's compete in NCAA Division II sports. The university offers basketball, soccer, tennis, baseball, golf, and volleyball.

Southwestern University
1001 East University Avenue, Georgetown
(512) 863-6511, (800) 252-3166
www.southwestern.edu

"Chartered as the state's first university in 1840, until the 1970s it was doing the conventional thing, providing the B.A. union card for its graduates' first jobs. Then with the catalysts of the new president's vision and the generosity of three Texas foundations, it was born again as a place to prepare for the 21st century." So writes Loren Pope in the book *Colleges That Change Lives.* This book, subtitled, *40 Schools You Should Know About Even If You're Not a Straight-A Student,* is one of several guides to colleges and universities that have taken note of Southwestern University in recent years. Called one of the best sleepers in the nation and one of the buried treasures among the nation's liberal arts colleges, Southwestern University may not remain one of Texas's hidden assets much longer.

Located 28 miles north of Austin in the seat of Williamson County government and even closer to our northern neighbors in Round Rock and Pflugerville, Southwestern University is a private Methodist four-year institute of higher learning that reflects the conservative values of Georgetown itself. Its fall 2003 enrollment was a little more than 1,250, a figure the university considers ideal.

Excellent leadership during the past two decades has helped Southwestern earn growing distinction as a university of academic excellence and high admission standards. Nearly 50 percent of the 2003–04 freshman class ranked in the top 10 percent of their high school. Twenty-two percent of the university's student body are racial or ethnic minority. The school has an endowment of more than $265 million, one of the highest endowments per student in the country.

Southwestern sits on a 100-acre campus filled with trees and dotted with beautiful Texas limestone buildings constructed in the stately Richardsonian Romanesque style. The university also owns 525 more acres plus a 75-acre golf course. Consisting of the Brown College of Arts and Sciences and the Sarofim School of Fine Arts, Southwestern offers more than 35 bachelor's degrees through its liberal arts curriculum and in preprofessional programs in medicine, law, business, theology, education, and engineering.

The university's seven men's and seven women's athletic teams compete in the Southern Collegiate Athletic Conference in sports that include basketball, cross-country, golf, soccer, tennis, volleyball, and baseball. Like the other colleges and universities in our area, Southwestern offers exciting programs for the public at large, including sporting events, fine arts productions, viewing nights at the on-campus Fountainwood Observatory, readings by renowned authors such as Margaret Atwood and Michael Chabon, and lectures by nationally prominent figures, including Desmond Tutu, former President Jimmy Carter, and Bill Moyers.

Concordia University at Austin
3400 North I-35
(512) 486-2000
www.concordia.edu

Concordia Lutheran College graduated to university status in 1995 when it became a member of the Concordia University System that spans the country. Founded as

i *The Texas Tomorrow Fund gives parents and grandparents the opportunity to pay for a future college student's tuition at today's prices. The fund, backed by the State of Texas, allows investors to buy college tuition in one lump sum or make regular payments. Contracts can be obtained for any public or private college or university in Texas or at www.texastomorrowfund.com.*

Concordia Academy in 1926 by pioneers who had Wendish and German ethnic backgrounds, the school originally trained young men for ministry in the Lutheran Church. Women were admitted for the first time in 1955, and in 1979 Concordia implemented a four-year liberal arts program for undergraduates. Concordia in 1998 took its first step toward becoming a graduate-level university when it instituted a master's degree program designed for working teachers. The university, which is owned and maintained by the Lutheran Church–Missouri Synod, has strong ties to the system's 12 other universities and seminaries. Students can transfer easily between schools and take classes offered at other campuses via the Concordia University Education Network, which uses video technology to transmit and receive courses. Concordia offers 16 majors in business, education and liberal arts, and sciences. The university also offers pre-professional programs in dentistry, law, medicine, and the seminary. The most popular majors at Concordia are in accounting and business administration. Education is another popular career pathway at the university, although students are enrolled in such diverse courses of study as behavioral sciences, church music, computer science, Mexican-American studies, and Spanish.

Lutherans make up less than half of the 1,000-member student body at Concordia, which also attracts Roman Catholics, Baptists, and students from other Christian and non-Christian denominations.

On a 23-acre campus along I–35 in Central Austin, Concordia has made great strides in serving the educational needs of Austin's working adults by offering evening classes and televised courses under its adult degree program. This centrally located university also opens its doors to the public for an extensive range of cultural and academic events, including art exhibits, lectures, theater, and music performances. The University's own OAKWILT Boys gospel group, made up of faculty and staff, perform at the school

and other Texas venues. Proceeds from their CD series support the OAKWILT Scholarship Endowment for Concordia students. Concordia sponsors an annual Ethnic Fair to celebrate the city's rich ethnic diversity. The event features live performances by many of the city's ethnic singing and dancing groups as well as the sale of ethnic foods, arts, and crafts.

Huston-Tillotson College
900 Chicon Street
(512) 505–3025
www.htc.edu

Huston-Tillotson College brings much more to Austin than merely its distinctions as the city's oldest institution of higher education and its only historically black college.

In East Austin on 23 acres of rolling hills that overlook downtown, Huston-Tillotson is a center of cultural and community involvement for Austin's East-side neighborhoods and one of Austin's largest minority businesses. The college is known locally for its participation in a number of cooperative relationships with the Austin Independent School District, the City of Austin, Austin Community College, and local business and community organizations.

This private four-year undergraduate college, affiliated with the United Methodist Church and the United Church of Christ, offers bachelor's degrees in arts and science to about 680 students from a variety of cultural and ethnic backgrounds. Within the college's five divisions—business, natural sciences, social sciences, humanities, and education—students can major in 20 areas of study, including the college's notable programs of chemistry, teacher preparations, sociology, and biology.

Huston-Tillotson College dates back to the 1870s, and one of its former buildings, Allen Hall, was, according to the college, the first building in Texas or anywhere west of the Mississippi constructed for the higher education of black students. Tillotson College was established by Congrega-

If your interest in higher education runs along less traditional lines, you should know that Austin also is home to a fine culinary school, the Texas Culinary Academy (www.txca.com), a Le Cordon Bleu program; the Texas College of Traditional Chinese Medicine (www.texastcm.edu); the Lauterstein-Conway Massage School and Clinic (www.tlcschool.com); and the Texas School of Bartenders (www.bartendschool.com). Cheers!

tionalists in 1875 (although it didn't open to students until 1881), and Samuel Huston College was founded by Methodists a year later. The two colleges merged in October 1952 to become the present-day Huston-Tillotson College.

While the campus has modernized over the past century and a quarter, two of its historic buildings remain as splendid landmarks and fine examples of turn-of-the-20th-century architecture. The Evans Industrial Building, built circa 1912, was completely renovated in 1984 and designated as a Texas Historical Site. The Old Administration Building, completed in 1914, is one of the few remaining examples of the Modified Prairie Style popularized by Frank Lloyd Wright. This building was entered in the National Register of Historic Places in 1993 and is slowly being restored.

Today's campus includes two residence halls, classroom and office space, a student union, a chapel/auditorium, a health center, an athletic field, and a library with more than 80,000 volumes.

Austin Presbyterian Seminary
100 East 27th Street
(512) 472-6736
www.austinseminary.edu

Known for its excellent preparation of leaders for the church, the Austin Presbyterian Seminary has graduates serving across the country and overseas. More than 300 students are enrolled in its various academic programs. Many live on campus in the seminary's housing units. The seminary opened in 1902 and has been at its present location, on about 12 acres along the wooded banks of Waller Creek, since 1908. Austin Presbyterian Seminary offers master's degrees in arts or divinity and doctor of ministry degrees. Additionally, the seminary offers classes for nondegree students as well as continuing education courses and a yearly series of lectures. An institution of the General Assembly of the Presbyterian Church (U.S.A.), the Austin seminary is one of 10 theological institutions related to the Presbyterian Church. The school is led by President Theodore Wardlaw, who heads 22 resident faculty representing a dozen disciplines. The Stitt Library on campus has more than 150,000 volumes, with a strong representation of material in biblical studies and archeology. The library also houses the Mission Presbyterian Resource Center and the McCoy Presbyterian Historical Research Center. In 1996 the seminary opened the James I. and Hazel McCord Community Center, which houses the Stotts Fellowship Hall and Student Life Area as well as the Continuing Education and Doctor of Ministry offices, additional classrooms, and guest facilities. The Austin Presbyterian Seminary opens its doors to the public for worship services, held weekday mornings except Wednesday. Many Austinites have been married in the chapel.

SCHOOLS AND CHILD CARE

SCHOOLS

Austin is a forward-looking place and that atmosphere, plus the city's worldwide reputation as a leader in the field of computer technology, has brought more and more high-tech industries to the area. And as employment soars, all the Capital City area's 10 school districts have been affected by growth in student enrollment, whether due directly to industries within the districts, to employees searching for suitable housing nearby, or to families fleeing the big city for the more peaceful suburbs. In recent years bulging school districts have passed bond issues to build, enlarge, and improve schools at a pace many of us had never before witnessed. Some smaller districts have seen their student enrollment more than double over the past few years, and other districts are growing rapidly. In 2003 more than 166,000 students from age 3 through 12th grade attended this area's schools.

The question "Which came first, the chicken or the egg?" as it applies to education and technology has interesting implications for Austin. High-tech companies cite Austin's high-education levels as one reason for locating here, and these same companies are competing with one another for well-trained, high-quality graduates at both the high school and college levels. As a result, many of the area's high-tech industries—and scores of other farsighted businesses and industries—are investing money, time, and expertise in local school districts to help propel education levels to new heights.

Texas as a whole faces considerable challenges in its huge public school system, and beginning in the 1980s state leaders from both political parties focused on improving the state's schools and, in response to lawsuits from poor school districts, changed the financing system. When then-Governor George W. Bush assumed the state's leadership, he proclaimed that education was his number-one priority. Working with Democratic and Republican leaders in the state legislature, he embarked on major education reforms. Almost half the state's schoolchildren are economically disadvantaged, and approximately 15 percent are not proficient in English, posing significant challenges to the Texas public school system. Business leaders have played a very important role in pressing for educational reforms, recognizing the need for a well-educated 21st-century workforce. Beginning with H. Ross Perot in the 1980s, major Texas figures in the business world have stepped up to the plate to lobby for improvement to Texas schools. The involvement of business leadership is not only on the political level; business leaders in the community have stepped forward to partner with schools to promote improvements.

Accountability is a watchword of the educational system in Texas. Testing has become a vital tool in the system, and, while there are complaints that schools "teach to the test" or that too much weight is given to the results, parents and teachers generally support the rigorous testing regimen. This is the model that President Bush took to Washington. One unique aspect of the testing system allows parents to readily access the information for their child's school or district on the Internet at www.tea.state.tx.us or by ordering a profile called a Snapshot (see our Insiders' tip in this chapter).

Since 1990 students throughout the state have been required to take a new

i

To find out more about literacy pro-grams in Central Texas, or to volunteer, just ask an armadillo. Will Read—yes, he's an armadillo—is the mascot that represents the Literacy Coalition of Central Texas, an umbrella organization formed in 2003 to assist all the region's learn-to-read projects. Call (512) 223-7975 or visit www.willread.org for information.

form of standardized test that shifted the focus of assessment from minimum skills to academic skills. First came the Texas Assessment of Academic Skills (TAAS). In 2003, under the federal No Child Left Behind Act, the TASS test was replaced by the broader Texas Assessment of Knowledge and Skills (TAKS). The tests in reading, math, and writing are used in part to measure a district's and individual school's progress in raising education lev-els but also can determine if a student passes a grade level or graduates.

Many schools in the Austin area are among the nation's leaders in providing high-quality education and setting high academic standards for youth. But at the same time, some schools have been iden-tified as low performing, a problem all the state's major urban districts have faced. When a school falls into that category, state law provides a specific regimen aimed at solving the problem.

That's not to say that Texas does not provide excellent educational opportuni-ties. By 2003, 362 public and private Texas schools, including 37 in the Austin area, had been named U.S. Department of Education Blue Ribbon Schools. Estab-lished in 1982, the Blue Ribbon program was updated in 2002 under the No Child Left Behind Act. The program honors schools "that are either academically superior in their states or that demon-strate dramatic gains in student achieve-ment," according to U.S. Education Secretary Rod Paige. Recipients, he said,

are "national models of excellence that others can learn from."

The Texas Education Agency (TEA) also rates schools and school districts on a four-tier scale of Exemplary, Recog-nized, Academically Acceptable, and Aca-demically Unacceptable. In our region, only the Eanes school district earned an Exemplary rating for 2001–02, the latest results published. Dripping Springs, Lago Vista, Lake Travis, and Pflugerville earned a Recognized rating; the other five dis-tricts in the area all received Academically Acceptable ratings. The ratings are based on schools' performance on standardized tests, annual dropout rates, and atten-dance rates. The TEA ratings are issued in the fall as the school year begins and can change from year to year. For the specific ratings for a district or for a campus listed below, call the agency at (512) 463-9744 or the individual school district.

One of the biggest issues facing the state's school system today is funding. In 1993—after nine years of court cases, pub-lic debate, and failed constitutional amend-ments—the Texas Legislature passed a school finance–reform measure that included the so-called "share-the-wealth" provision. The plan, dubbed "Robin Hood" by critics, requires the state's wealthiest school districts to share their property taxes with poorer districts. The Eanes school district, for example, has consis-tently been classified a "rich" school dis-trict and has contributed to the pool. In the past few years, however, other districts in Central Texas, including Round Rock, Pflugerville, and Lago Vista, also reached property tax levels that put them into the wealthy category. Surprisingly, the Austin Independent School District also falls into this category—even though half its stu-dents come from low-income families— making it the only urban school district in the state that must send money away.

Area school district leaders agree that the plan has served poorer districts well. They argue, however, that the state's ever-growing reliance on local property taxes to pay for public education will not solve the basic problem: not enough state money being dedicated to the Texas school system. At the same time, individual schools' costs are growing as they struggle to meet Washingon-mandated improvements. Revenues from the state lottery that go toward public education have not alleviated the pressure on school budgets, and the Legislature is forced time and again to revisit the issue of school finance reform.

Naturally, there is no comparison between the cost of sending a child to a private school versus a public school. But even in wealthy public school districts, the pressure on local schools to raise money to augment their budgets is intense. Although optional, parents in all the area school districts are urged to participate in fund-raisers. These much-needed additional funds go for a wide range of purchases and improvements, including books for the school library, computers, and even repairs. Parental involvement, through the area's Parent Teacher Associations or on an individual volunteer basis, provides vital additional resources in the classrooms, offices, and libraries of the area's schools. It is not uncommon to find a dozen or more parents on any given day offering their time and skills to improve their local educational facility. School administrators agree: Higher parental involvement results in an improved learning environment. Districts also supplement their budgets through programs that involve the local business community. The Austin and Del Valle districts' Adopt-A-School and the Eanes district's Joint Venture programs, for example, call on businesses to help out by giving money, making in-kind donations, or sending volunteers for special events.

All the school districts in the Austin area operate special schools and/or programs for both physically and mentally handicapped students and those with behavioral or emotional problems. Students who require more academic challenge are provided a number of opportunities, including honors programs,

advanced-placement classes, programs for talented and gifted youth, and, in the Austin school district's case, magnet schools. The region's many Spanish-speaking students are offered bilingual classes or so-called ESL classes, where they study English as a second language.

The school year varies slightly in Central Texas but generally runs from mid-August to the third week in May, for a total of 176 school days. Children entering Austin-area schools must be 5 years old by September 1 to enroll in kindergarten. Texas also requires that all children receive immunizations to attend school.

School Districts

Austin Independent School District
Carruth Administration Center
1111 West Sixth Street
(512) 414-1700
www.austin.isd.tenet.edu
The Austin Independent School District puts great emphasis on providing high-quality education for children of all races, economic levels, and English-speaking proficiencies. The district offers a solid core curriculum that stresses math, science, reading, and writing as well as special opportunities for a full range of students, from academically superior to those with learning difficulties.

AISD provides educational opportunities for about 76,500 students on 105 campuses, including 4 for special needs students. The district's commitment to children is evidenced by the number of national honors and rankings it has received in recent years. Austin has achieved a higher than average number of National Merit Scholars and has outperformed other Texas schoolchildren on the Scholastic Aptitude Test (SAT). Nearly 20 elementary, middle, and high schools have been named Blue Ribbon schools by the U.S. Department of Education. Fifty percent of the district's students are listed as economically disadvantaged, and 20 percent have limited English proficiency. The student population at individual schools within this huge district reflects the ethnic and economic makeup of the residents themselves. So within AISD, some schools have high concentrations of upper income families while other schools have a higher concentration of economically disadvantaged families. AISD is proud of its record of regularly increasing enrollment of minority and economically disadvantaged students in honors programs and advanced-placement classes. But in a large urban district, the challenge to continue producing top-quality graduates is staggering.

Del Valle Independent School District
5301 Ross Road
Del Valle
(512) 386-3000
www.del-valle.K12.tx.us

Once a region primarily of farms and ranches, the Del Valle Independent School District has witnessed major changes of late as more and more high-tech industries, and Austin's new international airport, moved into the area. The district, located in the countryside of Southeast Austin and Travis County, serves the urban communities of Montopolis, Frontier Valley, Sunridge Park, and Pleasant Valley as well as the rural communities of Garfield, Creedmoor, Mustang Ridge, Elroy, Pilot Knob, Webberville, and Hornsby Bend.

Del Valle ISD has about 7,000 students on six elementary campuses, two junior highs, one high school, and an alternative learning center. In 1997 voters approved a school bond issue to help fund expansion of Del Valle High School and to relocate three elementary schools—Popham, Hillcrest, and Baty—that were determined to be in the flight path of the new Austin-Bergstrom International Airport. As a result of the relocations, the district's elementary schools are no longer clustered in a central location but spread throughout the area to better serve neighborhoods and encourage parental involvement.

The bond issue also included funds to expand and renovate Hornsby-Dunlap and

Smith Elementary Schools and Del Valle Junior High. Smith and Baty Elementary Schools are U.S. Blue Ribbon schools.

Seventy percent of the district's students are listed as economically disadvantaged, and 17.5 percent have limited English proficiency. Del Valle offers an excellent range of courses from preschool through high school for students of all abilities and talents. Bilingual and English as a Second Language classes are in place throughout the district. Of special note is the district's technology program, which uses computers as an integral component of classroom instruction. Through its Adopt-A-School program, Del Valle enjoys strong support of the area's business and technology community, which provides scholarships, grants, and awards.

Dripping Springs Independent School District
510 West Mercer Street, Dripping Springs
(512) 858-4905
www.dripping-springs.k12.tx.us

Located 19 miles west of Austin in Hays County, the Dripping Springs Independent School District has seen explosive growth as a result of the 1990s economic boom in the Austin area. This small district of just four schools grew by 53 percent, to 3,311 students, between 1993 and 2002. The suburban district always receives good ratings from the state. All four individual schools, in fact, are often rated Exemplary. Dripping Springs Middle School is a National Blue Ribbon school. Students taking Scholastic Aptitude Tests score among the highest in an area that already beats the national average. The district sets high standards for its students and provides advanced placement and gifted and talented programs to its academically outstanding students. The needs of mentally and physically handicapped students are addressed within the schools themselves, with the assistance and guidance of the Hays County Co-op. To deal with the problem of overcapacity, the district has improved and expanded existing schools and built a new intermediate school. Eight percent of the district's students are listed as economically disadvantaged.

Eanes Independent School District
South Don Rogers Administration Building
601 Camp Craft Road
(512) 329-3600
www.eanes.k12.tx.us

Considered one of the finest school districts in Texas, the Eanes Independent School District has earned good ratings from the state. Eanes students taking the Scholastic Aptitude Test consistently score well above the national average. This district has about 7,250 students at six elementary schools, two middle schools, and one high school. The district is the largest in the state to have all schools and the district named Exemplary by the Texas Education Agency. Seven of its nine schools, including Westlake High School, are U.S. Blue Ribbon Schools.

Eanes is one of the wealthiest school districts in Texas, and 2.1 percent of its students are listed as economically disadvantaged. Just 2 percent have limited English proficiency. Eanes enjoys the benefits of having strong support from parents and the business community. In addition to its outstanding academic programs, the district is well known for its athletic programs for both boys and girls; the district has racked up state championships in golf, football, girls basketball, and girls swimming. The Eanes Independent School District encompasses 31.2 square miles in West Austin and in the municipalities of Rollingwood and West Lake Hills. In 1998 Eanes voters rejected a hotly contested proposal to build a second high school.

Lago Vista
Independent School District
8039 Bar-K, Lago Vista
(512) 267-8300
www.lagovista.txed.net

The smallest school district in the Capital City region, the Lago Vista Independent School District has just 1,000 students in its three schools. It makes for small class sizes—and excellent schools. The district covers 35 square miles on north Lake Travis and serves the communities of Lago Vista, Point Venture, and South Jonestown Hills. Although its communities are known primarily for resort and retirement living, the district is changing as more and more families with children move into the area, many to take advantage of the high-quality education the district provides.

The district emphasizes college preparatory programs and lifelong sports. Schools provide a number of learning opportunities for children of all learning abilities, however, including special education and English as a Second Language. Students needing more challenge and enrichment are offered a Gifted and Talented program as well as a number of advanced placement and honors classes. Fourteen percent of the district's students are economically disadvantaged, compared with 50 percent statewide. Lago Vista ISD, like most others in this region, is growing. The district receives strong community support.

Lake Travis
Independent School District
3322 Rural Route 620 South
(512) 533-6000
www.laketravis.txed.net

The Lake Travis Independent School District, one of the smallest in this region with just seven schools and about 4,350 students, is located west/northwest of Austin along Lake Travis's southwest shore. The district serves many nearby communities, including Apache Shores, Bee Cave, Briarcliff, Homestead, Hudson Bend, Lake Pointe, Lakeway, The Hills, and Vineyard Bay. Once largely comprising resorts and retirement communities, the district is seeing its profile change as more families move into the area. The Lake Travis ISD offers excellent educational opportunities at all levels and provides classes and programs for both academically superior students and those requiring special help. Lake Travis High School is proud of its reputation for providing rigorous academic programs for high school students, who are required to earn credits in core subjects as well as foreign language, technology, fine arts, physical education, and health.

In addition to overall good ratings, several schools within the district have received top marks from the state. High school students taking the national Scholastic Aptitude Test have scored higher than the national average. The district also produces a steady number of National Merit Scholars annually. Lake Travis ISD, once a component of the Dripping Springs Independent School District, was formed in 1981 with just 541 students in its kindergarten through 12th grade classes. Today the district is growing rapidly and already is experiencing overcapacity in the high school.

Leander Independent School District
401 South West Street, Leander
(512) 943-5000
www.leander.isd.tenet.edu

The Leander Independent School District is northwest of Austin in Williamson and Travis counties and educates students from the communities of Leander, Cedar Park, and a part of Austin. With more than 18,000 students, Leander is now the third-largest district in this 10-district region. This district, which covers 200 square miles, much of it still undeveloped, is in another fast-growing area of Central Texas. Leander is building schools to keep up with huge enrollment increases. In fact, more than half of the district's 21 schools have been built since 1994, including two of the three high schools. The newest high school, Vista Ridge, opened in the fall of 2003. Leander ISD also has 4 middle schools, 12 elementary schools, and 2 alternative learning centers.

Leander was among the pioneers in the state to develop an educational program aimed at better preparing high school students for college or the workforce by requiring them to take classes in a specific discipline. Leander ISD provides strong core curriculum classes and, for those requiring more challenge, an honors program. Individual schools within the district consistently receive Acceptable to Exemplary ratings by the state. The average SAT score in the district is above the state and national average. Sixteen percent of the district's children are listed as economically disadvantaged, and 3.6 percent lack English proficiency.

Manor Independent School District
312 Murray Avenue
(512) 278-4000
www.manorisd.net

This small district in Northeast Austin and Travis County doubled in enrollment from 1993 to 2003 to nearly 3,000 students. One of the poorest districts in the state in 1985, it made great strides during the high-tech boom of the 1990s. The Manor ISD is home to Applied Materials, the world's largest maker of computer-chip manufacturing equipment. Samsung is opening a $1.3 billion semiconductor factory in stages. Together the companies represent thousands of jobs and major tax revenue. A large industrial park in the district houses, among other businesses, Apple Computers.

What's happening in Manor demonstrates the benefits of having dynamic businesses that lend their support to schools. Among its many contributions, Applied Materials donated money to develop an up-to-date physics lab at Manor High School. Samsung and Applied Materials are working with Austin Community College to develop a curriculum in the district to begin training students interested in the technology field. That program could bring major opportunities for students in a district traditionally made up of working-class families, farmers, and ranchers that lists 60 percent of its students as economically disadvantaged. Manor has been working to improve its ratings and the SAT scores in the district. A new high school opened in the fall of 1998, and most of the district's other facilities were enlarged. Three elementary schools, one middle school, and

an alternative high school round out the district's facilities.

Pflugerville
Independent School District
1401 West Pecan, Pflugerville
(512) 251-4159
www.pflugervilleisd.net
Located in Northeast Travis County, close to several of the area's largest high-tech industries, the Pflugerville Independent School District has seen its enrollment more than double over the past decade to about 15,300 students today. That enrollment makes Pflugerville the fourth-largest district in the region. While the major high-tech companies are not within the jurisdiction of the Pflugerville school system, residential communities are springing up throughout the district to provide homes for families moving into the area to be close to jobs in Round Rock and Austin. As a result, the district has backed an aggressive expansion campaign over the past several years that led to the construction of several new schools, including Hendrickson High School, which opened in the fall of 2003. Today the district comprises 22 campuses: 3 high schools, 4 middle schools, an alternative learning center, and 14 elementary schools.

High school students taking the national Scholastic Aptitude Test have scored above the national average, and several schools within the system have been given Good to Excellent ratings by the TEA. Sixteen percent of the district's students are listed as economically disadvantaged, and 5 percent have limited English proficiency. Pflugerville offers a Spanish bilingual program for kindergarten through 3rd grade. High school students are offered foreign language courses in French, German, Spanish, Latin, and Russian in addition to a core curriculum that includes math, science, and language arts. High school students who desire can choose from among nine vocational programs, or they can choose from among advanced placement courses and honors classes.

For detailed information on a particular public school district, including demographic breakdowns, financial information, and student test performance, order Snapshot *from the Texas Education Agency at (512) 463-9744. For information about a specific school, ask the school for a copy of the* Academic Excellence Indicator System *report, or go to www.tea.state.tx.us. These reports are invaluable for parents who want to make informed decisions about where to educate their children.*

Round Rock
Independent School District
1311 Round Rock Avenue, Round Rock
(512) 464-5000
www.roundrockisd.org
The Round Rock Independent School District, just north of Austin in northern Travis and Williamson Counties, is a focal point of community involvement. Like several other districts in this area, Round Rock ISD has a fine reputation for offering excellent educational opportunities. The district has 42 campuses: 27 elementary schools, 8 middle schools, 4 high schools, and 3 alternative learning centers.

Students taking the Scholastic Aptitude Test in the district have outscored their fellow Texans and received marks above the national average. Additionally, Round Rock has a dozen national Blue Ribbon schools, including Westwood and McNeil High Schools. Several district schools have received the top ranking from the state, and the district regularly produces a number of National Merit Scholars.

About 16 percent of the district's students are listed as economically disadvantaged, compared with 50 percent statewide. Five percent of Round Rock students are considered to have limited English proficiency, compared with 15 percent statewide.

Round Rock, the second-largest school district in this area, with more than

32,500 students, spans nearly 110 square miles in southwest Williamson County and northwest Travis County. Only the Austin school district has more students. Like some other districts in this area, Round Rock experienced severe growing pains as high-tech industries moved into the area. A fourth high school opened in 1999. In fall 2003 the district opened Round Rock Stadium, a $20.5 million, 11,000-seat football and soccer complex that is easily among the finest in the country.

Charter Schools

University of Texas Elementary School
2200 East Sixth Street
(512) 495-9705
A grand experiment in educating inner-city youth was launched in the fall of 2003 with the opening of UT's elementary charter school. The East Austin school offers students access to some of the university's most innovative teaching resources and aims to become a model for other schools throughout Texas. Students have a slightly longer school day and year, and students who do not achieve benchmarks are required to attend after-school and summer programs. The school also provides teaching experience for UT education majors. Opened as a Pre-K to 1st grade facility, the school will add a grade each year until it includes 5th grade and totals about 300 students. The charter school serves students living in the area east of I-35, south of U.S. 290, west of U.S. 183, and north of Highway 71.

"This charter school will provide an unusual opportunity for the College of Education to determine what works in improving student performances and to share these findings with schools across the state of Texas," said Manuel Justiz, dean of UT's College of Education.

Texas Academy of Excellence
2915 Webber Bill Road
(512) 708-1888

The Texas Academy of Excellence serves children from Pre-K through 5th grade. The school in East Austin, a state-funded alternative to traditional elementary schools, integrates music, art, dance, and storytelling into its comprehensive educational program. The multicultural, multiracial school introduces children to foreign languages in preschool and continues with a program designed to engage all aspects of a child's development. In addition to the core subjects of math, language arts, and science, children are presented a world view through a diversity of subject matter, including history of Texas and the United States, ancient history, multicultural history, and the geography of North and South America. The Texas Academy of Excellence received its charter in 1996, but the school itself had been run for two decades under the name Capital Creative Schools, Inc. That non-profit corporation now runs Texas Academy. About 100 students attend the school, and enrollment is limited. The school is open to all children of appropriate age, although the half-day preschool program is limited to economically disadvantaged children.

Youthworks
216 East Fourth Street
(512) 472-8220, (800) 472-8220
www.ail.org
In 1996 the State Board of Education approved its first applications for charter schools. Among the first six authorized statewide was Austin's American Institute for Learning, now called Youthworks. The school provides education and job training to students ages 16 to 21 who have dropped out of traditional schools or are considered high risk for dropping out. Students work toward earning a General Educational Development (GED) diploma. The cornerstone of the year-round open-enrollment school is the Certificate of Mastery, which guarantees that the student has acquired the skills necessary to succeed in the workplace or in college. Students receive training in computers, business,

multimedia, and theater arts. Another aspect of the charter school is its involvement with the national AmeriCorps program. For persons ages 17 through 25, the Casa Verde Builders program teaches on-the-job construction skills, and the Environmental Corps program stresses education in water-quality testing, park maintenance, and other environmental areas.

PRIVATE SCHOOLS

Whether you're looking for a parochial school, alternative learning, a college-preparatory program, or an institute for academically gifted children, Austin probably has a private school that fits the bill. If the city falls short in any category, it would be in the scarcity of high-quality boarding schools similar to those found in larger cities, especially in the East. Only St. Stephen's Episcopal School, an excellent educational institution, provides room and board for high school students. All the private schools in the area are coeducational.

In Austin, many parents opt for private schools to round out their children's religious education, although the demand for all types of private schools is growing rapidly. In response, several schools in the Austin area are adding grade levels a year at a time or expanding existing facilities, although the pressure for space keeps mounting. Many schools have extensive waiting lists and require admissions tests and/or interviews. Some schools do not accept students based on a first-come, first-served system, choosing instead to accept students who meet their requirements. Some schools offer before- and after-school care and/or extracurricular activities; parents should check with the school if those extras are important.

One of the most important recommendations we can offer, based on our experience in researching the area's private schools, is that it is imperative to visit all schools under consideration before making a final decision. A particular

school can sound wonderful over the phone or in writing but seem unsuitable for any number of reasons once you've seen the campus. The agony of choosing a private school can be lessened by determining your own list of requirements before beginning the search: Religious or nonreligious? Cost? Location? Extracurricular activities? Those are just a few of the factors that must be considered. Parents who do their research should be pleased with the range of educational styles, school sizes, and programs available. With few exceptions, they will find administrators who are eager to discuss their educational philosophy and more than willing to offer tours of their facilities. Again, space is not always available, so it's important to plan ahead. Just as the city's public schools have increased in number, so have the area's private schools, particularly Catholic schools. For the latest developments check out the Austin Diocese Web site, www.austindiocese.org. In the listings below, we've included most of Austin's largest private schools as well as a representative sampling of the area's other private schools.

Central

Concordia Academy at Austin
3407 Red River Street
(512) 248-2547
www.concordiaacademy.org
A Lutheran school, Concordia Academy opened in the fall of 2002 as a 9th grade and is adding a grade level each year until it becomes a full senior high school by the fall of 2005. Affiliated with the Lutheran Church Missouri Synod, the school is currently on the grounds of St. Paul Lutheran School, an elementary and middle school. Concordia offers a college-preparatory program that, in addition to the core subjects, includes religion, Spanish, art, choir, band, and athletics. Enrollment is about 40 students. The school is not affiliated with Austin's Concordia University.

Huntington-Surrey School
4001 Speedway
(512) 478-4743
www.huntington-surrey.austin.tx.us
This alternative high school of about 75 students offers an academically stimulating environment for bright students who want a college-preparatory program, like to express themselves, and are willing to take on a great deal of responsibility. With a student-teacher ratio of 4 to 1, and sometimes 1 to 1, the school has no place for slackers to hide out. The educational focus is on writing, math, history, and science. Students sit around a table with the teacher to discuss lessons. The school has a morning session for freshmen and sophomores and an afternoon session for juniors and seniors. All students attend the school at midday to study foreign languages: French, Latin, Spanish, and German. The shorter-than-average school day allows students to work, perform volunteer services, or pursue outside interests such as music, dance, karate, swimming, and horseback riding for school credit. Huntington-Surrey is accredited by the Southern Association of Colleges and Schools.

Hyde Park Baptist School
3901 Speedway
(512) 465-8331
www.hpbs.org
Hyde Park Baptist School offers a Christ-centered educational program to about 900 students on two campuses. The campus on Speedway is for students from kindergarten through high school; the school in Southwest Austin, called the Bannockburn campus, is for kindergarten through 6th grade. Hyde Park is a college-preparatory, honors school that stresses educational achievement. The school aims to produce Christian individuals who are responsible, productive members of society. Hyde Park, established in 1968, is accredited by the Southern Association of Colleges and Schools. In addition to daily Bible classes, the teachings of Christ are integrated daily into the basic curriculum.

Additionally, students can choose from among three foreign languages: Latin, French, and Spanish. All elementary students are included in the schools' Excel program for gifted and talented youth. The school offers state-of-the-art computer labs for all students, a wide range of extracurricular sports activities and more than a dozen other after-school activities. The nondenominational school is sponsored by the Hyde Park Baptist Church.

Kirby Hall School
306 West 29th Street
(512) 474-1770
www.khs.org
One of Austin's most academically superior schools, Kirby Hall is an accredited college-preparatory school for students from kindergarten through 12th grade. One hundred percent of Kirby Hall graduates go on to college. Students rank three to four years above the national average on tests such as the Iowa Test of Basic Skills. In a historic brick building near the University of Texas campus, Kirby Hall is situated to allow students to walk to the university to audit classes and, with testing, achieve college credit. All the school's core curriculum classes for high school students are advanced placement classes, and many students graduate from Kirby Hall with college credit hours. This school is an independent, nondenominational Christian school for bright students who want to excel. It has no facilities for children with learning disabilities or for students with discipline problems. Entrance exams and uniforms are required. About 180 boys and girls attend Kirby Hall in classes that average 16 students in size.

Lycee Francais d'Austin
1507 North Street
(512) 302-3183
www.lyceeaustin.com
Founded in 2001, the Lycee Francais d'Austin aims to provide a quality French-American curriculum in a multicultural environment to students of all nationalities. Subjects are taught by native speakers in

both French and English. Spanish also is taught at all grade levels. The French curriculum closely follows guidelines set by the French Ministry of National Education. The school offers classes to students age 3 through 6th grade. Lycee Francais also offers a Summer Language Immersion Camp for children ages 3 to 8. The school is a local nonprofit association formed in response to demand by Austin's Francophone community.

St. Andrew's Episcopal School
1112 West 31st Street
(512) 452-5779
www.standrews.austin.tx.us

St. Andrew's was established in 1951, making it one of the area's oldest and best-known parochial schools. St. Andrew's serves about 700 students grades 1 through 12 and offers a strong college-preparatory program. Along with a challenging core curriculum, the school offers fine arts, foreign languages, and physical education. Admission tests and interviews are required. Entrance is determined through an "applicant pool" instead of by date of application.

St. Austin's School
1911 San Antonio Street
(512) 477-3751
www.staustin.org

This Catholic parish school was established in 1917 and today educates about 245 students from kindergarten through 8th grade. Daily religious instruction is an integral part of the curriculum at all grades, and students are prepared for the sacraments of Holy Communion, Reconciliation, and Confirmation. For students in kindergarten and 1st grade, teachers use a modified Montessori approach stressing basic skills and concepts, designed to encourage students to progress at their own pace. The middle school program reinforces basic skills and emphasizes higher-order thinking skills. In addition to a strong core curriculum at all levels, students study Spanish, computers, art, music, health, and physical edu-

Girls are encouraged to "Do the Math" at the Girlstart Technology Center, 608 West 22nd Street, (512) 916-4775, an effort by leaders in the Austin technology sector to boost girls' interest in math and science. The center offers after-school classes, weekend camps, and summer day camps. Fees are on a sliding scale to encourage participation by low-income families.

cation. The music program for students in kindergarten through 5th grade is integrated with religious instruction through preparation for weekly Masses at St. Austin's Church.

Sri Atmananda Memorial School
4100 Red River Street
(512) 451-7044
www.samschool.org

The learning approach used at the Sri Atmananda Memorial School was developed in southern India and brought to Austin by the school's director, Patty Henderson. She had placed her 5-year-old son in the Indian school while the family was there on business and was impressed with the results. Students at Sri Atmananda are not assigned a classroom or a teacher but instead are allowed to select their own area of interest from among the many labs available to them: math-geography, computer, art, science, and others. All subject matter is thoroughly integrated, and teachers present material and offer structured activities, especially for older students. Children do not receive grades for their work, although the learning material presented is appropriate for each student's abilities. About 40 students from kindergarten through 9th grade attend the school, although plans are in place to extend the curriculum to 12th grade by 2005. Sri Atmananda is the only school outside India to use this method, and several of the school's teachers have received their training in that country.

South Central

Parkside Community School
1701 Toomey Road
(512) 472-2559
www.parksidecommunityschool.org
About 145 students attend this Montessori school for children from 3 years old through 6th grade. Parkside was established in 1991 and focuses on the teaching methods developed by Dr. Maria Montessori in Italy. The program allows children to express their maximum creativity and to work at their own pace under the guidance of the classroom teacher. The core classes of language arts, math, science, and social studies are covered in all classrooms along with art, drama, sewing, and others areas of study. Preschoolers can attend classes full or half days, depending on the desires of their parents. Parkside also has an after-school program for its students of all ages.

St. Ignatius, Martyr, Catholic School
120 West Oltorf Street
(512) 442-8547
www.st-ignatius.org/school/
For students in pre-kindergarten through 8th grade, St. Ignatius educates about 230 students, both members and non-members of St. Ignatius Church. The school provides a strong Christian education that includes daily scriptural readings and reflection. Children gather at Liturgy to listen to God's Word and to learn to apply it to their daily life. Additionally, St. Ignatius offers a strong core curriculum that includes literature and the language arts, science, math, physical education, and the fine arts. Upper-level students are introduced to hands-on learning in the science lab and on computers. The math program includes pre-algebra and algebra for 7th and 8th graders. Students receive instruction in preparation to receive the Sacraments of Holy Eucharist and Confirmation in 2nd grade and Reconciliation in 4th grade. The school demands parent involvement and requires parents to spend a minimum of 20 hours each year in service to the school, either at the school or at any event sponsored by the Parent Teacher Organization. St. Ignatius is accredited by the Texas Catholic Conference Department of Education.

North

Austin Montessori School—Great Northern Campus
6817 Great Northern Boulevard
(512) 450-1940
www.austinmontessori.org
Great Northern, one of three Austin Montessori campuses, is for primary students through 3rd grade. The classic Montessori classroom design displays all learning materials on shelves and allows students to act on their own initiative in order to maximize independent learning and exploration. The Montessori approach is hands-on. Children work individually and in small groups and participate in whole-class activities. Teachers, known as guides, are trained to recognize a child's particular developmental stage and offer the appropriate learning materials in social studies, math, reading, writing, art, and music as the child becomes ready to use them. Ethics, social skills, and practical life are emphasized, as the school focuses on developing the whole child. The Austin Montessori Schools are considered models for the Montessori approach, and the school has hosted observers from all over the world. The school is accredited by Association Montessori Internationale. There is a waiting list.

Austin Seventh Day Adventist Junior Academy
301 West Anderson Lane
(512) 459-8976
www.austinsdaacademy.org
About 30 students from kindergarten through 10th grade attend this Christian school, supported by four Seventh Day Adventist churches in the region. The

school is on the grounds of the Austin First Seventh Day Adventist Church and accredited by the Seventh Day Adventist School System. Students attend multi-grade classes and study from Christian and Seventh Day Adventist textbooks. Students take classes in language arts, science, social studies, and math as well as computer science and physical education. The school stresses academic achievement, and enrollment is open to anyone.

Brentwood Christian School
11908 North Lamar Boulevard
(512) 835-5983
www.brentwoodchristian.org

About 580 students attend Brentwood Christian School, a pre-kindergarten through 12th grade college-preparatory school. The school provides a Christ-centered academic environment that gives high school students a choice of degrees to pursue: standard, advanced, or honors advanced. Brentwood students score above the 90th percentile compared with students nationwide on national achievement tests. The school has an extensive extracurricular sports program for boys and girls. Established in 1963, Brentwood welcomes students from all religious, ethnic, and national backgrounds if they are seeking a solid, Christian education. The school is affiliated with the Brentwood Oaks Church of Christ and is accredited by the National Christian Schools Association. Entrance exams are required.

Paragon Prep
2001 West Koenig Lane
(512) 459-5040
www.paragonprep.com

Weekly academic competitions, cooperative projects, and an emphasis on technology are just a few of the aspects of this college-preparatory school for about 135 middle school students. Founded in 1997, Paragon Prep seeks bright, motivated students who are aiming for higher education. The independent school for students in 6th, 7th, and 8th grades uses renowned

educational material, including the Chicago Math Series curriculum and the Junior Great Books program. Paragon calls itself "Internet intensive" and provides regular access to the World Wide Web through Internet classes that emphasize research and multimedia projects. The curriculum is designed so that students returning to public school for senior high will be exceptionally prepared. Paragon expects both student and parental commitments to excellence and offers in exchange a dynamic, fun, and stimulating environment. The school aims to produce students who are well rounded, concerned for others, and knowledgeable about democratic and entrepreneurial principles. Admission is selective, based on student testing and interviews with the student and parents.

St. Louis School
2114 St. Joseph Boulevard
(512) 454-0384
www.st-louis.org

This Catholic school, located on an 18-acre campus across the street from St. Louis parish, was established in 1956 and today provides religious and secular education to more than 470 students from preschool through 8th grade. The school's well-rounded curriculum includes daily religion classes as well as language arts, math, science, health, computers, social studies, music, physical education, Spanish, and the arts. Children attend Mass weekly and are given weekly sacramental preparation to supplement the program at St. Louis parish. The school provides a stimulating and progressive academic program integrated with Catholic values and traditions. Extracurricular activities include liturgical and bell choirs, team sports, cheerleading, student council, and altar servers. St. Louis School admits students of all religious, racial, and ethnic backgrounds. The school, affiliated with the Catholic schools of the Diocese of Austin, is accredited by the Southern Association of Colleges and Schools.

South

Christ Community Christian School
8210 South First Street
(512) 282-4263
www.cccs-mustang.com
A college-preparatory program combined with a strong emphasis on Bible study at Christ Community Christian School prepares students for higher education. About 200 students from several Christian denominations attend this independent school, established in 1982. Bible study is integrated into the curriculum at lower grades, and beginning in 7th grade students take a formal Bible class. Because the school is interdenominational, class discussions of the Bible raise diverse points of view, which serve to broaden students' understanding and challenge them to do research on their own. Christ Community is committed to helping all students reach their highest potential academically but at the same time stresses the development of positive character traits such as honesty and integrity. Students taking Scholastic Aptitude Tests score well above the national average. The school has a computer lab to complement its core subject material. Students can participate in the school's extracurricular sports programs, which include volleyball, basketball, and soccer.

Mirabeau B. Lamar, the second president of the Republic of Texas, is known as the "Father of Education in Texas." Under his leadership the Republic set aside land for schools. During the Republic, however, most education was provided by private schools and churches.

Strickland Christian School
7415 Manchaca Road
(512) 447-1447
www.stricklandschool.com

First graders at Strickland Christian School use the King James Version of the Bible as their basic reader. This religiously independent, nondenominational school was established in 1961 and today provides instruction for more than 250 students from pre-kindergarten through 8th grade. The school strives to provide academic excellence and a Christian foundation. The school, developed by Texan Corine Strickland, was a leader in teaching children to read phonetically, starting in preschool, and still emphasizes developing strong readers. Its core curriculum also includes writing, spelling, and math. Children also take classes in science, social studies, and physical education.

West

Austin Montessori School
Middle School Campus
5676 Oak Boulevard
(512) 892-0826
www.austinmontessori.org
This is the only school in the Montessori system that provides classes for students in 6th through 8th grades. The school extends the Montessori curriculum developed for elementary students by Italian Maria Montessori. The program stresses individual development and hands-on learning. Teachers act as guides to help lead children along a path of learning appropriate for each child. The middle school was established in 1993 and is accredited by Association Montessori Internationale.

The Children's School
2825 Hancock Drive
(512) 453-1126
This Montessori school for children ages 2 to 9 uses a progressive approach to learning that incorporates the classic Montessori curriculum with training in computer technology. For more than 20 years, computers have been an integral aspect of the Children's School, and today's youngsters are introduced to multimedia systems and language development through the use of

computers. The technology training adds to the fundamental teaching methods of the Montessori system, which allows for the physical, emotional, and intellectual development of each child. The Montessori curriculum consists of hands-on learning in all the areas of study, including language arts, music, Spanish, art, science, physical education, and math. The Children's School is extremely popular in the Austin area, and 90 percent of those who visit the school have been recommended by a parent of a Children's School student. In addition to its complete academic program, the school offers a variety of extracurricular activities. The Children's School is accredited by the American Montessori Society. There is a waiting list to enter.

Regents School of Austin
3230 Travis Country Circle
(512) 899-8095
www.regentsschool.com

In the fall of 1998 the Regents School of Austin welcomed its first sophomore class. The school added a grade level each year until it opened for seniors in 2000. Serving about 600 students beginning in kindergarten, the Regents School is a non-denominational Christian school that integrates a college-preparatory liberal-arts program with a strong Christian education. The school looks for students who are college bound and want to be challenged. Students begin the study of Latin in 3rd grade, which the school says helps them better understand English, science, and history. Students also study language arts, history, geography, math, logic, Spanish, and the arts. The Regents School of Austin opened in 1992 and is a founding member of the Association of Christian and Classical Schools. Admissions tests and interviews are required.

St. Michael's Academy
3000 Barton Creek Boulevard
(512) 328-2323
www.stmichaelsacademy.org

St. Michael's Academy offers a rigorous academic environment for about 400 college-bound students. The school, established in 1984 and located on 50 acres in Southwest Austin, challenges students to reach their full potential and helps them achieve that goal by offering a wide range of courses. Students desiring more academic challenge can pursue an Advanced Academic Diploma with Honors, which requires the completion of 10 semester hours of honors courses in addition to writing an honors thesis. The school's success in producing top-quality graduates is reflected in the number of students accepted to the nation's leading colleges and universities, in the amount of scholarships and awards seniors receive, and in the number of National Merit Scholars the school produces. The admissions process is competitive. The school is dedicated to serving a diverse student body and to that end offers a financial-aid program that allows students of all economic backgrounds the opportunity to attend. The school, which is owned and governed by a board of trustees, is accredited by the Texas Catholic Conference Education Department.

St. Stephen's Episcopal School
2900 Bunny Run
(512) 327-1213
www.sss.austin.tx.us

Austin's only boarding school for high school students, St. Stephen's also offers day classes for coed students in 6th through 12th grades. St. Stephen's is one of Austin's most academically superior schools. It regularly produces National Merit Scholars, its seniors score well above the national average on Scholastic Aptitude Test scores, and graduates are accepted to the world's most elite colleges and universities. The school stresses Christian and community values but welcomes students from all cultures, backgrounds, and religions. In fact, it was the first integrated boarding school in the South. Its range of academic offerings is outstanding and class sizes are small, both factors in its popularity. Additionally, St. Stephen's offers "Special Academies" in theater, soccer, and tennis. Admission is competitive and requires interviews, tests, and recommendations. On 428 acres, St. Stephen's has about 630 students, including 70 from 20 different countries. An observatory opened in fall 1998. St. Stephen's was established in 1950 and is affiliated with the National Association of Independent Schools and the Southern Association of Episcopal Schools.

St. Theresa's Catholic School
4311 Small Drive
(512) 451-7105
www.st-theresa.org/school
Four-year-olds through 8th graders attend this Catholic school in Northwest Austin. On the campus of St. Theresa's Catholic Church, the school offers a full, academically challenging curriculum designed to allow its 290 students to reach their full potential. St. Theresa's students score on average in the 90th percentile on national achievement tests. St. Theresa also provides enrichment opportunities for each course of study. In addition to daily religion classes, lessons from the Bible are integrated throughout the basic core subjects. Specially trained instructors provide classes in library skills, physical education, and computer training. Students begin using computers in preschool, with a program that reinforces reading skills, and continue their technology training through middle school on the school's classroom computers and in two Internet-connected computer labs. St. Theresa offers what it calls "mastery learning," which couples a well-trained faculty with the use of advanced technology and delivery systems.

Northwest

Austin Jewish Academy
7300 Hart Lane
(512) 735-8350
www.ajcds.org
The only Jewish school in the Central Texas area, the Austin Jewish Academy

opened in fall 1997. The independent school started with kindergarten through 3rd grade and has expanded over the years to the 8th grade. The approximately 140 students at the school are motivated, creative self-starters who can work within varying degrees of structure. A strong Jewish education is part of the school's curriculum, but the school does not embrace any particular arm of Judaism or require that students be Jewish. Students study Hebrew daily and also take classes in Jewish history, prayer, Bible, and the study of Israel. The school also offers a sound core curriculum that includes language arts, math, and science as well as social studies, Spanish, art, music, physical education, geography, and world cultures. Judaic and secular studies are highly integrated. Strong parental involvement is one of the school's greatest attributes. The school is a member of the National Association for the Education of Young Children and the National Association for Supervision and Curriculum Development and is housed at the Jewish Community Center in North Austin.

Grace Covenant Christian School
9431 Jollyville Road
(512) 345-7976
www.gccschool.com
This Christian school for children in nursery school through the 8th grade strives to promote academic excellence and spiritual growth in each student. Founded in 1978, the school is affiliated with Grace Covenant Christian Church and is on the church grounds. Grace Covenant integrates a Bible-based learning environment with a strong core curriculum that includes math, science, language arts, and social studies. The school also offers enrichment classes in computer science, the fine arts, music, physical education, library, and Latin. Grace Covenant students rank in the top 25 percent of students nationwide taking the Stanford Achievement Test. The school is a member of the Association of Christian Schools International.

Hill Country Christian School of Austin
12124 Rural Route 620 North
(512) 331-7036
www.hccsa.org

Founded in 1996, Hill Country Christian School in North Austin provides a Christian and classical education to children from kindergarten through the 12th grade. The school's educational philosophy is linked to the belief that Jesus Christ is the true foundation of all knowledge and learning. The nondenominational school, affiliated with Hill Country Bible Church, is a college preparatory institution that has about 450 students. Teachings from the Bible are integrated into the school's basic curriculum, which includes language arts, math, science, history, art, music, and physical education. The Bible also is taught as a separate lesson or course, depending on the grade level. Students in the upper grades can participate in the school's extracurricular sports program. The school is pursuing accreditation through the Association of Christian Schools International.

Redeemer Lutheran School
1500 West Anderson Lane
(512) 451-6478
www.redeemerschool.net

Redeemer Lutheran School is Austin's largest Lutheran school and one of the largest of its kind in the country, with a program that encompasses preschool through 8th grade. Founded in 1955, the school aims to share the Christian faith by assisting parents in providing opportunities for spiritual, intellectual, physical, emotional, and social growth for children in a Christ-centered environment. The school follows the Texas Essential Knowledge and Skills curriculum program found in most public schools but incorporates Christ in the daily education process. Although a Lutheran school, children of all faiths are welcome to attend the school. In addition to the basic core curriculum, Redeemer Lutheran School offers music classes, Spanish, and physical education. Computers labs give students daily access to computer technology and to the Internet. The school also has an active extracurricular sports program and choirs for children of all ages. The school is affiliated with the Lutheran Church–Missouri Synod and accredited by the Lutheran School Accreditation Commission.

Summit Christian Academy
2121 Cypress Creek Road (Pre-K to 12th)
1303 Leander Drive, Leander (Pre-K to 5th)
(512) 250-1369
www.summiteagles.org

Great Hills Christian School and Cornerstone Christian School in Leander merged in 2003 to form Summit Christian Academy, serving a total of about 330 students on two campuses. An accredited college-preparatory school, Summit provides an academically challenging environment based on a Christian world view. The school offers a varied but rigorous curriculum designed to develop and encourage the creative, expressive, analytical, and critical thinking skills necessary for college admission. Nearly 100 percent of the school's graduates go on to college, and a large percentage have received scholarships to prestigious universities. The school stresses a phonics-based approach to spelling and understanding of the language arts. Specially trained teachers introduce elementary students to computer programming skills. Middle school students who qualify can enter the advanced math track to begin earning high school credit in 8th grade. The school offers a nondenominational Bible program for all students. Bible classes are taught daily, and the study of religion is integrated throughout the school's programs.

Southwest

Austin Montessori School—Sunset Trail
5014 Sunset Trail
(512) 892-0253
www.austinmontessori.org

Sunset Trail is the main campus of the Montessori system's largest school in

Austin, providing education to students from age 14 months through upper elementary level. The school, founded in 1967, teaches children according to the method developed by Dr. Maria Montessori in Italy. She believed that children possess a natural and intense desire to learn about the world and that they can absorb knowledge effortlessly. The classroom is designed with all the learning material readily available on shelves in order to maximize independent learning and exploration. The school does not use textbooks but allows children to explore concrete materials, using their hands and their minds. Teachers, known as guides, are trained to recognize a child's particular developmental stage and offer the appropriate learning materials. Children work individually or in small groups in learning science, social studies, math, reading, writing, art, and music. Ethics, social skills, and practical life are emphasized, as the school focuses on developing the whole child. In addition to regular classroom activities, students can choose to learn violin or piano using the Suzuki method, which is based on the concept that children can learn music the same way they learn to speak—by ear. There is a waiting list. Austin Montessori also has a campus for young students in North Austin and a middle school campus in West Austin.

Austin Waldorf School
8700 South View Road
(512) 288-5942
www.austinwaldorf.org
The Austin Waldorf School, the only certified Waldorf program in Texas, offers an educational program to students from age 4 through the 12th grade on 12 acres in the Oak Hill area of Austin. Waldorf schools, also known worldwide as Steiner schools, are based on the educational philosophy of Dr. Rudolf Steiner, an educator, artist, and philosopher who devised a method of instruction based on the idea that children pass through distinct developmental stages. The program is designed to engage each child's innate creativity and builds on a strong academic foundation by integrating art, instrumental music, song, stories, and crafts into the daily curriculum. The independent school teaches according to the phases of child development, offering lessons at each stage that are designed to nurture a child's imagination. Mastery of the academic disciplines is of utmost importance at the Waldorf school, where students are introduced to all major fields of human endeavor through the study of mathematics, sciences, and language arts. Students are given the opportunity to explore all aspects of a subject matter and, with the guidance of their specially trained teacher, write and illustrate their own textbooks for each lesson. The school, founded in 1980, has grown to 370 students.

Hyde Park Baptist School—Bannockburn
7100 Brodie Lane
(512) 892-0000
www.hpbs.org
This is the Southwest Austin campus of Austin's largest private school. The Bannockburn campus for students in kindergarten through 6th grade has about 165 students. Hyde Park's other school in Central Austin is a K–12 school with more than 700 students. Building on a solid Christian foundation, the school aims to produce educational achievement and offers its elementary students a wide range of opportunities, including introduction to computer technology, foreign languages, and a strong core curriculum that integrates Bible study with all areas of course work. All elementary students are included in both schools' Excel program for gifted and talented youth. Students entering the upper grades begin a college preparatory honors program, and most go on to college. The nondenominational school is sponsored by the Hyde Park Baptist Church.

Cedar Park

Hilltop Christian Academy
1150 South Bell Boulevard, Cedar Park
(512) 258-0080
www.hbt.org

Hilltop Christian Academy provides educational and religious training in a Christian environment to about 250 students from preschool through high school. On a 40-acre campus in Cedar Park, the school has two instructional buildings, each with its own library, a full-size gymnasium, playgrounds, and an athletic field. The school integrates students' Biblical education with strong academic instruction, which has earned the school a reputation for providing high-quality education. In addition to a strong basic curriculum, Hilltop Christian Academy provides a wide range of computer training in the school's two computer labs. One lab is equipped to provide therapy for students and adults with learning difficulties. A well-equipped science lab, home economics lab, and a music hall help meet the school's goal of providing students a complete education. Hilltop's extracurricular program includes a variety of athletic, fine arts, and academic endeavors. Hilltop Christian Academy is accredited by the Association of Christian Schools International.

Round Rock

Round Rock Christian Academy
301 North Lake Creek Drive, Round Rock
(512) 255-4491
www.rrca-tx.org

Round Rock Christian Academy is a nondenominational school educating about 350 students from age 4 through high school. The school aims to cultivate a heart for God, develop the mind of Christ, and provide a distinctively Christian quality education. The school supports a Christian-based curriculum using primarily the Bob Jones and ABeka text books.

Math is taught using the Saxon method. In addition to core curriculum classes of math, history, science, and language arts, classes in American sign language, drama, choir, Spanish, and logic are offered. The academy's Discovery Program, for students in 1st through 4th grades, is an after-school enrichment program providing more academic challenge to qualified students. Under the Aim program, students with learning disabilities or other special needs work with a staff educational therapist. The school is affiliated with and accredited by the Association of Christian Schools International.

CHILD CARE

For parents, few decisions arouse more angst than determining who will care for their preschool-age child while they're at work. As Austin grows, that concern intensifies as more and more parents compete for existing high quality care. Area child care referral agencies insist that excellent care can be found, especially since more emphasis is placed these days on professional care, as opposed to just babysitting. Finding high-quality child care for infants seems to be the most difficult, according to the referral agencies. In fact, they say that people who are even thinking about having a child need to get on waiting lists at accredited child care centers. Parents often do not plan ahead for infant care, believing that because infants sleep so often, care shouldn't be difficult to find or cost too much. However, because state regulations require a higher ratio of providers to infants in licensed facilities than any other age group—4 to 1—it's often not profitable for a center to provide care for the very young, so they don't.

Finding care for toddlers is not as difficult, although in the fastest growing areas, especially in North Austin, Round Rock, and Cedar Park, the challenge to locate high quality care increases. Child care in downtown Austin, with its high concentration of state office workers, also seems to be increasingly limited. Although after-school programs are offered at most schools in the capital area's 10 school districts, waiting lists can be long, so it's important to register early.

Another option is to have a child picked up by an after-school-care provider. Again, it's important to plan ahead, as these also tend to fill up in some areas. For preschoolers, parents can expect to pay between $50 and $200 a week at any one of this area's licensed child care centers or registered family child care homes.

Austin faces serious challenges in terms of availability and affordability of quality child care. The continuous recruitment and training of qualified professionals, due to high turnover rates, is just one of the obstacles the system must overcome if Austin is to meet its child care needs. Austin's Fund for Child Care Excellence (FCCE), created in 1999 by the City of Austin and St. Edward's University, is a nonprofit organization that specializes in trying to solve those issues. A $3 million grant from the Michael and Susan Dell Foundation in 2001 provided an enormous boost to the fund's efforts to, among other things, recruit and train child care providers—for free. For more information about the FCCE's programs, check out the Web site at www.fcce.org.

Choosing a day care provider gets somewhat easier for parents once they know what to look for in a facility. The Texas Department of Protective and Regulatory Services (PRS), which oversees

day care providers, lists three categories of service: licensed, registered, and listed. The agency's Web site, www.tdprs.state.tx.us, also offers histories of violations at facilities in Texas. Facilities that care for 13 or more children are considered day care centers and must be licensed by the state. Registered facilities are home care centers that accept 4 to 12 children. The standards vary somewhat for these two categories, although they both are subject to unannounced inspections by the PRS. In 1997 the Texas Legislature created the last category: listed. According to new regulations, persons who care for one to three children in their home must be listed by PRS and are subject to the same records investigations as other providers. These homes, however, are not inspected unless there is a report of child abuse or neglect. The records of all child care providers are examined through the PRS's central registry to determine if they have a record of abusing or neglecting a child. Also, all providers must submit to a criminal history check. Anyone convicted of "crimes against the family" will not be authorized to work in child care.

In addition to receiving state authorization, more and more area child care centers and home care facilities are seeking accreditation through national agencies, which certify the standards at their facilities. Although accreditations are not required by the state, an increasing number of parents are seeking out accredited facilities. The accreditation agency for licensed centers is the National Association for the Education of Young Children. For family care providers, the National Association of Family Child Care is the accrediting body. One way for parents to ensure a safe environment for their children is to make sure that the facility is authorized by the state. Authorities at PRS, however, stress that parents are the most important regulators when it comes to child care. All parents, they say, need to accept the responsibility of inspecting their children's day care center regularly and to insist that any shortcomings be corrected.

Austin's Fund for Child Care Excellence honors "family-friendly" businesses and organizations that demonstrate leadership and innovation in creating family-supportive work environments. To see if your prospective employer has received this designation, check out the fund's Web site at www.fcce.org.

Finding reliable and affordable child care, for regular daily care, occasional drop-in care, or in-home sitters, can be one of the first tasks a family faces on arrival in Austin. Some neighborhood associations provide residents with lists of baby-sitters in their areas, while parents in other areas have formed baby-sitting co-ops, in which parents take turns at sitting responsibilities. Be sure to check with your neighborhood association for information.

Several referral agencies around town can help by offering experienced guidance in the child care search and by providing parents with lists of providers from their databases. Following are some of the sitter services and referral agencies for child care that can help get you off to a good start.

A Mom's Best Friend
4505 Spicewood Springs Road
(512) 346-2229
www.moms-best-friend.com

This popular business for the busy parent provides both sitters and nannies. A Mom's Best Friend can arrange for sitters to come to your home, hotel, or even your office for the amount of time you need. References and previous employers have been checked for all sitters, and a criminal background check has been conducted on all nannies. Clients looking for a certain age group in a sitter can, with enough advance notice, make a special request from among the staff, which ranges in age from mid-20s to mid-60s. A Mom's Best Friend also offers a service it calls Mother's Helper, which includes light house maintenance as well as child care—great for the new mom. Separate housekeeping services can also be arranged.

Austin Families, Inc.
1301 South Capital of Texas Highway, Suite 210
(512) 327-7878
www.austinfamilies.org

Austin Families is a nonprofit organization that has been helping families find child care since 1978. Their extensive database includes child care providers in 10 Central Texas counties, and they are remarkably helpful when it comes to providing information.

Kidcare Finder
(512) 451-5211
www.kidcarefinder.com

This business helps families locate just the right child care provider. The Web site is informative, and the staff is knowledgeable.

Kid's Space
13376 Research Boulevard
(512) 918-2562
1401 South I-35, Round Rock
(512) 244-7774

This center in the Galleria Oaks shopping center in Northwest Austin accepts children ages 1 to 12 for drop-in child care. Kid's Space offers plenty of entertainment for children of all ages. They're open daily at 8:30 A.M. and offer service until 12:30 A.M. on Friday and Saturday nights. It's a good idea to make a reservation, but that can usually be done the day the service is required. Also call to find out about immunization requirements.

Stepping Stone Schools
12 locations around Austin
1910 Justin Lane
(512) 459-0258
www.steppingstoneschool.com

Voted "Best Child Care" in 2003 by readers of *Austin Family* magazine, the Stepping Stone School offers early-chlldhood education and an "enhancement" program for school-age kids. The schools offer a progressive curriculum and accept children from 18 months to 11 years. Some of the schools take infants also. The locally owned business has been in Austin since 1979. Check the Web site or call the administrative office, listed above, for a location near your home or work.

UrbanBaby
www.urbanbaby.com

Austin is one of the original cities in the UrbanBaby network, which touts itself as a "network of comprehensive resource guides and interactive communities for urban parents in the top metropolitan cities." The on-line community was founded by Susan Maloney, a mom, former fashion editor, and stylist, who saw the Internet as a great meeting place and resource for busy moms and dads. In addition to on-line resources, the site also has message boards where Austin parents can offer tips and recommendations.

Work Source Child Care Solutions
2538 South Congress Avenue
(512) 326–1881, (800) 825–1914
Managed by the City of Austin, this organization provides child care subsidies for eligible families in Travis County and nine other Central Texas counties. Work Source also provides technical assistance and resources for child care providers.

HOME-SCHOOLING

Home schools might as well have been called "underground schools" back in the 1970s and early 1980s, because so many parents who chose to educate their own children guarded their secret as if they'd committed a crime. Indeed, many were prosecuted for failing to comply with compulsory attendance laws. A lot has changed. Today home-schooling is not only legal in all 50 states, the governor of Texas has recognized the value of home-schooling by proclaiming a Home Education Week. In Austin, parents can attend an annual book fair and convention for home-schoolers. The watershed occurred in 1987 when parents won a class-action suit

against the state, which stripped the Texas Education Agency of its authority over home schools. The Texas Supreme Court upheld the decision in 1994. Now attitudes toward home schools in Texas are among the most liberal in the country. Here the state asks only that parents pursue a course of study that includes math, reading, spelling, grammar, and a course in good citizenship. The curriculum, however, does not have to be filed with any government agency. An educational approach that was once largely the domain of Christian fundamentalists has spread to families of all kinds, and for many reasons. Certainly, many parents want to emphasize their children's religious education. Some choose to homeschool because they fear their children will be exposed to violence or the wrong influences in traditional schools. Others opt for home schooling to give their children more flexibility to pursue outside interests. Many aim to ensure that their children achieve academic excellence.

The Texas Home School Coalition, based in Lubbock, is a nonprofit organization that supports parents in their efforts to educate their children at home. The organization operates a database of home school support groups around the state, where parents can go to get information about available curriculums for home schools or about anything else they wish to know about educating their own children. Since 2001 the coalition has sponsored an annual state convention and family conference for home school families. For further information on home schooling, contact the coalition at P.O. Box 6747, Lubbock, TX 79493, (806) 744–4441, www.thsc.org.

MEDIA

Austin's long and rich media history goes as far back as the Capital City itself. The *Austin City Gazette,* a four-page weekly, made its debut on October 30, 1839, the same year that Austin became the capital of the Republic of Texas. Published by Samuel Whiting, a journalist from Houston, the *City Gazette* carried local, national, and foreign news; letters to the editor; editorials; and an occasional work of fiction. By the time the *City Gazette* folded in 1842 (some say due to the threat of invasion from Mexico) the frontier town of Austin had other publications to take its place. Austinites, it seemed, were eager for news, although getting it to this remote outpost was never easy—and definitely not quick. During the Civil War, one local publisher debuted his one-page bulletin, the *Texas Almanac Extra,* which he rushed into print three times a week after waiting for Pony Express riders to hustle in with the latest editions of the Houston and Galveston newspapers.

Decades later, during the Depression of the 1930s, the dean of American television journalism, Walter Cronkite, got his start in Austin.

"My first appearance before a microphone was during the college years at Austin," he writes in his book *A Reporter's Life.* Cronkite admits that his daily sports report on Austin radio station KNOW consisted of scores he memorized from a Western Union sports ticker at a Sixth Street tobacco shop while pretending to read the newspaper.

"Once out of sight of the smoke shop, I ran at breakneck speed back to the studio and typed out my daily sports intelligence before it fled my memory," Cronkite said.

He then moved on to work in print journalism in Austin, covering Texas politics. "It was a vast and diverse state, and the fight for dominance and privilege in Austin was never ending," wrote Cronkite.

The Austin media landscape has changed a mite since Cronkite's days here. Today's residents are bombarded with choices over what publications to read, where to land on the radio dial for programming that serves their needs, and which television news program to select. Austin cable TV giant, Time Warner Cable, launched Channel 8, a 24-hour local news channel in 1999. Residents also can order home delivery of the *New York Times* and the *Financial Times* and mail delivery of the *Wall Street Journal.* The fact is, there's a heck of a lot of news and information being disseminated around Austin. The bad news is that it's not all in one spot; you can't just pick up one or two publications or watch the evening news and feel as though you've captured the essence of Austin. The good news is that much of it is free! In addition to the radio and television news that's available at the flick of a switch, Austin has about as eclectic a selection of periodicals as one is likely to find in any city this size.

Without a doubt, one of the pleasures of living in Austin, one of the qualities that defines this city, is the abundance and diversity of reading material out there. It's not all award-winning stuff, but much of it is—and some of it deserves to be.

A sizable number of publications were started with the sweat, blood, and sometimes the rent of writers who saw a need for a particular kind of periodical in the city. As one writer/editor said, "We're writing the kinds of things we want to read." While many publications are making a go of it, others are struggling from day to day to survive. But it says a great deal about the local businesses that advertise, the public contributions some receive, and, of course, the readers themselves, that this volume of journals manages to stay afloat. William Sydney Porter, who gained international fame as short story writer O. Henry, didn't have as much luck. His 1894 Austin weekly newspaper, *The Rolling Stone,* displayed budding talent—but lasted only a year.

The list you'll find below represents a cross section of publications that make up the bedrock of the Austin print media. If your special interests lie elsewhere—in theater, business, technology, religion, public radio, or politics—take a look around; you're likely to find some publication that speaks to you.

NEWSPAPERS

Austin American–Statesman
305 South Congress Avenue
(512) 445-3500
www.statesman.com

As Austin's only daily newspaper, the *Austin American–Statesman* is in the unenviable positon of trying to satisfy all the news demands of a complex society. Editor Richard Oppel, in charge since 1995, helped improve the paper's scope of coverage in news, business, and editorials so much that the *Statesman* launched an advertising campaign using the slogan "It's not Your Same Old *Statesman.*" While Oppel has not been able to propel the staff to a Pulitzer prize—yet (his former paper, the *Charlotte Observer* of North Carolina, won three during his tenure there), the *Statesman* has come along nicely.

One highlight of today's *Statesman* is the weekly "XLent" entertainment section. Published Thursday and available free at area distribution points, this tabloid insert captures the eyes of young-at-heart readers who want a viewpoint besides the *Chronicle*'s (see listing below) for entertainment news and features. Kudos also to longtime columnist John Kelso, whose wry comments on current issues and events appear in the Metro section on Sunday, Tuesday, and Friday.

The *Statesman*'s main section features the top stories of the day, editorials, letters to the editor, and international news. Other daily news sections include,

Metro and State, Sports, Business, and Life & Arts. On Friday the Life & Movies section is published; Sunday delivers the Travel section as well as Insight, which includes coverage of local, national, and international issues, many written by the *Statesman*'s international staff. Show World, which includes the week's TV lineup, also appears Sunday. Available by request and at an additional cost is the Saturday supplement Weekly Business Review. Of special interest to many in the technology field is the *Statesman*'s Monday business page called Tech Monday, which focuses on the high-tech industry. The Techweek column in this section lists weekly meetings and events useful for those interested in networking. Published annually in July is *This Is Austin and Surrounding Communities,* a guide to the region that includes information on government, transportation, festivals, art, entertainment, recreation, education, business, and more.

In addition to news reported by its own staff and correspondents, the newspaper prints articles of interest from around the country and the world via international news services, including the Associated Press and the *New York Times.* Although many readers still feel the need to augment their daily intake of information by receiving national publications such as the *New York Times,* The *Wall Street Journal,* and others, the *Statesman* is, indeed, "not your same old . . ." The *Statesman* is owned by Atlanta-based Cox Enterprises, Inc., which includes daily and weekly newspapers in many parts of the country as well as a handful of Austin-area neighborhood newspapers. (See our In and Around Austin listing in this chapter). Daily circulation of the *Statesman* is about 183,000.

Austin Business Journal
111 Congress Avenue, Suite 750
(512) 494-2500
www.austin.bizjournals.com

Published on Friday, the *Austin Business Journal* is the only newspaper in the area dedicated exlusively to business news and information. Founded locally in 1980, the *Business Journal* was purchased in 1994 by American City Business Journals, Inc. Based in Charlotte, North Carolina, American City publishes more than 40 business journals across the country. The tabloid-format newspaper covers developments affecting the growth of the region and monitors the progress of new businesses coming to the area. It also promotes networking by publishing a listing of weekly events and meetings of interest to the business community.

Of special interest to many business-people and newcomers are the *Journal*'s annual guides and directories, most notably the *Book of Lists*. This massive volume, issued in December, provides information on more than 1,500 companies of interest to the business community. The *Business Journal* is available for delivery or can be purchased at newsstands around the area.

The *Austin Chronicle*
4000 North I-35
(512) 454-5766
www.austinchronicle.com

It's hard to plan an evening out on the town without first picking up a copy of the *Austin Chronicle*. The *Chronicle*, which will celebrate its 25th anniversary in 2006, stresses coverage of music, entertainment, and the arts but also provides a vital alternative voice on local political and environmental issues. The *Chronicle*, a big, fat, free publication distributed Thursday around the greater Austin area, was founded by six local entrepreneurs, several of whom had worked on the *Daily Texan*, UT's student newspaper.

Although at times a little rough around the edges, the *Chronicle* easily disappears from newsstands within a couple of days of publication. Editor Louis Black, one of the original godfathers (as the founders like to call themselves), has become a dynamic voice on the issue of long-range city planning. Take this from one of his past editorials: "I am tired of Austin being treated as a ridiculous environmental com-

munity run by crazies. . . . The issues facing Austin are serious issues—how we deal with a growing city and still respect the integrity of the environment. . . ."

But let's not forget the *Chronicle*'s main focus: Entertainment, with a capital E! Movie reviews, book reviews, record reviews, features on the fascinating figures that keep Austin interesting, art, theater and film listings, cartoons, and some insightful columns on everything from architecture to zydeco cram this 100-page-plus periodical. Of course the *Chronicle* knows the Austin club scene. You get the feeling that these writers don't just cover their beats, they *live* them.

The *Daily Texan*
(512) 471-4591
www.dailytexanonline.com

This award-winning student newspaper of the University of Texas is published Monday through Friday when school is in session. It covers largely campus news, but when the university is one of the largest in the nation, that's a big job. The *Daily Texan* is among the most recognized student newspapers in the country, and many of its graduates have gone on to win Pulitzer prizes with professional publications. The *Daily Texan* also provides some interesting local, state, and national news. Copies are distributed free in bright orange boxes on campus and at various locations around the downtown area.

MAGAZINES

Austin Family
P.O. Box 7559, Austin 78683
(512) 733-0038
www.austinfamily.com
This free magazine, published monthly
and available at about 500 distribution
points throughout the greater Austin area,
is an excellent resource for parents looking for news and information about summer camps, child care, schools,
family-friendly events, and much more.
While *Austin Family* has had several different publishers, this award-winning journal
has successfully met its goal of providing
information that promotes "smart parenting and healthy homes" since 1992. Don't
miss the great February issue that provides vital information on summer camps.

Austin Home & Living
505B Cypress Creek Road, Cedar Park
(512) 250-9023
This bimonthly magazine takes readers
inside some of the Austin area's most
beautiful and unique residences. With regular pictorial spreads and articles on
Austin homes, *Austin Home & Living* targets upscale readers. The magazine, a
four-color glossy publication, also includes
features on such things as gardening,
food, and home design. Owned since 1994
by Austin's Publications & Communications, Inc., the magazine sells by subscription or at retail locations.

Austin Monthly
P.O. Box 340927, Austin 78734
(512) 263-9133
www.austinmonthly.com
Started as a free publication in 1992 and
dedicated to the positive aspects of city
life, *Austin Monthly* has gone decidedly
upscale the past few years. Now a slick
four-color magazine, it is sold by subscription and at local newsstands around the
region. Yet it remains true to its origins.
Good features on the region's interesting
characters and on the events that make
Austin such a happening city are combined

with pictorial spreads, restaurant reviews,
an events calendar, and much more.

The *Good Life*
P.O. Box 4400, Austin 78765
www.goodlifemag.com
Award-winning Austin journalist Ken Martin
and his wife, Rebecca Melancon, debuted
this monthly magazine in 1997 as a publication for the 50+ crowd. Since then, the
Good Life has morphed into a fine publication for just about anyone interest in reading "compelling community journalism," as
its motto states. Published monthly, the
Good Life prints a broad range of well-
written news and feature articles for and
about the people of Central Texas, with particular emphasis on Austin. It also includes a
section called Gusto, which focuses on
health, wellness, and fitness. Apparently the
formula is working. The *Good Life* has
grown from a little 20-page publication in
the 1990s to well over 40 pages the past
few years. It's free at area distribution points
and is also sold by subscription for delivery.

New Texas Magazine
1512½ South Congress Avenue
(512) 462-1990
Established in 1979, *New Texas Magazine* is
now Central Texas's oldest magazine—and
it's still free at distribution points around
Austin, San Antonio, and the Texas Hill
Country. While it retains its "New Age"
image, especially with advertisers, *New
Texas* has branched out from its alternative
lifestyle focus to include a broader spectrum of articles on life in and around
Austin—and beyond. Published bimonthly
in tabloid format on newsprint, each edition
focuses on specific topics, such as Finance
and Careers, Environment and Gardening,
Food and Farming, Travel and Culture,
Health and Fitness, and Healthy Homes.

Southwest Cycling News
12702 Lowden Lane, Manchaca
(512) 282-1987
www.ccsi.com/~aca/
For many, many people in Austin, bicycling is not just a sport or a weekend

leisure activity—it's a lifestyle. If you happen to be one of those people, don't miss the *Southwest Cycling News*. This neat publication is published 11 times a year by the Austin Cycling Association and is distributed free at distribution points around the area. The *Cycling News*, a tabloid that averages about 16 pages per issue, grew from a small newsletter started in the 1970s called *Austin Cycling Notes*, then *Austin Cycling News*. The journal aims to promote bicycle safety, education, and access within Austin and includes articles on commuting, recreational cycling, touring, fitness, and health. It occasionally takes issue with city officials over bicycling policy decisions.

Texas Highways
150 East Riverside Drive
(512) 486-5858, (800) 839-4997
www.texashighways.com

Stunning color photographs and in-depth articles that celebrate the glory of Texas abound in this monthly magazine, published in Austin by the Texas Department of Transportation. This is the official travel magazine of Texas and provides current and accurate information on travel destinations throughout the state. It is a beautiful publication. And with circulation at 330,000, it's obvious that many people agree. *Texas Highways* started as an in-house publication of the Department of Transportation but has been exclusively a travel magazine since May 1974. The magazine clearly stresses protection of the environment and of the state's cultural heritage and has won awards from such organizations as the San Antonio Conservation Society, the Texas Historical Commission, and the International Regional Magazines Association. The December issue includes an index of all the articles written during the year and information about how to obtain back issues. *Texas Highways* can be purchased by subscription or at most major newsstands throughout Austin.

Texas Monthly
701 Brazos Street
(512) 320-6900
www.texasmonthly.com

Winner of numerous National Magazine Awards, *Texas Monthly* is the state's showcase magazine. And it's published in Austin. This full-color glossy magazine, which celebrated its 30th anniversary in 2003, offers lengthy news and feature articles and spicy true-crime stories of interest to its affluent, well-educated readers. It also provides frequently updated reviews of selected restaurants in Texas's major cities. Its regular column "Around the State," is a city-by-city guide to choice entertainment. The annual Bum Steer Awards, published in the January issue, take an irreverent look at the people and situations in Texas that the editors believe have been particularly weird or foolish over the past year; it's perennially one of the magazine's best-selling issues. The Best and Worst Legislators is another popular cover feature that comes out every other July (as the Texas Legislature meets biennially). Look also for the annual Top Twenty issue, which lists the magazine's choice of the 20 most influential Texans of the year. Publisher Mike Levy, who started the magazine when he was 26 years old, has found a formula that satisfies the majority of *Texas Monthly*'s readers, estimated at 2.5 million people each month.

With Levy as majority shareholder, Mediatex Communications Corp. published *Texas Monthly* until 1998, when the company was sold for a reported $37 million. *Texas Monthly* is now owned by Indianapolis-based Emmis Communications Corp., a subsidiary of Emmis Broadcasting Corp., one of the nation's major broadcasters. The Emmis publishing venture also includes *Atlanta* magazine, *Indianapolis Monthly,* and *Cincinnati* magazine. Levy and many longtime staff remain at the helm of this premier Austin production.

Texas Music
P.O. Box 50273, Austin 78763
(512) 472-6630
www.txmusic.com

This juicy, well-designed quarterly gets high marks for covering the Texas music scene. Insightful articles about contemporary bands and songwriters around the state combine with some interesting features on the state's long and varied history of music and music makers. Reviews of current CD releases and colorful photographs flesh out this glossy publication. There's also a great calendar of music-related events around Texas. Regular readers will soon have the Insiders' view on the wide range of Lonestar State music. We'd like to see *Texas Music* become a monthly. Incidentally, publisher/editor-in-chief Stewart Ramser says the idea for the publication came to him while he vacationed in Hawaii. The resulting business plan, written for an MBA class, earned him an A+. No wonder. The magazine is sold at newsstands around the country and is also available by subscription.

The *Texas Observer*
307 West Seventh Street
(512) 477-0746
www.texasobserver.org

Former *Daily Texan* writer Ronnie Dugger debuted the *Texas Observer* in 1954. Within six months the *Observer* established itself as a new voice in Texas media, becoming the first to report on lynchings in East Texas. For half a century this small biweekly magazine has struggled for survival while breaking the silence on story after story dealing with society's underdogs, the liberal movement, and Democratic causes. Dugger, who owned the paper until turning it over to the nonprofit Texas Democracy Foundation in 1994, called his magazine "A Journal of Free Voices," and wrote in the *Observer*'s mission statement, "never will we overlook or misrepresent the truth to serve the interests of the powerful. . . ." Today the small Austin staff that runs the magazine and the freelance writers from around the state who contribute articles continue to bring to light liberal/progressive issues not treated in the mainstream media. This publication, whose small but loyal following keeps it afloat through contributions, fund-raisers, and subscriptions, accepts advertising but doesn't actively sell space. The result is about 32 pages, just 8¼ by 10½ inches, of nearly solid black-and-white print. The *Observer* is available at selected newsstands around the state and can most easily be found in bookstores in the Austin area.

Texas Parks & Wildlife
3000 South I-35, Suite 120
(512) 912-7000, (800) 937-9393
www.tpwmagazine.com

This visually enticing, well-written magazine highlights Texas's great outdoors. Published by the Texas Parks and Wildlife Department in Austin and distributed all over the state, *Texas Parks & Wildlife* is a great source of information for newcomers and residents alike who love the open air. The magazine started publishing in 1942 under the name *Texas Game & Fish*. The name was changed in 1967 to reflect a broadening of its editorial scope to include all outdoor recreational activities, including hiking, backpacking, camping, bicycling, rock climbing, kayaking, hunting, and fishing. It also includes a great deal of environmental news and is an invaluable source of information on the state park system. *Texas Parks & Wildlife,* which has a statewide circulation of 150,000, has won awards for writing and photography from the International Regional Magazines Association, the Association of Conservation Information, and others.

Texas Triangle
611 West Sixth Street
(512) 476-0576
www.txtriangle.com

This publication based in Austin and Dallas provides information for the gay and lesbian community in Texas's major cities. Published by Angle Media, Inc., of Dallas, the *Triangle* also has bureaus in San Antonio and Houston. It receives the Associated Press news wire and publishes articles from around the world on issues and events relevant to the gay community. The weekly "Check It Out" column provides listings of selected events around the state of interest to the general population. The *Triangle* is distributed free on Thursday around the city and is also available by subscription. Averaging about 28 pages today, the periodical made its debut in 1992 but nearly closed down due to financial problems in 1997. The *Triangle* is on more solid ground these days.

IN AND AROUND AUSTIN

Hill Country News
103 Woods Lane, Cedar Park
(512) 259-4449

Published on Wednesday and Friday, the *Hill Country News* focuses on community news, business, and features in Cedar Park and northwest Austin. On Wednesday, the *Hill Country News* is a free publication available in Cedar Park. Also published on Wednesday, *Hill Country News Northwest* is aimed at the Northwest Austin area. That edition is sold by subscription and is home delivered. Friday sees the publication of the *Hill Country News Weekender,* which is mailed to subscribers. Of special note is the annual "Horizon" edition, an information and progress report published in March on businesses in Cedar Park and

the Texas Hill Country. Five times a year, the *News* also publishes a 30-page tabloid of upcoming activities in the Leander Independent School District, called "Education Express." The *News* was founded in 1967 and is owned by Granite Publications of Marble Falls, which publishes 17 newspapers in the Central Texas region.

Lake Travis View
2300 Lohmans Spur, Suite 186
(512) 263-1100
www.laketravisview.com

Even if you don't live in the Lake Travis area, don't miss the *View* in April when it publishes the annual "Lake Travis Summer Guide," a special section that details fun things to do at the lake, including camping, recreational activities, and dining. The rest of the year, the *View* focuses on local government, the Lake Travis Independent School District, and on community news along Lake Travis' sprawling south shore. Several local residents write regular columns, including the popular "Over 50, Going Like 60" by Dot Fowler. Once a month there's the special section called "Lake and Country Living." The paper, owned by Cox Enterprises, Inc., is sold by subscription and at newsstands. The special sections are available free at area newsstands.

Oak Hill Gazette
7200-B U.S. 71 West
(512) 301-0123
www.hometown.aol.com/OHGazette

Residents of the Oak Hill region in south Austin have a wonderful local newspaper that covers just about everything there is to know in their growing neighborhood. News and sports from the local schools; columns from the district's county, state, and federal government leaders; a column aimed at senior citizens and another on lifestyle combine, of course, with area news and business coverage to make a fine neighborhood publication. Published by the Oak Hill husband-and-wife team of Will Atkins and Penny Levers, the *Gazette* has been in business since 1995. It's published on Friday and is available by subscription or at news-stands in the area.

Pflugerville Pflag
200 West Main Street, Pflugerville
(512) 251-5574

Pfinding the *Pflag* isn't too hard in Pflugerville, the pfine community with the pfunny name. The *Pflag* is Pflugerville's pflourishing weekly newspaper. Published Thursday, it includes features of interest to local readers as well as community and business news about the town and the surrounding areas of Travis and Williamson Counties. Each issue includes sections on the Pflugerville Independent School District and on youth and school-sponsored sports and recreation. The "Faith and Values" section has infomation on area churches and religious activities. The newspaper's been owned since 2000 by Cox Enterprises, Inc.

Round Rock Leader
105 South Blair Street, Round Rock
(512) 255-5827
www.rrleader.com

Established in 1877, just a few years after the city of Round Rock itself was formed, the *Leader* has grown significantly from the four-page, hand-set publication of the early days. Today the twice-weekly newspaper reaches 7,500 homes in Round Rock and nearby communities and averages about 40 pages in size. The paper emphasizes community and school news, covers local and Williamson County politics, and also keep readers informed of the meteoric growth of the city, which has seen its population soar from 2,300 a mere 25 years ago to more than 61,000 today. Owned by the Todd family since 1972, the *Leader* includes a Bible verse on the editorial pages that the family says appeals to the conservative, family-oriented community.

West Austin News
5407 Parkcrest Drive
(512) 459-5474

Serving the neighborhoods of West Austin, Northwest Austin, Rollingwood and West Lake Hills, the *West Austin News* focuses on community, society, and school news. The weekly newspaper, published on Thursday, was started by local owner and publisher Bart Stephens in 1986. The paper publishes an annual sports guide in the fall and a shopping guide at Christmastime as well as biannual sections on Healthy Living and Home and Garden. In an effort to "Keep Austin Weird" (see the History chapter), newsroom execs say, the *News* sponsors an annual Art Car Parade in April. Artists(?) from all over Texas decorate their cars and show them off during the parade. The Art Car Ball proceeds the event.

Westlake Picayune
3103 Bee Caves Road
(512) 327-2990
www.westlakepicayune.com

Serving the community of Westlake, the weekly *Picayune* covers community and local government news and the Eanes Independent School District as well as local arts and entertainment. While the newspaper is sold by subscription and at newsstands, a monthly special section called "Distinct" is mailed free to 10,000 homes in the area, those with the zip codes 78746 and 78733. "Distinct" is the *Picayune*'s lifestyle section and regularly features an article on an interesting local resident. Founded in 1976, the newspaper is now owned by Cox Enterprises, Inc., the Atlanta-based company that owns the *Austin American-Statesman*.

ETHNIC PUBLICATIONS

Arriba Art & Business News
1009 East Cesar Chavez Street
(512) 479-6397

Austin's oldest newspaper for the Mexican-American community, *Arriba* was founded in 1980. This 8- to 12-page tabloid, distributed free biweekly, is written in English and Spanish, highlights community and business news, and goes to great lengths to cover the Hispanic cultural scene. In addition to regular features on Hispanic artists, it publishes listings of gallery shows, museum exhibitions, and other events of interest to the community.

El Mundo
2116 East Cesar Chavez Street
(512) 476-8636
www.elmundonewspaper.com
An impressive weekly publication for the area's Spanish-speaking population, El Mundo includes local, national, and international news and features, as well as sports and entertainment of interest to the Hispanic community. Owned and operated locally by the Angulo family, this newspaper is a strong advocate for area Hispanics and does not shy away from taking issue with the mainstream press over its coverage of the community. The paper is published Thursday and is sold in area newsstands.

El Norte
1823 Fort View Road
(512) 448-1023
This Spanish-language monthly newspaper provides information relevant to Austin's Hispanic population, including changes in U.S. immigration policy, news on Hispanic and community leaders, community support organizations, and activities within the area's Catholic churches. The 20-page newspaper is distributed throughout the Austin area. Journalist Gloria Montelongo Aguilar and her husband, Miguel, started El Norte in May 1996 in the back room of their home with two used computers and a printer bought at a pawn shop.

NOKOA
The Observer
1154-B Angelina Street
(512) 499-8713
Working out of his home, publisher Akwasi Evans debuted NOKOA in 1987 with the goal of creating a newspaper that reflected the interests and views of progressive political activists of all ethnicities. For more than a decade, the free weekly paper has championed the rights

of African Americans, Hispanics, Anglos, Asians, Native Americans, Women, Gays, Lesbians, and the disabled communities.

Evans calls the publication "a true progressive paper with an unabashed African-American perspective." The paper, published Thursday, covers Austin city government and the Texas Legislature when it is in session, as well as local, regional, national, and international news. NOKOA, which aims to be a voice of advocacy, addresses problems of discrimination, exclusion, cultural and political chauvinism, and the denial of opportunity. The paper is available at distribution points in Austin and Central Texas.

Villager Newspaper
1223 Rosewood Avenue
(512) 476-0082
This free weekly newspaper focuses on news of interest to Austin's African-American community. Owner T. L. Wyatt has been publishing the Villager since 1973 as a voice of advocacy with a focus on the positive events in the African-American community. Wyatt calls the Villager "the good news newspaper." The paper prints articles not often found in the mainstream press and analyzes news and events that pertain to its readers. Wyatt's weekly editorial column, "Rappin," appears on the front page. Newspapers are available on Friday at distribution points in East, South, and Central Austin.

YEARLY GUIDES

Austin Newcomer Guide
111 Congress Avenue
(512) 478-9383
www.austin-chamber.org
Published by the Greater Austin Chamber of Commerce, this annual guide provides information on housing, attractions, newcomer information, business, shopping and dining, arts and culture, retirement living, and other areas of interest to the recently arrived. It's sold on-line or at the chamber offices in downtown Austin. Also

available are the chamber's other guides: *Relocation, Business Relocation,* and *Job Search.*

Celebrate Austin
7514 North MoPac, Suite 200
(512) 346-6235
www.celebrateaustin.com
This four-color magazine has been giving visitors and newcomers the scoop on Austin for nearly 25 years. *Celebrate Austin,* found in 26,000 hotel rooms around the city, presents features on Austin personalities and places of interest and provides informatioin on myriad topics: home buying, government, education, health care, recreation, shopping, the arts, and the high-tech industry, to name a few. Hardcover versions are placed for permanent use in hotel rooms, but visitors can purchase the take-home softcover version either though the hotel or by mailing in a request card. The publication makes its annual debut in December.

Texas State Travel Guide
150 East Riverside Drive
(800) 8888-TEX
www.traveltex.com
Published in Austin by the Texas Department of Transportation's Travel and Information Division, this hefty guide of nearly 300 pages features highlights of tourist attractions throughout the state. Seven special sections summarize attractions around Texas's major cities, including Austin and the Central Texas area. Information on smaller communities and cities is listed alphabetically. Among the guide's many attributes are listings and descriptions of nearly 150 Texas lakes. The guide also lists national and state forests as well as state parks. Nature lovers can find information on the state's birds and flowers as well. The publication is free and can be requested at the toll-free number above. The guide, published in late January or February, can also be found at the Capitol Information Center on the grounds of the State Capitol building.

TELEVISION

Austin's television industry provides a strong and vital link among residents of Central Texas. Live local news broadcasts relay information and flash the latest images of events and newmakers around the Texas heartland and the world beyond. In times of tragedy and triumph, no other news medium rivals the awesome power of live television. None but television allows the faces and the voices of the participants themselves to illustrate the immediate events as a story unfolds.

If it's 24-hour local news or music you're looking for, you've come to the right town. In 2000 Time Warner launched Channel 8, its own news channel that broadcasts local and state news around the clock. There is also TXCN, a Texas-wide news network. Where else in the country can you go to watch a locally produced 24-hour music channel? The Austin Music Network on cable channel 15 is another of those wonderful little dividends we Austinites enjoy. Although in perpetual financial straits, this homegrown product features local musicians, presents local music shows, and airs music videos from all over the place. Don't miss it.

When it comes to television, however, Austin's national claim to fame is the long-running show, *Austin City Limits.* The *Austin American–Statesman* has called this program "the city's cultural calling card to the world." And indeed it is! The program, which debuted in 1975—six years before MTV—is all about music. It showcases local talent as well as nationally and internationally known performers. Taped live on the University of Texas campus and featuring the illuminated Austin skyline as a backdrop, *Austin City Limits* can be seen on PBS stations around the country. The weekly one-hour program airs Saturday at 7:00 P.M. and the following Friday at 11:00 P.M. on the local PBS station, KLRU. While tapings are supposedly open to the public, tickets can be as hard to come by as a cool day in July (see our tips in The Music Scene chapter).

Not many residents of a town Austin's size can tune in to a bit of home while they're on the road. Besides *Austin City Limits* our city also claims *King of the Hill*. The Fox network's popular cartoon sitcom about a family of Texans headed by Hank Hill was created by Austinite Mike Judge, who also created MTV's wildly successful *Beavis and Butt-head. King of the Hill* airs on Sunday night at 7:30.

Ranking 54th among the 210 largest television markets in the United States, Austin claims four network affiliates: CBS, ABC, NBC, and Fox. Additionally, Austin has a Warner Brothers–affiliated station, a UPN affiliate, and a Public Broadcasting Service station, which operates on two channels. Dozens of cable channels are available at a price through the area's largest cable provider, Time Warner, or from other cable, microwave, and satellite service providers in the area. The Austin Community Access Center offers public access programming produced by, for, and about the people of Austin on cable channels 10, 11, and 16. For those looking for Austin Independent School District information, there are cable channels 18 and 20. Travis County programming is on cable 17, and the Austin Community College access channel is cable 19.

In late 2002 Austin got its own full-power Spanish-language television station. Univision, running locally on KAKW channel 62, is the top-ranked Hispanic network in the United States. KAKW offers local news broadcasts in Spanish at 5:00 P.M.

Local Stations

KTBC, Fox, channel 7 (cable 2)
KVUE, ABC, channel 24 (cable 3)
KXAN, NBC, channel 36 (cable 4)
KEYE, CBS, channel 42 (cable 5)
KNVA, WB affiliated, channel 54
  (cable 12)
KLRU, PBS, channels 18 and 20
  (cable 9 and 20)

The locally produced **All Access Live** *television show features backstage interviews and live concert performances by Austin and national bands. The show, hosted by VJ Brian "B-Doe" Bymark of the Austin Music Network, debuted October 4, 2003. It airs Saturday at 10:00 P.M. on KNVA, channel 54.*

KBEJ, UPN affiliated, channel 2
  (cable 23)
KAKW, Univision, channel 62
  (cable 99)

Cable Providers

Time Warner Cable, (512) 485-6800
Grande Communications, (512) 878-4000
Heartland Wireless, (800) 880-0292
Cox Communications, (512) 930-3085

RADIO

Just as Austin's live music performers inspire fierce loyalties among fans—and ardent debates over favorites—so, too, do the city's radio stations. Radio is a hot commodity here in Central Texas, and the stations that fail to deliver the mysterious programming formula that quickly captivates listeners soon fade into thin air.

On the other hand, a few stations have withstood the test of time. KVET-AM, now an all-sports station, dates back to the post–World War II era and was started by a group of veterans that included John Connally, who was later to become governor of Texas. KUT, Austin's public radio station, began broadcasting on November 10, 1958, and continues to get great ratings for a noncommercial venue. It offers National Public Radio and a wonderfully eclectic mix of music, local bands, and original programming. KGSR, at 107.1 on the FM dial, is another long-shining gem in Austin radio. KGSR plays more local bands than any other area station and offers some excellent original programming. Additionally, KGSR releases an annual CD, *Broadcasts,* that features a mix of local talent and national acts, most in live performances from the studio. Proceeds from sales go to charity.

You can't discuss radio in Austin without mentioning the award-winning *Dudley and Bob* morning show on the rock 'n' roll station KLBJ-FM. Dale Dudley and Bob Fonseca won a *Billboard* magazine award for Local Air Personalities of the Year, and the show has been named Best Radio Program at the Austin Music Awards for the past decade.

The morning-drive duo of "Sammy and Bob" on KVET-FM is an Austin institution and a dominant force in the local radio market. Sammy Allred and Bob Cole team up to bring listeners a call-in show that doesn't screen callers and has managed to raise the ire of just about everyone in town at some point or another. Meanwhile, they manage to do some great interviews with local musicians and play some wonderful live music. Where else could you hear "Jingle Bells" sung by then Governor G. W. Bush and Larry Gatlin? This station is pure country.

Country music continues to be enormously popular around these parts, though it isn't the only sound in town—by far. Greater Austin radio serves up a 24-hour feast of music, news, talk, sports, and more music on an impressive number of stations. Rock, jazz, blues, urban, folk, Christian, and the increasingly popular Spanish/Latin beats are just some of the many musical offerings aired around the clock.

AM and FM Radio Stations

In a Class By Itself
KGSR 107.1 FM (Local bands, blues, jazz, folk, reggae, rock, interviews, live studio performances)

Alternative
KROX 101.5 FM (Rock alternative)

Christian/Gospel
KIXL 970 AM (Christian information, talk)
KFIT 1060 AM (Gospel)
KNLE 88.1 FM (Contemporary Christian)
KYCM 88.5 FM (Catholic Global Network)

Classical/Easy Listening
KKMJ 95.5 FM (Soft rock)
KMFA 89.5 FM (Clasical)
KNCT 91.3 FM (Classical, easy listening)

College Radio
KTSW 89.9 FM (College alternative)
KVRX 91.7 FM (Eclectic; 7:00 P.M. to 9:00 A.M. weekdays, 10:00 P.M. to 9:00 A.M. weekends)

Community
KOOP 91.7 (Community operated, eclectic music and talk; 9:00 A.M. to 7:00 P.M. weekdays, 9:00 A.M. to 10:00 P.M. weekends)

Contemporary Hits
KAMX 94.7 FM (Modern adult contemporary)
KHFI 96.7 FM (Contemporary hits, Top 40)

Country
KASE 100.7 FM (Country)
KFAN 107.9 FM (Country, blues, rock)
KHLB 106.9 FM (Country)
KRXT 98.5 FM (Country)
KVET 98.1 FM (Country, UT sports)

Hill Country Radio
KFAN 107.9 FM (Texas music from Fredericksburg)

Jazz
KAZI 88.7 FM (Jazz, R&B, blues, gospel, talk)

KQJZ 92.1 FM (Smooth jazz)
KQQT 106.3 FM (Smooth jazz)

Spanish/Tejano
KELG 1440 AM (Regional Mexican)
KFON 1490 AM (Norteno)
KHHL 98.9 FM (Tejano hits)
KINV 107.7 FM (Regional Mexican)
KKLB 92.5 FM (Tejano and dance)
KOKE 1600 AM (Regional Mexican)
KQQA 1530 AM (Regional Mexican)
KTXZ 1560 AM (Salsa, merengue, Spanish rock)
KUOL 1470 AM (Spanish Christian music, talk)
KXXS 104.9 (Spanish soft favorites)

News/Sports/Talk
KJCE 1370 AM (Talk, news)
KLBJ 590 AM (Talk, news, good local news)
KQQA 1530 AM (ESPN)
KWNX 1260 AM (News, talk, sports, ESPN)
KVET 1300 AM (24-hour sports)

Austin public radio station KUT began broadcasting on November 10, 1958, marking the beginning of noncommercial public service broadcasting in Central Texas. It was also the first broadcast from the University of Texas at Austin.

Public Radio
KUT 90.5 FM (Eclectic music, local bands, NPR news)

Rock 'n' Roll/Oldies
KEYI 103.5 FM (Oldies from the '60s and '70s)
KFMK 105.9 FM (Rhythmic oldies, R&B classics)
KHLB 1340 AM (Big Band; music from the '40s, '50s, and '60s)
KLBJ 93.7 FM (Rock 'n' roll)
KPEZ 102.3 FM (Classic rock)

Urban/Rhythmic
KQBT 104.3 FM (Urban, rhythmic)
KDHT 93.3/99.7 FM (nonstop hip-hop)

WORSHIP

When it comes to braggin' rights about whether Texas is God's Country, as many old-timers and newcomers will declare, the facts are clear: Texas has more churches than any other state in the Union. In 1997 the state had approximately 17,000 places of worship, according to that year's *Texas Almanac,* some 2,500 more than second-ranked California, and those numbers have grown. The state also boasts the largest number of church members, around 5.3 million, according to the almanac.

Among Protestants, the largest group belongs to the Southern Baptist Convention—4.5 million adherents. Roman Catholics make up the second largest group, with 4.3 million adherents. Survey data compiled by the almanac also suggests church attendance is higher in the rural areas of Texas than it is in the state's larger cities. In many of the state's smaller communities, the church or religious meeting place is the center of community activity.

When the Mexican flag flew over Texas, Roman Catholicism was the official state religion, and the parish church was the heart of the community. San Antonio's famous missions (see our Day Trips chapter) were established to bring Christianity to the Native Americans, and some of the mission sites were along creekbeds and riverbanks where Native Americans had gathered for centuries to celebrate their own sacred rituals. In the mid-19th century, Protestant preachers accompanied European settlers, although some groups, notably German, Czech, and Polish immigrants, were Catholic. No matter the denomination, church picnics and camp meetings were an important part of the social life in 19th-century Texas.

Many of the smaller towns around Austin continue to hold annual church picnics where family members gather, some coming in from their new homes in the city, to renew their ties with their ancestral homes (see our Annual Events and Festivals chapter). A visit to the local church and its accompanying cemetery is a great way to explore Texas history and offers visitors insight into various ethnic customs that have been preserved by immigrant groups and settlers. For example, some of the small Czech communities east of Austin preserve the custom of decorating gravestones with pictures of their loved ones. (See our Attractions chapter for more on Austin's historic cemeteries.)

DIVERSITY

Religion played an important role in both Austin's early life and its development. The log cabin that served as the first state capitol building also was home to a Presbyterian church, but the Presbyterians were not the only denomination in town. From the beginning, Austin had a diverse religious community. In his book *Power, Money & The People: The Making of Modern Austin,* Anthony M. Orum (see our Politics and Perspectives chapter) cites the city's first census, taken in 1840, showing that of the 900 residents 73 were "professors of religion." There were Methodists, Presbyterians, Episcopalians, Baptists, and a large number of Roman Catholics.

In the second half of the century the city blossomed, as did the variety of religious groups. Several of the city's landmark churches were erected in the central city in the latter half of the 18th century. St. David's Episcopal Church, 304 East Seventh Street, was begun in 1854 and completed 16 years later. The Gothic Revival structure includes several genuine Tiffany stained-glass windows. Legend has it that gamblers helped fund the construction, hence its nickname, the "gamblers' church."

St. Mary's Cathedral, 203 East 10th Street, is the city's oldest Catholic church, designed by noted Texas architect Nicholas J. Clayton and built in 1874. The cathedral sits in the shadows of downtown high-rises, but, inside, the beauty of its stained glass, imported from France and Germany, remains vibrant.

Just north of the University of Texas campus in Central Austin is All Saints' Episcopal Chapel, 2629 Whitis Avenue, a Gothic landmark built by Bishop George Herbert Kinsolving in 1899.

The first Swedish Lutheran church in Austin stands at 1510 Congress Avenue. Gethsemane Lutheran Church was built in 1883 in the Gothic Revival style, and builders utilized bricks from the state capitol building that burned down in 1881.

AUSTIN'S JEWISH COMMUNITY

Just two years after Gethsemane Lutheran Church was completed, the city's first synagogue opened. Congregation Beth Israel was serving the city's small, but very influential, Jewish community. Four of the city's leading businessmen and developers were members—brothers Phineas and Jacob De Cordova and German immigrants and brothers Henry and Morris Hirschfeld.

That tradition of civic leadership continues in the Jewish community. Austin's most famous business entrepreneur, Michael Dell, chairman of Dell Computer Corp., and his wife, Susan, have led the way in the development of the Dell Jewish Community Campus, a 40-acre development adjacent to the Northwest Hills neighborhood in Northwest Austin. The campus is home to several Jewish congregations. The campus also houses the Jewish Community Center and the Jewish Federation of Austin, plus cultural, social, and educational facilities.

The development of the campus did prompt debate and some opposition from neighbors who feared the complex would be too large and produce heavy traffic.

Each year, usually in June, members of 300 area evangelical churches hold the annual "March for Jesus" up Congress Avenue to the capitol. The march attracts thousands of participants. Call (512) 416-0066 for more information.

The debate is not a new one in Austin. Several churches have experienced significant growth, prompting some neighbors to voice concerns. There has been a long-running discussion over the growth of Hyde Park Baptist Church and the neighborhood in Central Austin.

On the positive side, the development of the Dell campus is evidence of Austin's flourishing Jewish population, now estimated at 8,000 members. Much of the growth has come as the city's high-tech center bring in professional workers from other locations around the country. Several local supermarkets have begun to offer kosher food handling and food products in response to the growth.

MULTICULTURAL TRADITIONS

Another impact of the high-tech boom has been the emergence of eastern religious temples in Austin. There are several Buddhist congregations in the city serving Chinese Americans, Japanese Americans, and other ethnic groups. There is also an Islamic center and several mosques in the city. While it is impossible to list every church in the Austin area, several religious organizations are listed at the end of this chapter. The *Austin American–Statesman* has a religion section on Saturday that lists local church and temple activities.

One of the most startling and beautiful sights in the Austin area is the Shree Raseshwari Radaha Rani Temple, the largest Hindu temple in North America, located on the outskirts of Southwest Austin. Built by Hindu artisans, this white-walled Indian-style temple with its colorful, intricate wooden decorations, sits near fields of golden marigolds on what once was a Texas cattle ranch. The temple, part of the Barsana Dham ashram, holds several important celebrations each year that evoke the spirituality of India. The Barsana Dham complex is approximately 5 miles south of U.S. 290 West, on F.M. 1826 (Camp Ben McCullough Road).

Many of the city's diverse religious groups welcome visitors to their celebrations. Chinese and Vietnamese New Year, Hindu festivals, Buddhist observances, Roman Catholic feast days, Greek Orthodox festivals, are windows into the multicultural soul of Austin. (See our Annual Events and Festivals chapter for festival days.)

HISPANIC TRADITIONS

One popular Catholic festival is held December 12 in honor of Our Lady of Guadalupe, the dark-skinned Virgin who appeared to a poor Mexican peasant on a hill outside Mexico City. The day is celebrated with dancing and street processions by parishioners of Our Lady of Guadalupe Church, 1206 East Ninth Street. Built in 1907, the Catholic church is home to Austin's oldest Hispanic parish.

Several churches in the diocese offer services in Spanish and conduct Mariachi Masses throughout the year.

Another annual tradition that reflects the rich Hispanic heritage in this region is the Christmas Posada. In the days before Christmas, children dressed as Mary and Joseph go from door to door seeking a refuge as their namesakes did more than 2,000 years ago. Named for the Spanish word for "inn," the nightly treks can take place for one night or several, but they always end at the parish church (see our Annual Events chapter).

The Catholic Church is a vital part of Austin's Hispanic traditions, and it also serves as a focal point of community and a central point for social groups and political grassroots organizations.

AFRICAN-AMERICAN TRADITIONS

Among the first churches in Austin were those serving the city's African-American population. The Metropolitan African Methodist Episcopal Church, 1105 East 10th Street, in the heart of East Austin, was built in 1923 and is the oldest African-American church in Austin that remains active.

In a time when social inequalities were the norm, the African-American church served a vital role in Austin, as it did throughout the country. One of the first African-American church leaders in Austin was the Reverend Jacob Fontaine, who founded the Sweethome Baptist Church in Clarksville (see our Relocation chapter), the historic, once predominantly African-American neighborhood just west of downtown Austin and north of West Sixth Street. The original church is gone, but its name and spirit live on at the new church, built in 1935 at 1725 West 11th Street. A historic landmark, the building now stands at the heart of a popular gentrified neighborhood.

The Reverend Fontaine also was instrumental in founding other historic African-American congregations, according to Orum's *Power, Money & The People*. Fontaine founded the First Baptist Church, which once stood on the site now occupied by the city's downtown library. Another pioneering churchman in the African-American community was Francis Webber, an Anglo priest from Detroit who came to Austin in 1935. Orum credits Webber with reaching out to the African-American community from his parish headquarters, Holy Cross Church, particularly in providing health care for the city's Mexican-American and African-American communities.

Throughout the dark days of segregation, into the civil rights era, and now into the 21st century, the city's African-American churches have been involved in all aspects of the community's growth and survival. Greater Calvary Missionary Baptist Church operates a life training program for African-American male teens called Rites of Passage. Once a week, boys ages 6 to 18 gather at the center to participate in the program. The program seeks to boost self-esteem and school grades and help participants learn the value of social consciousness, plus learn leadership and decision-making skills. The church members, many of whom are working poor, award small scholarships to the program graduates. The program, now being eyed by other churches in the area, receives no government funding.

SOCIAL ACTIVISM

Given the city's political life and history, it is natural that social activism has been a hallmark of several Austin churches for decades. Professor Orum cites the impact University of Texas campus church organizations and the Austin YMCA had on bringing students from diverse backgrounds together in the '30s and '40s.

Many Austin churches are committed to community causes, such as collecting food for the city's Food Bank or serving meals to the homeless. One young church member from an affluent and active West Austin church began a book drive for homeless men and women who pass through her church's soup kitchen. From the smallest effort to well-organized, major fund-raising campaigns, Austin's churches are engaged in serving the community. Some have taken their activism into the public-policy arena, representing both conservative and liberal thinking.

One of the most influential organizations, particularly on issues of education, is Austin Interfaith. Its membership is made up of church members from a diversity of congregations, many of them anchored in the city's working-class neighborhoods.

Interfaith was organized by Ernesto Cortes Jr., a legendary social activist who

A rare Gutenberg Bible is on display at the Harry Ransom Humanities Research Center, West 21st and Guadalupe Streets, on the University of Texas campus. One of only 48 extant copies, the Bible was printed in 1449 (see our Arts chapter for more on the center).

heads the Southwest office of a national grassroots political organization called the Industrial Areas Foundation, a network of mostly church-based coalitions aimed at community activism. The late Saul Alinsky, a community organizer from Chicago, created the foundation in 1940. Like Alinsky, his mentor, Cortes and his followers have been called radical by some, but there is no question the Austin Interfaith group has evolved into a potent force.

Like its sister organizations in Texas, Rio Grande Valley Interfaith and the very powerful Communities Organized for Public Service in San Antonio, the Austin group commands the attention of local politicians.

City council members and school board officials are particularly attentive. Although the group does not endorse candidates, it does query them at intense, detailed "accountability sessions." Austin Interfaith has worked on several ballott initiatives and is credited with ensuring strong support in the minority communities, where it is particularly active.

POLITICAL CLOUT

Texas is a Bible Belt state. Generally speaking, north of Austin is considered staunch Bible Belt country, home to many of the state's most conservative churches and denominations. South of Austin is generally considered to be less conservative, more likely Catholic than Protestant.

Occasionally, a church in Austin will find itself at odds with a national church

Several Austin churches celebrate October 4, feast day of St. Francis of Assisi, by holding blessing of the animals gatherings. Check the Religion listings in the Saturday edition of the Austin American-Statesman.

body over its stand on issues. Recently, one Baptist church was expelled from the Southern Baptist Convention because of its recognition of gay marriages. The incident is evidence of the city's liberalism, but other Baptist churches in the city are in step with their national leadership on such issues. Diversity is the keyword in Austin.

In general terms though, conservative religious views do manifest themselves north and east of Austin. In state elections on the lottery, for example, voters north and east of Austin tended to vote against gambling initiatives. The few dry counties in Texas are located north of Austin, also. In Travis County, home of the capital city, 48.4 percent of the churchgoers are Roman Catholic, according to the *Texas Almanac,* while immediately to the north in Williamson County, home of Round Rock, Southern Baptists make up 46.9 percent of the churchgoing public.

Williamson County politics, both at the school board and at city, county, and state levels, tend to be more conservative. Juries in Williamson County mete out harsher punishments, and the local newspapers are more conservative in tone. That same conservatism is reflected in community religious views.

PLACES TO WORSHIP

There are churches of all persuasions in Austin, some liberal, others conservative; some traditional, others decidedly New Age; some fundamentalist, some experimental. The *Austin American-Statesman* profiles a place of worship every Saturday.

A resource list of some of the religious organizations follows:

Austin Baptist Association, 1016 East 38th Street, (512) 454-2558, www.austinbaptist.org, is an Austin umbrella group for Southern Baptist churches.

Austin Metropolitan Ministries, 2026 Guadalupe Street, Suite 226, (512) 472-7627, austinmetromin.citysearch.com, is an interfaith group with 120 churches in its membership and works to coordinate community involvement in social issues.

Hillel Foundation at UT Austin, 2105 San Antonio Street, (512) 476-0125, is a Jewish center for university students that reaches out to convey aspects of Jewish culture to the community.

Church of Jesus Christ of Latter-day Saints, Institute of Religion, 2020 San Antonio Street, (512) 478-8575.

Episcopal Diocese of Texas, 606 Rathervue Place, (512) 478-0580, www.epicenter.org.

Friends Meeting of Austin, 3014 Washington Square, (512) 452-1841, www.austinquakers.org.

International Buddhist Progress Society, 8557 Research Boulevard, Suite 118, (512) 836-7459.

Islamic Center of Greater Austin, 1906 Nueces Street, (512) 476-2563, www.austinmosque.org.

Jewish Federation of Austin, 11713 Jollyville Road, (512) 331-1144, www.jfaustin.org.

Roman Catholic Diocese of Austin, 1600 North Congress Avenue, (512) 476-4888, www.austindiocese.org.

Texas District Lutheran Church–Missouri Synod, 7900 U.S. 290 East, (512) 926-4272, www.txdistlcms.org.

Texas Conference of Churches, 1033 La Posada Drive, (512) 451-0991, represents 51 religious governing bodies and is dedicated to promoting religious unity, www.txconfchurches.org.

United Methodist Church, Austin district, 3755 South Loop 360 (Capital of Texas Highway), Suite 150, (512) 444-1983.

INDEX

ABOUT THE AUTHORS

CAM ROSSIE

Cam Rossie is a journalist and freelance writer who started her professional career while still a university student, working as a reporter, copy editor, and editor for daily and weekly newspapers in the Midwest. A former domestic and foreign correspondent for the Associated Press news service, her news and feature articles have appeared in newspapers throughout the United States and abroad.

Her career with the AP began in Nebraska and later took her to New Mexico, Texas's Rio Grande Valley, and New York City. In 1984 she was chosen to open a new AP bureau in Northern Mexico. From her base of operations in Monterrey, Cam covered the U.S.-Mexico border from coast to coast, as well as other regions of Mexico and Central America. She is fluent in Spanish and is an accomplished public speaker who has lectured on journalism issues in the United States and Mexico.

An international journalism scholarship took her to Caracas, Venezuela, for nearly two years, sparking an interest in world cultures that remains to this day. In addition to living and working many years in Mexico and South America, Cam also lived for several years in Europe, where she wrote on education issues. While not at home in Austin, she travels throughout the United States and the world. Her passion for globe-trotting has taken her to more than 25 countries in Europe, Africa, the Middle East, and Central and South America. Her daughter, Quint Simon, was born in Mexico and has grown up as a third culture kid.

Cam first discovered Austin and the Texas Hill Country while on a camping trip to Lake Travis more than 20 years ago. She and her family spent many enjoyable vacations exploring the Capital City area, savoring the Austin music and cultural scenes and hiking the splendid hills before they decided to make Austin their home in 1993.

HILARY HYLTON

Hilary Hylton is a freelance writer and author whose work covers a variety of topics, including business, social issues, personalities, government, politics, cuisine, and travel. Her work has been published in national, international, and regional publications.

Hilary has lived in Austin since 1977, watching it grow and change. She has written about many aspects of life in Austin—its food, politics, lifestyles, and business—for both Texas and national publications. Hilary is a freelance reporter for *TIME* magazine and Reuters, the international news service. In addition, she has written for the Sunday magazines and feature sections of several major daily newspapers, including the *Los Angeles Times*. Her magazine articles also have appeared in major city, business, lifestyle, and airline magazines—features on food, travel, business, and political personalities.

Prior to freelancing, she worked as a journalist for several Florida and Texas newspapers. Her work was honored with a number of awards, including Texas Star Reporter by the Austin Headliners' Club. Hilary is also the author of a guidebook, *Texas Monthly's Mexico: A Completely Up-to-date Guide to an Extraordinary Country.*

Hilary is married to Peter Silva, an award-winning photographer represented by Zuma Press, an international photo

ABOUT THE AUTHORS

agency based in California. Peter and Hilary moved to Texas in 1974 after meeting while they were both working at the *Palm Beach Post* in Florida. Peter is a native of Manhattan, Kansas, while Hilary was born in Cheshire, England, and moved with her family to the United States as a teenager. They have two Australian shepherds, siblings Ben and Pepper, and several cats who serve as substitute livestock for the dogs.

Hilary's personal interests include reading history, armchair travel, gardening, cooking, and collecting cookbooks. Her culinary interests have led to stints in the local media as a food columnist for a magazine and a restaurant reviewer for the *Austin American-Statesman*.

HELP US KEEP THIS GUIDE UP TO DATE

Every effort has been made by the authors and editors to make this guide as accurate and useful as possible. However, many things can change after a guide is published—phone numbers change, facilities come under new management, etc.

We would love to hear from you concerning your experiences with this guide and how you feel it could be improved and be kept up to date. While we may not be able to respond to all comments and suggestions, we'll take them to heart and we'll also make certain to share them with the authors. Please send your comments and suggestions to the following address:

> The Globe Pequot Press
> Reader Response/Editorial Department
> P.O. Box 480
> Guilford, CT 06437

Or you may e-mail us at:

> editorial@GlobePequot.com

Thanks for your input, and happy travels!